Eleanor L. Mayer
1602 McDonough St.
Sandusky, Ohio

Hackman D - 229

Teaching
Elementary Reading

The World of Books

Teaching
Elementary Reading

By

MILES A. TINKER

UNIVERSITY OF MINNESOTA

and

CONSTANCE M. McCULLOUGH

SAN FRANCISCO STATE COLLEGE

Second Edition

APPLETON-CENTURY-CROFTS, Inc.

New York

PREFACE

The original edition of this book, written by Miles A. Tinker, was published in 1952. This edition, under the joint authorship of Constance M. McCullough and Miles A. Tinker, is more than a revision. Nearly all the material has been rewritten, its organization changed, and 10 new chapters have been added. New trends in the teaching of reading have been taken into account together with relevant research findings that have appeared since 1952.

The successful teacher, in addition to becoming familiar with the fundamentals derived from research and sound classroom practice, must apply these in his instruction. To equip him to do this, the materials presenting the basic principles are followed by chapters containing examples of practice recommended for kindergarten through grade eight. Thinking through these examples, the creative teacher will begin to invent other ways of obtaining the same results without violating the sound principles which she has studied in Parts I and II of this volume.

This book is written to foster improved understanding and better methods of teaching reading in the elementary school. The aim is to present a clear, simple, and straightforward exposition of the principles and practice underlying sound reading instruction in a balanced and sequential program. The materials are organized to assist both teacher-in-training and the teacher-in-service.

The appendixes will aid in the searching for certain kinds of information. Included are annotated lists of tests, books and monographs on reading instruction, sources of graded book lists and of materials, bibliographies of reading literature, a glossary of statistical terms, and tables of prefixes, suffixes, and root derivatives.

Many school systems, individuals, and publishers have contributed directly or indirectly to this volume. To them we give grateful acknowledgment. Specific recognition for permission to reproduce materials is given at appropriate places throughout the book. We are grateful for the suggestions of Dr. Theodore Clymer during the preliminary planning of the revision and also for prepublication information on some of his research. Thanks are due Harry Sartain for permission to reproduce his experimental report in our Chapter 2, to Mrs. Margaret Denmarsh for permission to include a description of the Torrance Approach to Educational Materials Distribution, to Helen Behn, for permission to reproduce her vocabulary count in the preprimers of eight basal reader series, to Dorothy Baruch, for use of her poem, "Rabbits,' the Macmillan Company, for the use of Rachel Field's "This Afternoon," and John Hersey for the quotation from *A Single Pebble* (Knopf), to Mildred Dawson and Marian Zollinger for the quotation from *Guiding Language Learning* Harcourt, Brace & (World), to Ginn & Company, for quotations of its interest inventory, skills tables, and monographs on reading, and to N.S.S.E. for the quotation from the 60th yearbook.

The writers are especially indebted to Dr. R. M. Elliott for his extensive, careful, and helpful editorial suggestions.

M. A. T.

C. M. M.

CONTENTS

PART I

About Reading
and the Reading Teacher

1

Concerning Reading

No one in this day and age is likely to put more emphasis on reading than it deserves. As a medium of communication and a means of learning, reading is indispensable. Through it we attain understanding and many forms of competence. Of course other means of communication such as television, radio, and motion pictures have their value, along with certain limitations. Gray and Rogers (114) have stated that reading satisfies needs which these newer inventions are unable fully to meet. They emphasize that reading is an indispensable component of modern life, intermingled as it is with work, recreation, and so many other activities of both children and adults. Actually, a large number of the values provided by what is recorded in print cannot be attained so effectively through any other channel of communication. It would seem certain that among educated persons reading will continue to be the paramount medium for the exchange of ideas and experiences.

Reading as Communication

Reading as a form of communication now plays a larger role in human affairs than at any time in the past. It has several distinct advantages over its rivals: (1) Printed materials provide the clearest and most varied records of human experience and attainments available. (2) In his searching for clear understanding and sound conclusions, a reader can pause to reflect, reread, and study as often as he wishes. He can weigh and deliberate at will. (3) Simply by turning to other books he may obtain a variety of information and find out what the judgments of experts on a difficult problem are. A person may choose what he wishes to read, whether for pleasure or for some serious purpose. (4) Reading tends to be a more efficient method of securing information than other means of communication in at least two respects: (a) Even an average reader, and certainly one who is better than average, can peruse printed material three to four times as fast as a person can talk intelligibly. This means that, in a given time, he can read several times as much material as he can hear spoken in a television or radio presentation. (b) The thoughts of the most creative minds in human history are there for any reader who is willing to go in search of them.

Many of these boons, of course, are available only to mature readers. Whether we think of personal advantages or of our nation's and mankind's goals, therefore, the teaching of reading, and especially of how to read well, is of tremendous importance.

Sociology of Reading

Of the various avenues of communication, reading is undoubtedly the most important in preparing an individual for the discharge of his civic responsibilties. The alert citizen is constantly receiving impressions from newspapers, magazines, books, conversation, radio, and television. To make sound judgments, he must attempt to discriminate fact from opinion. Otherwise he may not succeed in resisting the subtle influences of propaganda exerted on him. Among the skills possessed by the mature reader, the ones that are most effective for detecting propaganda are his store of concepts (word meanings), the readiness and depth of his comprehension, and his capacity for critical evaluation, such as distinguishing facts from opinions. To acquire the information requisite to understanding a proposition and to exercise sound judgment as to its truth and importance needs a relatively high level of reading ability. All this has enormous significance for the teaching of reading.

Reading ability in the USA

No one, whether parent, teacher, or citizen, should be complacent about the kind and amount of education that is acquired today by a large portion of our population. The following data are obtained from the *World Almanac* (1960 edition): Of adults 25 years or older in 1940, 14 per cent had either no education or less than 5 years of formal education; in 1950, 11 per cent; in 1960, 4 per cent (estimated). In 1950 the median length of time spent in school by adults 25 years of age or older was 9.3 years (i.e., one-half the population had been in school from 0 to 9.3 years); in 1960, 10.8 years (estimated). Unfortunately number of years in school is not a good measure of reading level attained, except in terms of averages. This is well illustrated by what Lazar (153) discovered. When pupils halfway through the eighth grade (8.5 grade) were measured, their reading score ranged from virtual "nonreaders," with little or no reading ability, to those who read better than the average high school senior. The percentage of pupils halfway through the eighth grade who had less than fifth-grade reading ability was 8.6; between fifth- and sixth-grade ability, 13.9. Thus, more than a fifth (22.5%) of the 55,140 pupils tested had less than sixth-grade reading ability. Many of these poor readers were destined to drop out of school before much further gain in reading ability was achieved.

The average measured reading ability of American adults is not high. Lorge and Blau (161) in 1941 found it equivalent to that of the average seventh- or eighth-grade pupil. If, as Gray and Rogers (114) suggest, the reading ability of adults corresponds closely, on the average, with the last school grade attended, the reading ability of adults (1960), as estimated, should compare with that of a typical high school sophomore who is part way through the 10th grade. This estimate has not yet been supported by actual findings.

To cite averages alone, however, is deceptive. Bond and Tinker (26, p. 37), for instance, show that while the average reading ability found in typical sixth-grade classrooms is sixth grade, the range of reading ability extends from grade 2.5 to 9.5. At higher school levels, the range is even greater. Bond and Bond (24, p. 20) cite data for 10th-grade pupils. The average reading ability was at 10.7 grade, with a spread from 5th grade to better than college freshmen. Approximately half the group had scores below average. And of course some of the poorer readers will have dropped out of school before this grade is reached.

Suppose the average reading ability of our adult population is in fact at the 9th- or 10th-grade level. Then approximately half of the individuals will be reading at levels lower than the average; a few will be nonreaders, and others will be functionally illiterate (with less than the typical 4th-grade ability). Many will read only at 4th- to 7th-grade level. Thus the statement of Gray and Rogers (114) that the reading ability of adults corresponds closely with the amount of schooling applies only to averages and tells us nothing about individuals.

Such data are not reassuring to one who is concerned over the strength and vigor of our democracy. They mean that the reading ability of a large segment of our population is so low that many citizens cannot profit much from anything that is printed. Although the level of reading ability does depend to some degree upon mental ability, many of these poor readers could improve markedly under proper instruction. This was shown by the high degree of success attained in the army reading program, as described by Witty and Goldberg (283). This program challenges us to further efforts in the schools.

Russell (213) and Gray and Rogers (114) summarize the literature describing what is read by adults. Details of this subject will be given in our chapter on interests and tastes. A brief statement will suffice here. Practically everyone reads a newspaper. Persons whose education is limited to grade and high school devote less time to reading magazines and books than to newspapers. Those with a college education spend more time reading books than magazines and newspapers. With few exceptions, the consensus of expert judgment is that the reading tastes of adults are relatively immature. The number and variety of "cheap" comic magazines and pulp magazines sold, the type of library books most commonly in circulation, and surveys of reading habits seem to indicate a relatively low level of discrimination in choosing what to read. There can be little doubt about the desirability of guidance to improve the reading tastes of Americans of all ages, in the interest of developing better-informed citizens in a stronger democracy.

Russell (213) distinguishes three basic factors which determine what a person will read: (1) his reading ability considered in relation to the difficulty of the material; (2) the accessibility of material; (3) the needs and interests of the individual. As might be expected, few people will read material they do not want to read.

Availability of materials

Access to libraries varies greatly. In Massachusetts and Delaware library service can be called available to all. But in rural areas in many states very few people have access to a library of any kind. Newspapers and magazines are much more available. With few exceptions the magazines and newspapers with large circulations are the ones that have a popular rather than an intellectual appeal. Thirteen of these magazines enjoy a circulation of over three million.

As we have implied, there are many indications that much of what is read by American adults and children is mediocre in quality: pulp magazines, glamorous and unrealistic love stories, detective stories, sensational newspapers, comics, and the like. Though we as a people have not achieved the reading abilities and habits of a mature society, there is evidence that the amount and quality of the reading done by adults is steadily rising. (For additional details on reading tastes see Chapter 14.)

Goals of Reading Instruction

In any attempt to formulate the goals of reading instruction, what is said should be neither too general nor too specific. If it is too general it will have few implications concerning how reading is to be taught. And if too specific it will sound like mere daily lesson planning. It seems best to present those goals which are relevant in formulating a balanced reading program at all grade levels. That is, a statement of goals must be broad enough to include present-day reading requirements in an up-to-date program.

Adjusting instruction in reading to individual differences

The degree to which reading goals will be achieved and how fast progress toward these goals will be made will depend upon the adjustment of instruction to individual differences. Pupils differ in many ways, in mental level, verbal facility, experience background, and emotional and physical maturity. For each child to progress at what is the optimal, or at least a satisfactory, rate for him, the reading instruction must be adapted to his individual capacity and needs. Some details on how this is done will be given in Chapter 13.

Word skills

Development of word skills involves building vocabulary, developing techniques of word recognition in a sequential program, and accumulating an ever increasing supply of words which are recognized at a glance, i.e., without analysis. Instruction in each of these three skills must continue throughout the grades.

Understandings: basic comprehension

As will be emphasized throughout this book, comprehension ability is basic in all reading. Comprehension depends upon grasping word meanings, grouping words into unitary thought complexes so that sentences, paragraphs, and the still larger units of material become intelligible. This involves grasping the relations between words in sentences, between sentences in paragraphs, and between paragraphs in larger wholes.

Comprehension and study skills

In addition to the basic understandings, the skilled reader has at his command a number of more complex comprehension and study skills. To fulfill the various purposes for which a pupil reads, he will need as the occasion arises, to skim, to read for merely the main idea, to follow and anticipate a sequence of events, to read to grasp relevant details, to read to follow directions or to draw conclusions, or to evaluate critically. He will also make use of such study skills as remembering what is read, locating information, and organizing and summarizing materials.

Adjusting reading procedures

To read well, the pupil must modify his procedure to fit the kind of material he is exposed to, as well as the purpose for which his reading is to be done. This involves selecting and applying the appropriate kind of comprehension skill, and adjusting his rate of reading to understand most effectively what is required. Some reading should be rapid, some slow, and in some instances rereading, even several times, is necessary.

Reading aloud

All pupils should be taught to read aloud well enough to communicate satisfactorily with their hearers, whether the purpose is to give pleasure, to provide information, to share an interesting item, or to illustrate some point under debate. Such reading involves proper phrasing, clear enunciation of words, voice control, and timing or rate of speaking, and with appropriate pauses.

Modifying behavior

Other important features in a broadly conceived program of reading instruction are instilling favorable attitudes towards reading, inculcating broad and varied interests, inspiring good taste, and nicety of appreciation and wholesome personal and social habits.

Habits and attitudes toward reading. Pupils should acquire the habits of demanding of themselves that they understand all that they read, of sensing the purpose back of reading each selection, and of being willing to seek information when it is needed. These attitudes towards reading should be positive: to want to learn to read better, to want to enjoy a story, to want to push further and find relevant references on a promising topic, and to want to share reading experiences with others.

Interests. The development of interests constitutes a vital part of the reading program. In reading, as in other activities, the interested pupil is the motivated pupil. His is the drive to accomplish something. If he is really interested, a child will find that he can read with understanding material that is more difficult than he has been accustomed to take in before. The instructional program to develop interests in reading has two aspects: (1) The teacher will be alert to use any interest patterns the child already possesses. (2) She will also provide guidance in broadening these interests while always seeking to stimulate the acquisition of new and more mature ones.

Tastes and appreciation. Practically all pupils can profit by a program aimed at improving their tastes and their appreciation of the meaning, and perhaps the beauty, of what they read. Good taste means being concerned with the quality of material that one reads, and appreciation means responding to quality when it is there. The goal here is to develop the ability to recognize excellence in what one reads and to prefer reading material of this quality. Improvement of tastes and appreciation involves the ability to discriminate between what is good and what is less good, or outright bad, and to develop a liking for the good over the less good, i.e., a matter of preferring the higher levels of excellence in any field of writing. Another value in reading lies in coming to feel what it can contribute to the enrichment of one's life, to the meaning or the fullness of living.

Personal and social development. Normal progress in learning to read is necessary if satisfactory personal and social adjustment is to be maintained. Two aspects of reading bear upon personal and social development: (1) The child who is a skilled reader escapes the feeling of inferiority, the heartaches, and various other unfortunate behavior deviations that may mark a disabled reader. All the while he feels the gratification that comes from success as a learner, whatever his educational level. (2) Reading should contribute to the development of desirable personal and social understandings, attitudes, and patterns of behavior. To achieve this there must be rapid improvement in the pupil's ability to carry through self-reliant and discriminating interpretation of what is read. To reach this goal, the instructional program must in turn establish a clear definition of pupil needs, both in relation to the personal growth of the individual and his adjustment to and participation in the social community.

Interrelations of goals. The goals we are discussing are intertwined. The child must possess certain reading abilities and skills in order to choose appropriate reading matter and to understand it when he does read. Moreover, any reading which will promote his personal and social development automatically contributes to raising his level of tastes and his appreciation of what is best in literature. And interests, habits, and attitudes enter into the development of tastes and both personal and social status.

The Mature Reader

With adequate instruction, many children who have successfully finished the eighth grade should have become fairly skillful readers. Some of them may in time become *mature* adult readers, the kind we are eager to develop. At present these expectations appear to fall short of what is hoped for. Although the study by Gray and Rogers (114) revealed that the reading behavior of our adult population ranges all the way from gross immaturity to a very high level of maturity, the number of highly mature readers is small. The hopeful aspects of this survey are that: (1) most adults expressed enthusiasm for reading, and (2) the superior readers were always able, when the occasion demanded, to interpret what they read with accuracy and penetration (p. 23). Further findings are that a college education does not assure maturity in reading, for apparently some pupils who have only finished eighth grade are mature readers, while many others possess the skills which will enable them to achieve maturity later. If the goals we have been upholding could be achieved, the following should be some of the characteristics of our adult population.

Characteristics of the mature reader

1. He will have mastered the essential techniques of word identification. Word-form clues, context clues (obtaining meaning from the rest of

a sentence), structural analysis, phonetic analysis, and dictionary skills are all employed appropriately and as needed. Their use has become so automatic or habitual that attention may be devoted largely to the thought of the passage being read.

2. His vocabulary will be extensive. A clear and precise knowledge of the meanings of words helps to form those concepts which are the tools of thoughtful and critical reading. Not only will his word knowledge be extensive, but he also will have learned how on his own to expand his vocabulary and thus be continually adding to his previous store.

3. His comprehension will be sufficient to meet any reasonable challenge as shown in reading sentences, paragraphs, and longer passages.

4. When required, he will be able to study, to draw conclusions after thinking things over, to locate and evaluate information on a topic, or to apply other comprehension and study skills.

5. He will be a versatile reader. He will know when and how to change his pace and to employ whatever skills are appropriate to the material to be read and to the purpose for which his reading is to be done. He will realize that effective reading is rapid reading in some situations and slow, analytical reading in others.

6. He will demand of himself that he understand what he reads instead of being satisfied with inadequate or partial understanding. He reads with a purpose which he recognizes and accepts. He knows why he is reading and his intention is to get a clear understanding in the light of his purposes.

7. Because good reading is thoughtful reading he will have learned to interpret, to evaluate, and to reflect upon what he reads. Reading has for him become a matter of thinking.

8. His reading interests will be extensive and varied. Because interests supply drive, he has formed the habit of reaching out and diversifying his reading interests into ever new lines.

9. His taste and appreciation will have developed along desirable lines. He can discriminate what is good from what is not good and really prefers the good.

10. He realizes that his personal and social adjustment can be promoted through self-reliant and discriminating interpretation of what he reads.

11. His skill in oral reading has reached a level that permits him to convey information and give pleasure when reading aloud. This requires good phrasing and timing, proper inflection of the voice, clear diction, accurate pronunciation, and the ability to achieve an emotional harmony between what and how he reads.

12. He knows how to use reading to satisfy whatever needs he becomes aware of. This may mean leisure reading for enjoyment, reading to find what he needs to know, or reading for his personal or social ends. Independence in the use of reading requires a whole repertory of reading skills.

13. He has built the foundations essential for developing further maturity in reading (Gray and Rogers, 114).

The degree to which a person will achieve the elements of maturity outlined here depends upon many things. In any large group there is a wide range of individual differences in every factor affecting reading proficiency. Intellectual level places a definite limit upon reading capacity. Among other factors which influence achievement in reading are: personal adjustment of the individual, the kind of reading instruction he received in school or after, his early home environment, and the availability of reading materials.

Nature of Reading

The goals of reading instruction cannot be achieved unless our techniques of teaching are based upon a sound understanding of the nature of reading. Although research in this area is not far advanced, the following discussion outlines what we have to go on.

Reading is one of the so-called language arts in the modern school curriculum. Customarily grouped as language arts are speaking, writing, listening, and reading. Reading benefits from and influences the other language arts.

Reading as talk written down

For the beginner, learning to read entails learning that printed symbols stand for speech. The child reads when he says the correct printed words and recognizes their meaning because of his previous experience in comprehending speech in meaningful sequence. He discovers that printed words "talk" sense. At an early age, the child is discovering an important aspect of reading, i.e., the interpretation of meanings is the core of the reading process. As he advances in school, he develops skill in word recognition, expands his vocabulary and his knowledge of concepts, learns to read by thought units, and reduces vocalization in silent reading. The child also has to learn that print is talk written down, but that reading is thinking (silent) and does not ordinarily involve vocalizing (oral).

Reading is a complex process

As the child progresses in reading, his store of sight words increases and word-recognition techniques operate with facility and speed. At the same time his reading material becomes more complicated in terms of vocabulary and concepts, sentence length and structure, and intricacy of language.

Furthermore, as he advances he encounters a greater demand upon his interpretation of meanings, his appreciation of style in writing, of vividness in description, and of humor. And more and more, work-type reading is encountered.

Reading and thinking

In addition to sensing an author's meanings, the child must learn to interpret, evaluate, and reflect upon those meanings if he is to become a competent reader. That is, mastering the mechanics of reading is not enough. Reading as a tool for learning will remain relatively ineffective unless he is equal to the thinking side of reading. The mature reader is a critical reader. He makes use of his accumulated experience and knowledge to interpret what he now encounters for the first time. He is on the alert to distinguish inconsistencies, faulty reasoning, and facts vs. propaganda.

Learning to read and reading to learn

An expanding curriculum and changing methods of instruction in present-day schools, as well as a world that demands more reading, have increased the need for a greater amount and a wider variety of reading. At all levels of education reading should be both a subject of instruction and a tool employed in studying in the subject-matter fields. During recent years the emphasis has been changing from learning to read to reading to learn. The extreme view has been upheld in some quarters that learning to read has no place in the modern school. The present writers tend to agree with Harris (122) that to put things in this way is not wise. The skillful teaching of reading is of the highest importance in the primary grades. And it remains important at all school levels where the maintenance of already acquired skills and the development of new ones are required if the pupil is to cope successfully with increasingly formidable challenges in his reading.

Definition of reading

Some have held that reading is getting the meaning from the printed page. But as pointed out by McKee (178), to say only this is misleading. There are no meanings on the printed page. There are only symbols which stand for meanings. Printed symbols as such merely stimulate one to recall some familiar concepts. All that the recognition of a word or a group of words does is to stimulate recall or the arousal of previously encountered meanings. Any new meaning comes from manipulation of the recalled concepts by the reader, not from the author or from symbols as such. If the reader already possesses concepts, they are readily recalled. But if the concept is new, manipulation of related materials and meanings in the construction of the concept becomes a kind of problem solving. It would appear then that reading in the full sense involves creative processes. It concerns all the complex mental processes involved in the interpretation of concepts and meanings aroused by recognition of the printed symbols. What the reader "gets from the page," therefore, is not exactly what any other reader would get or even what the author envisioned, but to some degree at least a personal re-creation on the part of the reader. And at times the process becomes highly creative.

The definition of reading here adopted may be summed up as follows: Reading involves the recognition of printed or written symbols which serve as stimuli for the recall of meanings built up through past experience, and the construction of new meanings through manipulation of concepts already possessed by the reader. The resulting meanings are organized into thought processes according to the purposes adopted by the reader. Such an organization leads to modified thought and/or behavior, or else leads to new behavior which takes its place, either in personal or in social development.

Changing Concepts of Reading

Concepts and methods of teaching reading have undergone a series of changes in America. At times a given emphasis has been overdone. Experience has demonstrated more than once that excesses of this kind seldom achieve the hoped-for results. Acquaintance with the ill-advised instructional practices of the past may serve to warn the present-day teacher against repeating the excesses which were harmful, or at least fruitless, in earlier days. One can disapprove of excessive emphasis in applying a principle which has a desired value when employed with discrimination and in conjunction with other supporting approaches. But a knowledge of the history of reading instruction should prevent a revival of procedures or emphases which have proved unsound. In addition, it will reveal the wisdom of the present-day balanced or composite program which consists of a combined, many-sided approach with an avoidance of extremes.

The alphabet-spelling system

In the colonial period, the strongest emphasis in reading instruction was upon furthering religious and moral education, either to prepare for the ministry or to enable the laity to read the Bible, prayer books, hymns, and other religious and moral materials. Pupils usually began to learn the letters by use of the *Hornbook*. The *New England primer* was the most famous of the early readers. Pupils first learned the alphabet, then syllables, starting with two-letter combinations such as *ab*, *ac*, and later progressing to more complex letter combinations. These were repeated over and over until memorized. Then came lessons in which sounds and fragments of words were memorized and chanted in unison. The droning, which may have sounded like the hum of a beehive, very likely had little more meaning than this to the pupils. The last thing the children encountered in their reading was connected material organized into sentences.

Reading was largely oral. Although the alphabet-spelling method of instruction was retained after the colonial period, greater emphasis began to be placed upon reading and speaking the English language correctly. This led to even greater stress upon pronunciation and oral reading. Attention was devoted to accent, emphasis, pauses, and gestures. Popular texts were *The blue back speller* and Webster's *American spelling book*. These were overloaded with rules in addition to the alphabet, syllables, and words to spell. When stories were introduced belatedly, the pupils had to spell them out word by word. It is not surprising that holding the pupil's attention and maintaining discipline were major problems.

The word method

About 1840, a desirable change in emphasis was introduced under the leadership of Horace Mann. Although this new emphasis represented an improvement over the alphabet-spelling method, it involved some of the same shortcomings: Comprehension of ideas came last. Isolated words were learned before sentences were read. This hindered reading in thought units. All words were learned by sight. A picture was shown to the children with a word below it. The children were told the word. In addition they were given the sounds of the letters and letter combinations. But Horace Mann helped to do away with the alphabet-spelling method with its false notion that a pupil recognizes a word by moving his eyes from letter to letter through the word. Horace Mann also condemned the stress on oral reading without comprehenison of what was read. For instance, he pointed out that 11 out of 12 pupils who read aloud glibly did not understand what was read. Another advance which began about 1840 was the introduction of a graded series of readers by McGuffey (*McGuffey eclectic readers*). Although these represented a definite improvement over the spelling type of readers, they too started with the alphabet and employed excessive repetition of relatively uninteresting sentences. The narrative element, so appealing to and therefore so valuable for beginners, was absent.

The first phonics era

The use of phonics for word analysis began about 1870 and was excessively emphasized until approximately 1920. Several elaborate systems, formal and mechanical, were developed. They involved practice isolated from meaningful material, such as identifying and sounding out the *ate* family (*date, mate, late*). Pupils were so busy sounding out words that they became slow, laborious readers who lost sight of meanings. In time, the unsoundness of this artificial method was recognized and it was abandoned.

But apparently the artificial phonetic procedures were not banished forever. Even today obvious descendants of these early phonetic systems are back with us in a vigorously promoted phonics system alleged to be the one and only "sure fire" system of teaching reading: Hay and Wingo, *Reading with phonics,* 1954 (124); Flesch, *Why Johnny can't read,* 1955 (88); and Terman and Walcutt, *Reading: chaos and cure,* 1958 (251).

The emphasis on look-and-say

Following disappointment with the results obtained from artificial phonics, the prevailing practice swung to another extreme. Teachers discarded all forms of word analysis for a time and adopted an equally unsatisfactory method. Every word was to be learned as a sight word by viewing the whole word and repeating it many times. Any phonetic training was prohibited. It was soon discovered that little progress in learning to read could be made by use of this look-and-say method alone. Notice that, again, schools went to an extreme instead of combining what was good in the methods of the past with the advantages of certain newer methods.

Shifting emphases

During the first 10 to 20 years of the 20th century there were few changes in reading instruction. Oral reading was dominant and continued for another 10 years or so. Phonetic analysis with some improvement in technique was stressed until the early 1920's. The look-and-say method was employed for nonphonetic words. Then the sentence and a little later (1915) the story method were beginning to appear. In the former, a whole sentence rather than a single word was presented together with a picture. And in the latter, the teacher told the story while the children followed in their books. Then the pupils dramatized or told the story, drilled on words and phrases, and at last were allowed to read the story by themselves.

Oral and silent reading. Just prior to 1920 the silent-reading concept was launched. This received extreme emphasis in the 1920's, while oral reading was neglected. During the following decades, particularly from 1940 to the present, authorities have advocated the teaching of both oral and silent reading as explained in later chapters of this text.

Research. Scientific investigations of psychological factors in reading began to appear prior to 1900. From that time on, studies of the reading process were reported with increasing frequency. During recent years, over 100 studies have been published annually, while perhaps as many as a thousand master's theses, doctoral dissertations, and independent studies have actually been made each year. These investigations, plus the reports of classroom experience, provided the basis for the major changes in the teaching of reading over the years. Some of the more important areas of this research are: various aspects of silent reading, individual differences in reading ability, remedial reading, reading readiness, reading interests and tastes, personality factors, mass-media effects, maturity in reading, teaching methods, use of visual and auditory aids, and development of special skills for reading content materials.[1]

Now that research studies have established the utility of certain methods for certain purposes in certain proportions, the teaching profession is no longer justified in swinging wildly to one extreme or another as new developments occur. Rather, its policy should be to undertake the careful experimental test of proposed innovations in procedure followed by incorporation of such new developments as the results of research warrant.

Reading tests. The development of reading tests deserves special mention. Beginning in the 1910-1920 decade, instruments for measuring reading abilities have appeared in increasing numbers up to and including the present. These standardized tests have made it possible to diagnose reading difficulties and to appraise progress in reading at various levels and using different kinds of material.

The composite method of reading instruction

A program of reading instruction that is both well balanced in its components and puts the emphasis where it belongs can be worked out by combining the results of research, reports of successful classroom practices, the statements of objectives, and the periodic evaluations of progress to be found in Yearbooks of the National Society for the Study of Education and such conference proceedings as those of the International Reading Association and the Annual Conferences on Reading held at the University of Chicago. The basic material in such a program is well organized and there is ample provision for individualized reading and the development of the specialized skills needed for work in the content fields. In the contemporary composite method certain mistakes of the past (see above) have been avoided. The teacher selects the good features of various methods. At all times maintaining the meaningful approach to reading, she adapts instruction to the individual needs of pupils. The consensus of authorities in the field is that such a composite method is the most effective one for reading instruction.

Plan of This Book

This book is written to bring research findings and examples of good instructional practice to teachers and others who provide leadership in

[1] For bibliography and summary of investigations related to reading, see annual reports by W. S. Gray in the 1960 and earlier volumes of the *Journal of Educational Research*. Also see our bibliography for the Traxler summaries of reading research.

school reading programs. The teaching method we recommend and describe is developmental. In it the child makes continuous progress in learning to read by a natural transition from one level to the next. What is learned at any one level becomes a foundation for what is to follow immediately after.

Chapter 2 is concerned with the reading teacher as herself a reader. It suggests how the teacher may keep her reading skills and experiences alive, discusses the selection of children's literature of high quality, emphasizes the value of reading aloud to children, and describes how best to read professional literature.

Chapters 3 through 16 present the basic principles of the reading program and their implications. These chapters include materials on reading readiness and the developmental phases of reading instruction upward through the grades. Separate chapters are devoted to concept building and vocabulary acquisition, word study and recognition, comprehension and interpretation, comprehension and study skills, oral reading, reading in the content fields, speed, individual differences, interests and tastes, appraisal of reading progress, and the materials needed in reading instruction.

Chapters 17 through 24 take up in detail the practices recommended in reading instruction. Separate chapters cover organization of instruction, the place of parents in the reading program, the instructional programs from kindergarten through the eighth grade, and remediation. Appendixes listing various materials are added.

Summary

As a medium of communication and a tool of learning, reading is an indispensable function in society. Educated understanding and the most valued forms of competence are unattainable by one who cannot read well. Reading satisfies needs in a way which the newer media of television, radio, and the movies cannot equal. Undoubtedly reading will continue to be the paramount means of exchanging ideas and experiences.

Most of the advantages of reading as a means of communication are available only to the skilled reader. Through his reading the individual is best equipped for discharging his civic responsibilities in a democracy. But as yet, as a people we have not reached the level of reading habits required in a highly developed society. A large portion of our population must be classified as poor readers and the majority of people are content to read materials of poor quality. Many do not have access to the best kinds of reading materials.

The goals of reading instruction are to develop skill in understanding words and their meanings at all levels of comprehension, from their basic uses to complex study, the ability to adapt reading procedures to each particular kind of material read and to every purpose for which reading is done, good oral reading, a broadened range of interests, and better taste.

Reading, especially on mature levels, should become an instrument of personal and social development.

In the early stages of his learning, a child discovers that reading is talk written down. Printed words "talk" sense. He also learns that the core of what he is doing while reading is grasping meanings. After the child has become familiar with simple words and reads more and more, he finds that reading can become a very complex process. After he has acquired the basic comprehension skills, he encounters the need to add the more complex comprehension and study skills, and learns that he must adapt his procedure to particular kinds of material and to different purposes. As he learns to be a critical reader, to think and evaluate as he reads, he is approaching maturity as a reader. Reading may be defined as recognition of printed symbols which serve as stimuli for the recall of meaning built up through past experience, and the construction of new meanings through the manipulation of those concepts already possessed.

Understanding the reading process has changed markedly for the better over the years. But even today we do not always do as well as we might in teaching reading. This is partly because the mistakes of the past get repeated and partly because we neither know as much as we should about reading nor do we make full use of the research findings and reported classroom experiences that are already available.

The plan of this book is to bring research findings and examples of good practice to teachers and others who provide leadership in school reading programs.

Vocabulary

Check your knowledge of these terms. Reread parts of the chapter if necessary.

critical evaluation *dist. Fact From opinion*	language arts - *reading, writing, speaki*
mass media *Large gp means of comm.*	vocalization
nonreaders - *Little or no reading ability*	sight words - *known at a glance*
average *norm*	work-type reading *demand interp, app*
range *classification from lowest Level to higher*	mechanics of reading
Level of comp maturity in reading	concepts - *word meanings - ideas*
reading taste	alphabet-spelling method
study skills *rem. what read - how to locate*	word method *isolated words Learne*
word analysis phonics *teaching words based on sounds*	look-and-say method *view whole word*
versatile reader *slow as well as rapid*	research *investigations* - *repeat*

Activities for Students

Observation: Visit an elementary school classroom or view a film of a reading lesson. Try to list the different methods you can detect the teacher using in teaching the lesson. From what part of the history of American reading instruction do you think each of these methods came?

Reading: As you read a newspaper, (1) analyze the purpose that makes you read one article as opposed to another; (2) when you come to an unfamiliar word, notice in what ways you work out its pronunciation and get its meaning.

Creative thinking: Analyze the reasons why the method of teaching reading in colonial times must have seemed highly satisfactory to the people of that day and the reasons why today they would be found totally inadequate.

Selected References

BOND, Guy L., and WAGNER, Eva B., *Teaching the child to read,* 3rd ed. New York: The Macmillan Company, 1960, Chaps. 1, 2.

DEBOER, John J., and DALLMANN, Martha, *The teaching of reading.* New York: Holt, Rinehart and Winston, Inc., 1960, Chaps. 1, 2, 3, 4.

DURRELL, Donald D., *Improving reading instruction.* New York: Harcourt, Brace & World, Inc., 1956, Chap. 1.

GRAY, Lillian, and REESE, Dora, *Teaching children to read,* 2nd ed. New York: The Ronald Press Company, 1957, Chaps. 1, 2, 3.

HARRIS, Albert J., *How to increase reading ability,* 4th ed. New York: Longmans, Green and Company, 1961, Chap. 1.

HESTER, Kathleen B., *Teaching every child to read.* New York: Harper and Brothers, 1955, Chaps. 1, 2.

HILDRETH, Gertrude, *Teaching reading.* New York: Holt, Rinehart and Winston, Inc., 1958, Chap. 1.

McKIM, Margaret G., *Guiding growth in reading.* New York: The Macmillan Company, 1955, Chaps. 1, 2.

RUSSELL, David H., *Children learn to read,* 2nd ed. Boston: Ginn and Company, 1961, Chaps. 1-4.

SMITH, Nila B., *American reading instruction.* New York: Silver Burdett Company, 1934.

The Reading Teacher as a Reader

Behind every child who becomes a reader is a teacher who is a reader. Sometimes that teacher is a parent, a sister or brother, an aunt, uncle, grandmother or grandfather, or an admired cousin or neighbor. But if it is none of these, and whether it is or not, it must certainly be you, the classroom teacher. In their book, *Guiding language learning* (56, p. 111), Dawson and Zollinger cite this incident as described by a friend:

One day (the teacher) was absent, and a substitute teacher came in. This teacher was direct and sincere in manner. She told us she could not teach the regular lesson and that she would like to share with us some of the things that she liked. So she started reading poetry to us, even some of the same poems that we had heard before; but this teacher was genuine in her liking. She didn't say much about the poems, but her reading brought out the mood, the meaning, the words that suggested pictures to our minds. And I have liked poetry ever since. Today the first thing I read in my new magazines is the poems I find in them.

How was the substitute teacher, who was not even "trying to teach," able to transmit this important message on the values of reading to the children whose lives she touched for only a day? She was herself an appreciative, able reader.

Behaviors of the Effective Reader

The teacher may not start out on a teaching career as a paragon, but at least she can be aware of the attitudes and kinds of behavior she hopes to encourage in the children she teaches, and can try to measure up to the goals she has chosen. The Sixtieth Yearbook of the National Society for the Study of Education (278, pp. 289-290) describes the effective reader as:

. . . a democratic and resourceful person, who not only knows how to help himself in reading and study activities, but how to help others, work with others, and learn from others. He knows his limitations as a reader and something about what to do about them. He reads efficiently for different purposes in many kinds of materials, using learning techniques which he has found effective for him. He follows written and oral directions for specific reading tasks. The level of his reading skills is proper for one of his ability, maturity, and opportunity. A broad variety of skills supports his reading performance. Through reading and discussion, he has become sensitive to the author's message both emotionally and intellectually, and has a growing awareness of the author's techniques, skills, and purposes.

Reading for pleasure and information is an established part of his school and home life. His reading interests are being broadened and refined, as well as extended along one or two lines of current interest. He is more adept at finding material in magazines and newspapers. He uses ideas gained in reading as a resource for his many activities, as information and entertainment for his friends, as a basis for comparing or developing his own ideas, and for critical appraisal. Television and motion pictures give reality to some of his reading and suggest other areas to explore through reading.

Through reading and through listening to the oral reading of well-written material, he has begun to look for more than surface value in a good piece of literature. Developing a personal standard of understanding what he reads and saying what he means, he is becoming impatient with vague or confused expression. He is curious about and interested in the use of words and of different literary forms. Gradually he is learning to note the style of a given author or illustrator and to anticipate the kind of product he will offer.

To provide leadership for such a child, the teacher herself must exemplify these same strengths. She keeps her own reading skills and reading experiences alive by making adult reading a regular and behavior-modifying part of her life. She keeps abreast of the new children's books and selects those of good quality and of interest to the children she teaches. She reads aloud to the children every day something "too good to miss" (9). And, like any other truly professional person in a field that is moving rather than static, she reads professional books and magazines for new insights into her work.

The Teacher as a Reader of Adult Literature

Most adults think of themselves as fast or slow readers, as readers who like this and don't like that, as readers who go to the dictionary or just figure it out when they come to a word they do not recognize. This is what remains of the fine public or private school education they had. Perhaps this is your case, too. If it is, you should do something about it right away. For a good reader today is taught to read rapidly for some purposes in some kinds of material, and slowly for other purposes in other kinds of material. He is led to discover that many kinds of literature offer many kinds of value worth his time. And he is made conscious of the variety of skills at his command, not only for the solution of the form of a strange word, but for the understanding of the interrelationships among words, sentences, paragraphs, and larger compositional units, for there are depths beneath the surface meaning of all material worth reading (216).

As he would use a saw, a chisel, or a hammer for different tasks in carpentry, so he selects his tools, his techniques, for achieving certain ends in understanding what he reads. When he becomes a skillful carpenter, he selects his tools less consciously. Still, if anyone should ask him, he could say, "Why, I'm using the saw because . . . ," and give a good reason. So with reading. He can tell you what his purpose is, what he is looking for, and how he is reading to obtain it.

Can you? If you can't, then you should know the many opportunities available to the adult who would improve his reading. For one thing, your educational television station may be offering a course in the improvement of reading for adults. This may give you a way to begin, and it has the advantage of appearing regularly and, in this sense, demanding your continued effort. (It is so easy to procrastinate.) The college or university in which you are taking this present course in the teaching of reading probably has a clinic or a reading laboratory which you can attend at odd hours or in the summer. The adult education program offered by your public schools may have a night course for adults which would suit your purpose.

Whether you do or do not engage in one of the courses suggested above, you can help yourself at home. You may instruct yourself through materials like those in Dr. Selma Herr's *Effective reading for adults* (127). Many people responsible for reading-improvement programs for college students have produced materials on which they can practice the various skills to be mastered. Examples of these are *Effective reading and learning* by Phillip B. Shaw (225), *Power and speed in reading* by Doris Wilcox Gilbert (104), and *The art of efficient reading* by George D. Spache and Paul C. Berg (237). Books such as these not only offer practice materials but give careful instructions in the way they are to be used for different reading purposes.

Or, if you are genuinely gloomy about the level of reading at which you suspect you have ceased to develop, you might start with a text from the high-school level, such as the series of three books by Nila Banton Smith entitled *Be a better reader* (228). Your university or board-of-education librarian can help you locate the material you would find most suitable to your present level of skills. Work on your problem for a short time every day. Doing something each day is better than trying to take the treatment in large, spasmodic gulps.

Far from being embarrassed about the need to improve your reading skill, you should realize that there isn't a healthy adult alive who could not improve his reading in one or more respects, and who, even though he may have had good teaching, has not allowed some of his skills to rust out from disuse. We remember how to subtract because we are always making purchases, but most of us have forgotten square root. We avoid trying to solve problems that involve it. Likewise, we have kept fresh certain skills which we apply habitually to the limited types of reading we do, but have lost those which we have neglected. Our reading habits are limited by these deficiencies. And many of these skills are far more useful than being able to take square roots!

Of course, it is easy enough to think that all this does not apply to you. You have "gotten along" in college, or you "have had" a remedial-reading course. This is a bit like saying, "They pulled me in with a rope. Why should I learn how to swim?" Or, "I've already had the flu once. This can't be it again." You may be perfectly right. But it might be worth your while to look over the following list of skills involved in reading—a list such as that frequently found in the index of a teacher's manual—just to see whether you feel informed and competent in each of these respects:

Word Meaning Through Knowledge of:

picture clues	related words
context clues	abstract meanings
figures of speech	enriched word meanings ("home")
idioms	synonyms
colloquialisms	definitions
multiple meanings	analogous words
homonyms (Do you need to consult the dictionary?)	connotation
	denotation
antonyms	effect of accent on word meanings

Word-Form Analysis Through Knowledge of:

consonants	contractions
consonant blends	how letter position affects accent
consonant digraphs (See dictionary again?)	plural forms
vowels	variant endings of verbs
vowel digraphs	adjective and adverb endings
vowel diphthongs	prefixes
phonograms	suffixes
compound words	stems or roots
hyphenated words	syllables
possessives	rules governing the above

Comprehension and Interpretation Through Observation of:

phrase meaning (including imagery, vividness, point of view, repetition as style technique, onomatopoeia, cadence, rhythm, stress by word order, phrasing; interpretation of colloquialism, idiomatic expressions, sentence fragments)
sentence meaning (including depth of comprehension)
main ideas (paragraph, section, chapter, story, or book)
details or facts
sequence
organization
manner of presentation of ideas
contrast
comparison

cause and effect
relevance or irrelevance
bases for evaluation or judgment of ideas, interpretation, organization, and
    author purpose
implications beneath surface facts

Study Skills Applied in:

card catalogue
table of contents
telephone book
encyclopedia
textbook
dictionary (alphabetical order, general location, guide words, base word as
    entry, pronunciation, derivation, part of speech, meanings, use of different
    dictionaries with different pronunciation keys)

index	maps
time tables	graphs
menus	charts
radio, TV, schedules	diagrams
posters for information	directions

signs
adjusting method of reading to purpose
adjusting method of reading to material
choosing topic for a report
selecting facts from material
taking notes
classifying material
outlining and planning report
making pictorial representations of data

Oral-Reading Skills Development Through:

setting standards
evaluating
noting effect of punctuation
studying stress appropriate to meaning
using breath control to accommodate phrases
altering voice for different characters, moods, and meanings
adjusting speed to the audience and subject matter
projecting and modulating voice to room conditions

Maintaining contact with adult literature

In their monograph, *Maturity in reading,* Gray and Rogers (114)
describe the mature reader as a person with catholicity of taste—a person
who reads a wide variety of material on diverse subjects in many kinds of
literature. He does not shun outer space to confine himself to the English
or American novel. He does not ignore drama just because he prefers the
essay or short-story form. Seldom if ever would he be caught thinking or
saying, "I *NEVER* read anything like *THAT.*"

Gray and Rogers go on to say that the mature reader is one who does have certain deep interests or preferences in reading, so that while he roams widely, he also goes deeply into one or two areas. Perhaps he reads everything he can find on photography; or perhaps it is American history. He devours far more difficult materials in this subject than he can stomach in the others, simply because he knows a great deal about it.

Further, Gray and Rogers determined that the mature reader does not read merely from force of habit, from a sense of duty, or to kill time, but for a variety of purposes related to personal growth. These are: to know and understand current happenings, for immediate personal satisfaction or value, to meet practical demands in daily living, to further avocational interests, to carry on and promote professional or vocational interests, to meet personal-social demands, to meet socio-civic needs and demands for self-development or improvement, including extension of cultural background, to satisfy strictly intellectual demands, and to satisfy spiritual needs (114).

A mature reader adjusts his method of reading both to the material in question and to his own purposes in reading it. For instance, he would sense that the first paragraph under the topic "Maintaining Contact with Adult Literature," which you have just read, contains one simple idea in the first sentence and elaborates it throughout the rest of the paragraph. If he understands the phrase "catholicity of taste," he doesn't have to read the rest of the paragraph. The same, he notes, is true of the second paragraph. But the third paragraph demands more careful reading, for it is packed with descriptive abstractions. The reader must think carefully what the practical meaning of "to know and understand current happenings" is, and must think what portions of his own reading would come under this classification. For the first two paragraphs he can read rapidly and actually skip sentences which merely illustrate what he already understands (provided he does understand); for the third his pace must be slow, probably with a pause after each phrase which describes a kind of purpose, while he thinks of its implications.

The mature reader will at times read "light" material but frequently challenges his ability with books and magazines which are intellectually demanding and rich in idea. For example, Gray and Rogers classify Selinko's *Desiree* as relatively light, G. B. Shaw's *Nine plays* as relatively challenging; *Life* and *Redbook* as relatively light magazines, the *Philosophical Review* and *American Political Science Review* as relatively demanding.

If one were to design a better reading program for himself as an adult, he might start by thinking through the variety of his reading purposes and the distinction between challenging and light literature. His reading of books would not be confined to book club choices or his neighbor's insistence. His magazine subscription list would be tailored to satisfy specific purposes rather than governed by what he can get at the bargain rate of three magazines for the price of two, if you sign now and help put the fellow who just interrupted your nap through college. He would think before he bought books; think with the book reviewer of his local newspaper, with the reviewers in a discriminating magazine such as *The Saturday Review,* with a bookstore proprietor who has discriminating taste and really knows his own stock. On the basis of these suggestions and the goals he sets himself as a reader, he would then make his choices.

The mature reader also knows that his experiences in a real sense become a part of him. If he reads mostly "cheap stuff," he can become mostly cheap. And so he finds himself looking for the worthy idea, for the author whose mind is worth associating with during many hours of a long lifetime. And just as he would prefer to see a great play by a distinguished company, so he seeks out the author whose style is equal to the idea. Let us set two poems side by side to illustrate this point, and read them to determine which is the more worthy in style and idea.

Now hills retreat in amethyst;
Peaked Sargent wears a cap of mist.
The sun has found a far white spire
And touched the tip to pagan fire.
In port the sea-turned windows twinkle
Like specks of mica. Lax sails wrinkle
As boats put in. Kelp ruddy shines
To mark the tide's last boundary lines.
In tattered ranks that storm the land
Dark on their point the spruces stand.
Gleaming as shells that shine through foam
Sunset is taking the sea-gulls home.

There is a bowling alley
   Away up in the sky,
Where every day it's plain to see
   A bowling ball roll by.

It glides without a waiver,
   And strikes with fearful might.
Oh, you should see the friction
   As it knocks them out of
   sight.

In the first poem (85)[1] we see the evening haze, the sunset coloring the windows, hills, and steeple; against the sunset the darkness of spruces and the bright light catching the wave tips on the water; sea-gulls black against the sky or rosy in the light (this we must see for ourselves). To assist our imagery the poet suggests retreat, a cap, fire, mica, an army (tattered ranks), shells. The poem gives the impression of the quiet of evening— little activity (sails wrinkle) except for the evidence of foam (which may have been made by the boats putting in). The atmosphere of quiet and peace in the scene is enhanced by the way the poet runs the sentences from one line into the next (Lax sails . . . Kelp ruddy . . .). The numerous *s*, *t*, and *l* sounds add to the feeling of hush.

The second poem likens the sun to a bowling ball—a ponderous, rumbling, wobbling bowling ball. Along with the bowling ball, in the reader's imagination, come the bowling alley, the cheering section, the smell of beer, the boys having a big time on their one night out. The streaks of colored

---

[1] "This afternoon" by Rachel Field, from *Poems.* Copyright 1934 by the Macmillan Company and used with their permission.

clouds at sunset, the bright rays of the sun, are likened to the tenpins, scattering after the strike. Those clonky, bobbling tenpins! The rhythm of the poem is full of pauses at the end of almost every line, making it impossible for the bowling ball to "glide without a waiver." This uncelestial comparison, then, is not only inappropriate to the subject but poorly sustained by the rhythm. There is a poverty of ideas. And we are happy to inform you that while the author of the first poem is Rachel Field, the author of the second is wise enough to make his living out of something else. Like textbooks.

Two contrasting pieces of prose will further illuminate the differences between well-expressed and poorly expressed ideas (129):

At length we erupted from the gorge. The limestone formations fell away, and we moved all at once into a region of plutonic rocks. In a valley nearly a mile wide huge boulders of gneiss and granite, larger by far than our junk, lay strewn about, and straight across the line of the river, relenting only enough to grant it a shallow channel, curious dykes of greenstone and porphyry rose up out of the other stone. It was a primeval landscape, and it seemed to have been arranged by some force of fury. I was deeply moved and humbled by the sight of the trackers scrambling like tiny, purposeful crickets over the rough and intractable banks. We were all hopeless insects in this setting.

Finally we came out of mountain country into a valley. The walls of the channel dropped away, and on either side we could see flat country strewn with great boulders. They were immense, and lying almost anywhere. They even blocked the river in spots, forcing us to pass around them. There was no sign of man here—only the violence of Nature. The sight made me feel very strange. The men who guided our boat from the banks looked pretty small in this country of great boulders. It was a place where people didn't seem to amount to much.

What principles of effective writing can be drawn from these passages?[2]
1. *Vividness.* The first passage, by John Hersey,[3] makes you feel that "you were there." Details have been selected to assist your imagery. The second passage might be about any one of many rivers; you could never tell which one.
2. *Suggestion.* Look at the first sentences in each passage. "We erupted" versus "we came." "Came" suggests nothing; it simply proclaims movement. "Erupted" suggests the suddenness with which the landscape changed. Further on, the word "relenting" suggests almost an evil intent of Nature toward man.
3. *Appropriate tone of mood.* In effective writing, a mood or tone is consistent and is clearly established. In the first passage, contrast of size ("larger by far," "tiny, purposeful crickets"), suggestion of strangeness

[2] One of the authors is indebted to Dr. Dora V. Smith for introduction to this type of analysis thirty years ago at the University of Minnesota.
[3] John Hersey, *A single pebble.* New York: Alfred A. Knopf, 1956, 15.

("curious," "primeval," "some force of fury"), support the mood of hope-less insignificance which the writer felt. The second passage offers only a vague "made me feel very strange" and "people didn't seem to amount to much." It offers no contrast between the size of the junk and that of the boulders.

4. *Uniqueness of expression.* The elements of vividness, suggestion, and creation of tone or mood are assisted by uniqueness of expression. If the author had said he was "scared out of his wits," that his way was full of "trials and tribulations," and that the sight "really sent" him, he would be using borrowed expressions from millions of tongues. "Some force of fury" is John Hersey's unique way of saying "violence of Nature," which is a common expression. It is unique because he thought carefully and said what *he* meant. "Pretty small" is a trite substitute for "tiny, purposeful crickets."

5. *Appropriate structure: clear, varied, forceful, suitable.* If Hersey had said, "At length, erupting from the gorge, the limestone formations fell away from us," he would have clouded his meaning; the limestone forma-tions weren't what erupted. If he had said, "I was deeply moved and humbled by the sight of the trackers," and had stopped his sentence there, the reader would not have known what about the trackers moved and humbled him. Hersey wrote with structural clarity.

Unless monotony is one of the impressions which the author is trying to convey, it should not be a mark of the author's sentence structure. Clearly, monotony is not true of the change of scenery recorded in this paragraph, and accordingly its sentences are varied in structure. Look at the variety in sentence beginnings, just for an example. Look at the third sentence in the first passage. It is a far cry from what it might have been: "The valley was nearly a mile wide. Big boulders lay in it. They were bigger than our junk. They lay all about, etc."

Hersey hit the reader with his philosophy in his last sentence. He could have dulled his point had he cluttered his final sentence with a trail of reasons: "We were all hopeless insects in this setting, I thought as I was deeply moved and humbled by the sight of the trackers scrambling like tiny, purposeful crickets over the rough and intractable banks." The Hersey structure was the more forceful. Further, it had a pleasing movement or rhythm.

Suitability of structure is achieved if the structure itself, whether it be that of a sentence, paragraph, chapter, or whole composition, reflects the subject matter and serves it efficiently. Hersey's paragraph proceeds from the gorge into the valley, and the sequence of observations culminates in the conclusions of the viewer. The reader feels that he has passed that way, too, and has arrived at the same philosophy that moves the author. Also, the third sentence particularly gives the reader a sense of the complexity of the scene and the mingling of the author's feelings with it, by the very

interweaving of modifying phrases. The "interrupters" are true to the interruption of the landscape by the randomly deposited boulders. In contrast,
a sentence about a smoothly flowing river would flow smoothly in its own
movement. The very rhythm of the phrases would suggest the movement of
the river.

6. *Appropriate choice of words: meaning, sound, rhythm.* In effective
writing the words provide exactness of meaning, and frequently convey
meaning through their sound. As the author of the first passage describes
the boulders, his sentences are filled with short, hard words—words that
sound like rocks—words that have the force of *g*'s, *d*'s. Later on, as he
describes relatively ineffectual man, his words have the lightness and pat-
tering quality of the idea: *t*'s and *s*'s are prevalent; words like "scrambling"
make light of the "insect" activities. The second passage shows no distinction in the selection of words. It might all be about Pablum!

7. *Sincerity.* The first passage gives the reader the impression that the
writer has had an unforgettable experience, the details of which remain
vividly with him. The writer's description justifies the mood he claims to
feel. The second passage gives no hint of the impressiveness of the scenery
until the last three sentences. Then the author makes a vague and relatively
shallow comment. How much depth and sincerity lie behind his words is
left in doubt.

8. *Truth to life.* In effective writing, characters talk and act like real
people; they are neither one-sided nor perfect. When one character is
speaking, you know that these are words he would say; that they are
distinctly not the style or thought of another. Situations and events in well
developed literature are also believable; so much so that the reader may
say to himself, "Yes, I've had this same feeling; this is the way it is."
Reading John Hersey's passage, even one who had not traveled in China
would know that, yes, Nature can be that wild, that overpowering. The
reader has felt just as helpless in a storm, an earthquake, a flood. Even if
his worst experience has been sweeping up the autumn leaves in a wind-
storm, he knows something of the author's meaning and says, "Yes, this is
true to my experience; it is life."

9. *Economy.* Notice how many images the reader receives from the
Hersey passage as compared with those of the cold record. Like the
"bowling alley" poem, the coldly recorded passage wastes the reader's time
with unrevealing verbiage. Economy in the use of language to create a
given impression is the mark of good prose or poetry.

10. *Depth.* Important literature has its deepest meaning below the surface. It deals with values and truth—important for civilized men to contemplate. The second passage makes the reader feel that man just hadn't begun
to operate in that part of the world yet. Wait till the bulldozers come. But
the first passage is permeated with the idea that there are some situations
in which man is a hopeless insect, "period." It suggests to the reader the

hopeless side of all man's endeavors, the greatness of the odds against him.

Perhaps a more helpful example of this quality of depth is an old Chinese proverb: "You cannot draw white cloth from a dyeing vat." Why should such a saying have survived for many generations among many Chinese, all of whom have not been in the dyeing business? Obviously, it has survived because of the additional meanings it has in many life situations. It is the general truth that environment has a profound effect. It is hard to believe that some people can read that proverb without getting the "depth" meaning, but it is true that this happens. They needed good teachers.

These, then, are some of the attributes the mature reader, who has developed taste as well as skill, savors in good literature. If you as a reader are aware of them, and you as a teacher learn ways of transmitting that awareness to the children and young people you teach, perhaps some day we shall be producing readers whose taste matches their reading skill (223, pp. 201-202).

The Teacher as a Selector of Children's Literature

As a teacher you are expected to "keep up" with children's books. You need to know what books are available for children's reference work, what books deal with ideas which interest children, what books are easy enough for them to read, what books they might read during vacations, what books their relatives might give them on their birthdays and at Christmas. (See Chapter on Reading Interests.) Graded book lists are a tremendous help in this task, but a question they do not always answer is the question of quality. Yes, this book is easy; yes, it is about dinosaurs. But is it worth living with? Is it good literature?

You can't always ask a librarian. (You were about to say that, weren't you?) Sometimes a child brings in a book for you to read to the class. Should you take much class time for it or shouldn't you? Sometimes you find in a bookstore a new book that would be timely. What is *your* answer to the question of quality?

Adults tolerate a great many sordid and depraved characters in their own reading, but they are pretty fussy about the values presented in children's books. If there is one issue more than others upon which librarians and specialists in children's literature often disagree, it is on whether a particular book gives children a proper view of the world. It isn't just truth to life that bothers them; it's the *kind* of life, the attitude toward life the book encourages. E. B. White's *Stuart Little* was a book which stirred controversy. Abhorred by some squeamish souls as a book reflecting abnormalities of birth, it was described enthusiastically by others as portraying a mouse with the best of warm, human qualities. Sometimes this kind of disagreement is merely evidence that the reader has missed the point and spirit of the book; sometimes, on the other hand, it reflects the awareness of some readers of a basic difference between the values of the author and those cherished by certain readers.

Though this is a controversial area, it is one in which the teacher should develop sensitivity and judgment. Perhaps the librarians and literary critics can be left to disagree over subtleties; but teachers should certainly feel responsible for distinguishing between the obviously unsuitable and that which, though unusual, by this very quality gives a lift to the imagination.

Examples of unsuitable material can be found at all levels of children's books, and in all types. In the scramble to produce easy books for children—books that would *appeal*—some authors have stooped to the most uncivilized impulses. While all the rest of the world is urging the child to conform, these authors are saying, "Go ahead and kick something." Or, they say, "If somebody does something mean to you, you can be just as mean." Or, they say, "If somebody misbehaves, paint him green and never have anything to do with him again." They deal with a world of "I will," "You won't," a world of meanness and retaliation in kind.

Contrast with such books the spirit of a book like Minarik's *Little bear*, in which a mother's patience reflects her love, or a book like McClintock's *A fly went by*, which says in effect, "Sometimes we get all worked up over things just because we don't understand them." These books are worth listening to; their authors help bring color into life, or a constructive philosophy. They add to living. They have something to offer to adults as well as to children, to the imaginative of all ages.

You ask, "Are some of the same elements of good writing which we noted in adult literature present in children's literature?" Let us see.

1. *Vividness.* In *Angus and the ducks,* Marjorie Flacks says, "Away the ducks scuttled and Angus lapped the cool clear water." She could have said, "The ducks ran away and Angus drank the water." But "scuttle" describes a rapid and somewhat noisy get-away, "lapped" makes us see and hear the tongue as it scoops up the water, and "cool, clear" suggests what a satisfying drink it must have been.

2. *Suggestion.* At the end of her story, when Angus has been pursued by angry, hissing ducks, and finally escapes into the house, she writes, "For exactly three minutes by the clock, Angus was not curious about anything at all." An inferior author might have written: "Angus was terribly frightened but soon forgot all about it." The skillful writer plants a little seed and lets the reader grow it.

3. *Tone or mood.* Joseph Jacobs retells the story of Dick Whittington with this introduction:

In the reign of the famous King Edward III, there was a little boy called Dick Whittington, whose father and mother died when he was very young. Since poor Dick was not old enough to work, he was very badly off; he got but little for his dinner, and sometimes nothing at all for his breakfast . . .

By the end of the first paragraph, Mr. Jacobs has worked up the reader's sympathy for the plight of "poor Dick." The reader feels at once that the situation is distressing and has half formed the question: "But can't he get somewhere even after a bad start like that?"

In *Pinocchio,* Carlo Collodi tells the reader that the old carpenter was about to make a table leg out of an old piece of wood, and had raised his axe to strike it, when a voice implored, "Do not strike me so hard!" Thus the reader is alerted to the fanciful nature of the story and is not disappointed from that point on.

In *The passing of the buffalo,* Donald Culross Peattie expresses consistently his appreciation for the place of the buffalo in pioneer days in the western United States. His sympathies are clear throughout. "To any American," he concludes, "Old Man Buffalo is a prized fellow citizen, and the memory of his former greatness will quicken our pulses, as long as bunch-grass grows and the west wind blows and a single horn is still turned up in the furrows of a prairie plowing." (Note the sound and rhythm of this style.)

4. *Uniqueness of expression.* Friends of Beatrix Potter's *Peter Rabbit* will always enjoy rereading, "but his sobs were overheard by some friendly sparrows, who flew to him in great excitement, and implored him to exert himself." A lesser writer might have said, "Some sparrows heard him crying and flew up and said, 'Get a move on, Buddie, or the jig's up.' "

In *Three kings, Uncle Herman's uniform,* and *Christmas night,* Ludwig Bemelmans describes the church decorated for Christmas: "It smelled like a cool forest at noontime when the sun shines through the tall pines." Again, he describes the sound of kettledrums: "It was a lovely warm sound that made Hansi feel hollow inside." How would you have said these things to make them uniquely yours?

5. *Structure: clear, varied, forceful, suitable.* In *Little pear,* Eleanor Lattimore divides a sentence neatly into three parts to show the three views she wishes her readers to grasp: "All around the village were flat fields of cabbages and beans and onions, and far away on one side was a great highway that led to the city, and far away on the other side was a river."

While variety is usually just as important in children's literature as in adult literature, sometimes repetition is cultivated for a special purpose. Rudyard Kipling made repeated references to the Elephant's Child's 'satiable curiosity, thus providing a unifying element to a series of events. In many of the old folk and fairy tales, events or characters come in threes, and the reader ticks them off appreciatively, feeling that the charm lies in the number three. In *A fly went by,* Mike McClintock achieves variety *in* repetition when he reiterates the flight of the frightened animals:

> The fly ran away
> In fear of the frog,

Who ran from the cat,
Who ran from the dog.
The dog ran away
In fear of the pig,
Who ran from the cow.
She was so big!

Forceful structure is well illustrated in the clout Big Claus gave Little Claus's horse, according to Hans Christian Andersen: "I'll gee up your horses for you!' said Big Claus, and he took the mallet for the tetherpeg, and gave Little Claus's one horse such a clump on the forehead that it fell down stone dead." Notice how that sentence falls down stone dead, just at the end when it should.

As for suitability of structure, watch and listen to the rhythm of this sentence which follows Little Pear's glance down to the sea: "He loved to stand on the high bank and look down on the swift muddy river and the ships sailing down it toward the sea." Note how the long *i* in *high* makes you pause on the bank. Then, from that point the rhythm yields a cascading effect. In *The Cyclops,* as retold by Charles Lamb, Ulysses' men were beaten in battle, and the few survivors returned to the ship with mixed feelings—sad for their defeat and their lost companions, but glad to be alive at all. This mixture of feeling, this interruption of sadness by gladness, is expressed in the very pattern of the sentence used to describe it: "Thence they set sail, sad at heart, yet something cheered that, with such fearful odds against them, they had not all been utterly destroyed."

6. *Appropriate choice of words.* Kenneth Grahame has the mole digging in *The wind in the willows:* "So he scraped and scratched and scrabbled and scrooged, and then he scrooged again and scrabbled and scratched and scraped . . ." Carl Sandburg tells about Pony Pony Huckabuck's squash: "In one corner of the corn crib, all covered over with pop corn, he had a secret, a big, round squash, a fat yellow squash, a rich squash all spotted with spots of gold." In *Whiskers* by Joel Stolper, the jungle is well described for those who may never actually see one: "Bamboo shoots rose stiff and straight near a clump of giant ferns, and the twisted stems of great climbing vines swooped down in long loops from tree to tree. Underfoot, the fallen leaves of a thousand seasons made a soundless, many-layered carpet for all the wild feet of the jungle."

7. *Sincerity.* In *The ugly duckling,* Hans Christian Andersen shows great understanding of human feelings, some amusement at human frailty, and concern over the tendency to condemn the one who is different. Repeatedly in little touches throughout the story one can see evidence that these understandings and attitudes of his are no veneer or temporary posture but an abiding characteristic. The mother duck tires of sitting on the eggs and wonders why no one comes to see her. As the strangeness of her ugly one becomes the talk of the community, she, with all of her own mis-

givings, becomes defensive. When the hen says to the duckling, "Well, if we don't understand you, I should like to know who would," the author is insisting on making the most of pain and provinciality. In the end, "He was too, too happy, but not a bit proud, for a good heart is never proud." The author is clearly telling his reader something he thinks he'd better begin to know.

8. *Truth to life.* Certainly the behaviors of the mother duck and the hen in *The ugly duckling* fit this category, even though not all of us turn into swans.

9. *Economy.* Andersen could have written an essay on the hen's attitude, but he condensed it into one sentence.

10. *Depth.* Certainly, again, the ugly duckling's story is an appropriate example. Superficially, an ugly duckling turns out to be a swan. More deeply, when we let appearances determine our attitudes, we are no better than the occupants of a barnyard. Still more deeply, how thoughtlessly we inflict unnecessary pain upon the unfortunate or different. These are only a few of the many implications which the thoughtful reader can draw from the work of as perceptive and wise a writer as Hans Christian Andersen.

So the answer is yes, children's literature of superior quality does offer values similar to those found in the best adult literature. One kind of story may serve to illustrate only one value. Another may illustrate several values. The teacher must learn to look for these values, recognize them, and use them as a basis for the selection of materials for reading.

The Teacher as an Oral Reader

For a little time each day, the teacher at every grade level should read aloud to the children something worth everyone's time. In this way she can keep alive the incentive to do better, in those who feel discouraged over their difficulties with the mechanics of reading. This is one way in which she can bring to children of limited skills the ideas for which they are very much ready. This is the way she can make children aware of the contribution of sound and cadence to the meaning of the well-formed English sentence. Through her reading, children satisfied with mediocre writing will have their ears tuned to a difference.

The first requirement is that the teacher be a person who really appreciates the material she is reading. The second is that she know her class well enough to choose something not only well-written but appealing to the children and perhaps even appropriate in some special sense, to the day or season or mood. The third is that she make a selection carefully on the basis of her own judgment and that of qualified critics. The fourth is that she be able to read well aloud.

Of course, real appreciation is a good beginning for effective oral reading; but it is not enough. There are ways of perfecting oral reading beyond the point of mere accuracy. Recordings of able story tellers and readers can provide much good listening education for the teacher. Educational TV programs often present people who read or tell stories to children. These examples of good expression are helpful in setting standards for what the teacher may hope to do herself. Making tape recordings of oneself in solitude and then (also in solitude!) listening to one's own voice reading can make the reader aware of such faults as a strained, or too highly pitched voice, improper phrasing, and monotony. When the teacher comes to the actual reading in class, she needs to watch her audience carefully, through frequent glances, to see whether the attention and understanding she hopes for are really hers. She should analyze failures, weighing every possible contributing factor, rather than take the easy attitude of dismissing it all: "Well, it just didn't go over this time."

The Teacher as a Reader of Professional Literature

There are several reasons why a teacher of reading should know how to read and interpret research reports in this field. The good teacher in any area is the well-informed teacher.

1. *Parent questions.* Parents are exposed to news reports, speeches, pamphlets, and books which declare with positiveness what is wrong with the current teaching of reading. So the parent asks why the alphabet is not taught early in the first grade, or why phonics are not taught early and thoroughly since this method is alleged to be fundamental and a "sure-fire" technique for learning to recognize words. Experimental reports of scientific investigations provide the teacher with answers to these questions and many others that the parent may ask. The alert teacher who has read the reports with *understanding* will be able to answer these questions and to justify the methods she is using, provided her instructional procedures are both up to date and well organized.

2. *Participation in research programs.* In many school systems the teachers will have occasion to participate in controlled experiments on teaching methods. If a teacher, through acquaintance with professional literature, knows how an experiment is designed and how data are to be interpreted, she will be better qualified to participate effectively in such investigations.

3. *New contributions.* Each year many scientific studies of one or another aspect of reading are published in journals available to most teachers. To find out what is new in her profession, based upon evidence from scientific studies, the teacher will want to know how to read and interpret these reports. She then has facts to go on, rather than opinions.

4. *Professional advancement.* Every person who takes his profession seriously looks forward to making progress in his chosen work. To achieve this a teacher must know among other things how to read and evaluate the

literature in her field. If teaching is to be regarded as a profession equal in status to such professions as medicine and law, teachers must keep themselves well informed through consulting professional literature of education, as are the doctors when they study up-to-the-minute medical reports and lawyers, important case abstracts.

5. *In-service training.* In many school systems, in-service study groups are fairly common. The teacher who knows how to interpret materials reported in journals can become a leader in such groups.

6. *Speeches.* Occasionally a teacher may be asked to give a talk on some aspect of reading instruction. If she is up to date on new scientific contributions, she can sift facts from opinions, and important principles from trivial ones, when she prepares what she has to say.

The design of a research report

An experiment is a planned procedure to be followed in testing the correctness of a *hypothesis.* A hypothesis is a hunch, a tentative but unconfirmed supposition concerning the relation between conditions set up by the experimenter (such as two methods of teaching) which are as alike as possible except in one respect, and the responses of the subjects (i.e., that children will learn better with one method than with the other). The statement of the *purpose* of the experiment tells how the hypothesis is to be tested. Often, as in the experiment given below, only the purpose is stated.

The organization or design of a scientific study and the report of the research follow the same general outline: (1) *The purpose or problem.* The investigator has a question which he wants answered. The statement of the purpose defines the problem to be studied. Sometimes the investigator reviews a previously reported study or studies to show the need for additional experimentation and then states his purpose. (2) *The design of the research.* This next step describes the plan or organization of the experimental procedures, i.e., how the experiment was conducted. (3) *Analysis of the data.* The data, having been collected according to plan, are treated with appropriate techniques such as statistical computations, summarization of verbal reports, and organization of the findings in tables and figures. (4) *Conclusions.* In this section of the report, the author sometimes summarizes the findings revealed by analyses of the data. Then he states the conclusions *justified* by the findings. These conclusions or generalizations bring out significant relationships and should answer the questions raised in the original statement of purpose.

An illustrative experiment

Read the following scientific report and try to identify each of the four parts. Note what each part contributes:

The Roseville Experiment with Individualized Reading

Harry W. Sartain[4]

The purpose of the experiment was to determine whether second-grade groups would make greater progress in reading skills when taught for three months by the method of individualized self-selection or when taught for an equivalent period by the method of ability grouping using basic readers plus a variety of supplementary books.

The experimental samples were ten classes of second-grade children attending six public schools in Roseville, Minnesota, a St. Paul suburb. In the fall of 1958 there were 660 second-grade pupils enrolled, and the median I.Q. on the Lorge-Thorndike Test administered seven months earlier was 114. The ten classes were randomly chosen from among those of teachers who expressed an interest in the study. Except for one beginner all of the teachers had had experience with group instruction and with a supplementary reading program utilizing the self-selection techniques. They prepared for the experiment by studying carefully the best references on the individualized method.

Procedure. The first week of the 1958-59 school term was a "warm-up" period in which the children read various stories in several readers to become refreshed in their reading skills. The teachers studied the children and tentatively grouped them for purposes of testing and later experimental work.

At the beginning of the second week of school the children who were classified as the "slower" group in each class were given Form 2 of the Gates Primary Tests of Word Recognition and Paragraph Reading. The average and faster students were tested with Form 2 of the Gates Advanced Primary Tests. All of the pupils were examined with the Word Elements section and the Letter Sounds section of the Developmental Reading Tests by Bond and others.

Five of the ten classes were randomly chosen to participate in the individualized self-selection program for the first three months of the study, while the other five classes were taught in three or four ability groups per room, using basic readers and supplementary books. This instruction began on September 9 and continued for fifty-six school days until December 1. The teachers scheduled approximately two hours and twenty minutes daily for reading work, with the time divided between morning and afternoon periods.

On December 3 a new period of teaching was begun. The classes that had used the individualized method first were now taught with basic readers in ability groups. Those that had been working in ability groups switched to the individualized plan. Instruction was continued for another fifty-six school days, through March 9, 1959. On December 2 and again on March 10 different forms of the Gates tests and the same forms of the Word Elements and the Letter Sounds tests were administered. Complete data were obtained for 171 pupils in the average and better groups and for 63 pupils in the lower groups.

The Individualized Program

More than one hundred different books were available in each of the classrooms at all times. Copies of the basic textbooks for all common reading series were provided, and every room had a library corner stocked with a wide variety of literary materials ranging in difficulty from pre-primer to fifth-grade level.

[4] Reprinted with permission of the editor and author, from *The Reading Teacher*, April, 1960, Vol. 13, pp. 277-281. The whole article is reproduced, minus footnotes.

Also the county bookmobile brought a box of thirty-five different books to each room every month.

Each child was aided in selecting the books which were most interesting and suitable for him, and he read at his own rate. Skills and oral reading were taught during conferences between the teacher and individual children, with conferences scheduled for approximately ten minutes twice a week. Small groups were occasionally called together to learn a skill needed by all.

Frequent sharing experiences included oral reading, telling about fascinating incidents, dramatizing, illustrating stories, "auctioning" books by exciting hints, writing descriptions of characters, showing action on a flannel board, making puppets, exhibiting objects described, making taped summaries, demonstrating experiments of story characters, nominating a "book of the week," explaining foreign words encountered, and innumerable other activities. All pupils kept detailed records of books read by using individual booklets, illustrated folders, etc. Teachers made adaptations in the individualized approach as required.

Enriched Basic Reading

During the alternate three-month periods the teachers divided every class into three or more ability groups. Each group read in a different basic textbook of suitable difficulty. The teachers' manuals were consulted daily for a thorough, sequential program of skills. Basic workbooks and various work-sheets were utilized in all groups to reinforce skills lessons.

In addition, a vigorous program of extension reading was undertaken. All of the books mentioned previously were grouped attractively on shelves, and after finishing their reading seat-work, the children were encouraged to read extensively in books of their own choosing. Occasional brief sharing periods were scheduled; pupils shared books in many of the same ways that were described in connection with the individualized method.

The Teachers' Observations

Before the data were summarized, the teachers listed the observations upon which they were agreed.

Strengths of the methods of individualized self-selection. (1) Individual conferences provide a valuable personal relationship with pupils. (2) Children are motivated to read more extensively. (3) There is a keen interest in sharing. (4) There is strong motivation for individual improvement. (5) Top readers are especially responsive.

Weaknesses of the individualized method. (1) All slow pupils and others who cannot work well independently become restless and tend to waste time. (2) There is no opportunity to teach new vocabulary and concepts needed before reading. (3) It is impossible to provide a systematic program of word attack skills. (4) It is exceedingly hard to identify pupils' difficulties in short infrequent conferences. (5) There is some doubt about the permanence of skills taught so briefly. (6) The method is inefficient because of the time required to teach skills to individuals instead of teaching groups who are progressing at a similar rate. (7) The conscientious teacher becomes frustrated in attempting to provide individual conferences for all of the pupils who need them each day.

Analysis of the Data

The data for the upper and middle groups were studied by a three-way analysis of variance. Because this showed that the gains achieved by the top and middle groups were not significantly different, the findings for these two groups were combined. The data for the lower groups were studied by a two-way analysis of variance and the effect of interaction was isolated.

The first comparison, incidental to the main purpose, was concerned with the differences in gains during the first three-month period and the second three-month period regardless of method. The findings are listed in Table 1.

On all tests except Advanced Word Recognition the groups made significantly greater gains during the first three months regardless of which method was employed. This finding offers a note of warning concerning the planning of other experiments in which all of the pupils are taught by one method at the beginning of the year and all are simultaneously subjected to another procedure later.

The second comparison was made between gains when the two different methods of teaching were employed. These findings are listed in Table 2.

In the first line one reads that the median gain of the more capable pupils in the ten classes under the individualized method was .46 of a year, with five classes following this method during the first three months and five using it for the second three months. The same groups made an identical gain during their three months of work under the basal reader group plan.

The differences obtained under the two methods at both levels on the Paragraph Reading tests and on the Visual Elements tests were not significant. However, the lower groups of pupils made an average gain of .35 year on the Word Recognition test under the individualized approach and .60 in ability groups. Both gains are remarkable for "slow" students, but it should be remembered that the average I.Q. for this grade was approximately 114 and mentally retarded pupils are not in the regular classes. Apparently the children made .25 of a year greater gain through basal reader instruction in ability groups than by the individualized method. This difference is significant at the .05 level ($F = 6.56$; with one degree of freedom $P < .05$). It could have occurred by chance only five times in one hundred.

A subjective study of the scores provides support for the belief that the individualized method is less profitable for teachers who have the least professional preparation and experience.

Conclusions

Combining the teachers' reactions with the statistical information, it was possible to reach several conclusions concerning the employment of the two methods in the second grades of this school district.

1. Obviously, second-grade children made greater progress during the first three months of the school year than during the second three months regardless of the method used.

2. Capable students made approximately the same gains in reading under both methods. Because of efficiency and the provision for readiness experiences and systematic skills instruction, the basic and supplementary reader method should be used as the backbone of the program for these pupils.

3. Because the slower pupils tended to make better gains in vocabulary when following the basic reader method, this method should be utilized for teaching them, also.

4. The individual conference procedure should be incorporated into the system of sharing and recording supplementary reading in each class because it provided strong motivation.

5. When capable children in a classroom have carefully completed the work

Table 1

Comparison of Group Means and Gains During First and
Second Three-Month Periods Regardless of Method

Test	Group	First Test Mean	Second Test Mean	Third Test Mean	Gain First 3 Months	Gain Second 3 Months	Difference
Gates Advanced Primary Word Recognition	Upper & Mid	2.81	3.27	3.74	.46	.47	.01
Gates Advanced Primary Paragraph Reading	Upper & Mid	2.63	3.63	4.25	1.00	.62	.38**
Gates Primary Word Recognition	Low	1.75	2.53	2.69	.78	.16	.62**
Gates Primary Paragraph Reading	Low	1.72	2.42	2.84	.70	.42	.28*
Visual Elements (Bond et al)	All Pupils	12.47	16.79	20.00	4.32	3.21	1.11**

* Significant at the .05 level.
** Significant at the .01 level.

The data from the Letter Sounds test were omitted because there were too many perfect scores.

Table 2

Group Means and Gains When Comparing Methods

Test	Group	Individualized Method			Basal Group Method			Difference Between Methods
		Pretest	Final Test	Gain	Pretest	Final Test	Gain	
Gates Advanced Primary Word Recognition	Upper & Mid	3.01	3.47	.46	3.08	3.54	.46	.00
Gates Advanced Primary Paragraph Reading	Upper & Mid	3.11	3.90	.79	3.15	3.98	.83	.04
Gates Primary Word Recognition	Low	2.24	2.59	.35	2.04	2.64	.60	.25*
Gates Primary Paragraph Reading	Low	2.14	2.62	.48	2.00	2.64	.64	.16
Visual Elements (Bond et al)	All Pupils	14.66	18.20	3.54	14.60	18.62	4.02	.48

* Significant at the .05 level.

for their grade in a basic reading series, they would profit from individualized reading for the remainder of the year.

6. Pupils in top reading groups may be able to master a thorough basic reading program if it is taught only during the morning reading periods each day with supplementary reading individualized in the afternoon.

In summary, because this study and others that have been carefully controlled show that the individualized method does not produce better reading gains than a strong basal program, there is no reason to forfeit the advantages of a well-planned basic system. Instead the benefits of the individual conferences should be obtained by their addition to the basic reader plan.

Did you, in studying this experiment, find the purpose stated in the first paragraph of description, the experimental design in the following 10 paragraphs, the treatment of the data in the next 9 paragraphs, and the conclusions at the end? State in your own words the hypothesis that was being tested in the experiment.

Experimental controls

If any two things, such as two methods of teaching reading, are to be compared scientifically, every condition in the experimental situation except the two methods must be the same. The children, the teachers, the length of time, the kinds of tests, etc. for the two groups must all be as nearly identical as possible.

An experiment is controlled observation. The term *variable* refers to any condition in a scientific investigation which may in any way affect the observations. And the behavior observed as the effect of the experimental conditions is also called a variable. Let us note some of the variables in the above experiment: (1) The variable whose effect we propose to study is called the *independent variable*. In Sartain's study the independent variable is methods of teaching. He is investigating the effect of varying the method of teaching on progress in learning to read. (2) All other variables (called *stimulus variables*) which may affect the responses we intend to observe (the resulting amount of learning) must be controlled, i.e., they are completely eliminated or else they are maintained in a constant state as far as any effects they may have on the learning (responses) are concerned. In Sartain's experiment, the following variables were controlled: (*a*) Motivation of the teachers: only those interested in the study were used. (*b*) Teaching experience: only teachers (with one exception) experienced in the methods of instruction employed participated in the experiment. In addition, all the teachers had studied procedures of the individualized method. (*c*) Bias of choice: the classes (with their teachers) to be used were *randomly* selected to avoid bias of choice that might otherwise creep in. (*d*) Practice effect: practice effects were equalized by having half of the classes (randomly selected) taught three months by Method I and then three months by Method II. The other classes reversed this sequence. Thus, when the methods are compared (Table 2), differences discovered cannot be contaminated by prior practice under one of the methods. (3) The responses (amount learned under the two methods of teaching) of the children constitute the *dependent variable*. That is, the experimenter tries to record any behavior or change of behavior due to the variation in the independent variable (in the present instance, method of teaching). In this way, one discovers any relationship that may exist between the independent variable (methods of teaching) and the dependent variable (amount learned).

Kinds of experimental design

Several different designs are employed in educational research. In the above study, a *comparative* design was used, i.e., the achievement under one method of teaching was compared with achievement under the other method.

The case study or clinical design. This method is used when an individual is studied in order to diagnose and treat a handicap such as a case of severe reading disability. This method consists mainly of verbal interviews, individual testing, and perhaps information from other sources such as the home life and data in a cumulative record. The case history based upon the data obtained provides information for diagnosis and plan for remedial treatment.

The control-group design. In this method, two equated groups of subjects are observed, each performing under the same conditions except for the influence of one factor. The presence or absence of this one specific factor represents the independent variable. The resulting difference in performance between the two groups is the dependent variable. We thus measure the effect of the independent variable upon the dependent variable.

It is important that the two groups possess equal potentialities to begin with. To assure this condition, the two groups are equated. Members of the group are selected so that all factors (as intelligence, level of achievement, sex, age) that might affect the results are equated, i.e., they are approximately the same in the two groups on the average. Or they are matched by pairs: for each person in one group, there is one in the other group with approximately the same score for each controlled variable. One group is termed the experimental group, the other the control group, whichever method of matching is employed. Difference of performance is revealed by comparing the scores of the experimental with those of the control group to discover the effect of the factor under investigation.

A study of Harrington and Durrell (121) illustrates this method of design. They studied the effect of each of four factors (phonics, mental age, auditory discrimination, and visual discrimination) upon reading achievement by matching (by pairs) the experimental group with the control group on three of these factors and creating a marked difference with respect to the fourth (experimental) factor. The difference on this fourth factor was the independent variable, the effect of which was being investigated.

The longitudinal design. Essentially, this method is one in which the performance or achievement of one, or more, groups is followed over a period of several years. If the study is to be comparative as well as longitudinal, the experimenter has two groups of subjects of approximately equal status whom he follows for a considerable period of time. (Sartain's study was comparative but not longitudinal). One group is exposed to one procedure (e.g., a method of teaching), and the other group to another (e.g., a different teaching method). This difference in experimental procedure is the independent variable. The same groups are studied for several years. The achievements of the two groups (dependent variable) are compared at periodic intervals and at the end of the experiment. Other factors (variables) are controlled. Sparks and Fay (238) employed this method to evaluate two methods of teaching reading. Actually, the longer a study continues, the more trustworthy are its findings. But it is difficult, as children become ill or transfer from school to school, to complete such a study unless the start was made with a very large population, and the records of those who drop out are discarded. Longitudinal studies are important because, often, short studies may favor a method while long studies may show its ultimate weakness.

The questionnaire design. Certain information can be obtained only by use of some form of questionnaire. Examples are: (1) the emphasis placed upon teaching the various techniques of word recognition in several school systems; (2) the kinds and amount of remedial teaching of reading in various school systems; (3) methods of school promotion in various parts of the country. A carefully constructed set of questions relevant to the problem is organized. This is printed or mimeographed and sent to the proper authorities or teachers. When the questionnaires are returned, the answers are tabulated and analysed. An example of the questionnaire is given by Dolch (64) in his self-survey of a school program for the teaching of reading.

Other designs. Several modifications of the above designs of research may be used. Some are different from the above. For an elementary discussion of scientific method and experimental procedures, see M. A. Tinker and W. A. Russell, *Introduction to methods in experimental psychology,* New York: Appleton-Century-Crofts, Inc., 1958, Chapter I.

Limitations of an Experiment

When a teacher reads the report of a scientific investigation, she should examine it carefully for any limitations in the applicability of its findings elsewhere. Are the results limited to the group used in the experiment or may they justifiably have wider application? Do they apply to *her* class?

Length of the study. It makes a big difference whether an investigation is carried out over a period of six weeks, a term, a year, or three years. The longer the duration of the experiment, the more likely it is that the results will hold up in other schools.

Nature of the population. The results from a small number of pupils tend not to be so valid as those from a large group (several hundred). In addition, the population (pupils) used in an experiment may not be representative of school children in general but biased as to economic status of parents, sex, age, intelligence, etc.

A sound experimental design is essential. The experimental design should be suitable to the purpose of the study. If any part of the experimental design is at fault, or adequate controls are not maintained, the results can be of little value.

Treatment of the data. Are the statistics adequate? Does the author present all of his data? For instance, if average (mean) scores and the significance of the difference between the means are given without the standard deviations (measure of the way the scores distribute themselves around the mean), the data are incomplete, or may be challenged. Large standard deviations usually represent much overlapping of scores in the two groups. Thus several scores in the group with the smaller mean may actually be equal to or above the larger mean. Such a situation reduces the importance of the difference between mean scores.

Statistical terms. See the Appendix for definitions of commonly used statistical terms. What is meant, in the Sartain tables, by "significant at the .05 level?"

Measuring instruments. In reading reports, the teacher will want to know whether the measuring instruments used are appropriate and reliable. To illustrate, are the reading tests employed at the appropriate grade level and adequate to supply the answers the experiment is set up to find? Survey tests and diagnostic tests are used for different purposes. The same is true for other tests such as those for vocabulary knowledge and paragraph comprehension. Does the experimenter give the reliabilities of the tests he uses, or do you know what their reliabilities are?

Author's conclusions. As already noted, the conclusions that are claimed should be based upon the experimental findings. They should not go beyond the results obtained. Examine again the conclusions in the Sartain experiment given above. Are all of his conclusions justified by the data obtained?

Summary

The reading teacher must actively work to prepare and maintain herself as one who is a reader worthy of becoming a leader of her pupils. This requires that she set for herself and work toward certain goals in her personal and professional reading.

As a person she should try to exemplify the characteristics of a mature reader: one who engages in many different kinds of reading, who delves really deeply into one or two areas of interest, who uses reading as a challenge to her intellect as well as a means of procuring information and finding entertainment, who is aware of what constitutes effective writing and has developed an enjoyment of and preference for it.

As a teacher of children she should know not only children's books but the elements which make them worthwhile. Her choices of material to read aloud to children should be governed by this knowledge. She should, furthermore, develop the ability to read aloud effectively in sharing with children every day a book or poem "too good to miss."

As a teacher of children and as a counselor of parents, she should be able to read and interpret the scientific literature in the teaching of reading. Just as she would not employ a doctor who failed to keep up with new findings in his field, so she should not expect the public to respect a teacher who cannot and does not read the new evidence in education.

The reader of this chapter who finds that she does not measure up should chart for herself a program of self-improvement. To be hopeful that the goals may be reached is to be hopeful for the children and ultimately for all we value as a society.

What Did These Words Mean?

word-meaning analysis	hypothesis *unconfirmed supposition*
word-form analysis	independent variable *methods of Tea*
comprehension *understanding*	stimulus variable *all other*
interpretation	dependent variable *amt learned*
study skills	comparative design *achieve of*
oral-reading skills	case-study design *ind study com*
maturity in reading *-wide level of interests*	control-group design *equal groups*
significant at the .05 level	longitudinal design *compared for*
elements of effective writing	questionnaire design *inform.*
reliability	means *averages*
	standard deviation *meas of way scores distrib. themselves around means*

Suggested Activities

Creative. Find one example of each of the elements of good writing in books for children. Bring them to class to compare and discuss. Choose one element and try to write a good and poor example of it, using the same topic for each. See whether anyone else can tell the difference! Your skill versus his ignorance!

Make a five-year plan of self-improvement containing something specific that you can do this week.

Further study. Look at recent issues of the *Journal of Educational Research* for an article on reading. Read it to see what kind of experimental design it describes. Note the statistical terms used and see the Appendix of this book for their meanings. Evaluate the study by the criteria given in the section of this chapter entitled Limitations of an Experiment. You will find the article hard reading, but it will give you an idea of what you need to master in order to read such material easily.

Selected References

ARBUTHNOT, May Hill, and others. *Children's books too good to miss,* 2nd ed. Cleveland: Western Reserve University Press, 1959.

FERRIS, Helen (ed.), *Writing books for boys and girls, a young wings anthology of essays.* Garden City, N.Y.: Doubleday & Company, 1952.

HAZARD, Paul, *Books, children and men.* Boston: The Horn Book, Inc., 1944.

PEI, MARIO, *The story of English.* Philadelphia: J. B. Lippincott Company, 1953.

TINKER, M. A., and RUSSELL, W. A., *Introduction to methods in experimental psychology.* New York: Appleton-Century-Crofts, Inc., 1958, Chap. 1.

PART II

Bases and Related Factors
of the Reading Program

3

Nature of Reading Readiness

Too many children fail to make satisfactory progress in learning to read in the first grade. This is not only disappointing to the teacher, but also baffling, because frequently she does not know why a certain child has failed. To the child, instead of its being a happy experience, trying to learn to read too often spells frustration, disappointment, and defeat.

Although one form or another of reading difficulty may occur at any grade level, the cause of many of the difficulties can be traced back to what happened in the early months of the first grade. In fact, the reading difficulties of some pupils are evident during the early weeks of the first grade. To a large degree, later success or failure in reading depends upon the experience of the child in these initial weeks of instruction. It is now generally recognized that many children beginning school need a program of reading-readiness activities. Baker (11a) notes the importance of a program of reading readiness for children at all grade levels. And Bradley (31) presents evidence that readiness-for-reading instruction in the early grades tends to make smoother progress later more likely. In a comprehensive study, Sister Mary Nila (190) presents convincing evidence for the value of this foundation for the success of the ensuing reading program. It is well established that an adequate reading-readiness program will prevent the occurrence of many reading difficulties and reduce the need for later remedial training.

Many people still have the notion that any six-year-old child or any child who begins first-grade work is ready to learn to read. Fortunately more and more schools and teachers are coming to recognize that reaching the age of six does not necessarily guarantee that the child is ready to read. In fact, Fallon (76a) has shown that in some school districts as many as 25 per cent of the children are not ready to begin reading when they enter the first grade. According to Hildreth (132), this estimate should be 40 per cent. Orme (197) found that about three-fourths of the pupils in her group were not ready for formal instruction in reading. The child is ready to begin reading only when he has reached a certain stage of intellectual maturity, is at least fairly well emotionally adjusted, has acquired certain attitudes, and has profited from some background experiences. Some children need more than others to develop this readiness for reading but the training can be profitable for all. Although the concept of reading readiness is basic to the development of good reading ability at all levels, from the kindergarten on, we shall concern ourselves here with its role in the elementary school.

Prior to launching into a detailed discussion of reading readiness it should be made clear that it is impossible to specify a precise level of mental maturity, or just the attitudes and amount of experience, and the qualities of social and emotional adjustment which are necessary for success in beginning reading. Children are fearfully complex and vary from one another in a thousand ways. Another thing is that readiness depends to some extent on the particular program of instruction offered in a school system. For instance, some programs start word analysis early in the first grade, others delay analysis until a certain number of sight words are mastered. In some countries such as Great Britain successful systematic reading instruction is begun with five-year-old children, which is earlier than in this country. And some children have already started to learn to read before they enter kindergarten. These and other factors, though they prevent us from stipulating rigid standards of readiness, will be discussed in what follows.

Nature of Reading Readiness

Marked differences among children already exist when they begin school. Take Jane as an example. Her parents are professional people who are sensitive to the needs of children of whatever age. Jane is told stories and read to a great deal during her pre-school years. She has numerous picture books and cut-out materials. Almost certainly her watching of television is restricted to certain selected programs. She has learned to use a pencil and crayons and scissors for cutting out things. Her co-ordination has advanced to the point where she can manipulate toys, ride a tricycle, and dress her dolls. When there are guests, Jane is allowed to mingle with them for a while and is encouraged to talk with them. Each summer she is taken on an automobile trip halfway across the country and lives for a few weeks on a farm. Jane, by the age of five, has had a lot of stimulating experiences. She talks well, and has acquired poise in her contacts with both children and adults. She shows a keen interest in places, people, and animals. She is eager and alert to learn more about almost everything.

Dick, who first came to school at the same time, has a very different background. His father is a laborer employed by a bus company. His home is small and not well furnished. Neither father nor mother is interested in books. Dick has few picture books or toys. He watches television whenever he wants to, no matter what the program is. He is seldom read to or encouraged to talk about his activities. He has never been far outside the city where he lives. Dick is shy and silent in the presence of people outside the family and even with children from his own neighborhood. In general, his experience is very limited in comparison with Jane's.

These are only extreme examples of the variation to be found among children in the same classroom. Such a range of differences occurs in mental development, verbal facility, physical health and development, personal and social adjustment, interest patterns, and amount and kinds of information picked up through experience. Templin (249) suggests that the greater talkativeness of the children in her study as compared with earlier reports is due partly to the amount that contemporary children view TV. Adequate guidance in preparing a child for reading must be based upon some knowledge of his level of development and his background of experience. There are many degrees of readiness among children at the beginning of grade one. Some have already begun to read, others are definitely not even prepared to begin reading. Durkin (66) found that 49 of the 5103 beginning first graders had learned to read in a nonschool situation prior to entering school. This represented almost one per cent of the population (0.98%). This calls attention to an important kind of precociousness which has been neglected up to now in the schools (see Chapter 19). The chronological age of entrance into the first grade also influences rate of progress in learning to read. Hampleman (118) studied children who were at school entrance (1) 6 years, 3 months of age or younger and (2) 6 years, 4 months or older. Intelligence was controlled. At the end of the sixth grade, the pupils in the older group were about ⅓ year ahead of the younger group. Though this difference could not be shown to be statistically significant it probably revealed a trend. In a similar study, Carter (40) compared the progress in learning to read of 50 children less than six years old at school entrance with 50 over 6 years. Sex and intelligence were controlled. At the end of the sixth grade, 87 per cent of the younger children had not equalled the school achievement of the children who entered at the normal age of six years. The differences were statistically significant. These two studies indicate that some children would tend to achieve better if they began school a few months later.

The success of the child in learning to read depends to a great extent upon his development and the amount and kind of his earlier learning. After evaluating the background of her children, the teacher provides a program to offset whatever deficiencies in reading readiness she has discovered.

Factors influencing reading readiness

Readiness is not an all or none proposition. It is not some one thing the child has or does not have. There are many factors involved in reading readiness. A child may possess any one of these in a trifling and ineffectual degree or much more adequately. The factors affecting readiness for reading tend to be complex and to interact with each other. Frequently these interactions are so intermingled in a total pattern that it is difficult to isolate and evaluate the separate factors in the order of their importance as determiners of reading readiness. Some of them are the product of maturation of the individual's potentialities. Others are acquired abilities that can be improved by training. Certain other factors are intertwined with the emotional adjustment of the individual. The latter, in turn, may be modified in a desirable or an undesirable direction by factors in the child's environment. Detailed summaries of studies dealing with reading readiness have been prepared by Smith (230) and by Williams (277). The influence of particular factors is set forth in detail by Hildreth (132) and by Monroe (184).

A child is ready to read when he has attained the necessary level of intelligence, his health is satisfactory, his experience has been wide enough and is adequately represented in his use of oral language, and his personal and social adjustment make it possible for him to progress at a normal rate in learning to read when exposed to good classroom teaching. In other words, he is ready to read when maturation, experience plus verbal facility and adjustment are sufficient to insure that he can learn in the classroom situation. For convenience in discussing the factors involved in reading readiness, they will be classified under the following: (1) intelligence and socio-economic status; (2) physical factors; (3) experience and language development; and (4) personal and social adjustment.

General Intelligence

To a striking degree, reading is an intellectual process. Level of intellectual development, therefore, appears to be an important determinant of reading success. It is a general observation that though relatively dull children can make some progress in learning to read, their progress is slow and the level they eventually reach is not high. And naturally, dull children are not ready to begin reading as early as children who are intellectually more mature.

Seeking to measure the relationship between mental development and reading ability, Monroe (183) found moderate but not high correlations. The correlation between Stanford-Binet mental age (maturity) and reading-grade score for elementary school children in regular reading classes was 0.60, for clinic cases 0.56, and for special reading cases 0.65. These correlations are in line with other findings. Morphett and Washburne (186), for instance, found correlations of 0.50 to 0.65 between mental age (Stanford-Binet) and ability to learn to read. Similar findings are reported by Anderson, Hughes, and Dixon (6). For elementary school pupils, the correlations between scores in the language factor on the California Test of Mental Maturity and reading-test scores run from 0.36 to 0.56 (Strang, 243). These data are somewhat misleading for two reasons (1) the correlations of reading with the language part of the test requires that the test items themselves be read and (2) the nonlanguage part of the intelligence test does not measure the same abilities as the individual Stanford-Binet Test (see Clymer, 45, 46). As will be emphasized below, the Stanford-Binet is the most satisfactory intelligence test that we now have for predicting potential reading capacity. Furthermore, care must be exercised in interpreting the correlations with Stanford-Binet scores given above. While they show that there is a general tendency for children of higher mental age to read better than those of lower mental age, the fact that the correlations are not higher indicates that there are a good many exceptional cases. That is, some children of lower mental age read relatively well and some of higher mental capacity read relatively poorly. It should also be borne in mind that the role of mental level in relation to reading readiness depends somewhat upon the nature of the program employed for beginning reading instruction (see below). Nevertheless, the correlations do indicate that mental maturity is related to ability to read. At the same time, we repeat, the correlations reveal that intelligence level alone does not insure success. But what we have said here and shall say later on does show that level of intelligence determines in some degree reading readiness at higher grade levels as well as in the first grade.

Mental age and reading instruction

In a recent study, Bevington (20) found that mental age at time of school entrance is more important than chronological age in determing progress in reading. It should be emphasized, as Carter does (40), that factors other than chronological and mental age operate to determine reading readiness (see below).

The stage of mental maturity which appears to be essential for success in beginning reading has been investigated by Morphett and Washburne (186). They studied the relation between progress in learning to read and the mental age of children in the first grade. The essential findings were as follows: Only a few children whose mental ages were below six years made satisfactory progress in reading. In case of higher mental age measured in months, a larger proportion did satisfactory work. At a mental age of six and one-half years and above, three-fourths or more of the children made satisfactory progress in reading. Only a few children with mental ages between seven and one-half and nine years failed to make satisfactory progress. Frequently we run across the statement, based upon the above findings, that there is a definite minimum mental age necessary for success in first-grade reading. This lower limit is placed at a mental age of six years by some writers, at six years, six months by others. Studies by Deputy (60) and by Woods (289) suggest that the minimum mental age required for success in first-grade reading is six years, four months.

That a child has reached a specific mental age, however, does not by itself insure that he will read satisfactorily. This is emphasized by Ilg and Ames (139) in their study of developmental trends in reading behavior. Nicholson (189), for instance, found that a high mental age does not insure a high learning rate in beginning reading. Though Harrison (123) in 1939 considered it safe to state that a child must have reached a mental age of at least six years before it is probable that he will be successful in learning to read, and that the chances for success are much more certain if the mental age is six years, six months, we consider that to set an exact requirement of either six years or six years, six months is hardly justifiable. Evidence from a variety of studies shows that some children with mental ages less than six years can be taught to read. Gates (98) concluded that, when modern methods of instruction, well adjusted to individual differences, are used, reasonable progress in learning to read can be made by most first-grade children whatever their chronological age. This does not mean, however, that the most opportune time to teach reading is before the child reaches six or more years in mental age. As a matter of fact, as noted by Harris (122), the evidence is against it. To teach reading at the lower mental ages requires more effort, a greater amount of individualized help, and progress is slower. Retention of what is learned is also likely to be less permanent. In fact there are few or no sound arguments for beginning reading while the child is mentally immature, and many arguments for postponing his reading. Even the postponing of reading instruction for one term or more for all pupils appears to produce favorable results according to Morphett and Washburne (186). In such programs, training in reading readiness can be much more adequate. The brighter as well as the less mature children will profit thereby. There are, of course, some administrative difficulties in postponing reading for individuals who are slow learners. Parents of slow learners do not understand the reasons for doing so, and are likely to feel there is injustice in the delay. This, however, is a problem of parent education, and should not be allowed to interfere with organizing the reading program in the most effective manner possible. Furthermore, exposure to the teaching of reading prior to adequate mental development may have unfortunate consequences. From the viewpoint of the teacher and the school it may turn out to be wasted effort. The relatively immature child does not learn to read and must be retaught. For the child himself, the effect may be more serious. He has tasted failure, which may be a bitter experience and leave him with a feeling of frustration which may develop into a distaste, if not for reading in general, at least for the reading instruction in school.

Mental age to begin reading

Summing up, the evidence indicates that it is impossible to set a minimum mental age at which all children will be able to begin learning to read and make satisfactory progress. Too many factors besides intelligence are involved. The accumulated evidence seems to indicate that children with mental ages appreciably below six years should not begin to learn to read in the ordinary classroom situation, i.e., in those classrooms which adhere rather strictly to the program specified in a basal set of readers. When such a program is supplemented by the use of certain exercises designed by the teacher herself, as pointed out by Durrell (69), mental ability is less related to reading achievement in first-grade reading. On the basis of measurements made at the end of grade two, Sister Harrington and Durrell (121) concluded that mental age is a less important determiner of success in primary reading than auditory and visual perceptual abilities. This finding is probably due to the fact that this group of children had systematic training in auditory and visual discrimination and in phonics. Also the mental test used was one that measured only ability to follow verbal directions and the reading tests measured only vocabulary. This indicates the emphasis in this teaching program was on acquisition of a primary-grade vocabulary and this in turn was what was measured by the reading tests. General or basic comprehension was not measured. Although Schmidt (222) found that beginning pupils of various mental ages could be taught to read, he also found that children with mental ages six years or over did better and failed less frequently than those with lower mental ages. In any case, if a pupil's mental age is at least six years and if other factors which we shall mention soon are favorable, the child can be taught to read, provided the first-grade teacher is alert to recognize and make adequate adjustments in the cases of fairly pronounced individual differences in ability which she will encounter. Many, or even most, of these children, however, can profit by further preparation for reading while they are attaining somewhat greater intellectual development. The soundness of such an approach finds experimental proof in Bradley's study (31). All children in the experimental group were given readiness training. No systematic reading instruction was given until a child was considered ready for it. Pupils in the control group were given systematic reading instruction from the beginning. At the end of two and three years, children in the experimental group equaled or exceeded the controls in reading performance. On the basis of her results, Nicholson (189) concluded that a reading-readiness program is entirely unnecessary for many children who are ready to read from the first day of school. This does not deny that such children would profit by reading-readiness activities. According to Gates (98), the mental age necessary for beginning reading will vary with the efficiency of the teaching, the materials used, the amount of individualized help, and the adequacy with which special problems are handled. Other things being equal, however, the chances for satisfactory progress in reading are greater, the higher the mental age when the child begins to read.

McLaren (179) investigated the relation between socio-economic status and reading ability among beginning pupils in Great Britain. Although children from families of higher socio-economic status learned to read more readily, he decided that this advantage could be attributed to the higher intelligence level and the greater verbal facility of such children. Sutton (246) also found a significant correlation of .56 between socio-economic status and reading-readiness scores.

Chronological age

Chronological age is ordinarily used as the sole basis of entrance to school for the first time. The child enters kindergarten at about age five and the first grade at about six. Actually so many other factors are important that chronological age has only a little bearing upon reading readiness. To some degree, of course, chronological age may indicate the amount of experience a child has had. Within limits, the older the child when he enters school, the better prepared he is to make a personal adjustment to the school situation. Nevertheless, under no circumstances should chronological age by itself be employed as an indication of readiness to read. On the basis of studies by Olson (192), and by Gavel (103), Durrell (69) points out that chronological age tends to correlate negatively with reading achievement in the first grade, i.e., it is the older children who progress less in learning to read well. Davidson (52) found that children of four years mental age could be taught to read. Her brighter (chronologically younger) children learned more readily and made more rapid progress than the older children even though the mental ages were the same for all. In fact there are many instances of bright prekindergarten children who learn to read before they are five years old, even though they receive only incidental help from parents. It is not uncommon to find precocious children who "figure out" how to read with almost no help from adults.

Physical Factors and Discrimination

Employing the longitudinal method of making periodic measurements on the same children over a period of years, Olson and his associates (193, 194, 195) have emphasized the unified character of growth and have employed the term *organismic age* to represent the average of all growth ages at ("a point in time") any particular chronological age. This average is derived by combining so-called height age, weight age, dental age, carpal age, grip age, mental age, and reading age. The pattern of the growth curves for the separate ages of any child tends to be unified (closely grouped) in most cases. And reading age usually falls within the area of total growth. It is to be noted that there are exceptions to this tendency, mostly cases of genuine reading disability. In general it is held that a child will learn to read without difficulty when his organismic or growth pattern reaches an appropriate level provided he also is given the opportunity to learn. At this level, children will tend to seek experiences which are compatible with their total growth patterns.

To postpone reading instruction until a pupil reaches an appropriate chronological or mental age, or organismic age (growth pattern) appears not to be substantiated in many experimental reports such as those by Sister Mary Nila (190). It appears that reading readiness is not something that comes of itself merely by delaying instruction in reading. Rather it involves the development of certain necessary abilities, skills, attitudes, and ways of adjusting. Contrary to the view of Olson cited above, a well-planned differentiated instructional program will not place the teacher or pupil under pressure to achieve fixed goals. Instead the teacher and pupil will experience the thrill of success.

Actually it appears that Olson and his co-workers are describing a reading-readiness program which emphasizes individual differences in physiological and mental maturation. They tend to neglect the educational side of building reading readiness. It is questionable whether physiological (physical) maturation as measured by weight, height, dentition, carpal growth, and grip is as important as represented. Anderson and Dearborn (5, p. 10) state that performance on mental tests remains the one best predictor of reading achievement. And Karlin (143) found no relationship between physical maturation (height, weight, and carpal development) and success in beginning reading. Karlin's study controlled intelligence, vision, hearing, and emotional adjustment. It would seem, therefore, that the concept of *organismic age* as an indicator of reading readiness should be viewed with skepticism. Obviously mental age is important. But experience, verbal facility, and emotional adjustment must also be considered. There must be, of course, adjustment to any physical deficiency present that may have an adverse effect.

Except for convenience in discussion, it is unwise to think of physical and mental factors separately, for they are to a large degree interdependent. The child functions as a whole. If his physical health is impaired, as by infected tonsils, malnutrition, and the like, he is not ready to direct his attention consistently to learning activities in reading or elsewhere. Physical fatigue, listlessness, and inability to see clearly or hear distinctly are all handicaps to the development of strong motivation toward learning. While correction of physical disabilities does not take the place of instruction, it seems obvious that every child should, if necessary, be aided in securing as good health and as high a level of physical efficiency as possible. The practice of giving a complete physical examination to every child as he enters school is to be strongly recommended. And at any time that the teacher notes signs of illness or physical disability, a medical examination should be advised. To expect a sick or physically handicapped child to take pleasure in learning is unrealistic. In addition to general health, physical factors that have a bearing on readiness for reading are eyesight, hearing, and speech.

Adjusting instruction to physical status

Many physical handicaps do not disappear merely with passage of time. There are cases of an appreciable per cent of hearing loss, and certain specific types of visual disability that cannot be eliminated by hearing aids, glasses, or any medical procedure. Gates and Bond (99) have emphasized that in such cases it is not desirable to delay beginning reading. The important thing is to recognize the deficiencies and then to adjust the reading instruction accordingly.

Auditory factors

Hearing may be a factor of vital importance in reading readiness. An appreciable percentage of children, on arrival at school for the first time, have hearing deficiencies severe enough to interfere with their learning. The teacher should be alert to detect signs of hearing deficiency (see below). An appropriate medical examination will disclose the nature of the difficulty and the degree of hearing loss. Some of these difficulties can and should be remedied, such as loss of hearing due to stoppage of the outer canal of the ear, closure of the eustachian tube by enlarged adenoids or infection, and certain infections of the middle ear. Immediate medical attention should be given to earache and abscessed ears to prevent permanent damage to hearing by rupture of the eardrum or penetration of the inner ear by the infection. Any permanent loss of hearing should be carefully evaluated and the indicated adjustments in instruction made. The pupil with even a moderate auditory deficiency should be seated in a place as advantageous as possible for hearing what goes on and also given individual help. Whatever method of instruction is best adapted to a hard-of-hearing child should be employed. In such cases greater use should be made of visual rather than auditory methods. Vernon (272) notes that a child with a mild auditory defect can learn to read normally if classroom instruction is adjusted to his particular handicap.

Children with hearing difficulties range from the slightly hard-of-hearing to the severely hard-of-hearing (partly deaf) and to the totally deaf. Special methods of instruction have been developed for teaching reading to partly deaf and totally deaf children. These have been described by Bond and Tinker (26) and will be referred to in some detail in a later chapter.

Hearing deficiencies and speech

Every teacher of children should be aware that the satisfactory development of speech in an individual depends to a considerable degree upon his being able to hear speech sounds clearly. The kind of speech defect which prevents clear enunciation may be due to inadequate auditory discrimination and this in turn is likely to lead to difficulty in word recognition. So retardation of speech development may be in the first place caused by hearing deficiencies and later lead to reading disability, especially in oral reading, as Bond (23), Monroe (183), and Robinson (211) have pointed out. An exhaustive survey of the literature led Vernon (272) to the same conclusion. The consensus is that defective articulation of speech sounds, rather than stuttering, is the type of speech defect most frequently associated with reading disability. All this has a bearing upon reading readiness since success in beginning reading depends a great deal upon facility in speaking. Furthermore, the general personal adjustment of a child may be seriously affected by inability to hear satisfactorily.

Auditory discrimination

The clear distinction between loss of hearing as such and defective auditory discrimination should be kept in mind. Vernon's extensive review of the literature (272) shows that some retarded readers are able to hear sounds perfectly well but are defective in auditory discrimination of the speech sounds of letters and words. He concludes that there is some inability in hearing the sounds of letters, letter combinations, and words clearly enough to remember them sufficiently accurately to reproduce them in association with the corresponding printed letters and words. This means that although a child possesses normal hearing he may at the same time have subnormal auditory discrimination.

Readiness for reading, therefore, requires that in addition to normal acuity of hearing the child be able to distinguish readily between the sounds of spoken words, especially of those words to which he will be exposed in his reading class. For instance, he should be able to distinguish the spoken sounds of *can* and *cane, car* and *care, pin* and *pen, where* and *bear, boat* and *coat, bat* and *bad,* and so on. In short, he should have learned that differences between words may occur anywhere within the words. They may begin with different sounds, end with different sounds, or have different middle sounds. Some children by the time they have entered school have developed sufficient auditory discrimination for learning to read, others have not. In studying the foundations of successful reading in grade one, Sister Mary Nila (190) found the four most important factors were: (*a*) auditory discrimination ability; (*b*) visual discrimination ability; (*c*) range of information; and (*d*) mental age. Of these factors, auditory discrimination ranked first in its influence on learning to read. And Durrell and Murphy (71) conclude that a child's ability to discriminate the separate sounds in words is a highly important factor in determining success in learning to read. A similar finding had been reported earlier by Durrell, Sullivan, and Murphy (72).

Training in auditory discrimination is indicated for children deficient in this ability on entering the first grade. Hildreth (132) cites experimental evidence which demonstrates the value of training in auditory discrimination for beginning readers. Fortunately most children deficient in this ability respond readily to appropriate instruction provided their hearing is normal. Durrell and Muphy (71) present similar findings. As will be discussed later, inability to discriminate between the sounds of words will result in difficulty with the letter and the phonetic sounds needed for adequate phonetic analysis in word identification and recognition.

Visual factors

Failure to learn to read can be due, in part at least, to visual inadequacy. It is obvious that a child who cannot distinguish the details of print clearly is not ready for reading. As demonstrated by Fendrick (82), visual defects may prevent successful progress in reading, particularly with those pupils taught primarily by the look-and-say (visual) method. It is not necessary to describe here all the various visual defects that may be involved. Some are obvious, as cross-eyedness and severe near-sightedness, others are not, such as astigmatism and certain difficulties in fusion (i.e., making a single image from what is seen separately by each eye). Even in cases where through a slight degree of muscle imbalance, fusion is made difficult, clear vision may be achieved by additional but undesirable tension on the muscles of the eye with the result that there will be eyestrain. Such eyestrain is frequently accompanied by headaches and perhaps digestive disturbances which interfere with the continued visual attention necessary in learning to read.

Every teacher should know the visual defects, if any, of every child in her room. Knox (146) identified 11 important symptoms of visual difficulty that may be noted by an alert teacher: facial contortions, book held near the face, tension during work involving fine visual discrimination, tilting the head as if to see better, head thrust forward, body tension while looking at distant objects like the blackboard or charts, moving the head excessively while reading, rubbing the eyes frequently, any tendency to avoid close visual work or to lose the place in reading, poor sitting position while reading. If classroom behavior like these or if screening tests by the school nurse indicate possible visual difficulty, the child should be sent to an eye specialist for examination. Difficulties that can be remedied by glasses or by special exercises should be taken care of. Where inefficient vision cannot be remedied, the teaching should be adapted to the child, as by emphasizing auditory rather than visual methods of instruction. Special provision must be made for any children with the more severe sorts of visual handicaps.

Bond and Tinker (26) have specified conditions for teaching reading to the visually handicapped child. Reading material should be printed in about 24-point type, certainly not less than 18 point. (Twelve-point type is adequate for children with normal vision.) Lines should be about 4 inches long (24 to 27 picas) and space between lines ample (with 4- to 6-point leading). For these pupils the goal is *ease* of seeing, *not speed* of reading. In addition, illumination should be relatively bright, at least 50 footcandles. And any reading period should be relatively short.

A developmental factor enters into any visual task such as reading which requires accuracy in binocular vision and co-ordinated eye-movements. According to Hildreth (132) the child normally acquires, between the ages of five and eight, adequate visual accommodation (i.e., the automatic adjustment by which the eye adapts itself for clear vision at different distances), and acuity for the visual requirements of reading. Apparently many children achieve adequate development of these visual functions prior to entering school. Perhaps a few do not. For them the increased demands upon near vision required in reading may result in eyestrain. This developmental factor receives little or no emphasis by most writers in the field of reading. However, it is mentioned by Vernon (272) in reviewing the literature. It cannot be too often repeated that any child who exhibits signs of eyestrain should be referred to an eye specialist.

Need of visual discrimination

Goins (105) studied visual perceptual abilities in relation to *early* progress in reading, i.e., in first-grade pupils. She used the general term "visual perception" to designate the processes by which objects are apprehended through the visual apparatus. Nonverbal materials (pictures and figures) were employed to measure perceptual abilities. Response to one or another of the 14 tests required discrimination of details, controlled association, orientation, visual memory, pattern completion, and recognition of incomplete picture designs. The results revealed marked individual differences among pupils. Most of the test scores were significantly related to reading progress, especially near the end of the school year. To some degree, the factor of intelligence is involved, for about half of the visual test scores, particularly discrimination of likenesses, correlated significantly with intelligence test scores. On the basis of the correlations, Goins concludes that visual perception as measured by her tests is related to reading progress in grade one. She further holds that "visual perception" is more important in the early stages of learning to read than in later grades. Since discrimination of details and of orientation (left-to-right-correct; reversals or right-to-left-wrong) are required in many of Goins' tests, which correlate significantly with early reading progress, the results appear to have a bearing on visual discrimination in reading.

Even though a child can see clearly, his visual discrimination may not have developed enough to distinguish adequately differences between all the words he will meet in beginning reading. He may not have learned to note many small differences which are present in words. For instance, while he may note the difference between *dog* and *wagon*, he cannot distinguish between *dog* and *day;* or between *were* and *wear*, and so on. Numerous words in first-grade reading have similar word forms or configurations. This is frequently a source of confusion to the child. It is imperative that he learn to discriminate the small differences which furnish clues to correct recognition of such words. Furthermore, he must learn that these differences may occur in different positions within the words, at the beginning (*bat* and *sat*), at the end (*bat* and *bad*), or in the middle (*bell* and *ball*). Some children "catch on" quickly, while others need considerable training in visual discrimination to prepare them for reading. From an analysis of her data, Goins (105) considers that efficient reading involves both the ability to hold in mind the wholeness of a word, phrase, or sentence and the ability to attend to individual words and to parts of words, i.e., visual discrimination. This means that those who are unable to discriminate clearly among letters, words, and phrases need special training.

Color discrimination

Most adults, in their sophistication, have overlooked the plain fact that colors are distributed among the objects of our world in far from arbitrary ways. Lights and darks, and colors, i.e., hues and their tints and shades, *mean* different things—browns are associated with the earth and with fall and winter, greens with growing things and with spring and summer. The use of certain colors on man-made objects generally follows traditional lines.

The development of meanings in relation to colors involves the grasp of both color name and color concepts. These concepts may be derived from experiences prior to school or in kindergarten and the early grades, or in all these situations. Some children have gained a considerable understanding of colors and their meanings and traditional uses prior to school, others have developed only the vaguest unclear concepts of colors before five years of age. Accurate understanding of color names and their use requires vivid and accurate concepts. These need to be developed or perfected after the child begins school.

Many activities in the kindergarten and connected with reading in the primary grades require ability to discriminate and use colors. Printed directions for the selection and use of colors occur frequently. Again the child may be required to match color names printed in black type with colored objects. Although some children upon entering school can identify certain colors by name, others cannot. To clarify color concepts and to improve color discrimination, all pupils require training. Obviously certain children will require more training than others. Furthermore, almost 8 per cent of boys on the average are partly color blind. They may have some difficulty distinguishing reds and greens or they may be unable to see reds and greens at all. Color blindness is inherited and cannot be corrected. These color-blind children need to be identified and, because of their disability, given special aid and consideration in any work that calls for identification, naming, and use of these colors.

Speech factors

Motor incoordination, which takes the form of a speech defect of some sort, is often associated with failure to make satisfactory progress in reading. Learning to read involves speech, for the sounds of speech are to be associated with printed symbols. The beginning reader must be able, therefore, both to speak and to understand speech. Monroe (183), for instance, considers that inaccurate articulation may be a hindrance in learning to read when it involves a confusion in the sounds of words that are to be associated with printed words. The child hears a word one way when the teacher says it and in another way when he speaks it himself. When a particular printed word is encountered there is a tendency for these conflicting memories of the way that word sounds to be aroused. This may result in confusion both in word recognition and in comprehension. And, according to Witty and Kopel (284), the emotional concomitants which inevitably attend defective speech may hinder learning to read by inducing self-consciousness, embarrassment, and general antagonism toward reading and other uses of language. Gates (97) also considers that immature speech development may have unfavorable effects upon learning to read. He states that the more severe speech disturbances, such as stuttering and clutches (temporary speech blocking), interfere with the reading activity, whether it is speech in oral reading or subvocal articulation during silent reading. It seems clear that, whenever oral reading and talking play a prominent part in teaching, speech disability is a hindrance to learning to read.

The treatment of speech difficulties should be a part of the reading-readiness program. A careful diagnosis should be made before any remedial efforts are begun. The most common speech difficulties can in fact be spotted by the teacher. Where they are serious, such as stuttering and spastic speech, the skill of a specialist will be needed to supplement the work of the teacher. Less serious defects, such as lisping and defective articulation, however, can often be successfully cleared up by the classroom teacher.

Lateral dominance

The rôle that lateral dominance plays in reading readiness is a subject of dispute. Orton (198) proposed a much discussed cerebral-dominance theory of laterality in relation to difficulty in learning to read. He claimed that learning to read involves selecting the memory images, or traces of letters and words of one hemisphere of the brain, the dominant hemisphere, over the other hemisphere. If such dominance is well established on one side, usually manifested by strong right-handedness or left-handedness, the child should have no difficulty in learning to read. But if the child has not developed either right or left dominance at the time he begins to read, difficulties will occur. Confusion appears, manifested, for example, in tendencies to mirror writing, in mirror reversals of words and letters, and in difficulty in associating these reversed shapes with the straightforward printed phonetic elements. Training to establish lateral dominance and in proper orientation in perceiving letters and words is prescribed. Orton's *theory* has been brought up to date and emphasized in a recent book by Delacato (58).

A number of relatively recent studies, however, have been unable to discover any relation between lack of lateral dominance and difficulty in learning to read. Noteworthy are the investigations of Bennett (16), Haefner (117), Gates and Bond (100), and Witty and Kopel (285). Vernon (272), after examining all the relevant literature, concludes that the claimed relationship between reading disability and incomplete lateralization and cerebral dominance is either lacking or extremely obscure (p. 115).

In line with these findings little emphasis is placed at present upon incomplete lateral dominance as a cause of reading disability. A few writers, like Vernon (272), consider that, at most, incomplete lateralization can only be a contributing factor, not the sole cause of reading difficulty. Nevertheless, it seems desirable that teachers in the kindergarten and first grade should identify the hand preferred by the child for skilled manipulation, as when he draws, writes, and uses scissors. To avoid emotional tension which may hinder effective learning, the naturally left-handed child *should not be forced* to change over to use of the right hand. The child should be allowed and even encouraged to use his preferred hand, whether left or right, so that it may become increasingly dominant.

It seems obvious that adjustment to all the physical defects we have discussed in this section must be made at all grade levels. Without such adjustments, the proper readiness to read and profit by reading cannot be maintained.

Experience and Language Development

Maturity in language development as manifested in the give and take of oral speech (talking and listening) is an important factor in reading readiness. A child's ability to grasp the substance of a story read or told to him, to relate a story represented in pictures, or to describe intelligently the events in his daily life are all instances of some degree, high or low depending on the quality of his performance, of linguistic facility in communication. The child who is able to converse well and understand the interchange of thoughts by spoken words has achieved a stage of language development such that most of the words he will meet in beginning readers are familiar to him. This knowledge of words and the concepts represented by the words are the fruits of his experience.

To be ready for reading, therefore, a child not only must have a broad background experience, but he must also have acquired a set of meaningful concepts from these experiences and the correct words for representing them. Typical of the experimental findings related to this ability are those reported by Hilliard and Troxell (134). They show that pupils who have a rich background of general information make more rapid progress in learning to read than do pupils whose backgrounds are meager. The information derived from varied experience furnishes material for the clarification of the concepts and meanings essential to success in reading. Furthermore, it is important that what he has experienced should be reconstructed in terms of his own store of concepts and refined by his own use of oral language. Only when printed symbols stand for words used meaningfully in his own speech, is the child ready to read successfully. To repeat, successful reading requires that the child come to the reading situation with a background of relevant information derived from experience. And the degree to which the child's experiences can be represented and recalled by use of oral language indicates the adequacy of the meaningful concepts upon which reading comprehension must be based.

Printed words are symbols. As emphasized earlier (Chapter 1), meanings are not obtained from these symbols. The symbols only serve to arouse concepts or meanings which the child has already acquired. In a sense one reads with his own experiences. Words read will convey ideas and stimulate thinking to the degree that they are related to and representative of what he himself has stored away in his mind. Most of what he gets from reading he brings to the reading situation, for reading is largely the association of symbols with meaningful experience. The understanding of what is read, then, depends upon a child's knowledge derived from his activities, his perceptions, his contacts with people and things, his emotional experiences, and his reactions to all these.

Russell (214) has given us an excellent discussion of the nature and developmental aspects of concepts. He points out that concepts develop out of related experiences and as a result of the child's reorganization of experiences in his thinking. An examination of concrete examples of concept development reveals the important role of words. But a concept is not itself a word. A word such as *teacher* represents a *class* of persons as *fun* represents a class of activities or ideas. However, the communication of a concept like *cross* requires a word or phrase or some other symbol, such as the design of a cross. Undoubtedly words help more than other kinds of symbols in developing the understanding which we call a concept. Although children rely partly on sensory perceptions in developing concepts, greater discrimination and precision are revealed by verbalizing such as saying "cows make my milk." Hence the development of most concepts and certainly their use in communication are aided by use of words, particularly if the words are employed in connected discourse.

In another report, Russell (218) points out that knowledge of concepts is involved in building vocabulary. The clarity and completeness of a child's concepts determine to a large degree his success in school. Certainly age, intelligence, socio-economic status, and experience are factors affecting the development of both concepts and vocabulary.

Experience and language facility

Stress should be placed upon facility in language as an important prerequisite for progress in reading. This facility is, of course, intimately related to intelligence, since any use of language requires some intellectual activity. But presupposing adequate intelligence, there are still other factors involved in verbal facility. One learns to talk by talking. Thus the development of oral language depends largely upon opportunity, stimulation, and encouragement to talk. The child who, in addition to having wide and varied experiences, also has both a home and a wider social environment which encourage him to talk about his experiences is fortunate indeed. He will have progressed far in readiness to read by the time he reaches school. The less fortunate children must be guided by the teacher in the development of oral language in the reading-readiness program. The children who have developed a reasonable facility in the use of oral language ordinarily will become successful achievers in reading. Language facility alone, however, does not assure success in reading. Other factors, such as mental maturity and personal adjustment, must be favorable.

There are other aspects of experience and the use of language that are involved in readiness to read. The child will need to acquire the ability to grasp ideas in proper sequences while he is engaged in sequential activities, while listening to stories, and when reproducing materials orally. And ability to follow directions is essential if the child is to function effectively in what goes on in the classroom. In addition, the child should become accustomed to handling school equipment such as books, pencils, scissors, and paper in approved ways. McCullough (172) has outlined methods of achieving these readiness skills and we shall say something about them later.

Children who come from a home where a foreign language is spoken may know little or no English. Since such children cannot understand or speak English well enough to participate much in ordinary classroom activities, they present a special readiness problem. Language-handicapped children need first of all a program designed to improve their knowledge of English. Such a program would involve building up a basic vocabulary for understanding and speaking, improvement of facility in oral communication, and building up a background of meaningful experiences. Words and concepts associated with the experiences must be in English. In this way a child learns to speak and understand a vocabulary before he encounters it in reading. Although the teaching of English and the teaching of reading can be done concurrently, they should be in separate class periods. Finally it may be noted that television may help to acquaint the child of foreign-language background with the sounds of English words.

Personal and Social Development

By the time children reach the first grade there may be among them as wide or a wider range in the sorts of personal and social adjustment they have made as in their differences in intellectual maturity. Feelings of insecurity, social inadequacies, and other emotional aberrations will characterize some of them and these may take a form that prevents a child from learning to read, a fact the teacher should be quick to detect.

When some children reach the first grade, they are already confident, well poised, cheerful, and co-operative. They get along well with other children and respond well to guidance in school activities. Other children are relatively immature emotionally. They are shy and timid, self-centered, unco-operative even in the most routine school activities. They are unable to get along with other children whether in play or at work, and are easily upset emotionally. Between these two extremes there are many degrees of wholesomeness in personal and social adjustment. The attitudes possessed by a child at the time of school entrance are also important (see below).

Three aspects of personal and social adjustment need to be considered in relation to reading readiness, as they are by Harris (122). *Emotional stability* is essential if a child is to learn to read easily and well. An unstable first grader has not yet left behind him the will-of-the-wisp flightiness characteristic of many pre-kindergarten children. The emotionally immature child is easily upset, crying at the least provocation. His moods change rapidly and he breaks out in temper tantrums.

Self-reliance is another sign of emotional poise. The degree to which a child is willing to take the initiative in directing his own activities is important in good school adjustment. Some children, either because they have been left to their own devices or because they have had positive encouragement have learned to take care of their personal needs, to organize their play, and to solve a variety of problems encountered in handling objects and getting on with other people. Many children, on the other hand, have been handicapped by having been fussed over too much. Over-solicitous parents insist on relieving the child of his responsibility by doing too much for him themselves, whether it be feeding him, dressing him, or later supervising all his contacts with both playmates and adults. Such supervision not only perpetuates infantile behavior, but may become extremely frustrating to the child who is naturally seeking maturer satisfaction. If given the right opportunity at the right time, most children will develop self-reliant forms of behavior.

The ability to participate easily and well in co-operative enterprises is an especially good indication of social adjustment. It in turn, of course, depends somewhat upon the personal adjustment of the particular child. A child who is well adjusted socially participates readily and with success and enjoyment in a large number of group enterprises both in and out of school. Ability to do this is especially important in the elementary grades, where much of the teaching is done in groups. On the other hand, the child who is too withdrawn, restless, or antagonistic to participate satisfactorily in group activities will miss much that is important for learning.

The causes for this can usually be found in the frustrations and conflicts present in the home or in its immediate neighborhood. The child may have been so overprotected that any moves he attempted to make on his own were stifled. Or the child may have suffered through lack of parental love, from tension and quarreling between his parents, by a broken home, by senseless and over-severe discipline, by favoritism shown by the parents to a brother or sister, or by sheer neglect. Rejection by playmates can also be frustrating. The child needs to feel that he belongs. For satisfactory development in adjustment, the child needs love, understanding, appreciation, and fair dealings. Otherwise he feels insecure, his emotional development is arrested, and all sorts of maladjusted behavior may result.

Measurements and ratings of emotional adjustment tend to be significantly related to reading readiness. Thus Orear (196) found that social maturity correlated higher (i.e., $r=.53$) with reading readiness than mental age (i.e., $r=.42$) for first-grade pupils. And Milner (181) found that pupils in the first grade who had higher scores in reading readiness had well-adjusted emotional relations with their parents. In a study of 150 kindergarten children, Sutton (246) found that ratings for social adjustment were positively and significantly related to reading-readiness scores.

If immaturity in personal and social adjustment characterizes the child when he arrives at school, he will not be ready to read. For one thing he will be incapable of the sustained attention necessary to get ahead in learning. And he will be unable to participate effectively in the essential group activities. Guidance will be necessary to develop a more satisfactory degree of adjustment. An immature child of this kind often makes excessive demands upon the teacher's time. He is unable to apply himself unless the teacher is there with him.

Attitudes toward reading

It is highly important that the child take a positive and accepting attitude toward his school, his teacher, opportunities to read, and all the other school activities. The way a child's parents react, what the children around him are doing, and the instructional program of the kindergarten itself tend to influence the formation of a child's attitudes toward his future reading. The whole pattern of readiness should be such that success in reading is possible from the first. Lack of satisfying success in activities preliminary to reading undoubtedly plays a prominent role in inducing dislike of reading in some children.

Some emphasis should be placed upon the fact that the attitudes of a child tend to influence what he sees, hears, and feels. According to Russell (214) they help to determine much of what a child perceives in his reading. Such attitudes operate especially where inferences are called for. The wise teacher, therefore, should be aware that different children will tend to perceive different things as they read the same stories and other materials.

Reading Readiness Beyond the First Grade

As already emphasized, the reading-readiness program should not be limited to beginning reading. The concept of reading readiness implies that at each stage of reading the child is prepared to carry out the activities which will result in further success in reading with understanding. As already stated, all the factors which influence reading readiness in the first grade are operating also at the higher levels. Additional factors which influence reading readiness at the higher levels have been competently discussed by Sister Mary Nila (190), Socher (232), Harrison (123), and Betts (18).

At any academic level and at any particular time reading readiness is highly complex. It is a composite of the various determinants of readiness and reflects a pupil's maturation, knowledge, past experience, and previous school work. In any particular child, these factors act together. They are interrelated. And in any group of pupils there will be individual differences in the strength or level of the separate factors. This will produce variation in the pattern of readiness from child to child.

Reading readiness should be developed and appraised not only prior to advance to the next reading level, as at the beginning of a grade, but also before each specific reading lesson or unit. Instruction will be needed to remedy any deficiencies that are discovered. Otherwise a child is likely to be unable to undertake the new work with self-assurance and success. This prerequisite of assuring readiness prior to each new reading unit becomes increasingly important as the pupil moves more and more into the reading of materials more complicated in content. Thus the subject-matter teacher, such as the teacher of arithmetic, history, geography, algebra, etc., is also a teacher of reading as such. If a child is not equipped with the essential concepts and techniques required to read a unit with understanding, he is not ready to read that unit.

To be successful in any specific reading task, therefore, the pupil must be equipped with the necessary concepts, the vocabulary, and the ability to handle the intricacies of the language involved. Without appropriate concepts, meanings will not be accurate; without a precise, extensive, and varied vocabulary there will be doubt, confusion, and gaps in the meaning. The pupil must be able to grasp each sentence, no matter how complex, for they are the building blocks of larger meanings. The need of guidance in developing each of these skills will vary from individual to individual. Later we shall in several places refer to the program of instruction in reading readiness at the higher levels.

Summary

Experimental evidence plus classroom experience indicate that a well-organized reading-readiness program is beneficial for most if not all first-grade entrants. Only some of the children who begin first-grade work are ready to start reading. Reading readiness depends upon a variety of factors which are interrelated. In general, the outlook for satisfactory progress in reading becomes more favorable, the higher the mental age when the child begins to read. Provided there are not special handicaps such as inadequate hearing or vision or speech, the child may begin to read in most instructional programs when he reaches a mental age of about 6 years. Satisfactory general health is a prerequisite and so are normal eyesight, hearing, and speech. Range of experience together with language facility are core essentials for reading readiness. Finally, there must be good personal and social development if adjustment to the learning situation is to be satisfactorily made. In general, a child is ready to read when he has attained an adequate level of mental maturity, possesses a sufficient background of experience, about which he can talk easily, and can be considered satifactorily adjusted personally and socially. When all these factors operate together he should respond to good teaching by progressing at a normal rate in learning to read. The instructional program must be one that is adjustable to the wide range of individual differences to be found in all but the most homogeneous—and therefore carefully selected—classes.

Vocabulary

Check your knowledge of these terms. Reread parts of the chapter if necessary.

mental maturity
emotional adjustment
verbal facility
reading capacity
auditory discrimination
organismic age
visual handicap
binocular vision

reversals
word form
partial color blindness
clutches
socio-economic status
emotional conflict
lateral dominance
social inadequacy

Activities for Students

Observation. Visit an elementary school classroom. Note differences in personality among the students who are being taught in a group. Watch for shyness, eagerness to respond and the forms this takes, tension, inattention, confidence or lack of confidence, etc.

Reading. Read in one of the selected references at end of Chapter 5 what is said about the mental age needed for starting reading. Compare what is said with the discussion in this chapter.

Creative thinking. Put in your own words the reasons for the strong emphasis upon reading readiness in most present-day schools.

Selected References

See Chapter 5.

4

Determining Reading Readiness

The reading difficulties of beginners in school can be largely avoided by proper appraisal of reading readiness during the first few weeks of school. Such an appraisal will ordinarily reveal marked individual differences in all those factors influencing reading readiness, as discussed in the previous chapter. The appraisal is a matter of using standardized tests, of observation and rating of a child's behavior by the teacher, and of securing information from various sources about the child's background.

Intelligence Tests

Since mental development is one of the more significant factors in reading readiness, it is obvious that a test of intelligence should be employed for determining the level of learning ability. There are group and individual tests devised for use with children in the kindergarten and the early grades. The group tests tend to be much used because they can be given and scored by the classroom teacher. In these, the directions are given orally by the teacher, and the children respond by making marks on pictures or diagrams. No reading is involved. Individual tests, which tend to give a more valid measure of learning ability, are given by a trained examiner. Because many schools do not have a trained examiner readily available, Harris (122) has a practical suggestion for getting along without one, at least in most cases. First give a group test to all children. To those with very low scores, or where there is reason to suspect that a child is brighter than his score indicates, a second group test may then be given individually or in a very small group. Where there is still doubt about the validity of a score, or when a child's score is so low that special class placement seems indicated, the child should be referred to a specially trained examiner for a more elaborate test.

All the tests listed below provide a measure of mental age (M.A.) and an intelligence quotient (I.Q.) The M.A. indicates the child's mental level in months, or years and months, and is the most valuable score for appraising reading readiness. The I.Q. is the mental age divided by the chronological age (C.A.) and is therefore an index of the relative brightness of a child. Thus $M.A./C.A.=I.Q.$ Ordinarily the M.A. and the C.A.

are expressed in months for use in the formula. An I.Q. of 100 indicates average brightness, where mental age and chronological age are the same. It is frequently useful to know the I.Q. as well as the M.A. of a child since brighter children tend to learn to read more readily than the duller children of the same M.A. (Davidson, 52). For instance, a child with an I.Q. of 120 and who is 5 years, 6 months of age has a M.A. of 6 years, 7 months. Such a child will be ready to begin reading provided his physical and social maturity are adequate. Certain schools permit some bright and apparently socially mature children under 6 years of age to enter the first grade provided they have a M.A. of 6 years, 6 months as measured on an individual intelligence test.

Below are listed several group tests which have been found useful in late kindergarten and first grade. These and additional tests with publisher's addresses are given with annotation in the Appendix. Full descriptions and prices may be obtained from the publishers.

Group tests

California Test of Mental Maturity, Pre-Primary Series. Hollywood: California Test Bureau.

Detroit Begining First Grade Intelligence Test. New York: Harcourt, Brace & World, Inc.

Kuhlmann-Anderson Intelligence Tests, Kindergarten or 1st grade. Princeton, N.J.: Personnel Press.

Pintner-Cunningham Primary Test. New York: Harcourt, Brace & World, Inc.

Otis Quick-Scoring Mental Ability Tests, Alpha Test. New York: Harcourt, Brace & World, Inc.

SRA Primary Mental Abilities, for ages 5 to 7. Chicago: Science Research Associates.

Individual tests

Stanford-Binet Scale, Revised. Boston: Houghton Mifflin Company.

Arthur Point Scale of Performance Tests, Revised Form II. Chicago: C. H. Stoelting Company.

Wechsler Intelligence Scale for Children. New York: Psychological Corporation.

An individual intelligence test is superior in general to group tests, especially during the early school years. It tends to be more reliable and gives more detailed information on a child's reactions and abilities than any group test does. Although time-consuming, an individual mental test should be administered to every newly enrolled child at the earliest opportunity. Some school systems periodically bring in an expert to test all pupils who have not previously been given an individual test. The data from such a test are sure to prove valuable throughout several grades.

Of the individual tests available, the revision of the Stanford-Binet, unless a child has some language handicap, is by far the best. If at all possible, this is the test that should be employed in appraising reading readiness. It is true that a majority of the responses which the child gives are verbal, but that cannot seem objectionable to those who are interested in determining readiness for reading since reading itself is verbal. The consensus of experts in the field is that the best single prediction of ability to learn to read obtainable from an intelligence test is that obtained by the Revised Stanford-Binet Test.

Neither the M.A.'s nor the I.Q.'s derived from different tests are strictly comparable. It is customary and desirable, therefore, in recording any M.A.'s and I.Q.'s, to designate which intelligence test was used.

Use of intelligence tests

Both the M.A.'s and the I.Q.'s derived from test scores are useful to the classroom teacher. Most children with M.A.'s of less than six years tend to have difficulty in learning to read with ordinary classroom teaching, i.e., instruction which follows a basal reading program. A child's I.Q. predicts fairly well not only the ease with which he will learn to read, provided his M.A. is adequate, but also the rate at which he will progress in the learning. Other things being equal, those with relatively high I.Q.'s tend to progress rapidly while those with lower I.Q.'s learn at a slower rate. With a knowledge of both M.A. and I.Q., the teacher will not only be able to appraise better a child's readiness for systematic instructions in reading but also to form a better estimate of his probable rate of progress and thus be in a position to adjust instruction to his needs.

The I.Q.'s of most children range from about 35 to 145. Idiots (I.Q.'s below 25) and imbeciles (I.Q.'s of 25 to 50) are uneducable in the usual school sense of that word. Morons (I.Q.'s of 50 to 70) are usually trained in special classes in the public schools or in special institutions for mental defectives. They can learn to read only a few words. Borderline defectives (I.Q.'s of 70-80) are usually taught in the public schools. They may attend classes with mentally dull children (I.Q.'s 80-90) or may even be permitted to stay in regular classes. The so-called average child will have an I.Q. somewhere between 95 and 104. Such a wide range of I.Q.'s indicates that, in an unselected classroom group, there are pretty sure to be several children below and many above the average. If the individual needs of all pupils are to be met, the teacher will have to adjust the instruction not only to the average children but also to those with lower and higher I.Q.'s.

The relation between I.Q. and progress in reading as pupils progress through the grades is shown in Table 3. The data show the reading achievement of unselected fifth-grade pupils for I.Q. levels from 55 to

Table 3

Scattergram Based on Stanford-Binet I.Q.
and Gates Reading Survey Level of Comprehension
Grade Score of 379 Fifth-grade Children[1]

Reading Grades	Intelligence Quotients									
	55-64	65-74	75-84	85-94	95-104	105-114	115-124	125-134	135-144	145-154
9.0 or above							1	1		1
8.5-8.9						1	3	2	1	1
8.0-8.4						4	7	7	1	
7.5-7.9					2	6	2	4		
7.0-7.4				1	3	7	9	6	2	
6.5-6.9			1	1	8	11	7	4	2	1
6.0-6.4				3	8	9	15	2	1	
5.5-5.9				3	14	8	5			
5.0-5.4		1		11	16	8	7	1		
4.5-4.9		3	4	11	12	5	4	1		
4.0-4.4	1	2	12	12	9	3	1			
3.5-3.9	2	7	9	14	7	4	2			
3.0-3.4		2	9	10	4		1			
2.5-2.9		2	2	3	2					

[1] Table 2, p. 69, from G. L. Bond and M. A. Tinker, *Reading difficulties*. New York: Appleton-Century-Crofts, Inc., 1957. Reproduced with permission of the publisher.

155. The reading grades obtained extend from 2.5 to 9.0 or above. The average I.Q. for the group was 105 and the average reading grade 5.5 (five months through the fifth grade). Two important trends stand out in the scattergram of the table: (1) There is a significant positive relationship between I.Q. and reading achievement. (2) Also a considerable range in reading grades is found among the fifth-grade pupils at any I.Q. level except the very low and the very high levels. In this instance the reading grades of children with I.Q.'s between 105 and 114 extended from 3.5 to 8.9. These data emphasizes the importance of intelligence-test scores for appraising reading readiness and for devising an individualized instructional program in grade one and later.

For the most part, the scores on any intelligence test should be kept confidential. This is especially important with young children who cannot be expected to understand what is involved, and with most parents, for only the exceptional parent will have the training and experience required to comprehend and make wise inferences from test results. As might be anticipated, in some cases parental reactions to this kind of information may have a decidedly unfortunate effect upon the child's personal and social development.

Color-blind Tests

The child who is color blind seldom finds it out by himself. Furthermore, neither the teacher nor the parents are likely to discover his color blindness without special tests. Since color blindness is likely to impose a handicap in the early stages of reading, all boys should be tested as early as possible. A color-blind girl is very rare. Although color-discrimination tests have not been specifically designed for use with young children, some may be employed with a fair degree of accuracy, particularly the following:

1. *Pseudo-Isochromatic Plates for Testing Color Perception.* Southbridge, Mass., American Optical Co. Designed for ages 7 and over but certain plates are responded to by tracing pathways and may, therefore, be used with younger children. The tracing should be done with a camel-hair brush which does not affect the chart.

2. *Farnsworth Dichotomous Test for Color Blindness.* Panel D-15. Designed for ages 6 and over. The score is either passing or failing and detects those grossly deficient in color discrimination. New York: Psychological Corporation, 552 Fifth Avenue.

Reading-Readiness Tests

Numerous tests have been devised for the sole purpose of appraising readiness for reading. They attempt to measure the more important abilities involved in beginning reading. There are scores for each part of a test as well as a total test score. Part scores are frequently more meaningful than a total score. Gates (94) and others such as Bremer (33) and Karlin (143) conclude that a total readiness score, while useful, is of less value than information concerning the strength or weakness of the child in each of the important abilities, skills, techniques, and interests that may influence progress in learning to read. In this respect, diagnosis by means of part scores on reading-readiness tests is a valuable aid to instruction at various stages in the first two grades and for use with reading disability cases where performance is below second-grade reading. However, this diagnostic information should not be misused. Ordinarily neither the artificial type of training derived from the formal exercises found in certain readiness workbooks nor drill confined to the type of materials included in the subtests of reading-readiness tests is to be recommended. Hildreth's (132) cautions are to the point. She notes that *formal* exercises aimed at improving auditory and visual perception may easily be overdone. Such exercises often tend to become artificial and meaningless to the child. It is more profitable to teach visual and auditory discrimination in the context of the child's immediate concrete experiences in which precision in seeing and hearing is required. In other words, a child should not be drilled on specific test items he has failed in a reading-readiness test. But if he is found especially deficient in such areas as language or visual discrimination, he should receive training through types of experience selected to overcome these deficiencies.

To illustrate, take the following example which is similar to an item to test visual discrimination in a word-matching test:

ball   dog

shoe   ball

The child is to draw a line connecting the two words that look just alike. If the child is found deficient in this kind of ability or skill, he should not be drilled on similar practice items. Rather, he should be given many sorts of experience in observing words in schoolroom activities—words on the blackboard, bulletin boards, or charts; names attached to objects in the classroom, in picture books or primers, etc. In these activities the teacher can also call attention to the proper left-to-right progression in perceiving a word, the function the word serves, and its pronunciation. Thus the child, while learning to discriminate details as well as the shape of the word, will learn some of the techniques of recognizing words and probably even learn to read some of the words. (See next chapter for detailed suggestions on developing reading readiness.)

Some children will have acquired considerable ability in the visual discrimination of word shapes or forms, and of the details of words and letters prior to entering the first grade. These abilities result from viewing or studying words in children's books, billboards, road signs, and magazines as well as from instructional activities in the kindergarten.

Any standardized measuring device, including reading-readiness tests, should be both *reliable* and *valid*. A reliable test is one that yields comparable results on successive administration to the same subjects, i.e., if a pupil takes a test a second time a few days after the first testing, he will, if the test is "reliable," make approximately the same score as on the first testing except for some slight advantage attributable to the "practice effect." Satisfactory reliabilities are assured in the cases of most of the reading-readiness tests in common use. Reliability coefficients are ordinarily cited in the manuals of directions of tests. A school official should take note of these reliability coefficients before money is spent purchasing a particular reading-readiness test. No absolute level of requirement can be set up for the reliability coefficients of those tests which are to be employed in individual diagnosis—the commonest usage of readiness tests. However, if the reliability coefficient is .90 or above, the reliability is excellent; in the high .80's, it is satisfactory; if in the low .80's, possibly satisfactory, though the results should be interpreted with reservations. Tests with reliability coefficient below .80 for the total score may be put down as unsatisfactory for individual diagnosis. (See chapter on appraisal for a more detailed discussion of reliability and validity.)

The *validity* of a test refers to the degree to which a test measures what it has been devised to measure. In the case of a reading-readiness test, this is the degree to which the test predicts ability to read in the instructional program of the first grade (or elementary grades). Such validity is ordinarily determined by correlating the reading-readiness scores obtained at the beginning of the school year with reading achievement scores obtained at the end of the first semester or at the end of the school year. Validity coefficients for total score of .60 or above may be considered excellent; those around .50, good; and those between .30 and .45 have some value but are not very satisfactory. A number of studies have been made of the predictive value or validity of reading-readiness tests.

Some caution should be exercised in interpreting the correlations between reading-readiness scores and reading achievement. They may vary considerably according to which readiness test or which reading achievement test is used. Furthermore if the range of ability among the pupils is relatively small, or if the administration of the tests is not well controlled, the correlation will tend to be low.

According to an analysis by Robinson and Hall (207), reading-readiness tests tend to yield highly reliable measures which fairly well predict success in learning to read. No one of the tests they studied could be recommended as consistently better than the others. In many of the published results, the correlations between reading-readiness total scores and achievement in reading range from about .45 to .60. Correlations between specific parts of readiness tests and reading achievement range mostly between .30 and .50 (the shorter the test, the lower the coefficient is likely to be). Apparently, as found by Moreau (185), reading-readiness tests given during the first month of the first grade predict reading achievement up to the sixth grade nearly as well as they do achievement in the first grade. A few researchers, like Bremer (33) and Karlin (143), tend to de-emphasize use of reading-readiness scores alone to predict reading achievement in grade one. However, even they found rather significant correlations between readiness and achievement (Bremer, .40, and Karlin, .36).

Apparently reading-readiness tests in general have not been found to be consistently better in predicting success in reading than intelligence tests, nor vice versa. In fact, the results reported by Gates (93), and by Fendrick and McGlade (83) indicate that all the mental tests and reading-readiness tests they studied predict ability to learn to read reasonably well. Although scores on intelligence tests correlate with those on reading-readiness tests, this relationship is not high and we cannot conclude that the two kinds of tests are measuring the same thing to any marked degree. As a matter of fact, when scores on intelligence and readiness tests are combined (multiple correlation), the prediction of reading achievement is increased somewhat. If possible, the appraisal program should employ both kinds of measures, as each makes a unique contribution.

No single test of reading readiness measures everything relevant to readiness. Emphasis varies from test to test. There are, moreover, certain relevant factors such as attitudes, interests, and the kinds of behavior that aid a child in his adjustment which must be appraised by other means. With some pupils it is advisable to employ more than one reading-readiness test in order to secure a more complete diagnosis. In the following list several representative reading-readiness tests are briefly described. Norms for use in classifying the child as to relative standing are ordinarily given in the test manual of directions. Prices and complete descriptions of the tests may be obtained from the publishers.

Since space is limited, instead of giving all the information for each readiness test, we shall describe rather fully only the first test considered. When ordering a test for use in his school, the purchaser will want to know in addition to its reliability and validity, how easy it is to administer, its cost, how clear the directions for its interpretation are, etc. These are given in all manuals of directions. A sample copy of a test with the manual of directions may be had for about 35 cents. All the tests described below are good. Some are longer than others and certain ones require individual administration in part of the test. The appropriateness of a test for a particular school system must be decided upon by the persons choosing the test.

Gates Reading Readiness Tests. One form. New York: Bureau of Publications, Teachers College, Columbia University. Working time about 40 minutes (two sittings). Kindergarten and first grade. Five subtests: (1) *Picture Directions,* in which the examiner gives oral directions and the children make designated marks on the pictures. Tested are the abilities to (*a*) listen to what the teacher says, (*b*) understand what is said, (*c*) remember briefly what is said, and (*d*) understand and make use of words and concepts about the country, the town, and a store. (2) *Word Matching,* in which four words are presented in an oblong area. The two words which are identical are to be connected by a line. (3) *Word-Card Matching Test,* in which sets of four words each are listed in the test sheet. The examiner presents for five seconds one word on a card and then the child tries to find among the four the word just shown him and draws a circle around it. Tests 2 and 3 reveal the status of a child's knowledge of and familiarity with printed words. Visual discrimination of word forms and details is involved. (4) *Rhyming Test.* In each item the children are given orally the names of four pictures in the test. The examiner then gives a word that rhymes with the name of one of the four pictures which the child marks. This test measures the child's familiarity with and sensitivity to the sound or phonetic characteristics of words, i.e., auditory discrimination. (5) *Reading Letters and Numbers.* Testing is done individually. The child is asked to read as many letters and digits as he can. A capital alphabet, a lower case (small-letter) alphabet, and digits 0 to 9 are presented. This is a test of the child's familiarity with printed letters and digits.

The *Gates Test* has high reliability and validity. Percentile ranks are given for testing at the end of the kindergarten and at the beginning of the first grade. Reading readiness is estimated in terms of percentile rank. Suggestions for readiness activities are outlined for children who are low in any one or all the areas measured by the subtests. Provision is made for use of other forms of information such as mental age, and visual and hearing status. It is suggested that intelligence be given about the same weight as one of the subtests.

Metropolitan Readiness Tests. Two forms. New York: Harcourt, Brace & World, Inc. Working time about 60 minutes. Kindergarten and grade one. Six subtests: Word Meaning, Sentences, Information, Matching, Numbers, Copying. Percentile ranks are given, together with ranges of scores, indicating superior, high normal, average, low normal, and poor readiness.

Lee-Clark Reading Readiness Test. One form. Los Angeles: California Test Bureau. Working time about 20 minutes. Kindergarten and first grade. Four subtests: Matching, Cross Out, Vocabulary, Word Symbols. The subtests principally measure visual discrimination, vocabulary knowledge and ability to follow directions. Letters, words, and pictures are employed. Scores are classified from high to very low with probable per cent of failure for each score, together with suggestions for interpretation.

Van Wagenen Reading Readiness Tests. Two forms. Minneapolis (1729 Irving Avenue South): The Author (Dr. M. J. Van Wagenen). Working time about 45 minutes. Kindergarten and first grade. Individual testing. Six subtests: Information, Verbal Relations, Vocabulary Knowledge, Memory Span for Sentences, Visual Word Discrimination, Speed of Learning Words.

Monroe Reading Aptitude Tests. Boston: Houghton Mifflin Company. One form. Working time about 34-40 minutes group; 10-15 individual. Kindergarten and grade one. The eight subtests provide measures of visual perception and discrimination, auditory discrimination, motor control, oral speed and articulation, vocabulary, and length of sentences. The predictive value of the test is shown by percentile ranks, together with the levels which tend to predict superior, average, or inferior readers. Suggestions for use with certain reading-disability cases are included.

Murphy-Durrell Diagnostic Readiness Test. New York: Harcourt, Brace & World, Inc. One form. Working time about 85 minutes. Grade one. Three subtests: Auditory Discrimination, Visual Discrimination, Learning Rate. Provided are: percentile scores, distribution of scores in high, medium, and low groups, and suggestions for instructional programs for different scores in auditory and visual discrimination. Learning-rate scores are divided into four groups to guide instruction.

Harrison-Stroud Reading Readiness Profiles. Boston: Houghton Mifflin Company. One form. Working time about 75 minutes. Kindergarten and grade one. Six subtests: Using Symbols, Making Visual Discriminations, Using the Context, Making Auditory Discriminations, Using Context and Auditory Cues, Giving Names of the Letters. The scores of a pupil are entered on a profile chart, the profile to be drawn. Percentile ranks may be read from the edge of the profile chart. Suggestions for interpretation for instructional purposes are given.

Diagnostic Reading Tests: Reading Readiness Booklet. Mountain Home, North Carolina: The Committee on Diagnostic Reading Tests. Two forms. Working time not given. Kindergarten and grade one. Subtests: Relationships in making figures and marking figures, Eye-hand and Motor Co-ordination, Visual Discrimination, Auditory Discrimination, Vocabulary. Quartile and median values are given for scores on each test with suggested scores which should be obtained to assure success in learning to read.

Using Reading-Readiness Tests

The teacher can readily learn to give both individual and group reading-readiness tests. In all cases the standardized procedures described in the manual of directions should be followed *exactly as given*. Otherwise the accompanying norms are valueless for interpreting the obtained scores. Where timing is required, it should be done accurately. This is best done by using a stop watch, which can be started at the moment the subject or subjects begin work. This avoids bothersome subtraction of time begun from time finished, which is necessary when an ordinary watch is used. The examiner must ascertain at all times that the children understand and are following directions. Authors of the group tests recommend that small groups be tested, less than 15 if possible, sometimes not more than seven. The smaller the group, the greater the likelihood that the results will be truly representative of a child's ability. The only advantage of group testing at the kindergarten and early first-grade level is to save time for the teacher and for the class. Any group test, of course, may be given individually. The teacher need not necessarily employ a test designed for individual use where individual testing is indicated, as with a retarded reader or when a case is questionable. A child should not be required to work continuously for more than about 20 to 25 minutes at one time. When tests require more time, additional sittings should be used.

Reading-readiness tests should not be given to first graders until the children have had at least two weeks to adjust to their teacher, the room, and to classroom activities in general. The tests are commonly given in the third to fifth weeks of grade one.[2] In any case, a readiness test should be administered only after a child has demonstrated sufficient growth in following directions and in handling a crayon or pencil to perform effectively in a test situation. The test should be given to groups only if the children have shown that they are satisfactorily adjusted to working in groups. If two forms of a test are not available, and a retesting is needed, the same form may be given after an interval of a month or more. Retesting after a child has had a period of readiness activities helps the teacher decide whether to start systematic reading instruction or to continue the readiness program.

Interpretation and use of reading-readiness scores

Having obtained the scores on a reading-readiness test, the teacher should make proper—and maximum—use of them as one form of help in

---

[2] A kindergarten teacher might better use one of the check lists of behavior rather than the formal test (see below).

appraising the readiness to learn to read of *each child* in her class. Although the other factors (physical fitness, mental age, emotional adjustment, etc.) we have discussed in the previous chapter also have their significance in determining reading readiness, the test scores are particularly illuminating in relation to these. In fact, Orme (197) found that pupils who reached or exceeded the norm (average) on the readiness test (Metropolitan), succeeded in reading and those who were poor risks remained poor risks until they had readiness training.

Suggestions for the interpretation and use of scores are available in the manual of directions of each test. These suggestions should be studied carefully. In addition, some manuals furnish illustrative cases, either in profiles or in tabular form. Practically all the tests include measure of visual and auditory discrimination in one form or another. Other measures vary with the particular test. See description of tests above.

The relationship between total readiness scores and reading achievement, as cited above, tends to be higher than for the scores on the subtests. Of the subtests, vocabulary, letter naming, visual and auditory discrimination generally correlate higher with reading achievement than the other measures.

When the percentile for total score is high (about 70 or above), the child is pretty likely to become a good reader. If the total readiness score is about average, the pupil should make about average progress in a basal reading program. However, such children will need readiness activities in those areas where the subtest scores fall much below the 50th percentile (or the median). In the cases of low total scores, percentiles below 40, systematic reading instruction should be delayed while the child is given appropriate readiness activities. Some of the pupils will need advance in mental maturity before much can be expected of them. In all cases, the percentile or score level in the subtests will indicate areas to be emphasized in the readiness activities. The analysis chart presented in Figure 1, taken from the manual of directions of the *Monroe Reading Aptitude Tests*, illustrates a satisfactory method of analyzing data on individual cases. Note that use is made of M. A. as well as the readiness scores.

All teachers should realize that there is no sharp dividing line separating the readiness scores of potential readers from nonreaders. And there is no need to bring a child up to a high percentile level on a subtest before he should begin reading books. As an instance, although the auditory discrimination of a particular child may be relatively poor, still he can begin reading because the kind of auditory discrimination tested is not required until he meets rhyming words or words beginning with the same letter. Meanwhile the teacher can help him acquire this skill. For most pupils, after two or three weeks of readiness activities, reading instruction may

SUGGESTED TYPE OF CLASS ANALYSIS SHEET—READING APTITUDE TESTS

PERCENTILES

Pupil	C.A.	M.A.	I.Q.	Visual	Auditory	Motor	Articu.	Language	Composite Total	Hand	Eye	Foot	Comments and Interpretation
Thomas T.	6–0	6–7	110	95	99	90	92	88	93	R	R	R	Potential. superior reader. Place in best section.
Mary S.	6–2	7–8	125	94	90	60	75	95	83	R	L	R	Potential superior reader. Since motor scores are lower than other scores and since she has left-eye preference, observe for reversal tendencies. Place in best section.
Billy J.	6–0	7–0	118	90	32	40	15	60	47	R	R	R	Place in average section. Refer for speech corrective work, and extra help in phonics. Says t for k, p for f, etc.
Tony A.	6–2	6–2	100	65	60	85	35	25	56	R	R	R	Place in average group with help in language. Foreign language spoken at home. Needs to develop wider English vocabulary.
Betty M.	6–4	6–5	102	5	30	25	40	50	30	R/L	L	L	Potential poor reader. Advise eye-examination. Place in special-help section. Encourage her to write with left hand if she finds it more comfortable to do so.
George T.	6–8	6–6	98	10	5	50	30	15	22	R	R	L	Potential poor reader. Place in special-help section. Encourage him in handwork since his motor abilities are good. Eye and ear examination.
Janet B.	6–5	5–7	87	63	50	65	65	60	60	R	R	R	Try in average section in spite of low M.A. since her other abilities are good.
Carl P.	6–3	5–3	85	20	15	10	5	'20	14	R	L	R	Generally retarded in all fields including M.A. Place in pre-1B with speech corrective work, postponing reading until next semester, then place in special-help section.

Figure 1. (Reproduced with permission of the publishers from *Marion Monroe's Manual of Directions, Reading Aptitude Tests, Primary Form.* Boston: Houghton Mifflin Company, 1935.)

begin. From then on, informal reading-readiness work should blend with the reading program so that it might be hard to say which is which (see Chapter 5).

Other Aspects of Measured Readiness

Poor visual or auditory discrimination and lack of satisfactory progress in reading may be due to deficiencies in these two senses.

Appraisal of visual efficiency

The visual efficiency of every child should be appraised before he begins reading. Some kind of *screening test* should be employed by the school nurse or other qualified person to detect those children who should be referred to a specialist for diagnosis and correction. The *Snelling Chart* and the *American Medical Association Rating Reading Card* are frequently used screening tests. Special charts are now available for testing children unable to read. The most common of these, the E-Test, is made up of block E's. The child merely indicates which side of the E is the open side. This the child can do by spreading the first three fingers of his hand and pointing in the proper direction, that is, up, down, right, or left. In all testing, a measure should be obtained for each eye separately and for binocular vision.

Any check of vision should include a test of near vision (about 12 to 14 inches) as well as distance vision (20 feet). A farsighted child will be checked as normal when looking at objects at a distance but be unable to see clearly at the close range required for reading. The nearsighted child, on the other hand, may be able to see distinctly at reading distance but be unable to see clearly what is on the blackboard.

A very satisfactory screening device consists of the Betts *Visual Sensation and Perception Tests* (18). These are designs mounted on stereoscopic slides and are viewed through the Telebinocular, a modified stereoscope. They provide measures of binocular vision, fusion in near vision and far vision, muscle balance, stereopsis level or depth perception, and sharpness of visual image in different meridians. The results are highly reliable and accurate enough for screening purposes. Another excellent device appropriate for visual screening in the school is the *Eames Eye Test*. It measures visual acuity, nearsightedness, farsightedness, fusion and astigmatism.[3]

---

[3] *Snelling Charts* and the *E-Test* may be obtained from the National Society for the Prevention of Blindness, 1790 Broadway, New York 19; the *Eames Eye Test* from Harcourt, Brace & World, Inc., New York City; the *A.M.A. Rating Reading Card* from the American Medical Association, 535 North Dearborn Street, Chicago; Western Electric Company's audiometers from the Graybar Electric Company, Graybar Building, New York City (offices in other large cities). Maico Electronics Inc., 21 North 3rd Street, Minneapolis, also manufactures dependable audiometers.

Many signs of visual discomfort which may be symptoms of visual disability may be noted by the teacher. Among these are excessive blinking and watering of the eyes, squirming about, contortions of the face, tilting the head when reading or attempting other visual discriminations, inflamed eyelids, and complaints of headaches after reading for a short time. When there is any suggestion of visual difficulty either in the behavior of the child or from the evidence obtained in screening tests, the teacher should see to it that the child is sent to a specialist for diagnosis.

Appraisal of auditory efficiency

The more accurate appraisal of auditory efficiency by school health services is made by means of an audiometer selected from among several which are available. Two recent models are the Western Electric Company's 4C and 6B. The 4C model is similar to a portable phonograph. Each child hears the sounds through a telephone receiver connected to the apparatus by wire. As many as 40 persons can be tested at one time. The test consists of a series of numbers which are written down by a child or other person taking the test. The chief advantages of this audiometer are its economy of time and the fact that it is more accurate than a whisper or watch-tick test for screening purposes. But, because of the response required, the 4C audiometer is unsuitable for young children who cannot readily write numbers.

When an audiometer is not available or when testing the younger children who cannot write numbers, the watch-tick test or whisper test may be used for preliminary screening. A loud-ticking cheap watch may be used for the watch-tick test. The normal child should hear the tick at about 48 inches. If the tick cannot be heard at a distance greater than about 16 inches, the child should be examined by a specialist.

Specifications for the whisper or low-voice test are given by Betts (18). The whisper test is given at about 15 inches from the child, and the low-voice test at 20 feet. The examiner pronounces words and numbers which the child repeats. If the child cannot hear, the examiner moves nearer until correct responses are possible. In all these tests, one ear at a time is tested. Only the more severe deficiencies will be revealed by the watch-tick or whisper test. Any children who do not pass the group audiometer test (model 4C) or who show signs of impaired hearing on the watch-tick or whisper test, should be given the individual and more precise test by means of the 6B or a comparable audiometer.

The 6B audiometer provides accurate measurement of hearing from relatively low pitches to high ones. Speech sounds ordinarily range from about 100 to 9000 vibrations per second in pitch. This range is covered by measurement on the 6B audiometer. The measurements are made in terms of significant hearing loss in comparison with the normal. Zero decibel loss means exactly normal hearing, in which, of course, there is some variation. However, when a decibel loss of 20 or more in either one or both ears is found, the disability is probably serious and the child should be referred to a medical specialist. Preferably this referral should be based upon a 6B or comparable audiometer test. Children should be free from colds when tested, since colds frequently produce some temporary loss of hearing. The most comprehensive and practical book on the measurement and evaluation of hearing among school children is Dahl's manual (48).

The alert teacher will notice signs of hearing deficiencies. The hard-of-hearing child may be inattentive and frequently asks that statements be repeated or he may misunderstand even simple directions. He may tilt his head, turn one ear toward the speaker, or report ringing and buzzing in the head. Hearing is affected by various abnormal conditions such as excessive accumulation of ear wax, mouth breathing caused by adenoids which block off the tube leading from the throat to the middle ear, frequent colds, and earache due to infection of the middle ear. A check on such symptoms may reveal the source of the hearing difficulty.

Teacher Appraisal of Readiness

According to Henig (126), many first-grade teachers are able, after having children under their guidance for a few weeks, to predict rather well their ability to learn to read. This does not imply that readiness tests are not important. Not every teacher is able to rate all of her children accurately. The tests do give a quick appraisal by standardized procedures. In general, the teacher's judgment should complement test results rather than replace them. In fact, certain aspects of readiness for initial reading instruction are best evaluated by the teacher. She should, of course, be experienced in making systematic observations of behavior and appraisals of development. Furthermore, certain factors concerned with emotional and personal adjustment are involved that are not readily assessed by standardized tests.

Use of teacher-made tests

Tests constructed by the teacher can be of decided help in checking ability to understand and follow directions in marking pictures, visual and auditory discrimination, and ability to identify letters and digits, etc. The techniques employed in standardized tests and in certain workbooks may be used, but the specific items in the tests must not be employed because of copyright laws. The teacher can easily make up the following types of items:

Marking pictures. Select pictures of the sort found in some expendable workbooks, and give the pupils directions so that their responses will demonstrate their ability to understand any concepts used in the directions and which apply to the content of the pictures.

Visual Discrimination. Matching exercises requiring recognition of like-nesses in words and letters may be used such as:

1.	baby	home	2. m	n
	dog	baby	u	n

The words or letters that are alike are to be connected by a line. Another type of item requires the child to draw a circle around the one word which is different from the other three in each line as:

1.	well	well	wall	well
2.	pin	pen	pin	pin

The exercises may be varied by printing a word (wall, pen) on a card or blackboard and asking the children to find the same word in a row of words. Rows of items like the above, each row different, can be duplicated for testing purposes. Since words in sentences are in rows along lines, it seems best to arrange these test items that way rather than in squares. A pupil can then examine the words from left to right as in a line of print.

Auditory Discrimination. This may be tested by asking the children to indicate which pairs of sounds are alike and which are different. Pairs of words or of single letters like the following can be employed:

1. fine, nine; boat, boat; pane, pan; mat, mat; cat, sat; etc.
2. b b; p,b; m,n; n,n; v,e; c,e; etc.

Another type of item involves asking the pupils which pairs of words begin with the same sound, as:

1. map, man; cat, sat; bell, ball; paper, pen; fell, tell; etc.

This procedure can be varied by asking the children to give other words which end with the same sound as a given word.

Teacher-made tests like the above may be employed to check the progress of pupils engaged in reading-readiness activities. At times the expendable materials found in certain workbooks may be used in place of the teacher-made items illustrated above.

Another problem in readiness development involves checking whether a child has mastered one step in the reading program sufficiently to go on to the next. Materials for such testing have been worked out and published for use with the Ginn Basic Readers (176). They start with the *Pre-Reading Test* and continue on through each part of the basic program to the end of the sixth grade. If such tests are not available in the basic series being used, the teacher can make up similar materials to check the level of vocabulary, word analysis, and comprehension, all for the purpose of appraising readiness for the next unit or book.

Appraisal of emotional and social adjustment

Emotional and social adjustment is not easy to judge. Nevertheless, there are several aspects of behavior which reflect personal adjustment and which may be noted and evaluated with some likelihood of success by the teacher. For instance, general withdrawing behavior may be accompanied by excessive timidity and self-consciousness. Or a child may manifest excessively aggressive behavior in his attempt to keep himself the center of attention by others. This may take the form of temper tantrums, the use of physical force to get one's way, or other varieties of blustering and disrupting behavior. Such a child is unable to complete assigned tasks. He lacks consideration for the rights of others. Other children, who are not happy in the school situation, may develop different ways of showing their disinterest in some or all classroom activities. All of these types have in common a tendency to tenseness, strain, and nervousness. Such children contrast with those who are cheerful, patient, responsive to guidance, and who complete assigned tasks. General maladjustment or lack of confidence as shown either by excessive shyness or by aggressiveness, both accompanied by nervous tension, are likely to produce negative attitudes toward reading.

Appraisal of interests and attitudes

Some evaluation should be made of a child's interests and attitudes, for they influence reading readiness. Note should be made of the types of games and leisure activities a child participates in, the degree to which he uses pencils and crayons, whether he enjoys examining pictures in books and magazines, and whether he likes to listen to and tell stories. The teacher should note any signs that the child is eager to learn, and what needs he evinces that may be satisfied through reading. Some children, of course, make perfectly clear that they are interested in the printed page and ask eagerly to be shown how to read.

In attempting to appraise the attitudes of the children in her room, the teacher will find it helpful to make an inventory which can be applied to each particular child by checking. She may list such groups of attitudes as reaction to authority, ability to get along harmoniously with other children, and willingness to accept suggestions. She may also note the degree to which the child likes school, the teacher, and the company of other children. Other clues to attitudes may be found in work habits such as care in use of materials (books, crayons), respect for the property of others, and ability to work quietly and co-operatively with others. The role of attitudes in developing reading readiness will come up again in later discussions.

Appraisal of experience

Experience is of many kinds, and, as noted earlier, breadth and variety of experience play an important role in reading readiness. The teacher evaluates the background and extent of a child's experience by gathering information about him in several areas. She may size up the nature of the child's home environment with respect to opportunities to tell stories and/or listen to stories read by the parents, the presence of books and magazines, kinds of language used at home, number of children in the family, recreational activities, and interest of the childrens' parents in their education. There should also be some inventory of the child's knowledge of urban versus country life, information about neighborhood and community businesses and services, kinds and uses of transportation in the neighborhood, and the extent to which he has traveled. It is particularly important to note the child's ability to verbalize the information gained through experience. Some children gain more rapidly than others in ability to describe their experiences.

This appraisal of experience should determine whether the child's information has provided him with a store of concepts adequate for understanding the material which he will soon encounter in his reading. For instance, children who start to read should always have fairly clear ideas about certain animals, some farm activities, what fire departments do, also mailmen, trains, playgrounds, food, and the like.

Other significant items to be noted

The list can be expanded to include other items the teacher may note. Does the child's vocabulary appear adequate or limited? Are there tendencies to lisp or stutter? Which is the child's preferred hand? This is usually readily determined by noting which hand is preferred for using scissors, crayons, and a paint brush. No matter how slight the preference, the child should be encouraged to use his preferred hand. When the child is ambidexterous, that is, shows no preference for either hand, he may be encouraged to write with the right hand, but not forced to do so. Such a child may develop of himself a hand preference as he grows older.

Appraisals made by the teacher

Appraisals derived from systematic teacher observations are highly important. They constitute an essential complement to the uses made of scores on readiness tests. However, it should be acknowledged that the rating of a child for emotional adjustment, background of experience, and

Check List for Reading Readiness
Physical Readiness
1. *Eyes*   YES NO

   a. Do the child's eyes seem comfortable (does not squint, rub eyes, hold   1. ☐ ☐
materials too close or too far from eyes)?

   b. Are the results of clinical tests or an oculist's examination favorable?   2. ☐ ☐

2. *Ears*

   a. Is it apparent through his response to questions or directions that he is   3. ☐ ☐
able to hear what is said to the class?

   b. Does he respond to a low-voice test of 20 feet, a whisper test of 15 inches?   4. ☐ ☐

   c. Do the results of his audiometer test indicate normal hearing ability?   5. ☐ ☐

3. *Speech*

   a. Does he articulate clearly?   6. ☐ ☐

   b. Does he speak in a group with some confidence?   7. ☐ ☐

   c. Does he speak without gross errors in pronunciation?   8. ☐ ☐

   d. Does he respond to suggestions for speech improvement?   9. ☐ ☐

4. *Hand-Eye Co-ordination*

   Is he able to make his hands work together in cutting, using tools, or bounc-   10. ☐ ☐
ing a ball?

5. *General Health*

   a. Does he give an impression of good health?   11. ☐ ☐

   b. Does he seem well nourished?   12. ☐ ☐

   c. Does the school physical examination reveal good health?   13. ☐ ☐

Social Readiness
1. *Co-operation*

   a. Does he work well with a group, taking his share of the responsibility?   14. ☐ ☐

   b. Does he co-operate in playing games with other children?   15. ☐ ☐

   c. Can he direct his attention to a specific learning situation?   16. ☐ ☐

   d. Does he listen rather than interrupt?   17. ☐ ☐

2. *Sharing*

   a. Does he share materials, without monopolizing their use?   18. ☐ ☐

   b. Does he offer help when another child needs it?   19. ☐ ☐

   c. Does he await his turn in playing or in games?   20. ☐ ☐

   d. Does he await his turn for help from the teacher?   21. ☐ ☐

3. *Self-reliance*

   a. Does he work things through for himself without asking the teacher   22. ☐ ☐
about the next step?

   b. Does he take care of his clothing and materials?   23. ☐ ☐

   c. Does he find something to do when he finishes an assigned task?   24. ☐ ☐

   d. Does he take good care of materials assigned to him?   25. ☐ ☐

Emotional Readiness
1. *Adjustment to Task*

   a. Does the child see a task, such as drawing, preparing for an activity,   26. ☐ ☐
or cleaning up, through to completion?

   b. Does he accept changes in school routine calmly?   27. ☐ ☐

Figure 2. (Reproduced with permission of the publishers from *Manual for Teaching the Reading-Readiness Program* by D. H. Russell and O. Ousley. Boston: Ginn and Company, 1957, pp. 55-57.)

Check List for Reading Readiness

c. Does he appear to be happy and well adjusted in schoolwork, as evidenced by relaxed attitude, pride in work, and eagerness for a new task?   28. ☐ ☐

d. Does he follow adult leadership without showing resentment?   29. ☐ ☐

2. Poise

a. Does he accept a certain amount of opposition or defeat without crying or sulking?   30. ☐ ☐

b. Does he meet strangers without displaying unusual shyness?   31. ☐ ☐

Psychological Readiness

1. Mind-Set for Reading

a. Does the child appear interested in books and reading?   32. ☐ ☐

b. Does he ask the meanings of words or signs?   33. ☐ ☐

c. Is he interested in the shapes of unusual words?   34. ☐ ☐

2. Mental Maturity

a. Do the results of the child's mental test predict probable success in learning to read?   35. ☐ ☐

b. Can he give reasons for his opinions about his own work or the work of others?   36. ☐ ☐

c. Can he make or draw something to illustrate an idea as well as most children of his age?   37. ☐ ☐

d. Is his memory span sufficient to allow memorization of a short poem or song?   38. ☐ ☐

e. Can he tell a story without confusing the order of events?   39. ☐ ☐

f. Can he listen or work for five or ten minutes without restlessness?   40. ☐ ☐

3. Mental Habits

a. Has the child established the habit of looking at a succession of items from left to right?   41. ☐ ☐

b. Does his interpretation of pictures extend beyond mere enumeration of details?   42. ☐ ☐

c. Does he grasp the fact that symbols may be associated with spoken language?   43. ☐ ☐

d. Can he predict possible outcomes for a story?   44. ☐ ☐

e. Can he remember the central thought of a story as well as the important details?   45. ☐ ☐

f. Does he alter his own method to profit by another child's example?   46. ☐ ☐

4. Language Patterns

a. Does he take part in class discussions and conversations?   47. ☐ ☐

b. Is he effective in expressing his needs in classroom situations?   48. ☐ ☐

c. Are the words used in the pre-primers and the primer part of his listening and speaking vocabulary?   49. ☐ ☐

d. Does he understand the relationships inherent in such words as *up* and *down*, *top* and *bottom*, *big* and *little*?   50. ☐ ☐

e. Does he listen to a story with evidence of enjoyment and the ability to recall parts of it?   51. ☐ ☐

f. Is he able to interpret an experience through dramatic play?   52. ☐ ☐

Figure 2. (cont.)

the like may often not be easy. Although the teacher may readily get an over-all impression of a child's competence, skill in more specific rating develops only with practice. Estimates or ratings should be made by comparing a child with other children in the same class with respect to whatever behavior, performance, or sort of adjustment is in question. For instance, the teacher in estimating the ability of each child to co-operate with other children in the school situation might choose to adopt a five-point scale. Its steps might be labelled: *quarrelsome, causes slight friction, indifferent, co-operates most of the time,* and *exceptionally co-operative.* Estimates of other traits may be made similarly.

A check list in outline form similar to that in Figure 2 can be helpful in reading appraisals. This *Check List for Reading Readiness* by Russell and Ousley (220), pp. 55-57, is part of the Ginn Basic Reader program. The following check lists for appraisal of reading readiness are recommended by Hildreth (133, p. 171):

1. Banham's *School Readiness Inventory.* Minneapolis: Educational Test Bureau, 1950.
2. *California Check List of Readiness.* Los Angeles: California Test Bureau.
3. General Appraisal of My First Grade Pupils, *My Weekly Reader* (Teacher's Ed.), 1954, No. 1, Vol. 32.
4. Guide to Teacher Judgment of Readiness, *Manual of the New York City Readiness Tests.* New York: New York City Board of Education.
5. Scale for Rating a Class for Reading Readiness, in A. J. Harris, *How to Increase Reading Ability,* 4th ed. New York: Longman's, Green and Company, 1961, p. 48.
6. Readiness Questionnaire, in E. Hurlock, *Child Growth and Development.* New York: McGraw-Hill Book Company, 1949, Chap. 20.
7. *Readiness Questionnaire.* California Principals' Association (Bay Section).
8. Readiness Questionnaire, in *Reading for Today's Children* (Thirty-fourth Yearbook of the National Principals' Association) Washington, D. C.: N.E.A., 1955, 38-41.

In addition to the judgments on the check list, the following should be listed for each child:

Chronological age (yrs. and mos.)
Mental age (yrs. and mos.)
I.Q.
Reading-readiness test scores
Tentative estimate of readiness for reading

From the data in a satisfactory check list which contains ratings on physical readiness, social and emotional readiness, plus the supplementary information obtained by measurement as discussed above, the tentative estimate of reading readiness can be made for each pupil. Then a summary sheet, listing all members of a class and noting the main strengths and weaknesses of each pupil, is easily constructed. The summary sheet should be revised from time to time as the readiness status of the children changes.

Summary

Reading readiness is determined through an appraisal of development in mental ability, general experience including language facility, visual and auditory efficiency, and personal and social adjustment. The appraisal is achieved by use of standardized tests of intelligence, standardized reading-readiness tests, and ratings based upon teacher observations. The most effective appraisal is derived from the standardized test results supplemented by teacher ratings. The appraisal of readiness for a specific child will reveal strengths and weaknesses in his pattern of abilities, experiences, and adjustments. These provide a guide for instruction in readiness.

Vocabulary

Check your knowledge of these terms. Reread parts of the chapter if necessary.

mental age	audiometer
I.Q.	zero decibel loss
individual tests	behavior inventory
validity	informal test
reliability	ambidexterous
word-matching	pattern of abilities
rhyming test	E-Test
standardized procedures	reading aptitude

Activities for Students

Observation: Confer with a teacher of a first-grade class. Obtain as much information as possible on how the teacher decides when a child is ready to begin reading.

Reading: Examine several reading-readiness tests. Note likenesses and differences in what is measured.

Creative thinking: Work out arguments for and against use of reading-readiness tests.

Selected References

See Chapter 5.

5

Development of Reading Readiness

Success in learning to read depends largely upon the stage of all-round development which the child has achieved. Involved in this growth is a complex of abilities, habits, and information. Some of its ingredients, such as intelligence, come with inner maturation. But many others are learned and are susceptible of guidance. To a large degree, therefore, reading readiness can be and should be taught.

There are three general periods in the development of reading readiness: *First* is the pre-school period. This begins soon after birth and continues until the child enters a school, either kindergarten or first grade. The *second* period includes the kindergarten year (in schools which have a kindergarten) and the early months of grade one. *Third*, there is the longer period inclusive of all the remainder of the grades, as explained at the end of Chapter 3.

Our aim at this point is to describe in some detail the readiness factors as they appear prior to entering school. In discussing development of readiness in the kindergarten and through the grades, only the fundamental features will be outlined. Then details concerning training in these two later periods will be introduced at appropriate places in the chapters on the kindergarten and on teaching in the grades.

The Pre-School Period

At present it is generally recognized that experience and guidance prior to kindergarten age can influence greatly the development of reading readiness. This is a period which has been stressed in the writings of Monroe (184), Bond and Wagner (27), and Larrick (149). The degree to which readiness develops during these first five or six years depends upon the relationship between the child and his parents, as well as upon the kind of home and the kind of neighborhood he is growing up in. Prior to school, the parents are the teachers of the child (see below), though, of course, other influences are involved. The child is getting valuable experience from his play with other children in the home and in the neighborhood and, if he is fortunate, in supervised playgrounds. And what he learns if he attends nursery school or Sunday school is not to be overlooked. The degree to which such pre-school experiences help to build readiness depends a lot, of course, upon the particular child and how intelligent he is. Other things being equal, the brighter child will naturally profit more from experiences and parental guidance than the less able child.

The development of reading readiness begins early in life, certainly by the end of the first year, usually somewhat earlier. In the five years (six years if no kindergarten is attended) before school the child develops countless aspects of readiness. He grows physically, mentally, and emotionally. In addition he acquires many of the habits, the interests, the vocabulary, the verbal facility, and a background of information, all of which prove essential when he begins learning to read.

The home environment

The differential effect on readiness of home environment is well illustrated by the contrasts between Jane and Dick, which we described in Chapter 3. A home, and all that goes on in it, including parental guidance, may be such that it fosters the development of excellent reading readiness, or only partial readiness, or hardly any at all. A number of ways in which readiness is likely to develop from home activities include the following:

1. *Growth of vocabulary and concept development.* The child begins early to learn the meaning of words and the concepts they embody. He hears words spoken in relation to objects, and to his activities and experiences. From this he soon appreciates the difference between the meanings of such words as *dog* and *cat, pig* and *cow, little* and *big, run* and *walk, up* and *down,* etc. From these learnings the child begins to develop more abstract concepts, the significance and limits of which gradually become clearer with added experiences. He comes to know that shepherds, spaniels, and other breeds are all dogs; or that hens, ducks, and turkeys, etc. are *not* all "chickies." Grasping of word meanings and concept building are guided constantly by parents and others. Questions are answered, mistakes corrected, and encouragement given.

2. *Verbal facility.* The development of verbal facility should progress hand in hand with growth in vocabulary and concepts. A child learns to talk by talking. Parents should not only encourage their children to put their experiences into words but should also steer them into the sorts of activities that foster talking. Clear enunciation is important. To discourage the persistence of baby talk, parents should set a good example by speaking clearly and guide his speech without nagging.

3. *Learning to listen.* Numerous activities encourage the child to listen: conversation with parents and others; stories told or read to him; receiving directions to run an errand such as taking a book to a neighbor, to bring in the evening newspaper, or how to play some kind of game.

4. *Auditory discrimination.* Skill in distinguishing likenesses and differences between word sounds is an important prerequisite for learning to read. Young children love to listen to the jingly repetition of words and rhymes, as in nursery rhymes. An opportunity to listen to word sounds and note how they differ and are alike occurs in many other situations such as in conversation and in hearing stories read by an older person.

5. *Visual discrimination* begins early and improves through the preschool years. The progress is from perceiving gross similarities and differences to ever finer discriminations between objects or pictures of objects and finally of symbols, figures, and words. Eventually the child learns that a printed word stands for a spoken word. He sees a word under a picture, he follows a sequence of pictures as his mother reads the accompanying printed story, he notes his dad reading something aloud from a newspaper or his mother reading the print in a book. Thus, even before he begins formal reading he may note the association between a printed word and the word spoken and its right meaning.

6. *Motor co-ordination* develops between eyes and hands through handling toys, scribbling with crayons, even turning a picture book right side up and turning pages of books and magazines. These co-ordinations are all helpful when the child begins to read.

7. *Personal and social adjustment.* The child whose personal adjustment is good has been at the same time developing his social adjustment, and both count as assets when it comes to learning to read. Personal adjustment is largely dependent upon a feeling of security inside and outside the home, a feeling of being loved and of belonging. Parents should provide opportunities, both in the home and outside, for a variety of social activities (play, parties, Sunday school, etc.) where other children are involved, so that the child will learn poise and co-operation when in groups. He should be encouraged to associate with the adults who visit in his home in order to develop ease in talking with grown-ups.

8. *Growth of independence.* The child who has everything done for him and all his problems solved by his mother has little chance to learn to do things by himself. This can become a serious handicap on entering school. He is far from ready to learn to read. Since his mother has not allowed him to take even the first steps toward growing up, he is still pretty much a baby. Two boys may be contrasted to illustrate how badly growth in independent behavior is needed:

a. Though Harry is a healthy and physically attractive five-year-old boy, he is almost totally lacking in self-reliance. Much of what he says is sprinkled with items of "baby talk." This supposedly "cute" but faulty enunciation has been encouraged by his mother who stands ready to interpret his speech to others instead of encouraging him to speak clearly. She bathes and dresses him, hangs up his clothes, puts away his toys, and directs all he does. Harry is never free to think for himself or act in line with his own purposes. His mother has unknowingly engineered Harry's complete dependence on her. On arrival at kindergarten or first grade, Harry is decidedly unready for learning on his own. The teacher must devote much time helping him to grow up and become to some degree self-reliant in the school situation.

b. Richard presents quite a different picture. Starting at an early age, his parents taught him to do things for himself and to think for himself. He was encouraged to dress and undress with as little help as possible, to keep his room in order, to put away his clothes and toys, to devise and play games by himself, and even to help plan picnics and other family trips. Richard also soon learned to run errands for his parents and to explore his immediate neighborhood on his own. He loved all this and made rapid strides in developing self-reliant behavior patterns. Each improvement in initiative was praised. Richard was well prepared and eager when he came to school and made rapid progress in all sorts of activities from the time he entered.

Some suggestions to parents

Bond and Wagner (27) have made some excellent specific suggestions to parents of pre-school children. They are given below in abbreviated form:

1. *Do all you can to insure the healthy physical development of your child.* A child who is undernourished, does not get enough sleep and exercise, or is subject to frequent minor illnesses, will lack the energy and vitality needed for learning, both in school and out.

2. *Note signs of sensory limitations.* Any defects in vision or hearing should be detected early and corrected if possible.

3. *Promote the development of many skills.* As your child gains skills, he achieves greater co-ordination, poise, and maturity in other respects which promote the kind of well-rounded development desirable for learning.

4. *Show that you recognize successful achievement.* Every child needs and wants approval when he is successful and encouragement when he is nearly successful or can do better next time.

5. *Join with your child in his activities and permit him to join in yours.* Co-operation between child and parents in family enterprises contributes much to development in following directions, assuming responsibilities, and feeling the emotional satisfaction of achievement.

6. *Assign tasks to be performed regularly.* In carrying out routine tasks about the home, the child learns that he has duties as well as privileges. The assigned tasks should be limited pretty much to caring for himself and his belongings. And they should be tasks which he can do.

7. *Encourage your child to explore his environment.* The main limitations on such exploration are those required for safeguarding the child and for avoiding destruction of property and cruelty to animals. A child uses all his senses in exploring: a cat feels soft, ice feels cold, some objects are of a size and shape to challenge lifting them, flowers look pretty and smell nice. Words and concepts are derived from these explorations.

8. *Extend the child's environment.* Without trips and firsthand experience, children cannot gain clear concepts of what are meant by such words as airport, depot, sleeping car, silo, freight yard, outboard motor, zoo, and innumerable other examples. A child should be prepared for trips beforehand and encouraged to talk about the experience before, during, and after it.

9. *Read to the child.* A child learns much from listening to stories, nursery rhymes, and poems. He comes to appreciate that pictures do not tell all the story and that much additional information can be obtained from the printed words. He gains a story sense from following a plot or from any orderly unfolding of events. He comes to appreciate the joys of reading.

10. *Provide books and other materials for your child's own use.* One aspect of readiness for reading is the ability to interpret pictures. Experience with picture books, some of which have a word or a sentence under the picture, builds readiness. Do not hesitate to read the sentence below the picture, moving your finger from left-to-right below the print as you read. A child may learn to recognize some of the words while a desire to read all by himself is forming. Cut-out and coloring materials should also be provided.

11. *Encourage creative activities.* Participating in creative activities in the home prepares the child for similar activities in school. Approval of what is accomplished *by the child himself* is ordinarily more effective than showing him how he could do it better.

12. *Encourage social participation.* Adjustment to group participation, both in free play and supervised games, equips the child for many school activities.

13. *Orient your child for the first day in school.* Prepare him so that he will anticipate with eagerness and pleasure his beginning school experiences.

14. *As a general rule you should accept your child's rate of learning.* Try to remember how long it has taken to teach your child the many skills, tasks and abilities he acquired during the pre-school years. Learning to read, which is a complex skill, will take longer for some children than others. Exhibiting irritation with the school or putting pressure on the child to get ahead faster should be avoided.

Kindergarten and Beginning Grade One

In many communities, children will spend a whole school year in kindergarten. Others will enter grade one on their first day of school. Details of readiness training in the kindergarten and in the first grade are given in the chapters devoted to those periods. We have space here only for certain basic information.

The kindergarten year

Teaching in the kindergarten is devoted primarily to preparing the child for systematic instruction in reading and other subjects in the primary grades, particularly in grade one. Experimental evidence demonstrates that this training is effective. Pratt (203) found that pupils who had had previous experience in kindergarten ranked higher than nonkindergarten children on reading-readiness tests at the beginning of the first grade and significantly higher in reading achievement at the end of the first grade. In a later study, Fast (78) discovered essentially the same advantage in reading readiness and reading achievement due to kindergarten training.

Obviously, because the children are less mature by a year, the readiness training in the kindergarten cannot be equal to that in grade one. Actually, however, the kindergarten teacher can provide beginning readiness training for all types of higher level activities in reading. Then the training begun in kindergarten is continued at a higher level at the beginning of grade one. The areas of training in kindergarten are essentially the same as in the first part of grade one: personal and social adjustment, identification of and adjustment to physical deficiencies, visual and auditory discrimination, supplying experiences and adding to information, developing language facility, developing desirable attitudes toward school and reading, interpreting pictures, learning to progress from left-to-right in perceiving, and experience with picture books and other materials. How all this is achieved will be explained in the chapter on the kindergarten.

Early grade-one program

The value of systematic instruction in preparation for reading at the beginning of the first grade has been demonstrated by Scott (224), Edmiston and Peyton (73), Orme (197), Jenkins (141), and Taylor (248).

As already noted, children enter grade one with various degrees of readiness for systematic reading instruction. Those best prepared, however, will profit from a brief period of orientation before beginning to read, during which they become adapted to a new teacher, to a new room, and to new class organizations, so that they feel comfortable and secure. During this time the teacher estimates, measures, and evaluates the pupils' abilities, backgrounds of information, and behavior patterns. Because of wide differences in degree of development, the readiness program will continue longer for some children than for others. As a matter of fact, certain pupils may be ready to begin the systematic reading program at the end of the orientation period of two or three weeks. As pointed out by Hildreth (133), the length of the readiness period will depend upon how readiness is interpreted, on the range in maturity of the children, how much grouping for instruction is advisable, and the number of slow learners in the class. As we have stressed before, the readiness program should be well organized and centered around definite objectives to promote growth according to the individual needs of the pupils. There will be some variation in emphasis according to local situations and to what is to be prepared for in a particular school system. Any tendency to confine the readiness program to formalized drill should be avoided.

Basic Program for Readiness Development

Readiness for reading is best developed in a stimulating class atmosphere which provides varied and well-organized activities. The nature of these activities is determined by what is needed by the child for success in learning to read. While several aspects of readiness are covered in the developmental program, they are not mutually exclusive since they are interrelated and overlapping. Hardly ever is a readiness activity confined to one aspect. The instructional program, if satisfactorily organized, co-ordinates the various aspects of readiness, is stimulating, and appeals to the child's interests. The program should provide enriched learning experiences that foster adjustment to school and supply information and skills needed for learning to read. The following discussion will cover the fundamental features of developing reading readiness. Details of co-ordinating the program in the classroom will be given at the appropriate places in the chapters on the kindergarten and grade one.

Personal and social adjustment

Other things being equal, the happy, well-adjusted child who feels secure in the school situation will make better progress in learning to read. Experiences should be so arranged that they encourage active interests and self-expression. Frequently special guidance is needed to develop confidence and self-reliance in a child. Participation and success in both classroom and play activities are important for developing a feeling of security in the timid, shut-in child. So are they for the child who is compensating for a feeling of inferiority by resorting to aggressive and bullying behavior. He needs sympathetic understanding as well as success in participation before he can gain enough self-confidence to co-operate easily and naturally in the school activities. Sometimes it is necessary to consult with and get the co-operation of the parents in order to help the child become better adjusted personally and socially.

A number of procedures are helpful to this end. Games can be so organized that each child will automatically expect to participate. Responsibility for a definite part of a group task, when the group is small, tends to develop confidence in a timid child. Feelings of warmth and security and a little pride may come from preparing and presenting something particularly useful to a group, or something it obviously enjoys. The effect of emotional attitudes on learning is ably evaluated by Monroe (184). In her analysis of reading cases, Ephron (75) shows how very important improved emotional adjustment is in the reading situation.

Adjustments for physical deficiencies

Whenever physical deficiencies are discovered, correction should be attempted, referring the child to a specialist if that is indicated. Some children need glasses, others should have their tonsils or adenoids removed to remedy impaired hearing. As we have said, minor speech defects can ordinarily be corrected by the teacher. This is true of mild cases of lisping, poor articulation, and too fast speaking. Relaxed attitudes should be encouraged. All severe and persistent cases of speech difficulty, however, require help from a specialist. Poor muscular co-ordination is much aided by *patient* effort and understanding, helping the child by showing him how to handle objects, and getting him to participate in the various rhythmic activities that occur in certain games.

Where defects cannot be corrected, as in some cases of deficient hearing and vision, instruction has to be adapted to give the child every possible chance to learn. The hard-of-hearing child should have a favored position close to the speaker and should be encouraged to watch the lips of the person speaking. For such a child the visual methods of teaching reading should be emphasized. Similarly, classroom adjustments should be made for the child who has poor vision. He should have a seat where the light is very good. Emphasis in his case is placed upon auditory methods of instruction. Reading need not be delayed because of either auditory (Bond, 23) or visual (Fendrick, 82) deficiencies, provided appropriate methods of instruction are employed. This does not mean that referral to a specialist should be delayed when trouble is suspected, for visual and auditory difficulties are bound to impose handicaps in learning to read.

When there is poor general health, care must be taken to avoid fatigue. Following a medical examination, the doctor's suggestions concerning the amount of work required of a child should be followed. Parents should be advised concerning the child's eating and sleeping habits. Adequate rest periods are essential.

Training in visual discrimination

Learning to read requires rather exacting visual discriminations. By the time a child has reached the beginning of grade one, he will of course be completely familiar with the differences between a chair and a stool, a box and a ball, a stone and an apple, a pencil and a crayon, and so on. To be prepared for reading, however, the child must be able to make much finer discriminations than these. He will have to be able to discriminate not only between word forms, but between details within word forms. Practically all reading-readiness tests have a section to measure perception of likenesses and differences in words and letters. Some tests include sections to measure discrimination of likenesses and differences in outlined pictures or geometric forms, though the uses of these are limited. Most children can readily distinguish between a triangle and a circle or square, and it is open to question whether training to discriminate geometric forms will have any important effect on ability to discriminate words. Only when there is an almost total lack of ability to discriminate between words or letters, should there be training with geometric forms and pictures as an initial part of the program in visual discrimination. The ordinary teacher will seldom encounter such pupils.

Improving discrimination of word forms and letters

Various kinds of exercises may be employed to improve discrimination of word forms. In such training it is not necessary, and the child should not be required, to pronounce the words. In organizing such exercises, the words used should be ones the child will meet in first-grade reading, the initial ones involving obvious likenesses and differences. As the training progresses, the discriminations required may become more and more exacting.

Formal exercises are to be used with discretion. For best results, they should constitute only a part of the readiness program for developing visual discrimination. The alert teacher will find many opportunities to emphasize visual discrimination during a variety of class activities. Nevertheless, some drill in word discrimination is desirable. McKee (178) stresses the need for training the child to distinguish between word forms, parts of words, and letters. It is likely that such training will become more effective as he begins to read. Hildreth (132) states flatly that exercises requiring the matching of word forms "should come after children have done some context reading" (p. 285).

With proper instruction, most children will improve rapidly in their visual discriminations. After beginning to read, practice in visual discrimination becomes an integral part of the reading process. At times, however, special training will be needed to meet individual difficulties and to assure clear perceptions of certain new words.

Training in auditory discrimination

By the time a child enters school he has gained considerable skill in ability to distinguish between sound patterns. Quite early he will distinguish between the sound of his mother's voice and that of other people, and between a word of approval and a word of command. Differences between ordinary sounds in his environment, such as an automobile horn and a barking dog, are readily detected. Many children will have learned to distinguish quite well the likenesses and differences in many word sounds through listening and talking, and through hearing and repeating nursery rhymes. It is doubtful, however, that all children will have learned to distinguish all the slight differences in sound needed in beginning reading, such as the differences between *wear* and *where,* and so on. Templin (249) investigated discrimination of speech sounds in children, ages 3 to 8. The *wh* sound proved particularly difficult for them to discriminate. Skill in distinguishing auditory patterns is extremely important in learning to read. While some children will need the training more than others, all will profit by some practice prior to and during beginning reading. For instance, the child will need to distinguish between the sounds of *dog* and *dig, big* and *bug, hat* and *hot,* and so on. Acquisition of the ability to distinguish not only between the more easily noted differences as *bat* and *bug,* but also between the more confusing sounds such as *broad* and *board,* is an essential part of preparation for reading.

Methods to improve discrimination of word sounds

Training in auditory discrimination in the reading-readiness program is concerned with the sounds made in pronouncing sounds of words that will certainly be encountered and used in beginning reading. It deals with discriminating sounds as they occur in different parts of words—the beginning, middle, and ending sounds. Various types of exercises have been devised for this training. Detailed suggestions are given in Betts (18) and in various methods books. As in the case of visual training, progress should be from easy to more difficult. Obviously all the exercises should be oral until after reading is begun. In all instances, *natural* pronunciation of words should be used, that is, without special sounding out of words.

Children are likely to profit more in learning discrimination if the words are in sentences rather than in meaningless sequences. Listening to rhymes and jingles is a good exercise and one that delights them. If they have become familiar with the material, or if it is repeated several times, they like to say the rhyming words aloud when the teacher comes to them. With encouragement, children also like to make up simple rhymes, such as "The *cat* caught the *rat,*" or "The little red *hen* lived in a *pen.*"

In all this work there are excellent opportunities to encourage clear and precise enunciation in speech patterns, with everything done in such a way that the child finds the experience pleasurable. After he actually begins to read, further training in auditory discrimination can be introduced as required. This will vary with the individual needs of pupils and should be modified to meet difficulties as they arise.

Training to cultivate oral word discrimination should be associated with language development. Such activities are most useful as an aid in learning to read when they are intimately integrated with experiences designed to develop linguistic facility. Hildreth (132) for instance, stresses the frequent use of familiar words in oral communication, together with clear enunciation, as aids in developing sensitivity to differences and likenesses in word sounds.

Informal grouping

The information obtained from tests and teacher ratings find two important uses in the reading-readiness program. They may be employed to good advantage in grouping the children for instruction, and for discovering areas for emphasis in the instructional program. Here we are concerned primarily with grouping for readiness instruction. As the school year progresses, readiness instruction will merge with systematic reading instruction.

In order to block out an effective instructional program the teacher must make a preliminary estimate of what particular children can do. It is customary to divide a beginning first-grade class into groups on the basis of their special instructional needs as these show up in the results of intelligence tests, the reading-readiness test, teacher ratings, and any other information available. Such a grouping will necessarily be *tentative and flexible*. A child may be shifted from one group to another on the basis of his growth in skills and any other evidence of the correct instructional level for him. In the average classroom about three main groups tend to be found practical. The following is suggested as a basis for the initial tentative grouping.

In the first group are placed the children who, in terms of available data, will probably make rapid progress in learning to read. A child placed in this group should have a mental age of approximately six years, six months or greater, a centile rating of approximately 65 or greater on total score of the reading-readiness test, above average language facility, a broad background of experience, and good personal and social adjustment. These children will need a minimum amount of reading-readiness training. They may be expected to gain rapidly in classroom co-operation, independent study, and reading skill.

The second group will consist of "average" pupils. The child in this group should have a mental age between about six years and six years, six months, a centile rating for total score in reading readiness between 35 and 65, an average background of experience and language facility, and be at least fairly well adjusted. These children will need up to about three months' training in reading readiness and may be expected to make normal progress in reading. Ordinarily reading instruction will be started prior to completion of the reading-readiness training.

The pupils in the third group will, for the most part, be decidedly lacking in reading readiness. The slow learners will certainly be found here. In other words, children in this group will fall below the standards of the other two groups. They will tend to be intellectually immature, those who seem to have inadequate background of experience and relatively poor language facility. Some will need training in reading readiness for a term. Others may not be ready to read for a year.

Classification into groups should be *flexible*. As soon as a child demonstrates improved development and skills, he should be shifted to the next higher group. Furthermore, there may be regroupings for different specific purposes. For example, a small group may be formed for training in auditory discrimination, another for practice in language facility, and so forth. This procedure will lessen the need for individual instruction. In some instances, therefore, it is advisable to employ relatively small groups for certain instructional needs. Suggestions for dealing with children who are already reading by the time they reach school will be given in Chapter 19.

The method of grouping and the number of groups it is found necessary to have should be varied to fit the local situation. In a residential district where the parents are competent, there may be no need for the slow group; in a distinctly less favored district there may be no high group, or the teacher may find it advisable to have a fourth or extra low group for relatively very immature pupils.

What is to be kept in mind is that the limits of intelligence- and readiness-test scores suggested above for forming the groups are only tentative. There is nothing sacred in a test rating of 65 or 70 centile score, or six years, six months mental age as the lower limit of group one. For instance, the teacher may find a child with a mental age of seven years whose background of experience and language facility suggests that he should be placed in the second group for a time. And another pupil with a mental age of only six years, three months may be so well developed in other respects that he should be placed in group one. The teacher will depend upon her appraisal of the total pattern of readiness in placing a particular child and in moving a child from one group to another as his development proceeds. (See Chapter 17 for discussion of grouping throughout the grades.)

Guides in readiness instruction

Test scores and teacher ratings are also employed to good advantage as guides in readiness instruction. Each of the abilities measured on a reading-readiness test, as well as degree of experience and language facility, may be improved by instruction. If a child is relatively deficient in language facility or obtains a low centile score on one or more aspects of measured reading readiness, he should be given training in the types of experience which will increase those abilities. The lower the score, the more need for special instruction.

Let us look at two contrasting cases. Jane, on entering grade one, has a mental age of seven years, manifests good adjustment in personal and social situations, has a good command of language and gets a centile rating of 81 on total readiness score. On all parts of the readiness test but rhyming she receives centile ratings of over 70. On the rhyming test she has a centile rating of only 38. Jane should make rapid progress in learning to read. Although she should be placed in group one, the teacher should provide special training in auditory discrimination. This may be done in part by including her in another group temporarily when auditory discrimination is being taught.

Jack's pattern of abilities is considerably different than that of Jane. He has a mental age of six years, five months, in talking he forms relatively simple sentences that are not well co-ordinated with each other, and his centile rating for total score on a reading-readiness test is 51. His scores on word-form and on letter-form matching are both low, 28 and 40 centiles respectively. The other scores range from 60 to 72. Jack should make about average progress in learning to read. Several weeks of training in the reading-readiness program are indicated. Special help should be provided in language usage, and in visual discrimination of words and letter forms. He will profit by both direct and vicarious experience as a basis for development of vocabulary and concepts. Jack should be placed in group two for instructional purposes.

Other children who are relatively low in all or nearly all scores on a reading-readiness test will need an extended period of reading-readiness instruction. The child who speaks a foreign language at home presents a special problem. He must learn English before much progress along other lines can be made. Manuals, such as that of Gates (95), give suggestions for the use of test scores as a guide to instruction in reading readiness.

Providing a background of experience and information

Earlier in our discussion it has been emphasized that printed words will have significance for the child in proportion to the degree that they stand for concepts and information related to his own experience. There are two avenues of experience, direct and vicarious. Direct experience is concerned with firsthand contact with things, such as a ride in a train, a trip to the zoo, or caring for a pet kitten. One gets direct experience through seeing, hearing, tasting, smelling, and feeling objects. Next best is vicarious experience, that is, secondhand or indirect experience. It consists of an extension of or a supplement to direct experience. It may come from pictures, maps, models, motion pictures, stories, etc. Reading, of course, is a source of vicarious experience and therefore must be a supplement to (or based upon) direct experience.

Experience and meanings. Concepts (or meanings) and information, together with the resulting enrichment of vocabulary that comes from experience, constitute the very core tools with which progress is made in the reading-readiness program. It is essential, therefore, that appropriate worthwhile experiences be furnished the children. Much careful thought has been given this problem. The consensus is that the experiences should be varied, that they be appropriate to the needs in the early reading program as well as provide a valuable and lasting enrichment of knowledge, that they fulfill the needs of the particular class being taught and be within the comprehension range of that class, and that they have value for developing desirable habits and attitudes. In general, the program should progress towards breadth of fundamentally enriching experiences which stimulate an enquiring attitude in the child. The enriching experiences will, of course, be pleasing in themselves as well as otherwise profitable.

Experience programs. Programs for providing and extending experience and information during preparation for reading are well developed. They include such activities as trips to the zoo, the post office, the fire station, stores, a farm, the library, railroad and bus stations, mills and factories. These firsthand experiences should be supplemented with appropriate vicarious experiences along the lines mentioned above, that is, pictures, discussion, stories, and so forth.

Children should be well prepared for such trips. In this preparation, the teacher explains the things that may be seen and what may be understood about them. Pictures are examined and related experiences shared. The trip is planned in detail. After the trip, the experience is discussed in detail and its meaning and value appraised. This will help to fill out aspects of the experience not noted by some of the children. Perhaps a second trip of the same sort will be advisable to satisfy interests and add further information.

Development of language facility

Readiness for reading is fostered by improved language facility. The greater the ability to comprehend material presented in oral form, and the greater the proficiency in the use of oral language, the more ready the child will be for beginning reading. Various influences improve language facility. For instance, by becoming a good listener, as Gates put it (97, p. 153), the child has acquired "story sense" when he has learned to listen to, understand, and follow a story told or read to him. Some children are deficient in this skill on arrival at school. Guided practice will improve the ability to select the most significant episodes as the story progresses and relate them to what comes before and after in the story. Thus a child may learn to anticipate what is going to come next. This use of context to anticipate what comes next in a story is a great aid to the child in learning to read. A part of the pre-reading program, therefore, consists of reading and telling stories to the children of a length and complexity appropriate to their needs and background. For the lowest group, the teacher should start with short, relatively simple stories and gradually work up to stories of the length and complexity of those which will be encountered in their early reading. The teacher can promote comprehension of related sequences of events in other classroom situations. Examples include the sequence of events to be followed in organizing a party, in reporting news and events in the community, in carrying out the teacher's directions for classroom activities such as how to set up a play store. An incentive to follow an organized sequence of events is provided by halting the story or account and requesting the children to tell what should come next. Often, a child will present a next step which does not come in the original account but which is after all perfectly logical.

Discussion improves language facility. Discussion periods foster improvement in a child's language facility. They provide opportunities for practice in using various forms of simple sentences, for broadening the speaking vocabulary, for clarifying enunciation, and for introducing new words. All this will promote accuracy and ease in oral communication. Munkres (188) furnishes a wealth of material designed to help children in oral communication. If carefully organized, even the shy and withdrawn pupils will learn to participate in the discussions and other talk. These situations may be concerned with the care of pets, a trip to the post office, the celebration of a holiday, the telling and acting out of stories, the organizing of a play store, and so on.

While a child's oral and listening vocabulary is based upon information and concepts derived from experience, readiness for reading occurs only when he has acquired some facility in the oral use of sentences. In addition to using single sentences, the child needs to use sequences of sentences orally that are logically related to each other as in storytelling or describing what happened on a trip. In other words, skill in seeing relationships and in expressing them in oral sentences reflect ability to think clearly and are prerequisites to beginning reading. An important aim in the reading program is, therefore, to develop sufficient command of oral language to speak fluently and with ease.

Developing habits of attention. Practice in listening to and telling stories, in discussion, in reporting events, and in carrying out instructions all furnish an opportunity to foster the habits of attention essential to effective learning. These habits would include the ability to sustain attention for an adequate length of time during regular work or play activities. In addition it is desirable that the child acquire the knack of thoughtful attention when new things are being introduced in the instructional program. Development of satisfactory habits of attention is possible only if the child also acquires the ability to disregard minor distractions while engaged in learning.

Various supplementary techniques aid in developing habits of good attention. These include forming intimate groups of children being taught something, voice inflections by the teacher, asking questions at appropriate places, holding the children to what is relevant in discussions, and clearly letting them see the purposes of a discussion. Closer attention is fostered also when children clearly understand what to listen for in a story, whether read or told. The teacher who understands pupil needs and organizes her programs to fulfill these needs will make good progress in developing the motivation and interest necessary for maintaining attention at a level satisfactory for learning.

Other training for readiness

There are a few additional points to consider in preparing the child for reading. We shall take up the roles of color experiences, interpreting pictures, perceptual orientation along successive lines of print, and growth in the desire to read.

Color experiences. Children need training in the perception and naming of colors, for contemporary children's books make a great deal of use of colored illustrations. Colored crayons are used in many activities both at home and in school, and color perception and interpretation (concepts) are necessary in many other activities. It is desirable that children become accustomed to assigning correct names to the common colors to promote appropriate interpretation of situations as they occur. This is best done in such activities as coloring with crayons, nature study, discussion of the color of animals, clothing, and traffic signals. The few boys who are color blind to reds and greens will need sympathetic understanding and special guidance by the teacher. Most color-blind persons can learn to assign proper names to the more common colors by attending to their brightness and texture differences even though they cannot discriminate red and green hues as such. Such children should be taught to interpret traffic signals in terms of brightness differences and placement (red is usually above green). As a matter of fact, most "red" and "green" objects, including traffic lights, are not pure spectral colors. Many are tinged with other hues, such as blue or yellow, to which red-green color-blind persons are sensitive. Thus the "green" traffic light is ordinarily bluish-green. This lack of purity aids color discrimination in many instances.

Reading pictures. Children should be taught to interpret, i.e., to "read" pictures. Interest in pictures develops at an early age and is maintained as the child grows older, hence the practice of illustrating children's books profusely. The imaginative interpretation of the pictures accompanying a story will furnish important context clues to aid word perception in reading. Ordinarily these clues do not attain maximal usefulness unless children receive considerable training in picture reading. When presented with a picture and asked to describe it, a child may merely enumerate the separate persons or objects present such as boy, girl, dog, mother, father, tree, and so on. He may be totally incapable of grasping the implication of the situation depicted. For such a child, training for interpretation should begin with relatively simple action pictures such as a dog and boy running. This could be followed by a dog running with a cap in his mouth and the boy after him. With some guidance the child will learn to perceive that the dog is running away with the boy's cap and that the boy is trying to catch the dog to recover the cap. By gradual transition the child will eventually be able to interpret a complex picture as meaning that a family has traveled in their car to a park for a picnic, the basket of food has been placed on the ground near a spread-out cloth for lunch, and while Dad is starting a fire, their dog has started to eat the lunch in the basket. Training in picture reading teaches the child not only to note the details in a picture but their interrelation in telling a story. There are abundant sources of appropriate pictures in magazines, newspapers, and posters as well as in books.

Training should be given also in interpreting series of pictures illustrating the unfolding of action in a story. The techniques of telling a story by sequences of pictures is employed in children's books as well as in comic strips and books. After gaining some proficiency in picture interpretation, children are delighted in reading them and rapidly gain in proficiency. In fact, many children learn to follow the story in comic strips before they can read. To foster picture reading, many pre-reading materials now contain stories in picture sequences.

Left-to-right progress in reading. The left-to-right sequence of perception accompanying eye movements along a line of print in reading has to be learned. Unless specifically trained to begin at the left and progress toward the right, it is just as natural for the young child to look at a picture or series of words from right to left as in the reverse direction. During the pre-reading period, the child needs specific training so that he will readily orient himself to attack individual words and lines of print in a left-to-right direction when he starts to read. To facilitate this, the child should be taught to identify his right and left hand, and to grasp the concept of right and left in relation to the sides of objects in the schoolroom such as the bulletin board, the blackboard, the desks, the page of a picture book, and so on. This can be accomplished largely through incidental learning or games rather than by formal drill. Thus the teacher can remark that she will write or draw something at the left side of the blackboard as she starts to do it. When the teacher asks the children to rearrange material on the bulletin board she can ask them to post the material from left to right. A sequence of action pictures can be drawn from left to right on the blackboard and interpreted in the same direction. Children can be trained to work from left to right in their readiness work books. Some picture books are designed for this purpose. The resourceful teacher will frequently bring in the notion of left to right in instructions, in play, in arrangements of material, and so on, so that the habit of proceeding perceptually in that direction will become well established. At every opportune place, therefore, as the child approaches the time when he will begin to read, the left-to-right sequence of perception should be emphasized. For example, when the teacher writes on the blackboard, the child can be shown that the words are formed from left to right, and that she then reads the material in the same order, following with a pointer. A very essential feature of pre-reading work is to set up this proper directional orientation.

Desire to read. Books are introduced early in the pre-reading program in order to develop an interest in them and a desire to read. There should be in the classroom a library corner with proper facilities for displaying various types of books. The children should be encouraged to examine the books and to make selections in them for the teacher to read aloud. Ordinarily, interest in a new book can be stimulated by reading selections aloud to the class and by showing some of its pictures. Children should be taught how to handle and manipulate a book. By discussion and example, the teacher instructs the children how to hold the book, how to turn the pages, and how to keep it clean and free from marks. As part of this training, the children should be frequently checked to insure proper habits in use of the books.

Work habits. During the readiness program it is desirable to develop good work habits with respect to both group and individual tasks. Effective learning in the group situation requires both participation and co-operation by each child. Children should learn to complete their tasks whether they have been assigned by the teacher or chosen by themselves. Guidance of the children to foster independence in their activities is also necessary. This training may involve care of materials in the classroom, or learning to complete a task with a few or no directions. The teacher should be generous with praise in approval of good performances. This is very important. Parenthetically it may be pointed out that in general it is better practice to praise the *accomplishments* of a child rather than the child himself. This draws attention to what is done well rather than to the youngster, who mustn't be encouraged to think of himself too much.

Reading-readiness materials

A great variety of pamphlets and books with instructions for using them in the reading-readiness program is now available. In addition, workbooks which accompany most basal series of readers contain materials organized to develop reading readiness. They contain pictures and exercises, arranged in developmental sequences, designed to foster the growth of the abilities essential for beginning reading, including the left-to-right progression of perception. Their main emphasis, however, appears to be upon developing perceptual readiness for reading. While many of these books are valuable, they do not constitute a complete reading-readiness program. Nevertheless the better ones do foster a more gradual introduction to reading, which is desirable, and they can be used to advantage as part of a well-organized reading-readiness program. There should be no wholesale use of readiness books as a substitute for a richer program of readiness activities.

Developing Reading Readiness Beyond the First Grade

Reading readiness plays an important role at all educational levels. Its presence cannot be assumed, it must be assured by appropriate appraisal, and supplemented by instruction when necessary for progress in the teaching program. Sochor (232) recognizes that since reading readiness is fundamental to all reading activities it is a basic concern of all teachers. It is important, therefore, that the teachers in all grades realize the problem and take steps to meet it. Individual differences in achievement become greater as children progress through the grades. Furthermore the reading task becomes increasingly complex from grade to grade. Not all children are ready for the reading tasks in the grades above the first. Here the readiness program must be geared to individual differences in addition to providing techniques for attacking new reading materials, especially in the content areas. Insuring reading readiness must necessarily involve a continuing program from the beginning of school through the successive grade levels.

Factors operating in the early months of the first grade as discussed above are also important throughout the grades: mental capacity, physical status, visual and auditory discrimination, experience and verbal facility, and personal and social adjustment. Individual differences in each and all of these factors must be considered in organizing the instructional program to meet the needs of the pupils in a class, i.e., to insure adequate readiness for specific reading assignments. Reading readiness is developmental, like reading ability. The two progress hand-in-hand. In her instructional program, the teacher must also make adjustments to differences in mental status at all grade levels. And with certain children, the program for improving visual and auditory discrimination, and personal and social adjustment must be continued at levels above grade one.

Other factors

As children progress through the grades readiness in other areas needs to be considered. These areas include experience, oral language, achievement, word perception, comprehension skills, and selection of materials.

Experience. If a reader is to understand, he must have an appropriate background of experience. In general, a rich and varied experience leads to better comprehension. For specific units of reading such as about a farm, a fire station, or a zoo, comprehension is maximum only when the child has had appropriate firsthand and vicarious experiences. As noted in an earlier chapter, there is no meaning inherent in printed symbols themselves. A background of knowledge which includes well-organized concepts is basic. Only then is the reader able to attach meanings to the printed symbols in his reading. Other things being equal, when a child possesses suitable information and concepts from experience and the English words attached, he is *ready to read.*

Oral language. To a large degree reading is based upon oral language. The child who has acquired verbal facility in relation to his thinking about experiences tends to be well prepared for reading material connected with the experiences. Precise and logical speech indicates that concepts related to experience are clear and well organized. Readiness for reading a specific unit, therefore, presupposes that the child understands the vocabulary and concepts involved and that he has the verbal facility to discuss materials at the complexity level in that unit.

Achievement. Readiness for reading a selection requires a level of achievement that is adequate for successful reading of the selection. Readiness is sequential in that each step depends upon previous learning.

Perceiving words. Learning the techniques for identifying and recognizing words begins soon after the child enters school and continues through the grades, step by step. Readiness for mastering each successive technique or skill depends upon having learned what came before.

Comprehension. The basic factors in comprehension are thinking, command of vocabulary and of the concepts for which words stand, and perceiving the relation between words in phrases and sentences. In addition, the child must learn to employ adequately the various comprehension and study skills. To be ready for reading a selection, the knowledges and skills previously covered in the developmental reading program should be mastered sufficiently for successfully reading the selection.

Selecting materials. To fulfill the requirements of reading readiness, reading materials are selected in terms of a pupil's readiness. That is, materials are adjusted to individual differences in ability and achievement. It is assumed that a sequential program of readiness has been carried out.

Russell (213) has listed the tasks of the teacher in diagnosing and developing readiness in the grades:

1. She must assure that the basic reading skills taught earlier have been learned. Any deficiencies discovered must be made up by teaching.
2. She should stimulate interest in the particular reading materials to be used. The stage is set for the unit by preliminary assignments, by discussions, by noting pupils' related experiences and how these may be amplified in the new materials, and by audio-visual materials.
3. She should familiarize the pupils with the vocabulary and concepts which occur in the reading material. This should be done by providing experiences related to the ideas in the unit rather than by mere dictionary study.
4. She should furnish a mental set for the specific material to be read.

5. She should guide the children to the most effective method for reading the selection to achieve the set purpose of the reading, i.e., whether it is to get a general impression, to note exact details, to draw conclusions, or something else.

Checking readiness

Appraisal of readiness through the grades is a continuing program. Readiness can be achieved at any level only when the teacher knows the strengths and weaknesses of her pupils. Appraisal is made at appropriate times to find whether pupils have achieved sufficient mastery of what has been taught so that the individuals in the class can progress to the next technique, skill, unit, or grade. This appraisal is achieved by tests designed for this purpose. Some basic series have tests to measure achievement when each book is finished. Teacher-made tests are employed for appraising day-by-day or unit-by-unit progress. Certain materials in workbooks may be used for such appraisal. See earlier material in Chapter 4.

Summary

Progress in learning to read is most rapid when all factors conditioning reading readiness are optimum. Many of these factors can be improved by instruction prior to and during beginning reading. Systematic training in the following areas is a legitimate part of the readiness program: personal and social adjustment, visual and auditory discrimination, experience and information, verbal facility in communication, desirable habits of attention and work, interpreting pictures, left-to-right sweeps of the eyes in reading, and development of a desire to read. Strengths and weaknesses in the various areas are appraised by reading-readiness tests or by teacher observations and ratings, or both. Appraisal of the total pattern of reading readiness of children (M.A., scores on readiness test, teacher ratings) will provide the bases for classification into groups for readiness training. In this way instruction is adjusted to meet the individual needs of each child. Through appraisal of progress in the readiness program, the teacher decides when a pupil has attained the mental maturity, the background of experience, the verbal facility, the behavior patterns, and the degree of adjustment which indicate that he is ready to begin reading with a good chance of success.

Reading readiness functions at all grade levels and in all reading activities. It is complex since it is made up of many interrelated factors. To achieve reading readiness for any reading unit, the teacher must know and adjust instruction to the strengths and weaknesses of the children in her class or subgroup of the class, i.e., individual differences in ability and achievement must be allowed for. Every pupil must be made ready to read.

Vocabulary

Check your knowledge of these terms. Reread parts of the chapter if necessary.

pattern of growth	average pupils
concept development	flexible grouping
motor co-ordination	vicarious experience
sensory limitation	consensus
creative activities	attention
basic program	reading pictures
feeling of security	sequence of perception
natural pronunciation	appraisal
teacher ratings	individual needs

Activities for Students

Observation: Visit a class in an elementary school and note in detail how the teacher prepares a group for reading a new unit.

Reading: Read through a unit in a fourth-grade basic reader. Then outline the things to be done to prepare pupils for reading the unit.

Creative thinking: State reasons for and against reading-readiness instruction in the intermediate grades.

Selected References

BETTS, Emmett A., *Foundations of reading instruction.* New York: American Book Company, 1957, Chaps. 8-13.

BOND, Guy L., and WAGNER, Eva B., *Teaching the child to read,* 3rd ed. New York: The Macmillan Company, 1960, Chaps. 6, 7.

—— and WAGNER, Eva B., *Child growth in reading.* Chicago: Lyons and Carnahan, 1955.

CAUSEY, Oscar S. (ed.), *The reading teacher's reader.* New York: The Ronald Press Company, 1958, 62-72.

DAWSON, Mildred A., and BAMMAN, Henry A., *Fundamentals of basic reading instruction.* New York: Longmans, Green and Company, 1959, Chap. 3.

DeBOER, John J., and DALLMANN, Martha, *The teaching of reading.* New York: Holt, Rinehart and Winston, 1960, Chaps. 5A, 5B.

DURRELL, Donald D., *Improving reading instruction.* New York: Harcourt, Brace & World, Inc. 1956, Chaps. 3, 4.

GATES, Arthur I., *The improvement of reading,* 3rd ed. New York: The Macmillan Company, 1947, Chap. 6.

GRAY, Lillian, and REESE, Dora, *Teaching children to read,* 2nd ed. New York: The Ronald Press Company, 1957, Chaps. 4, 5.

HARRIS, Albert J., *How to increase reading ability,* 4th ed. New York: Longmans, Green and Company, 1961, Chap. 2.

HEILMAN, Arthur W., *Principles and practices of teaching reading.* Columbus, Ohio: Charles E. Merrill Books, Inc., 1961, Chaps. 2, 3.

HESTER, Kathleen B., *Teaching every child to read*. New York: Harper and Brothers, 1955, Chaps. 3-10 .

HILDRETH, Gertrude, *Readiness for school beginners*. New York: Harcourt, Brace & World, Inc., 1950.

—— *Teaching reading*. New York: Holt, Rinehart and Winston, 1958, Chap. 9.

HUNNICUTT, C. W., and IVERSON, William J. (eds.), *Research in the three R's*. New York: Harper and Brothers, 1958, Chap. 3.

McKEE, Paul, *The teaching of reading in the elementary school*. Boston: Houghton Mifflin Company, 1948, Chap. 7.

MONROE, Marion, *Growing into reading*. Chicago: Scott, Foresman and Company, 1951.

RUSSELL, David H., *Children learn to read*, 2nd ed. Boston: Ginn and Company, 1961, Chap. 6.

6

Acquiring Concepts and Building Vocabulary

The definition of reading we prefer emphasizes meanings, comprehension, and thinking. Basically, learning to read involves the development of facility in grasping the meanings for which printed or written symbols stand. These meanings may be familiar, drawn directly from the past experiences of the reader, or they may be new meanings, products of a process of recombining and reorganizing concepts already in his possession. A child develops into a good reader to the degree that he enlarges his store of meanings and vocabulary and advances in understanding and interpreting printed materials.

Two skills are essential in vocabulary building. The first occurs when the child incorporates new words into his speaking and understanding vocabulary. Then second, he must identify and recognize the printed symbols with which these new words are to be associated. Proper co-ordination of these two aspects of vocabulary development produces comprehension, which is the purpose of reading.

To be most serviceable, these two aspects of reading must operate mechanically, i.e., promptly and habitually, so that the major portion of attention may be devoted to meaning and comprehension. Grasping concepts, meanings, is the primary part of the process; recognizing words, either old or new, is subordinate. Reading to learn springs naturally from the kind of learning to read in which understanding is primary.

Word recognition divorced from meaning, or when meaning is vague and unclear, results in mere *verbalism*, the pronunciation and use of words in context without comprehending their meaning, as contrasted with the manipulation and organization of meanings in purposeful reading. If the thinking side of reading is secondary or absent, true reading is impossible. Although the identification and recognition of words should be systematically taught, this relatively mechanical aspect of reading should be made secondary to the development of meaning, comprehension, and *usage* of words. Identifying and recognizing words should be co-ordinated with development of concepts in an integrated program in order to achieve

119

growth toward a reading vocabulary which will prove adequate to reasonable demands.

A child learns to read effectively only to the degree that he acquires a meaningful vocabulary correctly connected with an adequate stock of concepts, and progresses in ability to understand and interpret printed or written materials. Each word in the vocabulary is the label for some concept. A concept is a generalization about related data. It is derived from percepts, images, and memory. When sufficient generalization has occurred so that a single verbal symbol recalls some feature which is common to several different objects, we have a concept. For example, the word "chair" stands for a concept for a class of objects which may be sat upon. The child has had experience with kitchen chairs, dining-room chairs, upholstered living-room chairs, and others. There gradually builds up in his mind an accumulation of related concrete associations with the word "chair." As experiences with chairs continue, the child realizes that a chair is a piece of furniture (a cushion will not do), that has four legs and a back to lean against (a stool will not do), and is used to sit upon. All this need not be verbalized by the child, but the common characteristics must be appreciated.

The teacher should keep in mind that development of the abilities and skills involved in reading overlap in the instructional program although they may be discussed in separate chapters. How they are co-ordinated in the instructional program will be shown in Part III of this book. In this chapter, word meanings and concepts will be discussed more or less simultaneously. In general, the clarification and expansion of word meanings indicates also a better understanding of the accompanying concept. The acquisition of concepts is discussed in detail by Russell in two publications (214, 218), and by Burton, Kimball, and Wing (38). McCullough (173) summarizes the implications of research on children's concepts.

How rapidly children progress in vocabulary development will depend upon the particular teacher, upon how she organizes her program of reading instruction, upon the organization of the reading program in a school, and upon the individual abilities and needs of her pupils. The teacher, therefore, will adjust the vocabulary training described here to her program, keeping in mind basic principles, goals to be achieved, and the relation of reading to the arts allied to it.

Studies of Vocabulary Growth

Quite a few of the scientific studies of vocabulary deal with its growth during the pre-school years. Russell (213) has surveyed these and lists some of their implications for the school reading program. With some modifications they are given here:

1. Reading success depends largely on the size and usefulness of a child's vocabulary. Research during the last 20 years seems to indicate that the understanding vocabulary is much larger than was thought to be true earlier. Shibles (225a) confirms this finding in a recent study. Bryan (35a), who also agrees, urges that it is the responsibility of all educators to enrich the word power of children.

2. The rapidity with which vocabulary is acquired depends upon intellectual maturity and opportunity to engage in varied experiences. Shibles (225a) has found that the understanding vocabulary of bright children is much larger than it is in those low in intelligence.

3. By the end of fourth grade a child's hearing and understanding vocabulary is largest, his reading vocabulary is next in size, followed by his speaking vocabulary and, last, by his writing vocabulary. They all overlap each other.

4. The range in size of vocabulary found among the children in any class is great. This must be taken into account in the instructional program (Figurel, 85a).

5. Most children have a vocabulary sufficient for success in reading in the first two grades. It is important for other purposes, however, that vocabulary should continue to grow in these grades. Beginning with the third grade there is manifest an increasing need for clear concepts to insure adequate comprehension in reading.

6. Not merely the size of vocabulary, but the extensiveness and depth of meanings it embodies become increasingly important. Key concepts about which the child may know little need clarification. Elementary school children are likely to have vague or incomplete concepts of matters basic to modern living. Knowledge of concrete objects such as *mountain* or *house* tend to be more exact than for that of abstractions such as *government* or *laws*. Furthermore, Gammon (91) found that in the primary grades, where he conducted an experiment, words with multiple meanings also present special problems.

7. While the available "standard word lists" may supply us with the words most useful for reading, we must remember that the frequency with which a word is used does not necessarily indicate how easy it is to use or how meaningful it is.

8. Vocabulary building provides a most valuable tool. It contributes both to the development of abilities and to personal growth. The importance of the instruction in vocabulary building which a child receives must never be underestimated.

Acquiring a Vocabulary

The development of a repertory of meanings involves forming concepts or understandings. Becoming proficient in using these concepts in communication is an integral part of the development. That is, they must be used correctly in listening, talking, and reading. Only when concepts are vivid and accurate will there be satisfactory comprehension and interpretation in reading.

Words acquire their first meanings through association with some past personal experience. As language facility increases and words are used in connection with newly experienced objects, situations, and events, concepts become clarified and enriched. When a new word is met in reading, the meanings aroused depend upon all past experience associated with the word, especially upon whatever understandings have been present in hearing the word and when using it in similar context.

In general, three approaches may be employed for enlarging the child's repertory of meanings in reading: (1) varied and rich firsthand and vicarious experiences, (2) wide and extensive reading, and (3) study of words.

The experienced teacher realizes that development of meanings to the level where they are vivid and precise is a gradual process. Progress in learning word meanings is from no knowledge at all through a stage of vaguely apprehended meaning and then on to the greater clarity and enrichment that comes when a child can not only precisely use and understand one, but several meanings of the same word. All of this requires well-organized instruction.

The Role of Experience

Two general types of experience may be employed to develop word meanings. The first and most effective is direct or firsthand experiences. These should be supplemented by secondhand or vicarious experiences.

Firsthand experiences

Firsthand experience involves direct contact with objects, people, situations, and institutions in the child's environment. He hears, sees, touches, manipulates, tastes, and smells objects available. Words connected with the experiences take on meaning. Most of these contacts will be in the immediate and habitual environment but some may result from attendance at summer camps, or from traveling with parents, or from other special trips and excursions. To be instructive such an experience must have the right degree of complexity and richness if it is to attract and hold the child's attention.

One general class of firsthand experiences involves carefully organized and supervised trips to such places as the school heating plant, the post office, the fire station, a zoo, a city park or botanical garden, a grocery store, a department store, a manufacturing plant, a concert, a farm, or a dairy. These experiences should be as varied in scope as possible.

Another form of firsthand experience is provided within the school by demonstrations and laboratory work. Concepts that may be developed in this way include examining the structure of plants and the influence of different factors on plant growth, the effect of vitamins on health and growth in a white rat, the nature of a vacuum, or osmosis.

The value of firsthand experiences in developing and clarifying concepts probably cannot be overemphasized at any school level. It appears to be the most effective procedure in developing a vocabulary of meanings.

Vicarious experiences

It is neither feasible nor possible to develop the desired stock of meanings by direct experience alone. A tremendous enlargement of valuable experience can be brought to the pupils by means of secondary media. These include pictures, charts and maps, models, slides and film strips, motion pictures, radio and television programs.

Perhaps commonest of all the forms of vicarious experience is what is to be got through stories told or read by the teacher or pupils. Further enlargement can be had through the dramatizing of incidents by children, instructional talks by the teacher and outsiders, and so on. It should be noted that when a child is dramatizing or making drawings he is giving expression to his understanding of a concept. In addition, these activities may be means of building the concept for the child who is listening or watching.

Role of planning and discussion

If children are to achieve maximum profit from their experiences, whether direct or vicarious, the latter must usually be carefully planned. Since the meanings to be achieved in reading are determined by the nature and clearness of the concepts which are available, these experiences must be made to yield as varied and accurate meanings as possible. Children should be thoroughly prepared prior to being exposed to a particular experience so that they may attend to and comprehend as many of its aspects as possible. They should know what to look for and what questions will be cleared up. In other words, the acquiring of experience must all of it be seen as a purposeful activity.

Experiences become profitable to the degree that the child thinks about them, seeks out their meanings, and draws upon these in subsequent speaking, listening, and reading. To provide maximum encouragement toward this end there must be an opportunity both before and after participating in the experience for discussion under teacher guidance. During the exchange of ideas and the answering of questions there will be a chance to sharpen observation, to define purposes, to extend information, to clear up misconceptions, to clarify and enrich meanings, and to supply the new words that best convey the ideas that have been acquired. These advance preparations for an experience and the talks about it afterwards are highly profitable whatever the nature of the experience, whether it is a story told by the teacher, a movie, some projected slides, a story read by the children themselves, or a sight-seeing trip. Concept building is also promoted by the opportunity to exchange experiences in informal discussions. In all this planning and talk the child should be encouraged to seek meaning in everything he encounters and, when necessary, to ask frankly for additional explanations and further clarification of meaning.

An important aspect of concept development is the growth in meanings that comes with usage. A ready and proper use of vocabulary in speaking, and attentive and thoughtful listening to the talk of others is necessary for the development of a good speaking and comprehending vocabulary. There should be ample opportunity in all school activities, therefore, for children to talk about the concepts involved in the various kinds of experience mentioned above. Putting ideas into writing is also a practice which helps to clarify word meanings.

Any program for the acquisition of new meanings and ideas should be developmental in nature. Thus readiness to read any specific unit and to progress to new materials at a higher level necessitate the development of new concepts as well as the enriching and clarification of those already acquired. Experience, both firsthand and vicarious, together with plenty of discussion and everything that will aid these will find constant and legitimate use in developing concepts throughout the grades.

Wide Reading

The reading of interesting and relatively easy materials is a form of vicarious experience closely related to firsthand experience, close enough to provide enrichments of the same sort. Each new book, story, or article should introduce at least a word or two new to the reader and do so in a variety of contexts, and repeat many familiar words. Repetition of old words in a variety of contexts broadens and clarifies their meanings. The more important new words will be encountered with sufficient frequency in different contexts to acquire more and more meaning. Eventually, for the child who is making satisfactory progress in reading, their comprehension becomes commonplace. To a considerable extent the extensive meaningful vocabulary of the mature reader is acquired through well-motivated wide reading. Motivation is maintained by guiding the child to material which, while interesting, is pitched at just the proper level of difficulty so that the context will yield a maximum number of intelligible clues to the meaning of any new word.

Correct guidance in wide reading leads to exploration of many areas of experience, promotes extension of interests, and insures contact with many new words. At this stage, however, it is relatively unimportant to develop highly accurate concepts for words that are not key words and which are seldom encountered. Wide reading provides opportunities for the use of the dictionary and other reference sources needed to clarify meanings. Guidance and encouragement in doing this pay good dividends.

In the wide-reading program the proper use of clues from the meaningful context is essential if the concepts or meanings of the new words encountered are to be learned satisfactorily. In this respect, both the pictures and the verbal context may furnish helpful patterns of meanings. In reading of this kind, new words should not occur too frequently, probably not oftener than one in 100 to 200 running words. This is what is meant by supplementary reading of material that is not too difficult.

Evidence presented by Haefner (116) shows that normal pupils profit considerably in learning word meanings through wide reading with little or no guidance by the teacher. Nevertheless, some systematic training (see below) designed to aid children in developing ability to discover and use clues to the meaning supplied by the context in supplementary reading materials is desirable. McCullough (174) outlines several such clues. Thus the word may be defined in the sentence, it may be recognized as a synonym, or it may sum up particulars of the situation. Again a meaning clue may come from experience or from language patterns such as familiar idioms and sayings. Sometimes a clue to the new word comes from the mood or feeling reflected in the context. Artley (10) has suggested several ways in which the meaning of a word may be presented in context. Children can acquire new vocabulary from their reading more easily if authors will keep in mind certain simple stratagems. For instance, the definition or meaning of a word can be given in parenthesis, in a clarifying phrase or clause inserted in the sentence, in a synonym presented along with the word, in a simile or metaphor, or in an additional full sentence. Furthermore, with care sentences can ordinarily be so written that only one meaning is possible for the new word.

The number of different words which occur in books recommended for elementary school children is great. A large portion of the words occur only rarely. It is impossible, of course, to teach all or even most of the words a child will meet in his reading. According to Thorndike (252) the best solution to the problem of vocabulary building is to provide pupils with a wide variety of interesting and easy books. Many new words and concepts can be learned from context through wide reading in these books.

Although wide reading under the teacher's guidance contributes greatly to the development and enrichment of the child's repertory of meanings, it by itself is not enough. Word meanings should be taught as an integral part of the balanced program for vocabulary development.

The Teaching of Word Meanings

The value of teaching word meanings has been demonstrated by Gray and Holmes (112). It has been discovered again and again that direct, systematic, well-planned drill on words in context is valuable, whereas teaching of words in isolation is usually wasteful and ineffective. The exact meaning of a word very frequently depends upon the context in which it occurs. Furthermore, familiar words used in an unfamiliar sense are encountered. Teaching these new meanings of old words and the relation of the particular meaning to context is a considerable part of vocabulary training.

The vocabulary even in material written for children is enormous. Direct teaching of meaning, therefore, must necessarily be confined to the more important words. With material of appropriate difficulty, the new words can usually be taught as they are encountered in context. It is necessary to teach those words whose meanings are essential for understanding the passage. Compiled word lists are useful for identifying the more important words in the reading vocabulary at various grade levels (see Russell, 213). The words that are common enough to get into the word lists form a core that accounts for a large proportion of the words in reading matter ordinarily encountered at a given grade level. To be ready for proficient reading at succeeding grade levels, the child should know these common words of the preceding levels. Nevertheless, there are objections to using these word lists mechanically as measures of vocabulary difficultness. As noted above, they tend to represent *frequency of use* rather than difficultness of understanding. Some words not in the lists are more readily understood than some of those included. Lists of words satisfactorily graded as to difficulty of understanding are not yet available in published form.

At the end of each reader in all recently published basic series a list of the new words used in the book can be found. In addition to such lists, a dictionary or glossary section provides meanings of the more difficult words in books for grades beyond the fourth. Both workbooks and teachers' manuals furnish exercises and suggestions for teaching word meanings. The alert teacher will profit greatly by appropriate use of these materials. Full directions for such use are given in the manuals.

At the beginning of reading, the teaching of word recognition is dominant. As the child progresses from grade to grade the systematic teaching of word meanings becomes increasingly more important. A child must, of course, be able to identify or recognize a printed word before he can sense its meaning.

Emphasis in teaching word meanings

It should be re-emphasized that the study of words is only one approach to the learning of word meanings. Furthermore, the study of words should be well integrated with the approach through experience and with wide reading in the program organized for vocabulary enlargement. The report of Addy (3) reveals that teachers and supervisors favor methods which involve maximum use of context and experience. The most favored methods for fixing the meaning of a word involve some aspect of usage, as its introduction into conversation. Or pupils may be taught to select the one word which expresses a given meaning most effectively. The writers of this book consider that word study can be profitable in developing meaning only to the degree that it is integrated with use of the word in context, with experience, with oral and written usage, and with wide reading in a variety of situations. In the first place, therefore, word study should deal with new words met in context. Learning the meaning of a new word will make it fulfill a need at once, that is, the desire to understand the passage. Secondly, word study should involve use of the word in discussion and in oral and written reports. Finally there should be reading of considerable material in which the word occurs frequently. These techniques for keeping the development of word meanings in context and for fixing the meanings through usage are not sequential steps. They should be co-ordinated aspects of a single integrated program.

Teaching use of context clues

As noted above, the meaning of a new word can frequently be derived from the context in which it occurs. To do this the child will need to comprehend the rest of the words in the sentence or passage. A surprising number of children make little or no use of context in trying to discover the meanings of strange words. Children should be given practice in "guessing" or telling what their hunch about the meaning of an unknown word is as it occurs in context. They should be taught to read the rest of the sentence or passage and then look back and try to decide what the unknown word probably means. For instance note the sentence:

Mary's heart began to *throb* so much that she could feel it beat strongly in her chest.

The word *throb* acquires meaning from the context in the first and latter parts of the sentence. Take another example:

Even though Sally was surprised when Tom *glared* at her, she was not upset by his *angry look*.

If such a sentence is part of a paragraph in a story, certain other sentences may amplify and clarify the meaning. Some guesses may be worng. Nevertheless, training of this kind usually produces considerable skill in deriving meaning from context.

Clues to word meanings through their contexts often come from the author's definitions. Such a definition may be the explanation given in another part of the sentence, or it may come from another word or phrase in the sentence. At times it is in a separate sentence. A few examples follow:

1. When father did not like the *retort* Jack made, he asked Jack to *answer* him more politely.

2. The girls were delighted with the vacation *cruise—a voyage by steamship* along the coast.

3. Right after they got on the train for Chicago, the *conductor* gave the engineer the signal to start. Besides *directing the trainmen*, the conductor *collects tickets from the passengers.*

Children may have difficulty in choosing the correct meaning of a word that has several meanings. Thus the correct meaning of *paid* in the following sentence depends on the context of the complete sentence: "Sam paid dearly for missing the bus." Actually, the correct meaning of many words is sensed *only* in terms of information from the context. A wide variety of exercises designed to instruct children in use of context clues as aids to working out word meanings are given in workbooks. And directions telling how to teach the use of context clues are given in teaching manuals of all recent basic series of readers. Effective use of context clues is one of the better techniques for acquiring a vocabulary of meaning, especially when employed properly in wide reading.

The question method

Botel (29) states that "questioning" is potentially the teacher's most important tool for helping pupils to understand and to interpret what they read. How questions can be intimately related to improving a pupil's understanding of specific words is illustrated by the following:

1. What is the key word in this heading? Why?
2. What does _____ mean as used in this sentence?
3. What other meanings do you already know for _____?
4. What does the glossary in your book say about _____?
5. How many meanings does your dictionary give for _____?
   Which meaning is appropriate in this story?

Botel also lists under six headings the kinds of questions that may be employed to advantage in developing word meanings:

1. *The definition question.* Example: What does *foot* mean in the sentence: "They stopped to rest at the *foot* of the hill."

2. *The semantic question.* Example: What other meanings do you know for the word *foot?*

3. *The synonym question.* Example: what other word(s) may be substituted for *peculiar* without changing the meaning of this sentence: "The man walked down the street acting in a peculiar way."

4. *The antonym question.* Example: What word(s) can you substitute for *strict* to make the following sentence mean just the opposite of what it does now? "The new traffic law is *strict.*"

5. *The homonym question.* Example: Think of another word which sounds the same as the underlined word in the following sentence but which has a different meaning. "The farmers <u>sow</u> seed in the spring."

6. *The key word question.* Example: Give the meaning of the underlined word in this sentence: "The United States recovered the first nose-cone from a man-made planet in orbit."

Thus, one way to acquire word meanings is to ask carefully phrased questions about words which appear in the printed material that is read in every subject area. General comprehension as well as word knowledge is improved by this method.

In his analysis of the meaning vocabularies of children, Russell (218) takes up several ways in which knowledge of vocabulary develops. Some of these are listed below:

1. *Function,* or what does it do. Example: A butler is the head male servant of a household.
2. *Relationship,* or what it is connected or associated with and how. Example: An industrial area is a part of the country which has many factories making things.
3. *Characteristics,* i.e., traits or habits. Example: A frog is a reptile that moves by hopping. Its usual sound is a croak.
4. *Sensory aspects:* look, smell, taste, hear, feel. Examples: The apple is round and red. A lemon tastes sour.
5. *Association.* It is like something else, or reminds you of another thing. Example: Sculling is similar to rowing.

Acquiring meanings for basic sight words

No child can continue to make satisfactory progress in reading without acquiring a basic sight vocabulary. The Dolch basic sight vocabulary (see Chapter 25) of 220 service words constitutes about 65 per cent of all the words in the reading material of the primary grades and nearly 60 per cent of those in the intermediate grades. Some children have difficulty with these words. When recognition of such words is being taught, emphasis should be placed upon developing an understanding of their meaning when used in context. An effective way to do this is to organize exercises like the following:

Directions: Read the sentence on the left and then underline or indicate the word at the right that gives the idea or meaning of the word underlined in the sentence. If the words given as choices are difficult, the teacher may read them aloud while the pupil follows:

1. Jack sat under the tree.   (*a*) when   (*b*) where   (*c*) how   (*d*) why
2. Helen left on June 9.   (*a*) when   (*b*) where   (*c*) how   (*d*) why
3. Sam ran because he was late.   (*a*) when   (*b*) where   (*c*) how   (*d*) why
4. Sally has a brown dress.   (*a*) color   (*b*) wood   (*c*) cloth   (*d*) straw
5. Mary has the right pencil.   (*a*) odd   (*b*) wooden   (*c*) correct   (*d*) small

The meanings of some of these service words can be taught best in terms of usage in context rather than through a defining word. For instance:

1. When John and Bill reached home, mother gave *them* some cake.

Children are taught that *them* means the persons, animals, or things talked or written about. Similar ways may be employed to teach the meanings of many words that are hard to learn as *they, could, what.* It is a cardinal principle that those words are remembered best which carry the most meaning. Without specific instruction such words as *their, myself, by, where,* and the like are not particularly meaningful to many children.

Systematic study of words

Systematic, satisfactorily organized drill on words has value in developing word meanings when this drill is on words in context or is related to the usage of words in context. When the students are adequately motivated to take an interest in words in general it will be profitable to devote some study to the meanings suggested by common prefixes, suffixes, word roots (and to synonyms and antonyms as noted above). This approach to word study is used most profitably when a word that lends itself to analysis is encountered in context. A few examples will illustrate:

1. The visitors went *aboard* the ship (prefix and word root).
2. Mr. Kent has a *kingly* appearance (word root and suffix).
3. The yard was *unsightly* (prefix, word root, suffix).

Besides identifying the root word and prefix or suffix with their meanings, the pupils may at appropriate times try to make other words by adding other prefixes or suffixes to the root word. In this manner, the meanings of the more common prefixes and suffixes and many word roots may be worked out. Breen (32) lists the most important Greek and Latin root derivatives, suffixes, and prefixes with their meanings. The list is reproduced in the Appendix to this book. Instruction in word study (structural aids to meaning) is probably most effective when co-ordinated with instruction in the use of structural aids to word recognition (cf. next chapter), i.e., it should be introduced at the appropriate time in the developmental reading program and taught with structural analysis in word recognition. One approach to training in identifying and understanding roots, prefixes, and suffixes is illustrated by the following kinds of exercises:

1. Draw a line under the root in each of the following and tell what the root means:

        sailor   return   queenly

2. Draw a line under the prefix in each of the following and tell how the prefix changes the meaning of the root:

        reset   displace   unhappy

3. Draw a line under the suffix in each of the following and tell how the suffix changes the meaning of the root:

      rapidly   singer   thankful

After identifying roots, prefixes, and suffixes, their uses in developing meanings should be further emphasized through discussion and supplementary exercises. One way to do this is to rewrite sentences. Example:

Your coat is *unlike* mine.
Your coat is *different from* mine.

Many words with suffixes may be treated similarly. Example:

Mary sat *quietly* in the chair.
Mary sat in the chair *without moving or speaking.*

Working out in a similar way, synonyms (words of like meaning) and antonyms (opposites) of words met in context will enrich the meanings of words. Supplementary exercises like the following may be used:

1. Underline the word that means the same as *pretty:*
   lonely   beautiful   pale   thoughtful

2. Underline the word that means the opposite of *quiet:*
   rough   queer   noisy   funny

A great variety of exercises for developing word meanings along the lines discussed above are given in Russell and Karp (219), Durrell (70), Betts (18), Harris (122), Preston and Botel (29), Botel and Smith (30), Gates (97), Bamman and Dawson (13), and Strang, McCullough, and Traxler (244), as well as in the workbooks which accompany basic readers.

Use of the dictionary

Proper use of a good dictionary can be an important aid in developing word meanings. Relatively few children acquire the dictionary habit or know the wealth of fascinating information that can be found in a dictionary. Development of the dictionary habit depends upon a well-organized program of instruction carried out by a skilled and enthusiastic teacher. No child will enjoy using a dictionary to ascertain the meanings of words until he has become skillful in finding any desired word quickly. A favorable attitude, enjoying its use, is essential to developing dictionary skills. When a pupil habitually demands meaning from everything he reads, he will find he has to turn to the dictionary for enlightenment. The child who has established the attitude of insisting on getting his meanings clear is ready to make the most of his teacher's guidance in using a dictionary.

Learning to use the dictionary begins in earnest in the fourth grade. Certain activities in the primary grades provide preliminary orientation which is helpful. Many children learn to make and use a picture dictionary during the first grade. At the second-grade level, a good portion of the children know the letters of the alphabet and can use alphabetical arrangements at least according to the first letters of words. They may also have acquired some elementary knowledge of syllabication. During the third grade, many children understand what is meant by long and short vowels, are somewhat acquainted with the use of certain diacritical markings, and have some knowledge of the elementary principles of syllabication. These skills plus the ability to employ context clues effectively have prepared the child for introduction to a dictionary.

Introduction to use of the dictionary should be gradual and the teacher's guidance must be carefully organized. Using the dictionary should be encouraged in daily classroom activities. This implies that dictionaries should be available at all times. It is desirable that children learn to consult the dictionary when there is a genuine need for it, i.e., to ascertain a correct pronunciation or to clarify the meaning of the word met in context. In fact, the chief uses of a dictionary are to find out correct pronunciations, determine word meanings, note syllabic division, and check spellings. Training in dictionary use involves practice in locating words, ascertaining pronunciation, and selecting the correct meaning.

Locating words. In order to be able to locate words in the dictionary, children must know alphabetical order. Skill in this is gained by having them reorganize a jumbled list of words according to the alphabetical order of the first letters of the words. These lists should vary in the number of words involved. This may be supplemented by having a child tell which letter comes before and after a certain letter, or what letter comes between two others. A series of index cards with one word on each card can be used advantageously. Have the children put the cards in order according to the initial letter of each word. Such cards may be shuffled over and over and a certain number given to the child for alphabetizing practice. Later on, the pupils can be taught to alphabetize according to the first two and possibly the first three letters of each word.

After the child has learned to visualize the location of each letter's position in the alphabet, practice to speed up locating words in the dictionary may be introduced. This is facilitated by understanding how to use the guide words at the top of each page. Practice should start with words differing in the initial letter. Progress is then made to words beginning with the same initial letter but with different second letters. Another list could have the first two letters of the words identical, as with a common prefix as *un-, re-,* and *ex-*. The pupil should find the base word in the dictionary first and then look for the derived word he may have encountered in his reading. Thus for *screening*, first find *screen*, then follow down the column to *screening*. Observation of a child locating words often reveals his lack of skill in using the guide words at the top of the page or his faltering use of alphabetical order.

Learning pronunciation. To learn correct pronunciation from the dictionary, the child needs to know how to make use of diacritical marks, syllabication, and accent marks. Fourth-grade pupils should have acquired considerable skill in syllabication. All dictionaries and glossaries should have their keys to pronunciation repeated frequently at the bottom of pages. The pronunciation is indicated by diacritical and accent marks in a parenthesis after each word. Some training in the interpretation of these marks as used in cue words is usually necessary. Once these are known, getting the correct pronunciation should cause little difficulty. However, there should be a few exercises in which the pupil looks up and records (by diacritical and accent marks) the pronunciation of several words. Later each pupil should pronounce his words by reference to his copy. Durrell (70) suggests that learning correct pronunciation may be speeded up by some training on the vowel sounds and the variable consonants as designated by different diacritical markings.

Word meanings. After locating a word, the child must know how to select from the several meanings listed in the dictionary the one that fits the context from which the word came. This implies that the child must have a grasp of the meaning of the rest of the sentence or paragraph in which the unknown word occurs. One form of practice is to duplicate sentences containing unfamiliar words from material the children are reading. The unfamiliar word in each sentence is underlined. The child looks up the underlined word in the dictionary and chooses from the listed meanings the one most appropriate to the context of the sentence. Actually, comprehensive understanding of a word's meaning is achieved only when the reader meets it in many contexts rather than in his dictionary study alone. Some dictionary definitions, it must be admitted, yield meagre meanings to the grade-school pupil.

Exercises like those found in workbooks are easily constructed, for example:

Directions: Several numbered definitions are given for the word in heavy black type. Read the word and its definitions. Next read the sentences below the definitions. Write in front of the sentence the number of the definition in which that meaning of the word is used.

Grate (1) make a grinding sound
      (2) grind off in small pieces
      (3) have an annoying or unpleasant effect
      ——— Did you hear the door *grate* on its hinges?
      ——— His actions always *grate* on me.

Such routine exercises have only limited effect in teaching dictionary usage unless they are related to daily classroom activities. Additional dictionary exercises are found in Harris (122), Durrell (70), DeBoer and Dallmann

(57), Hildreth (133), Betts (18), Spache and Berg (237), and workbooks.

Cautions. Certain cautions concerning dictionary usage may be listed here: (1) As noted by Russell (213), before the teacher can profitably begin dictionary work, she must ascertain the "dictionary readiness" of her pupils. This readiness involves adequate ability to use an alphabetical arrangement, context clues to meanings, letter sounds, and syllables as parts of words. (2) A dictionary should be used to satisfy, and even bring pleasure to, the child who habitually demands to know what words mean. (3) An appropriate dictionary should be used, one especially prepared for school use (see chapter on materials). The glossaries in basic readers cannot take the place of a dictionary since their primary aim is to give only the meanings of the more difficult words in a specific reader. (4) The teacher should keep in mind that use of a dictionary is only one approach to the acquisition of word meanings.

Developing Sequences in Word Meanings

The principles and methods of vocabulary development discussed here are not all applicable at each reading level. They should be co-ordinated into a sequential program in which what has already been learned forms the basis for building and expanding what is new. In early stages, word meanings are cultivated by direct and vicarious experiences which bulk large in the reading-readiness program prior to and during beginning reading. An important aspect of reading readiness at successive stages of reading involves the development of the word meanings and concepts necessary for comprehending what is to be read in each new unit. This is achieved by a co-ordination of all the methods discussed above. The particular sequence of introducing and teaching words and their meanings will be determined by which basic-reader series is used, by the organization of the school program, and by the instructional procedures preferred by the teacher. The sequence will, of course, be based upon the logic of the situation and be guided by the teacher's experience. It is assumed that she will know what the instructional approaches on the preceding levels have been and just what in general the pupils have achieved.

Although the sequence for developing word meanings can not be separated into discrete and sharply defined stages, the need for a sequential program will be sensed by the teacher. Word meanings which are learned at the beginning stages are, of course, essential for giving the verbal context in which the newer words occur. For the meaning of a new word must fit the context in which it is found. There can be meaning context only when words and their relationships are comprehended, so new meanings are fixed by relating them to what has already been learned. The clearer the word meanings at any level, the more adequate is the foundation for acquiring new meanings and concepts at succeeding levels.

The facility with which children acquire word meanings varies greatly. In the case of a particular child, how fast he progresses will depend both upon his learning ability and upon what he has learned up to the time the new concepts are introduced. The clear inference is that teaching vocabulary sequences should be adjusted to individual differences.

Summary

To read means to read with understanding. Word meanings are essential for comprehension of sentences and larger units. This emphasizes the need for acquiring a considerable if not large store of meanings accompanied by clear concepts.

The development of a meaningful vocabulary involves building concepts and understanding the words associated with them. This is achieved ordinarily by an instructional program which provides experiences, extensive reading, and the study of words. These three approaches to teaching word meanings should be co-ordinated in a unified program. Both firsthand and vicarious experiences are used. Meanings derived from experience are enhanced by discussion and by incorporating items of vocabulary into both talk and writing. Word meanings are extended and enriched by extensive reading of varied materials which are interesting and relatively easy. The learning of word meanings by direct study of words has a place in the balanced reading program, but this form of approach is justified only for the study of the more important words encountered in context. Teaching words in isolation is as a general rule to be viewed with suspicion, for it is likely to be unproductive.

Vocabulary

Check your knowledge of these terms. Reread parts of the chapter if necessary.

mechanics of reading	root derivatives
verbalism	suffix
standard word lists	prefix
vicarious experience	synonym
wide reading	antonym
words in context	homonym
glossary	semantic
context clues	diacritical marking
basic sight words	guide word
dictionary readiness	base word
simile	metaphor

Activities for Students

Observation: Visit a class in an elementary school and note all the techniques the teacher employs to develop or clarify the meanings of words.

Reading: When you encounter a new word in your own reading, (1) list the methods you use to ascertain its meaning; (2) note any help the author who uses the word gives you.

Creative thinking: Work out a statement of (1) all the advantages of using context to arrive at the meaning of new words; (2) the possible disadvantages; (3) the supplementary techniques needed in certain situations.

Selected References

BETTS, Emmett A., *Foundations of reading instruction.* New York: American Book Company, 1957, Chap. 24.

BOND, Guy L., and WAGNER, Eva B., *Teaching the child to read,* 3rd ed. New York: The Macmillan Company, 1960, Chap. 8.

CAUSEY, Oscar S. (ed.), *The reading teacher's reader.* New York: The Ronald Press Company, 1958, 211-249.

DeBOER, John J., and DALLMANN, Martha, *The teaching of reading.* New York: Holt, Rinehart and Winston, 1960, 328-333; 380-395; 489-502.

DURRELL, Donald D., *Improving reading instruction.* New York: Harcourt, Brace & World Inc., 1956, Chap. 12.

HARRIS, Albert J., *How to increase reading ability,* 4th ed. New York: Longmans, Green and Company, 1961, Chap. 15.

McCULLOUGH, Constance M., Implications of research on children's concepts. *The Reading Teacher,* 1959, 13, 100-107.

RUSSELL, David H., *Children learn to read,* 2nd ed. Boston: Ginn and Company, 1961, Chap. 9.

7

Word Study and Recognition

Progress in learning to read requires word-recognition skills. To acquire these skills and to keep improving them constitutes one of the main tasks of reading instruction in the primary grades. And teaching to perfect them extends throughout the intermediate grades. The task is to equip pupils so that they may rapidly and effectively pronounce words and understand what an author says in a sentence, paragraph, or longer selection. In the case of the accomplished reader, these word-recognition skills must operate smoothly and automatically, so that his attention can be devoted primarily to interpretation of meanings.

Much of the instruction in the primary grades is devoted to the acquisition of a reading vocabulary that permits the child to grasp readily the meanings which the author intends to convey. Whenever a child has difficulty in recognizing words, his thinking and interpretation will be hindered. It is difficult for him to enjoy reading. So much of his attention must be devoted to word recognition that his comprehension becomes vague or is altogether absent. A satisfactorily flexible set of skills in word recognition enables a child to identify new words easily and independently.

This chapter will describe in detail the essential word-identification and word-recognition skills that should be taught. The development of concepts and of word meanings, discussed in the previous chapter, are of course integral parts of instruction in perceiving words, for there could be little sense in working out the pronunciation of a word unless the child understands what it means. Furthermore, to learn to recognize words by look-and-say methods would be impossible unless the child has the necessary basic ability to perceive the visual and auditory elements involved, and unless his understanding of meanings is adequate. Durrell (70) has stated this point bluntly when he says that unless there is satisfactory attention to meaning, attempts to read become mere word-calling. Also, without phonetic ability (see below), reading would become a guessing game. And if phonics alone are used, reading becomes just nonsense-syllable analysis.

To recognize a word means to identify it as a word previously known. That is, the visual form leads to correct revival of the sound of the word, with association between the sound and the sound's meaning and the visual form. Immediate recognition occurs only with well-known or "sight" words. This is comparable to identification of certain thoroughly familiar objects, such as one's favorite armchair or pet dog. Other words which one has encountered but which are less familiar are recognized less promptly but usually with only slight delay. In such a case, a little slower visual inspection with recourse to one or more of the word-recognition clues will usually result in ready recognition. Such, for instance, is the case of Jane seeing a neighbor's dog some distance from home. She might recognize the dog through noting his color, size, and markings and then clinch the recognition when she glimpses the dog's owner a moment later nearby. To identify and recognize a printed word that already has a place in one's comprehension vocabulary and that one uses in speech, but which has not been encountered in print before, requires application of recognition techniques, perhaps involving one or more clues (see below). At first the child must usually examine the word closely visually in applying such recognition clues. If a word has several different meanings, as the identification is made the one appropriate to the context is recognized. Then after repeated contacts with the same word in different contexts, recognition of the word and its correctly associated meaning becomes more prompt. Eventually a familiar word form, plus its meaning derived from context, provides swift recognition. Most of the reading done by the mature reader involves almost instantaneous word perception.

It should be noted that word identification and word recognition are two interrelated aspects of word perception. The initial inspection of a new word involves identification of its printed or written symbol in terms of its visual appearance, its sound, and its meaning. Additional contacts with the word develop recognition. Throughout this book, word recognition implies identification as the first step in the process. Eventually, through subsequent experience with a word in context, the printed word form is grasped immediately, i.e., it becomes what we call a "sight" word.

Word-Recognition Techniques

Some writers, such as Flesch (88), Terman and Walcutt (251), and Hay and Wingo (124), emphasize a single approach to word recognition, i.e., phonics. All contemporary authors who have a background of research as well as a broad experience in the field advise a combined approach for instruction in word recognition: Gates (97), Durrell (70), Bond and Wagner (28), Bond and Tinker (26), Hildreth (133), DeBoer and Dallmann (57), Harris (122), and others. The combined approach is designed to provide the child with the available techniques and to train him to be versatile in applying them. The versatile child will apply the most effective method to unlock a word in a particular situation. The objective is to employ the clue or clues which will bring quick and accurate recognition of a word. The slower techniques should be used only when the more rapid ones fail to bring recognition.

It will be difficult to make satisfactory progress in developing word recognition unless the child has acquired adequate auditory and visual discrimination. Basically, word recognition involves matching the visual symbol with the sound and meaning represented by the symbol. On the other hand, therefore, correct discrimination of the sounds represented in the word is essential. Going along with this there must be precise visual discrimination not only of the total word form but frequently also of its details. Sounds cannot be matched with the successive parts of a word until those parts are clearly perceived.

List of word-recognition methods

1. *Recognition of words as sight words.* In the reading field, the term *sight word* has at least two distinct meanings: (*a*) It refers to the method by means of which beginning pupils learn the names of printed and written words when acquiring the so-called basic sight vocabulary. This is the look-and-say method. (*b*) Another use of the term is to designate all words that a reader recognizes immediately when encountered in or out of context. This recognition is achieved without analyzing the word and usually without depending on the context in which it appears. The sight vocabulary in this sense refers to all the words a reader recognizes, irrespective of the method by which he first identified them. (Full description of this and other methods is given below.)

2. *Striking characteristics of words.* Certain children, during the early stages of acquiring a sight vocabulary, learn a word by noting a striking characteristic. These clues are pretty much individualistic. It has been reported that a child may recognize the word *monkey* by the "tail" at the end of the word. Such a clue may be noticed by one child but not by others.

3. *Word-form clues.* Many words have distinctive total shapes or configurations which may become important clues to recognition. Thus, such words as *apple, happy, story*, and *funny* are all five-letter words, each with its own distinctive visual form which may be discriminated in contrast with the others.

4. *Context clues.* Certain clues to word recognition are derived from meanings in the context in which the word appears. The context may be pictures or sentences or both. The child who can "read" or interpret pictures, and who knows most of the words in a sentence can learn to infer both meaning and pronunciation of a new word from the meanings of the picture or the verbal context.

5. *Phonetic analysis.* Phonics is the term which refers to speech *sounds*, whether sounds of letters, letter groups, syllables, or whole words. Phonetic analysis in reading consists of identifying by sounding out loud or to oneself

the letters and letter combinations which make up the pronounceable units of the word.

6. *Structural analysis.* Identification of those parts of a word which form units of meaning or units of pronunciation is structural analysis. These units may be parts of a compound word, a root, a prefix or a suffix, an inflectional ending, or a syllable—in short, any part of a word which is a unit of sound or meaning.

7. *Use of the dictionary.* When a word is encountered which is not in the speaking-understanding vocabulary of a child, he must ordinarily employ the dictionary to associate sound and meaning with its printed appearance.

Use of Clues and Techniques in Word Recognition

Further explanation of the methods employed to recognize words, as listed just above, will now be given. The teacher should keep in mind that one or more methods of word recognition may be employed as needed,

Recognition of words as sight words

Most currently recommended methods of reading instruction start with word wholes and later move on to consider parts of words. This is in contrast with the older ABC and phonic procedures which began with individual letters and built words out of them. To start with a whole word is sound psychologically, for young children are not prone to be very analytical in their perceptions. Their natural tendency is to perceive total patterns. Noting details and the relation between these and the whole develops gradually.

A child's first stock of sight words is learned by the look-and-say method. One way of proceding to teach these is to show him one word at a time with a picture of what it stands for. He looks at the picture and is told the word, or he "guesses" what the word must be. Materials which present words by means of pictures are found in workbooks, on picture-word cards, and in picture dictionaries. Again, as the pupil encounters a word in isolation, in a sentence, or a word list and is unable to recognize it, the teacher or other person tells him what the word is by pronouncing it. The pupil then repeats the word. Additional practice follows, preferably in the context of a sentence. This method can be used for new words, or for words previously identified but forgotten. Example: Suppose the visually new word *mother* is met in the sentence, "Mary ran to her *mother*." The child is told that the word is *mother*. For emphasis the teacher usually writes the word on the chalkboard so that its visual features will stand out more clearly from the context of the sentence. And as the child watches the teacher write the word he *has* to observe it from left to right.

At another time, a word may be presented to the pupils out of context. DeBoer and Dallmann (57) state that while it is generally agreed that words tend to be remembered better if studied in context, it is not essential that a pupil's first contact with a word should occur in this way. However, in dealing with children who need several exposures to the word in context before they associate meaning and form well enough to read the story containing the words, the teacher does well to write the words in phrases or sentences as the children watch and listen. Then the teacher can say, "Read the phrase that tells what the elephant did," and the child can find the word *trumpeted* again by remembering its location in the phrase "trumpeted loudly." When a word is presented in isolation, the teacher should be certain that the pupils know its meaning and the value of learning to recognize it. If a word is first presented in isolation it is desirable that the child should soon afterwards encounter it again in the context of a sentence. For instance, suppose the teacher refers to the word *good* written on the chalkboard and says that it is one of the new words in the story to be read. She then uses the word in a sentence as, "Flip is a good dog," which she writes on the board. The children repeat the word and one of them points it out in the written sentence. Ordinarily, the children are encouraged to use context clues present in the reading situation when learning sight words in beginning reading.

There is little consensus among authorities concerning how many sight words should be taught prior to any instruction in phonetic analysis. Some authors place the number between 50 and 100. As a matter of fact, it is difficult for most pupils beginning grade one to learn 50 or more sight words well enough to remember them by their appearance alone. DeBoer and Dallmann (57) state that it seems desirable to employ a few simple methods of word analysis before a sight vocabulary of even 50 words has been acquired. The present trend is to depart from a strictly look-and-say method early in grade one: Durrell (70), McKee (178). We suggest that as soon as the words the child is learning have common characteristics such as the same initial consonant (e.g., in *boy* and *ball*) the child should be encouraged to note this. Then you ask, how many words should be learned before making some use of phonetic analysis? Our answer is, "as many as are learned until common characteristics show up." Evidence from research and classroom experience indicates that a pupil can make only a limited amount of progress as long as he depends upon the look-and-say method, even with the help of context clues.

The value of sight words that are acquired week by week or month by month as the child progresses in reading ability is another matter. These words may have been identified originally by some other method or combination of methods. With repeated encounters they are recognized immediately, without analysis either in isolation or in context. The mature reader has accumulated an enormous stock of words frequently encountered. This makes it possible for him not only to read rapidly but also to devote, in effect, his full time to thinking and interpretation while he is reading.

The stock of written or printed words which a reader recognizes at a glance constitutes a sort of word bank (Hildreth, 133). The larger one's word bank, the more mature a reader becomes in a most valuable respect. Building the word bank is a cumulative process. It begins with the first contact with words and continues throughout the school years and as long thereafter as a person continues to read at all. The rate at which the word bank grows depends on a number of factors. We mention a few of these: individual differences; verbal facility; amount of reading done; nature of the program by which he is being taught; interest in words.

Words with certain values are easier to learn than others: (1) Emotion-arousing words such as *mother, father, dog, kitten,* or those referring to a strong interest such as *airplane, rocket, train, bicycle* are more readily learned than other words which lack such values. (2) The word *hippopotamus* is relatively easy to learn. Though long, it has rhythm, glamor, and a specific shape due to the alternation of ascenders (high letters), descenders (dropping letters), and short letters. (3) The names of concrete objects such as *cow, table, grass,* and *stone* are more readily learned than such abstract words as *time, where, when,* and *how.* To learn the harder words requires more repetition and perhaps special instructional techniques. Thus in writing out answers to questions, have the children write out the words that are hard to learn. To the question, "What did Dick say?" the answer might be *"Where is it?"* In contrast, to answer a question enquiring *who* did or said something that can be answered merely by writing a proper name such as "Dick" accomplishes little learning.

Recognizing words by striking characteristics

This is an individualistic procedure since the child ordinarily devises it himself. Furthermore, the characteristic noted and used by one child may have no special significance for another. As noted by Meek (180), since this method of word attack alone is not sufficient to meet new situations, the child may run into difficulties and become confused. For example, to recognize the word *monkey* because it has a tail at the end is effective for only a short time. As soon as the word *donkey,* which also has a tail, is encountered, confusion arises. A person does not ride a monkey and a donkey does not climb a tree and throw down coconuts. Similarly, the child who learns to identify *on* by noting the round *o* gets into difficulty when he comes to the word *one* or *or.*

The use of striking characteristics such as these for word recognition is a natural and initially helpful device. It is perhaps best to let the child use whatever works for him as long as it works. When such techniques are no longer satisfactory, then it is time to cut off the monkey's tail, i.e., to guide him to use some more enduringly dependable techniques. The main justification for employing distinguishing characteristics of words for word recognition is when the characteristic is an integral part of the word form or configuration, particularly at the beginning of a word (see below). Actually, most children will abandon the undesirable aspects of this technique soon after they become familiar with other and more efficient techniques.

Use of word-form clues

The visual structure and the spoken sound operate together in word recognition. As a word becomes more familiar, the visual clues become more potent. This is particularly true when a word has a characteristic shape or form. The presence and absence of definite word form are illustrated in Figure 3, which contrasts lower-case with all-capital printing.

Figure 3. Block outlines of the printed word "stopped" illustrate that lower-case printing exhibits characteristic shape or word form, whereas a characteristic total shape is absent when printed in all capitals.

The alternation of the long letters (ascenders and descenders) and the short letters provides a definite shape to the word *stopped*, but this is absent in all capitals when it is printed. Many words in lower-case printing have individual shapes or forms. Examples: *happy, help, false, hypertrophy, butterfly, buttercup.* The longer words tend to have more distinct word forms. There are of course many words that have similar shapes: *house* and *horse, these* and *there, beard* and *board.* In such cases, other clues to recognition besides general word form must be used. There are also words which do not have characteristic word forms. These are mainly words made up of all short letters: *cavern, convenience, manner, seen.* Word form is of little help in recognizing such words, although the length of a word sometimes helps.

Many early investigations, surveyed by Huey (137), indicated that mature readers employ word form as a clue to recognition of words. Other authorities, such as Vernon (272) and Anderson and Dearborn (5) also emphasize word forms as clues to recognition.

The initial sight vocabulary is usually acquired by learning to associate the total configuration of a printed symbol with its sound and meaning so that when the word is encountered later it is recognized in terms of word form. However, no child can become a proficient reader if he depends *solely* upon word form and the look-and-say method for recognizing words. He must learn to identify and recognize words largely through use of other techniques. Word-form clues are most useful in facilitating quick recognition of familiar words.

In general, word-form reading is employed extensively by the mature reader. When a reader becomes quite familiar with a word so that it is readily recognized by sight, the word form or configuration provides a sufficient clue for its recognition. As pointed out by Bond and Wagner (28), certain words that do not lend themselves to ready analysis tend to be learned as sight words more naturally than words that tend to fall normally into usable parts. Thus, such words as *taught, ability,* and *through* are more frequently recognized from their characteristic shape than a word like *therefore* which readily divides so that the child quickly sees it as *there fore.*

Learning to use word-form clues requires close attention to the visual characteristics of words. An habitual tendency to observe the visual characteristics of words becomes an asset in attacking an unfamiliar word. With guidance, likenesses and differences will be noted, not only in total configuration but also in parts of words. Thus the child who already has the word *came* in his sight vocabulary may encounter the new word *tame.* Habits of visual discrimination reveal that the two words end alike but that the new word begins with a *t* instead of a *c*. Context clues plus knowledge of the initial *t* sound can lead to identification of the word *tame*. Thus, "When the children *came* home Jack saw a *tame* rabbit."

The above suggests that if it is to be most effective, word-form clues must be combined with other aids to word recognition such as context clues and phonetic analysis. It is especially important that clues from word form be checked by context clues. Gates (97) has stated that in typical reading situations, prompt and accurate recognition of a word and an understanding of its meaning is best insured by employing context clues and word forms simultaneously.

It seems doubtful to the present writers that specific training in the discrimination of likenesses and differences in geometric forms and pictures, as this is sometimes employed, will show any appreciable transfer to discrimination of words. Working directly with printed words is certain to be more rewarding. The main problem is to develop sensitivity to total configuration, with some analysis of the factors which produce such characteristic word forms as are found in long words, in patterns composed of the alternation of short letters (*a, n, c,* etc.) and long letters (*l, t, p,* etc.). This analysis can occur both in class discussion and in the teacher's explanations.

Various kinds of exercises on the chalkboard, in dittoed material, and in workbooks are employed to develop skill in the use of clues to word forms. Thus with a series of words (doll, girl, doll, book, ball, doll) placed in a horizontal line, the child is asked to underline each word which is the same as the word at the left. It is probably best to avoid placing the series of words in a vertical column, since we are trying to establish left-to-right eye movements in reading. In a similar way the child may be taught to match two words only one of which is capitalized, or when one of the pair is plural, that is, singular versus plural.

Betts (18) describes other exercises which require the pupil to identify the word spoken by the teacher by examining two similar printed forms which may or may not sound somewhat alike (*there, three* or *send, sand*). Note that careful scrutiny plus accurate auditory discrimination are necessary. Identifying the right word or phrase in sentences, or selecting the right word to match a picture constitute other exercises. In all these exercises the words should be meaningful, that is, the child either knows the word already or in the exercise learns how to pronounce it and its meaning. For instance, the child should know the word *doll* when required to match the word with a picture or when required to choose a sentence to go with a picture of a doll if given the following:

> This is a ball.
> This is a doll.
> This is a bat.

To achieve effective use of clues to word forms, the following rules should be emphasized in the developmental program of instruction: (1) teach pupils the characteristic shapes of words; (2) instil the habit of combining context clues with clues to word form; (3) encourage closer visual examination of a word only when this is necessary for complete recognition of the word. Once a child has "caught on" to this procedure, little or no further training in the use of clues to word form is necessary. Extensive and rapid reading of material free from difficulties with words tends to encourage use of word form to develop recognition of well-known words at a glance. And as the child improves in reading efficiency, a progressively larger stock of sight words will be accumulated in this way.

Use of context clues

In general, there are two sources of context clues as aids in word identification and recognition. These are picture clues and verbal-context clues.

Picture clues

Actually, picture clues constitute a kind of context clue. An appropriate picture or set of pictures properly interpreted can contribute a great deal of contextual meaning to an episode or story. "Reading" or interpreting the pictures will supply such meaning as comes from closer acquaintance with its animal characters, with various objects in a street scene, with the appearance of a yard, a fence, a wagon, a bicycle, a doll or other toy, or it may show how the characters interact with respect to each other and how they relate to their environment, and so on. In short, the total pattern of action in a particular situation as portrayed provides vivid clues to word recognition.

Considerable guidance by the teacher is called for in showing how pictures are "read" and in the use of such interpretation as aids in word identification and recognition. Some attention was given to this activity in the earlier section on development of reading readiness. Here we repeat that few people realize the wealth of meaningful context that may come from "reading" pictures.

Though the child generally tends to limit his interpretation of a picture to the patterns of his own past experience, nevertheless, properly guided interpretation may greatly enlarge the amount of detail he will note and the related experience he can draw upon. At his first glance, only the total pattern will emerge. Then, with guidance, his attention is drawn to numerous details and relationships that otherwise he might have missed. Thus his attention may be directed to details of the clothing worn by a postman and how they differ from what other men wear, or to the relative size of dolls and children. Again the meaning of a dark cloud in the sky when a storm is approaching is made clear or the function of a fence around a yard may be explained in ways he had never thought of before. Objects in pictures may be merely variations of those already within his experience or he may be lead forward by associations with the words necessary to express them to surprisingly new combinations of ideas. In general, the "new" things that may be seen in pictures come from attending to details that he would have missed by himself and from understanding relationships that he would probably not have grasped without help.

Experience with "reading" pictures begins before school age. Though as an aid in recognizing words, reading pictures is useful throughout the primary grades, it is probably most helpful in grade one. In the intermediate and later grades, its primary contribution lies in developing and clarifying concepts. The effectiveness of the whole program of visual education can be increased by training in the reading of pictures.

In a well-constructed primary-school reader the pictures, intelligently used, open up paths of discovery among words. A picture, like that shown in Figure 4, may constitute an integral part of the story, depicting some of its most significant action. As reproduced on this page, the picture gives clues both to the objects named in the story and to the actions taking place, i.e., toy, children, wagon, go home, look (on discovering something at the house). A picture should complement the verbal text, not substitute for it. Therefore, in addition to being artistic and so interesting that it stimulates discussion, the picture should get the child looking for words that embody the context clues it provides. According to Betts (18), systematic guidance in the use of picture clues may be obtained from discussions in which pupils tell the story from a study of its illustrations, by making up suitable titles for pictures, by matching words with pictures, by finding sentences in the story which refer to items or relations depicted in an illustration, and by using picture dictionaries. Examples will demonstrate to the child how pictures may sometimes help to identify and recognize a new word in its

Susan Helps, Too

" Come, Betty and Susan," said Tom.
" We have to go home now."

Away walked the children.
Away they went with the wagon
and the toys.

Then Betty said, " Look !
Look, Tom ! Look, Susan !
I see something at the house ! "

183

Figure 4. Picture Clues. (Reproduced with permission of the publisher from Odille Ousley and David H. Russell's *The little white house*, rev. ed. (Ginn Basic Readers). Boston: Ginn and Company, 1957, p. 183.)

printed context. In such examples, the familiar meaning of the word is shown in the picture. Then the pronunciation of the new word may be guessed by reference to clues in the picture. In such exercises, verbal-context clues from the rest of the sentence and knowledge of the familiar initial consonant of the new word should be used along with the picture clues. Take the sentence, "Jack looked for his ball in the tall *grass*." Here a picture of the situation, the verbal context up to the last word, and a knowledge of the initial consonant blend *gr* operate to bring recognition of grass.

Although a child should be taught to employ picture clues to help get the full meaning that may be locked in a word, these clues should not be so unduly emphasized that he becomes too dependent upon them and memorizes the story from the pictures only. In other words, the goal in teaching the child is to get him to use picture clues himself, along with other clues, in recognizing new words in context.

The trend is towards more frequent use of pictures and diagrams in children's texts. Comprehension in reading subject matter in the fields of science, social studies, and elsewhere is expedited when the examination and interpretation of many pictures, diagrams, maps, tables, etc., is required. Frequently the grasp of what terms mean, the acquisition of information, and the development of appropriate concepts all depend to a large degree upon the interpretation of pictures and diagrams. Analysis of the results of six investigations led Malter (163) to conclude that without training and guidance, children experience definite difficulty in reading and interpreting diagrams.

Verbal-context clues

As McCullough has brought out (171), the *verbal* woods are full of context aids to reading. Do children by themselves achieve adequate techniques of deriving meaning from context? Early research revealed that the less bright pupils could not do this, nor the bright ones either. Like any and every other reading skill, "awareness and use of contextual aids are best effected by direct teaching and continuous attention." This is further stressed by Sister Mariam (165), who describes situations for developing the use of context clues in the kindergarten and through the primary grades. Use of verbal context through the higher grades as a means of inferring time and place is described by LaBrant (148). As a pupil gains proficiency in reading, he depends more and more upon clues in the verbal context to recognize a relatively unfamiliar word and to infer its exact meaning. Adults make constant use of this technique. In fact, if a pupil is making normal progress in reading, his use of verbal clues tends to provide him with a quick and effective method by which he can unravel the meaning of an unfamiliar or partially familiar word either in a sentence or a longer passage.

Context clues in familiar settings. If a child or adult is acquainted with a particular subject or environmental setting, either through direct experience or vicariously, he tends to *anticipate* familiar words and concepts when reading material dealing with it. For instance, Dick has spent a summer on a farm just prior to entering first grade. Soon he will read a story about the activities of children on a farm. In this reading, he is likely to anticipate many of its words, such as *cow, barn, hay, tractor, silo.* Dick is well prepared to recognize these words as they appear in proper context in the farm story. Bond and Wagner (28) emphasize the role of *expectancy* in recognizing words and concepts. They state that when a person reads in a particular field or on a given topic, he *anticipates* to some degree the words he encounters. This kind of anticipation is even more effective, naturally, in the case of the more mature reader.

Expectancy clues operate during pre-primer days and at all higher levels. During the initial reading period, anticipations are aroused by means of pictures specially chosen for the clues they provide. These are examined and discussed, characters are identified, and activities interpreted. Similarly, the preparation for reading a story or unit at successive levels builds anticipation for the words and concepts which it will contain. As a pupil's background of experience broadens, he will anticipate by himself many of the words and concepts he is going to meet as he moves in this familiar area.

Most teachers, of course, recognize that building expectancy for words and concepts in reading instruction is not new. The able teacher has all along planned exercises in anticipation of words and concepts that will be encountered in a new reading unit. Preliminary discussion, use of visual aids, experimental demonstrations, definition of terms, and making basic purposes clear are all relevant activities for building expectancy clues.

Clues from meaning in verbal context

The use of verbal-context clues derived from meanings of known words in a sentence or paragraph is one of the more important aids to word recognition. If reading is well taught, these clues begin to operate as soon as the child has accumulated enough sight words to read sentences in a little story pattern. Such clues operate quickly and effectively in many instances. For example, note the sentence:

Betty likes to *ride* on the train.

If the child knows all the words except *ride,* it is not difficult to infer from the context that the new word is *ride.* The verbal context operates by limiting the number of words which would fit into the meaning of this sentence.

Fairly early in the first grade, verbal context may be employed to confirm recognition of a word originally learned as a whole. In addition, verbal context may be used to identify by *inferring* what word already in a child's speaking vocabulary would fit into the meaning of the sentence. (Use of the word *infer* rather than *guess* is to be preferred if context clues are used properly. The term *guess,* even when in quotes, is apt to imply a wrong meaning.) Likewise, verbal context is helpful in differentiating between two familiar words that look the same in total form, when only one of them will fit appropriately into the given context. Thus, "Dick caught the (*hall, ball*) and threw it to Jack." During the early stages of reading, children tend to depend heavily upon context clues. As they advance in school, unless other clues are developed and appropriately used, inferring from context may tend to become a guessing game and thus a handicap.

Context clues alone are not enough. As far as meaning context goes, any one of several quite different words might fit the meaning. Or again, several words which are already in the oral vocabulary have similar meanings and any one of them would do. In such cases, therefore, use of context alone is seldom adequate because it provides only one aid to recognition. As these other skills are acquired, context clues should be combined with such aids as word form, phonics, and even use of the dictionary. Although dependence upon verbal context alone has many limitations, it is an invaluable aid. In fact, it probably provides one of the most important single clues to word recognition. A word must fit into the meaningful pattern of the sentence or larger unit of context. So children should be taught skill in its use.

As outlined by Gray (108a), the development of ability to infer meaning from context clues involves three things: (1) Reading material must be properly chosen so that both subject matter and vocabulary fit the experience of the pupils. (2) Children must be at the stage of development where they can attach suitable meanings to whatever new words they encounter. (3) The teacher must be able to push further the kind of training which produces more and more skill.

Proper selection of reading materials assures that pupils will be interested in what they are reading, otherwise the whole attempt will fail. It is this interest that motivates the search for clues to meaning. Material satisfactory for developing skill in exploiting the clues must consist of words and language patterns already familiar to the child who hears them spoken. The concepts also must be thoroughly familiar. In addition, whatever new words there are should be so distributed that the known words will provide a sufficiently meaningful context to permit inferring the meaning of each new word as it appears. Its pronunciation also must not present formidable difficulty.

Training in using context to recognize words should continue throughout the grades. Few children will be able to make all the use they might of these clues without such training. The procedures themselves may vary. When she is reading aloud, the teacher may pause at an appropriate place to permit the children to supply the next word that fits the context. Several types of specific exercises are to be recommended. These exercises may make use of the chalkboard, or of slips of paper with dittoed material on them, or they may be found in workbooks. At first simple sentences are used in these exercises. Gradually they are made more complex.

The ability to anticipate meanings so that appropriate words for them will be found may be promoted by *completion* sentences:

The cat can climb up a —————.
The monkey has a long curly —————.

In another similar form of exercise the child *selects* from a list the right word to complete a sentence which he must read through to make his selection:

At the ————— Mary saw some cows and pigs.
    store   *farm*   *house*

Jane was so ————— that she went to sleep.
    happy   *sad*   *tired*

The boy ran up the —————.
    street   *tree*   *string*

Some exercises should involve the discrimination of *word forms* by requiring the child to choose the proper word from two with shapes similar in appearance:

Tom swung his bat and hit the ————— over the fence.
    doll   *ball*

Completion exercises which furnish the initial one or two letters of the appropriate word may be used. This not only limits the choice when there are several possibilities, but also draws attention to visual clues that may be used as in the following:

Jane was pl————— in the yard.
Tom and Bob went to the lake for a sw—————.

Such items are made somewhat easier by employing a multiple-choice type of exercise as:

Dick thr————— the ball to Jack.
    thrift   *talked*   *threw*

When the teacher wishes to impress a part of a word upon the child, she arranges to have the child write that part so that it will make a greater impression. Example: The child is to write in the blank the proper letter he has chosen from those listed below it.

Give me the —all.
    l   *b*   *d*

Throw the b————— to Tom.
    all   *ill*   *et*

Varying amounts of guidance will be needed to identify and properly use the various clues furnished by the context, both in the primary grades and later. At times a new word will be defined in context as "Jack saw a *mallard,* a kind of wild duck, swimming in the lake." Again a word such as *lead,* one that has both different meanings and different pronunciations may be encountered. Example: "Please lead the way." "Jack was always in the lead." "The lead pipe is heavy." Also, when the child looks up a word in the dictionary, he must frequently select the definition and pronunciation which fit the meaning of the context in which the word appears.

Meaning-supplying clues derived from verbal context are most effective in aiding word recognition when they are used with phonetic analysis and structural analysis.

Other Word-Analysis Techniques

If a pupil is limited in his use of word-recognition techniques to the sight method, word-form clues, and context clues, he can never become a proficient reader. If his progress in learning to read is to be kept up, he must acquire skill in the following methods as well: visual analysis, phonetic analysis, and structural analysis.

The role of visual analysis

Perhaps more than other experts, Bond and Wagner (28) emphasize the role of flexible visual analysis in word recognition. We all realize that when we are trying to identify words for the first time we analyze them into segments or units which are often easily pronounced and recognized. The child, if he is to pronounce such a word, must know the individual sounds he recognizes visually in the units. Little is achieved by such a visual analysis unless the child can do this. For example, what would be gained by his separating the word *caution* into *cau tion* unless he knew how each part should be pronounced. With added maturity in reading, of course, he will need to use sounding less since he recognizes many words at a glance.

Visual *inspection* of words occurs at all reading levels. This holds when sight words are first learned since word forms and words furnishing context clues both require inspection. But with the introduction of phonics and thereafter, *visual analysis* becomes necessary. Prior to making such an analysis the child will not know what elements to sound out.

To develop the ability to analyze words visually up to the level of proficiency of which the average child is capable requires that instruction and practice be continued over a long period of time. In the beginning stages the child learns to locate usable elements at the front end of a word. Later he is taught to perceive variant endings, common endings, parts of compound words, prefixes and suffixes, syllables, etc.

Phonetic analysis

Definitions. The term *phonetics* and *phonics* are sometimes confused with each other. *Phonetics* is the science of speech sounds. *Phonics,* by way of contrast, is an *application* of phonetics as an aid to learning to read (and spell). As used in texts on reading, phonics is concerned with the speech sounds which correspond to letters, letter groups, and syllables in words. And the term *phonetic analysis* as used in texts on reading refers to identifying sounds in words, and progressing through words from left to right while saying the successive sounds aloud or subvocally to obtain clues to the pronunciation of the whole word. As noted by Hildreth (133), correctly pronouncing a word usually recalls the meaning of the word as used orally. Grasping word meanings through sounding occurs only when the word is in the child's speaking vocabulary or when he employs sounding and context clues together.

The co-ordination of the visual and auditory aspects of phonics warrants additional emphasis. Too frequently the visual analysis of words and phonetic analysis are considered to be two distinct and independent processes. This is unfortunate. Visual analysis and sounding are interdependent, since proper sounding cannot take place in reading without simultaneous visual analysis of the words. The visual and auditory elements of words correspond, as: *cer e mo ny; ex pe di tion.* As stated by Hildreth (133), a child would never learn to sound out words properly if his response was entirely oral or entirely auditory.

Readiness for phonics. It would seem self-evident that instruction in phonics should begin only when a child is ready to profit by that instruction. Several authors, such as Betts (18), Durrell (70), Tronsberg (269), Harris (122), and others have stressed phonic readiness. The following items are relevant:

1. *Auditory discrimination.* A child must hear the separate sounds in spoken words. Without the ability to hear similarities and differences in words he will be unable to connect or associate sounds with printed symbols.

2. *Visual discrimination.* The pupil must be able to perceive differences in printed symbols: letters, letter groups, word forms, etc. Lack of this skill will prevent correct matching of symbol with sound.

3. *Reading for meaning.* Prior to introducing phonics the child should have acquired the habit of reading sentences, phrases, and word wholes for meaning. That is, the child must have learned to read with understanding.

4. *Sight vocabulary.* Mastering a sight vocabulary large enough for generalizing about sounds is essential. As noted above, there is a lack of agreement as to how large this vocabulary should be. Suggestions range from 50 to 75 words, to less than 50, to at least three words that begin with the same sound as the *m* sound in *make, man,* and *mouse.* Now, with contemporary instructional practices which are more effective, it would seem that we need not wait until the child has 50 or more words in his sight vocabulary before beginning to teach him the elementary aspects of phonics.

5. *Use of context clues.* The child should be able to use context clues for word recognition with at least a fair degree of effectiveness.

6. *Left-to-right sequence of perception.* It is essential in phonetic analysis to perceive successive word elements from left to right. Prior to use of phonics the child should have acquired the habit of reading words in a sentence from left to right. With guidance this procedure can be transferred to perceiving elements within a word.

7. *Mental age.* The research of Dolch and Bloomster (64a) indicated that phonetic readiness is reached at about mental age seven. This finding has been cited by many writers. However, Durrell (70) states that it is the possession of an adequate perceptual background, not a "mental age of seven," that makes phonics effective. The evidence indicates that both mental age and perceptual knowledge are important for phonic readiness. Pupils with higher mental ages, as well as those with the better visual and auditory discrimination, tend to become better readers in programs which emphasize teaching letter names, letter sounds, and the beginning aspects of phonics: Nicholson (189), Olson (192), Gavel (103). These studies, however, have been carried out over a period of only about one year. In a carefully controlled study, Sparks and Fay (238) investigated growth in reading achievement over a period of four years. One group (A) was taught phonics from the beginning of the first grade. Only after a basic knowledge of phonetic analysis was acquired were other methods of word attack taught. The other group (B) was taught in a regular basic reading program. The pupils learned 50-100 sight words and then started to learn other methods of word attack. At the end of the first grade, Group A was superior to Group B in comprehension and vocabulary. By the third grade there were no significant differences between the groups. And at the end of the fourth grade Group B was superior to A in accuracy but there were no differences in other respects (speed, comprehension, and vocabulary). In addition, there was no evidence that either method favored the slow learner. On the basis of his survey of the literature, Witty (281) concluded that the notion that early systematic use of phonics produces perfect readers is not substantiated.

8. *Individual differences.* The time at which phonic readiness is achieved will vary from child to child. Some pupils will be ready to start word analysis soon after beginning grade one, others only later.

Learning to use phonics is a complex process. After a child identifies the word elements and their sounds, he must learn to blend the sounds so as to pronounce the word as a unit. The pupil *should always use the word in context soon after sounding it out.* Phonetic analysis of lists of isolated words is unprofitable and should be avoided. Encountering a word in context provides an additional clue to recognizing it and, of course, help is to be had from the meaning of the sentence in which it occurs.

The effectiveness of phonics depends to a large degree upon how one introduces and teaches it. A pupil may acquire a dislike of it if it is begun prior to phonic readiness and if the teacher presents the techniques too rapidly. Instruction should be adjusted to individual capabilities, including the degree to which the child is ready for phonics and the rate at which he can master each feature of the technique. The simplest technique (initial consonants) should be introduced first. Progress to the more complex aspects of phonics should follow in the most sensible order.

Subject matter in the phonics program

Experts who have recently written or revised their basic-reader series are in essential agreement as to the phonic elements to be taught. DeBoer and Dallmann (57) have listed these elements:

1. Single consonants in initial, final, and middle position in words. (Do not use words containing consonant blends when giving experience with the sound of the single consonant.)
2. Consonant blends or double consonants such as *st, bl, pl, str, tr, br, cr.*
3. Consonant digraphs (two letters that represent one sound) such as *ck, ng, ph, ch, sh.*
4. Single vowel sounds: short; long; sound modified when preceding *r;* and the *a* preceding *l* or *w;* remaining vowel sounds.
5. Vowel digraphs (one sound) such as *au, ai, ay, ee, ea, ie, oa, oe.*
6. Diphthongs (two vowels so blended that they almost produce one sound) such as *oi, oy, ow, ou.*
7. Letters that are silent.

Materials on phonics

Teachers should become thoroughly acquainted with all the material on phonics in the teaching manuals and workbooks of whatever basic-reader series they are using. Betts (18) and Durrell (70) give a detailed list of phonetic elements and their sounds. Feldmann and Merrill (80, 81), Roberts (206), and Durrell, Sullivan, and Murphy (72) devote adequate attention to the sounding of phonetic elements in their exercises.

Rules or generalizations

There is little agreement concerning the advisability of teaching pupils rules for word pronunciation. Hildreth (133) suggests that by the second or third grade pupils have had enough experience with specific words to note recurring sounds that conform to rules, and this makes them ready for generalized rules about them. She lists (p. 354) four groups of simple rules to be developed with the children through use of many illustrations. Betts (19) is in any case opposed to rote memorization of phonic rules, claiming that they contribute nothing to the functional generalizations based upon his own experience with words. Durrell (70) states that it is questionable practice to burden pupils with phonic rules. He believes that a child develops his own feeling for rules as his contact with words expands and as his perception of the visual and auditory elements becomes more acute. DeBoer and Dallmann (57) urge that when phonetic rules are taught, they be developed inductively. Pupils appear to understand and apply generalizations much better when they help to formulate them than if they first learn the rules and then try to apply them. DeBoer and Dallmann (pp. 88-89) list eight phonetic rules that stand out among those commonly recommended. Many teacher's manuals accompanying basic readers contain an abundance of phonetic rules designed to help pupils.

In this book, the position we take is that authoritarian imposition of *formal phonetic rules* by the teacher should be avoided. When a child has had sufficient experiences with words he should be guided to formulate generalizations (rules) in his own words and to note exceptions to those generalizations. In this way, he will arrive at the few essential and most dependable phonetic rules such as those for short and long vowels, the vowel digraphs, the role of the final *e*, the soft and hard sounds of *c* and *g*, etc. In the formulation of such rules, the wording need not be exactly like that in the teacher's manual provided the meaning is clear to the pupil and is accurate.

Other aspects of phonics

In a book of this kind it is impossible to give all the details needed for teaching phonics through the grades. As already noted, most of the manuals which accompany basic-reader series give a wealth of details for the systematic teaching of phonics at appropriate places in the developmental reading program. Because the individual needs of her pupils vary, the teacher may want to use additional exercises in the practice of phonetic skills as well as other word-recognition techniques. An abundance of these may be found in the references mentioned earlier (18, 70, 72, 206).

Combination of clues. Phonics are not infallible clues to word recognition. Context clues, of course, are to be used to identify the pronunciation of familiar words. When a word is outside a child's speaking vocabulary or when the context clue and sounding are inadequate, the teacher or some other person must step in to help him pronounce it.

An appreciable number of English words do not lend themselves to phonetic analysis. In others the phonetic clues are irregular or confuse the child (Pei, 201).

> The child you teach will want to know
> The why of *sew* and *sow* and *foe*.
> *Said* and *maid* don't rhyme you'll say
> Then how explain *say* and *weigh*.
> And *flood* and *food*, how can it be
> That sounds are not like what you see.

If this verse does not convince you that the child is often up against it, take the following words: bright, kite; John, on; beach, beech; shore, four, door; yacht, hot; breeze, trees; beard, heard, bird; here, hear; dozen, cousin; sail, gale; home, some; good, food.

Try to imagine to the full the skilled word recognition demanded of a child who attempts to read the following little story containing the above words:

One *bright* day *John* was on the *beach* flying his *kite*. It landed up in a *beech* tree. He climbed up to get it. From the tree he saw a big boat sailing towards the *shore*. He could see *four* men on it. He thought it was a *yacht*. The day was *hot* but there was some *breeze* in the *trees*. When the *yacht* reached the *shore* a man came out of the *door* of the cabin and John saw it was his *cousin* George with a black *beard*. Now he could see a *dozen* men on the yacht. Then John thought he *heard* a *bird* but it was his *cousin* calling him. George came whistling and calling, "Come *here*. Do you *hear* me?" John ran to the boat and climbed aboard. George showed him a torn *sail* and said they had been in a *gale*. Then George took John *home* with him to get *some good food* for lunch.

When all is said, however, phonics remains one of the most useful and the most consistently used techniques for word identification when properly supplemented by context clues. Phonetic analysis can also be a valuable aid in structural analysis, especially in syllabification.

Phonetic families and phonograms. Phonetic families consist of consonant-vowel or vowel-consonant combinations which may occur at the beginning of words as in *bed, bet, beg*, or at the end as in *car, far, tar*. In teaching, the tendency is to concentrate mostly on the ending families. But ending families should be taught only after initial consonants have been learned. Furthermore, if phonetic families are taught, they should be derived from sight words already in the child's vocabulary. Although much used in the past, the teaching of long lists of phonetic families is a practice of dubious value. More effective procedures are those which teach the discrimination of likenesses and differences in words. These may be concerned with single-letter sounds or with consonant-vowel or vowel-consonant blends. Various types of exercises may be employed as: underlining like elements in lists of words; matching words that begin alike, or end alike; matching or underlining words that rhyme; substituting initial consonants, or final consonants, or vowels. Exercises of these kinds are found in workbooks and these references (18, 70, 72, 80, 206).

In teaching phonics, the teacher must decide how much emphasis to place upon phonograms. A phonogram is a letter or group of letters forming a speech sound and constituting a word element. Dolch (62) notes that various authors have compiled lists of the "most common" or "most important" phonograms. These lists range from 24 to 203 phonograms. However, except for such common endings as *-er, -ed,* and *-ing,* these most common phonograms occur in relatively few words in the early grades. Also, phonograms taught in the primary grades (except the three common endings just cited) are employed to help recognize the endings of common monosyllables. Therefore, these phonograms are of little help in sounding out polysyllables. This is because, except for inflectional endings, they are not the same as syllables in the longer words. Knowledge of phonograms, however, is of some help to the pupil prior to learning syllables, and occasionally afterwards. Dolch (62) emphasizes that a more productive, but too frequently neglected, phonetic technique for unlocking polysyllable words is syllabification. Betts (19) also emphasizes the role of syllables and their use in phonics. This skill is acquired only through much practice. Guidance in syllabification, begun relatively early and continued through several grades, will provide an important aid in word analysis. It will tend to reduce some of the reading difficulties so frequently encountered in the upper grades and high school. And it will remain useful as long as reading is done.

Syllabification in word recognition. The use of syllabification permits the child to separate the longer words into relatively large elements for recognizing and pronouncing them as units, the latter meaning pronounced in one breath. His word analysis will become much more effective as he learns syllabification. The instruction, however, should be such that words which can be recognized at sight as wholes are not separated into syllables. If not overemphasized, syllabification is a useful technique for identifying the pronunciation of polysyllabic words. As the syllables are recognized, they must of course be synthesized in pronouncing the word. Another advantage of syllabification is that it is the system employed in dictionaries for indicating word pronunciation. In most cases, when syllabification is learned well enough to be useful, it becomes a more effective technique than the strictly letter-by-letter sounding phonics. The confusion that may arise from such piecemeal analysis is avoided in syllabification.

Two important prerequisites for syllabic division are training the ear to hear the syllables, and knowing vowels and consonants. Because these preliminary skills are drawn upon, the teaching of syllabification comes relatively late in the sequence of learnings. Systematic instruction begins about the time a pupil is in the third reader. Several methods may be used by the teacher to help children learn syllabification. Words, separated into syllables, are written on the chalkboard and attention directed to the syllables, progressing, as always, from left to right. When necessary the teacher should check in a dictionary how the syllables divide and the position of accents. Then lists of words to be separated into syllables may be given the children. At first, the number of syllables in each of these words may be indicated. The pupils divide each word into syllables by vertical marks. Exercises like these and additional ones can be found in teachers' manuals and workbooks or in other references (18, 206). Some authors classify syllabification with structural analysis.

Structural analysis

Structural analysis consists of identifying those parts of a word which form meaningful units or units of pronunciation. Actually phonetic analysis and structural analysis are two related aspects of word analysis and are

frequently combined in word identification and recognition. In this combination, structural analysis precedes phonetic analysis in words of more than
one syllable. Thus the initial visual analysis reveals which are the pronounceable units and this is followed by whatever phonetic analysis is
necessary to arrive at their proper pronunciation. In fact, division into
syllabic units usually indicates how the sounding is to be done, as with
la-dy and *lad-der*.

The units of meaning may be parts of a compound word, as when two
words make up *schoolhouse;* base words as *fall* in *falling;* suffixes as *-ing* in
falling; and prefixes as *re-* in *return*. Various inflected forms of nouns,
adjectives, and verbs are formed by adding *s, -ing, -er*, and *-ed* as in *dolls,
runs, eating, colder, looked*. In these illustrations the meaning unit is the
root in the inflected form of a word already known to the child, as *run* in
runs. The units of pronunciation are the syllables which make up the words.

Structural analysis and phonetic analysis are not only interrelated but
also must frequently be combined in unlocking a word. During the visual
survey which naturally precedes the sounding out of a word, the child if
properly trained looks for units of both meaning and pronunciation. Having
discovered the structural pattern by the visual survey, sounding out the
word follows naturally, provided the child has acquired systematic methods
of structural analysis and sufficient skill in phonics. Structural analysis
can become an extremely useful tool in word recognition when combined
with phonics and employed along with context clues. In fact, there is no
satisfactory substitute for these techniques for working out the identification
of new words.

When an unknown root with an inflected ending is encountered, such
as *skating*, visual analysis separates the known *-ing* from the root. After this
structural analysis, phonetic analysis of the unknown root gives its sound.
The procedure is similar with a compound word such as *playground* where
play is familiar but *ground* is new. Recognition of *play* may suggest that
ground is the second part of a compound word which is then sounded out
by phonetic analysis, and then the two parts blended.

When a new root word of two syllables which is already in the speaking
and understanding vocabulary is encountered, the word is divided into
syllables by structural analysis and then phonetic analysis will complete
the identification. The context serves as a check on the appropriateness of
the word. It is clear, therefore, that structural analysis is essential for identification when dealing either with inflected, derived, or compound forms of
known words, and with unknown root words of more than one syllable.

Little words in big words. At this point a word of caution may be
introduced concerning the practice of teaching children to find little words
in big words as an aid in identifying the latter. Little words in big words
tend to be neither complete syllables nor units of meaning. Furthermore,

the so-called little word may not have the same sound when incorporated into two different words. Thus the word *at* in *hat* and in *father* have different sounds. Or the child might note *fat* and *her* in *father*. Teaching the child to find little words in big ones is for most pupils a dubious kind of practice which may eventually turn out to be more of a handicap than an aid. It is better to confine the practice to identifying root words and parts of compound words. In any case, when the practice of finding small words in large ones is used, the child will get into less difficulty if the teacher tells him to look for *large* units rather than small ones: for instance, *soon* in monsoon, *motor* in locomotor, and *more* in Baltimore, rather than such small words as *so* and *on* in monsoon, and *or* in each of the other two words. Definitely, structural analysis is a more reliable technique. In it the child is taught to look for elements of meanings, and when syllabification is learned, he also looks for units of pronunciation.

Techniques of structural analysis. If the application of structural analysis is to succeed, certain skills and understandings must be acquired. These include the following: (1) The adding of *s* or *es* to nouns to form the plural. (2) The identification of such endings as *'s, -en, -er,* and *-est* which change the form of the word. (3) The analysis of derived forms involving prefixes and suffixes as *un-, re-, -less, -ly,* and so on. In all these, the root word is the meaningful element. When dealing with compound words, both parts are meaningful elements which by themselves are word wholes.

In words of more than one syllable that are not compound words, and where there are no prefixes, suffixes, or inflectional endings, analysis must proceed by syllabification. Good programs for teaching structural analysis are found in teachers' manuals accompanying such basic readers as the Ginn Basic Readers (Ginn and Company), Developmental Reading Series (Lyons and Carnahan), Betts Basic Readers (American Book Co.), The Alice and Jerry Reading Program (Row, Peterson and Co.), The McKee Reading Series (Houghton Mifflin Co.), The Sheldon Basic Reading Series (Allyn and Bacon), and others. Practice exercises are found in the workbooks of the same series. For an excellent presentation of the details of structural analysis including principles of syllabification see Gray (108a).

Choice of procedures

Having learned how to employ the various clues in "solving" words, the child should choose the one most effective in any specific situation. For instance, suppose he meets the word "luggage" in the following sentence: "After camping over night, all the *luggage* was packed into the boat." He might use the following methods in identifying and recognizing the word: (1) letter-by-letter sounding and blending of the sounds; (2) visually identifying the syllables *lug-gage* and then blending the pronunciation of the syllables; (3) using context and noting the initial consonant. Usually the last method will be effective and fastest. The first method is laborious and slow. If the child is skilled in syllabification, the second method is fairly rapid, especially if aided by context clues.

It is worth noting that word analysis, especially syllabification and structural analysis, are also aids in learning to spell. Hence, the spelling program is a good place in which to follow up the uses of word analysis.

Sequence for Teaching Word Analysis

At any grade level there are marked differences among pupils in each branch of reading achievement, including phonetic readiness, phonetic skills, and other techniques of word recognition. Obviously grade level cannot be a satisfactory criterion for determining an adequate phonetic sequence. The sequence to follow in teaching phonetic and the other recognition skills should be logically organized, progressing from the simple to the more complex. Also the sequence should be adapted to a pupil's level of achievement and rate of learning.

A satisfactory sequence for teaching phonetics is usually found in the teachers' manuals that accompany basic-reader series. These programs tend to be organized for the average child, so the teacher will necessarily introduce such departures from standard procedures as individual differences in skill may require. What is advised and suggested in them should not be followed slavishly.

Writers such as Betts (18), Durrell (70), DeBoer and Dallmann (57), and Gray (108a) have made proposals for a desirable sequence. The following sequence, which is only suggestive, draws upon the lists of all these authorities:

1. A first step in the case of each child is to make sure that he acquires a satisfactory degree of skill in visual and auditory discrimination.

2. *Single consonant sounds.* The sounds of single consonants are taught as they occur in the initial, final, and middle positions in words. At first emphasis is put on initial consonants.

3. After he has learned the use of initial consonants, he is ready to learn to substitute one phonetic element for another in words that are like a known word except for a single consonant at the beginning or at the end of the word. This device of *consonant substitution* avoids producing an unblended series of sounds. Known words form the basis for the substitution. Thus when the word *make* is known, the child should be able to derive the sounds of *bake*, *take*, and *cake* by changing initial consonants. He notes that *bake* looks like *make* except for the first letter, mentally substitutes *b* for *m*, and of course checks the meaning with the context. Note that in consonant substitution there is a separat-

ing out and identifying of the phonetic element *ake*. Clues to word form are used. The familiar word *make* is compared with *bake*. Similarities and differences are noted and then the consonant is substituted. Substitution of final consonants is done in a similar manner. As skill is acquired and reading progresses, consonant substitution may be employed with longer words.

It is easier for the child to learn consonant substitution as a method of word analysis than to learn long lists of phonograms. Furthermore, his attention is directed to complete pronounceable units instead of to vowel-consonant combinations. This is desirable because it fosters the perception of total word forms. Mastery of the substitution technique will facilitate the identification of many new words. The technique is applicable throughout the elementary grades.

At this level the child should also be taught to identify a known root word which occurs with the inflectional endings *-s, -'s, -ed,* and *-ing* as in *runs, dog's, looked,* and *looking.* The known root is then blended with the appropriate ending. The child will also begin to learn to identify the two known parts of a compound word, as in *sidewalk, backyard,* and *blueberry.* Pupils will have occasion to use this technique in the first as well as in subsequent grades.

4. *Consonant blends and endings.* At this level the child builds on and amplifies what he has learned at the preceding level. He will learn to attack four types of words encountered in context. After he has achieved some skill with single consonants, the sounding of initial and final consonant digraphs as *th, wh, sl,* and *st,* may be introduced. They are employed like single consonants and as in consonant substitution except that a blend of consonants is used instead of a single consonant. Unless these are recognized as special combinations, the child who is already working with single consonants will be in trouble. Since several consonant diagraphs occur at the beginning or end of many words, they will soon be noted by the child.

A second type is made up of words that resemble known words except for the endings *-es, -er,* and *-est.* The known root is identified and then this is blended with the inflectional ending, as in *wishes, slower,* and *slowest.*

In a third type, the final consonant of inflected forms of certain known words is doubled before *-ed* or *-ing* are added, as in *slipped* and *running.* The second or added consonant is usually silent. The known root word and its inflectional ending are identified and then blended.

The final type at this level deals with inflected forms of unknown words where the root is like a known word except for the initial or final consonant or consonant blend. After noting the root and the ending, the root is identified by consonant substitution and blended with the ending.

5. *Single vowel sounds.* Since the short vowel sound occurs much more frequently than the long, the short sounds are usually taught before the long. However, the short vowel sounds are less easily learned. Long vowel sounds are given by vowel names and are easily remembered.

6. *Vowel digraphs and diphthongs.* After the single vowels have been studied, the vowel digraphs as *ee, ea, oa* in such words as *feet, beat,* and *goat;* and vowel diphthongs as *ai, oi, ou* in such words as *air, oil,* and *out* are usually taught.

Also at this stage the child becomes familiar with inflected forms of known words where the final *y* is changed to *i* or the final *e* is dropped before the ending, as in *happier* and *making.* Similarly he learns to analyze known words in which the suffixes *-y* and *-ly* have been added to known root words, as in *rainy, slowly,* and *noisily.*

7. The child is usually taught the silent letters before he completes work on digraphs and diphthongs.

8. *Structural analysis.* Phonetic and structural analysis are employed for identification and recognition of polysyllabic words. It will be necessary to develop skill in syllabification. Principles which determine vowel sounds and knowledge of accent are involved. The child must also become familiar with a number of the simpler prefixes and suffixes to facilitate analysis of words made up of one of these plus an unknown root word. Many techniques learned at previous levels find important uses here, such as changing *y* to *i* before an ending is attached.

9. *Use of the dictionary.* When the meaning as well as the pronunciation are unknown, identification and recognition of a word must be aided by using the dictionary.

10. The learning of soft *c* and *g* has no definite location in phonetic sequences. After some acquaintance with other initial consonants, the soft *c* and *g* may be taught as they occur in such words as *city* and *gentle*. In teaching spelling, it will also be necessary to take note of these soft sounds, as in *central* and *gender*. Some children may discover how to handle these soft sounds during applications of their knowledge of single consonants.

Ordinarily most of the initial instruction of the phonetic skills is completed by the end of the third grade, or early in the fourth grade. But prefixes, suffixes, roots, and syllabification are taught extensively from third grade on. So teaching of phonetic skills should continue through the intermediate grades. Also, some children will not have learned all the techniques prior to the fourth grade. And all children need review and further application of what they have learned earlier.

Emphases in Teaching Word Recognition

To teach word recognition effectively certain cardinal principles must be kept in mind. The program for putting these principles into operation will be given in detail at the appropriate places in the chapters on reading instruction. At this point, we shall merely list some recommended practices.

1. Be familiar with all the word-recognition techniques, their most appropriate uses, their limitations, and the importance of employing more than one clue in a specific situation.

2. Teach word recognition in situations meaningful to the child. Teach it on known words; introduce exercises in it later on unknown words in context.

3. Be certain that the child understands the meaning of the word pronounced. Also make the child aware of what he knows and how he can use what he knows, i.e., what his skill is good for.

4. Adjust instruction to the individual differences of the children in terms of readiness for each successive step, and their different rates of learning.

5. Follow a logical sequence of instruction and progress from the simpler to the more complex techniques.

6. Teach word recognition in meaningful context, i.e., avoid drill on isolated word lists.

7. Make sure that each child moves from left to right in perceiving elements in words.

8. Train the child to co-ordinate visual with sounding analysis in recognizing words.

9. Employ reading material that is interesting to the child and appropriate to his reading level.

10. Teach the child to be versatile in applying word-recognition techniques so that he will use the most appropriate method or methods in each specific instance.

11. The wise teacher will accumulate an abundant supply of exercises for use and re-use in teaching word recognition.

Summary

The clues and techniques employed for developing word identification and recognition discussed in this chapter need not be evaluated in terms of relative importance. Although some may be used more frequently than others, all are important. The superior reader will have become *thoroughly familiar with all of the clues and techniques,* will be practised in their use, and will know how to select the proper combination of clues and techniques in unlocking particular words as quickly as possible.

An extensive and continuing program of teaching is necessary for mastery of these clues and techniques. In most instances, progress will be slow, involving much repetition. Patience and persistence, however, are certain to yield good returns in the final values—more and better reading.

Although different aspects of the program of word recognition have been discussed separately, the teacher will readily sense that there is much overlapping both in her teaching of the clues and techniques and in how her children use them in unlocking words. A given word may require more than one technique for its solution, and may be solved in different ways.

The program for developing word recognition outlined in this chapter is designed for application throughout the elementary grades. It will start when children begin to read in the first grade, and will evolve and expand as they progress through the grades. Most of the formal training will be completed by the end of grade three or early in grade four, but there will be occasion to review and give additional practice even through grades five and six. The clues and techniques will continue to be used by the reader as long as he does reading of any kind.

As emphasized at the beginning of this chapter, the development of vocabulary and comprehension is intimately related to development of word recognition. They have been distinguished here only in the interest of emphasis and for convenience of discussion. This relationship will become clearer as you study the chapters on reading instruction in the grades which appear later in this book.

Vocabulary

Check your knowledge of these terms. Reread parts of the chapter if necessary.

word identification	diphthongs
word form	vowel digraphs
structural analysis	consonant digraphs
consonant blend	formal phonetic rules
reading pictures	nonphonetic words
verbal context	phonetic families
expectancy clues	phonogram
phonetics vs. phonics	syllabification
phonic readiness	compound word
root	consonant substitution

Activities for Students

Observation: Note the techniques employed by a third-grade pupil in recognizing new words while he reads a passage aloud.

Reading: Skim parts of "The Story of English" by Mario Pei to find out something about how nonphonetic words got into the English language.

Creative thinking: Select a paragraph containing two or three *new* words, in the sense that they are probably not familiar to the usual child. List all possible methods a child might employ in working out the pronunciation of each new word. Indicate which method you consider to be fastest and most effective.

Selected References

BETTS, E. A., *Foundations of reading instruction.* New York: American Book Company, 1957, Chap. 14.

BOND, G. L., and TINKER, M. A., *Reading difficulties.* New York: Appleton-Century-Crofts, Inc., 1957, Chap. 12.

―― and WAGNER, E. B., *Teaching the child to read*, 3rd ed. New York: The Macmillan Company, 1960, Chaps. 9, 10.

CAUSEY, O. S. (ed.), *The reading teacher's reader.* New York: The Ronald Press Company, 1958, 173-212.

DEBOER, J. J., and DALLMANN, M., *The teaching of reading.* New York: Holt, Rinehart and Winston, 1960, Chaps. 6A, 6B.

DURRELL, D. D., *Improving reading instruction.* New York: Harcourt, Brace & World, Inc., 1956, Chaps. 10, 11, 12.

GATES, A. I., *The improvement of reading*, 3rd ed. New York: The Macmillan Company, 1947, Chap. 7.

GRAY, L., and REESE, D., *Teaching children to read*, 2nd ed. New York: The Ronald Press Company, 1957, Chap. 11.

GRAY, W. S., *On their own in reading*, rev. ed. Chicago: Scott, Foresman and Company, 1960.

HARRIS, A. J., *How to increase reading ability*, 4th ed. New York: Longmans, Green and Company, 1961, Chaps. 12, 13.

HEILMAN, Arthur W., *Principles and practices of teaching reading*. Columbus, Ohio: Charles E. Merrill Books, Inc., 1961, Chap. 7.

TRIGGS, F. O., *Reading*. Mountain Home, N. C.: The Committee on Diagnostic Tests, Inc., 1960, Chaps. 6, 7; pp. 135-141.

8

Comprehension and Interpretation

At all grade levels the teaching of reading is a matter of developing comprehension. The fundamental goal in seeking to produce mature readers is to have them able to comprehend whatever printed materials will serve their purposes, no matter how difficult these materials may be. The acquisition of a sight vocabulary and of skill in recognizing words, and of verbal facility in general, all are aimed at promoting the understanding and interpretation of the meanings embodied in printed symbols. The extent to which these meanings are clearly and accurately understood and interpreted by the reader represents the degree to which he is a good reader. As noted in the preceding chapter, to recognize the printed symbols merely as words encountered previously and to pronounce those words without understanding what is intended by the writer is not reading. Such *verbalism* inhibits or is a sham substitute for the *thinking* side of reading. The viewpoint of this book is that there is no such thing as reading without understanding and interpretation. Word-calling cannot be considered reading.

Interpretation in comprehending

Although comprehension and interpretation are not exactly synonymous, they are closely related and interdependent. By interpretation we mean the thinking side of comprehension, or, we might put it, *thoughtful interpretation.* In many situations satisfactory comprehension depends primarily upon how much interpretation is involved. Examples:

1. To arrive at conclusions or to draw inferences from what is read are marks of interpretation.
2. To obtain the intended meaning from graphs, maps, statistical tables, and certain pictures denotes interpretation.
3. To relate and co-ordinate information derived from different sources demands interpretation. The same is true for relating textual material to pictures.
4. To recognize the main idea of a passage and to marshal relevant supporting details is largely a matter of interpretation.
5. To recognize the problem and to efficiently seek its solution in reading for a specific purpose often involves considerable interpretation.

Speaking generally, all these five varieties of interpretation have to do with the kind of reading we would classify under comprehension and study skills. Krantz (147) emphasizes the roles of study skills, comprehension, and knowledge of vocabulary in reading in the content areas. There are other aspects of interpretation:

1. When a word has several meanings, if a pupil is to select the one that is appropriate he must think carefully and interpret the context.

2. Interpretation is required to ascertain the meanings indicated by such punctuation marks as the comma, semicolon, and exclamation point.

3. Interpretation of the meaning implied in such figures of speech as metaphor, simile, and hyperbole contrasts with literal meaning of the words used. It is important in reading nearly all kinds of material to be able to make this distinction between literal and figurative expressions.

4. Distinguishing between emotive and informative expressions requires interpretation.

5. To a large degree meanings are personal. The child, to an especial degree, interprets the meaning of a word or sentence in terms of his own related experiences. Also, as might be expected, the extent to which this is true of mature readers varies greatly depending upon the content. While interpretation tends to be involved to only a slight degree in grasping the meanings of the words that refer to concrete objects like *apple, chair, tree,* etc., it does come into play prominently in attempting to understand more complex and abstract concepts. Thayer and Pronko (251a) conclude that the experiences a reader brings to his reading are far more important than are the black marks on white paper that his eyes are tracing. A reader will react in his own individual ways to the reading matter and its wider references and implications in proportion as his background ("psychological history") is uniquely his own. These conclusions, which they reached in studying college students, are undoubtedly valid in some degree for younger pupils.

From the above discussion it should be clear that comprehension and interpretation are inextricably intertwined, and *not* to be discussed separately from each other. In this chapter, therefore, comprehension and interpretation are discussed together. At relevant places, the distinctive role of interpretation will be noted.

A few recent studies of interpretation may be cited. Gray (109) has summarized studies of interpretation in reading. He noted the wide variation in methods of studying interpretation. In a recent investigation, Piekarz (202) found that good sixth-grade readers maintained a relatively high level of interpretation. In contrast, poor readers in the same grade discovered only literal meanings in what they read. Mostly they ignored the implied meanings and failed to evaluate critically.

Comprehension essentials

In addition to the recognition of words and the understanding of word meanings something more is needed for comprehension. The elements of a sentence must be evaluated and their organization in relation to each other understood. Word meanings which are in harmony with the rest of the context must be selected. Furthermore, to comprehend a paragraph or larger unit, both the relations between elements in a sentence and the relations among its sentences need to be understood. Interpretation of these relationships involves thinking plus interpretation and is comparable to problem solving. If proficiency in interpretation is to be attained, the techniques for word identification and recognition must operate satisfactorily and be largely automatic. Either inadequate control over these techniques or a program of instruction which overemphasizes the mechanical aspects of reading will stand in the way of maximum comprehension.

Listening and Reading Comprehension

The processes involved in comprehending printed material are essentially the same as for understanding spoken words. In both cases, perception of words arouses meanings which lead to comprehension. The meanings aroused by the perceived words depend upon one's whole background of experience, including whatever facility in communication one possesses. At any given time, the length and complexity of a selection which can be comprehended varies greatly from child to child. Some may be limited to a sentence, others to a paragraph, while some may be able to comprehend longer units. According to Gates (97) the child, provided he is not handicapped by difficulties in the more mechanical aspects of reading such as word recognition, should be able to comprehend in written form as long and as complex a unit as he can comprehend in spoken form. The evidence from early research into the comparison of listening and reading comprehension has been summarized by Goldstein (106). More recent experimental reports have been published by Hampleman (119), Triggs (267), Webb and Wallon (273), Westover (274), and Witty and Sizemore (286, 287, 288). Although the findings are not uniform, the following trends are evident: (1) At the lower grade levels *auditory* comprehension tends to be *equal to or better than* reading comprehension. (2) For pupils of lower ability, *auditory* comprehension tends to be *equal to or better than* reading comprehension. (3) For more skilled readers and for those of higher ability, however, *reading* comprehension tends to be *equal to or superior to* auditory comprehension. (4) For college students auditory comprehension tends to be superior for easy material. *reading* comprehension for *difficult material*. This indicates the obvious advantage of going slowly and reviewing the difficult parts of what is read. (5) There is a general trend in all the studies that supports the view that *reading comprehension* becomes increasingly effective with increased age among those who read widely and finally comes to surpass listening comprehension in the case of good readers.

These results suggest that in the beginning stages, while children are in the process of mastering the mechanics of reading, listening comprehension tends to be superior to reading comprehension. As soon as the mechanics have become largely automatic, which occurs sooner for the more able child, the two modes of comprehension become equivalent. Then as greater proficiency and maturity are reached, reading comprehension may become greater than listening comprehension. This is an understandable progression. In the early grades considerable attention must be devoted to developing word identification and recognition. As these skills are acquired, more time is freed to devote to comprehending. Then with the richer background of reading experience, with the greater maturity and increased proficiency attained in the upper grades, there is equal or better reading than auditory comprehension, especially by the more able readers.

The implication of these trends for teaching seems clear. In the early grades, while word recognition and other mechanics should be developed effectively, they are to be relegated to an appropriate place which does not usurp the place of comprehension. That is, as soon as possible they should become automatic, while from the very beginning there should be a strong emphasis on comprehension. Then with the mastering of the mechanics, reading comprehension is freed from hindrance, and under guidance becomes more and more proficient. Thus instruction plays a dominant role in developing reading comprehension throughout the grades.

This stress upon development of reading comprehension does not imply any lessening in emphasis on oral language and usage. As noted earlier, increased proficiency in spoken language and in listening promotes improvement in reading.

Aspects of Comprehension

In organizing a program for developing reading comprehension there are several aspects that need to be considered. Various factors, to be considered below, determine the effectiveness of each aspect.

Size of unit comprehended

At any stage of a child's development, the amount of material that can be comprehended as a unit varies greatly from child to child. This is likely to be especially true in the primary grades. At any given time in any grade it is important for both the teacher and the child himself to recognize the largest comprehension unit that he can readily grasp. Light on this may be ascertained from the use of the *Durrell-Sullivan Reading Capacity and Achievement Tests* (see Appendix). Techniques for handling material within the limits of the child's abilities can then be organized under teacher guidance.

Degree of comprehension

At all grade levels, some children will, of course, comprehend more difficult and more complex material in a more thorough manner than the other children. The completeness of comprehension which is satisfactory for material at any level of difficulty is determined largely by the purpose for which the reading is being done. For instance, the elaborateness of detail which should be attended to varies greatly according to the practical requirements of the situation. On the one hand the relatively minor need for noting details simply to get the main idea of a story is to be contrasted with the exact and complete grasp of detailed directions which is necessary if one aims to bake a perfect cake. In many reading situations children tend to devote greater attention to details than is desirable. An important task of the teacher, therefore, is to develop in pupils the ability to sense the degree of completeness of comprehension required by the particular reading purpose. The efficient reader is not one who comprehends the most details, but one who comprehends just what is required by whatever purpose he has in reading at all and whose capacity to understand is equal to the difficulty of the material. The teacher's task is to guide pupils so that they will be able to sense by themselves the amount of detail they should grasp in order to satisfy some given purpose. A clear understanding of the purpose may originate with the child, as when he reads just for the thrill of a story, or so as to be able to understand the directions for assembling a new toy train and tracks which he has been given. In many instances teacher guidance may be very important. Through class discussion, with provocative questions and answers prior to reading a unit, the pupils may gradually become more proficient in sensing not only the degree to which details need to be attended to but also how to select the amount of detail relevant to their needs. This is highly important in the application of comprehension and study skills in reading content materials. Details will be discussed in the next chapter.

Depth of comprehension

Depth of comprehension refers to the degree of intellectual penetration achieved by the readers, i.e., the accuracy and completeness with which the pupil grasps the meanings intended by the author. Different children in reading the same selection will attain varying degrees of accuracy and depth of understanding. Depth of comprehension, as we mean it, involves more than degree of comprehension. It goes beyond this to include interpretation, the *thinking* side of reading. It can ordinarily be secured only by reading slowly and with marked concentration. The acquisition of a desirable depth of comprehension is difficult and comes slowly for most pupils. Much depends upon a child's background of experience and upon his capacity for realizing and holding himself to the achievement of what is required. The instructional program will involve much discussion, use of many illustrative examples, and questioning to clarify the kinds, amounts and depth of interpretation to be used at different times. The mature reader with more experience to draw upon will be able to dig deeply in comprehending what he is reading where this is desirable.

Speed of reading and comprehension

Undoubtedly much misinterpretation has arisen from a common tendency to treat speed of reading and comprehension in reading separately. In schoolroom practice this has frequently led to an overemphasis upon "speed of reading." Pupils are told of the need to increase their speed of reading and many exercises are devoted to achieving faster reading. As stressed by Tinker (258), the speed at which words can be identified can have little significance for reading unless the printed material is comprehended. It is much better, therefore, to use the term *speed of comprehension* rather than "speed of reading." When one thinks of speed he should be concerned with quickness of understanding. Since we realize, however, that people will continue to employ the term "speed of reading," we too will use it in this book but with the provision that the phrase means speed of comprehension. The topic of speed of reading will be considered in detail in a later chapter. At this place we wish to emphasize two points: (1) In the primary years, children are mastering the mechanics of reading. Little or no attention should be devoted to speed of reading. There will be some occasion to improve speed of reading with certain children in the intermediate grades. (2) In general, throughout the elementary school, proper emphasis should be placed upon development of comprehension, word meanings, and concepts. Then there will be little need for specific training in speed of reading. Speed will tend to take care of itself. When material is within the child's capacity for understanding, the more clearly he comprehends it the faster will his rate of progress tend to be.

Reader adaptation in comprehending

For most effective understanding the child must learn to adapt his procedures to what is required for comprehension in any reading situation.

Our goal is to develop versatile, i.e., flexible, readers, for the most proficient reader is also the most versatile one. He is a reader who, because he can discriminate certain differences, will adapt the thoroughness with which he seeks to comprehend to the requirements of his reading purpose. Such discrimination is taught, we have said, under "degree of comprehension."

Comprehension and Experience

Throughout this book it has been emphasized that meaning is built upon experiences. Durrell (68) in the *Forty-eighth Yearbook*, points out that comprehension in reading is reflected by the degree to which the child translates "the written word into images, ideas, emotion, plans, or action" (p. 194). Accuracy of comprehension is improved by constantly relating reading to observation, conversation, and other experiences. This not only provides a check on accuracy of comprehension, but also clarifies and enriches word meanings. Since meaning should be stressed at all levels of instruction, the desirability of relating reading to experience becomes obvious.

In very general terms, there are two kinds of reading material. One furnishes information, and the other evokes feeling and emotion. They are not mutually exclusive, of course. It is important for the reader to learn to distinguish between writing whose primary purpose is to furnish information or widen knowledge and that which is designed to arouse emotional response. One tends to be factual, the other imaginative.

The relations between experience and comprehension, therefore, will vary according to different kinds of reading material. These relationships are ably discussed by Durrell (68). The comprehension of imaginative literature is enhanced by those activities which build images, for example, through looking at and discussing pictures that take a child out of his usual orbit, or through dramatizing, and telling stories. Two dangers should be avoided in training aimed to deepen the comprehension of and feeling for imaginative literature: (1) The overanalysis of form should be avoided— something to guard against in requiring formal outlines and book reports, or the answering of objective questions. (2) It is equally hazardous to permit free reading with no supervision, no guided discussion, and no related activity. It can be unhealthy, for instance, to encourage imagery to an excess which results in the substitution of daydreaming for reality. To avoid this some help from the teacher may be needed. Guidance in reading imaginative literature requires understanding and careful thought and planning by the teacher.

When dealing with informative material it is comparatively easy to relate active experience to comprehension in reading. Whether the reading is a story about travel, or something in geography, science, or history, the development of concepts needed for more complete understanding is aided by direct experience as well as by the use of pictures, maps, models, and discussions. Preparation for a unit assignment is a relevant example. This is all part of the reading-readiness activities applied throughout the reading program.

Obviously, the meanings recalled in reading are those possessed by the child and necessarily must have been evolved through what he has had experience with in the past. As noted by Harrison (123), the meaning may be derived directly from those past experiences, or it may consist of a newly constructed meaning which results from combining and reorganizing meanings already in his possession. The author weaves such a striking constellation of ideas together that the reader senses the novelty above everything. Though the materials may be old, the whole idea seems new and pleasing. This is well shown by an example given by Bond and Tinker (26, p. 231). A fourth-grade child reads the following sentence: "The tired rider drooped in his saddle as his spotted horse walked along the mountain trail." Because the child had never seen such a rider, he may derive the meaning of the sentence from reorganizing a variety of remembered experiences such as: (1) his grandfather napping with his head bent forward as he sits in an easy chair; (2) a bridle path through the park; (3) a mounted policeman who sat erect on his black horse; (4) a spotted black and white dog; and (5) the scenery during a trip through hilly country. By fusing these memories, the child may well achieve a close approximation of the meaning intended by the writer of the sentence. It would appear that one reads primarily with experiences which come ultimately from sensory impressions of all sorts—touching, tasting, hearing, seeing, smelling, and feeling one's own muscle play.

Complexity of comprehension

The numerous skills which are involved in comprehension are interrelated in an intricate pattern. Included are such skills as word recognition, word knowledge and concepts, speed of comprehension, sentence and paragraph comprehension, and others (see below). Since some children have a good grasp of certain of these skills but not of others, the teacher will want to discover the strengths and weaknesses of her pupils in order to adjust instruction to their individual needs. Formal inventories for evaluating background of experience are given by Bond and Tinker (26, pp. 237-238), Dolch (63, pp. 121-123), and Witty and Kopel (284, pp. 185-188). Informal exercises which may be employed for either checking strengths and weaknesses or for practice in developing comprehension may be found in workbooks which accompany most basic-reading series. Teachers' manuals provide suggestions on use of such materials. Additional exercises may be found in Russell and Karp (219), and DeBoer and Dallmann (57).

Determinants of comprehension

Several factors determine how easily and how much school children comprehend. Some of the more important factors are: (1) Individual differences in intellectual ability. The correlation between mental age and both comprehension and knowledge of vocabulary is high. Maturity in intelligence comes with increasing age. All the other factors which follow may be improved by instruction. (2) Richness or meagerness of background. The child who has had many experiences, either directly or vicariously, will learn to comprehend more readily than those whose experience has been more limited. (3) The child who is preoccupied with the mechanics of word identification and recognition will be handicapped in comprehension. He will have little opportunity to think and interpret or in some instances to attend to word meanings. Thus the exclusive use of phonics for identifying and extracting the meaning of words may result in empty verbalism rather than reading with understanding. A similar effect may ensue when there is overemphasis on oral reading in which stress is on *how* the child reads rather than on *what* he is reading. At the Minnesota Reading Clinic, a ten-year-old girl could do a beautiful job of oral reading to an audience but at the end of the reading she could not cite a single idea from the passage "read." (4) Lack of a flexible approach hinders good comprehension. The child who employs the same style when reading a story for fun, a geography book, scientific material, or a mathematical problem cannot be a proficient reader (see chapter on content fields).

Conditions favorable to comprehension

McCullough (170) has described four general conditions favorable to comprehension. The points she emphasizes in her article are:

1. *Removing impediments.* The first problem of the teacher is to discover and eliminate the deficiencies which make it impossible for the child to profit by his attempts to read. Her guidance will be directed toward: (a) developing the confidence a child needs if he is to profit by his reading; (b) developing the new word meanings without which progress is blocked, (c) training to help the child grasp how sentences, paragraphs, and stories are organized, (d) aiding his interpretation and critical evaluation.

2. *Content.* Another condition involves the content of the reading, the sorts of ideas dealt with. Content ranges from easy to difficult for a particular child. The teacher must know what the topics are and how difficult they will be to understand. Only then can she assign to her pupils what is appropriate to their present level of proficiency.

3. *Preparation.* A third condition is to prepare the pupils for what is to be read. Involved are: the pronunciation and meanings of difficult new words, preliminary reading and discussion, audio and visual materials, a problem-solving approach, introducing supplementary materials from the library which

can be read, and, of course, explaining the purpose of the reading and arousing interest in it.

4. *Motivation.* Motivation is highly important. This may come partly from: the desire to do well, related past experience, previous acquaintance with a topic, curiosity over the answer to a question, a longing for approval, current interest in a subject, and the enthusiasm of the teacher or other pupils.

"Comprehension of material in any area of knowledge requires recognition of these four conditions."

In another report, McCullough (168) surveys relevant literature concerning practices for developing comprehension. A point stressed in several of the studies is that the various types of comprehension skills should be taught at successive grade levels and that adequate attention be given to individual comprehension needs. These emphases become increasingly important for reading in the content areas.

Sentence Comprehension[1]

In addition to knowing the meaning of words, the child must acquire many other skills before he can understand even a single sentence satisfactorily. These include grasping the relations between words and groups of words, reading by phrases or thought units, properly interpreting punctuation, understanding figures of speech and symbolic expressions.

Grade level in sentence comprehension is readily ascertained by means of standardized reading tests designed for the primary grades (see Appendix). Various types of exercises may be employed both for diagnosing lack of sentence comprehension and for training in what may be called *sentence sense* or the ability to understand the relation between the several parts of a sentence. For example:

Directions: Read each sentence. Then decide whether the underlined part tells when, why, how, what, or where. Draw a line under the one correct word which follows the sentence.

1. The small house belongs to Mr. Black.   when   why   how   what   where
2. Since Ann was ill, she remained at home.   when   why   how   what   where
3. Dick went into the house.   when   why   how   what   where
4. The tiny kitten came on the run.   when   why   how   what   where

A slightly different exercise is to find and copy the word or words that answer the question, "who" or "where." After the child is told that the

[1] Discussion of sentence, paragraph, and story comprehension is based partly on a chapter written by Tinker in G. L. Bond and M. A. Tinker, *Reading difficulties* (26). New York: Appleton-Century-Crofts, Inc., 1957.

sentences answer the questions "who?" and "where?," he is asked to write below the sentences the word or words that answer the question.

1. The girl went to the table to get the book.
2. "From home to school is only six blocks," said mother.

Sentence Number	Words that tell	
	who	*where*
1	_____	_____
2	_____	_____

The responses may be made by having the pupil draw a line below the words that answer the question, "who," etc.

Similar items may be constructed that answer the questions "when" and "what," or "why" and "how." Also the exercises may be varied by employing sentences to answer other combinations of questions as "when" and "who." Sentences are readily obtained directly from books or they may be made up from words in the pupil's reading vocabulary. Sample items are available in Russell and Karp (219) and in various workbooks. In using these materials, it is well to begin with relatively easy sentences and gradually work up to the level which is in other respects the instructional level of the child. In this way, the teacher will be able to adjust her teaching to the individual needs of her pupils.

Thought units

Development of ability to read phrases as meaningful units or thought units is essential for efficient comprehension of sentences. When a child reads word-by-word or tends to group words inappropriately, clear comprehension of the sentence as a whole is impossible. As the child becomes somewhat adept at word identification and as he builds a stock of words that he can recognize at sight, he is able to group some together.

The first grouping in phrases as thought units is in two-word combinations, as: "the boy;" "Mother said;" or "to run." Such grouping of words occurs only after the child is very familiar with each of the words and only when they are set off together by the typography. Thus in the sentence "Mother said, 'We can run,'" the punctuation makes the grouping of "Mother said" natural and easy. Somewhat later, at the primer level, when some two-line sentences appear, further aid is given to the child so that he may learn to read in thought units. A sentence would be printed like the following:

> Ann said, "Put the book
> on the table."

The form of such a sentence would almost force the child to read by thought units. Still later, as the child progresses in his reading, he is expected to be able to analyze a sentence into thought units rapidly as he moves along the line of print. This is a mature sort of reading which requires sight recognition of the words and phrases involved.

The simplest method for discovering whether a child reads by thought units is to listen to him read easy material orally. If he reads word-by-word or if he clusters words in meaningless groups, he is likely ineffective in recognizing and employing thought units in his silent reading. Obviously he is not grouping words into meaningful phrases in his oral reading. The teacher may also flash phrases before him to test recognition. If he reads the phrases appreciably less well than a child of equal general reading aptitude usually does, his ability to grasp thought units in isolation is limited. It is then probable that he would have difficulty in recognizing and grasping thought units in sentences. Since this latter test alone does not show the child's ability to analyze sentences into thought units, both oral reading and flash appraisals should be made. In fact, Gates and Cason (101a) have shown that the diagnosis of oral reading and the flash presentation of phrases are about the most practical and accurate appraisals of ability to read by thought units.

Instruction designed to help a child read in thought units should either be done in contextual settings or the phrases learned in isolation should be read immediately afterward in complete sentences. Exercises like the following will provide the child with instruction and experience in reading thought units. (Some exercises are stated in the form of directions to be given the pupil.)

1. Whenever the teacher introduces a new word it helps when she reads it in a phrase in which the child will encounter it.

2. Organizing material (containing phrases easily identifiable) which is to be read orally furnishes excellent experience in reading by thought units.

3. Multiple-choice exercises in which phrases are used as answers:

a. Draw a line under the correct phrase to complete the sentence.

(1) The bird flew (a) up the ladder, (b) over the trees, (c) under the water.

4. Quickly locating phrases on a designated page to answer specific questions.

a. On page ——, find the phrase that answers the question:

Question	Phrase
(1) What did Jane see?	(a tiny puppy)
(2) Where was the kitten?	(in the tree)

5. Mark off the thought units in the following sentences and tell which questions it answers (who, where, etc.):

a. The tall man walked quickly along the street.

6. Turn to the page I say in your book and find these phrases and tell what they mean.

black as coal	near the house
heavy as lead	a pretty flower

7. On page —— find a phrase that makes you:

    see something   (red roses)

    taste something   (a sweet orange)

8. The use of flash cards will aid children in grasping a thought unit at a glance. The phrases on successive cards should form a sentence, as:

The gray squirrel

sat up

with the nut

in his paws

9. Sentences may be separated into thought units to be read by the children, as:

He came running   with a ball   in his hand.

Sentence structure

The ability to sort out and correctly relate the meanings in different parts of a sentence is sometimes hindered by the way a sentence is structured. Difficulties may arise when the subject is last, or between two parts of the predicate, rather than at the beginning. Exercises like those described above for developing sentence sense may be employed here for instructional purposes. For instance, what word answers the question "who" in the following? "Seeing the light flash a second time, Dick remembered what had happened."

Pronouns

Some children do not readily identify the thing or person referred to by a pronoun. Exercises like the following may be used for instructional purposes:

Directions: In each of the following, the underlined word is used in place of the name of a person or thing mentioned in the same sentence. Draw a circle around the word or words that tell who or what is meant by the underlined word.

1. When the birds were freed, they flew up into the trees.
2. As soon as he arrived home from school, John went to deliver his papers.
3. Sally and Ann went to the park after they finished the dishes.

Punctuation

Improper interpretation of punctuation, or failing to notice it, tends to hinder sentence comprehension. Children should learn to appreciate the more common use of the comma: to separate words and groups of words written as a series in a sentence, to set off an appositive, or to set off a parenthetical expression in a sentence. Pupils should also be taught the role of the colon and the semicolon in sentences. The colon precedes an explanation of what comes before the colon, and the semicolon is used to separate clauses of a compound sentence not joined by a conjunction, or to separate co-ordinate parts of a sentence when the parts include commas. These are all listed by McKee (178, page 87). Sentences illustrating the above may be taken from readers used by the pupils. Most children (other than remedial cases) readily grasp the correct usage and meaning of a period, question mark, and an exclamation point. According to Strom (245), knowledge of grammar aids reading efficiency *only* when grammar is taught in relation to meaning. This suggests that grammar should be taught this way. Teachers should consult manuals and workbooks in basic series for additional exercises and suggestions.

Comprehension of Longer Units

To gain maturity in reading, the child must learn how to comprehend the material in paragraphs, stories, and other descriptive writing.

Paragraph comprehension

The comprehension of a paragraph requires comprehension of its sentences together with an understanding of the relations between the sentences which are all-essential for grasping the larger meaning of the paragraph. Extremely important, too, is identification of the topical sentence containing the key idea of the paragraph and interpreting how it is related to the individual explanatory or amplifying sentences.

To improve skill in locating the topical sentence, the child is given illustrations and explanations. He is also informed that the topical sentence may be the first or the second sentence, or it may be a summary sentence at the end. After a few examples and explanations, the child is requested to find and underline the topical sentence in new paragraphs. The pupil should also receive guidance in understanding how the other sentences in a paragraph develop the idea presented in the topical sentence: as by giving details, by stressing importance, by explanations, by contrast, and by repeating the same idea in other words. One way to do this is to number the sentences in a paragraph. Then through questions and analysis under teacher guidance, the role of each sentence in relation to the others can be made clear.

Any well-written paragraph deals with but one central idea. Instruction in how to identify this idea may be planned in various ways: (1) Give the child a paragraph followed by about three phrases, one of which may be considered a headline or title that best indicates the topic of the contents of the paragraph. Ask the child to state which one he considers most appropriate. (2) Or ask the child to write himself a headline or a sentence expressing the topic of the paragraph. (3) Submit a paragraph which is good except for one sentence which doesn't belong in it and blurs its sense. Ask the child to underline the topical sentence and then to cross out the sentence which does not belong in the paragraph.

Comprehension of paragraphs is important, of course, in all reading. It becomes absolutely essential for satisfactory understanding as a pupil advances into more extensive reading of the content subjects (Chapters 12 and 23). Usually some training for understanding paragraph unity is introduced by the time third-grade reading ability is achieved. More formal and extensive training to promote paragraph comprehension should become a regular part of reading instruction at the intermediate grade levels.

Larger units

To achieve full comprehension of longer units, the child should be able to sense the relation between paragraphs which make up the material. In good expository writing, the introductory paragraphs usually state what the article is about, or what is to be described or explained. Then the following paragraphs give the explanatory details in logical sequence. The final one or two paragraphs customarily state the outcomes or conclusions, or they sum up what has been said. In stories also, there are ordinarily three parts: (1) The introductory material identifies either the time or the place where the story happens, or perhaps both, and sometimes also the characters involved. (2) This introduction is followed by the main sequence of the story which tells what happens. (2) Then the last few paragraphs customarily relate how things turned out.

Instruction here will guide the children to understand better the relations between paragraphs whether in stories or in expository material. To do this the following suggestions may prove helpful: (1) Explain about the three main parts of a story or expository article, point out these parts in an illustrative example, and then ask a set of questions on each part (which you have previously written out). These questions should be organized to show the content that belongs to each part (introduction, what happened, outcome). (2) Instruct the pupils to recognize the transitional expressions that often start a paragraph. Such transitional expressions begin with phrases like: (a) *Then he turned to George* . . . (b) *But something else had occurred so* . . . (c) *When this job was done, he said* . . . (3) Provide the pupil with practice in writing a single sentence that expresses the main idea in each paragraph of a story or expository article. Then have him attempt to link these sentences together into a co-ordinated pattern of thought, employing transitional words or phrases where needed.

When a pupil is reading paragraphs or longer selections, his aim should be to grasp the essential thread of thought expressed in the material. To evaluate his proficiency in doing this, present him with a selection to be read silently and tell him why and how he should read it. At the end of the reading, check his comprehension by means of a series of questions. The teacher may ask these questions or the child may do the exercises by himself, as in workbook materials. If the pupil appears particularly deficient in this comprehension, the teacher may want to repeat the exercises orally in order to understand better what his difficulties are. The major portion of the training to comprehend longer units and to adapt basic comprehension to specific demands is usually associated with teaching of the specific types of comprehension (see below).

Materials designed to develop comprehension of sentences and longer units may be found in the workbooks accompanying basic series of readers. Also there are suggestions for teaching this in teachers' manuals. For additional materials see Russell and Karp (219), McKee (178), Strang, McCullough, and Traxler (244), and Thurstone (253).

Specific Types of Comprehension

As the child advances through school, he will also need to acquire skills in the more specialized techniques of comprehension. A firm foundation in the basic abilities of word, sentence, paragraph, and story comprehension plus the ability to apply appropriately the specialized types of comprehension produce the mature reader. In fact, mastery of the more complex comprehension skills constitutes the hallmark of the good reader.

Since the specialized techniques of comprehension overlap the essential study skills, both will be discussed in some detail in the next chapter. Here, the specific types of comprehension will be merely listed.

1. *Skimming* is a form of partial reading done rapidly to acquire specific kinds of information such as ascertaining a date, a name, or a relevant fact.

2. *Apprehending the main idea.* The purpose in such reading is to dig out the essential meaning, the central theme, or general import from reading a paragraph, a story, or a descriptive article.

3. *Following and predicting sequence of events* is essential for maximum enjoyment and sufficient understanding of narrative material.

4. *Noting and grasping details.* Proficiency in reading such materials as science and mathematics requires apprehension and assimilation of all relevant details.

5. *Following printed directions* is an important skill for both children and adults. Examples: Accurate grasping of directions for playing a game, constructing a model, or assembling a piece of machinery.

6. *Generalizing or drawing conclusions* is a skill that requires greater emphasis upon thoughtful reading and interpretation. So does the ability to think not only along with but *beyond* what is given in the printed material.

7. *Critical evaluation* involves the kind of judgment that selects appropriate data for generalizing. A reader's whole background of experience should be used in this skill. Example: Differentiating facts from opinion in a news article.

Summary

To read with understanding there must be comprehension of words, thought units, sentences, paragraphs, and longer units. Identifying words without understanding their meanings is not true reading. The development of comprehension and interpretation is fundamental in all reading instruction. As a child masters the mechanics of reading, his reading comprehension should become more nearly equivalent to his listening comprehension. With further progress in proficiency, reading comprehension should equal, or better still exceed, what is comprehended through listening. The aim in reading instruction is to have pupils reach this level as soon as possible.

The amount of material comprehended as a unit, the degree of comprehension, and the speed of comprehension or speed of reading vary from child to child. Skill in adapting procedures to the requirements of comprehension in specific reading situations indicates proficient reading. Certain conditions hinder comprehension, others aid it. Basically, comprehension depends upon a group of concepts or of meanings evolved through experience. Firsthand experience is best. This should, however, be supplemented by vicarious or secondhand experience, especially what can be got from books. The primary aim of such experience is to develop concepts which can be used by the child in thinking, speaking, listening, writing, and reading.

Standardized tests are useful for diagnosing grade level in sentence and paragraph comprehension (see Chapter 16). For determining specific needs of pupils, informal procedures are best. To comprehend sentences, the child must understand the words involved and the relations between these words and groups of words. He must also be able to read by thought units or meaningful phrases, correctly interpret punctuation, and understand figures of speech and symbolic expressions.

Paragraph comprehension depends upon comprehension of the sentences of which it is built and upon an understanding of their relations, one to another and to the whole paragraph. Similarly, the comprehension of larger units is based upon paragraph comprehension together with a large surplus of meaning to be gained by understanding the relations between the separate paragraphs and the larger whole.

Vocabulary

Check your knowledge of these terms. Reread parts of the chapter if necessary.

interpretation	use of commas
listening comprehension	use of semicolon
reading-capacity test	topical sentence
thinking in reading	expository writing
imaginative literature	transitional *expression
constructing meanings	comprehension skills
determinants of comprehension	skimming
sentence comprehension	word-by-word reading
sentence sense	flash presentation

Activities for Students

Observation: Visit a classroom in an elementary school and note the methods that are resorted to there in teaching comprehension.

Reading: Select a paragraph in one of your texts. Identify the topical sentence and then note how the other sentences enlarge upon the idea presented in the topical sentence. Point out the excellent structure of the paragraph, or how it falls short of this, if this is the case.

Creative thinking: State all the arguments you can think of for and against use of workbook exercises in teaching comprehension of paragraph material.

Selected References

BOND, G. L., and TINKER, M. A., *Reading difficulties.* New York: Appleton-Century-Crofts, Inc., 1957, Chap. 11.

—— and WAGNER, E. B., *Teaching the child to read,* 3rd ed. New York: The Macmillan Company, 1960, Chap. 11.

DAWSON, M. A., and BAMMAN, H. A., *Fundamentals of basic reading instruction.* New York: Longmans, Green and Company, 1959, Chap. 10.

DEBOER, J. J., and DALLMANN, M., *The teaching of reading.* New York: Holt, Rinehart and Winston, 1960, Chaps. 7A, 7B.

GATES, A. I., *The improvement of reading,* 3rd ed. New York: The Macmillan Company, 1947, Chap. 12.

HARRIS, A. J., *How to increase reading ability,* 4th ed. New York: Longmans, Green and Company, 1961, Chaps. 15, 16.

HESTER, K. B., *Teaching every child to read.* New York: Harper and Brothers, 1955, Chap. 12.

HILDRETH, G., *Teaching reading.* New York: Holt, Rinehart and Winston, 1958, Chap. 19.

9

Comprehension and Study Skills

Even the proficient reader will obtain from the printed material only what he is seeking. Jack, a fifth grader, barely glances at a newspaper article to find out how many runs his favorite baseball team made yesterday. At another time he may pore over every detail describing how to assemble a model airplane. In some instances he may be set to grasp only the general drift of a story. Again he may read every last clue of a mystery to learn just how the denouement is reached or to find out the grounds on which a scientific conclusion is justified. At all times, the efficient reader will make use of his comprehension and study skills to the degree required to attain his objectives.

Far too many pupils progress through the elementary grades without developing satisfactory proficiency in these skills. Moe and Nania (182) discovered that even the high achievers in junior high school may be deficient in how they go about understanding what they read and supposedly study. And Smith (231) points out that reading proficiency could be improved greatly if more attention were devoted in the primary and intermediate grades to the development of study skills.

Interrelationships of the skills

On its lowest level, acquisition of the more complex methods of study requires a knowledge of the words and sentence patterns encountered. Without such knowledge, there can be little learning of the higher level skills. Retention without comprehension can be of little value. While studying geography, Richard, in the fifth grade, read the sentence, "Minneapolis is at the head of commercial navigation on the Mississippi river." Although he remembered this sentence verbatim from his text, he could not tell what it meant because he did not know the meaning either of *commercial* or *navigation*.

Comprehension is essential in using reference materials. Even if a child is able to locate the material he needs, his reading is ineffectual if he cannot select its main points along with the relevant supporting details or if he wants to summarize some data but cannot comprehend the sentences and paragraphs in which the data are reported. Some children get the hang of stories fairly well but fall down when they attempt to read material in the content subjects. In general the *study skills,* such as locating information, using reference materials, interpreting graphs and tables, organizing material, and adjusting the rate at which unfamiliar material is tackled, play an important role when one or another *comprehension skill* is employed. This relationship is particularly obvious in reading in the social studies, in literature, or in science and mathematics.

The Comprehension Skills

As a child progresses in school, his reading in order to learn something becomes more and more prominent. This is because greater stress is placed on programs of reading organized to meet special needs and individual interests, and making use of a wide variety of source material, much of which is outside the regular texts. This kind of reading would seem to make heavy demands on the comprehension skills. But as noted by McCullough (168), there is considerable dissatisfaction with the extent to which schools develop reading comprehension. Her survey suggests that, while we have apparently developed readers who can ascertain *facts,* we seem to have failed more or less to develop *thinking,* i.e., *thoughtful* readers. Too often children fail to learn sufficiently the more complex skills required for comprehension as these must be used in making comparisons, in drawing conclusions, and in a hundred other forms of critical reading. McCullough also points out that, although the correlations are high between students' performances on various types of comprehension (listed by Davis, 53), the facts remain that students vary greatly in their mastery of different skills and can profit from special efforts to build up those in which they are deficient. The kinds of skills required to comprehend all sorts of subject matter are not adequately learned *once and for all at any one grade level.* And since different emphases are put upon them in different fields, they need to be studied in each separate field as the need is felt. It is unrealistic to expect wide, free reading, no matter how much discussion is added, to develop all the comprehension skills needed by the pupil in his work. If we wish a pupil to understand graphs, to make inferences, to summarize an argument, etc., etc., we must teach him these very skills.

Effective use of comprehension skills is selective in nature. As we have repeatedly stated, the choice of the skill or skills to be used must be made with certain ends in view. Only when the child has a clear understanding of his purpose can he seek suitable materials and choose just which procedures will best achieve the end he has in mind. To develop proficiency in using the comprehension skills, two important instructional tasks are encountered. *First,* the children need guidance and practice in defining what they are doing in reading and why. *Secondly,* the child must be taught to select the skill or skills for reading a particular selection which will achieve his purpose. This is accomplished only by carefully set up preparatory activities in which each of these is practiced in relation to a wide variety of materials and throughout the school year. An example may help to illustrate how to go about defining purposes.

Most manuals for teaching the units in a basic series give ample suggestions for clarifying a pupil's aims. Take "The Story of Johny Appleseed" in a basic fifth reader.[1] The accompanying Teachers' Manual shows how the reasons in reading such a story are made plain. Preliminary discussion tied the story in with preceding material about the wilderness. Questions were raised about Johnny Appleseed's attitudes and his relation to other pioneers. Then the story was read to find out why Johnny Appleseed has been so long remembered. This involved an understanding of his life of devotion to nature and to the needs of other people, i.e., the first reading was to grasp the general idea of the story. The reading was followed by a discussion of the main events in Johnny Appleseed's life. Then four questions were written on the chalkboard:

> How Johnny Appleseed felt about the wilderness
> How the pioneers felt about Johnny
> How he managed to live out in the open
> When and how he traveled

Each child chose one of these topics to work on for the purpose of presenting further information on the topic to the class. The steps to be followed were:

1. First, skim the story through to get information on your topic.
2. Second, jot down all the facts you find.
3. Third, prepare and plan how to present the information in a report to the class.

Here the comprehension and study skills to be used consisted of (a) skimming and (b) selecting and organizing information.

Another comprehension skill which might be employed is to *interpret the author's feeling* about Johnny Appleseed. To do this the pupils were to search out relevant places in the story. The teacher gives the pupils a start by indicating one such sentence.

It is time that we turn to consider what various writers list as the important comprehension skills. Although the lists are not identical, there is much overlapping and therefore agreement. We shall take up the ones most frequently stressed.

Applications of the comprehension skills will be discussed in several subsequent chapters. For teachers who wish to use supplementary exer-

[1] D. H. Russell, C. M. McCullough, and D. Gates, *Trails to treasure*. Boston: Ginn and Company, 1956, 86-96.

cises, Russell and Karp's little book (219) is an excellent source. Other exercises are listed in DeBoer and Dallmann (57).

Skimming

Skimming is a form of partial reading done rapidly to acquire specific kinds of information. It is a very useful as well as a specialized technique which must be carefully taught to avoid its abuse. In any and all skimming there should be a definite purpose and the reader should usually come out having acquired some precise and accurate information or impressions. The information may be a single item such as a date, a name, or a relevant fact. Or it may be the bold pattern or outline developed in an article, a chapter, or a book. Again it may be his intention to glean all facts relevant to one particular problem, or to locate an article or section of an article for more careful reading. Finally, a story, an article, or a book may be skimmed to get a general impression or overview of the material.

For the most part, skimming involves skill in skipping the irrelevant parts and judiciously selecting those that are relevant. The greater the background or familiarity in a field, the greater the facility in skimming. Most decidedly, skimming is an active process. It is guided by a definite purpose. The reader employs his own experience and information from other sources to check the relevance and accuracy of new acquisitions.

In the beginning, instruction in skimming should concentrate on methods of locating information. As some mastery is acquired in this, exercises may be introduced to speed up the process, such as recording the time taken to get the required information. Relatively short and simple material should be used at first. Then progress is made to longer and more difficult selections. Detailed procedures for training in skimming are given by Durrell (70).

Various exercises may be devised for practice in locating information. For instance, answers to specific questions like the following may be obtained by skimming:

On what date did Cornwallis surrender at Yorktown?
When was the first transcontinental railroad completed?
In what state is Yosemite National Park?
What state produces the most corn?
What four labor-saving devices are used in this model home?

The prepared set of questions is presented to the pupils who find the answers as quickly as possible, and write them down. The children are taught to glance rapidly over the material, noting only what they are looking for. With practice, the item sought will stand out as if printed in bold-face type. In many instances this skimming can be done with great speed. When a set of questions is finished, the answers can be discussed and, if desired, some sentences read in which they occur.

Skimming to grasp the pattern of discussion or over-all impression in a book, article, or chapter is somewhat different. The following procedures are samples:

1. Examining the preface, table of contents, and section headings in chapters of a book to note what is included, or to judge whether it is likely to contain the information you are seeking.

2. Sampling various pages in a story or a novel to decide whether it is easy enough to read, or if it appeals to you as worth reading.

3. Sampling the introduction, topical sentences of paragraphs, and conclusions of a controversial article to get the author's point of view.

4. Examination of the introduction, section headings, subheadings, illustrations or maps, and conclusions of a chapter to get the framework on which the topic is developed.

5. Examination of headlines, accompanying illustrations, and perhaps topical sentences in introductory paragraphs of newspaper articles to decide whether you wish to read the article. This procedure can be a great timesaver for the reader.

In all skimming the child must learn where to locate the source of information. In some instances the reference will be given by the teacher. In many instances, however, he must be able to size up the subject matter to be searched and then judge where it is most likely to be found. This necessitates acquaintance with source and reference works. He will need to be taught how to use indexes in textbooks and reference works as well as such general sources as the *Readers' Guide to Periodical Literature*. Probably the best training in the use of these indexes is through teacher guidance in finding materials and information which the child is going to need in achieving his objective.

Too frequently the ability to skim is not well learned. Grayum (115) studied this ability in six groups ranging from fourth graders to college students and well-read adults. The intelligence and reading ability of all in the groups were average or above. The results revealed marked differences among the individuals at each of the grade levels in ability to skim. Some readers, both average and superior, were very poor in skimming. In fact some adults were skimming as poorly as some fourth graders.

It would appear that greater emphasis should be placed upon teaching skimming. The expert skimmer has acquired a valuable asset. He has developed a distinctive skill which is quite different from other types of reading, one that is highly useful in several kinds of study.

Reading for the main idea

A relatively important subskill in comprehension is grasping the main idea from reading a paragraph, an article, or a story. The purpose in such reading is to dig out the essential meaning, the central theme, or general import of the material. This import may be an idea or it may be the feeling or emotion expressed. What results is the acquisition of a generalized impression that incorporates the central thought or impression. There is no attempt to remember details. Attention is concentrated upon selecting and understanding the essential implication of the passage as a whole. This involves discrimination and judgment. Consequently it is a relatively difficult skill to master, particularly by children of less than average ability.

Reading to extract the main idea is demanded in a wide variety of materials: stories, novels, most newspaper reports, magazine articles, and other informative writings. Much recreational reading falls into this class, but not all. This type of reading should be done at a relatively rapid rate though not inaccurately or superficially. Reading rapidly and accurately to apprehend the main idea is not an easy skill to acquire, partly because attitudes due to emphasis upon remembering details have tended to become habitual.

Development of skill in apprehending the main idea can be cultivated by a variety of exercises. Attention may be directed to the role played by introductions and conclusions, topical sentences, headings and subheadings and newspaper headlines. In discussing these roles, it is important that the pupil does not substitute the reading of conclusions, topical sentences, and so on, for reading the whole article. He should realize that they provide a pattern which is useful in directing his attention to the main idea developed in the entire text. Complete reading of the material is necessary for clarifying concepts and acquiring more complete understanding.

Another approach is to have pupils write a single sentence summary, or an appropriate headline to express the main idea or feeling expressed in a paragraph or in a longer article. Or the teacher may furnish several headlines or titles and ask the pupils to choose the most satisfactory one. Class discussion concerning the adequacy of choices provides helpful training.

Following and predicting sequence of events

Maximum enjoyment and sufficient understanding of narrative material depends upon the ability of the reader to follow a sequence of ideas and to anticipate what is coming next. In addition to noting the main idea, this skill requires appraisal of the cause-and-effect relations between successive events and the grasping of the implications of these for the future unfolding of the plot. Development of this comprehension skill begins relatively early from listening to stories that are told or read to the child. Further development comes with guidance and practice during the early grades. Following and predicting sequence of events in reading is dependent upon ability to do the same thing in listening. Practice exercises may include checking omissions, rearranging specific events in retelling a story heard or read, arranging in proper order events which have been listed in a wrong order, and completing an unfinished story which has been interrupted at a critical point. Supervised class discussion should show pupils how successful they are in doing this.

Reading to apprehend details

Proficiency in reading certain types of study materials requires apprehension and assimilation of all relevant details. This demands relatively slow, analytical progress and at times some rereading for fuller understanding. The goal, however, is not to remember isolated bits of information, which is what happens too frequently in teaching this exacting form of reading. The aim is to apprehend *relevant* details, with a full understanding of their relation to each other and to the main idea in the total pattern of the paragraph, article, or problem.

Although rereading is frequently necessary for full apprehension of details and their implications, instruction should aim at grasping as many of these as possible in a single reading. A common fault in dealing with study-type reading is to go too fast. This is particularly common with children accustomed to reading for the main idea. They have not acquired the versatility that leads them to change their pace to fit specific reading purposes and materials. More of the relevant details are apt to be apprehended when the reading purpose is clear and motivation is strong. For example, a boy who would like a bicycle will readily take in an article giving details of bicycle construction.

Many study-type materials should be read with precision, as in certain parts of history, geography, and science. Also, verbal arithmetical problems require precise accuracy in reading.

In exercises used to develop the skills of recall or recognition, the questions should be phrased to call for details related to the main idea. Furthermore, the work should be so arranged and supervised that through checking and discussion the errors are readily seen and improvement appreciated. The aim should be to develop motivation for increased precision and to inculcate an habitual attitude of striving for accuracy.

Following directions

An appreciable section of the reading of both children and adults is concerned with printed directions. Examples are directions for playing games, constructing models, making a cake, using a tool, carrying out a scientific experiment, and solving a mathematical problem, to mention only a few. Reading to follow directions is a relatively slow, painstaking process. All the pertinent details must be apprehended in a sequential order. Each step must be clearly understood and kept in its proper place in the sequence. It will be noted that reading to follow directions involves apprehension of details as discussed above.

Inability to follow printed directions is common among both children and adults. This is undoubtedly due to lack of appropriate experience and proper guidance in this kind of reading. Many of the difficulties encountered in science and mathematics may be traced to reading deficiencies of this kind.

Training in reading to follow directions produces the best results when an activity is involved in which the child has a definite interest. A wide variety of material is readily available in craft books, pamphlets, and magazines as well as in books and pamphlets on sewing, gardening, and cooking. The teacher can readily organize numerous situations for developing skill in reading to follow directions: instructions for conducting scientific experiments, and for constructing various items. She should be sure that the pupils clearly understand each step, and that the steps are kept in proper sequence. Checking the end product, as in a construction or sewing job, ordinarily will reveal to both pupil and teacher whether the directions were properly read and followed. Activities found in workbooks furnish practice in reading to follow directions. Because of their simplicity they are useful only during the early stages of training.

Generalizing or drawing conclusions

Certain comprehension skills require greater emphasis upon thoughtful reading or thinking along with and beyond what is given in the printed material. One phase of such reading is concerned with generalizing or drawing conclusions.

In reading to generalize or to draw a conclusion, the pupil exercises judgment in selecting and relating relevant facts found in one or more articles. This is done in such a way that the combined product points to, or indicates a general rule, a proposition, an inference, or a generalization. This product may be stated in the form of a conclusion.

Reading to generalize is purposeful reading in which the purpose is frequently set by a question that calls for an inference. Examples: (1) Why is there snow on the tops of some mountains in the summer time? (2) Why does the eating of fruit help to keep one healthy? (3) Why are there many cities located on the Mississippi river? To answer any one of these questions from reading requires the selection and relating of relevant information. Children should be taught that the first hunch or statement of a generalization is tentative. This is to be evaluated for adequacy in terms of past experience, other reading, and discussion. Thus, in addition to exercising judgment in selecting appropriate information and drawing conclusions, it is necessary to test the conclusions reached. Both the generalizing and testing of conclusions require further thinking.

Children tend to generalize readily. However, much of their generalizing is in error due to incomplete evidence and inaccurate thinking. Nevertheless, generalizing must be encouraged. The teacher, however, should guide the children to improve their skill in selecting relevant information and in evaluating the conclusions they form. In many instances the discussion of a conclusion may reveal the need for further reading to gain sufficient information to justify the tentatively formed conclusion.

Critical evaluation

In many situations, reading calls for critical evaluation of what is read. For instance, the judgment needed in selecting appropriate data for generalizing involves critical evaluation. This skill, as Gans (92) has shown, tends to be poorly developed even among the more able children. In demonstrating this she had measured the ability to discriminate whether a sentence or paragraph contained information relevant to a given question or topic.

As children engage in wide reading in quest of information on a specific topic, they will encounter conflicting views in different places. Reconciliation of such views demand critical evaluation. Contradictions may be found not only in newspaper and magazine articles but also in the presentation and interpretation of more scientific material. Critical evaluation may be in terms of such factors as an author's or publisher's prestige, the detection of his bias, or the out-of-dateness of a publication. For instance the background of a newspaper writer or the general policy of a magazine may be such as to lead to prejudiced statements. And the more recent of two informative articles on the same subject may make more facts, or better supported ones, available to the child.

In all critical evaluation the reader should make use of his whole background of experience. This drawing upon accumulated information will frequently make it possible to evaluate whether the new material seems plausible, is only partially correct, or appears biased. Conflict of the new with past experience may also lead to modification of the reader's earlier views. His earlier conclusions may have been based upon incomplete evidence. Supervised class discussion is very helpful in evaluating conflicting statements and views.

It is highly desirable that children learn to detect propaganda and to evaluate it critically. Propaganda, or systematic efforts to spread opinions or beliefs, is prevalent in many forms, good and bad. It is found in advertisements, speeches, and in many printed materials. Learning to detect and to evaluate propaganda is not easy. Nevertheless, children can be taught to recognize some of the more obvious propaganda techniques such as biased testimonials, name calling, and the frequently employed methods of associating views with "prestige" individuals and institutions. Furthermore, in our present society the attitude of questioning and sometimes becoming suspicious of appealing generalities unsupported by factual evidence should be cultivated. The more subservient one is to parent and teacher authority, the more receptive he is apt to become to propaganda. Although the satisfactory adjustment of the individual requires a proper recognition of authority and of the values of ripe experience, there should be a balance between this and independence in thinking. Neither slave-like submission nor complete rejection of authority is healthy. Children who learn to think for themselves by investigating or by demanding supporting evidence before making a judgment are more apt to resist insidious forms of propaganda.

Study Skills

As already noted, the skills required for comprehending and in studying operate together. If one is to be able to make effective use of the various techniques that aid comprehension, as we have described them, he must also acquire proficiency in using the skills that abet study. The following discussion will deal with the skills most commonly listed as aids to study.

Remembering what is read

There are marked individual differences in ability to recall the essentials of what has been read even among readers, all of whom understand fairly well what they are reading during the reading of it. It is a common complaint at all academic levels, elementary grades through college, that a student cannot remember later what he has read. Some pupils do remember better than others. But practically all individuals can learn to remember better if trained to employ correctly certain accepted principles of learning. The following set of principles will be found elaborated upon in most textbooks of psychology. It will be noted that many of the principles are related to the comprehension and study skills discussed in this chapter.

1. It is easier for you to remember material that you read with a high degree of understanding. When material is only partially comprehended, its recall is difficult or impossible. A pupil should be provided with material he can understand and which has some significance for him.

2. Read with a positive attitude, with intention to remember. Reading in a lackadaisical manner fosters inattention and daydreaming. It often helps concentration and you attend better, if you read at a rate slightly faster than you find comfortable.

3. Try to think while you read. Note ideas relevant to the reading purpose and their relationships. Material organized by the reader as he goes along promotes easier recall. Piekarz (202) noted that the readers who are more able grasped implied as well as literal meanings. The poorer readers had difficulty distinguishing between what the author said and what he thought. Again, this implies ability on the part of the reader to understand what he is reading.

4. Select items relevant to the reasons for which you are reading. Concentrate on these. Not all the facts can be remembered. The efficient reader is the one who tries to retain only essential points.

5. Outline in note form as you read, or underline topical sentences and relevant supporting facts, or make marginal notes of points considered important. Shortly after reading, go over the notes again, underline parts, and note continuities and relationships.

6. Reread your notes at least once, and afterwards review them periodically to insure retention.

7. After reading a body of material—not too much at once—pause and try to recall the essential points in it. Recite them to yourself and at the same time note how the ideas tie in to one another.

In general, if one is to remember he should (1) read actively with a definite purpose, (2) attend to relevant items and their implications, (3) outline what he reads, (4) review his notes periodically, and (5) recite to oneself the important points. Answering multiple-choice and true-false questions requires only that the correct answer be recognized. To develop ability to remember, a child should receive training in answering recall questions, i.e., he should be able to supply the gist of what he has read without rereading it.

Locating information

The ability to locate information in printed sources becomes increasingly important as the child progresses through school. It becomes an essential tool for the study type of reading encountered particularly in the content subjects. Unfortunately, large numbers of children finish elementary school, and even junior high and high school, with only limited skill in locating information. Fortunately, the schools are making greater efforts to improve this situation. The alert teacher meets the challenge by faithfully experimenting with the improved instructional methods which teach pupils how to locate information quickly and efficiently.

Importance of knowing the alphabetical order. Words and topics are arranged in alphabetical order in the dictionary, the index of a book, the card catalog in the library, encyclopedias, and many other reference books. Training in alphabetizing need not be described here, as it has been explained in the account of how to use the dictionary in Chapter 6. But since efficient location of information depends upon use of alphabetical order, teachers should check this ability in their pupils before beginning training in tracking down references. It is likely that some pupils in every class will be poor at alphabetizing and need special training in it. *It is unsafe for the elementary school teacher to assume that every one of her pupils is up to standard in this skill.*

Finding a specific page. In the initial stages of reading, children are taught to read numbers, to note the sequence of numbers from small to large, and how to open a book to the page they want. These pupils are told where to find the page number (which top or bottom corner, or middle of page), how to turn pages, and a little later how to open a book to approximately the right place and then turn the pages backward or forward as required to find the correct page. As an exercise, ask the pupils to guess about which page you have opened a book to when you open it near the beginning, about one-third the way through, etc.

Skill in using guide words. To locate a word quickly in the dictionary, glossary, encyclopedia and certain other reference books, the child must know how to employ the guide words at the top of pages. These give the first and last word on a page, or on two facing pages. Their use speeds up location of the sought word or item. Without adequate practice, many pupils will tend to neglect the guide words and this slows them considerably in finding an entry.

Key words and topics. Most indexes, encyclopedias, and reference books do not have guide words. But the entries and topics in them are usually in alphabetical order. So the child needs to know under what word or phrase to look for the information he is seeking. It is often difficult to decide under which key words or phrases a certain item of information is most likely to be found. Training in doing this should progress from easy to difficult. An early exercise consists of examination of an index with teacher guidance to note the key words and the sorts of subtopics under each. This can be followed by such exercises as:

1. Indicate the word or phrase in parenthesis which you judge is the most likely key word in an index or dictionary to give you the answer to the question:
   a. When was Thomas Jefferson president of the United States?
            (Thomas; president; United States; Jefferson)
2. Ask the pupils to suggest key words under which the following information might be found in a dictionary or reference book: *"Date of the outbreak of the Spanish-American War."* After several suggestions have been written on the chalkboard, eliminate through class discussion all but one or two that seem most promising.

Use of reference books. Most pupils need to learn the kind of information contained in various types of books and magazines such as history (*Encyclopedia of American History*), geography (Rand McNally's *World Guide*), science books, general encyclopedias for children, *World Almanac*, an atlas, a dictionary, and others. The acquiring of such information is a gradual process and skill in doing so can be built up indefinitely.

As pointed out by Bond and Wagner (28), skill in locating information is dependent upon the following abilities: (*a*) appraisal of the problem; (*b*) knowledge of likely sources; (*c*) locating a desired source in the library or other collection of reference books; (*d*) using the index and table of contents; and (*e*) skimming to locate the desired material within an article. The child will need to know enough about his problem to have some idea where to locate the desired reference books (library, shelves in the classroom, etc.). He should then employ the most likely key words or phrases in tracking down the information.

Library aids. These are best taught when a child needs them to reach some educational goal. They include use of the card catalog. This involves knowing how the Dewey Decimal Classification system operates, or how to use the *Readers' Guide to Periodical Literature* and various encyclopedias. Demonstrations by the teacher or the librarian are helpful.

Selecting relevant points. After locating the proper material, the child must learn how to select whatever points bear on his purpose. He will also have to know how to interpret any abbreviations, maps, charts, diagrams, and tables encountered in reference books. (See chapter on content subjects.) Cross references (see also . . .) will be met. Skill in finding and appraising these is developed through practice, guided by the teacher or librarian.

Aids in reference work. Pupils should be encouraged to examine reference books, noting how their sections are arranged, what they contain, how the indexing is organized, and the general nature and type of treatment of the material included. As another part of the training, pupils are asked to state what reference books they would go to for particular sorts of information, such as material on navigation, or data on the life of Thomas Edison. Methods books ordinarily include excellent suggestions for teaching how to locate and use information. Additional suggestions and practice exercises are given by Fargo (77) and by Mott and Baisden (187). Instruction in locating information should be kept close to the basal reading program where the sequential program for developing skills is being taught. The best time for such teaching according to Bond and Wagner (28) is while the children are doing extended reading in connection with a topical unit. There is ample opportunity to employ these skills while reading in the content fields.

Locating information in non-reference books

Pupils in the elementary school will make extensive use of textbooks and a variety of other books—"trade books," as they are called. Ability to find information in these books quickly depends upon applying certain sorts of knowledge:

1. *The preface, or introduction,* (or both) is located at the front of the book. It often tells the reader what topics or questions he may expect to find dealt with in the book.

2. *The table of contents* is useful at all grade levels. The listing gives the units, stories, or articles in the book with the page numbers at which they begin. By examining a table of contents, a pupil can discover quickly whether a certain kind of material is in the book.

3. Certain books, especially those in the content fields, provide a *list of illustrations, figures, and maps* and page numbers to show where they are located.

4. *Headings*. Pupils should be taught that when they are locating information they should use chapter, center, and side headings in both textbooks and reference books.

5. *The glossary*, near the end of the book, is a little dictionary—to be used like one—which gives the pronunciation and meanings of some of the more difficult or specialized words employed in the book. A glossary is a source of valuable information.

6. *The index* is usually the last thing in the book. The pupils should know that the entries are arranged in alphabetical order, that the sub-topics, if any, are found under the main entries and that the numbers opposite an entry refer to pages in the book. Illustrations are often entered in a different type face. Skill in using an index involves learning to (1) choose the most likely key word or entry when seeking information on a given topic, (2) locate an entry that appears as a subtopic in the index (as "*land grants*" as a subtopic under the entry "*railroads*"), (3) locate cross references quickly in the index, and (4) turn to indicated pages and spot the information you desire.

Organizing and summarizing material

A pupil does relatively little locating of materials in reference books without needing to take notes, and organize and summarize what he finds. Relevant facts and ideas are written down during the reading. Skill in note taking improves with practice. Key sentences may be copied verbatim but to an increasing degree the child should strive to paraphrase briefly the essential material. Instructions to pupils might be like the following: (1) First, read the article through and then go over it a second time to select and write down if possible *in your own words* the important points. Be sure to list the essential supporting details along with each important point. Note down only those details needed to clarify each main idea or point. (2) Make a notation of the reference source such as (*a*) name of the author of the article, if any, (*b*) title of article or section, (*c*) title of book, (*d*) publisher of book, (*e*) date of publication, and (*f*) pages covered by material read. (3) Organize your notes into an outline for reporting the information gathered. Use main headings for key ideas, with supporting details as subtopics underneath each main heading.

Making an outline. During the primary years the children begin to develop some skill in making simple outlines, organized in an elementary way from the material they read. For instance, they can sort out objects used in the kitchen from those in the living room. Also they have learned to sense the proper sequence of ideas in a story and even to list these in the right order. Perhaps they have already learned to make very simple outlines of what they read. All this constitutes a basis for organizing and outlining during the intermediate and higher grades. It is a sort of readiness program for the more mature aspects of classifying according to major topics and subtopics.

Early experiences usually consist of noting and outlining the sequence of events in a story, paragraph by paragraph. The main idea (topical sentence) is listed first, followed by the supporting or amplifying details as subheadings. After an initial reading of the entire story, each succeeding paragraph is reread and outlined. The outline might take this form:

Title of Story

I. (Main idea) _____
    A. (Supporting detail) _____
    B. (Supporting detail) _____

II. _____
      A.
      B.

III. (etc.)

Progress toward more elaborate outlines comes gradually. Several paragraphs may be organized under one main heading and its subheadings. The following example is adapted from a fifth reader.[2]

Christmas on the Yukon

I. Getting ready for guests
    A.
    B. etc.
II. The guests arrive
    A.
    B. etc.
III. Festivities at the cabin
    A.
    B. etc.
IV. A trip to the store
    A.
    B. etc.
V. Preparation for the Christmas party
    A.
    B. etc.
VI. Festivities at the school
    A.
    B. etc.

When information is gathered from reference books, the task of organizing and outlining in preparation for a verbal report or for a written paper becomes more complex. At times materials from more than one book must be combined and appropriately co-ordinated. Interpreting and using

[2] Russell, McCullough, and Gates, ibid., pp. 281-292.

such information involves activities like these: classifying ideas; making comparisons; making a time line; outlining; and summarizing. Teachers' manuals and workbooks describe how these activities are carried out and provide ample practice exercises for use as integral parts of the process of reading to learn. Such programs begin with the elementary tasks and gradually develop more complex ways of interpreting and using information, as the pupils move up through the grades.

Guided class discussions are extremely important in teaching organization and outlining, as well as for locating the information that goes into the outlines. By such means, pupils learn how to condense a long sentence into a few words, comparing various statements and choosing the clearest and most concise ones. Harris (122) suggests that pupils should learn to use a formal outline prior to making informal reading notes. If this is done, pupils are likely to make more orderly and intelligible notes thereafter because they have learned how useful they can be.

Preparing the summary involves the organization of a brief and comprehensive statement of the important ideas in a story or an article. The writer separates what is most significant from the supporting details. Then the significant elements are organized into a coherent whole. One approved way of teaching summarizing is to have the child identify the topical sentences in each paragraph of a story or article. Then these topical sentences are put in sequential order with just enough supporting facts to round out the summary and make it understandable by itself. Transitional words or phrases are employed to connect up the topical sentences where these are needed to establish continuity. Baker's *Reading skills* (12), and Russell and Karp's *Reading aids through the grades* (219) provide examples and exercises for teaching summarizing.

Material located in one or more sources, when the reading is for the purpose of preparing a topical unit, may be summarized in a somewhat similar manner. In doing this, it is best first to organize the material in an outline such as discussed above. Then the main ideas with a minimum of supporting details are written up in summary form. Material of this kind, however, is usually reported orally to the class or sometimes a written report is made. The outline forms the basis for such reports.

Adjusting speed of comprehension

Practice to increase speed of reading is common in many schoolrooms and in other programs for the improvement of reading. It has been erroneously believed that the speed of reading simple material provides an index of a pupil's speed of reading in all reading situations. If this should be true for a particular child, *he is certainly a very poor reader*. As noted earlier, the mature or efficient reader will adjust his speed to the kind of material read and according to the purpose for which the reading is done.

If he is to comprehend it as he should, every child must read some kinds of material slowly. Other kinds should be read relatively rapidly. The pupil who makes such adjustments is the one we recognize as a versatile reader. This matter is so important that we shall revert to it in greater detail in the chapter on speed of reading.

Summary

In addition to the basic tools he possesses, such as understanding words and concepts, the pupil must acquire proficiency in the more complex comprehension and study skills like reading to grasp details and to locate information. The efficient reader will make use of these special skills to whatever degree is required in order to achieve his objective. Unfortunately many pupils progress through the elementary school without developing satisfactory proficiency in these abilities.

Comprehension and study skills develop together. They supplement each other in most, perhaps all, types of reading which can properly be called study, especially in the content areas. Among the comprehension skills are skimming, reading for the main idea, following and predicting sequence of events, reading in order to unearth relevant details, following directions, generalizing or drawing conclusions, and critical evaluation. The study skills most commonly listed include remembering what is read, locating information, organizing and summarizing material, and adjusting the rapidity with which one tries to comprehend to the difficulty of the material and the depth of comprehension aimed at. Often subskills are also involved.

Studying is an art difficult to learn and even with the best of teaching it tends to develop gradually. It is unrealistic to expect wide, free reading followed by discussion of what is read to develop of itself all the skills the pupil is going to need in his work. These must be taught systematically, and throughout all the elementary grades. Many schools fail to push this training far enough to include, for example, making thoughtful comparisons, locating and organizing information, and many other forms of critical reading. Apparently a good many schools develop "fact readers" but fail to develop sufficiently thoughtful readers to insure that they will measure up to the demands our contemporary world is going more and more to put upon its citizens.

Vocabulary

Check your knowledge of these terms. Reread parts of the chapter if necessary.

comprehension skills	main idea
study skills	main headings
thoughtful reader	headline

sequence of events	daydreaming
supporting details	implied meaning
generalizing	guide words
subtopics	key words
relevant facts	library aids
critical evaluation	preface
propaganda	transitional words

Activities for Students

Observation: Visit an intermediate-grade class and note how the teacher instructs pupils in locating information in reference books.

Reading: List the steps you take to locate and summarize the following journal article: "Provisions for critical reading in basic readers" by Gertrude Williams.

Creative thinking: Organize a program for diagnosis and remedial treatment of those pupils in the fourth grade who may be deficient in reading to follow directions.

Selected References

BOND, Guy L., and WAGNER, Eva B., *Teaching the child to read,* 3rd ed. New York: The Macmillan Company, 1960, Chaps. 11, 12.

DAWSON, Mildred A., and BAMMAN, Henry A., *Fundamentals of basic reading instruction.* New York: Longmans, Green and Company, 1959, Chaps. 10, 12.

DEBOER, John J., and DALLMANN, Martha, *The teaching of reading.* New York: Holt, Rinehart and Winston, 1960, Chaps. 7A, 7B, 9A, 9B.

DURRELL, Donald D., *Improving reading instruction.* New York: Harcourt, Brace & World, Inc., 1956, Chap. 13.

GATES, Arthur I., *The improvement of reading,* 3rd ed. New York: The Macmillan Company, 1947, Chap. 15.

HARRIS, Albert J., *How to increase reading ability,* 4th ed. New York: Longmans, Green and Company, 1961, Chap. 16.

HEILMAN, Arthur W., *Principles and practices of teaching reading.* Columbus, Ohio: Charles E. Merrill Books, Inc., 1961, pp. 286-295; 299-321.

HESTER, Kathleen B., *Teaching every child to read.* New York: Harper and Brothers, 1955, Chaps. 12-15.

HILDRETH, Gertrude, *Teaching reading.* New York: Holt, Rinehart and Winston, 1958, Chaps. 14, 19.

MCKEE, Paul, *The teaching of reading in the elementary school.* Boston: Houghton Mifflin Company, 1948, Chaps. 12-16.

RUSSELL, David H., *Children learn to read,* 2nd ed. Boston: Ginn and Company, 1961, Chap. 11.

10

Reading Aloud

In recent times the amount of emphasis placed upon the teaching of oral reading has varied greatly. Around 1900 reading instruction in the elementary school consisted primarily of teaching to read aloud. But as early as 1908, Huey (137) pointed out that the chief form of reading in everyday life was silent. He held that the stress put on oral reading was unfortunate, since reading aloud would hinder thought-getting while reading. During a period beginning about 1920, a shift of emphasis occurred from oral to silent reading, a shift that showed up in the research conducted at the time, in educational reports and in school practices. More recently the true value of instruction aimed to produce good oral reading has been recognized, though without sacrificing emphasis on silent reading.

Importance of oral reading

Any survey will show that there is less reading aloud than there is silent reading. Nevertheless, when oral reading does occur, it is likely to be in a situation that is important to both reader and listeners. The purpose of reading aloud is to communicate ideas to others—to an audience of one or maybe many more. The value of such reading depends upon the skill with which it is done.

In a great many instances, oral reading is wretchedly poor. This is readily noted when reports or other material are read aloud at a church meeting, a parent-teacher gathering, a social club, a scientific meeting, or in a classroom. Of course the one who reads aloud in any of these situations would prefer to do it well, but too often he does not know how. An ineffectual presentation loses much of its value as a means of communication. In less formal situations, a child, a husband or wife, or a father or mother frequently likes to share with others in his household some item from a newspaper, a magazine, or a book he is reading. It is only natural that the reader would prefer to communicate such material in a pleasing manner when he reads it aloud. One surmises that there would be much more oral reading if there were more skillful readers. It is a matter for wonder why so many pupils are allowed to progress through school without adequate training in this skill.

Values of oral reading

The fact that oral reading is used only relatively infrequently should not lead schools to neglect teaching this skill. Ability to read aloud well is not acquired incidentally. Since it is relatively difficult to develop, it should receive specific attention in the instructional program. Hyatt (138) gives a number of examples of the use of oral reading in school and everyday life. Some of these plus a few additional ones are listed in a condensed form below. They are classified roughly as follows:

Technique-centered: teaching
1. *Prepare a part* in which you may participate in a dramatic activity such as a play, a puppet show, dialogue, and the like.
2. *Obtain criticism* of your oral reading of a story, a poem, or play for the sake of improving it.
3. *Try to set a good standard of oral reading to others,* whether of prose or poetry.
4. *As a teacher set an example* in your instruction at all grade levels that you know how to enjoy literature as well as to read well (see Chapter 2).

Information-centered: communication
5. *Tell an audience* about an interesting news item or a magazine article or some current event.
6. *Explain the composition and use* of a specific product by means of illustrative material from a pamphlet, newspaper, magazine, or book.
7. *Gather information from a variety of sources* that may contribute to the solution of a problem, and tell some group, enthusiastically, what you have done.
8. *Present material in support of or against* an important proposition under discussion.
9. *Present the facts to a club* of its present financial status, or the minutes of a previous meeting, or a report on some special activity engaged in by a group.
10. *Communicate instructions and make announcements* of concern to a group.
11. *Present part of a report* by reading it, and then continue with the remaining portions, speaking from notes.

Entertainment-centered: communication
12. *Share with another person* the entertainment you obtained from reading a story, a play, or a poem.
13. *Give verbatim the most interesting or exciting parts of a long story* in the hope of interesting your audience in reading the whole book for themselves.
14. *Share a complete story or poem* with the class or other audience.

Reader-centered: gratification and personal growth
15. Try to read so well that you *experience personal pleasure* in doing so.
16. *Give proper attention to motivating pupils to read aloud* to their class. You will find that many children in the elementary school desire to read aloud to their group. This also promotes exchange of ideas and induces

group unity. Other pupils will need to be specially motivated before they will undertake to read aloud.

17. Keep in mind what reading good literature aloud can do for your *personal growth*.

18. Try to maintain an attitude of quiet *self-confidence in presenting material orally* to an audience.

Relation Between Oral and Silent Reading

Reading aloud and silent reading are interrelated. Effective oral reading requires the use of most of the techniques and skills employed in good silent reading: word recognition, understanding of vocabulary and concepts, reading by thought units (phrasing), and comprehension. In a way, silent reading precedes oral reading. Words, phrases, and sentences cannot be read aloud with proper emphasis unless they are first recognized and understood. The processes involved in silent reading keep just ahead of oral pronunciation, with its phrasing. Degrees of progress are interrelated in both kinds of reading. If a child cannot recognize words and comprehend relations as fast in his silent reading as he can normally speak, he cannot become an effective oral reader. Proficient silent reading should be more rapid than oral reading. Ordinarily a pupil will read silently more rapidly than orally by the time he is in the latter half of the second grade. So the child, as he develops his silent-reading abilities, is actually preparing himself to read well orally.

Oral reading, however, involves certain additional abilities which come into play in situations specific to oral reading:

1. The pupil, besides recognizing each word and understanding its meaning, must know how to pronounce it accurately.

2. Voice control is essential. The pupil should articulate clearly, and speak in a pleasing, well-modulated voice.

3. The reader must keep contact with his audience whatever its size. And the listeners should understand and enjoy what is read. The reader himself must feel how important it is for him not only to comprehend what he reads but also to impart its meaning to others. He can do this by proper stresses, phrasing, and timing. The greater his depth of understanding and his feeling for the idea and the language in which it is couched, the better he will be able to communicate the full richness of its meaning to his audience.

4. Posture is important when one reads aloud. The pupil, though himself relaxed, should stand or sit erect. In most oral reading, therefore, he will give thought to how he looks as well as to how he reads. It is legitimate for him at times to become so concerned with the interpretation of what he is reading that, while making gestures and appropriate movements in the course of his interpretation, he ignores normal postural

requirements. Such spontaneous activities during oral reading should be encouraged.

5. Sight oral reading is frequently employed by the teacher to help her diagnose a pupil's instructional needs. When she does this so as to note the kinds of errors a child makes, she should work with the child individually and privately rather than in a group setting. There is little justification for oral sight reading in a group, one pupil reading after another around the circle. This practice will do little to improve skill in either oral or silent reading. It is likely to antagonize many children and become detrimental to their school adjustment, particularly in the reading situation. To require a child with limited reading ability to stumble along trying to read a paragraph while other children in the group follow the passage in their books can only promote feelings of frustration and insecurity in the not too competent reader that are harmful to his future progress. A pupil may even react so strongly that he rejects all further effort to learn to read. Frequently, serious reading disability results from repeatedly forcing a child to participate in oral-reading situations for which he is not qualified. A teacher may, however, have members of a group engage in sight oral reading when she knows her pupils' abilities well and is bent on improving their skills still more. In this case, the material should be relatively easy *for each particular child who reads*, as well as worth reading aloud. Moreover, the audience should include all pupils but the reader.

6. The eye-voice span is the number of words between the word being spoken and the one the eye rests on. In effective oral reading this span is relatively large. The eyes move on ahead of the voice, reading silently. This permits the phrasing and emphasizing necessary for fluent, meaningful, and well-organized communication. If the eyes are fixated on each word only as the pupil utters it (eye-voice span of zero), the reading will degenerate into mere word calling. The eye-voice span is easily determined for a particular child by noting how many words he can speak after the reading copy is suddenly covered.

Teaching Oral Reading

It is impossible to say exactly how much time should be devoted to oral as compared with silent reading at the different grade levels. Children who read silently at home may need less silent reading at school. Children whose knowledge and pronunciation of English are poor may need more than ordinary emphasis on oral reading at early grade levels. Thus in any given grade the proportion will vary from school to school.

There are at least two good reasons why a considerable amount of reading aloud is justified in the early grades: (1) These pupils ordinarily experience great pleasure whenever they read aloud to others or listen to others reading to them. Providing the group atmosphere is one of approval, the child welcomes any opportunity to read aloud to his class. Such a satisfying experience should be employed frequently since it promotes the desire to learn to read better. (2) Oral reading seems to fit in well with the young child's habits of responding. Oral language is the main avenue of communication with others prior to learning to read. Any pupil who has acquired the ability to talk to a group in a conversational fashion without embarrassment will move smoothly into oral reading as soon as he has some skill in silent reading.

The audience

Durrell (70) states that the attitude of the audience must be kept favorable if oral reading is to be beneficial. Two stratagems must be adopted to achieve this: (1) Avoid revealing the plot of a story during the preparatory work which is to be followed by its being read aloud. Children will listen to oral reading only when their attention is held. Usually the chief reason for this is lost if the plot has been prematurely disclosed. (2) Do not let the other pupils look at their books while one of the group reads aloud. Looking at the book to "keep the place" during oral reading has little or no justification at any level of reading instruction. Usually the slow learners are unable to follow along and attend to the individual words. The more able pupils, on the other hand, are forced to employ faulty silent-reading habits in keeping the place, or else they ignore the oral reader and read on ahead silently to themselves.

Introduction to oral reading is gradual. Bond and Wagner (28) have specified certain requirements that should be fulfilled in introducing a child to oral reading: (1) His first attempts should be integrated with the child's talking activities. A common practice is to have the child open his book at a marked place and read a few sentences in the story he is telling to the group. He will have prepared himself previously to read that small section orally. In this preparation, he reads the chosen selection aloud to his teacher (or to another pupil who is a superior reader) and is helped with any difficult words. (2) Oral reading of this kind should be enjoyable to the reader and to the listeners. (3) The pupil should look forward to reading and feel he is going to be successful in it. If he encounters difficulty with a word, the teacher supplies the word quickly and unobtrusively. Special attention to the unknown word can be a matter of a separate exercise later.

As the child develops poise and confidence in reading such short passages in the storytelling situation, he is able to undertake oral reading of easy and carefully prepared material before an audience, especially when what he reads is both new and highly interesting. As noted above, the teacher should help immediately if a difficult word is met. The class should be aided to listen attentively by the fact that all books and other possible distractors have been put away.

Oral sight reading before an audience is much more difficult than reading material that has been well prepared. It should be undertaken only after a pupil has acquired sufficient maturity in reading to guarantee his success. The reader must recognize words effectively and rapidly, comprehend quickly, and have an eye-voice span of five words or more. This enables him to anticipate what is coming next and to organize his phrasing and placing of emphasis so that he communicates meanings readily.

Admittedly in the early stages of oral sight reading, the child's task is a difficult one. The material he uses should be made up of words which he can identify readily and all the ideas in it should be perfectly familiar to him. Unless the materials are relatively easy, the child will betray his tension and embarrassment. A polished performance should not be expected at first. As further skill is achieved, more finished techniques of interpretation and refinement of expression may be developed through teacher guidance.

Mechanics of Reading Aloud

Durrell (70) notes that the basic abilities of phrase reading, voice pitch, expression, and enunciation are mechanical aspects of oral reading which call for the teacher's special attention. He outlines exercises to improve each of these.

Phrase reading. When a pupil needs to improve his phrase reading the signs are word-by-word calling, an expressionless voice, and an excessively slow rate of progress. Reading by phrases or thought units is essential for comprehension in both oral and silent reading. Also it helps to achieve proper speed of reading as well as promote communication with the audience. Techniques for improving phrase reading have been described in Chapter 8.

Voice, enunciation, and expression

The voice must be well pitched and enunciation and expression must be good if a reader is to impart meanings and give pleasure to his listeners. Durrell (70) emphasizes the importance of these factors. Poor enunciation, moreover, is an obstacle to perceiving similarities and differences in words. It is also associated with difficulties in spelling.

Only when a child reads with proper rhythm and emphasis can he properly take in the full meaning of a passage or the beauty of a poem. When a child enunciates clearly in oral reading, the pleasure and pride he takes in this accomplishment may well transfer to his conversational habits and to his speaking before a group. In fact, during practice to improve expression in oral reading, the teacher ordinarily points out what the desirable qualities of voice pitch and stress are, whether in reading aloud or in speaking. It is possible, however, for a child to have a satisfactory speaking voice while his voice control is poor when he reads orally.

How to improve voice pitch. A voice pitched too high is frequently the result of tension and insecurity in the reader. Feelings of this kind may spring from difficulties in recognizing words and in ability to read by thought units. The resort to easier materials and training in phrase perception will tend to reduce these difficulties. As tension disappears the voice drops to a more normal and correct speaking tone. Other causes of a high-pitched voice during oral reading are a lack of interest in what one is reading or undesirable pressures in the classroom situation.

The teacher can show the child how he needs to lower the pitch of his voice when he reads aloud. She can also demonstrate its advantages by reading first in an unnatural high-pitched voice and then in a conversational tone. Or she can demonstrate the differences in pitches by matching tones on the piano with those of the high-pitched and the conversational voice. The desirability of a conversational pitch cannot be overemphasized.

How to improve expression. Difficulties in voice pitch during oral reading are very likely to accompany inadequate expressiveness. Correction of the pitch will often take care of the other faults. Reading easy material which contains much conversation is a help in eliminating voice difficulties. Provided the child has some skill in phrasing, the reading of poems and plays will help overcome monotony of speech. The plays and poems selected for this training should not be too difficult for the reader either to interpret or to scan. Much of the fun in reading a play comes from proper timing and interpretation.

Children should learn how to emphasize particular words through voice modulation to indicate the exact meaning of a sentence. One way to teach this is to underline the word to be emphasized. Introduce the training by stressing different words in a simple sentence for successive readings: "*George* smashed the window." "George *smashed* the window." "George smashed the *window*." Gradually progress is made to reading paragraphs containing words underlined by the teacher. The pupil himself prepares by reading it silently before he reads it aloud. Later he underlines words to stress as he reads silently. Finally, during silent reading he selects the words he means to emphasize during his presentation, without underlining them. Actually there does not have to be agreement on the words deserving stress so long as the effect of the stress is suitable to the meaning of the passage.

How to correct faulty enunciation. First of all, the child should have sufficient training in auditory discrimination so that he habitually attends to all the sounds in a word. Particular attention should be devoted to accurate perception and pronunciation of each syllable in a word. Among the suggestions Durrell (70) makes is to have the child read for a short time in whispers. This requires unusual use of lips and tongue such that the voice then cannot obscure enunciation defects. Another useful resource is to give the child specific practice on the words he usually enunciates improperly. It is particularly helpful for a child to listen to his own reading voice as it has been recorded on tape. Then for comparison he can listen to the teacher's taped voice reading the same passage immediately afterward, permitting him to compare the two. By this technique the pupil's attention is directed to his faults, such as insufficient emphasis on the final sounds of words, slurring syllables within words, lack of proper phrasing, and ignoring punctuation. The desirability of overcoming these faults becomes obvious to every pupil.

Sources of Materials

At times during the reading session, bits of material—a few sentences from the basic text—are assigned for oral reading to illustrate an idea or give a description. Other good materials for oral presentation are provided by anecdotes, news items, announcements, letters, items from *My Weekly Reader*, children's magazines, poems, parts in a play the children are planning, and a variety of both humorous and serious materials, either fanciful or realistic. A wealth of material classified by subject matter and for different ages is listed and described in two excellent books by Nancy Larrick: *A parent's guide to children's reading* (149), and *A teacher's guide to children's books* (150).

One way of helping children improve their oral reading is to have them listen to good recordings such as Basil Rathbone's reading of Dickens' *A Christmas Carol.*

Relating speaking to writing motivates interest and develops skill in reading aloud. This may be promoted by class projects in developing a puppet show, or preparing a radio script for presentation to another class or to an assembly. TV frequently raises questions which children would like answered. The alert teacher with the help of the librarian can guide the children to books where they will find the answers, to such as "what is a seventeen-year locust?" Such information can be written down and later read to the class.

Evaluation of Oral Reading

Techniques for the appraisal of oral-reading performance may be classed as formal and informal. Standardized tests are employed for formal appraisal. Several of these tests are available (see Appendix). Analysis of the errors and the observations made during such reading provide the teacher with valuable information on specific difficulties in dealing with words and sentences such as: (1) how the child attacks strange words, (2) word-by-word reading vs. phrasing, (3) substitution and omission errors, (4) reversals, (5) repetitions, and (6) location of errors within words. This information helps the teacher to diagnose reading problems.

But evaluation of the specific skills of oral reading is best achieved by informal procedure.

Informal appraisal. Here the material to be read orally must be carefully selected. It should be interesting to the particular pupil tested and at a difficulty level which he can handle readily, which is to say it should be at least a grade lower in difficulty than his silent-reading level. As in any situation where there is an audience, the child should be well prepared by first having him read the material silently to himself and then aloud to the teacher to clear up word difficulties. As the child reads the prepared material to the class, the teacher takes notes on his performance. Under no circumstances should the other pupils in the class evaluate the performance by watching for points to criticize and then discussing them at the end of the reading. It is advisable for the teacher to use a prepared outline to facilitate her rating. These ratings should be made at periodic intervals throughout the year so that the teacher can appraise improvement in a child's oral-reading skills. A check sheet somewhat like Figure 5 may be used by the teacher.

Name of Pupil		Date:		
	Poor	Improved	Good	Comment
Phrasing				
Enunciation				
Voice pitch				
Voice expression				
Voice volume				
Rate: timing				
Posture				
Word attack				
Security manifestation				
Contact with audience				
Attention to punctuation				

Figure 5. Oral-reading check sheet

Since the teacher will be discussing his performance with each pupil, it is well to have a mimeographed check sheet filled out for each child. However, a somewhat similar class outline can be organized if desired.

To avoid pressure on the reader, it is best for the teacher to record the pupil's performance after the reading is completed or after class. The oral reading should be so conducted that no child feels put on trial when he reads aloud. At the end of the period, informal discussion of *group* progress in *general terms* is in order. Informal comments of approval by the teacher for improved performance by a pupil are desirable. But any suggestions given a particular child to improve his oral reading require a private conference between the pupil and teacher, in which the check sheet is used.

Summary

It is generally recognized that silent reading for the sake of grasping the full range of ideas presented by an author comes first, taking priority over oral reading. Authorities are agreed, however, that instruction in reading aloud should receive appropriate attention. The objective of oral reading may be to provide information on a specific point; to illustrate good dialogue; to share a favorite story; to improve the self-confidence and other desirable qualities of the reader; or merely to give pleasure to the listeners by the excellence of the reading be it a poem, a story, or selected parts of a play.

The conditions which make for satisfactory progress in oral reading are verbal facility and good social adjustment. The pupil who has learned to talk well and without embarrassment to a group will take to oral reading readily. First activities in reading aloud are a natural outgrowth of conversational experience. All oral reading should be before an audience and, except for sight reading, should be well prepared. Ordinarily sight reading should be undertaken only when the child has become a fairly skilled reader through many experiences in prepared oral reading. Instruction should be such that a pupil is successful in any oral reading from the beginning. His early performances will not be polished but they will be adequate for that stage of his development. The teacher must take great care to insure that the oral-reading experiences do not arouse negative emotional responses in the child, with unfortunate consequences.

To read well aloud the child should (1) attend properly to punctuation; (2) develop satisfactory voice control with respect to enunciation, volume, phrasing, and timing; (3) maintain contact with his audience; and (4) assume a good posture. The teacher's task is to guide individuals in their efforts to select reading material that is interesting and relatively easy, to provide the pupils with examples of good oral reading, and to see that the audience remains attentive.

Vocabulary

Check your knowledge of these terms. Reread parts of the chapter if necessary.

personal adjustment	voice volume
contact with audience	enunciation
timing	voice pitch
posture	expression
sight oral reading	tape recordings
eye-voice span	rating oral reading
communication with audience	punctuation
attentive audience	phrase reading

Activities for Students

Observation: Assign to some pupil in the upper grades or high school the task of reading aloud (1) a page which includes some conversation, and (2) a page of easy descriptive material. First allow him to read the materials silently and get help on difficult words if any are present. Then take notes on the good and less good features of his oral reading. In what respects does he need further training in reading aloud?

Creative: Assemble arguments for and against the view that all pupils should acquire the ability to read well orally by the time they leave school.

Selected References

BOND, Guy L., and WAGNER, Eva B., *Teaching the child to read,* 3rd ed. New York: The Macmillan Company, 1960, pp. 249-256.

DAWSON, Mildred A., and BAMMAN, Henry A., *Fundamentals of basic reading instruction.* New York: Longmans, Green and Company, Inc., 1959, Chap. 9.

DEBOER, John J., and DALLMANN, Martha, *The teaching of reading.* New York: Holt, Rinehart and Winston, 1960, Chaps. 10A, 10B.

DURRELL, Donald D., *Improving reading instruction.* New York: Harcourt, Brace & World, Inc., 1956, Chap. 8.

HARRIS, Albert J., *How to increase reading ability,* 4th ed. New York: Longmans, Green and Company, Inc., 1961, Chap. 8.

HESTER, Kathleen B., *Teaching every child to read.* New York: Harper and Brothers, 1958, Chap. 16.

HILDRETH, Gertrude, *Teaching reading.* New York: Holt, Rinehart and Winston, 1958, pp. 291-301; 432-445.

ROBINSON, Helen M. (ed.), *Oral aspects of reading.* Suppl. Educ. Monog. No. 82. Chicago: University of Chicago Press, 1955.

11

Speed of Reading

"How fast should Jim be able to read?" "How can I learn to read faster?" Questions like these occur at all levels: in elementary school, high school, college, and among adults. This concern about speed of reading is understandable. A person who is able to read material rapidly with understanding has a distinct advantage over a slow, plodding reader.

In elementary school, teachers have become much interested in techniques for improving the rate of reading of their pupils. In classroom practice this has frequently lead to an overemphasis upon rapid reading per se. Pupils are repeatedly urged to speed up their reading and various exercises are introduced to increase speed. The use made of certain standardized tests has promoted this movement toward faster reading. In many instances the results of this emphasis have been more rapid reading but with little understanding of what is read and also with neglect of other important characteristics of good reading instruction.[1]

Speed of reading in relation to rate of comprehension

To measure speed of reading by itself and divorced from comprehension is not a justifiable procedure. That is, to measure the rate with which words are recognized as words without reference to whether their meanings and their interrelationships are understood, produces scores of little or no significance in real life. Stated plainly, "reading" without comprehension is not reading. As noted in Chapter 8, any useful and adequate definition of rate of reading must also take into account how fast printed and written material is comprehended. But speed of reading, as the term is ordinarily used, does take comprehension into account. Therefore, we shall continue to employ speed of reading in our discussions with the understanding that the phrase means reading with comprehension. So to measure speed of reading is to measure the rate with which material is read and comprehended. And when comprehension itself is thought of it must always be considered in relation to the purpose for which the reading is done. In

[1] This discussion is based partly upon a chapter written by M. A. Tinker in *Reading difficulties* by G. L. Bond and M. A. Tinker. New York: Appleton-Century-Crofts, Inc., 1957.

practice, for instance, it becomes very important to know how quickly a particular pupil grasps the general ideas in a story, or how rapidly he comprehends material in history, mathematics, or science. In a reading test, what is measured is rate of comprehension of the specific contents of the particular test. Standardized tests of speed of reading (published tests which have standard directions and grade scores) have certain limitations because their contents, being limited to one kind of material, are an inadequate sample of all the different kinds of subject matter pupils must read. To assume that a measure of speed of reading is a general measure that somehow applies to the reading of a wide variety of materials is wrong. *There is no general speed-of-reading ability.* Rate of reading is fairly specific to a particular reading situation.

Every teacher should keep in mind that rapid reading in itself is not a cause of better understanding. A fast rate of comprehension becomes possible only because the pupil possesses the abilities necessary for clear and rapid understanding.

Appropriate Reading Rates

As noted in Chapter 8, the problem of speed in reading seldom arises until pupils are in the intermediate and higher grades. Then one task of the teacher is to help pupils read at appropriate rates. *Relatively* rapid reading is to be desired in any area of reading, i.e., the reading should be at as fast a rate as the material can be adequately comprehended. While the proper rate of reading mathematics is relatively slow, still it may be true that some pupils read such materials at an undesirably slow rate. The same can be true of subject matter such as science and the social studies. Whatever the material and the purpose in reading it, there can be an unnecessarily slow rate of reading or an appropriately fast rate. Though fast reading *in itself* has the value of saving time, the proficient reader will remember that he must not choose only speed as his goal. He must be versatile, i.e., flexible, in employing whatever rate the occasion demands (see "flexibility" below). In general, the goal is to *comprehend as rapidly as possible.* To teach a child to comprehend at an appropriate rate, the instructional program must supply him with the skills and concepts to understand properly what he is to read. When this much has been achieved, he will more and more rapidly understand what he attempts to read. Effort to increase comprehension that is successful makes greater speed possible.

Speed to avoid dawdling

Some pupils acquire a comfortable, meandering way of reading that is considerably below the rate at which they might read with both understanding and pleasure. Moreover, their habits are a handicap to proficient reading. Such easygoing dawdling permits attention to wander and encourages daydreaming. They cover too little material in a given time. We call it dawdling when the slow progress is not due to any one of the handicapping factors listed below. In the case of such pupils, incentives and exercises to promote an appropriately faster rate should be provided.

Adjustment to materials

Proficient reading requires a rate appropriate to the kind and the difficulty of the material. The kind of materials read by pupils varies widely. At one time they may be reading in science, perhaps a simple but challenging account of magnetism. Here relatively slow reading is called for to permit grasp of the ideas and relationships involved. A little later the same children may be reading an exciting story or an interesting newspaper item. For this, the appropriate rate is relatively rapid. Or if a child is reading to solve a mathematical problem, a very slow, analytical procedure is in order, with much rereading. In order to know the proper rate of reading to adopt, the pupil needs to exercise good judgment in sizing up both the nature of the materials and what its significance may be for his own purposes.

The child must adjust to variations in difficulty in a similar manner. Science and mathematics are more difficult to read than literature. And sometimes difficulty varies markedly within the same unit of a given subject. Difficulties arise when unfamiliar vocabulary and concepts are encountered or when sentences and paragraphs become complex. Any difficulty which demands increased attention to the content requires slower reading for satisfactory understanding. A pupil should read just as slowly as he needs to in order to grasp what is said, and should be prepared to reread whenever this is necessary. Easy material, of course, should be read faster than difficult material.

Adjustment to purposes

As noted in earlier chapters, all reading should be purposeful. Adjustment of rate of reading to the purpose for which the reading is done is perhaps most important of all. The speed should be relatively fast when a pupil needs to sense a general impression or idea, or when he is skimming to find a given item. But his pace will be relatively slow if he comprehends thoroughly the concepts in a given selection. This implies that, prior to any reading, the child should have a clear idea of the purpose for which he is going to read. The purpose may be formulated by the pupil himself or with teacher guidance. As the pupil becomes a really good reader, he will be able to size up the materials in the light of their difficulty and of his own purposes in reading them and then choose the appropriate rate to insure that he reads with understanding and without dawdling.

Relation of speed to comprehension

The exact relationships between speed of reading and comprehension are not firmly established. Various studies (Carlson, 39; Eurich, 76; Tinker, 255, 257, 258) have reported correlations (indexes of relationship) ranging from slightly negative to highly positive, with many of them insignificantly small. Examination of all the literature on the subject reveals the following trends: (1) For high school and college readers, and when rate of work and comprehension are measured on easy narrative material and comprehension on more difficult material such as geography, the correlations are low positive or negligible. (2) With elementary school children the relationship between speed and comprehension tends to be negligible. But the rapid readers of higher intelligence comprehend better while slow readers of lower intelligence comprehend better (Carlson, 39). In general, one is apt to find a higher relationship between speed and comprehension among the more mature readers. (3) Other factors which affect the degree of relationship between speed and comprehension include the nature of the reading task, techniques of measurement, difficulty of the material read, and the purpose for which the reading is done. Thus for mathematical material there is little or no relationship; the relationship is lower for more difficult materials; the relationship is lower in analytical reading (methodical, slow reading to grasp concepts in science or to follow detailed directions) than in reading narrative for the general idea. The basic reason for the differences in these correlations and for the generally low relationships discovered lies in individual differences among pupils in responding to any one of various reading situations. If all fast readers were good comprehenders and all slow readers were poor comprehenders, it would be simple. But some read fast and inaccurately; some slowly and accurately. Moreover, some could read faster with understanding, and some should read more slowly. And the material they are reading is not equally suitable to their reading comprehension level. (4) To increase speed of reading as such does not improve comprehension. The best indications from research are that a program to improve speed of reading is advantageous for most pupils who are well advanced in acquiring the basic reading skills, provided speed is not pushed to the point where adequate comprehension becomes impossible. Any general program for whipping up the speed of reading for all pupils in a class is inadvisable. It would seem that the child who has the necessary skills and abilities to comprehend well also has those necessary to read faster.

The role of eye movements

Numerous studies on the role of eye movements in reading have been published. Surveys of all this material up to 1958 are given by Tinker

(254, 256, 259). For over half a century, much emphasis has been placed upon the relationship of eye-movement patterns (regularity and number of fixation pauses) to speed of reading. In reading, the eye makes several stops, each a *fixation pause*, along a line of print. The eye moves from one fixation to the next with a quick jerk known as a *saccadic movement*. Perceiving occurs during the fixation pauses, these being the only periods of clear vision. The time required for these pauses totals on the average about 94 per cent of the entire reading time. The interfixation saccadic movements are so rapid that clear vision is impossible. Taken together they total about 6 per cent of the entire reading time, on the average. From these figures it will be noticed that the eyes during reading are motionless on the fixations for a very large proportion of the time. While reading a line, the eyes sometimes move backwards toward the beginning of the line and make fixation pauses to get a clearer view of material or to reread it. These backward moves are called *regressions*. When one line is finished, the eyes make a *return sweep* down to the beginning of the next line. (The *down* points out the fallacy in the metronoscope—see below.)

At an early date, writers pointed out that rapid reading is accompanied by few fixation pauses and few or no regressions per line of print. This has led to the use of many gadgets and techniques to train eye movements in order to promote rapid reading. Such training is designed to produce reading with few fixations and no regressions within each line. This training is the result of a misplaced emphasis on the eye movements themselves. "Good" eye-movement patterns are, as a matter of fact, symptoms of reading efficiency, not fundamental contributors to it. Moreover, exercises in "training" eye movements tend to be mechanical and throw the emphasis upon speed of reading per se rather than upon rate of comprehension. In fact, when speed and comprehension are improved by the fundamentally sound procedures described in this book, this improvement will be automatically reflected in improved eye-movement sequences.

It has been stated that there is a relationship between eye movements and speed of reading. As noted above, the pattern or sequence of eye movements changes with variation in rate of reading. But the teacher should realize that measurement of eye movements in reading is merely one method of measuring speed of reading. The average duration of fixation pauses multiplied by the number of fixations yields an accurate measure of speed. Further, the photographing of eye movements is an elaborate and expensive technique. Practically identical results are obtained by using standardized tests or informal tests as described below. Measurement of eye movements is primarily a research technique. Our conclusion then is that *the elementary school teacher need not concern herself with eye movements in any of her work in teaching reading.*

Speed of reading norms

As noted above, many people are anxious to know how rapidly they should read. The only truthful answer must be, "The appropriate rate of reading depends upon the capacity of the reader, the nature of the material, and the purpose of the reading." Consequently it is hazardous to specify rates of reading for successive grade levels. In the fifth grade, for instance, the average rate of reading in one situation could be 180 words per minute, in another situation only 92 words. The teacher should realize that when average rates are given, they are for reading a specific kind of material for a set purpose. Published averages are usually for reading relatively easy material in some reading test, standardized or informal. It should be obvious from the preceding discussion that such averages should never be interpreted as norms for all kinds of material read for different purposes.

For practical usage in answering questions concerning how fast should one read, a rough estimate for reading easy narrative material (i.e., easy for a particular reader) by high school students and adults is on the average around 250 to 300 words per minute. Since there are marked individual differences in rate of reading any specific material, it is futile to expect to bring all slow readers up to any average. With training, fast as well as slow readers gain in rate. The average of the group then moves up and there are still as many below as above this new average. But practically anyone can be sensibly advised that he can read considerably faster than he now reads, if he wants to, but without setting any precise standard for him to reach.

Measurement of Reading Speeds

Speed of reading may be measured by either standardized or informal tests.

Standardized tests

Several standardized tests provide measures of speed of reading (see Appendix). Some, such as the *Chapman-Cook Speed of Reading Test*, are primarily concerned with speed. Certain others, such as the *Iowa Silent Reading Test*, contain only one section devoted to measuring speed. In some other tests, such as the *Gates Basic Reading Tests*, a speed-of-reading score is obtained by noting the number of items attempted within a set time limit.

Standardized tests designed for measuring reading ability in the primary grades ordinarily are not concerned with speed. The first three years of school are devoted to the acquisition of the basic techniques and abilities upon which smooth, rapid reading depends (see Chapters 6, 7, and 8).

Most standardized tests which are designed to measure speed of reading contain easy materials to be read for a set purpose. Vocabulary concepts and sentence structure are simple. And comprehension is always checked. Such tests should provide an opportunity for pupils to show their maximum speed of reading *specific easy materials*. When the purpose is varied, as in the four types of the *Gates Basic Reading Tests*, speed scores will reveal to some degree the pupil's versatility, or flexibility, in adapting speed to purpose when the materials are relatively easy.

Measuring speed of reading on standardized tests has definite limitations. Special, rather easy material is used and the purpose of reading in a test situation is a narrow one. In addition, the scores are not related to speeds of reading other kinds of material. They are not appropriate for discovering the speed at which material is read in basic texts, supplementary books, or in the content areas. Informal tests will be needed for this.

Informal tests

What the teacher needs to know for instructional guidance she can ordinarily get from *informal* speed-of-reading tests. The teacher will want to know the rate at which a pupil can read with understanding material in the basic text or in units on science, or geography, or in some other field. She will also want to find out how well the pupil adapts his speed to changes in difficulty and to the varying purposes for which he reads.

It is easy for the teacher to devise these informal tests herself. She merely selects a few consecutive paragraphs of the difficulty and complexity desired from a text or a book used in a unit. The length of the test will vary with the kind of material, the reading level of the child, and the difficulty of the subject matter. It is customary to use about 400 to 800 words. The longer selections may be employed for the more able readers and for the easier reading tasks.

With each reading selection she should always prepare a set of comprehension questions for the pupil to answer when the reading is completed. Questions found in workbooks may be used as models. The purpose for which the reading is done should determine the number of questions used. For instance, reading for the main idea requires fewer questions (4 or 5) than when reading to answer specific questions (6 to 8). And when reading to note important details, there may be 10 to 12 questions. A pupil may skip through the material to make a good record and not understand it adequately unless comprehension is checked. The teacher, before beginning the test, must be sure that the child clearly understands why he is doing the reading.

In individual testing, the pupil may read directly from a book and then answer the questions. The teacher records the time taken to read the selection and then computes the number of words read per minute. When an entire class is to be tested at the same time, the selection will have to be mimeographed. All the pupils are allowed to finish the selection. As he finishes, each student copies on his test the last number, indicating the elapsed time, that the teacher has written on the blackboard. Meanwhile the teacher has been changing the figure on the blackboard at the end of each 10 seconds, beginning this before any pupil has time to finish his test.

The results obtained by standardized tests may be interpreted by consulting the published norms to discover whether a pupil in a particular grade is reading with undue slowness, considering the material used and the purpose of the reading. For instance, the four parts of the *Gates Basic Reading Tests* represent reading for four different purposes. The scores reveal both speed and accuracy of comprehension.

The teacher can also take into account both rate and degree of comprehension when informal tests are used. After testing several children in her class, good and poor readers, she can discover by examining the range of scores whether a child reads relatively fast or slowly in a given situation. Answers to the questions, scored by use of a key, provide data on comprehension. Good understanding is represented by about 85 per cent accuracy, fair by about 70 per cent, and poor by about 50 per cent or less. If a pupil's rate is high and comprehension low, or both rate and comprehension are low, he should *not* be given training immediately to increase his speed (see below). But if his speed is low or only average and comprehension high, the pupil will without question profit by a program to increase speed of reading.

The child's ability to adjust his rate properly may be ascertained (1) by determining through informal testing the rates for reading materials at several levels of difficulty and complexity, and (2) by ascertaining rates for reading a single selection for one purpose and then rereading it for another purpose. For instance, if the same rate, either fast or slow, is employed to read in order to grasp the general idea of the selection and also to note its important details or to find answers to specific questions, the pupil lacks ability to size up the situation and adjust his rate accordingly (see *flexibility* below).

Factors Affecting Speed of Reading

A number of conditions tend to produce reading at an unduly slow rate. When these handicaps are largely overcome, the child is more likely to grasp meanings accurately and as rapidly as he needs to for a particular purpose. Or he can be trained to do so with a minimum of instruction. It should be noted that no disabled reader should receive instruction to speed up his reading until any basic difficulties he may have have been corrected.

Sight vocabulary. The pupil whose store of words which he can recognize at a glance is limited cannot read at an appropriate rate. Sight vocabulary is measured by such tests as Test I in the *Bond-Clymer-Hoyt Silent Reading Diagnostic Tests* or Type I of the *Gates Advanced Primary Reading Test* (see Appendix). The norms which accompany the tests will indicate which pupils are deficient in recognizing words at a glance. An adequate sight vocabulary is one essential prerequisite for increasing speed of reading.

Vocabulary knowledge and comprehension. The greater the capacity of the reader to grasp the verbal concepts and the meanings in sentences and paragraphs, the greater is the likelihood of increasing his speed of reading. Knowledge of vocabulary and comprehension have been discussed in Chapters 6 and 8.

Word identification and recognition. Only when a child has the ability to recognize quickly and accurately words which he has previously encountered, and when he knows how to attack new words effectively, can he improve his speed of reading. Methods for developing word recognition are given in Chapter 7.

Overanalysis. Some pupils, owing to an overemphasis on phonetic analysis, have acquired the habit of sounding out a large majority of the words encountered in their reading. Their rate of reading is slower than is desirable because their habit makes rapid recognition of words and sometimes recognition impossible. The teacher can detect this unfortunate practice quickly by listening to the child read orally. Such habits can be broken by providing the child with other techniques of word recognition, while de-emphasizing sounding.

Context clues. The rapid reader tends to make maximum use of context clues in speeding up his recognition of words. At the other extreme is the child who, because he makes little or no use of context clues, finds it difficult to increase his rate of reading. Oral-reading performance reveals the degree to which context clues are employed. For methods of teaching the use of context clues see Chapter 7.

Phrasing. To read rapidly, the child must organize what he reads into clearly comprehended phrases or thought units as he progresses through a sentence. Without this skill, the pupil becomes a slow, plodding, word-by-word reader. Moreover, phrasing is just as important in silent as in oral reading. The knack of phrasing must be acquired before satisfactory reading is possible. For methods of detection and teaching phrasing see Chapter 8.

Vocalization. In the early stages of learning to read silently (primary grades), many children tend to articulate words rather precisely and fully. At this level a child reads silently no faster than he can talk. Later, as he picks up additional reading skill, his vocalization blocks the way to speeded up silent reading. Words may be whispered, or the lips and vocal organs may form the words silently, or the child may say the words to himself mentally with little or no movement of the speech mechanisms. In any case articulation of inner speech takes time. Until the habit of vocalizing is considerably decreased, there can be little improvement in rate of reading.

One way to detect vocalizing is to compare rates of silent and oral reading. Equal amounts (about one full page) of easy material from the same selection that has not been read before are read first silently and then orally. Pupils in the intermediate or higher grades will read three or four times faster silently than orally if there is no vocalizing (or other handicap). The nearer the time required for silent reading approaches that for oral, the more vocalizing is occurring unless other factors (see above) are involved.

Another way to detect vocalizing is to watch for whispering or lip movements during silent reading. Or the teacher can place the tips of her fingers against the child's throat half way between the chin and the collar bone. When the child reads aloud, movement is easily felt. When reading silently, it is difficult to feel any movement unless there is vocalizing.

By the time the child reaches the latter part of the third grade, the teacher can ask the pupils to try to read like grownups without moving their lips or whispering the words. Calling attention to these bad habits is ordinarily all that is necessary. When the vocalizing persists, lip movements and whispering the words can be prevented by having the child hold the tip of a pencil or an eraser between the teeth, or by chewing gum vigorously during the silent reading. Such strategical techniques should be discarded as soon as possible. Ordinarily vocalizing can be eliminated by providing the child with a quantity of *very easy* (even two grades below his reading ability) and *highly interesting* material which he must read fast. The motivation should be such that the child will want to tear through the story at a fast clip. He is urged to do this. At this stage, it matters little whether the child gets much meaning from his practice of rapid reading. This will come later.

Program for Improving Speed

If any of the handicaps we have been discussing are present, they should be mostly eliminated before any attempt is made to increase speed of reading. Otherwise the exercises may produce more confusion and discouragement than efficient reading. Any program to improve speed of reading must be carefully organized and become for the time being the major instructional objective.

Materials for use in speeding up reading

The material employed, particularly in the early stages of the program, should contain very few if any unfamiliar words. Books other than basic texts should be used. And, for a time, study-type of reading and especially oral reading should be curtailed or eliminated. Only after considerable progress has been made using easy materials is it safe to advance gradually toward more difficult reading. This transition is eventually necessary in order to prepare the child for reading regular classroom materials rapidly. The transitional introduction of more difficult material should be carefully guided by the teacher if it is to be maximally effective. In the early stages of the program, any checks on comprehension should be somewhat casual, such as merely asking the pupil what the story is about. After faster reading becomes habitual, better comprehension will be possible. At this stage more checking of comprehension is feasible and also necessary, since rapid reading with understanding is the goal sought.

Motivation

If he lacks a motive for doing so, the pupil will feel little or no urgency to read faster and is not likely to do so. Various factors which may well affect motivation include the following:

1. *Interest as an incentive.* Reading material that is highly interesting *to the pupil* encourages speed. The interested child is the motivated child.
2. *Pride in progress as an incentive.* A daily record of results reveals gains to the pupil and spurs him on to even greater effort.
3. Unless fatigue and boredom are avoided motivation will lag.
4. Cheerful and sympathetic guidance by the teacher is necessary. Exercises should be introduced with zest and gains greeted with enthusiasm.
5. The need for faster reading should be discussed with the child and he should be allowed to participate in planning the program for improving his rate.
6. The reasons for reading each exercise should be clearly understood by the child. Purposeful reading tends to be motivated reading.
7. When faster reading of special exercises has been attained, incentives should be provided to motivate a transfer of the rapid rate to leisure reading and to school subjects.

Natural ways of providing incentives for getting appropriate speed. These procedures may be introduced prior to use of special exercises but not until the teacher has assured herself that the child is not handicapped by any of the difficulties discussed above. First of all, the pupil must understand that he reads at an unduly slow rate and must want to improve his speed. In conference, the teacher explains the disadvantages of slow reading and the advantages of reading at an appropriately rapid rate. She also makes it clear that he will be perfectly able to read faster with understanding just as other children have done. Following are a few expedients that may be tried:

1. Assigning a limited time to read a short, easy story.
2. Emphasize that a book the child is reading with interest must be returned to the library at a certain time which is in the near future.

3. Be sure that the purpose of reading a unit of material is clearly understood by the child.
4. Ask the child to see how quickly he can find how Sam rescued his dog from the river by reading this page.
5. Tell the child that he may participate in a much desired activity as soon as an assignment is read.

Although some pupils will respond to these natural ways of improving rate of reading, many will also need specialized training.

Practically anyone who is not handicapped in word recognition, vocabulary, vocalization or some other way can learn to read faster if he desires to, if he is provided with enough incentive. In an appropriate setting, one which encourages a pupil to step up his rate of reading, and given proper material and well-organized practice day by day, real progress can be achieved.

A favored and effective technique for speeding up reading is to work against time. Relatively easy material (see above) is chosen for the beginning exercises. These exercises should be about 300 to 350 words in length and may be duplicated in a uniform manner for class use. If the teacher is working with a single pupil, the reading may be done directly from a book or magazine or perhaps a school newspaper of the proper grade level. At first, only one or two comprehension questions should be used, later five or six arranged on a separate sheet. These questions should be easy, dealing with the general ideas in the story. For instance, if the story is about a trip to the shore of a lake, river, or ocean: "What did Sally find on the shore?" "What did she do with it?" Although comprehension will tend to be poor during the early exercises, it will improve later.

Each practice exercise should be introduced under as favorable conditions as possible. After the child clearly understands the purpose for which he is reading, the teacher encourages him to read just as fast as possible with understanding. He should be eager and also expect to read faster than on previous exercises. The teacher times the reading (see informal tests above) and computes as the pupil's score the number of words he reads per minute. The pupil should be shown how to plot his own scores on a simple graph so that he can easily see his gains. If he reaches periods during which little or no gain is made, the teacher must be sympathetic and encourage him to expect further gains as practice continues.

To avoid too much pressure on the pupils and to achieve faster learning, there should be no more than two exercises per day, separated by an hour or so. Such *spaced learning* of a series of exercises is more effective than the same number of exercises given one right after another. After the program gets well under way no pupil should be pushed to read faster than his level of comprehension warrants (he should answer at least 70 per cent of the questions correctly). Transfer of the faster rate to regular school materials is gradually accomplished (see *materials* above).

Mechanical devices

Numerous mechanical devices have been constructed and vigorously promoted for use in increasing speed through "pacing" the reading by one means or another. The Metronoscope is an elaborate triple-shuttered device for exposing in succession three equal segments of a line of print followed in the same manner by succeeding lines of the same story. The apparatus may be set for a slow rate of reading and gradually speeded up on successive trials. Its aim is to control eye movements. Pupils are encouraged to employ only three fixations in reading each line and to eliminate regressive eye movements. The Harvard Reading films achieve the same end by a motion-picture technique. Phrases, grouped in thought units, appear in succession on the screen in bold-face type against a fainter printing of the remaining connecting material. The rate at which the phrases succeed one another can be varied from slow to fast. These films present a more normal reading situation in that the material is exposed in thought units and a whole page of material is present.

A variety of machines is available to pace the reader by moving a shutter, line by line, over the material being read. The shutter may be set to move from slow to fast rates. The reader tries to keep ahead of the shutter. In one of these pacers, a shadow from a wire moves down the page of print. The alleged advantage over the shutter type is that the whole page of print remains in sight. The trade names of some of these pacers are Reading Accelerator, Reading Rate Controller, Rate Reader, and Reading Board. Similar results may be achieved by an inexpensive push-card method described by Blair (21). The teacher or another pupil pushes a large card from top to bottom of a page while the reader tries to keep ahead of the card. The rate of moving the card can be adjusted to the needs of a particular pupil.

Another kind of machine is also employed to try to improve rate of reading. The Flashmeter and other short-exposure devices known by the common name tachistoscope are used to flash a series of numbers or words upon a screen for a brief interval, usually a fraction of a second. The aim is to develop quick perception and to increase span of recognition (number of items recognized at a glance). A few hundred dollars may be saved by using flash cards, for they can accomplish the same end. Material on each of such cards is exposed to a pupil for a brief instant by the teacher or another person.

Value of machines. Anderson and Dearborn (5) discount the value of tachistoscopic training to increase speed of reading. They conclude that time might better be spent on promoting growth in comprehension. Brown, on the other hand, (34) describes the alleged advantages of using the tachistoscope to improve reading, including rate. Reports of this kind, and there are several of them, neglect the role played by other factors in an experimental program: motivation to improve vocabulary, comprehension training, etc. In a carefully controlled experiment, Manolakes (164a) checked the influence of tachistoscopic training on improvement of eye movements and hence on speed of reading. When the effect of other factors was isolated, he found that use of the tachistoscope had no effect on reading performance. Evaluation of all relevant literature (Tinker, 259) suggests that tachistoscopic training to improve rate of reading is of questionable value.

In every experiment that has attempted to evalute the use of machines, it has been found that they are no more effective in increasing rate of reading than are less complicated but sound classroom procedures. Working with third-grade children Cason (41) obtained significant gains in rate when she used: (1) the Metronoscope, (2) well-motivated free reading in the library, and (3) exercises with special material divided by marks into phrase units. The gains proved to be just as good by one method as by the others. Her analysis indicated no special benefit from use of the machine. Westover (275) discovered that college students who used ordinary materials and methods in a well-motivated speed-up program achieved just as much improvement as students using a modified Metronoscope. Gates (97) questions the use of machines because of the artificial reading situation involved. And Harris (122) notes that the carryover to natural reading situations is sometimes disappointingly small and questions how much of whatever favorable effect appears may be due to motivation that could be secured by nonmechanical procedures.

An argument often given for use of machines is that pupils are tremendously interested in the use of the device and hence highly motivated. Yet such children make no greater gains than those taught by usual classroom methods. Possibly some particular child might improve under machine training who would not do so under ordinary methods. But to date no investigation has shown this to be so.

It would seem that programs for improving rate of reading can be just as satisfactory without use of the elaborate mechanical gadgets. This assumes careful selection of materials, a properly organized program, and competent instruction. If the teacher can provide the incentive which will motivate the pupil—*and most can*—machines or other gadgets are not necessary to achieve satisfactory gains in speed of reading. That is, the use of machines does increase speed of reading but their use is not necessary to get equivalent gains. Beery (14), speaking for the Yearbook Committee on Reading, censures the indiscriminate use of gadgets and machines in the teaching of reading. Instead, the Committee advocates more natural and informal methods closely related to actual reading. It believes that any funds available for purchasing the machines can be better used to furnish additional books for the classroom and library.

Two other drawbacks to the use of mechanical gadgets to increase the speed of reading are: (1) The machines are very expensive; (2) use of machines too often becomes a ritual and tends to overemphasize the mechanical aspects of reading to the sacrifice of proper attention to the more important processes of comprehension and thinking, which are the prime essentials in good reading.

Flexibility in reading speeds

It has already been noted that flexibility in adjusting speed of reading to the kind and difficulty of materials read and to the purpose for which the reading is done is necessary for proficient reading. When this is achieved, and as occasion demands, the pupil can tear along at a very rapid rate or he can employ a moderate rate if that is appropriate, or he can read very slowly, with rereading where highly analytical reading is in order. An appreciable proportion of pupils at all grade levels, even in high school and college, tends to read everything at approximately the same rate irrespective of the kind of material or the purpose for reading it. In instances where some slight adjustment of rate is made, it is frequently not of an appropriate sort. The following rates of reading are probably representative:

1. *Rapid reading.* The pupil should develop the habit of moving along at a fast clip: (*a*) in reading narrative material for the plot or main idea (stories of adventure, mystery, imagination, humor, real-life activities of various kinds, habits of animals, travel, news items of temporary interest, and others); (*b*) in reading easy informational material for pleasure; and (*c*) in rereading certain familiar materials for additional enjoyment or for further information, as in reviewing materials in content subject matter.

Skimming is a form of rapid partial reading (see Chapter 9).

2. *Moderate or "normal" rate of reading.* A moderate rate of reading is appropriate when one is reading: (*a*) to appreciate characterizations, literary style, people of other countries; (*b*) to grasp current events of social, civic and political import; and (*c*) to remember enough of a story to tell it to others later. Work-type materials of various kinds and of average difficulty (fairly easy) are usually read at a moderate rate.

3. *Slow rates of reading.* Relatively slow progress is more effective for reading much material, especially in the content subjects. Certain materials should be read very slowly and analytically (noting meanings and relations between successive words and phrases), and at times reread, e.g., in seeking to understand a mathematical problem or a new concept in science. Relatively slow rates are also required to read to remember all relevant details, to follow directions, and to evaluate and summarize. Ordinarily any material written in an unusual style, and containing many difficult vocabulary terms and concepts, must be read slowly to be understood.

To gain flexibility in rate of reading, the child must learn to choose the speed appropriate for a particular situation and learn to read at that rate with understanding. This requires systematic teacher guidance since every pupil reads many kinds of material for many purposes. The teacher will find that development of flexibility in speed of reading does involve her in a slow-moving and difficult instructional program. Such instruction becomes a perennial challenge at all levels from the third grade on. No teacher should attempt to develop flexibility at only one particular grade level. All teachers should understand that training to develop flexibility must be a continuing part of the reading instruction throughout the school years. Otherwise most pupils will never acquire it. We emphasize that the majority of pupils *slowly* acquire flexibility in adjusting rate of reading. But both teacher and pupil may be sure that whoever develops good flexibility possesses a most valuable asset—the hallmark of a mature reader.

Opportunities for guidance in adjusting speed of reading to different kinds of material are abundant in teaching units in the content areas. Preparation for every such unit should include discussion that leads to the choice of the right reading procedures to be employed, i.e., proper rate, comprehension skills, and study skills.

Another procedure to develop flexibility in rate is to have pupils read the same material several times, each successive time for a different purpose such as: (1) to grasp the main idea; (2) to note and remember the most important details; (3) to answer selected questions, which the pupils are given in advance; (4) to evaluate what is read. Witty (279, pp. 38-39) supplies a useful outline containing examples of reading materials, reading purposes, and reading methods. Two items are adapted in the illustration below:

Illustrations of Purpose, Materials, Methods

Reading Material	Purpose of Reading	Reading Procedure to Employ
1. A story magazine	To enjoy the stories	Examine contents, select story or stories, read rapidly for plot
2. Science textbook	To prepare for class discussion of a unit	Concentrate on slow, careful reading with rereading of difficult parts

Other opportunities for developing flexibility of rate occur in many situations such as teaching comprehension and study skills, reading for specific purposes, and learning to tackle materials varying in difficulty (vocabulary, concepts, and style). In general, any instruction designed to improve comprehension in reading will necessarily involve guiding the children to discover the most effective rate at which to read a particular sort of material.

Summary

Speed of reading, as the term is used in instruction in reading, means speed of reading with comprehension. Perceiving words as such without understanding meanings and relationships is not reading. An important task of the teacher is to develop reading rates appropriate to each kind and difficulty of materials, and each purpose for which the reading is done. In general, the goal is to comprehend at as fast a rate as possible. Some of the details discussed in relation to achieving this goal are: (1) speed to avoid dawdling; (2) adjustment to materials; (3) adjustment to purposes; (4) relation of speed to comprehension; (5) the role of eye movements; (6) speed of reading norms; (7) use of standardized and informal tests to measure rate of reading; (8) factors affecting rate of reading such as size of sight vocabulary, skill in recognizing words, skill in phrasing, and vocalizing; (9) program for improving speed which involves selection of appropriate materials, motivating the reader, natural ways of improving rate, working against time, use of mechanical devices; and (10) the development of flexibility in reading rates.

If a child has handicaps such as inadequate recognition skills, inability to read by thought units, or vocalization, these should be overcome so far as possible prior to instruction aimed at increasing speed. The best foundation for learning to read faster consists of adequate knowledge of vocabulary and good comprehension. With this foundation and after removal to the extent possible of any of the listed handicaps the child may possess, a program to improve rate may be begun with confidence.

Vocabulary

Check your knowledge of these terms. Reread parts of the chapter if necessary.

rate of comprehension	overanalysis
versatility	context
analytical reading	phrasing
eye-movement patterns	vocalization
fixation pause	articulation
saccadic movement	motivation
regressions	working against time
return sweep	tachistoscope
norms	metronoscope
correlation	spaced learning
range of scores	rate controller
sight vocabulary	span of recognition

Activities for Students

Observation: To observe eye movements in reading, sit facing another person, hold an open book about 14 inches from the person's eyes and, looking over the top of the book, watch the reader's eyes. Try to identify number of eye movements per line, regressions, and the back sweep. You will miss some of the movements because of the inaccuracy of your own observation.

Reading: Check the number of words you read per minute while reading (at your customary rate) (1) fiction, (2) textbook science, and (3) material in this textbook. To what extent are you flexible in your rate of reading?

Creative thinking: State as many reasons as you can for the popularity of programs for speeding up reading among adults out of school.

Selected References

BOND, Guy L., and TINKER, Miles A., *Reading difficulties*. New York: Appleton-Century-Crofts, Inc., 1957, Chap. 16.

DeBOER, John J., and DALLMANN, Martha, *The teaching of reading*. New York: Holt, Rinehart and Winston, 1960, Chaps. 8A, 8B.

GATES, Arthur I., *The improvement of reading*, 3rd ed. New York: The Macmillan Company, 1947, Chap. 14.

HARRIS, Albert J., *How to increase reading ability*, 4th ed. New York: Longmans, Green and Company, 1961, Chap. 18.

12

Reading in the Content Fields

Probably the term *content fields* stems from the prejudice that, when you are learning to read, you will have to be reading sawdust, but when you are reading to learn, the material is good red meat. Actually, of course, there has to be content in everything you read. When we speak of reading in the content fields we assume the reader has a work-purpose. The reader wants (or is supposed to want) to find out something, and the content is social studies or science or arithmetic, or one of the vocational branches of these. Or the reading may be related to art or physical education or music. This, too, is reading in the content fields. They may be con' tent (note accent) fields, but the children and teachers working in them are often anything but con tent'. That is the reason for this chapter.

The Role of Attitude

A certain advertisement[1] portrays a father and his little boy watching wild ducks flying in V-formation. The little boy says, "How do they know where they're going, Dad?" The father replies, "They're guided by instinct." And the little boy asks, "Is he the one in front?" This incident puts in a nutshell one of the biggest problems in reading in the content fields, or in thinking in them at all. Obviously, *instinct* is a word the little boy doesn't know. (It also covers up a lot his father doesn't know.) But the boy has an attitude problem as well as a vocabulary problem. He is used to thinking in terms of personalities—father, mother, book-characters. If he reads about a duck or a bear or steam engine, he likes to think of himself as that duck or bear or engine.

Unfortunately, the content fields are centered in another type of interest which he may not have developed. They may deal with ducks but may center logically upon a consideration of abstractions such as *instinct*.

The reader in the content fields frequently finds, instead of a story, a sequence of logical relationships. Instead of keeping an even pace, the material may describe one day on one page and a hundred years on the

[1] Advertisement for Prudential Insurance Company of America in *This Week Magazine*, January 8, 1961, page 22.

next, or deal at length with one animal on several pages and dismiss another with a phrase or paragraph. Reading materials in the content fields are also noted for abrupt changes of subject. The child scarcely becomes delighted with the subject of vitamins before he is catapulted into the common cold. This is a strain on whatever interest the child has managed to bring to the task of reading.

In addition, the child has been accustomed to asking about, listening to, or reading, something that interests him. The youngster in the advertisement was interested in ducks, not instinct. Chances are that his father soon lost his audience in the later discourse which, it should be noted, even the ad writers didn't bother to copy. But this little boy-king must learn gradually to become a subject, to read and get information from material because that is his job. The teacher may try to help the child feel that her purposes and the authors' purposes are his purposes. But essentially the child's will comes out slightly bent.

He was interested in people and things (and still is) but now must become interested in abstractions. He was delighted with stories (and still is) but must make the best of logical presentations. He had his own purposes for reading (and still has) but now he must learn to think in terms of author purposes and teacher purposes. He doesn't always know best.

Television and the exploration of outer space have apparently helped children develop an attitude of acceptance of factual focus and organization, earlier than before seemed possible. Publishers and librarians report increasing demands for books of factual content (156). So the present-day child may not find the reading of scientific material unpalatable at all. He will find, however, that he needs to notice different things if he is to read successfully in different fields.

Characteristics of Reading Material

Compactness

Material in the fields of mathematics, poetry, and, to a certain extent, science, is compactly written. Practically every word is important to the meaning. The child can skip over a few words, sentences, even paragraphs or chapters in a story and still perhaps derive the essential thought of the author. The same child can spoil a science experiment, misunderstand a poem, and get the wrong answer for the arithmetic problem if he skips in this way. He needs to know and say to himself, "In arithmetic, I read carefully." In scientific material he must recognize the kind of content that permits rapid reading for main ideas as opposed to that which requires careful observance of each fact and of the sequence in which the facts are given or of the logical relationships among the facts.

General structure

Each kind of material has its own nature which requires a distinctive type of reader approach. The arithmetic problem presents facts in a certain relationship to each other and asks a question. The reader needs to read this material several times, and think along different lines, such as these, though not necessarily in this order:

1. What kind of situation is it?
2. What kind of problem is it? (addition, subtraction, etc.)
3. What is the main question?
4. What are the other questions?
5. What are the facts?
6. How are these facts related to each other?
7. What is the statement of the problem in mathematical terms?
8. What would be a good estimate of the answer?

The problem may be such as this: "Oranges are 59 cents a dozen. How much will it cost to buy 3 dozen?" The reader must think to himself, "This is a buying problem, a multiplication problem. The question is the cost of three dozen. The facts I am given are that one dozen costs 59 cents and I am asked to find out what three dozen cost. Three dozen would be three times the cost of one dozen. The statement of the problem is $59 \times 3 = ?$ The answer will be more than 59 cents, more than one dollar, and less than three dollars."

While the arithmetic book is kind enough to ask the questions it wants answered, the social studies or science book usually leaves the questions to the reader. The material is usually written in chapters, each chapter starting with opening remarks to indicate what the general topic and purpose are, and continuing with titled sections dealing with the various subtopics. Finally, a summary statement or concluding idea reminds the reader that he has arrived at the end. As the reader reads, he has to ask himself questions.

When he reads a paragraph which begins, "Many things happen to the food you eat," he must ask himself, "What for instance?" Then as the paragraph proceeds to tell what the teeth, tongue, glands, and saliva do, he must think, "These are the things that happen to the food. The teeth grind it, the tongue rolls it, the glands emit saliva, and the saliva makes the food more digestible."

Lorge (159) found, in a study of compositions on the college-entrance level, that material tends to be more difficult to understand not only when the over-all organization is not clearly indicated, but also when the relationships of sentences to each other within a paragraph are not revealed by the wording. Sentence relationships within a paragraph may not be important when order or logical progressions are not involved. In a description of a room, it usually makes little difference what one mentions first. But relationships are important when an author goes from one thing to another with a certain plan, logical or chronological, in mind. Take the following paragraph from *From codes to captains* by Mabel O'Donnell and J. Louis Cooper (Evanston: Row, Peterson Company, 1960, page 146), a book designed to teach children in the intermediate grades how to read in subject areas. [The italics are ours.]

Scientists tell us that for hundreds of years after the arrival of the first Americans, early men in small groups wandered all over the part of North America now known as the United States. *As they wandered,* they discovered many different kinds of land climate. *In some sections* they found high mountains and deep valleys; *in others,* grassy plains . . . *All these sections,* or areas, were explored by some, though not by all, of *these early hunters.*

Notice how the second sentence starts with a reminder of the activity in the first (As they wandered . . .) *They* goes back to *early men in small groups.* The third sentence starts with a reference to the kinds of land mentioned in the second sentence. "In some sections *of land*" is the implication. *In others* and *All these sections* tell the reader that the sections are continuing to be described. *These early hunters* goes back to the first sentence. The teacher has to make the child aware of them by questions and exercises, so that he will learn to watch for them.

How to read the contents of a paragraph is only one problem. An additional one is how to determine the relationship of one paragraph to another. (The first two sentences here try to help the reader determine the relationship of the preceding paragraphs to this one by restating the topic of the preceding paragraphs in the first sentence, and in the second sentence telling the topic of the present paragraph.) If the subject is a familiar one, like *dogs,* it is fairly easy. For example, here is a hypothetical sequence of paragraph topics:

    1st Paragraph: Dogs are helpful.
    2nd Paragraph: St. Bernards rescue you from snowdrifts.
    3rd Paragraph: Police dogs bite burglars.
    4th Paragraph: Dogs are good companions.
    5th Paragraph: Since dogs are helpful and companionable, we should be
                     good to them.

It is not hard for the dog-oriented reader to sense the relationships among these paragraphs. He can see that the second and third paragraphs illustrate the helpfulness of dogs mentioned in the first paragraph. When he reads the fourth paragraph he realizes that this is a new point similar in importance and classification to the first (helpful, companionable). The fifth, he can see, draws a conclusion on the basis of the information offered in the first and fourth.

But, to put you, the present reader, into the position of a child reading in an unfamiliar field, it is now suggested that you try to comprehend the relationships among the following paragraphs:

1st Paragraph: Glomphs are snork.
2nd Paragraph: Igs blik you from cland.
3rd Paragraph: Barnds slock bists.
4th Paragraph: Glomphs are irt alks.
5th Paragraph: Since glomphs are snork and alks, we should be good to
                  them.

You should come out with the main idea of the whole selection (that we should be good to the snork and alks glomphs) but you won't have the slightest idea what it means. Now you know how it feels to read in the content fields without a teacher.

Worksheet structure

The child reading a worksheet or set of directions probably faces a sequence of things to do with certain amounts of material. A labelled illustration may be there to help him. For this task the child needs a different set of questions for himself.

1. What is being made or experimented with?
2. What materials are being used?
3. In what amounts are these materials to be used?
4. What are the steps in the experiment? (first, second, etc.)
5. What is the outcome I can expect?

He has to be able to interpret the illustration and read the labels on it.

A news article

In reading a news article for social studies the child has still another structure to analyze. The news headline is an eye-catcher, sometimes expressing the main idea and sometimes merely catching the attention of the reader while distorting its true contents. The article today may have a recognized authorship (a byline) which will suggest the slant. It may have a place and date (New York, October 6) which are important. It will then proceed to give the famous four types of information:

1. Who is concerned?
2. When did it happen?
3. Where did it happen?
4. What happened?

The reader needs to know that this information will be given several times in a long article, each time in greater detail. A very brief news account will give the information only once. A longer one will give it once and then add some details. A still longer story will say it once, go into some detail, and then go into still more detail. The child needs to look for the who, when, where, and what, and to read further to find what the remainder of the article has to *add* to what he already knows. He needs to be able to compare two articles on the same subject.

Types of paragraph structure

Dr. Stella S. Center in *The art of book reading* (42) lists and illustrates eleven patterns of writing frequently found in literature:

1. Question-answer
2. Repetition
3. Conclusion-proof
4. Opinion-reason
5. Problem-solution
6. Fusion of details: description
7. Contrast
8. Specific instances
9. Free association
10. Events in sequence
11. Systematic organization of related details

All of these, with the possible exception of Number 9, Free association, are important types of paragraph structure in the content fields.

The present writers wish to offer here a somewhat different classification. In order to make structure as clear as possible, the same content is being used in the examples below.

Five major types of paragraph structure occur repeatedly in factual writing:

1. Main idea stated first
2. Main idea stated last
3. Main idea implied
4. Main idea complex: central shift
5. Main idea: answer to a question

Examples of five types of paragraph structure

All of these structures occur and recur in the fulfillment of various purposes, such as making a transition from one idea to the next, showing cause and effect, or comparing or contrasting ideas.

1. Main idea first

Bad weather delayed both incoming and outgoing flights. Outgoing planes awaiting permission to go aloft occupied available gates. Incoming planes were stacked because of the delayed departures and occupied gates.

2. Main idea last

Outgoing planes awaiting permission to go aloft occupied available gates. Incoming planes were stacked because of the delayed departures and occupied gates. Thus bad weather delayed both incoming and outgoing flights.

This second type of structure illustrates a device commonly employed by the propagandist, who selects the facts for his readers to consider, thus determining their conclusion, which he states at the end, when they, too, have arrived at it.

3. Main idea implied

Outgoing planes awaiting permission to go aloft occupied available gates. Thus, only a limited number of incoming planes could land. Planes stacked aloft, waiting to land, further complicated the situation. Such were the effects of the bad weather.

In this third type of structure, the author leaves it to the reader to decide what to call these effects, how to summarize them.

4. Main idea complex: central shift

The flight for San Francisco was scheduled to leave at 4:45 P.M. However, at 4 P.M. an airline official made an important announcement. Because of weather conditions, immediate departure was imperative. Hence, passengers were urged to assemble immediately so that a departure could occur at 4:30.

This fourth paragraph actually contains two ideas: (1) the scheduled time of take-off was 4:45 P.M.; (2) passengers should help make an earlier departure possible. These two ideas are contrary to each other. The word *however* in the second sentence (often in the middle of such a paragraph) signals this difference and indicates that the second idea, the dominant one, is now to be given. The reader must gather the parts of the main idea together, selected from the subordinate information which comes first (Although the flight was scheduled to depart at 4:45 P.M.,—) and the material which follows the signal word *however* (—worsening weather conditions caused the airlines officials to urge the passengers to assemble for a departure fifteen minutes earlier.)

Note that the word *however* is a kind of turning point for which the reader should look in a paragraph whose first and last parts appear to disagree with one another. But the word might not be *however*. It could be *but, on the contrary, on the other hand, in spite of this,* or another way of signalling a reversal of thought. Sometimes collecting a list of such expressions helps the child to notice them when they occur in his reading.

5. Main idea: answer to a question

Why had the plane departed fifteen minutes before scheduled flight? Weather conditions were worsening. A blizzard was approaching from the north. Over the airport a thick, pea-soup fog was forming. Soon no plane would be able to leave.

The part of this paragraph which contains the main idea is the part which follows the question. To get the main idea, the reader must look for the answer to this question. The structure of the rest of the paragraph may be one of the four previously listed: that is, the main idea may be given first, then explained; the main idea may be supported, then given last; the main idea may be implied, the reader having to gather it from several sentences; or the main idea may be complex, with a subordinate and main clause in its statement.

The structure of this fifth paragraph, following the question, is of Type 2, with the main idea stated last. Why had the plane left early? Because soon no plane could leave. Why was this so? Because the weather was getting worse. In what way? A blizzard was coming and a fog was forming. Notice that in the three sentences preceding the main idea statement, the first sentence states a general condition, and the second and third supply details concerning this condition. An outline of these relationships might be:

Soon no planes will be able to leave
  Because of bad weather consisting of
    Coming blizzard
    Settling fog

Needless to say, a teacher who has not herself mastered the analysis of paragraph structure and the identification of types will be a poor assistant to the child in this endeavor.

Transitional expressions

Authors frequently try to help the reader sense the relationships between paragraphs. They do this by starting the second paragraph with a transitional word, phrase, or sentence. Observe these three examples:
With a word

Also, fog was sifting through the airport. Guide lights glowed more and more weakly through the veil. The waiting planes, at first so clear and vivid in shape and color, took on a ghostly appearance.

With a phrase

In addition to this hazard, fog had begun to sift through the airport. Etc. . . .

With a sentence

But there was something more. Fog had begun to sift through the airport. Etc. . . .

Here, the intention of the author is to show that this paragraph contains another point comparable in its significance to what preceded it. He is saying to the reader, essentially, "Add this point as number 2 (5, 8, or whatnot) in the list of points I've been giving you."

Transitional expressions, then, indicate the relative position of the new material in the outline of ideas or arguments of the material about to be given. These expressions vary because they signal in particular ways the direction (or place) the paragraph is taking. If a paragraph begins, for instance, with "But people were by no means in agreement on this," the reader is being given a signal alerting him that a list of points on the other side of the question is about to be given. If it begins, "First of all," or "The second characteristic," the reader needs to place the cited item first or second in the list he is keeping mentally or in his notes.

Transitional paragraphs

Transitional expressions are ordinarily followed by one of the five types of paragraph structure described earlier. However, a whole paragraph may, on occasion, be devoted to a transitional thought. The author wishes to whisk the reader from one century to another, or from one development to another, but he wants the reader to know what he is doing. Just as the musician, passing from one key to another to create variety in his composition, writes a transitional passage to connect the phrases written in one key to the phrases written in the other, so the author makes his transition in words. Here is an example of a paragraph of this type:

Transitional paragraph

However, there was something yet to come. Lame or infirm passengers still had to be hoisted to the level of the great new planes by truck elevator. The power of the new jet engines created a new risk for pedestrians on the field. Speedy boarding of as many passengers as the new planes could carry required broader corridors than the old narrow portable stairways provided. The situation called for a new invention.

Notice that the author is telling the reader why he is going to introduce the next idea. He leads him to the idea that a new invention is needed. The reader expects that it is going to be concerned with loading and unloading passengers on the jet planes. But the author doesn't tell what the new invention is. He holds that until his next paragraph. The transitional paragraph warns the reader of a new topic.

The signal words that indicate a change in direction in the Type 4 paragraph (Main idea complex: central shift) are often used as transitional expressions introducing paragraphs whose directions shift from the directions of the preceding paragraphs. In fact, an author could break a Type 4 paragraph into two paragraphs, one containing the first idea, and the second starting with *however* as the transitional expression.

Structure of comparative data

The child reading in the content fields must be ready to do what the author has not done, if he encounters comparative material:

Bill went to the store with a dollar to buy two dozen oranges. He found two kinds of oranges. A small kind was 49 cents a dozen, the bigger kind 59 cents a dozen. Which did he buy? Why?

Here in a sentence the reader is given the elements of a difference between two things, in this case the price of oranges. The reader's job is not simply to get the facts but to *compare* them.

In December the Southern Hemisphere is flooded with strong rays of sunlight. Spring is passing into summer. Grain is ripening in the fields. People crowd the beaches and lakes for a cool swim.

But north of the equator the rays of sunlight are slanting. Ice and snow and wintry blasts drive the leaves from the trees, and send people indoors. With shortened days and long, cold nights, spring seems far away.

Here again, the substance for the reader is not just the facts of these two paragraphs, but the sense of contrast in seasons of the Northern and Southern Hemispheres and the reason for the difference. Mentally, he has to be able to classify his data:

In December

	Northern Hemisphere	Southern Hemisphere
Sunlight	slanting	vertical
Days	short	long
Nights	long	short

therefore

	Northern Hemisphere	Southern Hemisphere
Season	winter: cold	summer: warm
Plants	grain ripening	trees bare
People	indoors	outdoors

Being low and flat, Denmark is different from Norway and Sweden, which you have just studied. It has few forests, but its meadows are covered with thick grass. So the Danes have many dairy cows for milk, cream, and butter. They are also famous for their beef, bacon, and eggs.

The author signals the reader that Denmark offers a contrast to Norway and Sweden. By noting facts and making inferences (beef = cattle; bacon = pigs; eggs = chickens) the child builds his mental picture of these differences:

	Norway Sweden	Denmark
Country	(here he fills in what	low, flat
Forests	he has learned earlier	few
Meadows	about these two coun-	many, rich in grass
Live stock	tries)	cattle, chickens, pigs
Products		dairy, beef, bacon, eggs

Sometimes within the same paragraph, contrast is presented from sentence to sentence, item by item:

The first airport provided a long series of shacks in which passengers might wait. The second airport, on the other hand, was spacious, with plenty of seating. The air in the shacks was stuffy and laden with smoke. Air conditioning made the second airport pleasant.

Again, the contrast may be offered through two separate descriptions whose parts must be matched for the contrast. In such cases, the child must remember details as classified material, to be matched with later offerings of the same kind. If the teacher gives him a form to follow in classifying the material he is about to read, he may be helped with this kind of reading. For instance, if the teacher suggests that the reader think in terms of buildings (architecture), furniture, air, and housekeeping, the reading of the material which follows may be easier.

The first airport was a hodgepodge of shacks, each one given over to a single airline. A few benches lined the walls. The air was thick with smoke, and the odors of tired hamburgers and stale coffee clung to clothing. Poor housekeeping left the floor cluttered with paper and cigarette stubs.

The second airport was a modern architect's dream, with beautiful high arches that suggested wings. Airlines had counters around the walls of the great central waiting room. Groups of benches formed a central island for passengers. Air conditioning both in the waiting room and in the restaurant made delays almost pleasant.

Structure revealing causality

Another common pattern for which the reader of content fields must watch is that expressing a cause-and-effect relationship. As you read the next two paragraphs, try to think what this relationship is.

The airplane left the airport fifteen minutes early because of bad weather. Another fifteen minutes and the take-off would have been impossible. Passengers were hurried into the plane and soon it rose through the thickening fog.

There was little gratitude for the quick action of the airline officials, which had made the flight possible. Some passengers complained that when they had phoned in advance they had not been told the flight would leave early. Others expressed anger at being hurried even though they had not been late. Still others said what they would have done to the officials if the plane had left without them.

Basically, the idea of the first paragraph is that the plane left early, while the idea of the second is that people resented the early departure. The reader has to see the relationship between the two, and arrive at the cause-and-effect idea that *because* the plane had left early, people were upset.

Some readers can read the facts and faithfully repeat them, one by one. Others can go beyond this to express the relationship between the two sets of facts. But many who can do this in familiar material—that is, in material about something they know well—cannot do it when the material contains strange concepts.

Jet engines use oxygen to burn their fuel. But difficulties develop as they travel farther away from the earth's surface. At high altitudes there is not enough oxygen to burn the fuel. Planes flying about 70,000 feet do not work well because of this. So rocket engines have been developed to fly at these higher levels. Such engines carry a tank of oxygen with them.

The cause-and-effect feature here is that because the supply of oxygen in the atmosphere diminishes at higher altitudes, ordinary planes cannot fly efficiently at these higher levels; and because they cannot, other engines which carry their own supply of oxygen have been developed to do this. This is perhaps simple enough to you, the reader. But notice how dependent this passage is on the knowledge that the atmosphere close to the earth contains oxygen, and on the knowledge of the effect of a draft upon a flame. Experiments showing the effect of the withdrawal of oxygen upon a flame, and diagrams of the jet and rocket engines would be a helpful preface to the child's reading. Perhaps a reminder how his father's own car balked in the mountains would help, too.

The Difficulty of Material

To the child, difficult material is material he has trouble reading with understanding. As far as the subject is concerned, if the child cannot read about it with understanding, he might use his time in some better way. One of the first tasks of the teacher in any subject field, therefore, is to find materials which the child can read.

Today there is an abundance of materials from which a teacher may choose. The problem is to discern which materials are suitable for which children. In the chapter on materials for reading (Chapter 15) you will learn several ways of assessing reading difficulty by study of the material itself: its format, organization, illustration, vocabulary, sentence structure and length, and other features. But in the present chapter we shall confine ourselves to an approach the teacher can make to the children themselves.

She looks over the available materials and selects three or four or five books which she thinks represent a suitable spread of difficulty. The ablest pupils, she believes, will be challenged by the most difficult one, and most of the poorest readers will probably be able to read the easiest one. But she doesn't know. She must test her hunches.

From each of these books, she chooses what she considers to be a representative paragraph or two. Perhaps one of the paragraphs runs like this one paraphrased from a social studies text:[2]

In old Rome there were two classes of citizens. One class was made up of people whose families had lived there a very long time. They were called *patricians,* from a Latin word meaning *fathers.* As nobles, the important people of Rome, they held all the public offices. Only they could be members of the Senate. The second class was called the *plebeians,* from a Latin word meaning *many.* They were the poorer people, the common people of Rome. Although they were free citizens, not slaves, they did not have the right to hold office. Therefore, they could never be senators. Many of them were small farmers and tradesmen.

[2] Grace Dawson, *Your world and mine.* Boston: Ginn and Company, 1958, pg. 59.

Studying this paragraph for the problem which it creates for the reader, the teacher sees certain social-studies words—actually technical words in this field: *citizen, Rome, patricians, nobles, plebeians, senators, Latin, tradesmen.* If she were teaching this paragraph to a group of children, she would have to make these concepts clear before expecting the children to read with understanding. However, note that *plebeian* and *patrician* are defined by the author. If the children can understand the explanations, they can understand these words.

Next she looks for words which are common in ordinary English but which have a special meaning in social studies: *classes, held office, small.* A small farmer is not a pygmy, in the sense that the expression is used here. She will have to make these meanings clear, too, before the paragraph will convey meaning accurately.

She knows, possibly, that some of the children will not be able to read beyond a general third-reader vocabulary. So she looks for those words which are beyond the third-reader vocabulary in the basal reader commonly used in her school. The words she finds are: *public, members, common, free.*

Instead of testing the children's knowledge of the meanings of all these words, she decides to sample the three types of words. She plans a test page, with the paragraph at the top, and with completion items such as these below:

In this paragraph, *citizens* means ———————————.
　　　　　　　　　classes means ———————————.
　　　　　　　　　free means ———————————.

Note that, by testing the word *free,* she will find out whether the children were able to profit by the author's clue, "not slaves."

If as a teacher she wants the children to get the main idea of a passage such as this, she will add an item like this:

The main idea of this paragraph is that:

—— the two classes of Roman citizens were called patricians and plebeians.
—— important people in Rome were called patricians. (partial meaning)
—— common people in Rome were called patricians. (partial and not true)
—— free citizens in Rome were not allowed to hold office. (only partly true)

If she wants the children to remember important facts, she adds an item on this:

Plebeians could never become

　　　　—— small farmers
　　　　—— senators
　　　　—— tradesmen
　　　　—— free

More than facts, more than main ideas, she may wish the children to think about the implications of the paragraph. She therefore sets up this type of item:

If you think this statement is true, finish it. If not, write NO after it.

There were more patricians than plebeians because ———————————

Our U. S. Senate is different from the Roman Senate because —————————

Plebeians were poorer people because ———————————————

If your father was a small farmer in ancient Rome, you could become an office holder because ————————————————————

By making such sample exercises based upon the materials she hopes to use, and by testing the children on them over the first few days of the term, she can soon identify the levels at which the different children will comfortably learn. She can make the same kind of assessment of their ability to use the illustrative material in the texts. (See Chapter 9.)

> Look at the map of Italy on page 57. Find Rome. Find Venice.
> In which direction from Rome is Venice?————————

In the case of each sample, she asks the child to do what she would ordinarily ask him to do during class. If he cannot do it, then she will have to do something to help him.

Concept Building

Before the children read an assignment, the teacher should introduce to them the important concepts they will encounter. Chapter 6 has dealt with the general requirements of concept building. Here are some suggestions frequently made to teachers dealing with the content fields:

1. Bring out as many facets of meaning as possible: appearance, sound, feeling, taste, smell; relationships to other things, to the child; function: how it operates, what it is good for; characteristics; habits, behaviors; cautions (porcupine).
2. Use firsthand experience as much as possible, encouraging children to observe the object outside school as well as in the laboratory.
3. Have children observe, handle, operate, discuss the object.
4. If firsthand experience is impracticable or not likely to be efficient, use mock ups, films, slides, pictures, or your own drawings or gestures and actions.

5. Have the children help or take leadership in explaining, defining, dramatizing, demonstrating, experimenting, illustrating.
6. Remember that with lower socio-economic status generally (but not
always) there will be a need for more concept building.
7. Don't tolerate the parrot-like response. Ask: "What is another way of
saying that?"
8. Speak clearly, facing the children. Have them repeat a strange name.
Write it on the chalkboard so that they can see how it looks.
9. Have the children study the word if this will help meaning. (For instance,
nucleus comes from a word meaning *nut*.)
10. After you believe the meaning of the concept and the form of the word
representing it are established, show a possible example and ask whether
it is a proper illustration and why or why not. Make the children give
detailed proof, showing that they know concept.
11. Have students use the new knowledge:
     making models
     labeling figures
     rewording worksheets
     using the new terms in subsequent discussions, writing, etc.
12. As much as possible, let the children arrive at these learnings inductively.
Give them examples and let them generalize. Everyone remembers his own
discoveries best!

Number 13 should probably be a "don't." Don't try to explain one
unknown by referring to another. A child needs to be taught how to read
a map before he can be helped to grasp the concept of South America by
referral to a map of it.

Word Analysis

The child will encounter many difficulties the teacher cannot anticipate
or prevent. But in some cases she can alleviate the pain.

One helpful offering is a chart listing all the details the reader can
observe in meeting a strange word:

Questions About a New Word

1. How does it start?
2. Is there a prefix I know? What does it mean?
3. Is there a root I know? What does it mean?
4. Is there a suffix I know? What does it mean?
5. Is it a compound word? What do the parts mean?
6. What are the syllables?
7. Where should the accent probably be? (open syllable or stem usually
accented)
8. Does my solution of it make sense in the sentence?

Another aid is to remind the child of the ways he knows to help himself.
If he forgets what *ph* says, as he tries to solve the word *phantom,* he can
remember that all he has to do is to think of words containing those letters

(*photo*, ele*ph*ant) and listen to the common sound of those parts. In the same way, if he remembers that *prepay* means to pay in advance and *preview* means to view in advance, then he will have some idea of what *presuppose* means, given the knowledge of the word *suppose*. This inductive thinking helps him both with the form of the word and with its meaning.

Guiding the First Reading

Frequently teachers gather together children who read in the same instructional group in reading, for instruction together in reading a piece of material in the content fields. This may be a newspaper or a textbook, for example. The children are guided to observe points about the material before they are ever expected to read such an assignment alone. First they learn as a group.

The teaching technique, in a nutshell, is, "Ask. Don't tell." The teacher says, "Look at page . . . What do you notice about . . . ? Read silently the first . . . and be ready to tell me. . . . Where in this sentence do you see a definition of a new word? How is it pronounced? How can we find out?" With regard to the structure of the material, the teacher is particularly concerned with designing questions which will draw attention to:

1. What the introductory paragraph does.
2. What the central headings mean and how they are related to the topic and to each other.
3. What the marginal headings mean and how they are related to the central headings and to each other.
4. The directions the material takes (headings, transitional expressions).
5. The kinds of thinking the contents require (comparison, contrast, summary, judgment, cause-and-effect).
6. The contribution of the illustrations to meaning.
7. The contribution of aids to typography.
8. What the conclusion of the chapter or section tells.
9. The vocabulary list, questions, additional readings at the end.

The Assignment

The assignment of independent reading in such fields as social studies or science partially determines the efficiency with which the child will read. Unless he knows what the teacher intends him to get, the chances are good that he will return with something else.

First, however, the teacher has to ask herself a serious question: "Do you want the child to get what you think is important or what the *author* thinks important?" If it is what the teacher thinks important, then she will have to present the child with specific questions to guide his selection of ideas to remember: "Compare. . . . Summarize. . . . Give an original illustration of. . . . Make a model of. . . ." If it is what the author thinks important, then the teacher must train the child to notice the ways an author indicates the importance of an idea: by using italics, making it a main heading, giving it much space, repeating it, illustrating it, asking questions at the first or at the end of his chapters about it, giving footnotes about it, including it in his vocabulary list. Again, lead the child to see these things. Don't tell him!

The reading assignment should usually result in a written record of what was obtained from it: written answers to questions, a dictionary note-book of terms, with indications of their pronunciation, definition, and use; original examples of what was discussed; a chart classifying the material covered; a map showing the movement of the people discussed; a brief summary of the sequence of ideas (stages in the life of the frog). In this way, ideas are secured through use, and the meaning and form of words are impressed through writing.

Sometimes, when the outcome of an assignment is particularly disap-pointing, a teacher may realize that the thinking skills themselves are at the root of the problem. By reading aloud simple examples of the same kinds of structure, she can get the children to see what the thinking process might be. Then, having them create such a structure orally, one sentence to a child, the teacher can have them build a paragraph or sequence of ideas similar to the one which baffled them. Listening activities and creative oral composition can be most profitable means of acquainting children with an author's style or point of view, or with the peculiar verbal features of a content field.

Research Justification for Practices

What is some of the research evidence which makes the reading specialist believe that such practices as those previously described in this chapter are important to success in the content fields? As early as 1930, McCallister (167), studying the reasons for difficulties encountered by seventh- and eighth-grade pupils of American history, mathematics, and general science, found these to lie in the pupil's method of attack (Who should help him alter it?), his inability to recognize relations (Who should make him aware of them?), his lack of knowledge of subject matter (Who should build this background?), his deficiencies in vocabulary (Who should intro-duce the new words?), his inaccuracies (Who will show him that certain kinds of material require slow, careful reading for details?), and lack of clarity in the directions he had been given (And whose fault is that?).

As long ago as 1938, Bond (22), in a study of the reading ability and subject-matter achievement of ninth graders, found that rapid reading was helpful in increasing vocabulary and broadening acquaintance with litera-ture, but that slow reading was associated with high achievement in science, Latin, and mathematics. There was evidence that pupils had developed habits of reading everything in one way, and at one rate, thus jeopardizing their chances of success in subjects requiring another approach.

Gans (92) reported in 1940 a study of critical-reading comprehension in the intermediate grades, in a variety of subject areas. She found that children who did well on tests of general-reading comprehension did not necessarily do well in reference reading. She identified reference abilities as including comprehension, skill in selection and rejection, and some pattern of delayed recall. Obviously there was a need for teaching the reading of reference material, and how to judge whether something was pertinent to the topic sought, and the ways of fixing the information firmly enough in mind to be able to retrieve it later from memory.

In arithmetic, science, and social studies, reading achievement makes a difference. Young's study (292) reported in 1941 showed the substantial relationship of reading-improvement achievement to improvement in achievement in the social studies. The investigator expressed the view that many difficulties in understanding written material in the social studies stem from lack of clear purpose or goal while reading and from lack of experience to bring to the grasp of what it was all about. He criticized the materials for using indefinite quantitative terms (largely, several, numerous) instead of more definite ones. Significantly, he urged that the language of the social studies be used orally in the direct teaching of this vocabulary. Materials, he believed, did not in themselves provide sufficient repetition of meanings to make those meanings familiar.

Swenson (247) similarly, in a report in 1942, found a close relationship between reading achievement and achievement in science. If a teacher wants students to learn her subject, she must see to it that they know how to read it. Treacy (266) reported in the same vein in 1944 that problem-solving in arithmetic was related to mental age and to the fourteen reading skills he measured. The same year produced a report by Hansen (120) that successful problem solving in arithmetic was associated with general language ability and the reading of graphs, charts, and tables.

Of course, the fact that two factors are related does not always mean that one is causal to the other. It remained for Rudolf in 1949 (212) to report a study of two methods of teaching social studies to eighth graders. One class was given definite guidance in reading the material, the other none. The class that had the guidance made significantly larger gains in knowledge of social studies during the time of the experiment. Howell in 1950 (136) reported that in grades four to eight, children who were taught map reading, use of references, use of the index, use of the dictionary, and the reading of graphs, charts, and tables became better readers through these experiences. Thus it was clear more than ten years ago that a teacher who helps her students read better in her subject area improves both reading skills and the students' knowledge and ability to function as thinkers in the subject area.

Since that time Maney (164) has established (1958) that literal reading of science material is closely related to verbal intelligence and general-reading comprehension, and that critical reading of science material is related (though not so closely) to these same factors. Fay had found out (79) in 1950 through a study of sixth-grade achievement and reading skills that the following skills were more closely related to the reading demands of the social studies than to those of arithmetic and science: predicting outcomes, understanding precise directions, comprehension, reading of maps, charts, and tables, using indexes, references, and dictionaries. This does not mean, of course, that these skills are *un*important in arithmetic and science reading; rather, that they are *less* important.

A child working a problem in arithmetic may have considerable trouble if he cannot predict a reasonable answer for the problem, if he cannot understand what he is to do, or he cannot interpret a chart or table included in the problem. What happens to the science experiment if the pupil does not understand the directions and cannot read the material? What happens to science reference tasks if a pupil does not know how to use a science dictionary, the index in his text, or the pictorial material which is there to aid his understanding?

Areas of Need

Thirty-five years ago McCallister defined the areas in which junior college freshmen needed to perform well if they were to live up to what was expected in the course of study designed for them (166). The general headings he used were: reading for pleasure and recreation, ascertaining the purpose of reading before study, rapid reading or skimming, assimilating and retaining information, amplifying understanding of a topic, interpreting and executing directions, proofreading written reports, apprehending relationships, comparing and contrasting, organizing information, evaluating materials, and drawing inferences from the reading. He found that the reading activities essential in one subject were not necessarily the same as those for another. For example, the kind of information a social studies or science student must assimilate and retain in certain of his reading tasks is different from that which he must assimilate and retain in arithmetic. He does not have to retain the fact that it was A who rowed twice as fast as B, after he has completed the problem. He has, rather, to retain the idea of making the comparison, and know that whenever he meets anyone doing something "twice as fast" as someone else, whoever it is and however fast or far, he must be able to recognize this pattern of language as indicating a problem of rate and multiplication. As far as retention is concerned, the pattern of the problem and the wording that signals it are of far greater importance than the facts themselves.

In recent years several authors of professional books and monographs have listed in detail the reading and study skills needed in their various areas. Courses of study have suggested ways in which the elementary teacher can foster these skills as she teaches the various subject-matter areas. Unfortunately, however, in many schools the teaching of reading in the content areas is still not very well done. Why should this be so?

It is so because many primary teachers still assume that reading in the special fields is an intermediate-grade problem. It is so because many elementary teachers on all levels still believe that good basal instruction alone can carry the whole burden. They believe that such instruction will automatically insure the grasp of concepts and vocabulary in a special field, the understanding of visual materials, symbols and abbreviations, and *know how* in the organization of materials in the different areas. Unaware of the good things that some teachers are doing in their school at one level, they fail to support them with comparable efforts at their own grade level. And because they are furnished a textbook in science, social studies, or arithmetic, they forget that all children cannot read it, and have not encountered the many fine materials of varied difficulty which publishers have been furnishing to meet the problem of individual differences in reading level in these areas.

The best thing that could happen for teachers who suffer these misconceptions would be, of course, orientation in what needs to be taught and how it needs to be taught in the areas and levels they teach. The best thing for the children would be that all the teachers in the school would know the kinds of contribution they could make at every level so that specialized skills would be gradually and soundly developed. Meanwhile, it is interesting to see that Science Research Associates, Inc., among others, is not waiting for the millennium. It is advertising a *Basic Skills Kit,* similar to its *Reading Laboratory,* containing three sets of graded materials in such skills as map reading, outlining, and organizing, for grades four through six. The cards on which exercises and tests appear in these sets are used individually by children, who progress at their own rates in their free time. Thus, if a teacher feels that she is not managing to build study skills properly and thoroughly, she can turn to these materials. She must, however, be aware of these pitfalls: (1) Something learned in isolation, and then never used, is usually lost. (2) Practice in making the same mistakes does not improve reading. The teacher will have to check on the child's progress and help him analyze his errors. (3) If a child advances rapidly through the material but the other activities in the class do not make demands on the skills he picked up in this brief exposure, he is going to forget what he learned sooner!

In other words, the writers of this book doubt that the responsibility for reading in the content fields can be sloughed off by the teacher, or that the "teaching machine" approach of itself will be sufficient to compensate for the things she might do. Teachers would do well to study the careful development of such materials as the *Basic Skills Kits,* to appreciate the sequence and techniques used in the presentations, and to see how many opportunities there are to support these same sequences and techniques in their own teaching.

Summary

The attitude of the child toward materials in the content fields may be unsuitable to success in reading in those fields. The teacher needs to tune his thinking to the new requirements and the new kinds of interests. The material of the different fields makes different kinds of demands upon the reader, and these should be recognized by the teacher as something the child must be taught to meet.

The structure of sentences, problems, paragraphs, and the larger units of composition needs careful study by the child, through ear training, creative oral composition, and guided reading. Common structures include those revealing comparative relationships among the materials, and those dealing with causation.

Tests sampling the materials and tasks expected of the child can show the teacher which materials and tasks the child can handle well, and which tasks will require special training.

The activities of concept building and word analysis loom as large in the content fields as they do in the basal reading instruction. Similarly, the first reading of a new kind of instructional material should be a guided experience with questions prefacing each observation. The assignment should be designed according to whether the teacher wishes to follow the emphases of the author or to motivate the children's reading through purposes of her own which she imparts to the children.

If there has been one weakest link in elementary-school reading it has been in the area of the content fields. We have assumed too much carryover from general reading instruction and have too seldom considered the necessity of suiting the reading material to the level of the reader in these fields. The unfortunate consequences have been evident in many a study of the children's critical competence and versatility in reading. If we will apply what we know, we can make it possible for each child to move toward his vocational goal without fear of failure in reading. Such an achievement will effect a profound transformation in our civilization.

Vocabulary

What did these terms mean?

content fields	transitional expressions
compactness	signal words
types of paragraph structure	mock-ups

classified material
structure revealing causality
technical vocabulary
special meaning for common words

hard words in general vocabulary
structure of comparative data
inductive method
guiding reading

Selected Activities

Creative. Using a central idea such as, "Saturday's football game was the best yet," write the five types of paragraphs discussed in this chapter.

Using a science or arithmetic text, make a test such as that described on pages 244-245.

Make a collection of interchangeable terms in arithmetic, such as *plus, in addition to,* and *increased by.*

Further study. Look for articles on reading in arithmetic, science, or social studies in the *Education Index.* Read these and take notes on any ideas not encountered so far in this text. What kind of reading will this be? How fast can it be? What will you ask yourself as you read? Notice the problems you face in carrying out this assignment. These may give you insight into the problems your own pupils will encounter later.

Selected References

ARTLEY, A. Sterl, Critical reading in the content areas, *Elementary English,* 1959, 36, 122-130.

BOND, Guy L., and TINKER, Miles A., *Reading difficulties: their diagnosis and correction.* New York: Appleton-Century-Crofts, Inc., 1957, Chap. 15.

—— and WAGNER, Eva B., *Teaching the child to read,* 3rd ed. New York: The Macmillan Company, 1960, Chaps. 13 and 14.

COLE, Luella, *The teacher's handbook of technical vocabulary.* Bloomington, Illinois: Public School Publishing Company, 1940.

DEBOER, John J., and DALLMANN, Martha, *The teaching of reading.* New York: Holt, Rinehart and Winston, Inc., 1960, Chaps. 7, 8, and 9.

—— and WHIPPLE, Gertrude, Reading development in other curricular areas, *Development in and through reading.* Sixtieth Yearbook of the National Society for the Study of Education, Part I. Chicago: University of Chicago Press, 1961, Chap. 4.

GRAY, William Scott (ed.), *Improving reading in all curriculum areas,* Supplementary educational monograph, No. 76. Chicago: University of Chicago Press, 1952.

KELTY, M. G., A suggested basic vocabulary in American history for the middle grades, *Journal of Educational Research,* 1931, 24, 335-349.

MCKEE, Paul, *The teaching of reading in the elementary school.* Boston: Houghton Mifflin Company, 1948, Chaps. 12-16.

METROPOLITAN SCHOOL STUDY COUNCIL, *Five steps to reading success in science, social studies, and mathematics,* 2nd ed. New York: Teachers College, Columbia University, 1960.

SPACHE, George D., Types and purposes of reading in various curriculum fields, *The Reading Teacher,* 1958, 11, 158-164.

STRANG, Ruth M., and BRACKEN, Dorothy K., *Making better readers.* Boston: D. C. Heath and Company, 1957, Chap. 5.

—— McCULLOUGH, Constance M., and TRAXLER, Arthur E., *The improvement of reading*, 3rd ed. New York: McGraw-Hill Book Company, 1961, Chaps. 5, 6, and 7.

—— *Teaching map and globe skills.* Curriculum bulletin, 1959-1960 series, No. 6, Brooklyn 1, New York: Board of Education of the City of New York, 1960.

13

Individual Differences

The organization of instruction in ways that provide for individual differences among the pupils in her class is a major task of the elementary school teacher. It is an ever-present problem at all grade levels beginning with the kindergarten. Nothing is more obvious about children (or other human beings, for that matter) than that they differ from one another. Children vary not only in weight, height, size, and appearance, but also in their behavior, intelligence, and personality. Even identical twins may be far from identical in conduct. In meeting a new class the teacher will first notice certain physical differences between the children, such as variations in stature, facial pattern, complexion, hair color, etc. But upon closer acquaintance she will come to appreciate that each child has a unique personality and way of behavior that is also his very own and which clearly sets him apart from all the others.

Suppose Jimmy is one of 30 children in kindergarten class and his teacher is trying to acquaint herself with his special abilities and needs as these show up in school. How does he differ from the other 29? Noting superficial differences such as his unusually light blue eyes, his missing front tooth and his slender build is not enough. Some important areas in which to look for differences relevant to her goal of individualizing her teaching include the following:

1. *Chronological age.* At the beginning of the school year, the age of the children in her kindergarten class range from approximately five to just short of six years.

2. *Intelligence.* I.Q.'s may run from not much above 60 to 150 (i.e., M.A. around 3 years to 7 years, 6 months).

3. *Background of experience.* As we have pointed out in the chapters on reading readiness, there will be very marked differences in the circumstances and experiences to which the children have been exposed.

4. *Verbal facility.* Some children in the class will show much verbal facility while others will have only meager ability to communicate what they would like to say either to grownups or other children.

5. *Physical vitality.* Some of the pupils will be healthy and almost tirelessly active. They will be eager to participate in every phase of the instructional program. Others will be listless, easily fatigued, and either unable or unwilling to join in many of the activities.

6. *Attentiveness.* Members of the class will differ greatly in capacity to keep their attention fixed on the task at hand. Flighty or faltering attention can be a serious handicap to a child and both a trial and a challenge to the teacher.

7. *Co-operation.* Due to their prior experience and training, some children will be ready and eager to co-operate with their classmates in all kinds of activities, others will show a strong preference for "going it alone"—which is another challenge to the teacher.

8. *Emotional adjustment.* Some children enter kindergarten inadequately adjusted, personally or socially or both. Fortunately others, probably a majority, will be well adjusted and eager to learn.

9. *Reading ability.* A few (perhaps around 1 per cent) will already be reading and a few others just ready to learn to read while they are in kindergarten. A few others will not even be ready to begin reading when they finish kindergarten (see readiness chapters and Chapter 19).

10. *Other behavior and personality traits.* In any kindergarten class of 30 children, there will be differences in numerous other aspects of personality and conduct such as timidity and shyness on the one hand, self-sufficiency on the other; leadership, actual or potential; ability to follow directions and finish assigned tasks; submissiveness and aggressiveness; and many more.

Now to return to the ways in which Jimmy may differ from the other 29 pupils in his kindergarten class. He is only one of the 30 children and yet he does not closely resemble any of the other 29 in any specific ability or behavior trait. Jimmy may be at the high end or the low in the range of any trait, or more probably he will be somewhere between the extremes. If he happens to be near the middle of the range on an ability or trait, he will be a good deal like several others because the distribution of scores on any ability or trait shows several individuals who are near the middle or *average.* But if the scale of measurement is fine enough it is unlikely that Jimmy will be in exactly the same position as any other child.

While the teacher is getting acquainted with Jimmy's traits and abilities, she will also be discovering in what respects each of the other 29 children differs from his or her classmates. To carry out her instructional job successfully, she must become familiar with as many as possible of the patterns of ability, personality traits, and individual ways of behaving of each pupil. Only then can she adjust her instructional program to meet the needs of each child in her class (see Chapter 19).

Differences at grade five

The task of adjusting instruction to individual differences is perhaps the most important problem at every grade level. For instance, if the teacher wishes to know how Dan differs from the other 30 to 35 pupils in his fifth-grade class she can be sure that to a greater or less degree, all the differences among kindergarten children that are mentioned are still present somewhere in the class. Perhaps some of the less favorable personality and behavior traits may have been modified in a desirable direction through teacher guidance. Nevertheless, the differences will still be there. In addition, several new differences will have developed during the earlier years in school. But here is a list of some of the skills and abilities that the teacher will want to watch for as she sizes up her pupils including Dan.

1. *Word-recognition skills.* Many of the pupils will have learned well what has been taught in prior grades while others have mastered the skills only partially.

2. *Growth in vocabulary knowledge and concepts.* Pupils will have grown at different rates in respect to both the words and the ideas they can handle.

3. *Other basic comprehension abilities.* These would include sentence, paragraph, and story comprehension (see Chapter 8).

4. *Comprehension and study skills.* Marked individual differences may be expected in these skills (Chapter 9).

5. *Level of reading achievement.* Differences here are large (see below).

6. *Interests.* By the fifth grade some children will have developed rather strong and varied reading interests; others will not.

7. *Tastes.* Reading tastes will have developed differentially by this grade, but will vary more in higher grades. At this level, children will like one story or poem better than another, but action, repetition, sound, rhythm, and subject matter will govern choice rather than sensitivity to values or style.

8. *Frustration.* Children who have fallen behind in reading or who are outright reading-disability cases will manifest varying degrees of frustration, which, if it is extreme, will often break out in undesirable behavior.

9. *Patterns of achievement.* In every aspect of reading performance, there will be marked differences among fifth graders.

How then does Dan differ from the other children in his class? Although he may be close to certain other pupils in some traits, he will tend to differ in others. He may be better or poorer than other pupils in achievement or emotional adjustment. What is true for Dan will tend to be true also for each of the children in the class. The teacher must try to identify these differences and to adjust her instruction to take care of the individual needs of each pupil. This sounds like a big job, and it is.

Similarities among children

Now we must speak of the other side of the picture. From the above discussion, one should not conclude that there are no similarities among children. As noted by Bond and Wagner (28), although children do differ, they are inevitably somewhat alike in many ways. Children are pretty similar in their need for physical activity. This means that a confining task should not be allowed to continue too long. While they may differ in strength of response, all children react rather similarly to success and failure. To become able readers, they must acquire much the same learnings, progressing through similar sequences even though at different rates. And under the usual rather uniform instruction, most children do learn to read in a fairly satisfactory manner. Moreover, as noted above, in any skill or behavior trait, several of the children in any class tend to cluster close to the average, i.e., they are *similar* in the skill or trait but not exactly alike.

Teacher attitude toward individual differences

Different children are bound to become proficient in reading at different rates. What is more, in any one group of children the individual differences in reading ability found among them tend to increase as children grow older. The fast-learning child gets still farther ahead and the slow-learning child drops even farther behind the average as schooling continues.

The teacher can neither eliminate these differences nor bring all children up to the same standard of performance. In fact, all authorities agree that differences in reading ability are to be expected and the good of teaching is to help each child achieve to the extent of his learning capacity and at his own optimal rate. The teacher who sees this will face the problem of individual differences realistically and adjust her teaching accordingly. To a large degree the success of any teacher depends upon her ability to provide for individual differences through adjustment of materials and instructional guidance to individual pupil abilities and needs. Skillful teaching of reading, therefore, implies a positive attitude towards individual differences in which instruction will seize upon and cultivate each pupil's potentialities, great or small.

Differences in Reading Achievement

Every teacher has a general awareness of the differences among her pupils in reading achievement and the factors influencing progress in reading. She is not immediately aware, however, of the precise nature and extent of these differences. This knowledge is attained only by systematic surveys and by study of the children. This requires the use of standardized tests (see Chapter 16) in addition, of course, to observing and rating the children on attitudes and personality traits related to reading performance.

Normal range of reading ability

The normal range of reading at different levels of instruction as we describe it here is what prevails in average classrooms, with ordinary children, employing the customary teaching methods and the usual materials. If, in a grade, one or more of the above conditions could be rated superior, the average reading capabilities of that grade will be increased and the range of reading ability extended. Or if the conditions, such as instruction and materials, are poorer than those ordinarily found, the class average will tend to be lower and the range of reading ability more restricted. Bond and Tinker (26, p. 37), present in Figure 6 the range of reading ability found in typical classrooms at grade levels two through six at the beginning of the school year. The classroom grades are given at the left side of the diagram, and the achieved reading grade along the baseline. The combined scores of children from several classrooms are used at each grade level.

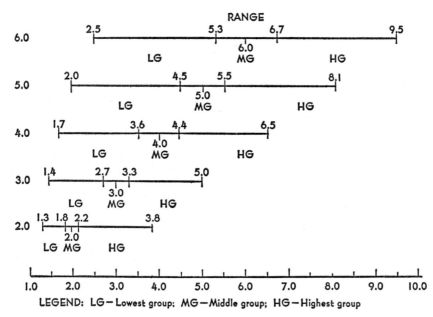

Figure 6. Normal range of reading ability found in typical classrooms of grades two through six at the beginning of the school year. (Reproduced with permission of the publisher from Guy L. Bond and Miles A. Tinker's *Reading difficulties.* New York: Appleton-Century-Crofts, Inc., 1957, p. 37.)

Figure 6 shows the median of the scores made by the best readers of all the classes at a given grade level; the median score of the poorest readers of the several classes at each grade level; and the median score for the grade which is the same as the grade level. For example, in the class beginning the second grade, the best is 3.8 reading grade ability; the middle score, 2.0; and the lowest, 1.3. The middle third of the second grade has a range of reading ability of 1.8 to 2.2, i.e., a four-month spread between the poorest and the best reader in the middle group of readers in grade two. At each grade level the distribution is divided into thirds, indicated by LG, MG, and HG, to show the typical make-up of the three groups (Low, Middle, High) the teacher has to handle, provided she employs the customary division into three groups.

Examination of Figure 6 shows that the range of reading proficiency increases as the children progress through the elementary school. The total ranges between the poorest and the best reader in the *generalized* classes are:

Second grade	2 years, 5 months
Third grade	3 years, 6 months
Fourth grade	4 years, 8 months
Fifth grade	6 years, 1 month
Sixth grade	7 years

As shown in the figure, there is a large amount of overlapping in the reading abilities of the children in the various grades. Thus some of the pupils entering grade two read as well as some of those in the upper third of grade three. And some pupils in grade two read about as well as some children in the middle group of grade four. The overlap of the low scores is also to be noted. For instance, the poorest reader in grade five reads no better than the average second grader, i.e., at grade 2.0.

The relatively great range in reading proficiency of the upper and lower groups shown in the figure for each grade has important implications for instruction. That the middle group is relatively homogeneous is also important. Thus the pupils in the middle group have somewhat similar needs. But in the high group of grade five, for instance, the difference between the best and poorest reader is two years and six months (2.6). While some of these pupils are only ready to read books suited for children halfway through the fifth grade, others are able to read with profit books appropriate for the early part of grade eight. In this high group, therefore, it will be necessary for the teacher to diversify the reading instruction. Similarly, the lower third of the fifth-grade class has a wide range of reading ability, i.e., two years and five months. While some of these children can read only second-grade material, others are capable of reading books suited to pupils halfway through the fourth grade. This is evidence that considerable diversification of instruction is also needed in this lowest group.

Adjusting instruction to fit the needs of pupils in the upper third of a fifth-grade class differs greatly from what is done in the lower third. Since children in the upper third of the class tend to be competent, assured, and independent readers, the teacher can lean heavily upon these characteristics in organizing her program of instruction. But in the lower third of this class the pupils can hardly be considered competent and certainly are not independent readers. This complicates the teacher's task. Moreover, suitable materials are much less plentiful for the lower group than for the highest group. Just how the reading instruction is organized to fit the needs of the three (more or less) groups in a given class will be described in detail in the chapters on sequences in reading in the latter part of this book.

Survey findings

A glance at some survey findings will help to clarify and support the statements we have just made. Comprehension, as noted in earlier chapters, is basic in reading capability. Bond and Wagner (28, p. 355), present the distributions of comprehension scores derived from standardized tests for children in grades two through six, with 30 to 33 pupils in each class. The median reading grade score and range of scores are given below:

School Grade	Reading Grade Median Score	Reading Grade Range of Scores
II	2 (10)	1.0 to 3.5 (31)
III	3 (8)	1.0 to 5.0 (30)
IV	4 (9)	1.5 to 6.5 (31)
V	5 (6)	2.0 to 8.0 (33)
VI	6 (7)	2.5 to 9.5 (33)

The number in parenthesis after median grade indicates the number of pupils at the median. The number after the range of scores shows the number of pupils in the class. Inspection of these data reveals: (1) that only about ⅓ to ⅕ of the pupils in the class achieved median scores although the median reading grade score was the same as the school grade. (2) A few pupils had made no measurable progress in reading at the beginning of the second grade and the same was still true of some at the beginning of the third grade (the reading grade is 1.0). (3) The range of scores (i.e., individual differences in reading comprehension) increases from grade to grade. (4) There is marked overlapping of reading-comprehension ability from grade to grade. For example, the best reader in the second grade is better than the poorest reader in the sixth grade by a full year. And the poorest reader in the sixth grade is not yet ready to read with understanding books suited for third-grade pupils. Comparison of these data derived from classes of moderate size with the normal range of reading ability to be expected in classrooms at grades two to six, as shown in Figure 6 above, reveals a surprisingly close agreement grade by grade. One cannot expect to find agreement as close as this always. Factors such as those mentioned in the preceding section can modify the pattern of a class's achievement. However, these findings as reported are fairly typical.

Another set of data presented by Harris (122, p. 100), emphasizes the enormous range of individual differences in the upper grades. Distributions of grade-equivalent scores for paragraph meaning (Stanford Achievement Test) are shown for grades 5, 6, and 7. There were 14,227, 13,679, and 10,327 pupils respectively in these grades. The grade-equivalent scores ranged from below 2.0 to 11.9 for grades five and six, and from below 2.0 to 12.9 in grade seven. In grade five, only 20.9 per cent of the pupils were reading at their grade level (5.0-5.9); at grade six, 22.5 per cent (at 6.0-6.9); and at grade seven, 15.6 per cent (at 7.0-7.9). This relatively small percentage of pupils reading at grade level stresses the important need of adjusting instruction and materials to individual differences. It is not surprising that there is often a lack of fit between the materials supplied for children in the upper grades and their capacity to read them with understanding.

A child differs from skill to skill

The above discussion reveals that children at any grade level differ markedly in reading capabilities. Any given child frequently shows a considerable range of differences in the degree to which he has mastered the essential reading skills. Although this may occur at any grade level, the variation is more apparent at the higher elementary grades. Bond and Wagner (28) present illuminating data for three children in grade four. A child may be approximately at his grade level in some reading skill or skills and above and/or below in others.

Case 1. This boy's age grade is 4 and mental grade 6. He is close to his actual grade level in isolated word recognition, synthesis of words, and visual analysis. He scores higher (by over one-half grade) than his grade level in vocabulary, comprehension, speed, total word recognition and words in context. His knowledge of word parts is at grade 3.5. Level of comprehension and speed were highest of all skills, grade 6.0 and 6.5 respectively. In terms of his mental grade level (6.0), this boy is doing satisfactory work in level and speed of comprehension but is poor in recognizing words. These basic incapacities will need attention if difficulties at the higher grades are to be prevented.

Case 2. This fourth-grade girl has a mental grade of 4.5. Her scores in comprehension, speed, words in context, and synthesis of words are relatively low. But in recognition of isolated words, visual analysis, and knowledge of word parts she scores relatively high. This means that she is an overanalytical reader, making little use of context. Her phonetic sounding of word elements is good but her pronunciation of whole words (synthesis) is poor. In short she is a word-by-word reader and comprehends less than she should. She needs less emphasis on phonics and special help in phrasing and use of context clues.

Case 3. This fourth-grade boy has a mental grade score of 3.0 but is a year older than the average pupil in his class. He is very low in comprehension and use of context clues. For his mental grade, his vocabulary knowledge is fairly good, also his recognition of isolated words, and his recognition of words in a running text. Apparently he had had much drill in word-recognition techniques. His major difficulty is comprehension, including use of context clues. This boy is a slow learner. And his progress will inevitably be slow, even with special help.

These three fourth-grade pupils illustrate well the unevenness of the reading skills that many children exhibit. They make clear that in order to adjust instruction to individual differences, the teacher must discover both the strengths and weaknesses of each child in her class. It is unsafe for her to try to adjust instruction to individual differences on the basis of a grade rating derived from the combined score on standardized tests alone. Such a rating, for instance, may indicate that a particular child's *average* reading grade is 4.2. But probably no one of his scores is exactly at grade 4.2. Analysis of his profile of scores, as described above, will probably reveal marked unevenness in reading skills. At least this is the commonest kind of case.

As already noted, differences in factors related to reading appear even in the kindergarten. As the child progresses through the primary grades many of these differences persist to a degree that requires adjustment in instruction. At the same time new differences which should be detected and adjusted to are beginning to appear. And as a child moves into the intermediate grades, additional differences associated with more mature reading may emerge.

The first step in adjusting instruction to individual differences is to become aware of the nature and magnitude of such differences as are present and to organize instruction in relation to them. Most of the more capable pupils will progress rapidly with a minimum of guidance. Slow learners, however, acquire reading skills slowly and will profit by much direct help. Although the process of individualizing instruction is complicated and difficult, the well-trained and conscientious teacher in any school system can achieve a degree of success which will reward her efforts many times over.

The consensus of such authorities as Betts (18), Bond and Wagner (28), Harris (122), Gates (97), and others is that the proper adjustment of instruction to individual differences can in many instances prevent the development of reading disability. Both classroom experience and research support this optimistic view. Dunklin (65) is one researcher who has demonstrated that most failures in first-grade reading may be prevented by means of adjusted instruction.

Causes of individual differences in reading

The rate of progress in learning to read is ordinarily conditioned by *a pattern of the interrelated factors* we have been talking about in the early parts of this chapter. It is a difficult matter to determine the relative importance of any single factor in the pattern. Among the factors which appear to rank high in importance as determiners of individual differences we may mention: (1) reading readiness at all grade levels; (2) learning ability, i.e., intelligence; (3) reading disability; (4) instructional procedures; (5) skill of the teacher; and (6) reading materials used. All of these have been or will be discussed at appropriate places in this book.

At this point we wish merely to emphasize again the need for thorough diagnosis of each child's strengths and weaknesses. Any indicated adjustment of instruction should be tentative and flexible, for it may require frequent re-evaluation to be followed, if and when indicated, by modifications. In doing these things, the teacher should keep in mind that practically never will two individual patterns of abilities be identical, and that individual differences in reading are caused by an interrelated pattern of factors rather than by any single one.

Providing for individual differences

Standardized tests, informal inventories, teacher-made tests, and the other devices described in Chapter 16 are employed in order to secure quantitative measures of individual abilities and needs along with other and less formal appraisals. The proficiency profile or pattern of achievement, abilities, and personality derived from these tests, and the teacher's observations, indicate strengths and weaknesses of the individual. These supply the basic information for adjusting instruction to meet a child's needs.

Methods of providing for individual differences may be concerned largely with instructional organization or with variation in teaching techniques and materials, or both. Several of the more frequently recommended or used procedures will now be considered.

Remedial reading

Remedial reading in the classroom will be considered in some detail in Chapter 25. At this place, discussion will be confined to a few remarks on the principles involved. In the extreme theoretical sense one might feel inclined to say that if the reading program were sufficiently individualized from the beginning of instruction there would be little need for remedial teaching. However, in practice things work out differently. No school system has yet provided for such *sufficiently individualized instruction*. Moreover, a goodly portion of the program for meeting individual needs depends upon discovering and correcting difficulties *just as soon as they appear*. Even in any well-organized instructional program, it is not surprising that one child or another will on occasion fail to master a specific skill satisfactorily, perhaps such a skill as use of context for word recognition. With frequent appraisals of the progress to be hoped for as the result of good instruction, any such difficulty will be promptly noted. Analysis indicates the nature of the difficulty and the procedure necessary to remedy it. In the ideal case, then, when the difficulty has been noted at an early stage, it can usually be readily corrected by individualized attention. Troubles when they do come, consequently, are due to one or more of the hundred factors which make it impossible to achieve the ideal.

Another reason why individualization of the reading program cannot eliminate all remedial work is that now and then a child is so seriously in trouble that he fails to make the expected progress in reading despite the best efforts of the teacher. The difficulty may be too complicated or deep-seated for the classroom teacher to handle. In such cases, the child requires the services of a specialist.

Diagnostic and remedial reading, therefore, is a legitimate adjunct of adjusting reading instruction to individual differences. It is, in fact, one of the more important ways of taking care of individual needs as they arise. When the remedial program is viewed in this way, it provides a unique opportunity for individualizing instruction. When well organized and executed, such a program will prevent severe reading retardation in all but a few special cases.

Reading readiness

Providing for readiness to read at all levels of instruction throughout the grades is an essential aspect of individualized instruction in the developmental program. Each new step in reading is built on what comes before. The teacher makes certain that each pupil has at his command the specific skills and concepts necessary for successful reading of the new assignment.

Administrative provisions for individualization

Certain promotion policies have been adopted by various school systems in order to cope with differences in learning ability. It has become rather common practice to accelerate facile learners by letting them skip a grade while the slow learners are held back to repeat a grade. In the early grades, this most often means acceleration or retardation in terms of reading proficiency. Another practice followed by some schools is to eliminate all grade divisions in the three primary school years. Nevertheless, the problem of promotion to grade four or remaining longer in the primary grades must be met eventually (Bond and Handlan, 25). And contrary to certain assumptions, acceleration or retardation of pupils on the basis of reading proficiency makes neither the pupil's adjustment nor the teacher's instructional job any easier. One cannot expect every child to fit automatically into every preconceived notion of what children at a specific grade must do. As emphasized by Cook (47), the crucial issue with regard to the pupil's achievement and his personality development is how well his needs are met wherever he is placed. Consequently, any general policy of promoting pupils cannot by itself insure satisfactory adjustment to individual differences. (Also see Chapter 17.)

Grouping

The principal aim of grouping for reading should be to produce a situation which facilitates the adjustment of instruction to individual differences. Apparently there is no one best method of grouping pupils for reading instruction. It is obvious, as shown by Betts (18) and by Harris (122), that opinions differ considerably concerning the basis on which grouping should be made. This problem will be considered in detail in Chapter 17.

Materials

Any program organized to take care of individual needs of pupils in a class requires that the teacher have a thorough knowledge of the materials to be used. Specifically, she must be familiar with the degree of difficulty of the vocabulary and the concepts in these materials, with their interest value, and with their literary quality and particular content. Evidently the teacher must read the material herself and also get the valuable help that can be had from such sources as Larrick's two guide books to children's reading (149, 150), Arbuthnot's *Children and books* (8), and Hollowell's book on children's literature (135). Various lists of books, graded as to difficulty, are available (see Appendix on materials). Methods of appraising the readability (difficulty) of materials are discussed in Chapter 15. Numerous studies of the interest children take in specific books are available (see Chapter 14).

Many new books for children are published each year. A list of the more noteworthy books published during each preceding year may be found in the *Proceedings of the Annual Conference on Reading Held at the University of Chicago*. These books are classified according to appropriateness for primary grades, middle grades, and upper grades. Previews of new books appear weekly in certain major newspapers and periodicals. All these are good sources of information on new materials to add to the classroom and school libraries.

Experience units have an important place in individualized reading instruction in the elementary school. They are most appropriately employed to supplement other forms of instruction rather than to take their place. Illustrative teaching units for use through the elementary grades are available in two volumes (270, 271) prepared by the teachers at the University of Minnesota Demonstration School. The alert teacher will, of course, accumulate her own unit-resource file. Some such units will parallel the topical units in basal readers. Others will treat of topics known to appeal to children. The teacher will need to know something about their contents and difficulty in order to be able to organize such topical units. When the teacher knows her material well and the interests, abilities, and needs of her pupils, she should be able to assign materials to different individuals with great appropriateness and correspondingly good results.

The Individualized Reading Program

There is a trend, known as *individualized reading instruction,* which has been promoted by some experiments in the classroom and by various journal articles and books, that is creating considerable interest in several areas of the country. This program goes all out for individualized teaching of reading. The pupils choose what they read. Instruction is completely on an individual one-to-one basis. There is no dependence on a basal program for the systematic development of essential skills. Darrow and Howes (51) explain at book length what individualized reading is and how it may be applied in the elementary school classroom. Another volume edited by Stauffer (240) discusses several of the issues involved. While some educators give enthusiastic support to "individualized reading instruction," many others are inclined to doubt its efficiency as the sole method of instruction. It would seem that the heart of the problem in organizing a program for teaching reading is to evaluate the various methods or approaches according to how well each of them stands up under classroom experience and research investigation. On the basis of this kind of evaluation, soundly conducted, whatever proves effective can be worked into a balanced program of instruction. This is what we believe we have done in Chapter 17.

Special Problems

Special problems arise in adjusting instruction to such extreme individual differences as are found among slow learners and gifted children. Each of these groups have very special needs.

Slow learners

Children with I.Q.'s from 50 to 89 are classified as slow learners. Reading instruction for children with I.Q.'s below 50 is futile since they can learn only a few words. But, with proper instruction, those with I.Q.'s between 50 and 89 can make progress in reading up to the grade level corresponding to their mental age. As stated by Kirk (144), slow learners cannot be expected to begin learning to read at chronological age 6. The consensus of educators is that systematic reading instruction for them should begin only when they reach a mental age of at least 6 years. Moreover, they need a prolonged reading-readiness period. According to Gates (97), the readiness program for slow learners should be broader and richer than normal in order to reduce to a minimum the new learnings required when the pupil actually begins to read (See Chapters 3, 4, 5). During the pre-reading training and when the child's mental age is between 5 and 6, he can learn to recognize his name and a few words used as labels and signs. Before pupils have attained at least 6 years mental age, the reading instruction ordinarily given them in a classroom can result only in a tremendous waste of time and energy on the part of the teacher, because they learn so little from it. None the less, if special instructional methods are employed, these children can make a little progress in reading before 6 years mental age.

The following suggestions for adjusting reading instruction to slow learners are derived largely from Gates (97) and Brueckner and Bond (35). Instruction in reading for such children should begin later than for normal children. The slow learner is ready to begin formal lessons at a somewhat later chronological age than the normal child. The beginning of instruction should be deferred as long as is required to make some progress in the prerequisite learnings.

Slow-learning children develop reading ability in much the same way as normal children, but at a somewhat slower pace. This holds for growth in word-recognition techniques, vocabulary growth, and basic comprehension abilities. These children need many more repetitions of a word in the context of basal reading material before they can learn it. This is over and above such encounters as they may have with the same words in appropriate supplementary reading. The reading materials used are the same as those which have proved satisfactory with regular normal pupils. But there is more exposure to such material, and the instruction is more highly individualized and more intensive. Repetition, explanation, demonstrations, plenty of experience units, and a lot of recreational reading are what is needed. Thus there must be more review of the basic words, the explanations must be more detailed and simplified, and the illustrations should be concrete and related to the subject of the reading. In contrast with an average child, the slow learner is handicapped in generalizing and in thinking abstractly about what he is reading. The word-recognition skills prove to be particularly difficult for slow learners to acquire. Thus they profit from additional drill in analyzing words and in learning the sounds of different word elements. Incidentally, rapid reading should not be attempted with these permanently slow learners. In short, the program for the slow learner is broad, detailed, simplified, and *slow-moving*. In other respects, the program of reading instruction is the same as for normal children. The attention and interest of slow learners can be held and their motivation maintained if they are exposed to a lot of interesting and exciting material pitched at an appropriate level of difficulty. But in general it remains true that they enjoy approximately the same kind of reading material as more able children of their age.

The teacher may have some slow learners with I.Q.'s of about 70 and above along with the brighter children in her classroom. Those with lower I.Q.'s should be taught in special classes. Even the child with 70 I.Q. can be expected to learn to read up to grade 4.8 under average instruction and up to grade 5.2 with superior instruction. The same is true of the slow learners whose I.Q.'s are higher. Superior instruction leads to an eventually higher reading level. Superior instruction means adequate adjustment to individual differences by an able teacher whether children are slow learners, average, or superior. The above suggestions are intended to help the teacher to discover the strengths and weaknesses of slow learners and to organize her instruction to meet their needs.

Gifted children

Gifted children who read well also constitute a special problem. Special guidance by the teacher is necessary in order to meet their unusual needs and to provide them with educational experiences that will prove challenging. Frequently the regular classroom work is too easy for them, or they finish such work in a much shorter time than other pupils in the class. As noted by Witty (280), it is unsatisfactory and undesirable simply to have the gifted child do a larger amount of work of the same kind as that engaged in by the more nearly average class members. Having ascertained the capabilities of a gifted child by standardized tests and systematic observation, the teacher should set about supplying him with educational experiences that are gauged at his level. Right here in the field of reading lie probably the greatest possibilities for enrichment in his education. Reading is "precisely the area in which such children usually excel, but in which they also need guidance and encouragement" (Witty, p. 149).

Although they may tend to read a good deal, gifted children are at times inclined to restrict what they read to their special interests. Robert may read only material on baseball, or about airplanes. And Jenny may insist that she wants to read only stories about dogs. At the same time, such children may manifest little or no discrimination as to the quality of materials they read. And some are disinterested in school readers and textbooks.

The reading ability of the gifted child should be recognized, developed, and guided in the school. Rather than requiring them to read materials already mastered, the teacher should encourage them to read widely and to contribute to class projects from such reading. As the gifted child ranges about in a variety of reading materials, he may discover new and emerging interests. These can be fostered by guiding him toward more good books along the lines of each awakened interest. Pupils, no matter how gifted, are likely to require help in finding books that will satisfy what they particularly feel are their personal needs. These needs are usually for such things as learning to understand oneself, to get along better in a complex social environment, and to decide upon a satisfying way of life—what they may later hear called a "philosophy of life."

Gifted pupils tend to become independent readers at an early stage. For this reason, perhaps, such children do not acquire incidentally all the skills they need to become mature readers. In addition to the word recognition and basic comprehension skills, which they usually learn readily, they must have systematic training in the proper use of comprehension and study skills (Chapter 9). They will also need to practice the skills previously taught them. It is also likely that they will profit by instruction in the specialized skills required for most effective reading of materials in the content fields.

The general methods for dealing with gifted children most commonly used are acceleration, special groupings, and enrichment. These are discussed in some detail by Dawson and Bamman (55). The enrichment will include thorough training in skills—not just more reading. The most serious drawbacks that may be the consequence of acceleration and special grouping are the harm they may do the social development of the child. The accelerated child is thrown with children chronologically older than himself who may have interests and engage in activities he is not ready for. And in the special grouping, a gifted pupil's social development may be hampered for lack of contact with children from the different socio-economic classes, and especially with children who differ widely from himself in abilities and past experiences. It is unfortunate if segregation of gifted children prevents them from ever understanding and appreciating many sorts of people. Terman and Oden (250), however, have shown that school achievement of gifted children is maintained whether accelerated or not, and that the risk of social maladjustment from acceleration is less than commonly believed.

It is a notable fact that during recent years a great deal of thinking, research, and experimentation has been devoted to education of the gifted child. The monograph edited by Robinson (210) is devoted entirely to a discussion of ways of promoting maximum attainments in the field of reading among the most able pupils.

Various school systems have organized programs of enrichment specifically designed for bright and talented pupils who remain in the regular classroom with the other children. These procedures aim to develop basic and higher level skills and to promote effective individual and small-group projects. They also open up *avenues* of expression for special talents such as writing and performing skits based on books read, or other forms of dramatics. Or the gifted who may have other sorts of potentialities for leadership are led by reading to feel in how many different channels it is possible to live interesting and useful lives. After all, imagination is the nursery of accomplishment. The reading program for gifted children should be varied, extensive, imaginative, and thought provoking.

Hildreth (131) describes clearly an effective program for teaching gifted children in the Hunter College Elementary School. She recommends a permissive atmosphere in a workshop setting, an intelligent answering of questions to foster self-direction, and emphases on personal responsibility, thinking for oneself, and trying to achieve on one's own. The teacher always stands ready to give individual guidance. The gifted children are held to high standards of performance. Like the less gifted, they are given systematic instruction in the various reading skills but relatively fewer repetitions are required for learning the skills.

To adjust reading instruction to individual differences, therefore, the teacher will have to give special attention to the patterns of achievement, interests, and personal needs of the gifted pupils. As with other less able children, their strengths and weaknesses must be identified and adjusted to.

Summary

Perhaps the most complex as well as the most important task confronting the teacher is adjusting instruction to individual differences in reading and in activities related to reading (as readiness). At any level in the elementary school, from kindergarten through all the grades, children vary greatly in physical characteristics, emotional and intellectual maturity, habits, interests, background of experience, and previous learning. For effective progress in learning to read, the teacher must organize the class and instructional procedures so that each child has the opportunity to achieve up to his capacity. This holds alike for slow learners, average pupils, and the gifted. To make this adjustment to individual differences, it is necessary to know just how children differ, which means knowing the strengths and weaknesses of each and every pupil in the class.

The range of reading capabilities found in any classroom is great. When the instruction is excellent, the average reading performance of the class will be raised and the range of differences in reading ability within the class will become greater. Then with each succeeding year of instruction, the range of difference within the class will increase still more. In grade two the range may be only about two and one-half grades. But in the sixth grade, the difference in reading ability between the best and the poorest reader will amount to about seven years. There is inevitably extensive overlap in the reading capabilities present in the various grades. In fact, the overlap is so great that the teacher at any grade level must also be able to provide for the instructional needs of children who read at the level of the grades below and above the one she is teaching. In general, adjustment to the more able pupils is somewhat easier than it is to those of rather low ability because of the reading competence and independence of the more able pupils and the greater availability of suitable materials.

The program of individualized instruction involves a co-ordinated pattern of those procedures which have been found to be efficient and sound. Instruction should be so organized that the basal program and individualized procedures are co-ordinated into a well-balanced program (Chapter 17). Reading readiness and day-by-day correction of reading difficulties play a role in adjusting to individual differences. The well-trained teacher who knows her materials and sees to it that there is an ample supply available will be able to organize her class and instructional program to meet the individual needs of her pupils. For applications in the classroom, see Chapters 19-25.

Vocabulary

What did these terms mean?

adjusting instruction	consensus
interests	pattern of causes
tastes	reading disability
frustration	remedial reading
behavior trait	enrichment
slow-learning child	acceleration
gifted child	experience units
overlapping	individualized reading
median score	supplementary reading
range of ability	abstract thinking
workshop	self-direction

Suggested Activities

Further study: Compare and evaluate the suggestions in two of the references below (as Bond and Wagner, and Harris) for grouping as a means of individualizing instruction.

Observation: Talk with a teacher in the elementary school. Find out all you can concerning her methods of adjusting instruction to the needs of the more able pupils in her class. To what degree do her procedures seem adequate? What else might be done?

Selected References

BOND, Guy L., and WAGNER, Eva B., *Teaching the child to read*, 3rd ed. New York: The Macmillan Company, 1960, Chap. 17.

—— and TINKER, Miles A., *Reading difficulties*. New York: Appleton-Century-Crofts, Inc., 1957, Chap. 3.

BETTS, Emmett A., Adjusting instruction to individual needs. *Reading in the elementary school.* Forty-eighth Yearbook of the National Society for the Study of Education, Part II. Chicago: University of Chicago Press, 1949, Chap. 13.

DARROW, Helen F., and HOWES, Virgil M., *Approaches to individualized reading.* New York: Appleton-Century-Crofts, Inc., 1960.

DAWSON, Mildred A., and BAMMAN, Henry A., *Fundamentals of basic reading instruction.* New York: Longmans, Green and Company, 1959, Chap. 13.

HARRIS, Albert J., *How to increase reading ability*, 4th ed. New York: Longmans, Green and Company, 1961, Chaps. 5, 6.

HILDRETH, Gertrude, *Teaching reading.* New York: Holt, Rinehart and Winston, Inc., 1958, Chap. 24.

KIRK, Samuel A., *Teaching reading to slow-learning children*. Boston: Houghton Mifflin Company, 1940.

ROBINSON, Helen M. (ed.), *Promoting maximal reading growth among able learners*. Supplementary Educational Monograph, No. 81. Chicago: University of Chicago Press, 1954.

RUSSELL, David H., *Children learn to read*, 2nd ed. Boston: Ginn and Company, 1961, Chap. 15.

14

Interests and Tastes

The acquisition of skill in reading can benefit a person little until he puts it to use in spontaneous and voluntary reading. The child, therefore, after having achieved independence in reading through the acquisition of good, sound reading skills, must be motivated to read, and read widely, for enjoyment, profit, and the enrichment of life. In this process, how much he reads, how widely he ranges, and the quality of what he reads all have their importance. Reading can contribute enormously to understanding oneself and others and the great wide world. To achieve what it intends to do, the instruction a child receives in school must provide him with broad and permanent interests, and an appropriate level of taste. These are concerns of teachers at all grade levels. The right kind of guidance, from the beginning of reading instruction, can do much to cultivate interests and tastes, even though not all influences involved in their development occur as parts of school experience. Despite the fact, also, that growth in these respects can only come gradually, much can be accomplished before the end of elementary education.

Reading Interests

Interest patterns are learned tendencies to respond selectively, positively, and with accompanying satisfactions to certain features of one's environment. They may, for instance, induce a person to participate eagerly in a particular form of play activity, a hobby, or in reading a good book. Interests tend to produce pleasant anticipation followed by action, which in turn ordinarily brings more pleasure. One interested child plays baseball, another goes as often as he can to the airport, a third listens to a favorite radio or television program, or the same boy does all these things at different times. Interests can grow tremendously in intensity and breadth, or they may fade and die out altogether. Ordinarily, a person will tire quickly of an interest in which his activity becomes restricted or in which he can do nothing at all, though this is far from always true, as unsatisfied longings prove.

No factor is more important in teaching reading than maintaining strong motivation. There is ample evidence from research and classroom experi-

274

ence—which was hardly needed—to show that children make greater progress in their reading when they read about things that interest them greatly. Larrick's (151) claim that, as she puts it, under conditions of interest 50 per cent of the battle is won, may well be an understatement. Interest breeds motivation, the will to do something, including the drive needed for learning. This is true in learning to read—the interested child becomes the well-motivated child, the child who is on his way to becoming an habitual reader. Since the converse is true, we can be sure that the child without motivation sparked by interest will tend to learn little and read less.

Knowing these things, it is no wonder that authorities on reading emphasize a vital relationship between interest patterns and both reading activities and progress in reading. The contemporary trend is to base reading programs upon pupils' needs as these are reflected in interest patterns. Experience reveals that these patterns can provide strong motivation to achieve in school reading and then widen into lasting habits of reading, both recreational and useful. In all this the teacher has a twofold role: In order to provide the most effective instruction in reading, it is imperative that she make the most of the dynamic mainsprings which each child's interests essentially are. In addition, the teacher should take the lead in strengthening the better interests of her pupils and in stimulating new ones. This means that the reading interests which the children bring to school supply the teacher with her initial opportunity. Yet she must always keep in mind the possibility that the reading interests with which they leave school may be in great part her own creation.

To take advantage of the interest patterns of children, it is necessary to know what these patterns are. Summaries of interest investigations are to be found in periodic surveys of research in reading by Traxler (263), Traxler and Townsend (264, 265), Traxler and Jungeblut (262). Another source of references are the summaries of reading investigations by W. S. Gray published yearly in volumes of the *Journal of Educational Research* (up to 1960, since then by Helen M. Robinson). The studies summarized cover many areas. Several deal with differences in age and sex with respect to reading interests in such subjects as games and sports, making collections, pets, use of leisure time, and so on. Mackintosh (162) obtained valuable and illuminating information about the reading interests of pupils in grades one through eight from the answers of 628 children to two questions: (1) "Which book that you have read this year did you like the best?" (2) "Why do you think another girl or boy would like to read it?" The following generalizations, given here in abbreviated form are supported by an analysis of these data:

1. Chance influenced some choices, as certain pupils reported they had a difficult time choosing just one book.
2. Some choices were influenced by the chance availability of certain books.

3. Children expressed a keen interest in books containing factual information.

4. Children tended to prefer stories of real animals rather than "talking" animals.

5. Interests in distant places and in the ways in which other people live appeared early, by the beginning of second grade.

6. Only in the first three grades was a strong interest in family relationships evident.

7. In general, interest in vocations did not appear before the eighth grade.

8. Interest in mystery stories was confined largely to pupils from grade five on.

9. Starting in the primary grades and on through the higher levels children expressed increasing interest in science, particularly in trucks, machines, airplanes, rockets, jets, and space travel. Also, the fact that children are interested in the most recent developments in science tells us that contemporary children's interests are expanding in this day and age.

10. Biographies, mainly of famous Americans, and stories of pioneers and explorers were frequently chosen, especially from grade five on.

11. The reasons the children gave for believing that other girls and boys would like a certain book were characters, incidents, and situations.

In addition to the above findings, it appeared that primary school children enjoy fairy stories, and that Bible stories are favorites up through grade six. Surprisingly enough, books on how to make things and books about sports received low ratings.

This survey reveals where there is emphasis and where there is lack of emphasis upon certain kinds of material in the school program. In some places the program is strong and in others weak. The most important recommendation the author makes is that many books and many titles, covering a wide range of reading difficulty, should be available.

Information from various published studies can be of value to the teacher. For instance, certain findings indicate the kind of books (whether adventure, rocketry, biography, mystery, romances, animals, other people, etc.) that *tend* to appeal to children of a given age and sex. The usefulness of such information, however, has its limits for it can only specify the areas within which the interests of a particular child *may* lie, never what the interests of one particular child actually are. Interests vary greatly from child to child of the same age and sex, and only an inquiry or actual trial will disclose individual interests.

Methods for ascertaining a child's interests

Various methods[1] and stratagems may be employed to get at the specific interest patterns of a child. Since no single method can tell the teacher all she would like to know, she may want to use more than one procedure.

[1] Some of the following discussion is based upon Chapter 17 written by M. A. Tinker in G. L. Bond and M. A. Tinker's *Reading difficulties*. New York: Appleton-Century-Crofts, Inc., 1957.

Questionnaires. Detailed questionnaires may be very helpful. Sample interest blanks are given by Harris (122), and by Witty (282). Such questionnaires ordinarily consist of check lists covering such interests as work done outside of school, play and other forms of leisure activities, hobbies, and reading interests. Check marks by a child may indicate either a preference or actual participation. Or answers to questions may be written in, as illustrated by Bond and Tinker (26, page 237). After noting how these questionnaires are organized, the teacher can readily prepare her own for use with her pupils. Or a group of teachers may co-operate in preparing such a questionnaire. A unique advantage of a teacher-constructed questionnaire is that it can be changed at any time to make it more complete or more applicable locally. A carefully organized homemade questionnaire can be as good or even better than the printed commercial ones. And it is inexpensive.

The interview method. After the teacher has become well enough acquainted with a pupil so that a sympathetic relation has been established, she can have a quiet, confidential talk with him about his interests. Such an interview may supplement the use of the questionnaire, or in some instances take the place of it. During the interview, the teacher should strive to shape things so that the child will feel at ease and talk freely about his activities in and out of school, the kind of reading he enjoys, and his favorite radio and television programs. The teacher will find it useful to employ a mimeographed outline to guide her interview. But this should not be done if there is a risk that it may interfere with good rapport between her and the pupil. Ordinarily it will not disturb the child to have her jot down such items as favorite sports, movies, books, or suggestions for the child's future reading. The essential thing is to achieve a relaxed personal give-and-take in a quiet interview. Even though such an interview tends to be time consuming, so much information is usually gained that it is very valuable.

Observation of activities. Another fairly effective and relatively simple way to discover what a child's interests are is to observe closely his daily activities in school and out. In practically all situations where children are free to express themselves in talk, play, drawing diagrams and pictures, and many other activities, the alert teacher will find opportunities to jot down an anecdotal note for later reference. It is likely that the child who draws boats will be interested in reading about sailing. And the girl who loves to play nurse is pretty sure to be eager to read about nurses. A number of leads pointing to possible reading interests are uncovered in this way.

The hobby club. Much worthwhile information on interests can be provided at the regularly scheduled meetings of a classroom hobby club. Each pupil in the club has the opportunity to relate the things he likes to do best during his free time. An enthusiastic report by one child may encourage several other children to take up the same hobby. And frequently the teacher can suggest some specific reading to deepen the hold of a given hobby on a child.

Possibly the well-conducted interview will provide more information on interests than any other technique. Even so, the teacher will ordinarily find it profitable to gather data by more than one method. After accumulating data on a child's interests and activities, the information must be evaluated. Witty (282, p. 306) suggests how this can be done. The child's attitude toward the interview, his responsiveness, and co-operation are rated. Other aspects of the interest pattern are appraised by rating the strength of the appeal of an activity or an expressed interest on a three-point scale, such as (1) strong, average, or present but slight, or (2) as likely to profit from strengthening, curbing, or directing. Strengths and weaknesses are rated in order to estimate a child's needs. The final step is to note specific activities that might broaden the child's interests and particular reading he might do to enrich and expand them. Any teacher should be able to organize a satisfactory evaluative guide to employ with her pupils. Its use will in the case of most children reveal the areas where the development of interests will lead them to read more, and where the interests already awakened can be expanded and enriched.

Ways to Develop Interests in Reading

Both home and school can promote interest in reading by creating situations that favor it. At home, reading is encouraged by such things as: (1) positive attitudes of parents toward reading; (2) availability of books and magazines of a suitable level of difficulty and relevant to the child's interests; (3) talk about books, magazine and newspaper stories and articles in which the child is welcome, and if necessary urged, to take part; and (4) storytelling and reading aloud of stories, poems, and other good matter. If they are to be effective, activities of this kind in the home must be spontaneous, rather than something staged in an effort to snare the child into reading. Children tend to want to be like their parents, and also to be active in ways that are obviously genuine and worthwhile. When the home provides such favorable circumstances, nearly all children will spend more leisure time in reading and broaden their reading interests.

At school, favorable conditions for encouraging reading include a reading corner or classroom library which is colorful, attractive, and comfortable. The reading material, the books and children's magazines, should vary enough in difficulty and content, and be abundant enough so that each child in the class can find something interesting that he is able to read with pleasure. If the reading corner is to serve its purpose, time must be allotted in the daily schedule for browsing about and for individual silent reading. With such arrangements and a small amount of teacher guidance, the use of the reading corner will stimulate and broaden reading interests of most children.

The scheduled *free* reading period should be one in which the pupils are completely free to read by themselves any book or magazine they choose. If a child needs help in selecting a book on the right subject and appropriate in degree of difficulty, the teacher will be available to help him. And the teacher who has a knack of reading stories aloud with real enthusiasm so that they fascinate the children will have little difficulty in stimulating interest in reading (see Chapter 2). An entertaining story which the teacher has read to the class will be reread by many pupils when it is placed in the classroom library and when attention is called to it. Similarly, when some of the good readers among the pupils read aloud to the group selections which have been carefully chosen and which they have prepared to read, interest of the listeners is stimulated.

Interest in reading may also be stimulated by (1) a book club having its own pupil officers, (2) displays of book jackets and book advertisements, (3) an attractive wall chart on which each pupil can list the books he has read, and (4) carefully organized and regularly changed book exhibits on a special shelf in the classroom or in a corridor case. When the enthusiastic teacher plans systematically for developing interest just as she works at developing other aspects of reading, she will be rewarded by the responses of her pupils. It is undoubtedly this enthusiasm of the teacher, together with that of other pupils, for a variety of stories and books that awakens effective motivation in other children to broaden their reading interests. A judicious balance of all the methods discussed is to be recommended. A particular pupil may respond more readily to one method than to others. Knowing her pupils, the teacher will sense when and how to emphasize a particular method.

One more point, a controversial one, should be noted. A few teachers consider it good strategy to give the child a book in line with his interest but a grade or so above his securely attained reading level. The assumption back of this practice is that his interest will motivate him sufficiently to read such a book with understanding and pleasure. This is not usually the case. Perhaps the child persists in wading through the material, but with difficulty. His attempts to identify some of the strange words and to dig out the meaning of new terms and concepts may prevent his reading smoothly and with as much understanding as needed for enjoyment. Such a method of "guiding" children to books cannot be expected to broaden interests or even to maintain those interests which they already have. On the other hand, children need not be denied access to books which others may consider too difficult for them. Certain children may find an unusually gratifying challenge in digging out material of special interest to them, even though it is somewhat beyond their reading level.

Reading Tastes

As noted above, interest determines largely the area or field where and how much a pupil tends to concentrate his reading activities. But the characteristic quality of what he chooses for reading determines the level of his *taste*. For instance, whether Jerry prefers to read about pirates in *Treasure island* or in *Black Silver pirate crew*, which he bought in a ten-cent store, certainly reveals his taste.

It is not easy to establish a criterion of excellence. The quality of writing varies in every field whether it is animal stories, adventure stories, scientific or other factual material, or imaginative stories. Whatever the subject matter, to improve one's taste requires a swing upward in preferred materials from a lower to a higher level of excellence. To prefer or choose the good implies discrimination. And to achieve discrimination is possible only when the child has had a rather wide range of reading experience. Tastes evolve or grow out of past experience and growth in this respect tends to be slow and uneven. Thus it is entirely possible for a person's taste to be good in one area of reading and poor in another.

What is good taste and where the road to it lies are highly individual matters. Reading taste in children has to be appraised in terms of the increased satisfactions, increased happiness, and the all-around increased welfare of a particular youngster. Appraising his improvement (or the opposite) in taste requires turning a searchlight on his present level as compared with the former level *of this same individual*. That is, the teacher must think in terms of this specific child's growth through experience. For what will pass as "good" literature for one child may not be at all worth reading by another. We say this without raising the thorny issue of the general criteria of excellence in literature.

Level of reading tastes

If we accept at face value the comments of many writers, based upon surveys and opinions, the reading tastes of both children and adults in America are decidedly immature. Some of the stronger terms employed to describe the general level of reading tastes are "deplorable" or "appalling;" milder terms are "mediocre" or "leaves much to be desired." The great variety and numbers of comics and pulp magazines sold, the types of library books that are popular, and surveys of reading habits do seem to indicate a relatively low level of discrimination in the choice of reading materials by many people. It is generally recognized by thoughtful people that improved tastes as well as broadened interests in reading among both children and adults would add greatly to our country's strength in the difficult decades ahead. The race for world leadership may well be won by those nations in which the contributions of sheer intellect to civilization are most highly esteemed and cultivated.

Actually, the conditions are probably not as black as often pictured. Undoubtedly, the possibilities for improvement with proper guidance are good. In spite of the competition from other leisure-time activities such as using the car, movies, radio, television, and all sorts of things, a surprisingly large amount of reading gets done by a majority of the population. In addition to large newspaper circulation, there are tremendous weekly and monthly circulations of many magazines. For instance, the *Reader's Digest* had over twelve million circulation per month in 1959, *Life* over six million, *National Geographic* over 2¼ million, and even the *Atlantic Monthly* over ¼ million. Further testimony to popularity of reading is revealed by the numerous commercial book clubs such as the *Book-of-the-Month Club*. Book sales are increasing by leaps and bounds. In 1959, over 800 million books were sold. A contributing factor is the tremendous sale of inexpensive reprints of books in paperbound editions. These include children's books as well as adult books. In addition to the public libraries, there are thousands of commercial loan libraries located in corner drugstores, bookstores, and department stores. Various reports show a marked increase in public library circulation. For instance, Harold L. Hammill, Los Angeles City Librarian, reports (*Los Angeles Times*, February 20, 1961) an average monthly increase of 5.6 per cent during 1960. He also points out that people are reading more serious books today than they have in the past. Similar reports come from other centers such as Minneapolis. Taking into account all the competing activities, it is gratifying that so many people read so much. In addition, much that is read in books and magazines is of fair to good quality. For instance, discrimination is exercised in the choice of books for many subscription book clubs, and many of the inexpensive reprints are of good quality.

The trend in the reading of children is equally promising. Nancy Larrick's article "But Children Do Read Nowadays" in the November 14, 1954 issue of the *Saturday Review,* its issue for National Children's Book Week, is illuminating. It is concerned with publication, sales, and circulation of children's books. While in 1920 there was one editor of children's books among the publishing companies of the United States, by 1954, there were 60, all working to see that our children get more and better books. And a quarterly survey printed in *This Week Magazine,* March 12, 1961, reveals that high school pupils are now reading more good books and liking them. Actually, there is ample evidence that American children never had so many good books as they have today, and never read so many. Still, many children need a program of guidance to increase the amount of voluntary reading, to broaden interests, and to improve tastes.

It is quite probable that practically all the survey type of reports of the reading habits of the population give an inadequate picture of the amount of reading done. Perhaps the findings of Link and Hopf (158) should be counted on the side of gratifying evidence rather than as one more sample of the familiarly encountered indictment of reading habits. Thus, 50 per cent of the population, they found, were active book readers. And, of the books read, 37 per cent were nonfiction and 58 per cent were fiction. And the fact that more time is spent reading newspapers and magazines than books does not seem so bad when one remembers that much magazine and newspaper writing is of good quality.

The reading of comics

Unquestionably the wide-spread reading of the so-called comics is a disturbing symptom of our immaturity as a people. Many survey data and much comment on them have been published. Fairly comprehensive analyses of these data and views with implications for guidance in reading are given by Russell (213), Smith (227), and Witty (282). The comics are tremendously popular with elementary school children and are widely read by high school students and even by adults. It is generally agreed that little is gained by wholesale denunciation or prohibition of comics. This does not mean that nothing can be done to stem the tide of their influence. Presumably the comic magazines and comic strips are here to stay, at least during the forseeable future. There can be no doubt about their popularity. Comic strips appear in nearly every daily newspaper, and many millions of copies of comic magazines are sold each month. In terms of interest and tastes, the mere reading of comics is not the more serious aspect of the problem. Worse is the handicap of interests and tastes produced by the tendency among some children to limit recreational reading to the comics.

The possible effect of comics on the personality and adjustment of children is ambiguous. Even among psychiatrists, juvenile court judges, psychologists, and child specialists there is lack of agreement. Some claim that much juvenile delinquency and crime is caused by the crime and sex comics; others claim that this is unlikely. As Smith (227) points out, the possible harmful effects of comics seem to depend upon which comics and which child we are thinking of. The child with a well-balanced, wholesome personality will probably be unharmed by any comic material. But excessive reading of the extreme sex and crime comics by severely maladjusted children may undeniably be harmful. It is also possible that the youngsters who are already emotionally disturbed and maladjusted are the very ones who are drawn to the gory crime and sex comics.

Usually the reading of comics is a reading problem when it becomes so excessive that it limits or prevents a broadening of interests and a whole-some development of tastes. Thus many children who read comics also read large numbers of books of different kinds and of good quality. These children are not handicapped by reading several comic books each week. On the other hand, children who do practically no voluntary leisure reading except comics neglect reading the materials needed to enrich and extend their interests and the materials suitable for cultivating tastes.

It is generally agreed that what is needed is guidance rather than a denunciation and/or prohibition of comics. There are a number of positive things the teacher can do in a program of guidance concerning comics. An initial step is to establish some degree of discrimination towards them so as to build up a preference for the better or more acceptable comics. A second approach consists of relating the subject matter of comics to subject matter in books of recognized worth.

It has been demonstrated that guidance can lead to appraisal and dis-crimination in evaluation of comics by children in the intermediate grades. For instance, in Denecke's investigation (59), the children examined comics for such things as interesting points, monotony, degree of whole-someness, accuracy, and relation to reality. These pupils, through discrimi-nation and evaluation, identified three relatively unique types of comics: those giving wholesome information; those providing humorous or amusing material; and those stressing crime, hatred, and revenge. Discriminating analysis of this kind can provide a good basis for guiding children's prefer-ence for the more desirable comics.

Since the content of comic magazines varies greatly in quality, and consequently in desirability as reading matter for children, it would seem self-evident that comics which employ better language, and which avoid emphasis upon crime and sex, while giving wholesome information, some of which is organized to improve reading proficiency, are the more desirable kind for children to read. The teacher can cultivate transfer of interest from undesirable to the more desirable comics by providing for a wide sampling of such material and by guidance in discrimination and evaluation. Fre-quently, getting the child acquainted with a more desirable comic plus social approval will furnish sufficient incentive to get him to choose and read the better ones.

Conspicuous among the elements that are attractive in comics are sur-prise, action, pictures, excitement, and sometimes humor. So guidance should also be concerned with providing children with a variety of good literary sources which are rich in the same features that attract them to comics. Most children would rather read *Pinocchio* than *Dennis the Menace* if they had the chance. Phyllis R. Fenner, in *Our library* (John Day), advises us to give the children the adventure they crave, but to give them books written with sincerity and honesty. There are many short stories and books which have stood the test of time that contain characters, settings, and plots just as attractive, and depict episodes just as exciting as those in comics. When a seven-year-old demands a murder mystery, Miss Fenner suggests (ibid.) *Freddy the detective*. This usually fills the bill although there is no murder and Freddy is only a pig. In fact, the almost universal interest in comics among children (over 90 per cent of elementary school children habitually read them) affords an excellent opportunity to provide guidance for the development of tastes. The teacher who knows both comics and good literature can frequently motivate a child to seek additional related stories in better books by calling attention to the intriguing plots and episodes in the latter. Thus moving from comics to other sources which yield satisfying reading experiences can be a first important move toward better tastes.

Development of tastes

The first step in any program to develop a child's reading tastes requires an appraisal of his present level of taste. This may be achieved through questionnaires, interviews, and observation as in the appraisal of interests. If any program to improve tastes is to succeed, the teacher should start where the child is, recognizing that his present pattern of taste is where she must begin. Then a sound program of guidance, necessarily highly individualized, will lead him by *gradual* steps to a sampling of a wide variety of material so that he may come in contact with writing of better quality. One child may confine all voluntary reading to the comics; another may read anything and everything on animals; another may read only factual material to gain information about a hobby; another may confine her reading to sentimental stories; and so on. No matter how much material is read, if the child fails to practice discrimination of quality, either by confining his reading to the relatively "poor" literature or by exercising no choice between "poor" and "good" materials, he will fail to make progress in developing taste.

Although taste is suggested by *what* a child reads, it is shown even more perhaps by what he is *aware of* as he reads. Clues to a child's reading taste may be revealed during instruction periods. For instance, how well a child can state what the author made him *see* or *feel* or *sympathize with a situation* are clues to taste. Further information on taste is gained when the child senses what made a character in a story seem real, and what made him more or less real than a character in some other particular story. Thus much information on the development of taste may be gained by observing a pupil's reactions in class discussions of the literary qualities of what they have been reading. When the material read varies in quality, pupil reactions during these class discussions will tend to reveal whether a child is exercising discrimination between poor and good literature.

Incidental growth in reading tastes is seldom constant or rapid. Opportunities and guidance must be organized if pupils are to improve satisfactorily. In kindergarten and the early primary grades, the teacher furnishes the stimulation that promotes enjoyment of good children's literature by reading aloud carefully selected materials. Then, as the pupils improve in reading ability, they do more and more leisure reading of books and other materials which they choose for themselves. While the extensive variety of stories and descriptive articles in the basic texts can initiate growth toward good tastes, the availability of proper supplementary materials, together with guidance in their use, are needed if this growth is to be maintained.

A variety of conditions favors the development of reading tastes:

1. *A child must be a proficient reader in order to permit his tastes to improve.* Whatever the nature of the material, it must be read with facility and a satisfactory degree of comprehension if it is to instill enthusiasm and give keen enjoyment. This means that materials of the proper level of difficulty must be supplied for each child. Furthermore, since there are proportionately many more books of good quality as their difficulty increases, the child has greater opportunity to read better books and so improve his tastes as he gains in reading proficiency.

2. *The child who reads a great variety of material and who has broad reading interests encounters more opportunities to improve his tastes.* The development of reading interests and improvement of tastes progresses hand in hand. In fact, some writers make no clear distinction between reading interests and tastes. Obviously they are reciprocal in action, each working on the other.

3. *Favorable environmental conditions encourage the development of reading taste.* Appropriate reading materials must be conspicuously accessible, for children tend to read what they can most readily obtain. Moreover the child must have sufficient time to read uninterruptedly. At school there should be regular periods for leisure reading. And parents should encourage leisure reading and endeavor to organize home life so children have plenty of time for it.

4. *The role of the teacher is of prime importance.* To promote growth in tastes, the teacher should know her pupils individually, be well read herself, and become enthusiastic over the fun of bringing children and books together. Smith (227) emphasizes this, pointing out that the understanding teacher senses which are the appropriate times for introducing new books, occasions for getting the right book to the right child at the right time. The teacher who has a wide knowledge of children's literature and shares this with her pupils through discussions, oral readings, and calling attention to good books that are right there to be read stands a good chance of developing tastes in her pupils.

5. *The school has an important role to play.* The classroom reading corner should be co-ordinated with the school library if the school has a library, and loans of books from the city or county library at periodic intervals can supplement the books in the school. Pupils should be taught how to use both the school and the public library. In this, the classroom teacher and the librarian should work together to aid in getting appropriate books to children as they are needed.

6. *Improvement in taste is slow.* Building taste is a continuing process, one that should last as long as the child is in school. Not much progress is to be expected in a day, a week, or a month. Exposure without cessation to a variety

of good materials is mandatory. This allows progress to occur, step by step, in a steady sequential order, gradual and sliding, one step into another higher one. Not until a child is ready for it will he read such materials as *Treasure island*, *Caddie Woodlawn*, or children's books in science, or listen to the poetry of A. A. Milne. Growth in discriminating taste accompanies the formation of good reading habits and interests. There will be gradual progress from a relatively low level of taste to materials of better quality.

7. *Direct teaching.* Ordinarily the materials in basal readers are of good quality. Direct teaching of this material with an emphasis on those qualities (sensing and feeling what the author intends) will promote improvement of taste. This is also accomplished by presenting contrasting good and poor materials to the pupils (see Chapter 2).

Objectives: Interests and Tastes

Any teacher is naturally concerned with what would be the best program for developing interests and tastes if it could be achieved, and she is concerned also with how much can be expected in practice when undertaking such a program. In general, it is a good thing to guide the child to the stage where he will of his own accord read extensively a wide variety of materials with understanding. Such a program should move from relatively narrow interests to broader ones, and from a relatively low level of tastes to materials of better quality. With well-organized help, all children will progress, but some will advance farther than others. *The main thing is to get children to read widely with enjoyment.* There will always remain wide individual differences in taste. And it is neither possible nor desirable to set up one level of taste as if it could be achieved by all children.

The classics. To force a child to read classics is an unfortunate procedure. Although opinion varies with regard to reading of the "classics," their value for developing taste is apt to be destroyed if reading them is made compulsory. Moreover, the books, stories, and poems which are considered classics now may be considerably different from those so designated by an earlier generation. Also, even with the best of teaching, many of the so-called classics become meaningful only to the more able children. In general, it seems sensible to urge that pupils should be exposed to good literature, classical and other, under the most favorable circumstances. This means that with expert teacher help the children may be introduced to the classics when they are able to read them with understanding and when there is a good probability that they will be genuinely interested in so doing. It is a good plan for the teacher to introduce some classics by reading aloud from them.

Summary

The well-rounded reading program aims to furnish the kind of instruction that will develop broad and permanent interests and an appropriate level of taste. Guidance to achieve these aims should continue throughout all grade levels. In addition to providing strong motivation for learning to read, interests determine what is read and how much is read voluntarily. And the level of taste of a reader depends largely upon his interest patterns. Teacher leadership can broaden these interests and stimulate new ones. To do something for a child's interests, it is first necessary to find out what they are at the time one starts to try to change them and to add new ones. Data are available concerning which interests tend to be shared by children of a given age and sex. But when it comes to identifying and appraising a particular child's specific interest patterns, it is necessary to resort to questionnaires, interviews, and observing his behavior.

In the home, interest in reading is promoted when the parents themselves read and want their children to do the same, by having plenty of books and other reading material available, and by storytelling and reading aloud stories and poems. In the school, interest in books and reading is fostered by an attractive reading corner adequately supplied with books of many kinds, by oral reading and storytelling by the teacher, by free reading periods, by displays of book jackets and advertisements, and by organizing among the pupils book and hobby clubs. Of greatest importance, perhaps, is the guidance given by the enthusiastic and well-read teacher.

A criterion of good taste in reading is not easy to establish. Improvement in taste is relative to a pupil's present level of taste, which the teacher has to discover. Although progress is always slow, well-organized teaching can lead to improved discrimination and choice of reading materials by all children. The gains will be great for some pupils, small for others. But for most children, taste is not going to be improved in school unless the teacher knows what good taste is and unless she works both directly and indirectly to develop it. How this may be done is shown in Chapter 2.

Among the factors which have effects on the development of tastes are level of reading ability, strength of interests, amount and variety of voluntary reading, availability of materials, sufficient time for considerable leisure reading, and the skill of the teacher. It has been demonstrated that well-organized and well-executed programs can bring about remarkable improvement in reading tastes.

The reading of comics presents special problems in reading interests and tastes. Those children who do practically no voluntary leisure reading except comics are of course missing the materials which they need to enrich and extend their interests and to improve their taste. The teacher can provide a program to instill some degree of discrimination even among comics so as to bring about a preference for the more acceptable ones. She can also direct pupils to similar subject matter in books of recognized worth.

Vocabulary

What did these terms mean?

reading interest	discrimination
reading taste	comics
motivation	pulp magazines
questionnaire	subscription book clubs
interview method	comic strip
leisure reading	evaluation of comics
book jacket	classics
incidental growth of tastes	hobby club

Suggested Activities

Observation: Visit an intermediate-grade class. Note all the techniques you can that the teacher employs to stimulate interest in voluntary reading. What can you suggest that might improve her methods of stimulating these interests?

Further study: In what ways can television and radio programs stimulate reading interests? Look up some articles along this line in several issues of *The Reading Teacher, The Elementary School Journal*, and *Education*.

Creative: Select a good and a poor piece of writing from children's books. Plan questions which would make children aware of and able to distinguish differences in quality.

Selected References

Bond, Guy L., and Tinker, Miles A., *Reading difficulties.* New York: Appleton-Century-Crofts, Inc., 1957, Chap. 17.

—— and Wagner, Eva B., *Teaching the child to read*, 3rd ed. New York: The Macmillan Company, 1960, Chap. 15.

Dawson, Mildred A., and Bamman, Henry A., *Fundamentals of basic reading instruction.* New York: Longmans, Green and Company, Inc., 1959, Chap. 8.

DeBoer, John J., and Dallmann, Martha, *The teaching of reading.* New York: Holt, Rinehart and Winston, Inc., 1960, Chaps. 11A, 11B.

Gans, Roma, *Reading is fun: Developing children's reading interests.* New York: Bureau of Publications, Teachers College, Columbia University, 1949.

Gray, Lillian, and Reese, Dora, *Teaching children to read*, 2nd ed. New York: The Ronald Press Company, 1957, Chap. 14.

Harris, Albert J., *How to increase reading ability*, 4th ed. New York: Longmans, Green and Company, 1961, Chap. 17.

Hildreth, Gertrude, *Teaching reading.* New York: Holt, Rinehart and Winston, Inc., 1958, Chap. 21.

Lazar, May, *Guiding the growth of reading interests.* New York: Board of Education of the City of New York, 1945.

McKee, Paul, *The teaching of reading in the elementary school.* Boston: Houghton Mifflin Company, 1948, Chap. 17.

Robinson, Helen M. (ed.), *Developing permanent interest in reading.* Suppl. Educ. Monog. No. 84. Chicago: University of Chicago Press, 1956.

Russell, David H., *Children learn to read,* 2nd ed. Boston: Ginn and Company, 1961, Chap. 12.

Witty, Paul, *Reading in modern education.* Boston: D. C. Heath and Company, 1949, Chap. 2.

15

Materials

Satisfactory progress in learning to read depends upon the quantity and quality of what is read, as well as upon good teaching. In every classroom an ample supply of varied materials of fine quality should be available. The degree of difficultness of these materials should be appropriate to the range of reading ability among the pupils (Chapter 13). When the teacher is competent, she is able to provide a systematic developmental program of reading instruction just in proportion to the excellence of the material available. The enrichment of the program, the adjustment to individual differences, the well-handled unit instruction, and the providing of incentives for recreational reading all depend to a large degree upon availability of appropriate materials.

The trend today is for schools to see that the children have access to many books besides their textbooks. Even so, it must be admitted that the supply of books in many school systems is at present too meager to insure that all pupils are learning as much as they might. According to Whipple (276), who was writing in 1949, both the number and variety of books available at that time tended to be much less than the best authorities were recommending. This deficiency showed up in classroom libraries as well as in school libraries. Both teachers and administrators were aware of these needs. It is still true today that wherever funds are available, a first step towards improving conditions for teaching reading should be to increase the supply of reading materials both in the classroom and in the school library.

Fortunately conditions have been changing for the better during the past 12 years. Great numbers of children's books of good quality are being published every year, many of them relatively inexpensive (Chapter 14). Though Hildreth (133) claims that in any school the bare minimum is not less than one book per pupil, exclusive of textbooks, there should be many more—20 to 30 books per child.

Role of the library. It is difficult to exaggerate the importance of library facilities in the reading program. For effective teaching of reading, it is likely that next in importance to the classroom teacher is the role of the trained librarian in the school library. The classroom library or reading nook, the school library, and the community library are all indispensable. And close co-operation must be maintained between the classroom teacher and the librarian if the best provision is to be made for the reading needs of pupils. Whenever good materials suitable to children's needs are available, more recreational reading is bound to occur, and when the enjoyment to be had from this is great enough, children tend to become habitual readers. Both the teacher and the librarian, supplementing each other, should make certain that they have thorough knowledge of the reading materials available. Only then is full use of the materials in the reading program going to be made. For more about how to use this knowledge in guiding pupils, see especially Chapters 13 and 14.

The materials center

Some schools are now organizing a materials center. Its purpose is to pool all of a school's stock of instructional materials and make them available as requested by classroom teachers. For instance, the Iowa State Teachers College Laboratory school has a book room where all the books for class use except library books are kept for distribution as needed. The College of Education Reading Clinic at the University of Minnesota has a similar arrangement. When a school has no room organized and staffed as a materials center and no school library, it should have book stacks in some central location where the books can be lent to classroom teachers and pupils.

A very effective program for use of books and other educational materials has been organized by Torrance, California, Unified School District.[1] The Educational Materials Building supplies material to 30 elementary schools and 3 high schools. Any teacher may select what she needs from 200,000 library books and supplementary textbooks, 700 films, 4,500 filmstrips, 6,000 records, 300 sets of study prints, and other instructional aids. Selected materials are delivered daily to all schools in the district. Facilities are available to preview films, listen to records, and examine filmstrips. The Educational Materials Building has a well-equipped professional library for teachers. It also serves as the instructional center of district activities such as extension courses, district workshops, institutes, and committee meetings. The Torrance set-up, for what it provides, is economical both in cost and in the space and staff it requires.

In addition to a knowledge of materials immediately available, the teacher will need to be familiar with other sources of information and of supply in order to direct children to proper materials for both recreational and work type of reading. She may also have occasion to recommend

[1] The authors are grateful to Mrs. Margaret Denmarsh for a description of the Torrance Approach to Educational Materials Distribution.

purchase of new materials. Various avenues of approach to a knowledge of materials are discussed below.

Types of Reading Material

Many types of material are needed for use in the developmental reading program. Detailed examination of these needs may be found in the *Proceedings of the Annual Conference on Reading* held at Chicago, 1957 (Robinson, 209), and more recently in Part I, Section III of *The Sixtieth Yearbook* of the National Society for the Study of Education, 1961 (226, pages 165-253). Anyone who is responsible for a balanced reading program must know what its characteristics are in the case of every type of material, and he must find out just what is available and where it can be obtained. The information we can find room for here will *not* be sufficient for those teachers who serve on those committees that actually make the highly important selections of books for purchase by the school system. Such teachers will need to know a lot more than this minimum. However, it is the job of *every* teacher to have enough information about materials to organize and carry out her own program of instruction, and what we include here is intended to help these teachers.

An up-to-date analysis of what is involved in basal reading and what basal instructional materials in reading offer is given by Herrick, Anderson, and Pierstorff (128). They note that there is general agreement that *basal reading* refers to reading systematically developed by means of a series of books and other materials particularly suitable for each successive stage of reading development. Basal reading materials should foster continuity in reading development so that there will be no gaps in a child's reading experience. Herrick and his associates examined 12 series of basal readers to discover what materials were commonly used at different grade levels, what the stories they contained were like, and how vocabulary and difficulty were controlled at successive levels.

A note of caution is in order concerning any analysis of the contents and methods of teaching in basal reading series. Such analyses are quickly outdated as new editions of the basal series are produced. Consequently a new analysis has to be made periodically to keep teachers informed on content and methods of teaching incorporated in the revised materials.

Method of instruction. Each basal reader in a modern series has an accompanying workbook for children, a teacher's manual, and an edition of the reader for the teacher. Functions of workbooks vary somewhat with the particular reader series. Ordinarily they introduce vocabulary and review background material related to reading in regular books. Also they provide supplementary practice exercises to develop the skills, vocabulary, and concepts met in the reading lessons. Some workbooks put the major emphasis upon sequential skill development. Although published evaluations of workbook materials have included questions as to their effectiveness, they can become an important integral part of the developmental instructional program. This is possible when the workbook material is well organized and carefully co-ordinated with the textbook material and the whole instructional program. Teachers using workbooks must be alert to see that what the workbooks are doing for the pupils is in step with the rest of the reading program. Moreover, it should be obvious that use of a workbook is no substitute for the kind of instruction which a resourceful teacher can provide better.

In any good basal series, the teacher's manuals provide detailed and complete directions on how to use all the instructional materials needed to insure a well co-ordinated developmental program. Every teacher can profit greatly by careful study of the manual both to make her teaching effective and to save time. This does not mean that she has to follow the manual slavishly. Every resourceful teacher will at times want to deviate from the suggestions in a manual, and will do so to advantage. The pattern of instruction laid down in the manuals usually includes for each unit: (1) a preparatory phase, which includes hints on how to provide for motivation, the teaching of new words, the clarifying of purposes, and the reviewing of background material; (2) guided reading and oral reading followed by questions and discussion; (3) a study phase to clear up difficulties in vocabulary and word attack, with individual help where needed; (4) extension of experience through reading of related material and participation in other relevant activities.

Use of more than one reader. There are instructional hazards involved in the use of more than one basal reader at a given level, particularly at the lower primary levels. In comparing seven widely used pre-primers and primers, Behn (15) found that only ⅓ to ½ the words are common. And McHugh (177) found only two-thirds of the words common in a similar study of second- and third-grade readers. This means that the child who switches from one book to another can read: "The _____ _____ in the big red _____ every day." In addition to his difficulties in recognizing words, the child will run smack into other obstacles. The program for developing skills is not exactly the same in the different readers since they are tailored to different vocabularies. This means that children switched from using one series as a base to another series as a base are confronted with different sequences in building vocabulary and other skills unless the teacher takes it upon herself to bridge the gap by co-ordinating learning in the two (or more) sets of material.

Other contributions. Specific application of materials for basic instruction will be given in Chapters 20 through 24. A few additional contributions which all sets of basal materials aim to make should be mentioned. What these are has been excellently stated by Whipple (276), and Herrick, et al (128).

1. *Control of readability factors.* The level of difficulty in materials is meant to increase gradually, so that the sequence of progress becomes truly developmental. Careful attention is devoted to the rate at which new words are introduced, to repeating words, to making new concepts clear, to helping when sentence structure is becoming complex, to the length of stories, and so on. Continuous and satisfying progress in learning to read is assured for the majority of children only when there is proper gradation of difficulty in these basic materials. For details of application, see Chapters 20-24.

It is probable that control of readability or difficulty is most important in the primary grades, especially in grades one and two. Rigid control of readability is likely to decrease in importance at each successive level, starting at about the third or fourth grade. Apparently these controls are most valuable for the slow learner and least needed by the more able and gifted children. In fact, it is possible that a rigid control of vocabulary and sentence length throughout the grades may well act as a brake upon the reading growth of average as well as gifted children. It might well appear to some educators that the elaborate precautions taken to insure that the slower learners get the help they need will often work to the disadvantage of average and superior pupils. Every teacher should be aware of this possibility so that she may provide adequate stimulation and facilities for the more able pupils (Chapter 13). Their achievement will do much to maintain her spirit and spontaneity.

2. *Nature of reading units.* The stories and reading activities in the primary grades deal with the lives of young children at home, in school, and in the community: i.e., units about home, a circus, a farm, picnics, animals, trains, the post office, and a fire station. When the units introduced deal with experiences and interests common to children, they can be of greatest assistance to the teacher who is alert to the values of good motivation. For example, she then finds it easy to use the unit as a point of departure to stimulate additional reading of related material.

In the intermediate grades, the basic materials extend the themes that have been encountered earlier to include people all over America, or anywhere in the world, and including what has happened at other times. This pattern of extension follows the social studies and science materials sequences of the elementary school with added emphasis on literary material which is likely to be imaginary, folk tales, and stories from the classics. As the children move into the seventh and eighth grades the basic books deal almost exclusively with literary items, biographies, folk tales, humor, science, and poetry. At this level the basic readers tend to be collections of stories and articles that will be read for their personal or intellectual appeal.

3. Modern basic series provide for an orderly *development of comprehension and study skills.* When material has been especially prepared for the purpose, instruction designed to develop the following of a sequence of thought is facilitated. Likewise the search becomes relatively easy,

whether it be for supporting details, the locating of some specific information, or the development of some other comprehension or study skill.

In general, the modern series provides a well-controlled basic *core* of materials for instruction. Such materials can play a valuable role in the balanced reading program. Russell (217) has expressed this view well. His analysis reveals that the modern basic series of readers is constructed so as to provide: (1) continuity of growth; (2) wide variety of reading activities; (3) a complete organization of reading experiences; and (4) worthwhile ideational content. He stresses the point, however, that even though the books are carefully written in line with these principles, they should be relied upon as only a part of the whole reading program.

When the teaching is good it is possible to achieve normal progress in reading proficiency without using basic readers at all. However, since no one denies that normal progress also occurs when basic readers are used, there seems to be no advantage gained by not using them. Moreover, as Lazar (152) has emphasized, when reading units are organized in the primary grades without the use of basic readers, it is up to the teacher herself to select, organize, and control the vocabulary properly. In fact, no advantage over the basic readers could be expected unless the substitute materials organized by the teacher proved to be better than those available in the basic series. This is not very likely to be the case.

Supplementary reading materials

A well-conceived reading program requires much more reading material than what is provided by a basic series used in connection with workbooks. Supplementary reading materials will include the following: (1) readers designed to supplement and enrich materials in a specific basic-reading series, or those planned to supplement any basal reading program; (2) collections of stories organized around a specific geographic location, cultural period, topic, or person; (3) collections of stories, descriptive prose, and poetry; (4) trade books of children's literature (see below). All these kinds of material are needed to widen experience, enrich vocabularies, clarify concepts, and satisfy individual interests and demands for information.

Materials in the content fields. Reading of content materials begins in the primary grades and expands rapidly in the intermediate and upper grades. The role of reading to develop new knowledge, understandings, appreciations, and interests in the content fields is outlined by Whipple (276). Additional discussions are presented in the monograph edited by Gray (108). There are now available at all grade levels excellent science and social studies books and pamphlets with controlled vocabularies. Both easy and more difficult biographies of great scientists and other leaders are also published (see Appendix). When children have attained sufficient proficiency in reading, they should find out for themselves how much valuable information is to be found in children's encyclopedias, dictionaries, reference works, and selected magazines (see below).

There are many worthwhile series of books containing content materials. The following are interesting and useful (for additional sources see Appendix):

1. "All about" series: *All about radio and television, All about the sea, All about volcanoes and earthquakes, All about dinosaurs*, etc. New York: Random House.

2. The "first book" series: *The first book of snakes, The first book of stones, The first book of space travel, The first book of science experiments*, etc. New York: Franklin Watts, Inc.

3. The landmark series: *Mr. Bell invents the telephone, The Wright brothers, Clipper ship days, The Vikings,* etc. New York: Random House.

4. The Unitext series (Paper-covered booklets): *The basic science education series*—over 50 titles; *The basic social education series*—15 titles; *Real people*—24 titles. Evanston, Illinois: Row, Peterson and Company.

5. The world geography readers: *British Isles, Australia and New Zealand,* etc.—20 booklets. Columbus, Ohio: Charles E. Merrill Company.

6. The world landmark books: *Napoleon and the battle of Waterloo, Mary, Queen of Scots, The adventures and discoveries of Marco Polo*, etc. New York: Random House.

7. *Follett Picture Stories*—35 booklets dealing with science and social science topics, third- to fifth-grade difficulty. Chicago: Follett Publishing Company.

8. *Community of Living Things* (5 vols.). Nature study, conservation, science materials. Mankato, Minn.: Creative Educational Society.

9. *Creative Science Series* (4 vols.). Physical science: planets, atoms, weather, earth. Mankato, Minn.: Creative Educational Society.

Newspapers and magazines

Magazines and newspapers are a good source of supplementary reading material for elementary school pupils. Besides furnishing current and timely articles, they provide enjoyable recreational reading, for broadening experience, and for supplying valuable material for certain unit projects. Magazines and newspapers have a special appeal to children and are eagerly read by those who have progressed sufficiently in reading ability. A few of them are listed below:

My Weekly Reader, American Education Press, Columbus, Ohio. Suitable for grades one to five.

Current Events, American Education Press, Columbus, Ohio. Suitable for grades five and six.

Young Citizen, Civic Education Service, Washington, D.C. Suitable for grades five and six.

Junior Scholastic, Scholastic Magazines, New York. Suitable for grades six to eight.

Young American, Eton Publishing Corporation, New York. Suitable for grades six to nine.

Child Life, O. H. Rodman, 136 Federal Street, Boston, Mass. Suitable for young children.

Children's Activities, Child Training Association, 1018 South Wabash Avenue, Chicago, Ill. Suitable for young children.

Jack and Jill, Curtis Publishing Company, Independence Square, Philadelphia, Penn. Suitable for children 6 to 12 years of age.

Highlights for Children. Highlights for Children, Inc. Columbus, Ohio. Suitable for elementary grades.

Open Road for Boys. Don Samson, 136 Federal Street, Boston, Mass. Suitable for intermediate grades.

Story Parade. Story Parade, Inc., 200 Fifth Avenue, New York. Suitable for primary grades.

Playmates. A. R. Mueller Company, Cleveland 4, Ohio. Suitable for primary grades.

A number of other magazines contain interesting material which can be read by the more proficient readers in the intermediate grades. Examples are: *American Boy, American Girl, Audubon Magazine, Boy's Life, Popular Mechanics, Popular Science Monthly, Nature Magazine, Read, Outdoor Life, Scouting, Mechanix Illustrated, Handbook for Boys, Children's Digest, Junior Natural History.*

Children with at least ninth-grade reading ability (there are several in the upper elementary grades) will be able to read with understanding much of the material in daily newspapers, *National Geographic Magazine, Life, Readers' Digest*, and *Time*. For a detailed list of juvenile periodicals see *Magazines for school libraries*, by Laura K. Martin, New York: H. W. Wilson Company.

Dictionaries

The use of dictionaries constitutes a necessary aid in developing reading proficiency. In the primary grades, children become acquainted with picture dictionaries. From about the fourth grade on, children use regular dictionaries of appropriate content and difficulty. Representative dictionaries for use in the elementary grades are listed below:

Picture dictionaries. Construction of word-picture dictionaries by primary school pupils is a rather common practice. Some of the ready-made dictionaries of this type follow:

WALTERS, G., and COURTIS, S. A., *The Picture Dictionary for Children*. New York: Grosset and Dunlap, 1948.

WALPOLE, E. W., and REED, M., *The Golden Dictionary*. New York: Simon and Schuster, Inc., 1944.

WRIGHT, W. W., and LAIRD, H., *The Rainbow Dictionary*. New York: The World Publishing Co., 1949.

SCOTT, A., and CENTER, S., *Dictionary for Boys and Girls*. Garden City, N. Y.: Garden City Publishing Co., 1949.

MACBEAN, D. W., *Picture Book Dictionary*. Chicago: Children's Press, 1946.

GRIDER, Dorothy, *My First Picture Dictionary*. Chicago: Wilcox and Follett Company, 1948.

MOORE, Lillian, *A Child's First Picture Dictionary*. New York: Wonder Books, 1948.

OFTEDAHL, Laura, and JACOBS, Nina, *My First Dictionary*. New York: Grosset and Dunlap, 1948.

SCOTT, Alice, and CENTER, Stella, *A Picture Dictionary for Boys and Girls*. Garden City, N. Y.: Doubleday and Company, 1949.

REED, Mary, and OSSWALD, Edith, *My Little Golden Dictionary*. New York: Simon and Schuster, 1949.

DeWITT, C., *The Golden Book of Words*. New York: Simon and Schuster, 1949.

WATTERS, Garnette, and COURTIS, S. A., *Illustrated Golden Dictionary for Young Readers,* New York: Simon and Schuster, 1951.

CLEMONS, Elizabeth, *The Pixie Dictionary*. Philadelphia: John C. Winston Company, 1953.

PARKE, Margaret, *Words I Like to Read and Write*. Evanston, Illinois: Row, Peterson and Company, 1955.

Dictionaries for the intermediate grades. Care must be exercised in choosing regular dictionaries for the elementary school. "Bargain" editions are likely to be inadequate and disappointing in many ways, since construction of a reputable dictionary is a long and costly undertaking. Supplementary instructional aids to dictionary use are available for pupils and teachers. Several of these are listed by Betts (18, p. 670). Examples of dictionaries especially designed for use in the elementary school:

Webster's Elementary Dictionary. New York: American Book Company, 1956.
Thorndike-Barnhart Beginning Dictionary. Chicago: Scott, Foresman and Company.
Thorndike-Barnhart Junior Dictionary. Chicago: Scott, Foresman and Company, 1959.
Funk and Wagnalls Standard Junior Dictionary. Evanston, Ill.: Row, Peterson and Company, 1957.
Thorndike-Barnhart Senior Dictionary. Chicago: Scott, Foresman and Company.
Webster's Junior Dictionary. Springfield, Mass.: G. and C. Merriam.
Thorndike-Barnhart Advanced Junior Dictionary. New York: Doubleday, 1957.
Webster's Student Dictionary. New York: American Book Company, 1956.
Webster's Biographical Dictionary. Springfield, Mass.: G. and C. Merriam.
New Winston Dictionary for Children. Philadelphia: The John C. Winston Company, 1953.
New Winston Dictionary for Young People. Philadelphia: The John C. Winston Company, revised annually.
Junior Book of Authors, rev. ed. New York: H. W. Wilson Company, 1951.

Reference materials for work-type reading

As children move into the intermediate grades and concentrate more upon units requiring work-type reading, children's encyclopedias and other reference works are needed. The following are valuable sources of information for pupils who are proficient enough to read them:

Compton's Pictured Encyclopedia. Chicago: F. E. Compton Company.
Britannica Junior. Chicago: Encyclopedia Britannica.
World Book Encyclopedia. Chicago: Field Enterprise.
Book of Knowledge. New York: Grolier Society.
Oxford Junior Encyclopedia. New York: Oxford University Press.
Golden Encyclopedia. New York: Simon and Schuster.
The Children's Illustrated Encyclopedia of General Knowledge. New York: Philosophical Library.
Columbia Encyclopedia (for more able readers). New York: Columbia University Press.
World Almanac. An up-to-date edition is useful on many occasions.
Collier's Encyclopedia. New York: P. F. Collier.
Childcraft. Chicago: Field Enterprises.
Children's New Illustrated Encyclopedia. (Pageant of Knowledge Series.) Toronto, Canada: Collins.
Golden Book Encyclopedia. New York: Golden Press.
Our Wonderful World. (An "encyclopedic anthology.") Chicago: Spencer Press.
Richard's Topical Encyclopedia. Chicago: Field Enterprises.
The Space Encyclopedia. New York: E. P. Dutton and Company, 1958.
Lincoln Library of Essential Information (content subjects). Buffalo, N. Y.: Frontier Press, 1953.

Children's literature

The teacher who is responsible for reading programs will need to keep up to date on books recently published. The following reference works on children's books, containing much specific information, should be available to every teacher of reading. They contain extensive annotated bibliographies, each book classified as to difficulty.

ARBUTHNOT, May H., *Children and Books*, rev. ed. Chicago: Scott, Foresman and Company, 1957.
HOLLOWELL, Lillian, *A Book of Children's Literature*, 2nd ed. New York: Holt, Rinehart and Winston, Inc., 1950.
LARRICK, Nancy, *A Parents Guide to Children's Reading.* Garden City, New York: Doubleday and Company, Inc., 1958. (Also published in paperbound edition by Pocket Books, Inc.)
—— *A Teacher's Guide to Children's Books.* Columbus, Ohio: Charles E. Merrill Books, Inc., 1960.
Subject Index to Poetry for Children and Young People. Chicago: American Library Association, 1957.
Index to Children's Poetry. New York: The H. W. Wilson Company, 1942; First Supplement, 1954.
Subject and Title Index to Short Stories for Children. Chicago: American Library Association, 1955.

Subject Index to Books for Intermediate Grades. Chicago: American Library
Association, 1950.

Subject Index to Books for Primary Grades. Chicago: American Library Association, 1950.

Numerous other sources provide information on children's books (see
Appendix). Burton and Larrick (37) give an up-to-date discussion of
literature for children and youth.

Children's book clubs

In 1960 nearly 10,000,000 children were receiving books periodically as
members of book clubs (Larrick, 150). Two clubs, *Arrow Book Club* and
Teen Age Book Club, distribute books (paperbound) directly to schools.
The books are delivered in bulk, five and eight times respectively, during
the school year.

Parents, school librarians, and teachers are eager for book club information. Details on membership and costs may be obtained from the following
clubs:

Arrow Book Club, 33 W. 42nd Street, New York 36, N. Y. For ages 9-11 years.
Teen Age Book Club, 33 W. 42nd Street, New York 36, N. Y.
Catholic Children's Book Club, 260 Summit Avenue, St. Paul, Minn. Five age
groups: 6-9, 9-12; 10 up; girls 12-16; boys 12-16 years.
Catholic Youth Book Club, Garden City, N. Y. For ages 9-15.
Junior Literary Guild, Garden City, N. Y. Five age groups: 5-6, 7-8; 9-11;
girls, 12-16; boys, 12-16.
Parent's Magazine Book Club for Beginning Readers. Bergenfield, N. J. For
ages 8-11.
Weekly Reader Children's Book Club. Education Center, Columbus 16, Ohio.
(Five books per year plus a dividend book sent.) For ages (*a*) 5-8; (*b*)
8-12.
Young People's Book Club. Spencer Press, Inc., 153 N. Michigan Avenue,
Chicago 1, Illinois. For ages 8-13.
Young Readers of America (Division of Book-of-the-Month Club). 345 Hud-
son Street, New York 14, N. Y. For ages 9-14.

Appraisal of reading difficulty

The materials in trade books vary in ease of reading with enjoyment by
children in various stages of reading proficiency. Many of these books are
not classified as to level of *readability*, or relative difficulty. When a teacher
states that a certain book is about right for a typical third grader, she is
referring to its level of readability. The principle of readability is incorporated in every well-graded basic-reader series where successive books
gradually increase in difficulty.

Measuring readability. Several formulas have been devised to measure
the relative difficulty of reading materials. Among the more widely used

formulas are those of Dale and Chall (50), Gray and Leary (113), Flesch (86, 87), Yoakam (291), and Lorge (160). But Dolch (61) and Spache (233) have worked out formulas for use with primary materials. All the formulas require analysis of samples of reading material. The two language factors most commonly taken into account are vocabulary load and sentence structure, especially the former. Since the formulas differ, the results from the different methods are not in complete agreement. Sampling errors (variations due to chance, i.e., due to the fact that the samples selected for analysis are not perfectly representative of the whole) also produce variation.

The uses and limitations of readability formulas are examined in detail by Klare and Buck (145). Certain relevant factors are not measured by the formulas now in use. As noted by Hildreth (133), easy-to-read material is characterized by "concreteness, easy vocabulary, and simplified sentence structure with few dependent clauses and a small proportion of prepositional and adverbial clauses" (page 375). Long sentences, complicated paragraphs, and uncommon polysyllabic words all increase the difficulty of reading material.

The application of readability formulas yield results that roughly approximate the grade levels in basic-reader series and also agree with the judgments of experienced teachers and librarians. Although their use is to be recommended, slavish adherence to any formula is not justified. Other values need to be considered, as we shall point out.

Ordinarily the readability of materials will be determined by specialists in children's literature, such as research workers, textbook authors, and librarians. However, the classroom teacher should understand what is involved in such appraisals. She will, of course, need to know how difficult materials are in order to utilize them properly in adjusting instruction to individual differences. Moreover, the teacher who understands the basic principles of readability is better able to make informal judgments concerning the suitability of a book for a particular grade or an individual child.

Audio-visual and other aids

Much equipment besides books is used in teaching reading. A large portion of this equipment consists of audio-visual aids such as pictures, film strips, and recordings. These aids may be employed at all grade levels to broaden experience, to clarify concepts dealt with in reading, and to stimulate a desire to read. When firsthand experience is not possible, they provide informative vicarious experience. Also these aids constitute highly effective supplements to actual experience, as when animal pictures or a film of animal life are shown following a trip to a zoo. In a recent publication, Spache (234) has emphasized the widespread use and significance of audio-visual aids. He also notes how these aids are co-ordinated with the reading program at the different grade levels and the limitations and advantages of each kind of aid. Although auditory and visual materials are effective for certain purposes (mentioned above), "they can never possess the flexibility and personal elements of the teacher-pupil relationship" (page 213). The teacher should always remember that these audio-visual devices are *aids*. They supplement rather than take the place of teacher instruction. For instance, the aids can be helpful in developing interests and tastes as well as reinforcing the desire to read. A rather complete list of sources and descriptions of audio-visual aids is given by Leestma (154) and Spache (236).

The audio-visual aids which may be employed advantageously on one occasion or another include flat pictures, slides, filmstrips, silent and sound pictures, models, specimens, exhibits, graphs, maps, globes, radio and television programs, and phonograph recordings. Material chosen for a particular group should be suited to the children's stage of development and maturity. Simple flat pictures, mounted or unmounted, constitute one of the most practical and effective visual aids. They are readily found and well adapted to use in almost any reading activity. Teachers can assemble and file pictures, post-card illustrations, pictorial maps, etc. The pupils themselves often can bring to school the same sorts of materials and will be happy to do so. Other audio-visual materials may be borrowed from the school library, a public library, a visual-education department, or a museum.

Teaching machines. In addition to short exposure devices, eye-movement cameras, and reading pacers (Chapter 11), teaching machines are now entering the educational field. Several organizations are developing so-called teaching machines for learning a variety of subject matters such as arithmetic, areas of biological and natural science, algebra, calculus, electronics, and so on. It is to be expected that various applications to reading will be forthcoming. A teaching machine may be described as a device which presents to each learner individually bits of subject matter organized in small sequential steps. Each item or bit is followed by a question. The machine informs the learner at once whether his answer to each question is correct. A program, such as material from biology or electronics, consists of hundreds of bits (items) or even thousands. The items are carefully selected and arranged in a developmental order. Such auto-instruction has three distinctive features: a learner may be continuously active; he knows at once whether his response is correct (and is corrected if he is wrong); the learner proceeds at his own rate. Teaching machines and programs are described by Allen (4). The machines are being tried out in pilot programs in several places. They are not intended to take the place of the classroom teacher. But they may well find an important use in individualizing the instructional program. For instance, they could probably be employed with some pupils who are ahead and with others who are behind the middle group in a class. It is too soon to know how effective teaching machines will become in the school situation.

Appraisal and Choice of Books

The careful appraisal and wise choice of books for the reading program in a school system can undeniably become a complicated and difficult task. The availability of a wide variety of reading materials does not eliminate the necessity for fine discrimination in their selection. All books published are not equally satisfactory. Some are dull. Some may be attractive in appearance but lack suitable content or style or vocabulary control. Thoughtful appraisal and choice of books is necessary if the books selected are to serve specific purposes in the reading program. And, as noted by Whipple (276), books should be selected for individual children rather than for children in general. The choice of suitable books necessitates the use of proper standards and methods of evaluation.

Selection of books for the reading program is ordinarily done by teachers who will use them or by a committee composed of teachers, school officials, and the librarian. Suggestions of criteria and procedures to aid appraisal and selection of books are given by Whipple (276), Spache (235), Storm (242), Edman (74), Russell (213), Gray and Reese (107), and Clement (43). Clement (44) has also devised a score sheet for recording the results of evaluation. The best brief summary of data on readability is given by Dale (49). The teachers serving on a committee for appraisal and selection of books should study the specifications listed in these references. Other teachers should become familiar in a general way with the basic factors involved in appraisal and choice of reading books as outlined below.

Standards and methods of evaluation

It is desirable to keep the work of evaluation at a minimum and at the same time take enough pains to insure a satisfactory choice of books. The number of items or factors that are eligible as a basis for selection is large. Whipple (276) suggests that the teacher choose from these items or factors several of real importance in terms of meeting the reading needs of individual children. The teacher can then use the time and effort available to make as objective an evaluation as possible in terms of this limited set of items. When the list of items to be considered is long, the tendency is to spend too much work on appraising minor factors. At the same time the minor factors tend to receive undue weight relative to more significant characteristics. Then, too, use of a short list of items avoids the confusion which is apt to result in summing up ratings based upon a long list, many items of which are trivial. Quite often each teacher or committee will want to make out a list of items related to the task at hand.

In evaluating a particular kind of reading material such as basic readers or dictionaries, reference can be made to the relevant parts of the above discussion of "*types of reading material*." The items to be considered will vary, of course, with the type of book to be selected. For example, it may be a primer, a picture dictionary, or a workbook. Some of the following items will need to be considered in all ratings. Others only for specific types of books. No teacher, however, in her evaluation need feel restricted to the items listed below:

1. *Nature of content:* Appropriateness with regard to the needs of the children who will use the book, purposes to be achieved by its use, range or variety of subject matter, interest appeal, literary quality, and style of writing.

2. *Level of difficulty:* Appropriateness in terms of vocabulary control, sentence and paragraph structure, complexity of concepts, and literary style.

3. *Typography:* Appropriateness of quality of paper, size of type, length of line, leading, margins, and so on in relation to readability.

4. *Illustrations:* Suitability in terms of simplicity, context value or information relevant to textual material, coloring, size, and number.

5. *Instructional values:* Appropriateness in terms of promoting specific reading objectives, stimulating thinking, providing opportunity to develop word-recognition skills, vocabulary knowledge, concepts, comprehension skills, and study skills. Clarity and completeness of directions to students and to the teacher in workbooks and teacher's guides.

Miscellaneous Materials

In addition to books and the audio-visual aids mentioned, the teaching of reading requires certain other supplies and equipment. Children's experiences and activities ordinarily lead to constructing a vast amount of informal materials, especially in the primary grades. Various kinds and sizes of cardboard and of paper will be needed. Every schoolroom should have ample facilities such as a bulletin board, tack boards, and chart holders for displaying materials. Duplicating equipment and a typewriter should be available. In the primary grades the typewriter type should be of primer size if possible.

Other materials needed at one or more grade levels include paints, crayons, paste, scissors, blocks, clay, toys, and perhaps plants and pets. Construction work in certain teaching units will make use of building materials, a hammer, and other simple tools. The children themselves may bring in important contributions of materials for such units. Ordinarily, empty wooden boxes and crates can be obtained from local stores. Materials necessary for elementary school activities are discussed in method books or pamphlets such as the *Iowa Elementary Teachers Handbook*, Vol. II (140). Lists of commercial materials such as cards, games, and booklets are given by Dawson and Bamman (55). Also see Appendix.

Summary

The supply of reading materials available in schools tends to be much less than what is necessary for good teaching. The degree to which a competent teacher is able to provide a satisfactory developmental program of reading instruction is in direct proportion to the *quantity* of *good* material available. Effective use of materials requires, of course, that the teacher should have a thorough knowledge of what she has on hand, or could get, or make herself.

For best results in any reading program, materials should be ample in amount, varied in subject matter, and of the proper level of difficulty. The kinds of reading material needed include basic series of readers, practice materials such as workbooks, supplementary books, and pamphlets for intensive and extensive reading, subject-matter texts, newspapers and magazines, dictionaries, and reference books. The basic readers ordinarily provide for the core of the instructional program. Various sources of descriptive information on books are available to the teacher. Audio-visual and a variety of other materials and equipment are also needed.

Careful appraisal is a prerequisite to wisely chosen books for the school. This appraisal is likely to be more satisfactory when the teacher concentrates her efforts upon a relatively small number of highly important items dealing with content, level of difficulty, typography, illustrations, and instructional values in the books.

Vocabulary

What did these terms mean?

materials center	juvenile periodicals
basal readers	picture dictionary
teacher's manual	encyclopedia
readability	annotated bibliography
reading units	readability formula
supplementary materials	audio-visual aids
controlled vocabulary	typography
sampling error	polysyllabic

Suggested Activities

Further study: Read Chapters 9 and 10 in Nancy Larrick's *A teachers guide to children's books.* Outline the material for your future use in teaching.

Observation: Visit a third-grade class. Note what visual or auditory aids the teacher employs in teaching a reading unit. Can you suggest additional aids?

Selected References

DAWSON, Mildred A., and BAMMAN, Henry A., *Fundamentals of basic reading instruction.* New York: Longmans, Green and Company, 1959, Appendix A.

GRAY, Lillian, and REESE, Dora, *Teaching children to read,* 2nd ed. New York: The Ronald Press Company, 1957, Chap. 15.

HENRY, Nelson B. (ed.), *Development in and through reading,* the Sixtieth Yearbook of the National Society for the Study of Education, Part I. Chicago: University of Chicago Press, 1961, Chaps. 10, 11, 12, 13.

HILDRETH, Gertrude, *Teaching reading.* New York: Holt, Rinehart and Winston, Inc., 1958, Chaps. 16, 22.

ROBINSON, Helen M. (ed.), *Materials for reading.* Suppl. Educ. Monog. No. 86. Chicago: University of Chicago Press, 1957.

SPACHE, G., *Resources in teaching reading.* Gainesville, Florida: The author, University of Florida, 1955.

STRANG, Ruth, McCULLOUGH, Constance M., and TRAXLER, A. E., *Problems in the improvement of reading,* 3rd ed. New York: The McGraw-Hill Book Company, Inc., 1961, Chap. 16.

16

Appraisal of Reading Growth

In order to adjust a child's instruction in reading to his specific needs it is necessary to evaluate his reading abilities at intervals, such as when he enters grade three and then subsequently as the program of instruction develops sequentially. This evaluation should be comprehensive, detailed, and concern itself with the objectives the instruction is designed to meet. In such an appraisal, consideration must be given to reading attitudes, and reading interests, tastes, and study skills. Besides these there are the basic and special reading abilities. In other words, if one is to know how well the reading objectives have been achieved, and how well the teaching program is planned to meet individual needs, there must be periodic measurements of reading ability, in addition to day-by-day observations and checking by the teacher. The techniques employed at any given time will depend upon what is to be appraised. For instance, one method may be more useful for appraising skill in some aspect of word recognition, another for vocabulary knowledge, another for a specific study skill, and still another for reading taste. As far as possible, the appraisal should be in situations which closely approximate actual reading conditions. The alert teacher will sense how much the quality of her instruction will depend upon her securing a thorough-going appraisal of how her pupils are progressing in their reading.

Careful appraisal should promote consistent as well as balanced growth in reading proficiency. It is not a one-time event but a continuing process. With the data obtained in the appraisals (see below) and her evaluation of them, the teacher will be able to select appropriate materials and shape her instructional program to take care of the individual needs that are disclosed by the initial appraisal, the subsequent appraisals, and day-by-day or week-by-week testing and observation. The teacher will soon discover that appraisal of growth in reading and adjusting instruction to individual needs are complicated processes because reading itself is a highly complex skill.

Appraisal is Necessary

There are many reasons why appraisal is necessary for best progress in the development of reading proficiency. These reasons may be grouped into two categories: those concerned with achieving reading goals; and those concerned with guidance or adjusting teaching to individual needs.

The well-organized reading program has clearly defined aims or goals to be achieved at each successive stage in development. In general, appraisal is concerned with progress, which is, at least in part, the outcome of instruction. More exactly, appraisal of growth in reading is undertaken to determine the degree to which the goals specified at successive levels have been attained. This periodical appraisal is necessary if instruction promoting steady progress toward the next level in the sequential program is to be competently planned and carried out.

Appraisal is equally concerned with promoting guidance in individualized instruction, that is, in promoting best adjustment of instruction to individual needs. These needs vary from child to child and in the same child from time to time. The ideals of successful guidance cannot be achieved unless the teacher ascertains the level of proficiency that has been attained by the child in each specific skill. She can then adjust her instruction to insure that the child may proceed naturally in gaining just those proficiencies which experience specifies are requisite for progress to subsequent levels in the sequential program.

Appraisal and the class program. In Chapter 13, adjustment of the instructional program to the needs of individual children within the class was emphasized. Knowledge of the wide range in reading proficiency to be found in any ordinary class, and knowledge of just where each child stands within that range, will provide information necessary for guidance in organizing the teaching program, for these reasons: (1) It helps the teacher to see clearly the instructional problems she faces, and at the same time provides information to guide her in the adjustments of her teaching which she is certain to have to make. (2) It furnishes the chief data necessary for grouping pupils in her class for reading instruction. (3) The adaptation of instruction to individual differences within a group cannot be done without this knowledge. (4) Intelligent selection and use of reading materials in a classroom is possible only when the teacher knows the distribution of reading proficiency of her pupils. (5) It helps the teacher to maintain a balance in instructional emphasis. For instance, it will reveal lack of satisfactory progress in some area or skill such as skimming, vocabulary meaning, or reading arithmetical problems, whereupon a shift in emphasis can remedy the deficiency (also see Chapter 13).

Appraisal for adjustment to individual needs. Once the selection of materials and organization of classroom instruction to fit the range of reading talent among the pupils is guaranteed, it is still necessary to utilize guidance in providing for the specific needs of each pupil. These needs are identified by appraisal. Thus one child is found to be deficient in sight vocabulary, another has failed to profit much from instruction in phonetic analysis, and still another does not phrase properly in oral reading. Remedial teaching to help those children with difficulties is possible only after diagnosis based upon appraisal which defines the nature of the disability and indicates the corrective measures needed (see Chapter 25).

Techniques of Appraisal

A technique of appraisal of reading proficiency is a method for (1) discovering the grade level at which a pupil can read effectively, and (2) obtaining knowledge of a child's reading status in each of a number of areas discussed below, such as vocabulary meanings and concepts. Evaluation of the information from the different areas will reveal the child's pattern of growth in reading since the previous appraisal was made. The types of information found to be most useful for evaluation are derived from standardized tests, informal tests, teacher observation, questionnaires, and records of various kinds.

Standardized tests

Standardized tests are measuring devices of proved reliability and validity. They furnish norms or standards of achievement for a specific series of school grades. Ordinarily they are readily scored and usually, after a moderate amount of experience, the scores are easily interpreted by the teacher. A reliable test is one which yields highly consistent performance when the test is repeated, that is, a child achieves about the same level of performance if he repeats the test within a short space of time. A test is valid when it yields a true or accurate measure of that aspect of reading for which it was designed, such as vocabulary knowledge. Norms are established by giving the test to sufficiently large and representative groups of children. Then the mean scores achieved at successive grade levels are computed and listed in tables. When a standardized test is used, it is possible through reference to the norms to ascertain the grade level of achievement of a pupil or of a class. By this means, strengths or weaknesses are revealed in word recognition, vocabulary meaning, reading for details, speed of comprehension, and the other aspects of reading performance. Norms represent average performance. Deviation from average performance can be expected from many pupils.

Two general types of standardized reading tests are available: the *survey test* and the *diagnostic test*. The survey tests, such as the *Gates Reading Survey* (see list of tests in Appendix), are used primarily to ascertain a pupil's level of achievement in such basic reading abilities as vocabulary, comprehension, and speed. The diagnostic tests, which furnish data for guidance in reading instruction, enable the teacher to discover a pupil's strengths and weaknesses in such specific skills as word perception, understanding sentences, and noting details. The *California Reading Tests* by Tiegs and Clark, and the *Diagnostic Reading Tests* sponsored by the Committee on Diagnostic Reading, are diagnostic tests. Actually, there is no clear-cut division between the survey type and the diagnostic type of *group* reading tests. Many survey tests provide information useful in individual diagnosis and vice versa. For instance, the *Gates Basic Reading Tests* which measure four specialized kinds of reading ability are useful both for survey and diagnostic purposes. However, certain *individual* diagnostic tests such as the *Gates Reading Diagnostic Tests* are highly specialized for diagnostic purposes.

The use to which scores on standardized tests and informal tests (described below) are put is important. Although it is necessary to know the grade levels of individual pupils in reading ability, the main use for test results is teacher guidance in adapting instruction to individual requirements. In other words, the most valuable uses of data obtained with standardized reading tests are for diagnosing needs of pupils. In fact, most manuals of directions which accompany reading tests contain helpful suggestions on how to use the test results for diagnostic purposes. Any user of a test can profit by a study of these suggestions.

The directions for administering a standardized test have been carefully, even painstakingly, arrived at so that the child taking the test can operate under the most favorable conditions for eliciting a valid measurement of his reading ability. All published norms have been obtained under the conditions of use prescribed by the standard directions. To make sure that the obtained scores are meaningful, therefore, it is necessary that the directions for administering the test be followed exactly as given. Too frequently, a teacher may deviate from the standard directions, not realizing the possible adverse effect of such changes upon the results and *therefore upon her interpretation of their significance,* when she uses published norms.

Many standardized reading tests are on the market. A list of representative tests will be found in the Appendix. While not necessarily the best tests for every situation they are all commonly used tests. Other rather extensive lists of reading tests may be found in Bond and Wagner (28), Betts (18), Bond and Tinker (26), Harris (122), Traxler (261), Triggs (268), Wrightstone (290), and Witty (282). An exhaustive list of tests with evaluations is given in The Fifth Mental Measurement Yearbook (36). Any school planning to use standardized tests might well consult these descriptions of the tests. Sample copies, with a manual of directions, should be ordered and examined for suitability prior to ordering in quantity.

Informal reading tests

The two most common kinds of informal reading tests are workbook tests and teacher-made tests. They are informal in the sense that they are not standardized. These tests are employed for the day-by-day appraisals needed in individualized teaching. The workbook tests are concerned largely with measurement of word identification and recognition skills and vocabulary knowledge and comprehension. For the most part they measure the skills, vocabulary, and meanings presently taught in the accompanying basic reader. An analysis of responses to the test items will frequently furnish important information on sources of reading difficulties so that prompt remedial measures may be taken.

Workbook tests measure success with workbook materials. Since the workbook materials ordinarily constitute only part of the pattern of any daily lesson, the most satisfactory appraisal of daily progress can be made only if additional informal testing is done. This is accomplished by use of tests made by the teachers themselves. The types of items in these tests depend upon the individual teacher. To a large degree the make-up of these tests approximates that in workbooks and in standardized tests. Teacher manuals, which accompany series of readers, usually provide helpful suggestions on construction of test items. Aids of this kind with samples of items are given in the *Iowa Elementary Teachers Handbook* on reading (140), by Gray (111), and Stanley (239). The test items are usually mimeographed or dittoed for use in class.

Due to manner of construction, the teacher-made tests are readily adapted to checking daily, weekly, or monthly progress in learning what is taught. Both workbook tests and teacher-made tests reveal strengths and weaknesses of pupils and thus provide information for guidance in adjusting instruction to individual needs.

Informal oral reading tests are especially useful for guidance in reading instruction. In fact, most teachers note and correct some errors in oral reading almost daily. A more systematic informal measure of oral reading proficiency can be obtained readily by observing performance while reading aloud selections in a carefully graded series of basic readers. The teacher works with the child individually and notes accuracy of pronunciation and degree of comprehension as the child reads selections in successive books in the series, progressing from easy to more difficult levels. Betts' different levels (18) are readily ascertained by this method. The level appropriate for extensive free reading requires accurate pronunciation of 99 out of 100 words, with at least 90 per cent comprehension in the case of factual and inferential questions. The instructional level requires accurate pronunciation of 19 out of 20 words and at least 75 per cent comprehension. When the child can pronounce only 9 out of 10 words and comprehends less than 50 per cent of the material, he is considered to be at a frustration level in reading.

In addition to evaluating the level of reading proficiency, the informal oral reading test can furnish information useful in guiding day-by-day instruction. In fact the informal oral reading test is almost a necessity for adjusting instruction to individual needs. A record of errors is made as the child reads materials orally. Analysis of the errors will disclose individual needs by revealing such sources of difficulty as inadequate use of verbal context, lack of skill in phonetic and structural analysis, insufficient use of clues to word form, and determination of whether the difficulty tends to be at the beginning, middle, or end of words. In addition to revealing the source of difficulty, the informal oral reading tests when repeated will indicate how fast the difficulty is being eliminated.

The use of workbook tests, supplemented by teacher-made tests, makes it possible for the teacher to maintain intimate contact with her pupils' progress in learning to read.

Teacher observation

Teacher observation of pupil behavior and pupil responses in the reading situation provides extremely important information for appraising growth in reading. As a supplement to test results, the information obtained by a direct study of the child is of great value not only for exploring reading attitudes, interests, and tastes, but also for following day-by-day proficiency in reading.

The teacher by direct observation readily evaluates a variety of attitudes connected with reading. She perceives signs of eagerness and joy with which reading is approached, or, on the other hand, the indifference and distaste which spell avoidance reactions. Degree of anticipation for the free reading period which is ahead, for trips to the library, and for examining new books is noted. Participating in discussions and group projects is significant. Tendencies to demand meaning, to go to books for desired information, and to engage in wide reading for pleasure are also good signs to watch for. In general, attitudes connected with reading are best evaluated by the teacher who is alert in her observations.

Close watching shows the teacher how proficiently a child employs study skills. For instance, she can note how effectively he locates information and selects materials. She can also employ observation for more or less continuous appraisal of pupil success in learning what is being taught at the time. The knowledge obtained provides a basis for the shifts in emphasis required for adjustment to individual needs.

Through accumulated observations and test data a teacher becomes acquainted with members of her class. She comes to know much about each pupil's strengths and weaknesses, his attitudes, interests, and tastes. Occasionally the teacher, to better understand a pupil, will make use of one or more personal conferences. Such talks provide an opportunity to follow up leads derived from more general observation, to become better acquainted with the child, to fill in gaps with information not detected in earlier observation, to gain more complete information on attitudes and

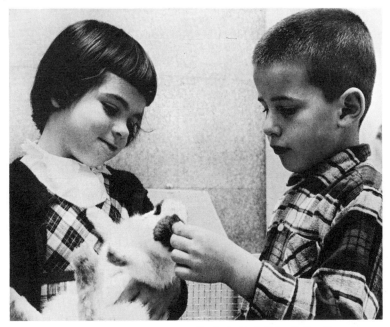

Frederic Burk School, San Francisco

Experience is something to think about, talk about, read about, and write about.

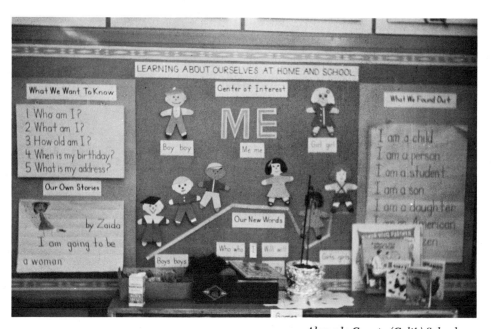

Alameda County (Calif.) Schools

In first grade the children become acquainted with the school and introduce themselves. Words about themselves are highly interesting.

Alameda County (Calif.) Schools

A good beginning in the reading process is to be able to
find the same sentence in another place, and to know what
it says.

Sonoma County (Calif.) School

Word form is associated with word meaning

Children discuss objects that interest them, and classify
them by initial consonant sound.

These are the letters that make the common sound in these words

All about Indians

Our Trip
What shall we look for at
the wholesale market?
1 The kinds of fruit
2 The kinds of vegetables.
3 How the produce is arranged
4 How the trucks are

Preparing to visit a market

These fourth graders find their science textbooks easier to understand after they have prepared for a topic by finding and identifying the concept involved. See the different kinds of leaves and cones in the display behind the teacher.

Story Time

Frederic Burk School, San Francisco

Two students in the sixth grade compare
the map in the atlas with the representation on the globe

Whittier School, Phoenix, Ariz.

Making selections for use in a group project

interests, and to build for herself a place of confidence in the child's mind as his or her friend. The additional information that can be gained in personal conferences is particularly important for guidance in dealing with the shy, retiring child, with the over-acting, frustrated child, or with any other child in difficulty. Occasionally the teacher may co-operate with specialists such as a physician, a social worker, or a psychologist, in a case study. A case study consists of a more elaborate investigation of strengths and weaknesses involved in a child's adjustment to the school and other situations. Ordinarily case studies are made by specialists. The teacher can improve her guidance by using the recommendations derived from a case study of one of her pupils.

Use of questionnaires

A variety of questionnaires may be employed to evaluate attitudes, interests, and behavior patterns that are concerned with adjustment to the reading situation and with progress in reading. Certain standardized questionnaires or inventories are available. In general, however, the informal questionnaire made by the teacher herself provides a more useful source of information for guidance purposes. This is because such a brief teacher-made questionnaire can be specifically related to the very aspects of reading which are at the moment at the focus of the instructional program.

Kinds of information which may be obtained by use of questionnaires include the following: (*a*) data concerned with social and emotional adjustment, (*b*) attitudes toward the school, teacher, other children, reading, and books, (*c*) nature of leisure-time activities with likes and dislikes, (*d*) preferences for kinds of books and other reading material, (*e*) kind, variety, and amount of reading done, and (*f*) impressions obtained from and reactions to different kinds of reading.

These and a number of other aspects of attitudes, interests, and tastes related to reading may be measured by teacher-made questionnaires. Even though they are not standardized, they can provide a pattern of information of great value to the teacher. This may be employed for guidance in adjustment of instructional procedures and for obtaining evidences of desirable growth in reading interests and tastes.

Records

It is not safe for any teacher to depend entirely upon memory for co-ordinating and appraising the strengths and weaknesses of 30 to 40 individual children in her class. For this reason she should keep records, preferably of two kinds: anecdotal and cumulative.

When the significant aspects of informal observation are noted in anecdotal form, the result is called an anecdotal record. These notations deal with a particular child's behavior pattern. They describe some specific episode, or a reaction to a specific situation. For the most part such anecdotes are concerned with reading situations, or behavior related to reading. Although the anecdotes may later be employed in appraisal, they are written down merely as description of an incident. Examples: "Today for the first time Mary brought a book from home and shared it with the class;" "John is now making real progress in combining verbal context clues with phonetic analysis when he identifies new words;" "Nancy still refuses to try to sound out new words not readily identified by other clues." A series of these notes may provide an important supplement to other observations and measurements used in appraising growth in reading. In particular, they often aid the teacher is such evaluations as a child's adjustment to group work, to specific learnings (as to use of context clues), to reading before a group, or to the wide reading program.

When accumulated in usable form, certain data on a child constitute cumulative records. These data may consist of a teacher's records and observations, reports of conferences with parents, results of mental and educational measurement, anecdotal records, the report of a physical examination, information on interests, or records of special strengths and weaknesses. Summaries of growth trends in reading inserted periodically by the teacher are valuable. When kept up to date, material in the cumulative record may be co-ordinated to evaluate patterns of behavior related to reading and to appraise growth in reading. Especially important is the long-term pattern of behavior changes and reading development revealed by the cumulative records. It is in them that continuity of growth is readily discerned.

Teacher use of evaluation information

Various techniques of evaluation employed to obtain data for appraisal of growth in reading have been described. It is possible that no one technique is the most important. To some degree, different techniques of evaluation are used for different purposes. Nevertheless, appraisal of the total pattern of growth in reading is best achieved by co-ordinating the information from all sources of evaluation, for each technique of evaluation yields information which supplements what can be derived from other sources.

The important thing is not a test score, specific data from a questionnaire, or an anecdotal notation, but rather the integrated appraisal based upon these sets of information and the use to which that appraisal is put. The most important values of appraisal, as indicated at the beginning of this chapter, are ascertainment of the degree to which reading objectives are achieved, and provision of a sound basis for guidance in instruction to meet individual needs. There is little to be gained by collecting in a cumulative-record folder test scores, questionnaire results, and notes on observed behavior unless these data are used in appraisals. In addition to checking on progress toward achieving class objectives, the teacher is interested in the growth in individual patterns of reading, the strengths and weaknesses in these individual patterns, and in finding out whether her individualized teaching is producing progress toward elimination of the weaknesses.

Areas of Appraisal

Since achievement in one area of reading proficiency may not be closely related to achievement in other areas, it is not sufficient to measure one alone. To obtain a satisfactory picture of the pattern of reading development, there should be appraisal of growth in each of the main areas. The formal classification into areas and the terms employed to designate each of the main areas vary according to local usage. Here the classification of areas we employ is that used in the preceding sections of this book. They are: (1) vocabulary meanings, (2) word identification and recognition, (3) comprehension and interpretation, (4) comprehension abilities, (5) study skills, (6) speed of reading), (7) specialized reading skills in the content fields, (8) oral reading, (9) attitudes, and (10) interests and tastes.

Appraisal of Vocabulary Growth

It is ordinarily possible to appraise growth in understandable vocabulary and in word recognition simultaneously because these two most essential aspects of vocabulary building are intimately related. The techniques of their evaluation and measurement are similar. As in the case of word recognition, teacher observation, informal tests, and formal standardized tests all contribute to appraisal of vocabulary growth.

It seems probable, however, that teacher observation is not so satisfactory for evaluating vocabulary knowledge as for word-recognition skill. This means that in day-by-day evaluations, there is greater dependence upon informal vocabulary tests, whether made by the teacher or found in workbook exercises, in adjusting instruction in vocabulary to individual strengths and weaknesses.

The importance of vocabulary development is reflected in the heavy emphasis its measurement receives in formal standardized reading tests. Representative samples include: *Gates Reading Survey; Metropolitan Achievement Tests—Reading;* and the Bond-Clymer-Hoyt *Developmental Reading Tests.* In the *Durrell-Sullivan Reading Capacity and Achievement Tests* what they call meaning vocabulary is isolated from word recognition. The information accumulated from informal tests and observation should be supplemented periodically by results from such standardized tests as these. Tests for use in the primary grades ordinarily measure general vocabulary meanings. A few vocabulary tests in subject-matter fields are available at the higher grade levels.

Appraisal of Word Identification and Recognition

The appraisal of progress in the child's ability to employ word-identification clues and techniques is for all practical purposes a continuous affair. The day-by-day adjustment of instruction to individual needs is guided by such appraisal.

In these appraisals the teacher seeks information on progress in mastering use of the clues and techniques discussed in Chapter 8. These include evaluation of skill in using picture clues, word-form clues, verbal-context clues, various aspects of phonetic and structural analysis, and use of the dictionary. At any specific time the appraisal is usually confined to those aspects of the clues and techniques then being taught. For example, when syllabification is being taught, much of the appraisal is concerned with discovering how well the children are mastering syllabification as a tool for unlocking new words. At the same time the teacher will, of course, take note of other deficiences that she may run across. Periodically the appraisal will be concerned with evaluation of progress over a longer period of time.

Techniques employed for appraising word identification and recognition include teacher observation of pupil responses during class work, use of workbook tests and informal tests made by the teacher, or exercises appropriate for evaluating mastery of what has just been taught, and formalized standardized tests. The items in both the formal and informal tests consist largely of matching and multiple-choice questions. Matching a word with a picture is one common type of item. The picture may represent an object, a situation, or an action. Many exercises in workbook tasks may be profitably used in evaluating word-recognition skill. Both workbook materials and the suggestions in teacher's manuals which accompany series of basic readers provide examples of kinds of items and procedures to guide the teacher in constructing homemade tests for evaluating proficiency in identifying and recognizing words.

One of the best methods for evaluating efficiency in the use of word-recognition clues and techniques is the oral-reading test. Observation of procedures used in attacking new words, in the self-correction of errors, together with an analysis of the types of errors made by the child during his reading will provide a wealth of information on how well the child comes to grips with the text unaided. Data are readily obtained on the child's degree of proficiency in his use of context clues, work-form clues, phonetic analysis, and structural analysis. Most satisfactory results are obtained with such standardized tests as the *Gray Oral Reading Paragraph Test,* the *Gray Oral Reading Check Tests,* or the oral-reading section of the *Gates Reading Diagnostic Tests.* Informal oral-reading tests also may be used. Or much information useful for appraisal of word-recognition skill can be procured by observing oral reading of basic text materials which are somewhat more difficult than the child's general instructional reading level (see above). The observation and recording of errors for analysis should follow the procedure used in the standardized oral-reading tests.

The role played by development of a sight vocabulary is important throughout the grades. A good measure of word recognition for the sight vocabulary in the primary grades can be obtained by the *Dolch Basic Sight Word Test.* Many standardized reading tests include sections for measuring word recognition. These tests provide information on level of maturity in recognizing words. They should be employed in evaluation at appropriate intervals, not only to ascertain grade level in word recognition, but also to appraise amount of growth over a period of time. Three representative tests which measure word recognition are: *Manwiller Word Recognition Test, Gates Primary Reading Test,* and the Bond-Clymer-Hoyt *Developmental Reading Tests.*

Appraisal of Growth of Comprehension

Although all techniques of evaluation may be employed to appraise growth of comprehension, results from informal and formal tests are most useful. Some aspect of comprehension is measured in almost every standardized reading test, and in various tests, several aspects are measured. In addition to sentence and paragraph comprehension, other aspects of comprehension fall under such headings as "ability to understand directions," "comprehension of details," "larger meanings," "interpretations," and so on. As in other areas of reading, the formal standardized tests are most useful for appraisals of growth over an interval such as three months, a semester, or a school year. An accumulation of scores makes it a simple matter to trace growth in each of the comprehension skills measured. Relative proficiency in the different kinds of comprehension is revealed by reference to norms. Entering a child's measured reading abilities, including comprehension, in tabular or profile form is helpful and quickly indicates where needed acceleration might be secured by additional instruction.

The teacher, however, will need more frequent evaluation of progress in comprehension skills than she is likely to secure by the use of standardized tests. In order to adjust emphases in her instructional program, to move ahead at a satisfactory pace, and to adapt her instruction to individual needs, the teacher will have to carry on a more or less continuous evaluation of the degree to which the children are acquiring the comprehension skills. Although she depends somewhat on her observations, her evaluation will be obtained mainly by the use of informal homemade tests and workbook tests and exercises. This day-by-day evaluation will reveal how well the class is mastering the comprehension skills they are being taught, in addition to disclosing individual difficulties which require additional individualized guidance for their elimination.

This continuing appraisal process may be facilitated by a check list covering various aspects of the comprehension skills. The skills represented by the items on the check list can be rated as frequently as desired and the successive ratings consulted in making appraisals. Thus the standing of a child in the item "Understands relation between sentences in a paragraph" can be rated 1, 2, or 3 to indicate that the child is making less than adequate, average, or unusual progress in this aspect of a skill. The number and variety of the items to be rated, as well as frequency of rating, depend upon the teacher and the reading objectives she chooses to emphasize in her teaching.

The basic comprehension skills requiring appraisal are those discussed in Chapter 8, such as sentence and paragraph comprehension. A large variety of standardized tests measure one or more kinds of comprehension. Examples are the *Gates Advanced Primary Reading Test* and *Traxler Silent Reading Test*.

Appraisal of Comprehension Skills

Many kinds of techniques may be used to appraise skill in comprehension. A large number of standardized tests aim to do this. The list of such tests in the Appendix will reveal tests to measure reading to predict outcome, reading to get the general idea, reading to follow directions, reading to note details, reading to evaluate, reading to interpret, etc. Such tests should be employed for periodic appraisals. Their use will enable the teacher not only to ascertain a child's proficiency in a particular form of comprehension at any given time but also to follow his growth in each of these abilities over several terms and years. This requires, of course, that the scores on the tests be entered in a cumulative record and kept in the child's folder. When a pupil's comprehension abilities are posted on a profile (see below), the teacher can in a glance identify and evaluate individual needs. And by examining the profiles of members of her class she can see what the class as a whole needs, i.e., areas where the whole class tends to be deficient. All this provides the teacher with information she needs to plan and, if necessary, modify her instructional program.

In addition to these more formal appraisals the teacher should make less formal day-to-day or week-to-week appraisals of growth in the comprehension abilities. She needs to discover, as instruction progresses, which abilities the child needs further experience in to prepare him for what is coming next. The teacher will gain some information along this line by examining the workbook exercises completed by each child, as well as from the results of the tests she makes herself and her own general observations (also see Chapter 9).

Appraisal of Study Skills

Study skills, such as those discussed in Chapter 9, are reading skills and should be appraised. All the techniques discussed above are useful on occasion for this evaluation. In general, however, observation by the teacher and the informal tests she constructs tend to be most useful and, therefore, the most used, for this kind of appraisal. In the primary grades only observation and informal testing is possible at present since the standardized tests of study skills have been worked out for use in the higher grades only. As with other areas of reading, there should be fairly continuous evaluation of growth in study skills through use of informal observation and teacher-made tests as well as periodic evaluation (in upper grades) by means of standardized tests where the latter are available.

Appraisal of study skills through informal observation occurs at all grade levels. Observation of day-by-day performance indicates the quality and the promptness of the choices which the child makes in using the table of contents or the index in books, and how skillfully he adjusts to library usage when he wants to find material pertinent to his interests or to select books and subject matter relevant to a specific topic.

In addition to observation the teacher may present a practical test situation which requires one of the specific study skills, and check the proficiency with which the child adjusts to the situation. Use of a table of contents, an index, or selection of pertinent references for use in a study unit may serve this end.

As the child progresses beyond the primary grades, evaluation of study skills can become more specific. Speed and accuracy may be checked as he uses indexes, library card catalogs, the dictionary, or an encyclopedia. It is also possible to note a child's proficiency in finding a specific fact in a textbook or a reference book, or his skill in selecting and evaluating pertinent information.

Much workbook material is designed to develop one or another specific study skill. The exercises may be concerned with use of an index, or a dictionary, or with the selection of relevant information. When these exercises are co-ordinated with class instruction, checking of day-by-day performance reveals the degree of progress in use of the particular skill. Similar exercises or tests may be constructed by the teacher. In the upper grades, the practical test situations presented to the pupils can become more complex. Development of skill in reading tabular material, graphs, charts, and maps may be evaluated day by day through observation, teacher-made tests, and practical situations.

A few standardized tests are available for evaluating grade standing or relative ability in several, but not in all, of the basic study skills. This type of evaluation, besides being highly objective, is desirable for periodic measurement of progress and for appraisal of individual and class performance in relation to norms and objectives. Samples of standardized tests which include measures of study skills are: *Iowa Silent Reading Test; Iowa Every-Pupil Tests of Basic Skills, Test B; SRA Reading Record.*

As with other areas of reading, appraisal of study skills is most useful for teacher guidance. Strengths and weaknesses of pupils are discovered and the indicated adjustments are made by means of group instruction or more highly individualized teaching.

Appraisal of Specialized Reading Skills

Evaluation of the specialized reading skills required for successful reading of material in the content fields must be made largely by observation and other informal techniques, since few tests are available for measuring these skills. The aspects of reading in a content field that are ordinarily measured in standardized tests are vocabulary knowledge, comprehension, and interpretation.

Observation of daily performance, use of teacher-made tests on acquisition of skill and understanding, and standardized achievement tests will reveal whether a child is making satisfactory progress in arithmetic, in geography, or in some other content subject. Lack of satisfactory progress in a content subject may be due to deficiency in the special reading skills required. In seeking out the cause of the difficulty, the teacher should check the pupil's ability to read the subject-matter material. It is understood that the teacher will also keep an eye on other factors such as motivation or clarity of purpose.

Reading difficulty in a subject-matter field may merely reflect inadequacies in the mastery and use of the fundamental and specialized reading skills, abilities, and procedures such as word-recognition techniques, general vocabulary knowledge, comprehension skills, or study skills. If these skills, abilities, and procedures have been satisfactorily developed in general reading, the difficulty in the special subject matter is more likely to be due to either one or two other factors. The pupil may be deficient in the ability to adjust these skills, abilities, and procedures to the specific requirements and purposes of the particular subject matter. Or he may lack the necessary meaningful technical vocabulary and related concepts. The requirements of a technical vocabulary and some of the difficulties involved in developing such a vocabulary have been considered in Chapter 12. Observation of pupil responses in classwork, in teacher-made tests, in workbook exercises, supplemented if necessary by personal conferences, will reveal the degree of proficiency in technical vocabulary and in the handling of related concepts. If standardized tests of technical vocabulary knowledge are available, they may be employed for periodic checking to ascertain grade standing of the pupils.

The adjustments required for effective reading in the content fields vary greatly. The child who attempts to read science or mathematics as rapidly as he reads stories, will get into trouble. The former require slow analytical reading. The pupil's knowledge of how and when to apply skills to satisfy the requirements of the materials and to achieve the purpose of a particular reading situation must be noted by the teacher. Appraisals should be frequent enough to detect deficiencies before they become serious.

Both the teaching of reading and the evaluation of reading progress in the content fields tends to be far from satisfactory. This is due to the lack of a thorough knowledge of teaching and measuring techniques appropriate to this area. For the present the teacher must depend largely upon her own efforts and ingenuity in devising and using informal techniques of appraisal.

Appraisal of Speed of Reading

As noted in Chapter 11, the rate at which printed words can be identified can have little significance unless identification is accompanied by comprehension. The term *rate or speed of reading* as used in this book signifies, therefore, *rate or speed of comprehension*. Factors which influence rate include clarity of comprehension, difficulty of the material, and reading purpose. Flexibility in adjusting rate of reading to the material and the purpose for which it is read is the mark of proficient reading. It should be emphasized that reading at a rate unduly slow for any specific kind of material is a handicap.

The teacher's task in evaluating speed of reading is threefold: She must appraise whether (1) the rate is appropriate for the material and the purpose, (2) reading in a particular situation is so slow that it represents dawdling, and (3) the pupil has sufficient flexibility in adjusting his speed to fit the requirements of the material and the purpose of the moment. In other words, it is not enough not to dawdle; the pupil must be able to read rapidly when that is appropriate, and slowly and carefully when the latter is called for.

Speed of reading one kind of material cannot be counted on to be a good indicator of speed in another kind. The chances are not great, for example, that the pupil who is fastest in reading a story is fastest in reading geography or science; or that the one who is next to fastest in one is also next to fastest in another, and so on. To ascertain speed of reading in content material such as history, science, or geography, it is necessary to measure speed while reading material in the specific field in which one is at the moment interested. In other words, rate of reading relatively easy material like that measured in most standardized "speed of reading" tests for elementary school students is not a good indicator of rate of reading other kinds of material. Standardized reading tests, therefore, are of relatively little use to the teacher in appraising speed of comprehension in reading.

The teacher must depend for the most part upon teacher-made or teacher-selected tests for evaluating speed of reading. It is a relatively simple task to pick out representative passages from different kinds of material to be read for one specific purpose or another. The test is timed and the number of words read per minute is obtained. A sample of three to five minutes in length is desirable. The pupil should clearly understand the comprehension requirements before starting on the test and his reading should be checked for comprehension. Testing should be frequent enough to provide guidance for instructional procedures.

When a pupil is reading too rapidly or too slowly for the requirements of a specific material, or for a particular purpose, instructional procedures to correct the situation should be instituted. One of these is to inform the child of his scores (number of words read per three minutes) on successive tests, a procedure which usually motivates children to read faster. To slow reading down to a pace which is proper for the requirements of the material or for a particular purpose, the teacher can insist upon a high level of comprehension. At the same time she takes pains to point out to the pupils that such a level of comprehension can best be achieved by reading more carefully and more slowly.

Ordinarily, training at the elementary-school level to increase *speed of reading as such* probably is not justified. When a child reads at a rate considerably less than optimum for a given material and a particular purpose, it is best to seek the causes of the excessively slow reading. The best way to teach a child to read at an appropriate rate is to furnish him with the concepts and techniques by which he can fully understand what is to be read. In general, the emphasis should be upon developing clear comprehension in reading. When this is achieved, and a child reads a given material with the accuracy and understanding demanded by the purpose, in most instances the rate of reading will reach a satisfactory adjustment more or less automatically. In summary, the emphasis ordinarily should be upon achieving accuracy and understanding, while adjustment of rate is allowed to take care of itself.

Appraisal of Oral Reading

A large proportion of high school students give a mediocre performance, or worse, when they attempt to read orally. This may be due largely to their failure to enjoy the benefits of periodic appraisal and guidance in this kind of ability during the elementary school years. The desirability of developing skill in oral reading has been stressed at several places in this book (see Chapter 10). The guidance necessary in adjusting instruction to individual needs in developing oral reading is possible only if there is frequent appraisal.

The use of standardized oral-reading tests to locate difficulties in word recognition have been touched on above. Scores on these tests do not show up certain factors of great importance in reading aloud to an audience. The teacher must depend mainly upon informal observation and testing situations which she devises herself for evaluating skill in oral reading as a form of communication. The day-by-day observation of performance will provide much useful information. This should be supplemented by information derived from more systematic observation and rating of performance while reading selected passages aloud. These passages should consist of relatively easy material and should contain considerable conversation, as in stories. For the most part evaluation should be made upon the reading of materials which the child has prepared for the oral presentation.

In oral reading before an audience the aspects which need to be observed and rated in appraisal of proficiency vary somewhat. The following list may be considered representative but not inclusive: accuracy of word recognition, enunciation, phrasing, volume or loudness, posture, expression, fluency, tension, rate, poise or confidence, voice quality, and rhythm or timing.

To note progress in proficiency in oral reading, it is desirable to record the results of periodic ratings. Anecdotal records derived from daily observation can provide valuable supplementary data for the appraisal. For details see Chapter 10.

Appraisal of Attitudes

The initiation and development of attitudes which will promote growth in reading constitute an important aspect of training in reading. Since the growth of these attitudes is gradual, they are of concern to teachers at all grade levels. In fact, guidance for developing desirable attitudes must be based largely upon information derived from more or less continuous evaluation throughout the grades. This evaluation will be concerned with all the attitudes referred to at different places in this book. The list includes attitudes towards the school, books, the teacher, the reading situation, and toward class activities. Various habits developed in learning to read, such as thoroughness in work-type reading, also must be considered.

The teacher, in evaluating attitudes, must depend largely upon day-by-day observations supplemented by occasional anecdotal records. In this way she can detect the presence or the bare beginning of undesirable attitudes and, repeating the process later, appraise the stages of development of desirable attitudes. At the same time, if necessary, steps can be taken to counteract or modify the undesirable attitudes. And where progress in developing desirable habitual attitudes seems unduly slow, instructional procedures can be modified to speed up progress. The appraisals will frequently reveal, naturally, that the rate of development is entirely satisfactory in the case of some attitudes. Observations for these appraisals may take place during regular class work or during a special assignment devised especially to get clear light on an attitude or group of attitudes which are judged significant. For instance, an assignment may be devised to reveal a pupil's thoroughness in work-type reading, or his degree of independence in working on a unit project.

Appraisal of Reading Interests and Tastes

The nature of interests and tastes in reading and their interrelationships were discussed in Chapter 14. Evaluation of interests and tastes is neither simple nor easy. Nevertheless, evaluations are necessary if pupils are to receive teacher guidance in broadening interests and in developing more satisfactory tastes. The first step in any such program is to ascertain the present breadth and intensity of interests and the level of tastes. Subsequent appraisals will reveal the degree and quality of changes which may occur as a result of further experience and guidance.

Evaluation of interests and tastes is necessarily informal. The teacher employs day-by-day observation, individual conferences, anecdotal records, and teacher-constructed check lists of activities and preferences. Useful systematic inventories or check lists of preferred activities and interests have been organized by Hildreth (130), Witty and Kopel (284), and by Witty (282). Teacher-constucted inventories should provide for the listing of work and play activities, in addition to reading activities and preferences.

Much information can be obtained from reading lists kept by the child. These records may include what the child reads over a period of time, what books he owns, what stories he recommends to others for reading, or what books he takes from the library. Some evaluation is possible through observation of children's choices during free reading periods either in the school room or in the library.

Analysis of the data derived from these check lists and the various aspects of observation noted above will yield considerable information on interests and tastes in reading. Breadth of interests will be indicated by the varieties of activites and of reading carried out. Strength of an interest pattern is revealed by the time and effort expended upon a given type of activity or reading material. Although these appraisals of breadth and strength of interests are largely subjective, they are based to some degree upon quantitative data, for example, number of books owned or read or withdrawn from the library, or time devoted to certain kinds of material. Appraisal of reading taste, however, is entirely subjective. Standards or criteria of taste or quality of reading are themselves established by subjective estimates. How well a pupil measures up to these standards also involves subjective appraisal. Nevertheless, the teacher's evaluation of pupil's reading interests and tastes will aid guidance in the instructional program. Also see Chapter 14.

Keeping Records

At various places in this book emphasis has been placed upon the keeping of records to facilitate guidance in teaching reading. A picture of a pupil's pattern of reading abilities and skills is obtained more readily when the results of tests, observation, check lists, and the like are organized in a record form. A sample form (Figure 7) is given on the following pages. Each teacher will probably wish to organize a somewhat different outline form to meet her specific needs and then duplicate it so as to have a copy for each pupil in her class. Data and evaluations are entered at appropriate places. Under "Standardized Reading Tests" any desired number of oral or silent reading tests may be entered with results. In Section II, brief notation can be made of initial and subsequent evaluations. In Section III, brief summary statements derived from informal observations, teacher-made tests, check lists, and so on may be entered from time to time. Under each part of Section III, subheadings may be used. Observations on general trends, special difficulties, and so on can be made on the back of the record form or on additional sheets.

It is sometimes helpful in evaluations to enter results of standardized tests in a profile. Any teacher can construct a profile outline to fit the needs of individual pupils in her class. A sample (Figure 8) is shown following the outline for the reading evaluation record. Dots or small crosses are entered in appropriate columns according to the pupil's actual school grade level, grade derived from chronological age (CA), grade derived from mental age (MA), and grade equivalents of the test scores. Successive points across the outline are then connected by lines. Inspection of the resulting profile will reveal trends which should aid evaluation of proficiency and appraisal of growth in reading.

In constructing the outline for the profile, note that provision can be made for two (or more, if desired) tests in each area such as vocabulary or comprehension. Perhaps the teacher will have some test scores other than reading which she would like to show on the profile. These may be entered under "Others." The particular tests and the time at which they are given are identified below the outline as indicated.

The systematic keeping of records and their use for guidance purposes

Pupils Reading Evaluation Record Form

Teacher_____

School_____

Name_____ Grade_____ Date of Birth_____

Record begun on (date)_____ at age_____

Mental Test	MA	CA	IQ	Date
_____	_____	_____	_____	_____
_____	_____	_____	_____	_____

I. *Standardized Reading Tests*

Test	Date Given	Score	Grade Equivalent
1._____	_____	_____	_____
2._____	_____	_____	_____

II. *Appraisal Based Upon Standardized Test Results*

Initial Evaluation:_____

_____

Subsequent Evaluations:_____

_____

III. *Informal Evaluations*

Word Recognition:

Vocabulary Development:

Comprehension:

Rate of Reading:

Study Skills:

Specialized Reading Skills:

Oral Reading:

Attitudes:

Interests and Tastes:

Additional Related Information:

Figure 7.

pay good dividends in promoting effective teaching. Some system for accu-mulating records in individual files is helpful.

Selection of Standardized Tests

As already noted, standardized tests, when well constructed, yield fairly accurate and reliable measures of various aspects of reading such as vocab-ulary and comprehension. They are employed to evaluate relative reading proficiency (that is, scores in grade equivalents) at periodic intervals such

Profile for Reading Achievement

(Name of Pupil)

Grade Level	Actual Grade	CA: Grade	MA: Grade	Grade Equivalent: Reading Test Scores							
				Vocabulary*		Compre-hension		Special Skills		Others	
				Test 1	Test 2	Test 1	Test 2	Test 1	Test 2	Test 1	Test 2
9.0+											
8.5											
8.0											
7.5											
7.0											
6.5											
6.0											
5.5											
5.0											
4.5											
4.0											
3.5											
3.0—											

*Vocabulary: Test 1——————————————————Date——————————

Test 2——————————————————Date——————————

Comprehension: Test 1——————————————————Date——————————

Figure 8.

as at the beginning and end of semesters or school years. While specific learnings are appraised daily by informal evaluations, the broader aspects of progress in reading are evaluated by means of standardized tests.

A well-organized testing program is an essential part of reading instruction. Careful consideration should be given, therefore, to the selection of standardized tests so that a maximum amount of information may be obtained by their use. The over-all school program of reading instruction should be considered. This means a co-ordination of the testing program from grade to grade. Tests should be selected accordingly. Other factors to consider in selecting tests: (a) aspects of reading measured by a test; (b) grade range in reading ability covered by a test to insure its appropriateness for the range of abilities in a given grade; (c) cost; (d) testing time; (e) availability of norms. Grade equivalents of scores are very useful.

In addition to what may be found in catalogs, descriptions and evaluation of reading tests are given by Traxler (261) and by Buros (36).

Summary

Appraisal of growth in reading is required to determine how well reading objectives are achieved and to provide the teacher with information to guide her in organizing her instructional program so as to meet pupil needs. The more formal appraisal should be repeated periodically, while less formal appraisal goes on continuously. Periodic appraisal measures progress toward achieving instructional goals, while day-by-day appraisal provides information for adjusting teaching to individual needs. Several techniques are employed to obtain the information needed for appraisal. The more important of these are standardized tests, informal tests, teacher observation, questionnaires, and records of various kinds. Appraisal of the total pattern of growth in reading is best achieved by co-ordinating the information from all these sources.

To adjust instruction to the individual needs of pupils in her class, the teacher must appraise the reading proficiency of each child in the following areas: vocabulary meanings, word identification and recognition, comprehension and interpretation, comprehension abilities, study skills, speed of reading, specialized reading skills, oral reading, attitudes toward reading, interests and tastes in reading. Information for the appraisals is obtained by means of teacher observations and ratings, informal tests and check exercises, and standardized tests. Appraisal is facilitated by organizing the data from various sources on record forms and in profiles.

Standardized tests should be selected so that a maximum amount of information can be obtained from their use. The over-all school reading program should be integrated with a co-ordinated testing program from grade to grade. Other information needed to facilitate the selection of suitable tests includes knowledge of just which aspects of reading are measured by a test, the grade range in reading ability it covers, what the test costs, testing time, and availability of norms.

Vocabulary

Do you know the meaning of these terms?

technique of appraisal	day-by-day evaluation
standardized test	basic comprehension skills
survey test	profile
diagnostic test	study skills
informal tests	specialized reading skills
questionnaire	test norms
anecdotal	test reliability
cumulative record	test validity

Activities for Students

Reading: In the Robinson reference listed below, read the sections on reading in the content areas. Make an outline of the material for use in your future teaching.

Creative: Work out in detail an informal test to check progress in mastering word-analysis techniques in a third-grade class.

Selected References

AUSTIN, Mary C., BUSH, Clifford L., and HUEBNER, Mildred H., *Reading evaluation*. New York: The Ronald Press Company, 1961.

BOND, Guy L., and WAGNER, Eva B., *Teaching the child to read*, 3rd ed. New York: The Macmillan Company, 1960, Chap. 16.

BRUECKNER, Leo J., and BOND, Guy L., *Diagnosis and treatment of learning difficulties*. New York: Appleton-Century-Crofts, Inc., 1955, Chaps. 4, 6.

GATES, Arthur I., *The improvement of reading*, 3rd ed. New York: The Macmillan Company, 1947, Chap. 3.

GRAY, Lillian, and REESE, Dora, *Teaching children to read*, 2nd ed. New York: The Ronald Press Company, 1957, Chap. 16.

HARRIS, Albert J., *How to increase reading ability*, 4th ed. New York: Longmans, Green and Company, 1961, Chaps. 7, 8.

NOLL, V. H., *Introduction to educational measurement*. Boston: Houghton Mifflin Company, 1957, Chaps. 6, 7, 8, 14.

ROBINSON, Helen M. (ed.), *Evaluation of reading*. Supplementary Educational Monograph No. 88. Chicago: University of Chicago Press, 1958.

RUSSELL, David H., *Children learn to read*, 2nd ed. Boston: Ginn and Company, 1961, Chap. 16.

TRIGGS, Frances O., *Reading*. Mountain Home, N.C.: The Committee on Diagnostic Reading Tests, Inc., 1960, Chaps. 7, 9, 11, 13, 14.

PART III

Recommended Practices in Reading Instruction

Parts I and II of this book have introduced you to the major research findings affecting the various aspects of the teaching of reading. They have also attempted to reflect the best thinking of leaders in the field in areas which are still unsettled or unexplored.

You need now, however, to put this information to work. What does it mean in the kindergarten, in the first grade, in the sixth or eighth? Of course, there are curriculum guides in your city or county which itemize for you the many facets of the instructional program, telling you exactly what to teach. Whole books have been written on the organization of the school day and the classroom. Other books have been written entirely about a single level of instruction. Teachers' manuals have shown in detail what the teacher should do to develop language power and reading skills.

It is not the intention of the authors to duplicate the offering in these excellent references. We wish rather to try to bridge the gap between what a teacher knows in theory and what she does in practice, to suggest to her, taking only samples of her total responsibility, approaches which are sound and practical. Our aim is to install a better transmission system.

You can visit a school for a day and see for yourself what an entire day in it is like—in summer school if not during the regular school year. You can keep a check list of all the skills you must develop. These are valuable things to do. But they are no insurance policy for the children you teach.

The insurance policy rests somewhere in the marrow of a teacher who has so saturated herself with practical application of sound theory that she does not even *think* wrong when she plans her work with the children. The best practice seems natural to her. This is what we hope will happen to you.

17

The Organization and Administration of the Reading Program

A process as complex as reading and an organism as complex as a child cannot be handled by a simple formula. Sort children into grades by age, and you find in one grade a range of abilities too extensive to treat simply. Put them into classes according to mental age, and again you find the reading levels and needs varying widely. Organize classes according to reading level, and, after a few weeks, children whose levels seemed initially the same are now surprisingly different; meanwhile their needs at any given level are widely diverse.

Interclass Grouping

But perhaps you persist in the belief that some one kind of administrative adjustment will work. You say, "All right. I shall have classes heterogeneous except for age, then a special reading period. Each day during that period, all children who read at a given level will go to one teacher who teaches that level. Then if, during the year, some children progress more rapidly than others, the teacher can form more groups within her class; but at least she won't be teaching at four levels at the beginning of the year and fourteen at the end."

So you try this system. And what happens? At the beginning and end of the year, you test the children by a survey reading test. Their reading growth may be the same as, or may exceed, what they would normally have achieved. The parents, feeling that the school has been striving boldly to improve the reading program, favor the new system. Children, spurred by parent interest and new teacher zeal, put more effort into their work. The teachers, even though they may be working just as hard as before, feel less frustrated.

If you take parent and teacher opinion, children's enthusiasm, and survey-test results as your criteria of success, you may conclude that the system is worth continuing. Besides, having instigated it, you have a proprietary interest in your brain-child and would be loath to back down now. Yet you have a nagging conscience which asks, "Why haven't many authorities in reading and child development promoted this long and enthusiastically? What is holding them back?"

Evaluation

What is holding them back? For one thing, they know that reading growth can occur outside the reading period as well as within it. Reading growth takes place when a child writes or tells a story like the one he has read, draws a picture or develops a dramatic interpretation of the story, makes up a song or rhythm to go with a little rhyme in the story, tape-records an interview with the supposed author about his reasons for describing or organizing the content as he did. How can the teacher who has the child for the rest of the day be aware of these possible relationships and make the most of them?

Furthermore, the child may need certain kinds of skill development, such as getting the main idea. His need may not be primarily to get the main idea during reading, but to get the main idea at all. He could profit by having to summarize or entitle situations that occur during the school day. If his teacher knew his need, she could throw main-idea tasks his way. But she doesn't know this because she isn't his reading teacher. Besides, she has 25 to 45 reading problems of her own during the interclass grouping period.

For what other reasons do some reading authorities "hold back" in giving their blessing to a special reading teacher plan? In studies which have been made of the plan (2, 89, 215), they suspect that teachers have been doing a better job of teaching reading than they previously did, and that better teaching rather than the administrative design effected the reading improvement. Perhaps, too, in most of the studies the classes were not really homogeneous. Children grouped together because of similar *total* scores on a survey test of reading are not necessarily reading at the same *level* (175). If the classes in the studies were grouped according to total scores, the experiment involved simply an exchange of rooms and teachers rather than a true reduction of heterogeneity.

It is suspected, also, that if parents and teachers had been as well briefed on the virtues of the previous system as they had been on the new one, they might have been less enthusiastic about making a change.

In addition to these considerations there is doubt that a survey-test score reflects truly the children's grasp of the many facets of the reading process (1). Skillful driving of a car under simple road conditions does not prove the driver's skill under challenging or hazardous conditions. Careful, thorough teaching may not be able to show itself as superior to a superficial job of teaching if the testing instrument hits only the high spots. Also, the results at the end of just a year do not prove the long-term benefits or penalties of the administrative design.

For these reasons, while interclass grouping has its enthusiastic advocates, many students of reading development doubt that its adoption will usher in the millennium.

Team Teaching

Another design (7, 205), again a bold administrative stroke, has attracted considerable interest lately. In it, the first step (though not necessarily) is to tear down the wall separating two classrooms. The second is to have two teachers man the two classes as one class in the now larger room. Instead of two teachers teaching several children on the same level in different rooms, one teacher instructs all the children of that level, thus releasing the second teacher to deal with another group. In theory, twice the number of groups may be thus served. The teachers can pursue their reading goals with the children all day in various situations. The particular strengths of each teacher may be utilized. In some cases, a more skillful teacher can be training a less skillful one. Class control is supposedly more effective. The teachers can make better judgments about the children because they can confer with each other on problems.

A disadvantage is that, although there are more adults to handle the children, there are more children to handle the adults. Also, the commonness of children's needs may not be dealt with efficiently unless the teachers spend professional time conferring with each other. This usually takes longer than talking to oneself. More records have to be kept to support this communication. And the two teachers must be very congenial to endure each other's housekeeping and continuous presence.

The truth is that any one administrative design creates some kind of trouble as well as some kind of advantage. If you adopt one design, you must be ready to meet and counteract its peculiar disadvantages. It is through failure to establish safeguards that administrative designs for teaching reading break down.

The Self-Contained Classroom

Many administrators prefer to have one teacher know well the needs and abilities of 25 to 45 children and let her have all day to work on them. If more than one makes the broth, someone may forget to put in the meat. What is the trouble with having one teacher teach all children of a certain age and grade level? Mainly, that differences in reading level and reading need are too numerous for any one person to meet. The better a teacher is, the more she is aware of these differences, the more she feels conscience-stricken that she cannot accommodate all of them by direct teaching, and the more she wishes for a one-way ticket to outer space. Having gone around in circles and come down to Earth with a thud on many occasions, she feels well qualified as an astronaut.

The administrative program

Are there administrative ways of coping with this challenge? A sound administrative approach will include several steps:

1. The level of each child should be determined at the first of the school year. This can be done by:

    a. Individual oral testing on passages from successively harder selections from pre-primer, primer, first reader, etc. (229).

    b. Administering a silent-reading test containing passages of increasing difficulty. The teacher will note the hardest passage the child seems able to comprehend with few errors, compare it with the reader-series books, and so determine the book level at which the child can probably learn with the teacher's aid.

    c. Noting the reader level just completed, according to the cumulative record or previous teacher. (See Reading Record, San Francisco Unified School District.) Of course, many things can happen during the summer interval to make this an unreliable index of proper instructional level.

    d. Ascertaining the free book choices of the child. Most of his selections will ordinarily be somewhat easier than the level at which it would be reasonable to expect him to learn. However, when it comes to his hobby or special interest, a child may be able to read material somewhat more difficult than he will accept in other areas.

2. A frequency distribution of the class should be made to show how the children group themselves at the various levels. In a small class of 19 sixth graders of relatively high ability, a teacher found the following groupings:

> Pupils A, B, C, D, E, F, G, J, M—Sixth-Reader Level
> Pupils H, I, K, L, N, O, P   —Fifth-Reader Level
> Pupils R, S   —Third-Reader Level
> Pupil Q   —Second-Reader Level

    And, by the way, the pupils had been listed from A to S according to total score on the reading test. Notice that the total score did not in every case reflect the true level of the child. By total score, H, I, K, and L would have been put into a reader too hard for them; and so would Q. (See Chapter 16 on Appraisal.)

3. A decision should be made on a *feasible* plan of grouping for instruction. By "feasible" is meant that the children put into any one group can learn on that level, and that the teacher does not divide the class into so many levels that she cannot meet with any one group long enough to teach it.

DIRECTIONS TO TEACHERS:
1. Use one copy of the record for each child.
2. As a child completes each reader, record the date of completion in the column next to the list of readers (i.e. 10/61). If partially completed indicate the last page the child has read.
3. Record unlisted books in the blank columns on the back.
4. Keep the record in the child's cumulative folder.

READING RECORD
SAN FRANCISCO UNIFIED SCHOOL DISTRICT

PUPIL'S NAME: _____
　　　　　　　 LAST　　　　　　FIRST

SCHOOL: _____
　　　　　(PENCIL)

READER LEVEL	STATE ADOPTIONS (BASIC)			STATE ADOPTIONS (SUPPLEMENTARY) (effective September 1961)					
	(effective September 1961)		(until September 1961)	AMERICAN BOOK	GINN	L. W. SINGER	CHARLES MERRILL	ROW, PETERSON	
	GINN	ALLYN & BACON	LYONS & CARNAHAN						
Readiness	FUN WITH TOM & BETTY	PICTURE STORIES	STORIES IN PICTURES						
PRE-PRIMER	MY LITTLE RED Story Book; MY LITTLE GREEN Story Book; MY LITTLE BLUE Story Book	AT HOME HERE & NEAR HERE & AWAY	THREE OF US PLAY WITH US FUN WITH US		COME WITH US				
PRIMER	THE LITTLE WHITE HOUSE	OUR SCHOOL	MANY SURPRISES		UNDER THE APPLE TREE	STORY WAGON			
FIRST READER	ON CHERRY STREET	OUR TOWN	HAPPY TIMES		OPEN THE GATE	STORY TIME		I KNOW A STORY	
SECOND READER I	WE ARE NEIGHBORS	FIELDS AND FENCES	DOWN OUR WAY			STORY TRAIN		IT HAPPENED ONE DAY	
SECOND READER II	AROUND THE CORNER	TOWN AND COUNTRY	JUST FOR FUN						
THIRD READER I	FINDING NEW NEIGHBORS	MAGIC WINDOWS	STORIES FROM EVERYWHERE			STORY CARNIVAL	TREAT SHOP	AFTER THE SUN SETS	
THIRD READER II	FRIENDS FAR AND NEAR	STORY CARAVAN	ONCE UPON A STORY TIME						
FOURTH READER	ROADS TO EVERYWHERE	BELIEVE AND MAKE BELIEVE	MEETING NEW FRIENDS	PATHS TO FOLLOW		ALONG THE SUNSHINE TRAIL	MAGIC CARPET		
FIFTH READER	TRAILS TO TREASURE	FINDING THE WAY	DAYS OF ADVENTURE	FRONTIERS TO EXPLORE		ACROSS THE BLUE BRIDGE	ENCHANTED ISLES		
SIXTH READER	WINGS TO ADVENTURE	ARRIVALS AND DEPARTURES	WINSTON MOVING AHEAD	WIDENING HORIZONS		ABOARD THE STORY ROCKET	ADVENTURE LANDS		
SEVENTH READER									
EIGHTH READER									

READER LEVEL	DISTRICT SUPPLEMENTARY					ADDITIONAL BOOKS				
	AMERICAN BOOK	HOUGHTON-MIFFLIN	ROW, PETERSON	SCOTT, FORESMAN	READER'S DIGEST (Skill Builders)					
Readiness	THE ABC READY! GO! ABC BIG BOOK	GETTING READY		New BEFORE WE READ WE READ PICTURES WE READ MORE PICTURES						
PRE-PRIMER	THE ABC ON OUR WAY THE ABC TIME TO PLAY THE ABC ALL IN A DAY	TIP TIP AND MITTEN THE BIG SHOW BIG BOOK		New WE LOOK & SEE New WE WORK AND PLAY New WE COME & GO						
PRIMER	THE ABC UP THE STREET AND DOWN	JACK AND JANET		GUESS WHO New FUN WITH DICK AND JANE						
FIRST READER	THE ABC AROUND GREEN HILLS	UP AND AWAY		New OUR NEW FRIENDS						
SECOND READER I	THE ABC DOWN SING-ING RIVER	COME ALONG		New FRIENDS & NEIGHBORS						
SECOND READER II	THE ABC OVER A CITY BRIDGE	ON WE GO		New MORE FRIENDS & NEIGHBORS						
THIRD READER I	THE ABC BEYOND TREASURE VALLEY	LOOKING AHEAD		New STREETS & ROADS	PART I PART II PART III					
THIRD READER II	THE ABC ALONG FRIENDLY ROADS	CLIMBING HIGHER		New MORE STREETS & ROADS						
FOURTH READER	THE ABC AMERICAN ADVENTURES	HIGH ROADS	IT MUST BE MAGIC	New TIMES & PLACES MORE TIMES & PLACES	PART I PART II PART III					
FIFTH READER	THE ABC ADVENTURES HERE AND THERE	SKY LINES	THEY WERE BRAVE AND BOLD	New DAYS & DEEDS MORE DAYS & DEEDS	PART I PART II PART III					
SIXTH READER	THE ABC ADVENTURES NOW & THEN	BRIGHT PEAKS	THESE ARE THE TALES THEY TELL	New People & Progress More People & Progress	PART I PART II PART III					
SEVENTH READER										
EIGHTH READER										

Figure 9. (Courtesy of the San Francisco Unified School District.)

One point needs to be understood clearly: The sequence of reading instruction consists of two things: repeating old learnings on new material, and introducing new learnings at each book level within a series of readers.

For instance, at third-reader level, the children may review long and short vowel sounds (second-reader learning), using the new words they are learning, and may learn for the first time how to divide a word into syllabic units. Both the review and the new learning utilize relatively easy words.

The pupil can learn about dividing words into syllables by using words as easy as *return* or as unusual as *abstruse*. He can analyze the structure of a paragraph whether it is a relatively short, simple one made up of easy words and sentences, or a fairly long one made up of harder words and more involved expressions. Therefore, for the purposes both of review and of new learnings, the pupil does not have to be reading the hardest possible material for him. Although he may be able to read a fifth reader, if there are skills in the fourth reader that he has not developed well enough, he can be put into a fourth reader and spend part of his time with the work of the group operating at that level. If he is at third-reader level, however, he should not be put into a fourth reader, for he would be expected to review what he has not yet finished, grasp new learnings on material whose vocabulary, organization, and concepts are too advanced for him.

Because of the fact that a child can learn principles at a lower level and apply them at his higher reading level, the teacher does not have to have eight or ten reading groups in order to provide profitable instruction in reading for all of her pupils. Once a group of teachers recognizes this fact, a school can provide a profitable sequence of learnings for all individuals in classes throughout the school without sending children from teacher to teacher each day or driving a given teacher beyond her endurance in an effort to recognize subtleties of level within a given class.

After all, basal readers mark arbitrary divisions in the reading program. Because there have been ten little books in the series by fourth-reader level, a teacher does not have to have ten groups; nor, if there had been sixteen books, would she have had to have sixteen groups. Her motto should be: Keep the children progressing but don't skip learnings.

Another point that should be understood is that a basal reader labelled "fourth" does not mean that only the average child in the fourth grade should study it, while the more able should study a fifth, sixth, seventh, or eighth reader. A fourth-reader manual typically assumes that the book is to be used with the average and more able children of a fourth grade. The varied activities suggested for each lesson in the teacher's manual are designed to meet such a range of differences. Ordinarily, a principal who would improve reading in the fourth grade would do less well by ordering fifth-, sixth-, seventh-, and eighth-grade readers for that grade than he would by helping the teacher of that grade interpret and use the manual of the fourth reader, build reading skills in the subject areas, and develop a strong recreational-reading program.

4. Specific reading strengths and needs of individual children should be assessed. These can be determined in part by:

   a. Analysis of pupil success on individual items in a diagnostic test, such as some of the basal-reader tests of readiness for different reader levels, tests from the manual of the preceding level, and standardized tests of specific skills. (See description of tests in Appendix.)

   b. Charting pupils' skills, noting needs by marking items missed. One part of the chart might concern a test of eight types of syllabic division, for instance, and a cross (x) would indicate a child's error:

PUPILS	EIGHT TYPES OF SYLLABIC DIVISION							
	1 let-ter	2 la-bor	3 an-chor	4 peo-ple	5 scoop-ing	6 ex-cuse	7 mail-man	8 pes-ter
Julie							x	
Beth								x
Star			x					
Jay							x	
Dorene						x		x
Kay		x					x	x
Randy				x	x	x	x	x
etc.	etc.		etc.			etc.		etc.

It is apparent that certain children need the same kind of help and can be worked with as a group; some need only one kind of help, which no one else needs to share; and some, like Randy, need to sit in on everything. Of course, if a test has only one item of a kind in the test, the error or the correct response might be a matter of chance rather than a matter of true knowledge or ignorance. The results of such a test are suggestions of probably needed training, and a suggestion is better than nothing. At the same time, suppose there were five items of a kind in the test. If the child missed one of the five, you wouldn't be likely to insist that he had sufficient skill in that area, would you? Any time a child makes a mistake, it is worth investigation.

   c. A determination of which skills may best be handled in routinely formed groups at the different instructional levels, which ones in a special group or on an individual basis, and which ones in connection with the teaching of social studies, science, arithmetic, or other classroom activities. Perhaps, for example, Julie's regular instructional group will be having quite a bit of emphasis on Type-7 syllabification. No special arrangement will have to be made for her in this regard. Jay, on the other hand, who missed the item on Type 7, is in a group which has mastered Type 7. He will have to be drawn into Julie's group when it works on Type 7. Perhaps Randy is reading on a much lower level than others in the class and has never had instruction in syllabification. Possibly he still knows so little about consonants and vowels that instruction in syllabification would only confuse him. In his case, you would not be concerned because he knew so little about it. If you had been sure of his reading level prior to the testing, you might not even have had him take this test.

But, again, suppose Randy will be sent to a school next year that does little to help students who are below average in reading skill. You may feel that the present is the time for considerable help in building knowledge of consonants and vowels with the words he does know, followed by work in syllabification, even though ordinarily these learnings would have been spread out over a period of years. In this case you are glad he took the test, for you see that, fortunately, he has no trouble with Types 1, 2, and 3, and so you may concentrate on the other five.

Suppose our test example had been the use of the index, and you had found that many children were poor at the task. If the use of the index is prominent in your work in social studies and science, you might use the time allotted to those areas to introduce this necessary skill to all the children. Those who already knew how can act as leaders in demonstrating how they proceed to use the index. The fact that the skill is taught when interest is high and the skill is necessary makes the learner more receptive and the learning more efficient.

d. Ascertaining whether the lacks of a given child are evidence of earlier failure or insufficient opportunity to learn.

The skills which are developed sequentially in the reader series are outlined, book by book, on large charts or in pamphlets which the publishers furnish gratis to teachers and administrators on request. On them can be seen, for instance, that long and short vowels are taught at second-reader level in a given reader series. If the chart of skills described in b shows practically all fourth graders deficient in this skill, it can be suspected that, if it ever was taught by the second-grade teacher, it was not sufficiently maintained by the third-grade teacher. It needs reteaching, and all children from high second-reader level on, who show this lack, should be given further training. Suppose a fellow like Randy, however, is at beginning second-reader level, and lacks both consonant sounds and vowel sounds. He needs reteaching of consonant sounds immediately, and as he proceeds through the second reader he will be exposed to the vowel instruction, too.

By the way, it is always a cheerful discovery for the teacher proud of her school to note that a child who did worst in a test is a transfer from another school, preferably from another county, ideally from another state. But we should remember that transfers from school to school are not always very good examples of the effectiveness and continuity of an instructional program. Sometimes they only reflect instability within the family, which makes good school performance difficult; and always transfer means that much of the child's energy and attention is involved in making friends and becoming accustomed to the new environment.

e. A comparison of the child's development in special skills, with his level of reading. If a child's vocabulary and comprehension scores suggest fourth-reader level but his development of subskills (word analysis, study skills, etc.) suggests third-reader level, the teacher must decide whether he might best be put into a fourth-reader group and given the missing skills on an individual basis, put into a fourth-reader group and invited to participate in third-reader activities when the group at third-reader level deals with the missing skills, or put into a third-reader group entirely, to build the skills carefully and thoroughly at this easier level. This last choice would be made only if his lack of skills at third-reader level were quite extensive.

5. The tentative assignment of individuals to groups for instruction at the different levels (3 above) should be altered in accordance with the comparison just made. Occasionally a personality problem may require further alteration of the plan. Two children at each other's throats do not study well together. However, if a big, burly teacher sits between them and demands concentration on work, the problems that loom large on the playground and in less formal classroom situations are some-- times minimized and even forgotten. And perhaps even this is part of the education for an adult life in which we often have to accept as fellow-workers people we would not have chosen as partners in kindergarten rhythms. But if in the teacher's judgment the presence of a certain child in an instructional group will have a deleterious effect upon the progress of the group as a whole, the teacher may have to decide in favor of the majority, who also have needs, potentialities, and tax- paying parents!

Of course, as a child's needs and achievements alter, so must the decisions change regarding the best grouping for him. Some teachers like to make these decisions with the child rather than for him. If so, the child should be as well-informed as the teacher on the determining factors, so that the decision will be just as wise.

In summary, the steps in determining the grouping for instruction in a classroom might well be these:

1. Determining the reading level of each child.
2. Listing the children by apparent reading level.
3. Deciding on the number of groups to be attempted initially.
4. Noting the strengths and weaknesses of individual children to determine special needs and wisest instructional grouping in view of these needs.
5. Tentatively assigning pupils to instructional groups, keeping in mind personality patterns and unrevealed needs which might alter plans as the year proceeds.

Time and Kind of Reading Instruction

Schools vary both in the amount of time they devote to reading instruction and in the way they schedule children for it. Some say they teach reading all day, and have a relatively short period for direct reading instruction or none at all so specified. Others admit that reading is used throughout the day and, on occasion, taught in connection with other subjects during the day, and yet allot a relatively long period to reading instruction. At the primary level some schools devote as much as two hours and fifteen minutes a day to reading, perhaps half of the time to direct instruction and half to recreational reading or the reading of factual materials. Others at this same level have half the children come for instruction from nine to ten in the morning, leaving at two in the afternoon; the other half coming at ten and having reading instruction from two to three in the afternoon. In this way the teacher has only half the class to manage and instruct at one time. (This, again, has its administrative advantages and disadvantages.) Still other schools allot perhaps an hour for reading instruction at the primary level, forty or fifty minutes at the intermediate grade level, and even less at grades seven and eight.

Factors to consider

Perhaps one might say that the amount of time is not so important as the quality of teaching and study for reading purposes during that time. Still, one is bound to wonder at the differences in achievement between the child who has good instruction and reading experiences for two hours and fifteen minutes a day and the child who has good instruction and reading experiences for an hour or less a day.

Both the amount of time scheduled for reading activities and instruction, and the scheduling of these reading experiences, should be determined not so much by a hard and fast administrative decree as by a careful look at the pupils we teach. Suppose you have a classful of children who can't sit still any appreciable length of time. How long and when should your reading instruction take place? How much and what kind of variety in instruction and activities should you provide? And what can you do, through your reading program, to help the children *learn* to sit longer and pay attention or concentrate longer? If you take your children as a kind of barometer and watch where and when and how the pressures build up, you can not only predict your classroom weather, you can *create* it.

Imagine that you are teaching a group of youngsters who are encouraged to read at home, have a place there to read, and books to enjoy; whose hobbies have enticed them into such out-of-school activities as reading directions for making a model rocket or a bird house; whose families are interested in the results of their children's reading, and discuss with them as equals the information or fun they derive from it. How much time will you have to spend with such children to develop recreational reading interests and out-of-school uses of reading? How much time will they need to spend reading recreational materials *in school?*

Then suppose you have children, on the other hand, who lack encouragement, place, time, and anything readable at home. Will your emphases be different for these children? Will your work with the parents be different?

Again, suppose something true of many classroom situations: that you have both kinds of children, and all gradations and varieties of such differences in children in your classroom. Are you going to give them all the same diet?

Basic to planning the amount of time and to scheduling reading activities and instruction of each child is the teacher's knowledge of his out-of-school life. The previous teacher's notes on the child will be helpful; but, as family circumstances change, they must be reviewed along with new evidence from the child himself. The first few days of the new school year should be a time of intensive getting-acquainted. Too often the pupil finds out more about the teacher than vice versa. But the teacher can use some more effective devices than chance informal chats and fortuitous eavesdroppings to gain the information she needs.

Here, for instance, is a questionnaire attached to a reading test for intermediate-grade children.

Interest Inventory[1]

1. How much time do you spend helping your parents? ⎯⎯⎯⎯

2. What work do you do for them, or for other people?⎯⎯⎯⎯⎯

3. When do you work? ⎯⎯⎯⎯
(before school, Saturdays, other times)

4. What games do you like best? ⎯

[1] Page 11 in *Fourth-Grade Readiness Test*, Ginn Basic Readers, Ginn and Company, Boston, Mass. Reproduced with the permission of the publisher.

Interest Inventory (cont.)

5. Do you go to the movies?
Yes— No— How often?——————
Name the movies you like best ——
————————————————————————

6. Check places you have been:
A farm— Picnics— Church—
A Zoo— Fairs— Lakes—
A Museum— A Circus—
Mountains— A Library—
Beaches— Others——————

7. Do you do any gardening?
Yes— No—

8. What do you make or build for fun? —————————————————

9. Do you have any pets? Yes——
No—— What?——————————

10. Do you listen to the radio?
Yes— No— Do you see television?
Yes— No— What program do you enjoy most? ————————————
————————————————————————

11. Have you made a special study of birds?— butterflies?— rocks?—
shells?— stars?— animals?—
trees?— flowers?—

12. Check the kind of reading which you enjoy most:
Poems— Stories— Funnies—
True books (science, etc.)—

13. Check how you like to read best:
Orally— Silently—

14. About what do you like to read best?
Animals— Knights— Fairies—
Inventions— Automobiles—
Pioneers— School— Adventure—
People of other lands— Birds—
Farmers— Indians— Airplanes—
Others ————————————

15. Name the best book you ever read ————————————————
————————————————————————

16. Name some books you have read recently ——————————————
————————————————————————
————————————————————————

17. How many books do you yourself own? ——————————

18. Do you read the newspapers regularly?— Sometimes?— Never?—
What sections? ——————————

19. What are your favorite magazines? ——————————————
————————————————————————
————————————————————————
————————————————————————

For younger children, a discussion based upon each of these questions or the drawing of pictures about these activities can reveal a great deal to the teacher. Younger children can also tell what they did last night, last weekend for fun, for work, with or without their parents; how big their families are and what they do together; how they help their families. Older children can keep a log of out-of-school activities for a week, which will reveal the amount and kind of responsibility, free time, and recreational activity which fill the child's life.

Log of Out-of-School Activities

Time	*What I Did*
3:00-4:00 P.M.	_____
4:00-5:00	_____
5:00-6:00	_____
6:00-7:00	_____
7:00-8:00	_____
_____	_____

Meanwhile, of course, the keeping of the log, the reading of each other's logs, and the tabulation of class results give the class an experience in reading charts, and insight into chart construction.

From these pieces of evidence you can discover many relevant items: (1) the amount of reading which is going on or is possible outside the school; (2) the need for getting the child acquainted with his neighborhood library and planning frequent visits to it; (3) the kinds of reading skill which are needed to support out-of-school activities (reading the minutes of a club meeting, reading do-it-yourself directions, reading the grocery list). You will also sense the opportunities the child needs to discuss his outside reading, the need to probe for deeper meanings, to clarify ideas and utilize them. The data will also reveal what help he needs in finding books and other reading material to suit his purposes or to broaden or refine his reading interests.

Procedures in primary grades

At the beginning of the first grade you may find that your class falls naturally into two groups: those ready to read and those who need experiences to build readiness for beginning reading. If so, your schedule will often involve this kind of daily plan:

1. Instructions to reading group (what to do while you are working with readiness group).
2. Teaching the readiness group.
3. Giving the readiness group independent work.
4. Teaching the reading group.
5. Starting reading group on independent work to be continued next day.
6. Checking on independent work of readiness group.

In chart form, your activity will look like this:

Readiness Group	Reading Group
1. Teaching Assigning individual work.	1. Instructions to group (Children work alone.)
2. (Children work alone.)	2. Teaching Assigning work to start now and complete next day.
3. Checking on work.	3. (Children work alone.)

As the semester progresses, you find that some of the children in the reading group are capable of progressing faster than others (who may after all need some readiness instruction), so much faster that you probably should divide the children into two groups. Or perhaps the big break comes instead in your readiness group, where some are now ready to start reading and others still need preparatory work. Either case will entail the addition of a new group and a new schedule, and teacher time with each group is cut down. The chart may now look something like this:

First Reading Group	Second Reading Group	Readiness Group
Instructions to All Groups at First of Reading Period		
(Children work alone.)	Teaching and assigning individual work.	(Children work alone.)
Quick look and suggestions. (Children work alone.)	(Children work alone.)	Teaching and assigning independent work.
Teaching and planning follow-up.	Quick look and suggestions. (Children work alone.)	(Children work alone.)

(Children complete checking on work of the three groups.)

A weekly schedule will look similar, extending over the five days. But you will alter the program for various purposes. For one thing, on some days you may wish to spend part or the full time in the school library, helping children select books to read for pleasure or for study. (The readiness group will concentrate on books with many good illustrations.) For another, while the regular instructional groups take care of *level* needs, they do not take care of *peculiar* needs. You may spend part or all of some days meeting children individually on individual problems or meeting a succession of groups of children who have a common difficulty or need or interest.

Again, there will be times for sharing the results of the reading of different groups or individuals, or for teaching the whole class a skill which is new or rusty, which all need.

Procedures in intermediate and upper grades

If you are a teacher of intermediate or upper grades, you may have less time allotted by your school system for reading instruction than there is in the primary grades. If this is the case, you must spend more time on reading problems when you teach social studies, science, health, and mathematics. But during the time officially allotted for reading instruction, you may do something like the following.

If your class falls into two or three or four instructional groupings, and if you have fifty minutes a day for reading instruction, you very likely will attempt to meet only two of your groups in two twenty- or twenty-five-minute periods, while the others work on other reading assignments. If you have seventy-five minutes a day, you can schedule meetings with three groups, and your general plan may be like that of Mrs. John Bixler at Frederic Burk School in San Francisco:

	4th-Reader Level-2 Group	4th-Reader Level-1 Group	3rd-Reader Level-1 Group
9:00-9:25	Read silently.	Read with me.	Work independently.
9:25-9:50	Work independently. Do related reading.	Work independently.	Read with me.
9:50-10:10	Read with me.	Do related reading.	Work independently.
10:10-10:15	Hand in papers, collect reading books, etc.		

The fourth-reader level-2 group first reads an assignment silently, then writes answers to questions on the assignment (or whatever the follow-up is), then reads other materials on the same subject (such as another pioneer story in another basal series or in a trade book or magazine), then works with the teacher, discussing answers to questions, and the information obtained from the related readings.

At intermediate grade (4-5-6) levels and upper grade (7-8) levels the organized program for systematic, sequential development of skills (represented to a large extent by the basic readers and teaching materials related to them) may be allotted only two or three days a week. The remainder of the time is devoted to other reading situations in which the teacher and librarian can give reading guidance. If you have a school library, each of your instructional groups may have the opportunity of visiting during reading time once a week, to discuss reading choices with the librarian, have instruction in reference skills, or hear the librarian describe some books she feels would interest the group. If you have recreational reading material or reference material in your classroom, individual children may pursue individual reading activities and obtain your help.

At the primary level, these same opportunities for independent reading and library guidance should be available to the children but, typically for most children, a greater proportion of the time is devoted to instruction through a sequential program such as that offered by a basal reader and its teaching materials.

Instructional grouping, as illustrated in the examples above, is a week-in, week-out insurance policy for teacher and student that positive challenge is being given and positive growth effected in many different facets of reading development. But this is not the only way of managing the reading program. In fact, if the teacher were to be satisfied with only this type of organization, she would only be solving some of her instructional problems while other untended problems multiplied. Like any one type of organization it must be balanced by other types.

Grouping for different purposes

You as a teacher must know that at times it makes very good sense to teach something to all your children at once. When you deal with your whole class at once, you have to remember that some children will fail to learn anything unless you have chosen materials easy enough for the poorest readers in the class. Sometimes also, when you see that a few children need help of a particular kind, it is wise to stop to see that they get it. And sometimes, when an individual is evidently floundering, that may be the time to rescue him, either doing it yourself or drawing on the services of another pupil. Again, you may recognize that two children who need the same help can learn together as a team. Perhaps feeling they have a pal in the same boat is all they need for courage to pull the oars.

Suppose you came to school some morning to find several children fascinated with an idea new to them. Now may be the time to explore it— perhaps not at the cost of all the other ongoing activities which have engaged the interest of the rest of the class—but at least to give these children the opportunity to visit the library together, to find materials on the subject, and to use their free time to pursue their common interest. Perhaps, again, the interest may not be an unpredictable mushroom that sprang up overnight, but an outgrowth of something picked up in the social studies or science. Someone asks a question. What is the answer? Fortunately (we hope) you don't know, or, wisely, you don't give it. You let the children who want to know form a committee to investigate through reference materials and return with the answer. This may take five minutes, a week, or still longer. And then there are Susie and Billie, and Joe and Frances, all crazy about dogs or poetry or outer space. You give them chances to find books on the subject, share their findings with each other, and have the satisfaction of setting up a display in the room, making a scrapbook, reporting to the class about some of the books they have enjoyed on the subject, or giving other concrete evidence that they have achieved something.

So it should be clear that the teacher has eight ways of organizing the children:

as 1. a whole class
   2. an individual working independently or with the teacher.
   3. an instructional group organized by level.
   4. a group organized by a special need they have in common.
   5. a group teamed for moral support and mutual help.
   6. a tutorial group, aided by a child.
   7. an interest group, organized by common interest.
   8. a research group, organized by curiosity about a question.

These are ways the teacher can meet the individual needs in her classroom. If she is a really fine teacher, she tries to avoid mechanical, routine methods in using them. Rather, she draws upon them and blends them as an orchestra director draws upon the various sections in the orchestra and blends them for something more personal than a mechanical rendition of a score. And, believe us, the result can be real music and real art. And real learning.

Here are two examples of the way teachers can plan and execute the lessons given on days when instructional groups meet with her or work independently on such special assignments. The first is a primary grade example. The teacher has three groups—a high group using a reader at the grade level, an average group using a somewhat easier book, and a low group reading a grade or so below the grade in which they are.

A Primary Reading Day[2]

Monday morning, bright and cheerful, Miss Jones appeared armed with work for the whole class. She asked all the children what they were planning to do when they had finished work, and, with halos faintly visible, they all replied that they would go quietly to the cupboard for a game or to the library table for a book.

First she gave her assignment to the low group. She had taken one of five paragraphs from a workbook page and had devised several questions requiring identification of the main idea (Which is the best name for this story?); details (What did the house look like?); and sequence (What happened first?). She asked these children to draw a picture showing what they thought would

[2] Reproduced with permission of the publisher from *Independent reading activities* by Constance M. McCullough, Boston: Ginn and Co.

happen next in the story beyond the paragraph which they were given. She had gone to this trouble because she had found that this group was too slow to do as much on a workbook page as an average group, and she had found this a good way of adapting the material to suit their needs.

The average group on this particular day did not all need the same work. Some of them could profitably study the review page in the workbook on initial consonants, so she assigned this to them. The others related to her what she had previously told them to do. Two of them were going to work together on their sight vocabulary file, testing each other. Three of them, who were to report in the Tuesday reading club meeting on books they had read and liked, were going to go into a corner to read aloud to each other the passages they planned to present to the class and plan what they would say about the books. What was the average group to do when they had finished all this work? They were to go to the library table for a book of their choice and read it at their seats.

Miss Jones, with this group thus taken care of, returned to the front of the room and asked the high group—John's group—to bring their chairs quietly. She commented as they were doing it, "I like the way John holds his chair— the way Sally walks so softly."

Sometimes Miss Jones pushed two small tables together and gathered her group around it, but today she needed the blackboard. She introduced the new story to the children, stirring up a fine curiosity about pictures and title, and guiding silent reading with questions on things to be found out.

On the blackboard she had put a number of questions about the story which the children were to answer at their seats. These questions emphasized different kinds of comprehension and required the child to think about what he had read and to find the places in the story which gave the right answers. For instance: "How did Peter feel after Grandfather spoke to him? Write the words of the story that make you think this."

One question made him think about the use of words.

"What words in this story helped you to see how the farm looked?" The last item in the assignment asked the child to write about what he would have done if he had been Peter, or about a time when he was in a like situation.

Miss Jones sent John's group quietly back to their seats, then took a quick look at the work of the average group to see how it had been faring. Next she called the low group together at the front of the room. First she allowed them to display the pictures which they had drawn during their independent work period and made a brief check of their understanding of the paragraphs. Then she introduced them to their new story, taking care to forestall vocabulary and comprehension difficulties and to challenge their best efforts by helping them set a purpose for reading. Before the children in the low group went back to their tables, Miss Jones gave them each a big sheet of paper with lines cutting it into four squares for four pictures. She asked them to find four sentences in the story that told four important things, to write a sentence below each square, and then to draw a picture illustrating each sentence. This assignment would take some of these children into Tuesday.

As these children were returned to their seats, she retained Bill and Esther from the group and called two other children from the other groups to join them at the blackboard. All these children, although in different groups, happened to suffer from the same ailment. All were making reversals on the same small, common, troublesome words.

The children watched Miss Jones put these words on the blackboard, saying them as she wrote them. Then they traced a word with their fingers on the blackboard while saying it and watched her retrace it. Next they wrote the word with chalk, saying it again as they wrote. When successful, they wrote it in a sentence. Miss Jones now sent these children to their seats with the assignment to write these words in sentences during their next free time.

Next Miss Jones called up the average group for its new story. First, however, each child reported briefly on his progress during the independent work period. The story which this group was reading would make a good play. At the end of the lesson, Miss Jones suggested that in tomorrow's independent time the children read to decide how many scenes the play should have, name them, and put down what should happen in each scene. If the children worked well together, she might have them work in small committees during the second part of Tuesday's reading time, preparing dramatizations of different scenes for presentation on Wednesday.

Before or during this reading day the teacher had had to hectograph one set of papers, draw lines dividing another set of papers into four squares (she could have had the children simply fold the paper two ways instead of drawing lines), and write questions on the blackboard for another assignment.

An Intermediate Reading Day[3]

In another consolidated school the teacher in the fifth grade is Mr. Zane. He has three groups in reading also: a group reading at fifth-reader level, another reading at fourth-reader level, and a third at high second-reader level.

Because it was Monday, Mr. Zane started the reading period by asking if everybody knew what to do. The children made two types of response. One was to point out that a member of each group had written on the blackboard on Friday a reminder of what that group was to do with its two reading periods of twenty-five minutes each on Monday. The other was to designate the chart which the class had made listing the things that could be done during any free time in the reading periods.

Mr. Zane told the low group—not using that term, of course—that he had brought from the public library some books in which they might be interested, for he had tried to remember everybody's favorite subject in choosing them. These books could be kept for a limited time only. He had some of them classified and grouped on the shelves at the back of the room, under such headings as "Fun," "Animals," etc. The aviation books were displayed on the reading table. Mr. Zane had tried to recognize in his selections the fact that these children had mature interests even though they were reading at the high second-reader level. When the children finished reading the books they now had, they were to look over these new books quietly and select one to read.

The low group spent the first part of the reading period in a variety of ways. Those who were still reading books on topics of special interest to them individually, continued this activity. Those who had just finished their books made preparations for the Tuesday Reading Club meeting where they would report on their reading. Some drew pictures representing high points in the story which they were reading. One added a picture to his poster on adventure stories. Some wrote short recommendations of their books for the class card file of good stories. One reread the part he wanted to read aloud to the class. One recorded his book on a map of the world which the class had made to show how many

[3] Reproduced with the permission of the publisher from *Contributions to Reading No. 10* by Constance M. McCullough. Boston: Ginn and Co.

parts of the world they could read about. Gradually as the boys and girls completed these activities, they went quietly to the reading table or the shelves for another book.

The main job of the high group in this first period was to classify the facts which they had obtained from a story about two different animals. Under headings such as "food," "home," and "appearance," they were to list in separate columns the characteristics of the two animals. Then they were to write a summary of their findings, telling how the animals were alike and how different and what one could expect from them because of these character differences and likenesses. Two of the children worked together on this job because the teacher had agreed that they would benefit by each other's help. The others worked independently.

The second half of the reading time the high group devoted to committee work. It had divided into committees to plan to present to the class and possibly to another room the unit of stories just completed. Two or three children comprised each committee. They sat together at this time and quietly talked over what might be an interesting way to give their part of the program. Some started writing scenarios, some planned a series of pantomimes for a guessing game, and so on.

Mr. Zane worked with the average group. He introduced the background of the new story in their reader, and a vocabulary committee reported on the new words which they should know in order to read it. The group planned the things they would especially look for in the story, listed these as questions on the blackboard, and went back to their seats to find the answers and write down their impressions. Each pupil also was to write a question of his own which, in the subsequent reading period with the teacher, he would ask some other pupil.

Because the story which they were to read was of considerable length, this activity would take most of the second period on Monday as well as the first period on Tuesday. The rest of the time, if they had extra time, individuals would work on their special needs. Each one knew what his greatest difficulty was and had planned a special attack to make upon it. Jim and Peter, always troubled with sight vocabulary, worked together on the new words. Esther drew a picture of a descriptive passage, trying to record all the details, because she was poor at reading for details. Adeline studied the new words to see whether she could add any to her list of words of various phonetic types. And so it went.

Mr. Zane next introduced a new story to the children in the low group, presenting vocabulary on the blackboard as it was needed. Here his technique was to ask a question. The children read to find the answer, discussed the answer, and read to answer the next question. In this way they proceeded through the story. As an assignment for the ten remaining minutes of their reading time and for their first period on Tuesday, Mr. Zane suggested that this story would make a good play. The children should decide how many big scenes it required, who should appear in each scene, what should happen in each scene. Then they should reread the parts carefully, each deciding which of several parts he might take successfully. Mr. Zane gave each of the children in the group a sheet to fill out which provided the following outline.

Title of Scene One————————————————————————

Characters in Scene One————————————————————————

What happened first————————————————————————

What happened next————————————————————————

Title of Scene Two————————————————————————

And so on

In the last ten minutes Mr. Zane had several children from each group come up to the blackboard. All these children were still having trouble with the long and short sounds of single vowels. He first gave them an ear-training exercise to make sure that they could hear the sound correctly.

Which of these words has different sounds of the vowel "a" in it? Hold your finger up if you hear it.

Bad   Watch   Make   Run

The fingers went up for the first three.

Then he listed words containing the long "a" sound and had the children name others which he put on the blackboard. The children then underlined the part of each word that made the long "a" sound. They had found several different ways to get the long "a" sound: ai, ay, ei, ā, ey. Mr. Zane next sent them to their seats with sheets of paper on which were columns for these different spellings of the "long-a" sound. In their free time the children were to find words familiar to them which illustrated these different spellings.

For this day of reading Mr. Zane had planned independent activities for everyone. Two of these activities called for a hectographed sheet but actually could have been written on the blackboard. Directions for some of the activities had been given the previous Friday. Still other activities, the individual jobs in the average group, were the result of a series of suggestions, made to different children over a period of days and weeks, which were designed to take care of demonstrated needs in reading skills.

One of the best features of Mr. Zane's program was his treatment of his low group. He did not ladle out "sulphur and molasses" to them, trying to rush them through a reader to catch up to some mythical average which they could never maintain. They were having just as good a time as any other group. They were not struggling, yet they were learning. Their independent activities were enjoyable, yet they involved real reading jobs.

The two examples just given of primary and intermediate grade teaching might be typical of two or three days each week, or two-fifths to three-fifths of the reading time. Research has not revealed what the ideal proportion should be for any given population. The essential development of this organization is *through* the group work at levels of instruction, *toward* individual work as the teacher sees the need for it. The chief strengths of this type of organization are: (1) that the pupil has the benefit of teacher instruction from one-half to one-fourth of the time instead of his individual share of perhaps one-thirtieth; (2) that the pupil can learn through other children, as group study of any one piece of material brings the child to facets and depths of understanding which he alone or with only the teacher would not reach; (3) that the teacher can depend upon the continuity and comprehensiveness of carefully prepared commercial materials, such as the basal reader materials, and concentrate on evidences of individual needs.

Individualized Reading

The remaining days of each week, or the remaining portion of each day given to reading instruction—whichever way seems more profitable—may be devoted to a type of organization which has come to be called "individualized reading" (51). Actually, this is as much a misnomer as the title "grouping" is for the organization just described. Individualized reading, starting with a primary concern for individual work, continues with a recognition of opportunities for group and whole-class activities. The children spend most of their time during these "individualized reading" periods reading materials which they individually choose from a classroom collection. These may be factual or fictional, reference materials, newspapers or magazines, or exercises chosen for their specific benefit to the individual child. Part of the time is spent recording activities and reacting to what has been read, discussing with other children, or engaging in other creative activities. Here opportunities enter for team grouping on common problems, tutorial grouping for special help, and interest and research grouping. Each child may look forward to having, once every two or three weeks —or more often if the class is smaller—a private conference with the teacher for about ten minutes more or less, according to need and feasibility. Or the teacher may also meet with him and a few other children on a need they have in common.

In the private conference the teacher notes what a child has read, attempts to find out the quality of his reading comprehension and interpretation, notes growth and deficiencies in word meaning and word attack, etc. She helps him select materials to read, both in view of his current interests and in view of her ultimate goals for him as a reader in breadth and depth. If the school has a librarian, the teacher may arrange with her to give library help to half the class while she works in the classroom on this individual basis. The librarian has been informed about the interests and levels of reading of each child, and, by her own observation becomes aware of each child's need for growth in library skills. On some of the library visits, certainly, the teacher should go along.

Some share of the class time may be devoted to meetings of the whole class, in which children tell the whole class some of their reading experiences, in narrative, graphic (drawing, painting, etc.), or dramatic form. However, since time is precious, the teacher canny, and the type of presentation artistic or oral, the teacher in a school which counts its minutes may call this "art time" or "language time," which, indeed, it is. Presto! More time for reading!

The chief strengths of this "individualized" type of organization for reading instruction are that (1) the pupil has the benefit of individual conferences with the teacher, during which both concentrate on his reading progress; (2) the pupil can read materials of his own choice, at his own pace, and in his own way; (3) the teacher is guided in her instruction by all the concrete evidence she is able to gather of the child's reading needs, and can constantly look for opportunities to group children for instruction according to the needs they have in common.

Evaluation

If you study research papers in the field of reading, you will discover that almost every idea about teaching reading has been initially presented and supported and tested as though it were the one way to achieve a good result. However, if you follow through the history of such research, you will also see that usually each idea has had its value and ultimately has had to accept its relative place in the reading program rather than to dominate. If you measure the chief strengths of the "grouping" organization against the chief strengths of the "individualized," you will see that the strengths of one are the weaknesses of the other. Like man and wife, they may have difficulty getting along together but they need each other.

There are those educators who believe that a compromise should be made between these two systems. Some say, "Use the basal reader the first part of the year and have your instructional grouping for it. Then spend the rest of the year with individualized reading." This is a fine, simple idea but it will not work. For half the year, the benefits of the one system pile up, but so do its weaknesses. The children may be reading the basal reader twice as fast as Nature or the authors intended. During the rest of the year, the initial benefits of a forced draft peter out, while gains in other respects seem striking.

Advantages of combining both systems

It makes a great deal of sense to have both systems operating at once. Some schools are experimenting with morning sessions of "grouping" and afternoon sessions of "individualized reading." Others schedule "grouping" two or three days a week, during which they develop a story in the basal reader, with its attendant skill-building activities, and then turn to "individualized reading" the remaining days. The effect of the one system upon the other is to increase the effectiveness of both systems. The child works more efficiently during "grouping" time, for he knows that the "individualized" reward lies at the end of instruction. He feels closer to the teacher because she has conferred with him personally. In the group meetings he is eager to show her what he has learned, and he knows she will throw tasks his way during these meetings to give him practice in the areas of his special need. The "group" instruction gives him many ideas to follow during "individualized" time, if he chooses. Because he does not have all week to read at his own pace, in his own way, material of his own choice, he takes books home more readily. Thus, the desirable habit of reading at home is more likely to become established.

In a combination of the two systems, the teacher's morale and efficiency tend to be higher for a number of reasons. The individual conferences help her know individuals better and make for better rapport both in the class and in the groups. She can see the practical effects of group and individual instruction upon the child's skill in making his own choices and in his eagerness to read. Seeing individual needs during group instruction, she can work on them in individual instruction, and vice versa. Realizing that she is not a master of all the facets and gradations of reading instruction, nor even a walking encyclopaedia of reading techniques, she appreciates the comprehensive guidance in systematic instruction which she obtains from the basal-reader manuals. Being able to depend upon it, she is free to devote her energies to unmet problems.

The fact is that many good teachers have organized their work in this way for years, without labelling it. It is not the brand name that makes the product good; it's what is in the can.

Administering individualized work

How does the teacher administer the "individualized" work? First, she must know or anticipate the needs and interests of her children and provide materials and activities to fulfill them. There are various estimates of the number of books representing the interests of children that should be available in the classroom—some say roughly five times as many books as children. But, of course, even more important is the provision that every child will find in this classroom collection several books he will want to read and will be able to read.

These books she groups or designates in some way so that children know roughly the location of the books they will have the ability to read. The teacher knows, and so should the pupils, that they can read a somewhat harder book on a familiar subject and stand it. She also has a table or shelf where children's newspapers and magazines can be displayed, read, or borrowed. In another location she has reference tools—dictionaries for the different reading levels of the children, a simple encyclopaedia, a globe and maps, books that settle arguments on what kind of leaf, what kind of dog, or what kind of bird it was.

She also organizes and puts where the children can obtain them, various exercise materials to develop reading skill. There may be some flash cards and some little pocket charts in which children can build their own stories with the cards. The teacher may resort to some booklets which have been designed commercially for the development of a particular skill. Also she may have a nicely organized collection of workbook pages, mounted on cardboard, covered with a clear plastic sheet, and clipped to an answer key. The child can choose from the group of such exercises the ones he feels he needs, write his answers on the plastic sheet, check his answers with the answer key, record his results, and clean off his answers.

The reading time, then, is a time of reading descriptive and fictional material, or brushing up on a needed skill. This means there must be records. So the teacher has a special file, with an individual folder for the child. The record of the books he has read may be as simple as this:

Reading Record

My Name———————————————————— Date————————
Author——————————————————— Title————————————
Main characters or subject————————————————————
What happened or what the book told about————————————

Or the record may be more demanding, requiring such items as the *kind* of book it was, the part of the world it dealt with, the times it was concerned with, what it was especially good for, what other book it compared with and why, and to whom else in the class it would probably appeal.

The child also keeps a diary of his independent activities. It states briefly what he did on a certain day and what the result was, such as:

Date	*What I Did*	*Results*
Oct. 13	Read story about Halloween.	Drew a picture of the best part.
etc.	etc.	etc.

The teacher, too, keeps a record about each child, jotting down the date on which she conferred with him about his work, what was accomplished, what assignment was made, and what she noted about further needs. She keeps a checklist of the whole class, noting the dates on which she sees each child individually, so that during a certain period of time she knows that she has conferred with every pupil.

Good organization of such a program of independent activity requires also that materials and equipment for creative activities should be available and easily found by the children: e.g., paper for writing comments on stories, paper for drawing pictures, paints, etc.; at lower grade levels a file of cards containing words commonly needed in writing; perhaps a tape recorder for the rehearsal and criticism of a panel discussion on a book; a puppet stage or shadow-show stage for the dramatic presentation of something several children have happened to read and enjoy; a table around which a committee may confer quietly on a panel discussion or on another program to be presented to the class as a whole. The more the children's help is enlisted in planning the arrangement of materials and equipment, and in setting up procedures, the more fruitful will the outcome be.

Summary

Whether it is the principal with his staff organizing the reading program for a school, or a teacher with a particular child organizing his reading program, he or she must recognize that organization is merely a means to an end—a means with shortcomings which must be constantly watched and balanced by other methods. Interclass grouping, team teaching, departmentalization, homogeneous grouping, the self-contained classroom, even private tutoring, all have their drawbacks as well as their advantages. The ways by which a teacher can manipulate children—as a whole class, in groups with special purposes (instructional level, special needs, team, tutorial, interest, research), or in private conference—have their special values for parts of the reading program, and their limitations if they are exclusively depended upon.

The reading development of a child requires complex organization and administration not only of individuals and groups but of many kinds of material and equipment. (See Chapter 15.) It requires the co-operation of pupils, parents, librarian, teacher, and principal. Beyond these there is another ingredient without which all may add up to sawdust. Parents, librarian, teacher, principal, and children must believe—must be sufficiently informed so that they do believe—that their co-operative program is, so far, the best conceivable program for progress in reading. If all of these persons know what their aims are, if they know how important it is for themselves and for their country that their goals be attained, and if they know that the way they are working for them is a good way, then they will have the confidence, the will, and the pride in teamwork to make the program effective.

What Did These Words Mean?

interclass grouping	weekly schedule
heterogeneous class	independent work
team teaching	readiness group
administrative design	special-needs grouping
self-contained classroom	team grouping
instructional grouping	tutorial grouping
frequency distribution	interest grouping
reader level	research grouping
instructional level	individualized reading

Suggested Activities

Creative. Using the floor plan of a classroom you know, plan the placement of tables, chairs, reading materials, and equipment, for efficiency in carrying out group, individual, and whole-class activities.

Decide what supplies you would order to assist your determination of the reading level of each child in a particular grade at the first of a school year. Defend your choices with quotations from this book.

Further study. Read a recent article in *The Reading Teacher, Elementary School Journal,* or *Elementary English,* on the organization of the reading program. Try to ascertain the background of the author, to see how his experience qualifies him for making sound judgments in this area. Editorial notes help. A biographical reference, such as *Leaders in Education,* and the *Education Index* will suggest something about his activities. Is he a crusader for one idea or is his view objective? How can you tell?

Selected References

BARBE, Walter B., *Educator's guide to personalized reading instruction.* Englewood Cliffs, N.J.: Prentice-Hall, Inc., 1961.

BURTON, William H., and others, *Reading in child development.* Indianapolis: Bobbs Merrill Company, 1956, Chap. 15.

DARROW, Helen F., and HOWES, Virgil M., *Approaches to individualized reading.* New York: Appleton-Century-Crofts, Inc., 1960.

DEBOER, John J., and DALLMANN, Martha, *The teaching of reading.* New York: Holt, Rinehart and Winston, Inc., 1960, Chap. 15.

DURRELL, Donald D., *Improving reading instruction.* New York: Harcourt, Brace & World, Inc., 1956, Chap. 6.

FOX, Lorene K., and BROGAN, Peggy, *Helping children read.* New York: Holt, Rinehart and Winston, Inc., 1961.

GRAY, William Scott, Role of group and individualized teaching in a sound reading program, *The Reading Teacher,* 1957, 11, 99-104.

GOODLAD, John, and ANDERSON, Robert H., *The non-graded elementary school.* New York: Harcourt, Brace & World, Inc., 1959.

HANNA, Geneva R., and McALLISTER, Mariana K., *Books, young people, and reading guidance.* New York: Harper and Brothers, 1960, Chap. 8.

LAZAR, May (ed.), *A practical guide to individualized reading.* Bureau of Educational Research Publication No. 40. New York: Board of Education, City of New York, 1960.

MEIL, Alice (ed.), *Individualized reading practices,* Practical suggestions for teaching, No. 14. New York: Teachers College, Columbia University, 1958.

ROBINSON, Helen M. (ed.), *Materials for reading,* Supplementary Education Monograph, No. 86. Chicago: University of Chicago Press, 1957.

—— (ed.), *Reading instruction in various patterns of grouping.* Supplementary Education Monograph, No. 89. Chicago: University of Chicago Press, 1959.

RUSSELL, David H., *Children learn to read,* 2nd ed. Boston: Ginn and Company, 1961, Chap. 15.

STRANG, Ruth M., and LINDQUIST, Donald M., *The administration and the improvement of reading.* New York: Appleton-Century-Crofts, Inc., 1960.

VEATCH, Jeannette, In defense of individualized reading. *Elementary English,* 1960, 37, 227-234.

WITTY, Paul A., Individualized reading: a summary and evaluation, *Elementary English,* 1959, 36, 401-412; 450.

18

Parents as Partners in the Reading Program

Parents do more than provide the grist for the education mill. They have been giving storage space, and a lot of care, to that grist for five years before the school receives delivery on it, and they continue to do this for a part of each 24 hours throughout the school years.

Parents not only endow their children and surround them with powerfully influential environment, but they are normally unusually interested observers of their children's development. Since much of the teacher's success with the learner depends upon thorough understanding of him and his reactions, his parents can be valuable sources of information which the teacher needs.

Parents as people

Children are not the only human beings bristling with individual differences. Parents manifest them, too. There are busy parents, tired parents, nervous parents, parents with physical or language handicaps—in short, parents who, in their different ways, are not ready or not equipped or not willing to help the child become a proficient reader through the kind of out-of-school influences they provide. Then there are over-anxious parents, laissez-faire parents, and punitive parents, whose attitudes make their co-operation a doubtful blessing. Also, there are militant parents who would like to see the school made over in the image of their early recollections, or after a supposedly ideal pattern they have gleaned from a meeting, a television program, a magazine article, or a book. And finally there are, we may be thankful, parents who have time or take time, and are willing, interested, and eager to make their end of the parent-school relationship contribute to a team approach to this overwhelmingly important task of education.

One of the teacher's jobs is to "size up" the parents of the children she teaches, to know that if she sends a note home to Billy's parents, Billy will get the help he needs; while if she sends the same note home to Ernie's parents, Ernie won't be able to sit down for a week, and perhaps that wasn't what he needed.

What Parents Need to Know

If with every baby bonnet sold to proud parents, a pamphlet on parent education could be given, some children might be better prepared on arrival at kindergarten. Most parents need to know how to act as the earliest teachers of their children, and at the outset many of them really want to know badly. After awhile, when they have made enough mistakes, habits become more important than information. What are some of the facts and information that parents should be given?

The parents as a model

The parent sets an example for the child, not only because the child is basically imitative but because, as the child develops, he is apt to view his father and mother as people whose example is worthy of emulation. If the parent is careful about his speech, the child may also speak correctly. If, in advance, some parents know the importance of this, they can actually do something about their faulty speech habits as a preparation for parenthood.

A parent is also a model in the standards he sets for himself. The child can observe that he keeps his tools in order, that he works systematically, with concern for the quality of the product, and that he cleans up the work space afterwards. Perhaps he lets the child join him in the work, holding a tool, putting the finishing tap on a tack, or selecting or carrying objects. The child learns to take pride with him in the completed task. He is not likely to view his father's standards in a critical way; rather, he thinks, "*This* is the way you *do* it." That is a good start.

The parent is a model, too, in the way he obtains information and entertainment. If he looks at every television program indiscriminately, the child joins him in being a human sponge. If he reads only the headlines in the newspaper and only picture magazines, these become the child's idea of home reading. But if he reads books, magazines, and newspapers with apparent enjoyment and with a desire occasionally to share his findings in discussion or reading aloud, the child knows that these are among the rewards of growing up.

Relationship with the child

Parents who can provide regular, balanced meals for their children and who see to it that the children have enough hours of sleep are building good readers as well as healthy bodies. But such physical provisions are only part of the picture. Almost certainly, even more important than these is the relationship of the parents to their children.

Parents who make decisions together and present a "united front" in dealing with crises in the child's life give the child no excuse for "working one parent against another" and then making the decision himself. The Stewart study (241) showed that children from homes in which the joint chiefs of staff disagreed, using the child as another way of not getting along with each other, often produced a retarded reader.

The family that expects a child to do his best (but not achieve the impossible) is likely to be the family of an achiever. The Stewart study found, also, that the inferior reader was often an overprotected, overindulged child who could afford to do inferior work. An interesting parallel is found in the study by Heil, Power, and Feifer (125), which reported that teachers whose classrooms and programs were work-oriented and businesslike, who expected much of themselves and their pupils, seemed able not only to obtain better educational results according to tests but to have a friendlier relationship with pupils. Especially interesting was the finding that children of all personality types responded to such a teacher. We can gather from this that the family that takes pride in achievement—in the work of the father, whatever it is, in the work of the mother, and in the school successes of the other children—the family that believes in doing its best in whatever it attempts and that respects every person who does his best, is the family that will send Junior to school ready to work and to do his best, too.

Adverse comparisons and anxiety are twin evils in the family's attitude toward Junior's school work. If one child is compared with another, he frequently develops a dislike of the other child and an attitude of "What's the use? He's always ahead anyway." Comparisons do not have to be put into words to be felt. Junior is probably keenly aware of the difference between himself and the neighbor's boy or an older brother or sister (or, worse, a younger child who is doing better in work Junior no longer has a chance to do over), and might better be out of earshot when the parents remark on the achievements of the other child.

There is a fine line between expressions of interest and expressions of anxiety. The interested parent makes the child feel that his efforts are recognized and appreciated by people whose respect he especially desires. The anxious parent discovers that Junior is having trouble with reading, or thinks he will have because Junior's grandparents did. He or she meets Junior at the door each afternoon with the same greeting: "How did you do in reading today? Did you ask the teacher to move you into the top group? Did you get to read? How was your seatwork?" The child becomes tense when reading time comes around each day, knowing that this is the most crucial part of his success, according to the family signals. Being tense, he does less well than he might; and pretty soon the parent has the satisfaction of knowing that Junior is a chip off the old block—Grandfather's reading block.

The teacher can relieve the anxious parent by putting him to work. If there are games or exercises or other activities which the parent can supervise at home, which will aid the child's school progress, the parent can feel that he is helping him along. He doesn't have to spend all of his energies in anxiety. Gradually, as he sees evidence of results, his anxiety is further relieved. However, the activities must be easy enough for the child to do well, and the parent must be the kind who has enough self-control not to make the child tense in this situation, also.

Preparation for work at school

Parents can prepare a child for working co-operatively with a teacher in at least two ways. The *first* is that they, themselves, demand and deserve respect. The child learns that he speaks to his peers as equals and to his parents and other adults with deference. That deference is born partly of the family rule that "this is the way it is" and partly from experience which shows the child that adults do have judgment superior to his own and can be trusted as guides to his learning. If the parents are sending the child to a school in which corporal punishment is forbidden, they should not express their authority invariably in physical terms. If they do, the child becomes accustomed to doing what he likes until he senses a physical threat.

Overindulgent parents and parents who view their lot with helpless levity are prone to chortle over "Dennis the Menace" with his pranks and impertinences. They fail to see that they are rewarding impertinence and inviting more of it. The teacher of their product has a long row to hoe, all uphill.

The *second* way the child can be prepared to work co-operatively with the teacher is by having the parents take a supportive attitude toward the school. Whatever misgivings they may secretly have about new methods, young teachers, old teachers, male or female teachers, they should voice before the child only positive, appreciative views. Then the child will see that he cannot work one side against the other.

Another contribution to the child's success in school is the building of self-reliance. The child, prior to school entrance and thereafter, should be able to take responsibility and to see a task through to the end. Mother can teach this with little jobs around the house—setting the table for dinner, putting groceries away, bringing in the newspaper, the mail. Helping with tasks can gradually develop into complete responsibility for performing them. The child learns to take care of his own room, his own clothing, and to do his share in maintaining the common living quarters of the family. Father can teach Junior this self-reliance by having him help with odd jobs. Junior learns that work comes before play, and that it must be work well done. It is important that the jobs be geared to the abilities of the child, and that they increase in complexity and difficulty as the child develops.

If the child comes from a home in which he has not learned to take responsibilities, the teacher must gradually teach him by giving him similar tasks in the maintenance of the classroom.

Getting along with other children is another very important form of learning which the home can foster. Through home, neighborhood, church, and supervised park activities, the child must learn how to share materials as well as take care of them. He needs to be eased into the appalling truth that life is a long series of ego-assailing experiences and that no one can for long have all the cake and eat it, too, in this world. Parents who spare him this realization by purchasing ten of everything so that sharing is unnecessary, are dodging a crucial issue in the education of the young child.

Building concepts and language facility

Parents should know that both work and play provide experience in learning the meanings of words. When they work with the child, they should discuss what they are doing, see that he uses the proper names for the tools, appropriate verbs for the actions, and accurately descriptive words. When he has worked alone, they should invite him to tell what he has been doing, and supply for him any words he does not know.

Play activities often require phrases or sentences which the child picks up from other children. Often these borrowed expressions are mispronounced or misunderstood. The parent can by example correct the child. "Aw faw dow" can be translated into "all fall down," thus providing good language experience for the child who will someday read these words.

Visits to a farm, zoo, fair, or circus; trips to the mountains, a beach, a lake, or a park; watching television and motion pictures can enrich language. But the dividends will scarcely justify the outlay of effort if discussion does not accompany such experiences. (See Chapters 3, 4, 5 on readiness for reading.) In discussing objects, the parent can comment on how something looks, feels, smells, tastes, sounds; what its behavior is—how it works and what it is good for—how it is related to other things; what it is like and what another name for it is. In the years during which the child often asks more questions than he wants to hear answered in full, the parent may intersperse explanations with, "What do *you* notice about it?" so that the child helps answer his own question by a guided reasoning process and has language experience to boot. After the trip or whatever the experience is, the child may be encouraged to act it out, play it out, talk it out, or draw a picture about it and tell what the picture says.

Guessing games during or after the experience can sharpen a child's observation and recall. "I saw something that had long hair on its neck and a long tail and four thin legs. What was it?"

Family puppet shows or shadow shows, or use of a section of the attic or utility room as a gallery of paintings by the child, can give importance to these evidences of language power and recall.

Children can become interested in patterns. Some houses look as though they are smiling, by the arrangement of windows and doors. A tree becomes a nose for some. Curtains can suggest a worried look. Clouds can look like continents, boots, ducks, ice cream cones, feathers. These observations draw attention to pattern and use the characteristics of other concepts. Two children standing on opposite sides of a big puddle can see each other's reflection, darker, upside down, and shaking. Differences between right side up and upside down are important to reading.

When a parent talks to a child, he can help him with logical organization of ideas—the type encountered in factual writing—by this kind of procedure:

"This morning I saw the wren. Guess what she was doing."

"Eating?"

"She was flying to her nest with something in her beak. Can you guess why she was doing that?"

"She was going to feed her babies!"

A very young child will repeat this news as a kind of language ritual, to a neighbor or another member of the family who has not heard it. The parent may prompt with, "Tell about what I saw this morning and what you decided about it." In this way, the parent has guided the child through a sequence of who, what, and why.

Similarly, when the child comes in with, "Guess what Jack is doing. He's going to New York." The parent replies, "Why is he going there?"

"He's going to see his grandmother."

"What will he do when he's there?"

"He says he gets to go to the zoo and gets to see the ships."

(What, why, where.)

The procedure can be developed into a game of what, how, and where:

"I see something green," says the child.

"What is it doing?"

"It is eating some lettuce."

"How is it holding the lettuce?"

"With one foot."

"Where is it?"

"In the cage."

"Now I know. It is the parakeet."

The child gradually picks up the pattern of interrogation and engages in it himself.

When the child receives gifts on his birthday or at Christmas he can dictate 'thank you's," even before he can write. He can watch Mother write the words he says (in lower-case manuscript letters) and see her use the friendly-letter form. He should be beside her or on her lap, so that he views the letter right side up. He can be the bearer of oral messages to neighbors, to the grocer, to the person who telephones while Mother is washing her hair.

In department stores, drug stores, and supermarkets, parents see drawing and painting books for children. Grandmother gives the child lots of paper and a set of crayons when he comes to sit out the football game his parents attend. On another occasion, Father strips his son to his underdrawers, and puts him and the easel in the bathtub where it won't make much difference—he thinks—until she comes home. Yes, this is art, it is muscular co-ordination, and it is also language and recall. The child should be encouraged to talk about what he has drawn or painted, or what he is drawing or painting. He begins to think of pictures, both those he draws and those he sees in magazines and advertisements, as telling stories.

Language is made up of sounds and forms which must be recognized as alike or different. Hence, the parents can build meaning and sensitivity to sight and sound by having a child notice that Rover has a happy bark, a hungry bark, a burglar bark, a pained bark. Which bark is Rover barking now? One ring is the back door and two rings are the front door. And there is another "Burgie" ad, just like the one downtown. It has the same man on it. And here is another dog, but he has long hair and Rover has short hair.

Perhaps this is too good to hope for. But wouldn't it be wonderful if parents realized the importance of left-to-right observation in reading? They can encourage it by having children look at rows of objects from left to right. Even when window-shopping, they can call attention to and name objects from left to right instead of the reverse or helter skelter.

Provision of a reading environment

In the long-gone pretelevision days, when dinner was over and the dishes washed and dried, some families had a nightly ritual. One by one, they assembled in one room—the living room, or if they had one, the library. There they sat in special places—each knew which his was—and read a book of his choosing. Occasionally they would be interrupted by a hearty guffaw, and would listen appreciatively to the reason. Sometimes they understood and sometimes they didn't; but the young one growing up knew that this was expected of him, too, and looked forward to something funny enough or interesting enough to engage the attention of the whole family.

Dinners in such families were not times of "Joseph, I wish you'd eat just one more spoonful of that delicious soup," but times of discussing books and magazine articles and current news. The young one forgot how much soup he was eating as he listened and participated. Although not permitted to leave the table until dismissed, he sometimes was allowed to go to look up a word in the dictionary. Was there such a word as "normalcy?" The dictionary, published twenty years before, was the authority, and President Harding's new word was considered out of line.

What chance had a child in such a family to be a nonreader?

The youngest one had special treatment accorded only those who weighed lightly on the paternal lap. Early in the evening, before the others were assembled or could be disturbed, he sat on his father's lap and was read to. Some things he understood and some he didn't, but here he met stories from the Bible, Hans Christian Andersen, and the stories of King Arthur. Each night he was asked how much he remembered from the night before, and disappointed his father with the clear evidence that he had been asleep on the last several pages. Probably that is the reason Father chose to read things he could bear to read again.

It was a good time, having the attention of a whole father, feeling his arm around the side, smelling the tweed and the tobacco, looking down at the pages that turned and turned, and waiting for the wonderful pictures. This early association of affection with reading, and reading with family pleasure, is a priceless beginning for the young reader. It should not be entirely lost in the age of television.

There were also the memorable trips to the library, the excursions with Father or Mother, or as the younger ones came along, with the older sister or brother as shepherd. While the grownups chose small, thick books, the littlest one picked out all the big, thin books with lots of pictures. And one fabulous afternoon he was allowed to choose one from all the rest to take home for a whole week. As he grew up and became a real reader, it was here that he exhausted the supply of dog and horse stories, learned to use a library card and how to avoid fines.

In those days a reading family had books in every room in the house. House cleaning took a long time, for cleaning the book shelves meant a chance to look again at old favorites. Frequently there was more reading than cleaning. The good provider did not buy single books; he bought sets of books nicely bound; and for long weeks afterwards, one became immersed in all of Mr. Poe or Mr. Dickens or Mr. Shakespeare. A side effect of this expenditure was that the children learned to have clean hands and to open and handle a book with care. "Your Father paid good money for it." Nobody ever wore a book on his head or scribbled on the flyleaf or tore a page. The children learned early to worship at the same shrine.

The modern reading environment

Today the modern reading family has a wealth of material from which to select. Adult reading materials come in hard and soft covers and are produced by competitive companies. Father does not buy *the* atlas, *the* dictionary, *the* encyclopaedia; he browses and discusses and then selects the one or more of each he can afford and wants. Book clubs assail him with introductory offers, and he often chooses one and becomes, for a shorter or longer time, a monthly reader of the selections. There are hundreds of magazines to chose from in planning the family subscription list. There is often more than one newspaper in his locality.

Bookstores are not the only places in which books are sold. He finds himself browsing at the airport, in the drugstore, at the supermarket. And Junior trails along and wheedles for his comic book.

There must be children's reading material in the reading home, and here, too, a wealth of material is available. Recently when a bibliography of the best books for children was to be assembled, competent authorities nominated 15,000 books for the honor of inclusion (17). The child reader need not starve.

Parents should know the magazines, encyclopaedias, atlases, and dictionaries for children, and the book clubs through which they can build their own juvenile libraries (149).

Parents can take the responsibility of conducting library visits with their children, help their children to obtain a library card, and help them to learn what it means, in terms of the weekly allowance, to let a book become overdue. Parents of different families can take turns shepherding the neighborhood youngsters to the story hour which the neighborhood library offers. Story-hour broadcasts on television can be made special events in the home, followed by discussion, reading the book, and dramatization.

When a child brings a book home from school, there should be interest in what he is reading and provision for a quiet time and place for him to read it. There should be a special shelf where his personal library may be kept. In "reading time" at home, interruptions should be at a minimum, for the child cannot learn concentration by being called away from his book.

What should be the reaction of the reading family when the preschool child points to a word on a page and says, "What's this word?" A child should be told what the word is. Similarly, if he asks the name of a letter, he should be told. Some children, watching the page as the parent reads aloud, "reading" the ads as the television announcer speaks them, looking at billboards and signs along the highway or street, looking through picture books by themselves, learn to read before they enter school. The Durkin study found 49 such children among the 5,103 first graders in the Oakland public schools (67). Parents who answer questions about pictures, letters, and words foster such early growth.

How Parents Can Co-operate With the School

A reading program cannot be entirely successful if it is left completely to the school. Most of the school time must be spent in instruction; but instruction loses its potency when it is not accompanied by practice. The home can provide the time and place for some of the practice. Furthermore, reading skills are lost and the whole purpose of the reading program is defeated unless the child establishes a habit of reading for information and entertainment. The home, the public library, and the community centers should offer the situations and the reading materials to entrench this habit. Of course, if these are nonexistent or unsuitable, the school must carry the entire burden; but in this case the program is necessarily less effective.

In addition to a time and place for practice, the home can furnish the appreciators who make reading progress seem important, the listeners to ideas gained from reading, and the holders of cards or the suppliers of words in practice exercises for word recognition.

What are some of the ways in which the parent can give positive support to the school reading program? *First,* he must be informed by the school. At parent-teacher association meetings he can learn something about the philosophy of the school and the conduct of the reading program. He can support the drives that this organization sponsors to obtain books for the school library, classroom collections, and the tape recorders and record players. Remembering that organizations do not thrive on dead wood, he can participate on committees planning programs of interest to parents.

"Open house" nights are occasions for seeing the setting in which his child works, and for talking with the teacher about classroom activities. Because so many parents and children come, it is not always the ideal time to discuss problems and make plans for a joint attack on a particular difficulty. If possible, the parent should be willing to attend a separate conference with the teacher for such discussion.

Especially at kindergarten and primary grade levels, some schools conduct "teas." The parents come to see a demonstration of the class activity. First, they are told what the purpose of the activity is and some of the points to watch. After the demonstration, the class is taken over by an administrator or another teacher, while the teacher and the parents have refreshments together and discuss what they saw. This is an opportunity for the parent to see what actually happens in the reading program instead of depending upon alarmist articles and books or neighborhood gossip for his information. Now he can ask the questions that he has wanted to ask, and get the answers firsthand.

The parent should read, or have someone read to him, the reports and requests and announcements that the school sends regarding his child. Some schools send bulletins to their kindergarten parents, giving general information and suggesting ways the parents can help. The Tulsa Public Schools in a ten-page bulletin of this kind list the following ideas relating to reading (155):

Be friendly with the teacher. Tell her anything which will help her to know and understand your child better.

Visit the school so that you may understand what the teacher is trying to do for your child.

Make appointments either before or after school with your child's teacher to talk over important problems.

Attend group meetings for parents, such as P.T.A. meetings, and other school events.

Read and answer promptly all notes sent from the school to you. Be interested in the materials your child brings home from school. Discuss his day in kindergarten with him and let him know that you enjoy listening to his experiences. Have a place for your child to keep his school materials. Show him that you appreciate them.

Some parents find themselves fascinated with the work of the school. They give loyally of their time and talents. Not waiting always to be asked, they volunteer help which they see is needed: chaperoning field trips, making a box for the class card file of sight words, building a puppet stage, finding discarded industrial material which is valuable for school activities.

Exercise for specific purposes

In these days parents are reading and hearing a good deal about the use to which other countries are putting education. They are told that education is a part of national defense. And so it is not only a concern for Junior but a desire to see their own country progress that motivates their eagerness to "do something at home" to help Junior learn to read. More commonly now, even in first grade, children are taking home simple types of homework which do not take long to complete. These are valuable because (1) the child may establish a serious habit of study at home, (2) he knows that learning to read is his business and that he is expected to work at it, (3) the parents sense that modern reading programs do have "teeth" in them, and (4) they can observe their child's performance. If he is doing badly, the teacher does not have to be the bearer of the bad news.

When the child is learning to hear likenesses in letter sounds, he can be given a sheet of paper with a picture of a box and a ball at the top. The homework will be to draw all the things he can think of that begin like those words. A note to the parent can suggest that he have the child repeat all the words he portrays, to make sure that they all do begin with the same sound. Additional work may be to write down words (lower-case letters in manuscript writing) the child mentions that he does not portray, but that also begin the same, or a game may be played while Mother fries the potatoes: she is to say three words, and the child is to tell which one begins like *ball*, and prove it by saying both.

There are many such activities in which parents can engage the child if the teacher will only tell them what will be helpful. Trips to the grocery shelves can require the matching of pictures and shapes, counting, and colors. On the way there and on the way home, guessing games can be varied to suit the need: I see something red. I see something round. I see two things exactly alike. I see two things that rhyme. I see something big and something little right next to it. I see something that says (make the sound).

If the child needs help in oral reading, the teacher can send the child home with a story he has already read, to read aloud to the parent. If he misses a word, the parent can supply it. If the child needs help in silent reading, the teacher can suggest material which he would find interesting and profitable. The child can read silently and the parent can then ask him such questions as: "What was the story about? What did you find out from it? What person did you like best in it? Why?" A game could be played in which the child draws a picture about the story or a sequence of pictures, and then the parent looks at the picture and asks the child to find in the story the actions and objects he put into his picture and read those parts aloud. Then the child can identify the things in the picture which he added to the meaning of the story in his interpretation of it.

Once a teacher begins to think in what ways parents can help, the ideas multiply.

In purchases for their children, parents can select toys which help the reading program. A child who is learning the sequence of letters in words may be entertained and helped by a toy typewriter or printing outfit. Word building games can foster acquaintance with letter sequences and the structural aspects of word analysis—how a compound word is formed, a verb ending, etc. A chalkboard can be a place for family announcements, a pad for needed groceries, and the child can be the one to write the messages. Another consideration in purchases of toys is that the child who is interested in something will be more ready to read about it. Toys involving science experiments make him read directions and make him want to read more about science. Model-airplane construction requires the reading of directions and stimulates interest in reading about planes, about which much has been written at every level of difficulty. Construction and experimentation should not be done once but many times. Sometimes the child builds as the parent reads the directions, and sometimes the reverse. A purposely forgetful parent can require more than one reading of a difficult sentence.

The Teacher's Relationship With the Parent

Probably the most important principle for the teacher to remember in her relationship with parents is: *Don't be bad news.* If the teacher communicates with the parent only in case of disaster, the relationship will be entered into with trepidation. The teacher will be on edge, wondering, "How shall I lead up to it?" The parent will be growling, "NOW what?" The best idea is to get acquainted early, make clear the common goal and good intentions of everybody, and keep the channels of information open. Even before the teacher knows her class well, she can send home to the parents news of class activities.

During the latter part of kindergarten and beginning of first grade, the teacher can give the parents suggestions for home activities directly related to the printed word:

Show the child how to write his name. (Send home lower-case alphabet with directions of strokes indicated.)

Supervise the writing of his name. Watch direction of strokes.

Write from the child's dictation a caption for a picture he has drawn.

Supervise the copying of the caption at the bottom of his picture.

Record in manuscript writing the stories he dictates to you. If you have him "reread" the stories, he will dictate short ones!

Thumb through a magazine with him and answer his questions about objects and words. Ask whether he sees another word on the page like the one you said. If he does, ask how he knows it is the same, or to point to the parts he sees are alike.

A classroom newspaper, compiling children's creative writing over a period of from two to four weeks, can be read by the child in school and read by or to the parent at home. Notes accompanying report cards can cite evidences of the child's progress. The teacher can add suggestions for help by the parent or for home activities. Since these are not easily invented on the spur of the moment, the teacher should keep a file of such ideas, organized by purpose: ear training, visual discrimination, main idea, classifying, etc.

When the holidays and vacations come around, the teacher can make book lists for the children. Part of the list for Junior will be made up of books his group might profit by reading. The rest will be special books to meet Junior's particular interests.

If the class subscribes to a newspaper, such as *My Weekly Reader* (see Chapter 15), the teacher may use the newspaper in class as a reading lesson, then send it home. On the first occasion, a note should accompany the newspaper, telling the parent to let the child share his news, much as Father does, and receive similarly serious attention.

If one of the parents is a writer, a reporter, or an editor, he may create a good deal of class interest in reading. The children can plan an interview with him about the way writers (reporters, editors) work. Or they may correspond with him, writing their own letters and reading the reply.

Sometimes as part of the writing program and as a way of impressing the child with his reading endeavors, the children can write letters to their parents, telling about the kinds of books they are reading and what they are learning about reading: "Here are some of the ways we solve new words." "These are the things we look for in a good story."

Parents and Criticisms of Education

Teachers, principals, supervisors, and superintendents of schools have to be ready to answer the criticisms levelled at modern education. Parents, reading or hearing about these criticisms, bring their worries to the school; or, feeling that the school is probably wrong, they try to do something at home or through a tutor. What can the school do about such criticism?

For *one thing*, it can use the criticism as a reason to re-evaluate its program. "We are criticized as being deficient in this way. Let's find out whether we are." *Secondly*, it can say, "What is the research evidence on this subject?" If the research does not support the parents' request, then the parents should be given the findings of the research so that they, too, can understand why the school resists the change.

Thirdly, it can examine the materials and techniques the parents are proposing or resorting to, in the light of what is known about good education in reading. An example of this is a book on phonics which parents and teachers are purchasing in great quantities. How good is this book? It has three characteristics which make it less desirable than the program of word analysis which most reader series present: (1) In its effort to teach the child quickly all the things he needs to know to analyze words, it actually misinforms the child about the sound certain letter combinations make. For instance, the *ou* sound is described as a short *o* sound. (2) In order to have the child learn the sounds before he knows words by sight, it tells the child the sound a letter makes. It fails to teach him how to determine the sound in case he forgets the rule. He is completely dependent upon memory, because he has not learned an inductive approach to word analysis. (3) The child is given a set of steps to use in analyzing all strange words, all of which steps are centered on phonics. He is not encouraged to solve words in shorter ways when this is possible. His mind is chained to a relatively slow and frequently unrewarding method.

When the school has examined and analyzed these materials, it should report its findings to the parents. But it should also tell the parents what it is doing instead. If parents get the impression that the school substitutes nothing for something, they will turn out to vote for something.

A *fifth* step the school can take, not necessarily in this order, is to examine the source of the criticism itself. It may be a subversive group. Or it may be a person who knows only half-truths about a situation and is therefore honestly disturbed by what he thinks is serious neglect. Sometimes it is a person who has misinterpreted the evidence, like the person who was alarmed because only fifty per cent of the children in a school were at or above grade norms in reading. And sometimes it is a person who is right. The school board, the parents, and the community should be apprised of the outcome of this investigation.

Communicating With Parents

Parents should be able to count on educators to show skill in communication. Educators are supposed to know that technical language discriminates against the uninitiated. They should avoid using technical words unless they explain their meanings. Even the word *phonics* needs to be defined for parents, who use it without knowing its specific meaning. Grandiose abstractions such as "providing meaningful experiences for the development of skills, attitudes, understandings, and knowledges" leave a glaze over the eyes of the lay listener, and should be avoided in expositions to parents.

It would be a wise educator who would say to himself before a conference or presentation of material to a parent audience, "What practical examples can I give instead of using vague terms? Can I draw upon the parent's own reading experience to illustrate points? What clues to meaning must I plant in my sentences if I use technical words? What pictures or charts can I use to make my meaning clear? Can I start with a parallel home situation or other illuminating analogy?" Then, he would be wise to tape or write out his talk, and prune it of all needless, bewildering technicalities.

He should also say to himself, "What do I need to know from the parent? How can I ask my questions in a way that will not make the parent defensive or defeat the purpose for which I ask it? How can I remain objective about something over which I can easily become defensive, too? How can I give him the satisfaction of feeling that his contribution is valuable?" The answers to these questions should promote good communication.

Summary

The teacher must learn to know the parent as an individual and as a partner in an important task—the education of his child. If possible, the school should encourage early parent education so that parents can make the most of the first five years of being home teachers. In their role as educators, parents set the child an example by their own conduct. Their relationship toward the child and toward each other helps or hinders reading progress.

Certain work habits learned in the home, and certain attitudes toward work and responsibility contribute to success in reading in school. A child who fails to learn how to share and get along with other children has difficulty in the classroom. The child who does not learn respect for his parents often carries this handicap over into his relationship with the teacher.

Through activities in both work and play, through trips and games, through drawing and painting, the child can learn much at home that will prepare him for reading in school.

A parent can create an environment that will reinforce the desire to read, by being a reader himself, by reading to his child, and by giving him a time and place and materials for uninterrupted reading. Appreciation of the child's efforts to read goes far to encourage him in a difficult task. It is very important that the parent answer the child's inquiries about words.

By making the most of his opportunities to get acquainted with the school program, and by offering his services and information about his child, the parent can support the reading program. The school which tells him what he can do to help his child at home is providing a channel for the efforts many parents wish to make. The teacher needs to make suggestions for home assistance.

Through notes, letters, reports, classroom newspapers, and pupils' products, the teacher keeps the home informed about what is happening at school. Book lists and suggested exercises and questions on home reading help the parent become a better home teacher.

Criticisms of the reading program should be met with positive action rather than defensiveness. And parents should share in discussions of the school's effectiveness and needed improvements.

If educators mean to be understood in dealing with parents as partners, they should speak in terms that laymen can understand.

Suggested Activities

Creative. Write an explanation of the inductive method of teaching word analysis (See Chapter 7) in terms that the lay public can understand.

Plan the contents of a folder of samples of a child's work, by means of which you could show a visiting parent the child's reading progress. Assume a first-grade level.

Further study. Read one of the following books which parents may have read, to determine the differences between its point of view and that in Chapter 7. Plan how you would explain the differences to a parent.

FLESCH, Rudolf, *Why Johnny can't read.* New York: Harper & Bros., 1955.

SPALDING, Romalda B., and SPALDING, Walter T., *The writing road to reading.* New York: Morrow and Company, 1957.

TERMAN, Sibyl, and WALCUTT, Charles C., *Reading: chaos and cure.* New York: McGraw-Hill Book Company, Inc., 1958.

Selected References

For the teacher:

DeBOER, John J., and DALLMANN, Martha, *The teaching of reading.* New York: Holt, Rinehart and Winston, Inc., 1960, 345-349.

HILDRETH, Gertrude, *Readiness for school beginners.* New York: Harcourt, Brace & World, Inc., 1960, Chap. 12.

ROBISON, Eleanor G., *Helping parents understand the modern reading program*. Ginn and Company Contributions in Reading No. 3. Boston: Ginn and Company.

RUSSELL, David H., *Children learn to read*. Boston: Ginn and Company, 1961, Chap. 17.

For the parent:

ARTLEY, Sterl, *Your child learns to read*. Chicago: Scott, Foresman and Company, 1953.

GRAY, William Scott, *On their own in reading*. Chicago: Scott, Foresman and Company, 1960.

LARRICK, Nancy, *A parent's guide to children's reading*. Garden City: Doubleday and Company, Inc., 1958.

McKEE, Paul, *A primer for parents: how your child learns to read*. Boston: Houghton Mifflin Company, 1957.

MONROE, Marion, *Growing into reading*. Chicago: Scott, Foresman and Company, 1951.

ROBISON, Eleanor G., *A letter to parents*. Ginn and Company Contributions in Reading No. 8. Boston: Ginn and Company.

19

Recommended Practices in Kindergarten

Drawing by CEM;
© 1961, The New Yorker Magazine, Inc.

The kindergarten teacher's contribution to the teaching of reading is to discover what the child brings with him from his home and after five years of life, and to prepare him for formal reading instruction. Chapters 3, 4, and 5 have described the behaviors which the teacher analyzes in her contacts with the child, and the activities and practices through which the teacher and parent can improve the child's chances for success in reading.

The thesis of the present chapter is that nothing is expected of the eighth grader in reading which is not fostered in some way by the kindergarten teacher. There is nothing that will not be better in eight years for her having worked on it or toward it during the prereading period. The kindergarten teacher does not have to teach words in books in order to be helping a child become a good reader. But she does have to keep many different goals in mind in order to make the most of kindergarten opportunities.

At the present time there are two views of the kindergarten program which are completely at odds with one another. On the one hand is the view that the kindergarten should not expose the child to the visual symbol of a word at all, that the activities relating to reading should deal with objects other than visual word forms. On the other hand is the view that the kindergarten should use the materials of the basal-reader program to introduce the child to as much learning of beginning reading as he can master at that time.

The authors of the present volume reject both of these views. It does not stand to reason that a child of the present reading environment should be housed several hours a day in a room devoid of verbal symbols. On the covers of books and magazines at home, along with the pictures in his books, on the television commercials, and along the street as he walks to school, the child encounters and to some extent interprets verbal symbols. Certainly the kindergarten environment, which is supposed to help him toward reading competence, should not be completely lacking in this ingredient.

The second view essentially imposes upon the child materials which were designed for a child of twenty per cent more life experience and maturity. It does this despite two important findings of research: (1) that a half year or year later a child can learn the same things faster, and (2) much reading growth can be effected through casual contacts with verbal material throughout the school day.

The kindergarten year includes children who are far from learning to read, some children who are ready, and other children—perhaps one in the average-sized class—who are already able to read simple materials. Whatever is offered by the kindergarten teacher should provide help and challenge for every child. This is the guiding principle upon which the following suggestions for the kindergarten program are made.

Verbal Facility

What to say and how to say it—this is a big problem for children. Partly it is learned by example, partly by strongly motivated attempts at expression.

"Do we get time fo' one mo'?"—big eyes pleading—

"Do we have time for one more?"—teacher helping—The basal reader will not contain sentences with "do we got's," "fo's," and "mo's" in them.

Then cautiously, "Do–we–have–time–for–one–more?"

Broadcasting time, the microphone plugged into the record player, is a time for us all to sit together and take turns speaking at the mike.

"Who is first?" the teacher asks, looking for the most attentive, straightest sitter of all. "Marvin?"

Marvin rises and takes the microphone. "This is Station ABC, Room One, Marvin Pilf speaking. Good morning, boys and girls."

A supporting chorus replies, "Good morning, Marvin." Then Marvin, impressed into his best speech, reports: "My dog Suzie had pups yesterday."

The microphone is passed temporarily to an eager hand.

"How many do she have, Marvin?"

The teacher says, "Can you say that in a better sentence?" if she knows the child knows better. Otherwise she repeats the preferred form and the child tries again.

"How many does she have, Marvin?"

Marvin takes the mike and replies, "She have—she has four puppies, Oscar."

Singing time, similarly, is a time for excellent enunciation.

"Let me hear that crac*k* in crackle," the teacher says, and she gets it. Her approval and the feeling of accomplishment are the children's reward.

Concept Building

The rabbit in the classroom is a wonderful opportunity for concept building. "What do we notice about him?" He is round, someone says, and fat and white and long-eared. His eyes are pink and so are the insides of his ears. (So far, shape and color.) Fortunately, he moves. "What can he do?" He can wiggle his nose and cock his ears. "Why does he move his ears like that?" He hears something and moves them in its direction. "What do *we* do when we hear something?" Why, we have to turn our whole heads and look.

"What does he look like?" (This brings out the poet. We are after relationships now.) He looks like a big snowball, like that fluffy cotton candy, like a white muff. What do his ears make you think of? A shell, a (veined) leaf, a piece of lettuce.

All of this and the rabbit has scarcely moved. He is nowhere near exhaustion, and neither is the subject. "Let's pretend with our hands that we have rabbit ears and are listening over this way and listening over that way." (Getting the concept with creative activity and taking care of some restlessness.)

"Has anyone seen him move his hind feet? What does he do with them? (action) Can you show us? How are those hind feet different from the front feet? (contrast) Who can point to his front feet? His back feet? (concept of *front* and *back*) When you pretend you are a rabbit, what are your front feet? (Now perhaps *front* and *back* are straight.)

"Let's think how the rabbit feels. (tactile impression) Each one of you, one at a time beginning with Albert, gently run your hand down his back. Then tell us how he feels." (adjectives) He feels smoove, says Albert. "Yes, he feels smooth. What else is smooth? Does he feel like this sandpaper? (Building concept by contrast.) No. Let's all say smooth and let me hear that ending: smoo*th*."

In such a lesson there are a hundred directions the teacher may take. Shall she pursue appearance, touch, sound, and the like? Should she dwell on opposites: rough—smooth, front—back? Should she turn the rabbit into a speech lesson? She does what she thinks is needed most, and she calls on the child who needs the practice, to learn to speak or to think or to act or merely to pay attention for longer periods of time. These are all reading-readiness activities. At the end of rabbit time, she is not quite sure that she has made the right choices, but this is a good sign. It means she sees the many possibilities and will turn to them another time.

The teacher has been working for *kinds* of observation about the rabbitness of the rabbit. The children have been producing nouns (ears, eyes, feet), adjectives (smooth, fat, white), verbs (hops, moves), adverbs (forward, back), and sentences without knowing it. They have been kept to topics (appearance, movement, feeling) as someday they will read topics, each in its own paragraph.

And then to help the children extract rabbitness from Peter's individual characteristics, the teacher pulls out some pictures of rabbits. "What are these?" More rabbits. "How do you know?" Well, ears, hind feet, little tail, etc. "How are they different from our rabbit?" They are different colors, of course, different patterns. Bobby, the travelled one in the group, tells about a rabbit show he attended in Chagrin Falls, Ohio, where he saw rabbits with fur likes foxes' and beavers'. "Well, you do have to be careful that the next foxy beaver you see isn't a rabbit! What do all these rabbits have? (Children enumerate common traits.) So you will know it's a rabbit if what?" (Here a child *summarizes* the rabbit gleanings of the day.)

The little girl who speaks only Chinese—what has she gotten out of this lesson? She knows rabbits, of course, but not by that name. The teacher needs to say *rabbit* many times for the child needs to hear it many times associated with her old acquaintance with a Chinese name. "Let's all say it together: rabbit," will help her get the feel of the word without embarrassment. Ritualistic talk about what we know will give the needed ear and speech training: Our rabbit is a white rabbit. Our rabbit is soft. If the child tends to ignore word endings (Our rabbi i sof), the teacher makes much of the endings herself and has the children repeat with emphasis.

What about the child who entered kindergarten already reading?. He can find rabbit pictures in books, to show the other children. When children are finishing their work, those who are already finished can sit around him to hear him read a rabbit story. They listen carefully because they may be able to take parts in playing it, or retell the story with hand puppets the next time.

If a note to the parents requests that the child be helped to find pictures of objects that are smooth (or the child may be told this), extra thought will be given to the concept. Or the adult may list the things the child thinks of in this category, or the child may draw pictures and tell what they are.

What is in this lesson for the child who already has a large vocabulary? He will bring up the level of the whole discussion and observation, for the rabbit's nose will be *moist* and his ears may even be *gradations* of pink. The teacher will translate him to the others. (Yes, they go from dark pink to light pink. The veins are really red.) Sometimes she will have him translate himself, for he will have to learn to do this to make himself clear, all his life. (How else could you say this? What other word means the same thing or almost the same?) And she will throw a challenge his way, and let others benefit as best they can. (Your father didn't want you to pick up the wild rabbits because wild rabbits sometimes have an illness that human beings can get from them. The sickness is called *tularemia*. Can you say it?)

Word Recognition

As each new kindergartner tells his name, the teacher writes the first name on the chalkboard in manuscript letters for all to see. She stands aside as she writes so that she does not obscure the writing for any of the watchers. They can see that writing is done from left to right. She may even say, "I am starting every name with a capital letter, a big letter," just in case an advanced child will remember. Another day she may say, "What kind of letter do I use to start your name?" and be surprised with a favorable response. Now she knows something about the child.

She will make cards with the children's names on them, to be put up with their belongings—on the front of the box or above the coat hook. This is an opportunity to find out who can already match forms. Every child is given the card with his name on it. Can he match it to his name on the chalkboard, holding it below to show everyone that it does match? The children who cannot do this are helped to do it and then are permitted to put the card in the place to mark their possessions.

A small picture of a flower or a small snapshot of the child himself is an extra clue to those who are far from recognizing their names. But the teacher encourages them. "Bill, how did you know your name?" Why, it's short and tall. And how did Betty? It begins with a *B* and goes tall and then way down. The children's answers cue the teacher to what they know. Listening children raise their sights. Tony, emulating a pattern of success, says that his begins with a *B*, but finds that what works for Betty doesn't work for him.

The children come into the classroom from a world of signs. Many of them already know the general pattern of *Maxwell House Coffee* or *Lipton's Tea*, from packages, signboards, and television commercials. Some can actually read these, independent of picture clues. Certainly the kindergarten should not be an environment devoid of signs. So that visitors can know what is going on, signs are planned. "What shall we call the box where our rabbit lives?" *Our Rabbit House.* "And the box with the food in it waiting for feeding time?" *Peter's lettuce.* We are always mixing up the two cupboards." On one we put in manuscript letters a sign: *paper;* on the other, *crayons and paints*. The paper sign is made on a piece of the paper. The crayon and paints sign carries a color sample of the two media. Mothers and fathers who come to visit are shown around. Some children will say, "Here's where we keep the *paper*." Others will say, "This sign says paper." Some of those who say the latter really can read. Others just know that the paper sign is a short one and the crayons and paints sign is a long one. Still others lean on the color clues.

While the teacher makes the signs, she has the children watch. She stands aside so that they can see, and she says the words (pa-per) as she writes them. She involves the children. What is the word she is to write? Who knows how it should begin? (If she is pretty sure someone does.) Betty thinks she can write it already. Betty tries it out on the chalkboard. Sure enough. Grandmother has been working overtime on this able grandchild, with the letter forms on page 71 of Nancy Larrick's *A parent's guide to children's reading* (Doubleday, 1958), so that the child is making the letters with the proper forms and sequences of strokes. Betty may make the sign herself. If it isn't good enough the first time, she will certainly work to get it right.

"Who thinks he can go to the paper cupboard today and get one sheet of paper for each person at his table?" Unconsciously the child who does not read finds himself aiming for that *paper* sign. The lower-case letters three-quarters of an inch high (upper-case would be twice that), written boldly with a thick black crayon or another instrument such as the Speedball B1 pen, carry across the room. Many such experiences may begin to impress the shape upon him. One would think this association had been planned by the so-called "Madison Avenue" boys. See it enough and you begin to believe it.

The lid is not down on the gifted child. He can read the signs. He can write his name. He signs his pictures. And when he asks what something says, he is told. If he does well enough, he may even help the teacher put names on the pictures by children who do not know how to write them.

At home the children are encouraged to tell the story of their rabbit or about a rabbit they know or about something they care about more. As the parent writes down what the child dictates, he uses the same manuscript letters that the teacher does, making the strokes in the same sequence and direction. He signs the child's name. At school the teacher reads these stories aloud to the class. Some of the children "read" their own from memory. Others really read them. At home, too, parent and child leaf through a magazine together. The parent answers the child's questions about the words.

Word Orientation and Sounds

In reading, concepts such as *long, tall, short, straight, round, before, front, end, curved, middle, left, right, first, last* help in the observation of words. These are mostly relative ideas, best conveyed by contrasts and many occasions for their use. "When does the rabbit stand tall? When does he look very short? Show how long his ears are. Is his tail as long as his ears? Show with two fingers how his ears can stand straight up. Show with your arms how round he is when he sits hunched up."

The children study the flannel board picture as it develops. "Where did Milton put the lettuce?" (in front of the rabbit's nose, before Peter's nose) "The rabbit is where?" (in the middle of the picture) "What is on the left side? On the right?"

"Who would like to take the tall tree and put it into our picture?" Someone selects the tall tree from the assortment of objects lined up in a row before the children. "Who would like to take the first thing in the row, the first thing on the left? Who will take the last thing in the row? Who will find two things just alike?"

By sampling in various situations over a period of time, the teacher finds out which concepts are confusing, such as *left* and *right*. For the children who have this confusion, the teacher designs special exercises. The children who do not have the difficulty derive another kind of experience from the same exercise.

"In this picture, who can find the rabbit that is facing left? Susie? Who can show Susie which way left is in the picture? Is he correct?" (Getting everybody involved in the thinking.) "Who will tell us what he thinks the rabbit is going to do?" (Someone who is not confused by direction has experience listening to and speaking in sentences.)

A similar opportunity arises when the teacher is writing before the children, on a chart. "Where should I start my sentence?" (way over at the left) "What was the first word in the sentence you gave us, Jonas?"

Auditory Discrimination

The little girl who speaks Chinese notices that the writing goes from left to right instead of from top to bottom or right to left, but in her speech she makes no distinction between the *l* and *r* sounds; they are both the same to her ear; and she tends not to attend to final consonant sounds, such as the sound of the *t*'s at the ends of the words. With few exceptions, the words in her language end with vowels. The teacher exaggerates the sound of the *l* in *left*, and has the child look as she places her tongue to produce the sound; so with the final *t* sound.

A certain amount of the work on the *l, r* and *t* sounds is good for everyone, as a check, if nothing else, on the children's ability to hear and reproduce these sounds.

"I am going to say some words, some that begin like *left* and some that do not. When I say one that begins like *left*, hold up your left hand (put out your left foot). When I say one that begins like something else, keep your hand down. Here are my words: *long, look, lift, rock, ring*, etc." Different children are given an opportunity to call the words.

As soon as the teacher knows the children can hear the difference between the *l* sound and the *r* sound, she gives them practice in reproducing the sound. "Look at my mouth. Listen to the word I say, and watch my mouth as I say it. Then say it after me, just as I did: *left* (left), *lost* (lost), etc." If some *refts* and *rosts* remain, she must do special work with this group while other children are otherwise occupied. She may use a mirror for the child to see that his lips and tongue are placed like hers for the initial sound. Some children practice at home with mirrors or parents or both. (It is useless if the parents have the same handicap.) Their greeting to the teacher each morning is a special one. "Good morning, Mrs. Merron. Rook at me." And someday it becomes *Mrs. Mellon* and *look*. They make collections at home of *l* words they hear on TV, *l* objects they see on the way to school, and report their findings. There is a big *lump* of butter in every serving. The *line* formed outside the school. The *leaves* were turning brown. The children are getting sentence practice while they have sound practice. The teacher slyly throws practice their way, in connection with other activities during the school day. "What did you want to do for the rabbit this morning, Mae?" "I wanted to give him his *l*ettuce!"

The child who is already reading can participate in this program in a slightly different way. Instead of just remembering a few words from home, he writes them and reads them. Instead of listening to TV for a sound he already knows, he watches for words beginning with it. Writing them in columns, he can generalize. What does he notice? They all begin with the same letter. It's *l*, according to his grandmother. The teacher shows him what power this knowledge can give him. A l____ looks like a cat and has spots. What's more, whenever he wants to know what sound a letter makes, all he has to do is to think of two words he knows beginning with that letter, and listen to the sound they make. It is an almost fool-proof (*c*ircus, *c*at) method of getting on with your reading without always asking for help. In about two minutes with a bright child, the teacher has removed a roadblock to his progress toward independence.

Without touching the more formal first-grade teaching materials, this teacher is helping each child advance according to his ability, in knowledge that will be useful later in word-analysis techniques.

Comprehension and Interpretation

"I have a new story for you today." The teacher has the children gathered before her, close together but not so close that Jerry *must* keep shoving Isabelle. All can see the cover of the book she holds up for them to see. "The title is 'Snipp, Snapp, Snurr and the Red Shoes' and the author is Maj Lindman. Are we all ready to listen?"

The children are encouraged to discuss what they see if there is a picture on the cover of the book, or if there is an interesting picture on the first page. "Snipp, Snapp, and Snurr were three little boys who lived in Sweden." As each page is turned, the children are shown the new picture. If there is suspense, they are asked, "What do you think he will do?" Thinking children will give good answers. "They'll ask their father for money." "They'll run errands for the neighbors." These interruptions should not be numerous; but if they do not occur, at all, some children do not think *with* the story. They let it wash right off. Their minds wander. They learn to daydream when they are supposed to attend. And what does that mean for comprehension? For next year, and all the years ahead?

It requires no genius for a teacher to know that the children are rapt in attention and need no comments or involvement. If they are so engrossed, she reads on, showing the pictures and encouraging the mood of complete concentration. But if they are restless, distracted, she is careful to choose as the next story one that is short and on a topic highly interesting to them, and the chances are that she will see the need of keeping them thinking. "What did Tommy show us this morning? (The new shoes he got for his birthday.) Here is a story about a birthday and something that someone wanted very much as a present. Let's see whether that person was as lucky as Tommy."

There is more to this story than the surface meaning the child is likely to gather from hearing it the first time without interruption. The next day, "Who remembers the story we heard yesterday?" One child may tell the whole, or several individuals may help each other through, as the teacher turns the pages to show the pictures without text.

Picture interpretation is good exercise for children who will learn to read partly by dependence upon pictures for clues to new words. It is also good for keeping fresh the kinds of thinking they should apply when they read.

The teacher shows the picture of the boys raiding their piggy bank to see whether they have enough to buy Mother a birthday present. "What is happening in this picture? Who are in the picture? What are they doing? What do they want to find out? How do they do it? What do they find? Who else are in the picture? (dog and cat) What do you think they are waiting for? There is something important on the left side of the picture. Who can see what it is? (A picture of mother—the one whose birthday it is going to be.) How do you think the boys are feeling? How can you tell from the picture?" (postures of puzzlement) The artist has put as much meaning and feeling into his illustrations as the author put into the words. His work deserves careful reading, too.

Recall of details and sequence of ideas may later be further exercised with hand puppets or dramatic re-enactment of the story. Or all of the children, as Snipps, Snapps, Snurrs, can show their puzzlement, paint the fence, clean the chimney, and carry the flour sack, in dramatic play. They may also make big pictures of the story sequence, under each of which the teacher writes a dictated sentence: *Snipp painted the fence*. These are made into a movie on a roller, with a narrator. Or they may make a series of pictures individually into a booklet and take it home to retell the story to their families, turning the pages just as one does with a book, and learning to be careful, for these are *their* drawings.

Rereading a favorite story, or reading a story which has much predictable repetition ("Gingerbread boy"), the teacher pauses in the middle of a phrase and the children join in to finish it. This can be done also with the refrain in poetry. Sound and phrasing have a way of suggesting what comes logically or rhythmically next. A sensitivity to sentence patterns is being developed, along with the ability to think with the author and look ahead.

Children's creation of stories like the stories they have heard is another means children have of confirming sentence sense and story sense. "When you shook the piggy bank and couldn't find enough in it, what did you do? Did you work with flour, or paint, or soot? Did you come home white or red or black? Who would like to tell the story as though he were Snipp, Snapp, or Snurr?"

Similarly, the children can draw story pictures and each child can dictate to the teacher what he wants it to say. The teacher writes it on a sheet below the picture and displays it in the room. The child who is already reading and writing may write his own: "My dog is on my mother's bed. My dog is a Pekinese, and my Pekinese is black and brown. and we feed our dog airvry night. and we half to feed her our food thats on the table. and my dogs name is monkey. Michael.Thomas."

Study Skills

The ability to summarize seems to be strengthened as memory fades. After some days, the details of a story fade away, and it is easier just to say that this was a story about three boys who wanted to get their mother a birthday present and worked at jobs to do it. Guessing games can foster this ability, after the children have shared several stories together.

"Let's think over some of the stories we have all heard together. I'm thinking of a story about three boys who wanted to get their mother a birthday present. How many of you think you know which story it was?" A child is selected to tell. After a few examples, "Can you think of a story that I have not mentioned? Can you tell us in a sentence what it was about, and see whether we can guess which story you mean?" Sometimes quick sketches of what the child has said, help the children to keep these ideas in mind as they try to think of the story: three stick figures of boys, a stick figure of a mother, and two shoes.

The reverse exercise can be done. The teacher shows the children the front cover of a book they have heard read. Somebody tells what the title is. (The one who can read, reads it. The one who can remember, remembers it.) Someone else tells in a sentence what it was about. The teacher draws the stick figures rapidly. If the child leaves out something important, it will be obvious from the drawing, and other children will volunteer to fill in. Or the child himself may remember.

Someday these children will be expected to take notes on what they read. How can a readiness for this task be created in the kindergarten? Apropos of interest in where food comes from and what farmers do, a question may come up such as: What kinds of farms are there? Meta says her father raised tobacco where he came from. Gerald says all he sees is chickens when his father takes him to farms. Out comes the little book, *Ten big farms* by Dahlov Ipcar (Knopf, 1958). The teacher says, "Let's look at the pictures very carefully to see all the kinds of farms there are, and what they raise."

As she shows different pictures, the children say what kind of farm it is. In the picture file in which the teacher keeps alphabetically classified the pictures which she frequently uses, she finds what she is looking for, saying as she looks, "Vincent says this is a chicken farm. Chicken begins with a *C*, so I'll look back behind the *C* in the file . . . and sure enough." She pulls out a picture of chickens. "Who will put it on the chalk tray?" Someone proudly does. "So what is one kind of farm? Yes, a chicken farm or poultry farm. Let's say *poultry*. (They all do.) Now let's look through the pictures until we come to another kind of farm. Tell me when you think the picture is something different." The children observe the pictures carefully. Mentally, they are having to rule out chickens and look for something else. When they find it, they want to put another picture on the chalk tray. At the end, "How many different kinds of farms have we found out about? Who can come up here and name them?"

If the teacher has pictures of turkey farms and duck farms and chicken farms, as she comes to each example she says, "A turkey farm is a poultry farm, too. Poultry are birds that we raise to eat." In this way she builds the idea of the general term. Ultimately, the children can classify. "Who can find all the pictures of fruit farms? Of poultry farms? Of truck farms?" The children are learning the rudiments of outlining, main and subordinate headings, keeping to a subject.

Reference reading can be the perusal of pictures in books on farms. Each child has a different book. "All of these books tell us something about farms. We can learn much from studying the pictures. Maybe we shall find a book so interesting that we will all want to hear it read aloud. But we haven't time to hear all of them. Look through the book you have, from front to back as I am doing mine, and be ready to tell what you found out about farms."

When the teacher herself is stumped on a question, she does not scurry away into privacy to cover her ignorance as she finds out. She shows the children how she finds out. They accompany her to the school library with the burning question for the librarian. They watch her and listen to her decide out loud which volume of the encyclopaedia to use. They see her put the pictures back under the right headings into her file. They are learning about study skills. And housekeeping!

Occasionally there will be a need to look back into a story which has been read aloud. "How far in the story would you say it was? Was it right at the first? If I look halfway through the book, will that be about the right place?" A child ceremoniously shows where he would open the book. Is he right? There is great interest in the good guess and the outcome. The children get the idea that you can find things faster if you think where to look before you act.

The Content Fields

All that the teacher can do to develop concepts, comprehension, interpretation, and study skills will help children read in the content fields. Some children in their free time will not be painting the usual neckless figure with the thin legs, the peaked house, and the tree. Their creations may be pictures of dinosaurs or space ships. Their world is wide. As one kindergartner said, "I know Denmark, Sweden, France, China, Mexico, and Chicago."

Since children's interests are tremendously influenced by what happens to be on television, there is no telling from week to week what the hot issue will be. The teacher is ready for anything. Her long-term insurance is the school librarian. Her immediate references are recommended book lists for children and a few very simple reference books in the classroom. A simplified encyclopaedia, while it gives limited information, presents data in language the children can understand, with pictures that are colorful and realistic.

If it must be dinosaurs this week, the teacher is ready. She finds the D volume of the encyclopaedia and opens up the dinosaur page, where seven types of the monster are portrayed in various unbecoming postures. "The word *dinosaur* means terrible lizard," the book says. "From the end of its nose (the longest of the dinosaurs) to the tip of its tail it was about 70 feet long" (200, pp. 420-421). Stepping off the room, perhaps adding the hall, the children can imagine what a monster it was. Lizard? What is a lizard? The book says they weren't really lizards at all. But whoever made the mistake of calling them lizards must have had a reason. Perhaps if we look at pictures of lizards, we'll know. The school librarian can locate for the kindergartners a book their teacher can read to them or show them, on old beasts for young people. Meanwhile Colbert's *The dinosaur book* (Whittlesey, 1951) has good illustrations.

The teacher explains that we don't call a dinosaur a terrible lizard. We call him a dinosaur. We use technical terms in science to say exactly what we mean. In this way, the habit of calling the object by its proper name is built up, and a spotty but dependable scientific vocabulary grows.

Now that we know so much about dinosaurs, maybe we should send the big news to our parents, who imagine that kindergarten is a combination of sand pile and bead stringing. The teacher takes dictation on a letter:

January 15, 19——

Dear Parents,

This week we learned about dinosaurs. There were more than 5000 kinds of them. We saw pictures of only seven kinds. Some of them were bigger than our room.

Please send us any news you have on dinosaurs.

Your————————,

The teacher duplicates the letter, helps the children insert their names or writes them herself, and sends the young scientists home to pump their parents.

Children of this age do not have to be encouraged to ask questions, but they do have to be encouraged to answer them themselves. Why should the teacher answer what other color a pig can be but off-pink, when there is the picture file full of pigs after P? If there is a reference in the room that answers the questions, the child should be helped to find his information in it. If the question can be answered by interviewing parents, by looking at pictures in magazines, by finding books in the library with the aid of the librarian, this should be done. Pretty soon the child is very proud of knowing where he will probably find his answers for himself, with a little help, of course.

"Why did somebody think a dinosaur was a kind of lizard? Well, let's look at lizards and dinosaurs in the encyclopaedia and see. What would you say, looking at the Diplodocus and the Chuckwalla? What about the head, the neck, the legs?"

"How many dinosaurs did we read there were? Listen to what it said about the lizard: 'There are about 3,000 kinds of lizards.' How big was the biggest dinosaur? Listen to this: 'The biggest lizard is the dragon lizard. It is found in Indonesia. This lizard may be 10 feet long and weigh 250 pounds' " (Ibid., p. 820). The brighter children's reasoning is used: Five of anything is more than three of anything (Five children, three children illustrate.). Five thousand dinosaurs are more than 3,000 lizards. The Brontosaurus was 70 feet long (the length of the hall), and the dragon lizard 10 feet long (from here to the desk). In size, then, the dinosaur was much bigger. Here the children have listened to straight factual information to find an answer (comparable to reading for a purpose and taking notes), used simple proportion to determine the difference in size, and generalized to the conclusion that in appearance (picture reading) and statistics, the dinosaur was not a lizard.

What if the teacher, fresh out of a college course on prehistoric life, had *told* the children the answer? From the point of view of creating a scientific approach to problems and teaching the rudiments of later reading reference work, it would have been sheer tragedy. It is not the business of a teacher to limit a class to what she knows. It is, rather, her role to teach a pupil skills which will continue indefinitely to give him greater knowledge and control over his environment.

Interests

With rabbits in the classroom, Dorothy Baruch's poem, "Rabbits,"[1] has an appreciative audience. "Here is a poem by someone who watched her two white rabbits in her yard, just as we are watching ours. And this is what she says:

> My two white rabbits
> Chase each other
> With humping, bumping backs.
>   They go hopping, hopping,
>   And their long ears
>   Go flopping, flopping.
>   And they
>   Make faces
>   With their noses
>   Up and down.
> Today
> I went inside their fence
> To play rabbit with them.
> And in one corner
> Under a loose bush
> I saw something shivering the leaves.
> And I pushed.
> And looked.
> And I found—
> There
> In a hole
> In the ground—
> Three baby rabbits
> *Hidden* away.
>   And *they*
>   Made faces
>   With their noses
>   Up and down."

[1] "Rabbits" from *I like animals* by Dorothy W. Baruch. Copyright 1933 by Dorothy W. Baruch. Reprinted by permission of Dorothy W. Baruch.

This can become a favorite poem, one the children want to hear again and again. Pretty soon they are joining in to say the lines. Sometimes, as a way of calling the children to attention and settling them in preparation for another activity, the teacher simply starts softly, "My two white rabbits chase each other—," the children one by one join in, and soon the entire group is unified by the charm of something they all quietly enjoy. Genuine hypnotism sets in when a child with his hand-puppet rabbit under some leaves in a box "shivers the leaves" and at the right moment with the words of the poem has the rabbit appear.

The interest in dinosaurs can lead the teacher to read excerpts from *Dinosaurs and other prehistoric reptiles* by Jane Werner Watson (New York: Golden Press, 1960). The very bright child who is already reading may be up to the fanciful *Danny and the dinosaur* by Syd Hoff (New York: Harper and Brothers, 1958) and tell the children about it. In general, it is to be hoped that the books especially designed for children to read for themselves in the beginning stages of reading will not be read aloud to them by the kindergarten or first-grade teacher or by their parents. There is plenty that the children will not be able to read for themselves at the age of their greatest interest: Mother Goose, animal and folk tales, simple books on science and machinery are in the main well beyond the reading ability of those who can appreciate them most.

One book can lead to another. Interest in boats can lead the children to explore *Boats on the river* by Marjorie Flack (New York: Viking, 1946) and make them want to listen to a story with a boat hero: *Little Toot* by Hardie Gramatky (New York: Putnam, 1939). Landlubbers may remember and tell from the pictures, stories they have heard before, such as Marie H. Ets *Little old automobile* (New York: Viking, 1948), another personified means of transportation.

As the teacher makes her choices, she remembers that the story must not be allowed to elbow out all factual materials. Both should be represented in the child's reading diet. The fanciful and the realistic, the humorous and the sober, in fact, the entire range of topics and feelings that children's literature offers should be sampled during the year.

In addition, it must not be forgotten that depth of exposure is a teaching purpose, also. If it is dogs that the children adore, the little library table in the corner will have a rash of dog books on it. "Bowsers for browsers": *Finders keepers* by Will and Nicolas (New York: Harcourt, Brace, 1951), *Barkis* by Clare Turlay Newberry (New York: Harper and Brothers, 1938), *No roses for Harry!* by Gene Zion (New York: Harper and Brothers, 1958), and the Angus books by Marjorie Flack. Dog fanciers can visit the school library on a special mission: to bring them back alive, between the covers of books. Drawing pictures of their favorite stories and retelling them briefly to the class or to visitors, or dictating explanations to be attached to the pictures and displayed, are ways of requiring recall and extending interest.

Everything fascinating in the world seems to have a "catch" to it. With books, it is that they must be handled with respect. We don't wear them on our heads or use them as pedestals. So this is the way we hold a book, and open it, and turn the pages from the upper right-hand corner—carefully so that we don't tear or crease the paper. We practice it and are complimented on doing it well. We are careful of books because we like them and because other people are going to be using them, too.

The teacher supplies the parents with lists of books they can read to their children and also books that are mostly pictures, for the children's personal libraries.

Taste

While children's interests at this level are varied and changeable, their tastes—the grounds upon which they like or dislike stories or poems— are fairly predictable. Action and repetition are what beguile them most in stories. The sound and rhythm of poetry attract them. They enjoy a surprise and humor. Such characteristics determine in part the choices the teacher makes in recordings, storyreading, storytelling, and poetry reading and telling. But if these are the sole determinants, the bars are let down to admit much that is trash or very nearly so. In such a case, the children's time is wasted as far as the development of taste is concerned. One learns to appreciate good things partly by being exposed to them. One learns to be satisfied with the mediocre or worse, by having such a diet.

Recordings of songs or stories which are used should be chosen for the faithfulness of the singer or storyteller to the spirit of the song or story, not for the fact that the person is funny or that the children are familiar with the person on television. Recordings by Gudrun Thorne-Thomsen, distributed by the American Library Association, and those produced by Caedmon are suggestive of the quality available to the teacher who wishes to offer the best. Ideally the teacher or librarian tells the stories and reads the poems, and the recordings can be used to show her the possibilities in her own rendition. But sometimes there is a good reason for the teacher's not telling the story herself. When the children re-enact the story with puppets, for instance, it is good for the teacher to be free to watch the billy goats Gruff.

The selection of suitable stories and poems can be guided by the materials included in the better anthologies, such as the *Arbuthnot anthology* (Scott, Foresman) and *Through golden windows* (E. M. Hale Co.), and also by suggestions in selective bibliographies. (See Chapters 14 and 15.) *The Horn Book* is an excellent guide to new, worthwhile material. Reviewing the literary values discussed in Chapter 2, the teacher herself can develop the ability to choose well for young listeners.

The artists who illustrate the stories and poems are not to be overlooked. They, too, put the stamp either of the cheap and degraded, or of quality upon the product. Some of the same values which apply to literature apply to them. For instance, good art suggests rather than shows everything. Although it may appear simple, there is more to observe than can be taken in at a superficial glance. The colors do not shout and fight for dominance but create a design which emphasizes the important meaning of the picture. The movement in the illustration, too, draws the reader to the main point, whether it is an object or a mood.

Sometimes the mood created by the story or picture has so obviously enveloped the children that it is best to say nothing. Sometimes, however, awareness can be prodded with a question: "How does this picture make you feel? What does it make you want to do? What sounds do you think are in it?" Imagination and appreciation are cultivated by guided observation of this kind.

Summary

The kindergarten teacher fosters reading by offering guided observation and discussion of objects and ideas which interest the children. Her questions provoke remarks on appearances, functions, actions, relationships, and the like. Word recognition is motivated by the presence of signs around the room and children's name cards. Experience basic to word analysis is undergirded with ear and speech training and left-to-right observation of words and objects. Storytelling provides opportunity for training in comprehension and interpretation of the meaning of English sentences and story form. Study skills are developed in the use of picture files, reference books, and rudimentary experiences in outlining, led by the teacher. Factual materials are listened to for purposes similar to those later used in studying the content fields. Poems and stories read to the children, in which they often join, meet their varied interests. Careful selection of materials for quality of content, illustration, and rendition means a beginning in the development of taste.

The point of view of this chapter is that the kindergarten teacher makes a beginning in all the aspects of learning that are important in the complicated reading process, that she provides an environment which reflects the reading world in which the child lives outside the school, and that she makes casual contacts with reading possible for the able child. It is not proposed that workbooks and books intended for the six-year-old in a more formal setting be used in the kindergarten.

Suggested Activities

Further study. Select a "center of interest" (The rabbit in this chapter was one.) and plan the kinds of questions you might ask the children, to guide their observation and to help them develop a vocabulary with regard to it.

Observation. Visit a kindergarten class. Write an analysis of the reading-readiness contributions made by the activities and the teacher's suggestions and questions. Consider what advances were made through these activities, suggestions, and questions.

Selected References

ARBUTHNOT, May Hill, CLARK, Margaret Mary, HORROCKS, Edna Marguerite, and LONG, Harriet Geneva, *Children's books too good to miss,* 3rd ed. Cleveland: Western Reserve University Press, 1959, 14-20.

—— *Time for poetry.* Chicago: Scott, Foresman and Company, 1961.

DALGLIESH, Alice, *First experiences with literature.* New York: Charles Scribner's Sons, 1937.

FERRIS, Helen, *Favorite poems old and new.* Garden City: Doubleday & Co., 1957.

HILDRETH, Gertrude, *Readiness for school beginners.* New York: Harcourt, Brace & World, Inc., 1950.

KIRK, Samuel A., *Teaching reading to slow-learning children.* Boston: Houghton Mifflin Company, 1940, Chap. 3.

MOORE, Eleanora Haegele, *Fives at school.* New York: G. P. Putnam and Sons, 1959.

ROBINSON, Helen M. (ed.), *Promoting maximal reading growth among able learners.* Supplemental Educational Monograph, No. 81. Chicago: University of Chicago Press, December, 1954.

20

Recommended Practices
in First Grade

The writers assume that the reader will derive ideas about the organization and sequential procedures in first-grade classrooms from Chapter 17 (Organization and Administration of the Reading Program). Visits to classrooms, student-teaching experiences, the reading of basal-reader manuals, and language-arts guides will also develop this knowledge.

The present chapter samples the activities which one might see if one followed a first-grade teacher around all day and even into the night. It is organized by the topics which have been considered in Part II in this book. Each major topic is considered separately here, and practices regarding it are described. The practices are selected for their adherence to the findings of research which have been discussed in Part II. The creative teacher will think of additional ways to act upon these research findings, measuring the value of the activity not so much by immediate results as by its accordance with our knowledge of learning, of children, of reading, and of the goals which we value for the individual and the citizen.

Other practices which the first-grade teacher will find useful are described only in Chapter 19, on the Kindergarten, and in Chapter 21, on second and third grades, in order to avoid needless repetition. The first-grade teacher will find the description of teaching the reading of a story, which is given in detail in Chapter 22 (Recommended Practices in Fourth, Fifth, and Sixth Grades), also applicable to her grade level. In fact, the wise teacher will not read solely about her grade level, for she, of all people, should know what the child has experienced before and what will be expected of him in succeeding classes, and should realize that children sitting in the same classroom may be grades apart in their levels of development.

Readiness to Begin Reading

The first job of any teacher at any grade level is diagnosis. What do the children bring in attitudes toward reading, in understandings about what reading can do for them, in skills and abilities to apply to the work of learning to read well?

It is a long time from June to September; yet the kindergarten teacher's word that certain things have been achieved by June are better than no hint at all to the first-grade teacher. If something has been achieved before, then perhaps a brief review is all that is necessary. If nothing has been achieved, then the teacher must start at scratch.

At the same time, it must be appreciated that summer may have meant growth instead of backsliding. The child who had no farm concepts in June has spent some time on a farm during the summer, or has followed a television program dealing with farm life. During the kindergarten year the teacher had made the family aware of the importance of parent example and parent reading to the child. Perhaps in the summer father or mother has started the habit of reading something aloud to the child each evening. What pictures, what ideas has the child gained through this experience?

The questionnaire

Back in February the first-grade teacher gave the kindergarten teacher a list of things she would like to know about each child. This list was duplicated so that there would be one for each child. During the spring the kindergarten teacher tried to observe as many as possible of these points about each child, and in June she turned over the lists to the first-grade teacher. What with accidents and transfers, all of these children would not be in this school in September, but those who would, would have a real welcome. All summer the first-grade teacher is hatching ideas in the back of her mind.

In planning the list for the kindergarten teacher, the first-grade teacher does not simply copy some well-recommended list from a textbook such as this or from a curriculum guide. She examines the pictures, vocabulary, and exercises in the basal materials she will teach, determines what understandings and skills will be basic to success in dealing with these tasks, and asks about these. *Perhaps* her list is like this:

Name of child————————————————— Sex—— C.A.—— I.Q.——
Can see likenesses and differences in shape.————————————————
Can recognize and name all colors except————————————————
Can speak in sentences.————
In using English, makes these characteristic errors in structure and usage: (*Do he eat cake?*) —————————————————————————
In using English, makes these characteristic errors in pronouncing words: (other than speech difficulties) (*kilt for killed, pitcha for picture, youse for you*) —————————————————————————
Makes these substitutions in speech: (*rittle for little*) (*dis for this*)————
Can hear likenesses and differences in the beginning sounds of c, r, j, g, b, w. (These are the first to be taught in the series of books the first-grade teacher expects to use as basal.)
Can produce orally a word beginning with the same sound as two spoken words starting with c, r, j, g, b, w.

Can remember in order (*number of*) things to do.
Works well in a group with the teacher._____
Works well in a group working alone._____
Has this major problem when working with a group:
_____

Can work alone._____
Has this major problem when working alone:
_____

Has been able to give full attention for as long as_____minutes when
   (*activity*)_____
Can count up to_____
Knows the meaning of numbers up to_____
Can recite the alphabet._____
Recognizes his own first name._____ Writes his first name._____
Can read (*what he can read, if already reading*)_____
Can remember what a sign says from one day to the next._____
Has these physical handicaps:_____
Likes to hear these kinds of stories:_____
Can retell a simple story in sequence._____
When given free choice of subject, tends to draw or paint (*objects*)_____

Has spoken this original sentence (one of his longest, most complex in structure):_____

Knows what is meant by these words illustrated in the pictures of the first basal
   book he will read in first grade:

dog	—	hats	—	marbles	—
bear	—	wagon	—	blocks (toy building)	—
tree	—	skates	—	screen door	—
flag	—	jump rope	—	ball	—
chair	—	shoe	—	wheel	—
stick	—	fence	—	box	—
		hammock	—		

Under no circumstances, of course, should the kindergarten teacher use
the basal book or show the pictures from it. If, however, in kindergarten
activities, children may become acquainted with these ideas, a major part
of the concept readiness will have been achieved.

If the child comes from another school in which such a record of his
pertinent readiness achievements has not been made, the first-grade teacher
must discover them herself during the first several weeks of the term.

From the parents, either through questionnaire, telephone calls, home
visits, or talks with the child, the first-grade teacher tries to learn:

Name of child_____
Plays (*what games*) with other children.
Plays (*what games*) alone.
Likes (*something to do*) best of all.
Likes (*place to go*) best of all.

Has been to a zoo____ a circus____ a farm____
    the ocean____ a lake____ the mountains____
    a library____ an aquarium____ a pet shop____
Enjoys doing these things with his father or mother:_____

Enjoys doing these things with an older brother or sister:_____

Enjoys doing these things with the whole family:_____

Watches these television programs: (Here the teacher lists programs which she
    hopes he watches and leaves spaces for filling in the names of others. For in-
    stance, the story-telling programs on educational TV would be listed. These
    serve as a hint to the family to see that the child has the opportunity to watch
    them.)
Does these things to help at home: (*Here the teacher suggests* things a young
    child can do to learn responsibility.)
Has a pet _____ named _____
Is read to by (*member of family*) every _____ for (*length of time*).
Has heard these stories read recently:_____

Looks through newspaper or magazines or books with (*member of family*) and
names the objects in the pictures.

    This will not be the only contact the teacher will make with the parents
early in the school year. If the answers to her questions suggest that the
parents are willing to read to the child, she may soon send home a list of
books which they may read to him. "Since Jimmy has a duck named
Oscar, he would like to hear someone read some stories about ducks. He
can go to the neighborhood library with an adult and ask for duck stories.
Then the adult can take out one or two stories at a time, to be read to him
at home. Here are some good duck stories he shouldn't miss:

> *Make way for the ducklings* by Robert McCloskey
> *Angus and the ducks* by Marjorie Flack
> *Cock-a-doodle-do* by Berta and Elmer Hader
> *Two lonely ducks* by Roger Duvoisin"

If the parents do not speak English, the teacher will suggest through an
interpreter (an older child in the school is often a helpful volunteer) which
television programs the child should be encouraged to watch, the library
story hours he should try to attend, and other activities which she feels
will increase his acquaintance with the sound and use of English words and
sentences. If the kinds of homes the children come from are quite different
from the homes pictured in the pre-primers to be used, the teacher will
encourage the watching of programs which show "pre-primer life." With
the extensive observation of television by children of all cultural and
socio-economic groups, this problem of accustoming children to the so-
called upper-middle-class life in the reader series at the early levels is no

longer what it once was. Actually, some children by the age of six have spent almost as many hours watching people in model kitchens, etc., on television as they have observing carefully the details of their own dwelling. (Like many another oft-repeated chant in the teaching business, this one about the reading difficulty created by the different type of life portrayed in the books has largely outlived its verity.)

How does the teacher get information about a child's home if for some reason the adults (the parents or relatives responsible for the child) cannot be reached? In the first few weeks of the term, the child is supposed to be getting acquainted with the school and the school with the child. He draws pictures of himself, of his family, of what he likes to do, of how he helps at home. Under the first picture, the teacher writes his name, "Joe," and puts it with others above the chalkboard. For the second, he tells her to write, "This is Joe's family." For the third, he has her write, "I like to watch my dad fix the car." For the fourth, he dictates: "I bring things from the store." Oral opportunities are given also to tell more about what these pictures mean, and about other activities not portrayed. A booklet on "Me" may be the result, with sections on family and fun and work. Each child has his own booklet of his own pictures and remarks. Some children have been able to write the comments themselves. Others have dictated and copied. Others have dictated and watched as the teacher wrote. The non-English speaking child is given the sentence and repeats it. Some children can read what the comments say. Others can remember and recite. They all take them home to be admired.

Interpreting a reading-readiness test

The teacher wants more than her own opinion to support her plans for teaching the first graders to read. Perhaps she administers a standardized reading-readiness test, such as the *Gates Reading Readiness Test,* or perhaps, if she is using the Macmillan Readers, she prefers to use the readiness test which was designed for that series. (Many reader series have their own tests.) When she suspects that several of the children are really ready to start reading, and a period of getting acquainted has passed, she administers the *Reading-Readiness Test* for the Macmillan Readers (Copyright 1955 by the Macmillan Company).

Scoring these tests in the way the manual of directions directs, she finds that several of her youngsters made top scores. (Sixty-four is the highest possible.) But she knows that it is important to discover what the other children need to do to improve their readiness. She has not, of course, attempted to administer the test to the child who has just arrived from Germany, speaking and understanding only German. His first hurdle is obvious. She looks inside the tests of each child, and matches what she knows of his background and behavior, with what he has done in the tests, to decide what he needs.

Test 1, Following Directions. A child with minimal recall missed Item 1 but had Item 3 right because the teacher showed him exactly what to do and he did it immediately. Gloria, from a skyscraper jungle, marked the skyscraper for a toy shop. Pierre, who has obtained his toys from a trading post, mistook the school building in Item 2 for the toy shop. The child who needs to be shown everything, who doesn't catch on very well by just listening, missed Item 4 entirely. Ellen got Item 5 because everything was told her simply in sequence, but Item 6 stumped her when she had to "translate"—to know that the wagon was "the toy that a child can ride in."

Test 1, page 3. A child who answers correctly all four items relating to the first picture on this page can remember as many as four things to do in succession. The first answer requires knowledge of the meaning of *bigger*. The second requires the child to remember that Father is in the barn, even though he is not visible in the picture. The third requires that the child be able to recall three things to do in succession. All these items require knowledge of the general shapes of farm animals, mothers, children, pets, and barns.

The second picture on the page is of a circus. The first question gives one direction, the second also one, the third two directions and the fourth four. Children who can follow directions in the first picture may fail this test because of not being familiar with circus concepts. *In order to take this test at all, the children need to know how to draw crosses, lines, and circles.*

"Well!" says the teacher. "Even if Zelda had only the first and third picture right on page 2 and the two first questions for each picture on page 3, she has a toe-hold on following directions. If I ask her only one thing at a time and have her act on it immediately, I can start her reading. But she will be a bother when I am working with other children, unless I can find some way of extending her recall of several directions at once."

Test 2, Auditory Discrimination. The teacher makes a chart of the items in this test and indicates on it which items were missed by which children. Item 1 was a sample, so the chart looks like this:

	Test 2 page 4				*Test 2 page 5*				
Names	Item 2	Item 3	Item 4	Item 5	Item 1	Item 2	Item 3	Item 4	Item 5
	-ouse	-all	-ose	-oat	-eep	-ill	$\overline{oo}$	-orn-	-upboard
Jimmy	x		x						x
Bjorn				x	x	x			x
etc.			etc.		etc.			etc.	

The teacher can see at a glance which children missed which rhyme endings. This suggests to her which children she will help with the *-ouse* ear training. The child who had nothing right does worry her. Has he a hearing loss? Did he do just the opposite of what he was told? But the teacher does not plan to keep children from beginning the reading program on the basis of that test alone. The vocabulary of the first pre-primer does not require such fine discrimination. She will, though, as she starts them reading, work on rhyme endings in which these children are deficient. She thinks she will try some ideas from *Let's listen* (Ginn and Company), the recordings in ear training. They stress initial consonant sounds. She can make up similar exercises for the rhymes that they do not cover.

Test 3, Visual Discrimination (*pairs of words alike or unlike*). This test, too, the teacher charts. The first item is a sample, but the others she lists like this:

Names

Item	2	3	4	5	6	7	8	9	10	11
	car	pig	then	tree	on	boots	like	run	very	toy
	far	pig	them	tree	on	boats	like	ran	very	boy
	B		E			M		M		B
Jimmy						x		x		
etc.	12	13	14	15
	but	good	eat	red
	but	good	cat	bed
			B	B

She puts B for "beginning of word different," M for "middle of word different," and E for "endings of word different." She sees that Jimmy missed only the items whose middles were different. Apparently he doesn't look carefully at the middles of words. She can start him reading, but she will have to give him special exercises on observing word middles. Introducing writing along with the reading will help this.

Test 4, Problem Solving. Charting the results of this test, the teacher sees that some children got the first four items right and the last one wrong. The first four require that the children know the ingredients of a cake, the tools used to build a house, the materials and equipment used in sewing, and what people wear when it rains. They also have to know that a cake is its ingredients before it is a cake, that a house is boards and nails before it is a house, etc. In the last item, however, there is a different kind of problem. Here are animals. Which one would be fun to play with? A lion? A puppy? A giraffe? Anita had the first three wrong and the last two right. Her mother buys the cake, moves into an old house, and buys the clothes ready-made. But Anita knows what she wears in the rain and what pet she'd like to play with. Anita can solve the problems she knows about. Civilization has just solved too many for her! Anita's school will have to give her the experiences that she has been cheated out of, but she is a good enough problem-solver to start reading.

Test 5, Test of Story Sense. This test shows whether a child gets the sense, the direction, the logic of a story, or just some details, or nothing really accurately. Charting the results of this test, the teacher wants to notice the kinds of wrong choices as well as the right ones. In the first row of pictures, the right choice shows that the child can draw a good conclusion for the story. The next choice shows he has garbled the sequence of events in the story as well as missing the point. The last choice shows he added a detail which wasn't in the story at all! The second row, first picture, is chosen by a child who mixes the sequence of events; the second picture by the child who mistakes firemen for policemen. The third row, first picture, is chosen by the child who adds too many dogs to the story, with the wrong appearance; and the last picture by the child who forgets that the chicks were too little to play with (detail). The last row, first picture, is chosen by the child who remembers details but not the point of the story; the second by the child who forgets that Mother, not the boy, wrote the note to the grocer. Esther, then, who marks Item 3 Row 1, Item 2 Row 2, Item 1 Row 3, and Item 2 Row 4, needs experiences in recalling specific details in a story, as well as activities which make her draw conclusions in chronological development. Suzie, who marked Item 2 Row 1, Item 1 Row 2, Item 3 Row 3, needs to remember events *in the order of their occurrence.* "What happened first, next, next?"

Other ways of determining readiness

In addition to the reading-readiness test, the teacher uses other means of deciding what the children need in order to be successful in reading. In one of the basal-reader manuals she finds a checklist of the ways children behave when they suffer from: ocular discomfort; poor hearing; speech difficulties; poor co-ordination; poor health; inability to share, to co-operate, to be self-reliant; inability to see a task through, to face disappointment or failure; lack of interest in books; poor memory and poor reasoning processes; inability to interpret pictures; unstable left-to-right observation; inability to profit from the mistakes of others; lack of effective means of expression in language, art, and dramatic play. Needless to say, the teacher does not add up the total number of positive things she observes in order to judge the child's readiness; rather, she decides whether the presence of any particular one or more disabilities precludes an immediate start in reading.

The experience chart as a means of determining readiness

Can the children read and remember what they read, from one day to the next? The use of the experience chart to find the answer has the virtue of involving all the children while it differentiates their tasks. At first this may be only a one-line sentence: "The leaves are falling," which the children dictate as the teacher prints it before their eyes, and recognize later on a strip of tagboard elsewhere in the room. After the children show that they can remember and recognize the wording of single sentences, longer stories are dictated and recorded, as described below.

The children have had an experience together, such as a walk in the park. They have had such a good time that they really should record what they did. "What shall we call our story?" The teacher asks this first, because you can't teach children to stick to a topic unless they select a topic to stick to in the first place.

Jane suggests "Our Walk." Matt says, "The Park." Mortimer says, "What We Did." The teacher writes each down, one under the other, in manuscript letters, standing so that all can see the writing, and saying the words as she writes. Then she repeats the titles: "Let's read them."

She runs her hand from left to right under each title as she and the children say, "Our Walk. The Park. What We Did."

"Let's think about these good ideas. If we call it 'Our Walk,' what might a visitor not know? (Pause for participation.) He won't know that we went to the park, will he? He won't know which of our walks it was."

Irrepressible Isadore says, "That goes for 'What We Did,' too."

"If we call it 'The Park,' what won't the visitor know? (Pause.) Will he know we went to the park, took a walk in it? Who thinks he can put these good ideas together so that the title will be more exactly what we want to say?"

Isadore says, "Our Walk in the Park." (If he doesn't, the teacher is ready to prime the pump with the question, "What shall we call our walk in the park?")

"Will that tell that we took a walk? Will it tell where we went? Yes. Now how many like our title better?" The amiable children are vastly pleased.

The teacher writes the new title on a piece of unprinted newspaper which she has taped with masking tape to the chalkboard. "I wonder who will be ready to read our new title for us." (Better pay attention, Junior. You might be it.) She says the title carefully as she writes. Then she selects different children to come up to the paper, place an index finger on either side of the title (This is called *framing* the title.) and read it to the class. "Now let's all say it." Everyone says it, even the timid, the tongue-twisters, and the non-English speaking children, as she runs her hand below it from left to right.

If she suspects that some of the children can read already, the teacher asks, "Who can find the words that say 'Our Walk'?" Alice does. "How many think she is right?" Alice is practically always right. Mortimer places a shaky bet on Alice, but the teacher reads his face and knows pretty well what isn't going on. She jots a mental note on Mortimer in her head, to be transferred to her anecdotal records later on: "Mortimer still at sea." It will be some time before she can record, "Land ho!"

"Now, what are some of the things we would like to tell about our walk in the park?"

Araminta contributes, "We seen a squirrel."

"Could you say that in a different way?" If it is certain that she can't, the teacher supplies, "We *saw* a squirrel," and has the child repeat it after her. Araminta must *taste* the new way as well as hear it. "How many think that is a good sentence for our story?" The sleeping dogs are not to lie undisturbed. In fact, if restlessness or inattention is obvious, the teacher may have all stand to indicate their acceptance, or all stand to read a portion of the story.

The teacher writes on the chalkboard (not the newspaper) and says, "You tell me the words as I write." The child says, "We–saw–a–squir-rel." The children then read the sentence smoothly in unison. (The teacher insists on smooth reading, showing by example what she means.) In the same way, other sentences are added until the teacher has written two or more. Ordinarily, the first story will be short; but for the sake of illustration of the technique, we shall assume that these are now the sentences:

> We saw a squirrel.
> We tried to find where
> he buried the nut.   (The teacher indents sentences,
> First he buried it.   breaks them *between* phrases.)
> Then he ran away.

"Let's look at these sentences. This seems a little mixed up to me. Which sentence should we start with? First, what did we see?—Then what happened?—And then what? I'll put a number 1 in front of the sentence which belongs first. I'll put a 2 before the sentence which belongs second. What shall I do for the third sentence?" Here comes Alice with the number 3.

"Now let's read our title again. 'Our Walk in the Park.' The first sentence of our story should tell where we went. Does it? No, it tells what we saw. Can anyone think of a good first sentence to tell where we went?"

The teacher then starts writing on the newspaper, having the children tell what comes next and next and next. When she comes to the second reference to the nut, she says, "We don't have to say 'the nut' again, do we? We didn't keep saying 'the squirrel.' What did we call him? (He.) We don't call a nut 'he.' What do we call it? (Dead giveaway.) Yes 'it'."

The ending of the story is unsatisfactory because it leaves the reader with an unanswered question. "Do you think anyone will wonder something at the end of our story? Let me read it to you again. . . . What will somebody wonder. We *tried* to find the hole. . ."

Eric explodes. "We couldn't find it at all."
The final story is:

> Our Walk in the Park
>
> We took a walk
> in the park.
> We saw a squirrel.
> First, he buried
> a nut.
> Then he ran away.
> We tried to find
> where he buried it.
> We couldn't find it
> at all.

The teacher would not use such a long story as a readiness test for children of low ability. In such a case, she would settle for two or three sentences. But if she had an unusually able class, she might try five sentences.

The children draw pictures of themselves walking in the park. Each figure is then cut out and pasted into a composite picture to illustrate the chart. That night the teacher makes a chart and extra strips of chart paper reproducing the sentences in the same size of manuscript writing and the same spacing. An extra inch of space is left at the bottom of each strip so that the letters will appear whole when the strip is placed in a pocket chart. She places these strips in the pocket chart (a holder for sentence strips) and when the children come in the morning, the chart is displayed in one place, the pocket-chart story in another. Who will discover that both are the same story?

Who remembers from yesterday?

The teacher asks, "Who remembers what our chart was about? Who remembers what the title was? Who can read the title for us?" She proceeds this way and watches the volunteers. One child may say, "I can read the whole thing by myself," and proves it. Another may remember the title and subside. Araminta remembers her own sentence, complete with 'seen,' and is again corrected. The millennium does not come with only one reminder.

"Can anyone find our story any place else in the room?" If no one can, readiness is a long way off. The abler children read the strips in the pocket chart, sentence by sentence, as they have the chart.

At another time, the teacher says, "Who can find the two sentences which say, 'We took a walk in the park'?" A child frames and reads the same sentence on the pocket chart and on the chart itself. He proves that they are the same by taking the strip from the pocket chart and holding it under the right sentence on the chart itself, for everyone to see the likeness as he reads aloud.

Later the teacher makes it harder. The children must think of the meaning of each sentence, not just parrot the memorized parts. "Who can find the sentence which tells what the squirrel did first?" She skips around among the sentences so that the sentences are not given in the original sequence, thoughtlessly.

By this time it is pretty clear that some children are not ready for reading. They do not remember sentences from one day to the next, or identify the same sentence in two places. For this unready group, however, there must be experiences which help build readiness. The teacher plans a booklet with them—their own booklet of the story. Each day she brings a sheet of paper for each child, at the bottom of which she has written the title or one sentence from the story. They "read" what is there, discuss how the idea might be illustrated, and draw a picture on the paper above the wording. When each picture is completed, the child can show it to the group and the group reads the wording again. Finally, all the pages are stapled like a booklet, and the children read them in unison, turning the pages. They find the sentence about the squirrel by their own picture clue, and "read" it. The teacher alerts the parents to be delighted when the child brings the booklet home to "read" and not to push him for identification of words and letters which he does not yet know.

With such children the teacher sends home suggestions similar to those made by the kindergarten teacher. Of course, special suggestions are made for children with special problems, just as they were the year before.

The group of children that seems ready for reading is pushed a little farther. These children, too, may make a booklet, but their sessions with the teacher are not used in reading and showing the booklet but in trying to identify the phrases and words in the chart and pocket chart material.

"Who can find the strip which says 'in the park'?"

The teacher cuts the strips into phrase units. (We took/ a walk.)

"Who can read the strip which tells what the squirrel had?"

The strips are placed along the chalkboard ledge in mixed order. The children rebuild the story with these strips, proving their correctness by matching strips to the chart. If they can do this, the teacher may say, "Some words are repeated again and again in this story. Do you see a word which is used more than once? Can you read it?" She notes mentally that one child noticed that *walk* and *park* were both repeated, even though one of each began with a capital letter. The children notice this difference, and the teacher has them see that the title has capital letters in it and so have the first words of each of the sentences. "And a period at the end," says Isadore. His grandmother has not been idle.

If the children do not see the repetition of words, the teacher may say, "I see the word *we* in this story several times. Let's read the sentences and listen and watch for the *we*." They hear it in the first, second, fifth, and sixth sentences. They see which it is. A child frames *we* with his fingers in the four places, saying it each time.

The next day, the teacher says, "I think we learned several words yesterday. Let's see whether you know them." She holds up a card: *we*. On other cards she has the other repeated words. The children who know these are the ones who probably could start formal reading immediately. Some of them may have such a good sight vocabulary already that they could easily spurt through the series in the pre-primers. The teacher plans, however, to see that they get the skill-building exercises which the manuals accompanying these books offer, for her reading purposes consist of more than building sight vocabulary.

Isadore and Alice are taken through the oral-reading test in Nila Banton Smith's *Graded selections for informal reading diagnosis* (New York University Press, 1959) just to see how much they can read.

In the group instruction exemplified by this chart experience, children who do not learn readily learn something from the leadership of those who progress rapidly. They may not know the answers on the first or second chance, but they may have them by the nth. Helpful comments are made by the keen observers.

"What makes you know that that word says *we*?"

"It's the short one."

"It starts with that long, funny-looking letter."

There will be many more occasions for chart making and reading during the year. Children will begin to pick up a vocabulary of words they know by sight from seeing them so often and reading them with so much pride.

Verbal Facility

The kindergarten teacher worked on clear enunciation and speaking in sentences. She taught the child who didn't know how to excuse himself to say the magic words in the acceptable way. She worked on intonation and pitch with the child of foreign language background, who transferred the music of his first language into the English equivalents. First she had him listen and recognize the difference or likeness in two things that she said. Then, when he could do that, she had him reproduce the sounds that she made, after her, and listen to himself on a tape recorder. These activities the first-grade teacher continues. If she does not, the child slips back into his old grooves, and the kindergarten teacher's effort has been for naught.

"Ah ain' gonna do tha' no mo'."

"Listen: I'm not going to do that any more. Now let me hear you say it."

Through choral speaking, poetry recitation, puppetry, singing, and the use of the microphone, the children have enjoyable experiences with careful production of English phrases. "How nicely we did that!" The icing on the cake is the teacher's approval. They know they did well, but it is good to hear about it.

Concept Building

In a book which one group is reading is the new sight word *home*. Of course, everyone knows what a home is. His home is where he lives. We all drew pictures of our houses and our families. But there are ideas about the concept of home that may not have occurred to the children. The teacher approaches this in several ways.

"My home is in a tree. It is made of sticks and mud. It is round. It has no roof." She continues until the children can guess who she is.

"My home is made of glass. It is round. There is no roof. It is full of water."

"My home is lined with fur. It is in the ground. It is hidden with leaves so that no one will steal my babies."

Isadore has his own idea. "My home is in the sand. When people throw a rock, I squirt water up out of my home." He is only temporarily a clam.

When we say we feel at home, what do we mean? When the baseball player talks about home, what does he mean? On television the other night, some of us saw a program about homing pigeons. What are they?

If we are not careful and it is the right time of year, we may get into a discussion of what home is to a migrating bird. Home is where she can find food and enough safety to build a nest. Home is where the climate is favorable. How do we make the climate right in our homes? How do we make them safe? (Here is another concept! Safe.)

One day a desert tortoise is presented to the class, thanks to a wandering uncle. What kind of home would he like us to make him in the classroom? By the time of his arrival, the concept of home is so well developed that we know enough not to give him the same kind of home that we made for our duck and our rabbit and our goldfish. We know that we have to find out what home means to a desert tortoise.

Word Recognition

In the picture on the page of the pre-primer, Jane wants Billy to watch her, but Billy is busy with his own interests.

"What do you think Jane wants Billy to do?"

"Look."

"Could you say that in a sentence?"

"She wants Billy to look."

"Here is her sentence." The teacher writes, "Look, Billy," while she

makes sure that all are watching. "Who can read what Jane said?" Someone reads, "Look, Billy."

This is the first look at *look*. It will take a lot more before *look* is a part
of the sight vocabulary of each child in the group. How can the teacher
provide this repetition?

Play and *come* are in their sight vocabulary. So the teacher writes directions on the chalkboard, and the children do what they are told.

> Joe, play with Bill. (They dance around.)
> Millie, come to me. (Millie approaches the teacher.)
> Look at me, Ellen. (Ellen looks.)

"Who can frame and say the word that makes you jump? The word that
makes you use your eyes? The word that makes you use your feet?"

With word cards the teacher builds sentences in the pocket chart and
calls on children to do what the sentences say. She puts the cards in carefully from left to right, and sits at the right so that her arm doesn't hide the
left-hand side of the sentence from the children as she builds it.

When she makes worksheets, she does not fall into the trap of making
half the work a guessing game. Also, she sees to it that the children have to
look carefully at the word which requires the most practice.

> ——————— at me.
> Billy, ——————— at Jane.
> ——— and play with me.
> Come and ——— at Billy.

She puts "elastic" into the work periods, so that a child who finishes
filling in the blanks quickly will have something constructive to occupy his
time. Elastic may be to draw a picture that tells someone to look at something or someone, and to write the word in a sentence at the bottom of the
picture.

There are games containing sentences with blanks to fill, and small cards
with the possible missing words on them: *come, play, look*, etc. A child
may play such a game when he finishes the other work. Then it is important that he read what the sentences say. He may read to Isadore, who can
tell him when he is wrong, or to the teacher when she comes around.

The teacher knows that some words are harder to learn than others.
For instance, little words like *at* and *to* look much alike and have little to
make them stand out in meaning. *Billy* is easy because the form is unusual
and the idea of a boy is interesting. *Airplane* is easy because of the odd
form and the glamor of the idea. *Mother* is easy because of the emotional
appeal of the idea. *Hippopotamus* is a pushover because of its great, odd
length. *Where* has an odd shape, yet is easily confused with *there, here*, and
several other words. And it lacks concreteness in meaning. Several days
before *where* is introduced as a word to learn, the teacher dramatizes its
meaning. She loses something and dramatically writes on the board, "Where

is it?" Then she hunts around in exaggerated fashion. Or, we are to get the ball for recess. "Where is it?" the teacher writes.

We need to get some food for the tortoise. "Where?" the teacher writes and says the word while she writes. The children see and hear the word and know what it means. "Let's all say it." They say *where* and see it and hear it. The teacher knows that the simultaneity of sensory impressions is important to the learning. *Where* is not such a hard word by the time the book reading requires it.

The teacher knows, also, that every time a new word is learned which resembles old words in the sight vocabulary, the old words have to be relearned in a way they were not learned before. The child has to observe something about them he didn't have to notice before. *Run* is easy as long as it is juxtaposed with different looking shapes like *play* and *jump*. But when *sun* comes up, *run* is temporarily under a cloud. The teacher writes *run* and *sun*, one below the other, on the chalkboard so that the child can clearly see the difference. "How are these two words different?" They begin differently. We are going to have to look carefully to tell which is which. Now we must have exercises which require the insertion of these two words in sentences. If the children have to write the words they will remember them better; and if they have to think which one is appropriate in meaning to the sentence involved, they will associate the meaning with the right form.

run   sun

Billy can ——— fast.
The ——— comes up.
See the ———.

The children invent other sentences of their own and illustrate them.

As children write their own stories, they ask again and again for the same words. The teacher makes a class file of words the children constantly request. The words are written on separate cards and given to the children to copy in their stories. Later the children file each word behind the right alphabet card. Next time they want to write these words, they will know where to look. Meanwhile, some of the words should be learned, for they are used so often. The teacher shows the children how to trace and say the word (84), then trace and say it from memory, then write it from memory and check to see whether they are right. Children keep a personal file of words they have learned well enough to spell and write.

By keeping track of the words the children are learning besides those in the pre-primer they are reading, the teacher knows when it is safe for a child to read a pre-primer from another series all by himself. The following chart, which Helen Behn of San Francisco has made of the words appearing in the first, second, and third pre-primers of eight modern reader series, helps the teacher to determine quickly whether the child's present vocabulary is adequate for a safe excursion into a particular book.

Words Appearing in the First, Second, and Third Pre-Primers of Eight Series, Exclusive of Those Used as Proper Nouns[1]

Word	Betts 1958 ed.	Bond 1949 ed.	Burton 1950 ed.	Gray 1956 ed.	McKee 1949 ed.	Russell 1957 ed.	Sheldon 1957 ed.	Gates 1951 ed.
a	2	3	2	3	2	2	3	3
airplane	2	2				1		
and	1	1	1	1	1	1	1	1
apple/s						1		
are				3	2			
at	2	1					1	1
away		1	2	3			3	
baby				2				
ball/s		2	2	3	1	2	3	
balloons			3					
be					2			
bed					2			
big	2		2	2	3	3	3	2
birds			2					
blue	2		3	2		3	2	
boat			2	2			2	2
box					3			
cake						2		
call					2			
came		2						
can	3	1	3	2	3	1	1	
car			2	2			3	
chair						2		
chirp			2					
come	1	1	1	1	1	1	1	1
cookies				3			2	
Daddy		3	3		3		1	
did		3						
dinner						2		
dish					2			

[1] Reproduced by permission of the author.

Words Appearing in the First, Second, and Third Pre-Primers
of Eight Series, Exclusive of Those Used as Proper Nouns (cont.)

Word	Betts 1958 ed.	Bond 1949 ed.	Burton 1950 ed.	Gray 1956 ed.	McKee 1949 ed.	Russell 1957 ed.	Sheldon 1957 ed.	Gates 1951 ed.
do	3				3			3
dog					2			
doll			2					
down	2		2	1	2	3	2	2
eat			3					
fast		3				1	1	
Father	3			2		1		1
find			2	1				
fish							3	3
flower/s			3					
for	2	3	3	3	2	2	2	
fun	3							
funny				1		3	2	
get		3	3		2	1	3	2
give					2			
go	1	1	2	1	1	2	2	2
good		2	1		2			
got		3						
green						2	2	
has					2			
have	3				2	3		
he		3					2	2
help			3	2		2	1	3
her					2			
here	1	2	1	3	1	2	1	2
home					1		1	
house	3		2	3		3		
I	2	2		2	1	2	2	2
ice-cream							3	
in	1	3	3	3	2		3	2

Words Appearing in the First, Second, and Third Pre-Primers of Eight Series, Exclusive of Those Used as Proper Nouns (cont.)

Word	Betts 1958 ed.	Bond 1949 ed.	Burton 1950 ed.	Gray 1956 ed.	McKee 1949 ed.	Russell 1957 ed.	Sheldon 1957 ed.	Gates 1951 ed.
is	2	3	2	2	1	2	2	2
it	2	3		3	2		2	2
jump	3	1	3	1			3	1
kitten					2			
lake								3
let			3					
like	3	2						2
liked		3						
little	2		1	2	3	3	3	2
look	2	1	1	1		3	1	1
looked		2						
make	3	3		2		3	3	
man	3							
may		2			2			
me	3	1		3	1		1	3
milk					2			
mitten					2			
Mother	3	3	3	2	3	1	1	1
my	2			2	2		2	2
near							2	
no					1			
not	3	2	2	3	1	3	3	
Oh	3		1	1				2
one				3				
our							3	
out	1							
park			3					
penny					3			
play/s	3	1	1	2	1	3	3	1
played		2						

Words Appearing in the First, Second, and Third Pre-Primers of Eight Series, Exclusive of Those Used as Proper Nouns (cont.)

Word	Betts 1958 ed.	Bond 1949 ed.	Burton 1950 ed.	Gray 1956 ed.	McKee 1949 ed.	Russell 1957 ed.	Sheldon 1957 ed.	Gates 1951 ed.
playhouse		3						
ran		2						
red	2		3	2		2	2	
ride/s	1	1	1			1	3	2
run/s		1	1	1			1	1
said	3	2	3	3		2	3	2
saw		2						
see	2	1	1	1	3	1	1	2
she		3						
show					3			
sleep					2			
something	3			2		2	2	
splash								1
stop	1	2				2	3	
surprise						2		
that					2			
the	2	2	2	2	1	1	2	2
there							3	
this					2	2		
three				3				
to	3	1	3	3	2	2	1	1
too					2			
toy/s	2					1		
train	2	3	2					
two				3				
up	2		2	1		3	2	2
us			3					
want/s	3	1	3	3		2	3	2
water		3						
we	2	3	3	3	2	2	3	2

Words Appearing in the First, Second, and Third Pre-Primers
of Eight Series, Exclusive of Those Used as Proper Nouns (cont.)

Word	Betts 1958 ed.	Bond 1949 ed.	Burton 1950 ed.	Gray 1956 ed.	McKee 1949 ed.	Russell 1957 ed.	Sheldon 1957 ed.	Gates 1951 ed.
what	3		2			3		
where			2	3	2			
will	3				1			2
with	3	1			1		2	2
work		3		2		2	1	
yard		3						
yellow			3	2			2	
you	3	2		3	1	2	2	2
your					2			
TOTALS	51	54	52	53	58	56	58	42

Word Analysis

Studying the word-recognition program for the basal readers she is using
(Many publishers print a separate booklet on this.), the teacher sees that
ear training must precede visual training.

Structural analysis

"See the dog . . . How many do I say to see? (one)"
"See the dogs . . . How many now? (more than one)"
The children begin to hear the sound of the letter that makes the difference between one and more than one. When they can do this, and when the
following words are in their sight vocabulary, the teacher writes:
"See the apple."
"See the apples."
And the children dutifully draw one apple after the first sentence, several
apples after the second, and underline the *s* to show that that is the letter
which is making the difference. This is the technique of contrast, which
the teacher uses over and over again. Gradually she makes the children
aware of the way they can find these things out for themselves: "How can
we see the letter that is making the difference?" Write the two words under
each other and see what the difference is, the children say. Now some of
the brighter children can learn much on their own, with this knowledge of
technique.

"Listen to this word and tell me what two words you hear in it: pancake. (pan cake) Someone. (some one) Postman. (post man) Can you give us a word like this and let us tell you what two words make it up?"

Later, when these words are in the sight vocabulary, the children can divide them visually. "Watch as I write these words on the chalkboard. Be ready to tell me what two words are in each word." A child is permitted to find a card in the pocket chart and match with one of the words, find the second and match it to the second part, then place the cards in proper sequence to reproduce the compound word on the pocket chart. In "matching" the words, he places the card under the part of the word that is the same, and says the word so that all can hear. "How many think he is right?" asks the teacher. If the children have sat a long while, "Stand if you think he is right." Learning takes place when there is active involvement.

Endings must be heard and spoken clearly before chalkboard comparisons are made: "Today Jack plays. Yesterday what did he do? Jack played." Children fill in the words as the teacher starts the sentences. A child jumps. "Today Eva—(The children say, "Jumps.") Yesterday she— (The children say, "Jumped.")

Phonetic analysis

Kindergarten ear training on rhymes and initial consonants is continued. "I am thinking of a word that begins like *big* and *box*, and Tommy is one and so is Everett." Oh, they all think they know. "Big—box—" One is chosen to say, "Boy." "I am thinking of something that begins like *big* and *box* and *boy* and it is about to ring." Someone says, "Bell." "Let's say the words over to see whether he is right: *big box boy bell*. Is he right?"

When these words are in the sight vocabulary, children will confuse them unless they begin to learn more about their structure and sound: The teacher writes these words, one above the other, and says, "Watch what I write and be ready to tell me what you notice about these words." She writes:

big
box
ball

(It takes at least two words to apply generalization, which is the technique used here. Notice that the words have only one letter in common, and preferably consist of one syllable, so that the task is clear and simple.)

"Let's read these words together as I put my hand under each one: big, box, ball. What do you notice about them?" Bernard says, "They all begin alike." "Show me," says the teacher. Bernard comes up and puts his finger under each of the *b*'s. "Let's all say the words again and see whether we notice anything about the way they *sound* at the beginning." Benita says, "They sound alike at the beginning." Isadore says, "They all begin with the same letter and that letter makes the same sound in all of them." Do the other children agree with Isadore? Do they know what he means?

"If that letter makes the same sound in those words, let's see whether you can discover what the new word in this sentence is. It is going to begin with that letter, too." The teacher writes a sentence, all of the words in which are known sight words except the new one: Mother can *bake* a cake. The children know what the word is. They know that whenever they see a word beginning with a *b*, it will begin with that same sound.

They reinforce the learning by filling a chart with all the *b* words they know, and adding to the chart as they learn new ones.

When they come to confusion of words like *now* and *not*, the teacher says, "How can we tell which is which?" They put one word below the other and see that they begin alike but end differently. They hear the sound and see the letter *n* that makes the common sound. Do they know a word like *now?*

now

cow

how

What makes that sound that is the same in all three words? *Ow. Now* ends with *ow*, like *cow* and *how*. That's why it isn't the same as *not*.

"Whenever we want to know what sound a part of a word makes, what can we do?" We can find another word we know that has the same part in it, and listen to what it says.

Another trick that the children learn is to leave off a known part and listen to what is left: cow—ow. The children practice as the teacher writes a word and has them pronounce it, then erases the first letter and has them say the remainder. Children build new words with the ending (ow—how) by putting the first letter on it and having other children pronounce the whole.

Whenever they solve a new word by sounding out the parts, they try the meaning of the new word in the sentence to see whether it makes sense. *Not* really says *not*, and *now* really says *now*, because the sentence is: "Not now," said Tom. He wouldn't say "Now not."

Comprehension

In the picture in the basal reader Jane is jumping off the log which Billy was balancing himself on, according to the previous picture. Billy is making motions of protest to the two dogs, Skip and Rex. Picture comprehension is basic to meaningful reading of the page.

"Is Jane playing the same game in this picture that Billy was playing on the last?" No, she is not balancing; she is jumping. "Why do you suppose she is not balancing?" She is the little sister. Bet she can't do it. Jumping over the log is not too easy, either, but she can do that. "What is Billy doing?" He is shooing the dogs off. "Why do you think so?" His hands look as though he is pushing them away. "Why is he doing this, do you suppose?" The dogs get in the way of the games Billy and Jane are playing. "What might happen if the dogs play with them?" Jane might get her two front teeth knocked out, stumbling over them. "What do you think the dogs want to do?" They want to play, too. "If you were Billy, what would you be saying to the dogs?" Go away. Go away and play somewhere else. That is just about what Billy is saying, too. "Does anyone know of a good word for what Billy is trying to do for Jane in shooing the dogs off?" Perhaps someone does. "He is trying to protect her so she won't get hurt." "Protect is a good new word. Let's all say it: *protect*. How do you protect your sisters and brothers?" (The point to observe here is that the limitation on the children's sight vocabulary does not hold for their oral vocabulary. The latter can be expanded during the discussion of the limited sight vocabulary.)

Another picture in the basal reader shows a boy running with a toy airplane whose propeller whirls as he goes. More is in this picture than meets the dull eye of the unimaginative adult. "What is making the propeller go? (The boy is running with it.) Why does that make it go? Would it go if he stood still?" (Only maybe. The wind would have to blow. The air would have to move. The boy is moving it through the air, and the air is pushing against it.)

A few pinwheels in the classroom and a few volunteer runners or blowers can show that the pinwheel moves when the air moves, stops when the air is still. Isadore may say that the difference between a propeller on an airplane and the pinwheel is that the airplane propeller goes around thanks to a motor, and moves the air, while a pinwheel goes around thanks to the movement of the air, and does not itself cause the airplane to move. These comments surround the language of the text with more meaning than the few words the children yet know by sight can carry by themselves.

Attention should be drawn to the beginnings of paragraph structure. A greater space is left between sentences of different paragraphs than between sentences within these early paragraph forms made up of single-line sentences, one under the other. "What are the first four sentences about? (They tell how two children are playing together.) What do the next three do? (They tell what the boy said.) What do the next four do? (They tell what the girl said.) What do the last two do? (They tell what the dog did.)

Routine matters around the classroom require comprehension, when a chart proclaims:

Our Good Helpers

(picture)   Michael and Linda
            will feed the fish.
(picture)   Marie and Karl
            will feed the lizards.
(picture)   Ricky and Gail
            will feed the snake.
(picture)   Judy and Michael D.
            will feed the birds.

The first-grade teacher continues the work which the parents and the kindergarten teacher started on logical organization of ideas. If she is taking dictation from the children on something that is a matter of record, she guides the selection of content logically with questions.

"First, we should tell what happened. Who will give us a good first sentence?"

"Our hen laid an egg."

"*How* did we find out?"

"Charlie heard her cackle."

"How else?"

"Billy found her nest under the bushes."

"How does the egg look?"

"It is a big brown egg."

"*What* are we going to do now?"

"We are going to wait for it to hatch."

For a sense of sequence, the teacher may say, "What really happened first? Who can read the sentence that tells the first thing that happened?"

"Charlie heard her cackle."

"And then what?"

"Billy found her nest."

"And what did Billy see in the nest? What sentence tells that?"

"It is a big brown egg."

"Now what does the hen have to do?"

"She has to sit on the egg to keep it warm."

"And then what will happen, we hope?"

"It will hatch."

"A little chicken will come out."

Pictures recording the different stages of the story are drawn by different children, identified, and displayed in chronological order.

For an experience in comparative composition for the children, the teacher builds upon an incident.

Esmer says, "Jimmie and Archie look just alike."

"Let's look at Jimmie and Archie," says the teacher. "Are their eyes alike? (No.) Is their hair the same color? (No.) Are they the same height? (No.) Then what is alike about them?"

"They both have on red sweaters and blue jeans."

Other unsolicited contributions come in, such as their having two arms, two legs, heads, ears, etc.

"Their sweaters and jeans are the same colors," says the teacher. "That's what makes them look so much alike. Who can finish this sentence: Jimmie and Archie look just alike because—?"

Interpretation

First graders are no exception to the rule that human beings often exert only a minimum of effort in directions others demand they take. They may read and think just the facts of a story, just the action, if that is all that is asked of them. But the teacher pushes them with questions which make them think beyond the facts. When Billy has protected his little sister, she asks, "What does that show about Billy? What kind of person is he?" He is a good brother, helpful, etc. "How does Billy treat the dogs?" It is to be noted that he didn't kick at them or take a paper or stick to them. He likes the dogs and is kind to them, too. He is only telling them what he wants them to do. "Are the dogs bad dogs? (No.) Why?" They aren't biting anybody or growling. They just want to play. (Notice that the teacher doesn't ask a "yes, no" question without a follow-up of "Why?" She makes the children think and be ready with a reason for their statements.)

Acting out the story incident and saying things the way the characters must have said them shows the degree to which the children have grasped the situation and understood the feelings involved.

Study Skills

The acquisition of a desert tortoise sends the children to books about tortoises. The teacher reads to them the information about their tortoise. It is a desert tortoise and has four claws on its front feet and five on its hind feet, according to the book. The children count Cactus Pete's claws. Cactus Pete has five claws on his front feet!

Further research is necessary. The second-grade class has a tortoise, too. The children decide to look at *his* feet. *He* has five claws, too. They plan a telephone conversation with the curator at the museum and take turns interviewing him over the phone. He reports that he has counted five claws on the front feet of the desert tortoise. But the children know that good research isn't based on one case. "Did you count only one tortoise's claws?" a child asks. No, says the man, he has counted six tortoises' feet, just to be sure.

They dictate a letter to the author of the book.

Dear Mrs. Huntington,
   We like your Desert Book.
   We have a desert tortoise.
   His name is Cactus Pete.
   Your book says, "His front feet
have four claws."
   Our tortoise has five claws
on his front feet.
   We looked at the Second Grade's
tortoise. That tortoise has five claws
on his front feet.
   We called Mr. Sampson at the
Junior Museum. Mr. Sampson
looked at six desert tortoises.
   Each tortoise had five claws
on his front feet.
   Are there different kinds
of desert tortoises?
      Low First Grade, Farragut School

In due time the author replies that it was an error in the book. Cactus Pete is a worthy member of the breed, all right.

A newspaper picture of a three-hundred-pound tortoise in a zoo raises the question of Cactus Pete's relative size. A scale shows that Cactus Pete weighs four pounds. How much bigger the tortoise must be! Five of the largest children weigh in to add up to the big tortoise's weight. The teacher makes a chart of the names and weights of each child. The children can find their names and weights, the smallest, the largest.

Oral Reading

The temptation in early attempts at reading is to read aloud, since language is initially an oral experience. However, from the beginning, the teacher tries to make the oral-reading experiences purposeful ones, not rituals which simply entrench a habit.

"Who can read it the way Dick said it?"

"How did he feel? Who thinks he can say it to show how Dick felt?"

A good audience is important to oral reading.

"Let's listen to hear whether this is the first step in our experiment."

"Let's listen to hear whether this is a good proof of Jim's opinion."

The teacher reads about desert tortoises. "Raise your hand when you hear anything about the number of front claws a desert tortoise has."

Her audience is not simply alerted. It is held responsible. "How many think you heard something about . . . ? What was it?"

Choral reading gives every child a chance to sound wonderful by association. Even the poor reader does not stumble. The child of foreign language background mimics the intonation and phrasing of the strange English wording.

The class decides that certain behaviors are characteristic of the good oral reader:

> "I stand facing my audience.
> I hold the book so that people can see my face.
> I read so that all can hear.
> I try to sound like the person who is talking in the book."

The audience has to be worthy, too:

> "We look at the speaker.
> We listen for a special reason.
> We are quiet until he is finished."

Silent Reading

Silent reading is not learned unless it is practiced from the first.

"Let's open our books to the first picture. You know who this is because we have talked about him before. He is the boy in our story. Don't tell me his name. Just think his name. Look at the word below the picture. It is his name. Look at the word and think the name to yourself. Who thinks he can read it to us?"

Silent reading upside down and backwards is worse than none.

"Watch as I write his name. Think the name as I write it." The teacher writes "Billy" slowly and carefully, in well-formed manuscript letters, standing so that all can see the development of the word from left to right. "Now who can say his name for us, reading the word I have written?"

Silent reading is fostered by action responses to sentences on the chalkboard: The teacher runs her hand under each sentence, calls on a child to act out the sentence, has others tell whether he is right, and read the sentence aloud to prove that he is.

Independent silent reading of worksheets and stories gives children an opportunity to read without the necessity of speaking. Yet many children will still, at this stage, mouth their words silently. A limited time allotment will discourage dallying and encourage efficient silent observation of the words.

Efficient Reading

Rapid reading is practiced in reviews for other purposes.

"Let's look at page 10. Who can find the sentence that tells . . . ?"

"On which page does Bill speak again?"

"Jackie, you found that very fast. How did you do it? What did you look for?" Jackie tells her secrets of skimming to the rest of the group.

"Let's see how quickly you can match the endings of sentences to the beginnings I put on the pocket chart."

The teacher has: "Bill came" on the pocket chart. A child quickly finds among the phrase cards in the chalk tray "to the playhouse" to complete the sentence. Then someone is asked to read it aloud, and someone else has to find the picture which shows this action. "Is he right?" Why should the teacher give away the answer, when it is the children's education?

When the teacher says, "When you have finished, you may draw a picture of . . . (or) you may go to the reading table and select a book to 'read,' " she is encouraging rapid completion of the worksheet. This is another way to accustom children to a more rapid pace in reading than dawdling and early uncertainty might seem to warrant.

Content Fields

All around the room are the results of activities in the content fields. In science, the children have studied air, and have come to conclusions which the teacher has recorded from their dictation, in outline form, one of the first exposures to this form for the children:

Air Pushes Up

I. What we did:
1. We filled a glass with water.
2. We put a piece of paper on top of the glass.
3. We pressed the paper tight on the glass,
   so that no air could get in.
4. We turned the glass of water over.

II. What we observed:
1. The paper did not fall off.
2. The water did not run out.

III. What we learned:
1. Air was pressing against the paper.
2. When we turned the glass of water on its side,
   a. The paper stayed in place.
   b. The water did not run out.

Classification is experienced in a study of animals:

What We Learned

Names of Farm Animals

Family	Mother	Father	Baby
cattle	cow	bull	calf
sheep	ewe	ram	lamb

The hard life of a modern whale appears in the local news:

The Poor Whale

A whale came into the bay.
He swam under the pier.
He could not get out. He was
stuck.
He was bumping the ship.
The ship moved out into the ocean.
The whale was still stuck.
S.P.C.A. shot him.

In a study of magnets the children list some of the things they think they want to try with a magnet:

Do magnets attract these?

(picture)	(picture)	(picture)
"tin" can?	cloth?	staples?
(picture)	(picture)	(picture)
string?	nails?	steel lid?

Interviewing is one way to obtain information in the content fields. Stephen Rojas takes the microphone, which is attached to the classroom record player, and announces to the class: "This is Stephen Rojas speaking. My brother showed me what a magnet can do."

Individuals in the class take the microphone to ask pertinent questions: "Do it pick up pins?"

"Can you say that better?" The teacher has spoken of this before.

"Does it pick up pins?"

"Yes, Alfreda, it does," says Stephen.

"Does it pick up cloth?"

"We didn't try cloth, Boris."

Isadore asks the best question: "What does it pick up, Stephen?"

When the interview is over, a summary of findings is necessary, so that what is known about magnets is clear to all.

"Who can tell us all the things that Stephen found that magnets attract?" (*Attract* means pull, pick up, draw toward. A good word!)

Ultimately, all that they find out from books, interviews, pictures, and experiments, they summarize in a chart which all can read:

Our Science Learnings

Magnets

Magnets have different shapes.
Magnets are different sizes.
Magnets attract metals with iron.
Magnets attract other magnets.
Magnets pull and push each other.
Magnets attract through glass and paper.

Interests

Over in the corner beside a shelf full of books are four chairs. When a child is finished with his regular work and wants to read quietly or browse for the right book, he comes, selects a book, and sits down to read it. The books are arranged alphabetically by topic: Animals, Fun, People, Science, and Transportation. Some of these books have been read to the children and are here to be enjoyed again mostly through the picture sequence. Some are new and belong to the category of "Please read this one," when it is time to hear another story. Especially popular are the animal books, such as *Curious George takes a job* by Hans A. Rey, *The camel who took a walk* by Jack Tworkov, *The travels of Babar* by Jean de Brunhoff, *Theodore Turtle* by Ellen MacGregor, and *Chouchou* by Francoise. Fun is represented by *500 hats of Bartholomew Cubbins* by Dr. Seuss. Stories about people—neighbors and adventurers—scarcely ever succeed in keeping the animals out. *Wait for William* by Marjorie Flack and *The biggest bear* by Lynd Ward are such books. *Sun up* by Alvin Tresselt and *See for yourself* by Nancy Larrick sit above the "Science" sign. And, of course, because Eddie brought a magnet to school, books about magnets are there for their pictures and for whatever anyone can read. *The boats on the river* by Marjorie Flack, *Clear the track* by Slobodkin, and *The first book of airplanes* by Jeanne Bendick are some of those on transportation. A few children may be able to read "beginner" books without help, to enjoy them, and to tell about them or read parts to the other children. (See next chapter.)

As new topics are raised in class, as new questions are asked, new books appear. The children visit the library and bring back several books for the classroom collection. They decide where in the shelf the different books belong.

The teacher puts a card for each book in a card file. The card has the title and the author. Alphabet tabs (Aa, Bb, etc.) indicate location of cards according to the first letter in the title. When a child wishes to take a book out overnight, he finds the card that matches the title and writes his name on it. When he returns the book, he crosses his name off. In this way the teacher and children always know where the book is and the children learn something about the practical use of the alphabet. At first, everyone has to clear with Alice, who knows how to read everyone's name and knows the alphabet pretty well; but, if the class is an able one, the system soon works smoothly without requiring a hyper-active child librarian.

Once a week the class visits the school library for a storytelling time with the school librarian. She not only tells a story but miraculously seems to know just what other books to suggest that the children will like. New areas of reading interest are constantly being opened up in this way.

Each child has a little booklet he is making himself. It is called *Stories I like*, and each page gives the title and author and a picture the child has drawn to represent the story. These are stories he has read himself or has heard. In this way, all children, whether or not they can read, have a booklet of book friends in which they can take pride. Gradually they are able to write more than the name of the author and story. "I liked the bear in it."

Authors are interesting people to know. When the children like their books, the teacher tries to find out something about the authors by looking in references such as *The junior book of authors* by Kunitz and Haycraft. "Listen to this and see whether you can tell me why he was able to write such a good story about bears."

Taste

A chart in the room reads:

Little Spider

Little spider on the block
                    Around
Around   Around
                    Around
He went
Just
    like
        the
            clock.

Another chart announces:

Something that is shiny

the moon
the stars
a dime
a bracelet
a car
a new truck

By having children hear poetry and make up poetry, the teacher is helping them enjoy and understand it. By having them think together about sensory impressions ("See how this glass shines? What does it remind you of? What else do you know that shines?") she is encouraging them to think like a poet.

Another chart says:

Songs We Know

Jack-in-the-Box
Let's Sing a Little Song
Big Bass Drum

Singing gives a feeling for rhyming, for the sounds of words. Clear enuncia-tion, gestures, and bodily movement with the wording, increase the child's awareness of the effect which language can have upon thoughts and feelings.

The voice of the teacher can have a magical effect upon the listeners. Thirty-five wigglers, squirm by squirm, become quiet as she reads Jack Tworkov's *The camel who took a walk:*

"The forest was dark and very quiet. Not a creature was stirring."

"Not even a mouse," interrupts Joel. A glance settles him.

"Even the wind had stopped breathing. Not a leaf was falling, not a blade of grass was moving."

The tigers in the class are alerted when she reads, "And when a tiger's eye is open the tiniest crack, then you know that the tiger is not sleeping as he would have you believe." How good it is to outsmart a tiger, when he is in the book and you are under the spell of it.

The movement of the camel is in the teacher's voice as she reads, "A very beautiful camel, with soft brown eyes, was just taking her morning walk. She walked—oh, so slowly, so gracefully, with her head way up in the air. Her nose smelled the early morning sweetness, and her eyes took in all the blue and pink colors of the sky."

Reporting to Parents

In October a hectographed letter goes out to the parents:

October 18, 1957

Dear Parents:

I am a busy first grader. In these first six weeks I have been learning many things . . . how to be a good listener and quiet worker in the classroom.

And most important of all, I am learning to read, to write, and to do numbers . . . See all the new words I've learned: (These are listed.) Please save this list and help me study these words so that I won't forget them.

Just see how nicely I'm learning to write my name. (A sample of the child's writing is attached.)

In the next letter, in December, the child reports:

I have my own A to Z spelling box, and in it are the two words I've just learned to spell: *me* and *see*. I'll be learning new words and putting them into this box all year long. Soon I'll be writing my own stories with these words.

In January the child reports:

In addition to reading in our books, we spend some time each day studying phonics. Isn't that a big word? It means I'm learning the sounds the different letters of the alphabet make. We listen to records using these sounds, and we're learning some poems that have these sounds in them. This helps us in both our reading and our speaking. Soon I'm going to make my own alphabet book.[2]

Summary

The first grade continues the activities for reading readiness initiated in the kindergarten and includes, as the child can master them, the activities suggested in this chapter. Diagnosis of each child's status, needs, and characteristics is the first duty and the continuous concern of the first-grade teacher. Children who need more ear training, more speech experience, more knowledge of their environment, are given them. Children who are already reading are helped to read and to express themselves in writing. They are also given opportunities to help other children.

Experience charts provide reading and thinking experiences. Individual booklets give children a sense of accomplishment. Concepts such as that of "home" are explored to the extent of the children's experience in and out of the classroom. Word recognition is aided by signs in the classroom, labelled displays, dramatic interpretation of meanings, and numerous appearances of words to be learned, in different contexts. Structural analysis, including -s and -ed endings, and phonetic analysis, including consonants and rhyme endings, start with ear training and proceed to the arrival at principles through comparison and inductive reasoning. The alphabet is learned by the use of files and writing.

Comprehension and interpretation are fostered in discussion of what is read. Vocabulary development is extended through the oral use of harder oral vocabulary than the children can master in visual form. Oral reading enhances interpretation. Study skills are sharpened through skimming to answer questions, classifying material, and doing various types of reference work relating to social studies and science topics. Efficient silent reading comes with careful cultivation of silent observation of words, worksheets, and time limits. Reading speed is a natural outgrowth of only so much time to do many interesting things.

Reading interests are extended through the content fields, through incidental matters which children express interest in, and through deliberate library exposure. A classroom collection teaches the care of books, a simple library procedure involving the alphabet. Reading taste is tuned by the ear as the teacher reads aloud and engages the children in poetry making, singing, and observation of nature with emphasis upon associative thinking.

Parents are kept informed of the child's progress in language and reading, and are given things to do to help if they are able.

Obviously, although this is a long chapter, it is only a suggestion of the many things the teacher, the parents, and the librarian can do to help a child learn to read.

[2] Thanks to Helen McDonald of Lockwood School, Oakland, California.

Suggested Activities

Further study. Take the manuals for the pre-primers, primer, and first reader of a good reader series. Study the skills index and make a chart of all the skills you are expected to teach through these books, but, even more important, during the first months of teaching a child to read. Study also the lists of books which the children can read or the teacher can read to them, which are in an appendix or at the end of each lesson plan. See the filmstrip and film and recording recommendations accompanying each lesson and get acquainted with some of them in your audio-visual library. See the test file in your education library and become well enough acquainted with one readiness test to know how you think you might administer and interpret it. Look at the vocabulary lists in the first-grade readers and then look at the books recommended as first-grade reading. See which ones you think a child could read, knowing primer vocabulary; first-reader vocabulary; which ones you think would be just for Isadore and Alice.

Creative activities. Review the activities under each subheading in this chapter. Think what other activities you might undertake with the children which would cultivate the type of learning desired and would be in keeping with what you have learned about good reading methods.

Suppose you were the teacher of a neighbor's child whom you know. What books would you wish to read to him throughout a year to give him a love of books, a sense of their variety, a greater understanding of his world, a more thoughtful approach to living? Remember that he is not just a statistic. You must meet his intelligence level, his interests, and his attention span!

Selected References

ALSTETTER, Mabel, *Adventuring with books.* Champaign, Illinois: National Council of Teachers of English, 1960.

ARBUTHNOT, May Hill, *Children and books*, 2nd ed. Chicago: Scott, Foresman and Company, 1957.

ARTLEY, A. Sterl, *Your child learns to read.* Chicago: Scott, Foresman and Company, 1953, Chaps. 2 and 3.

Best books for children. New York: R. R. Bowker Company, 1960.

BETTS, Emmett A., *Foundations of reading instruction.* New York: American Book Company, 1946, Chap. 20.

DEBOER, John J., and DALLMANN, Martha, *The teaching of reading.* New York: Holt, Rinehart and Winston, Inc., 1960, Chap. 13.

DUFF, Annis, *Bequest of wings.* New York: Viking Press, Inc., 1944.

DURRELL, Donald D., *Improving reading instruction.* New York: Harcourt, Brace & World, Inc., 1956, Chap. 2.

FRANK, Josette, *Your child's reading today.* Garden City, New York: Doubleday and Company, Inc., 1960, Chap. 7.

GRAY, Lillian, and REESE, Dora, *Teaching children to read*, 2nd ed. New York: Ronald Press, 1957, Chap. 7.

GROFF, Patrick, Recent easy books for first-grade readers, *Elementary English*, 1960, 38, 521-527.

HARRIS, A. J., *How to increase reading ability*, 4th ed. New York: Longmans, Green and Company, 1961, Chap. 3.

HEILMAN, Arthur W., *Principles and practices of teaching reading*. Columbus: Charles E. Merrill Books, Inc., 1961, Chaps. 2, 3, and 4.

MATHES, M. N., *Basic book collection for elementary grades*. Chicago: American Library Association, 1959.

McKIM, Margaret, *Guiding growth in reading*. New York: The Macmillan Company, 1955, part 2.

—— Reading in primary grades, *Development in and through reading*. Sixtieth Yearbook of the National Society for the Study of Education, Part I. Chicago: University of Chicago Press, 1961, Chap. 15.

MONROE, Marion, *Growing into reading*. Chicago: Scott, Foresman and Company, 1951, Chap. 9.

RUSSELL, David H., *Children learn to read*, 2nd ed. Boston: Ginn and Company, 1961, Chaps. 6 and 7.

—— and RUSSELL, Elizabeth F., *Listening aids through the grades*. New York: Bureau of Publications, Teachers College, Columbia University, 1959.

Films

Individualizing reading instruction in the classroom. New York: Bureau of Publications, Teachers College, Columbia University, 1956.

Newstime in first grade reading. Iowa City: Bureau of Audio-Visual Instruction, State University of Iowa, 1956.

Reading with Suzy. Los Angeles: Churchill-Wexler Company.

Skippy and the 3 R's. Washington, D.C.: National Education Association, 1953.

Using a reading readiness book. Iowa City: Bureau of Audio-Visual Instruction, State University of Iowa, 1956.

Filmstrips

Children learn to read printed symbols, grade 1, *Reading*. Detroit: Jam Handy Organization, 1955. (with 33⅓ rpm recordings)

It happened in the first grade. Boston: Ginn and Company, 1957.

Learning to read. Valhalla, New York: Stanley Bowmar Company, Inc.

21

Recommended Practices
in Second and Third Grades

The techniques which have been described in the chapters on the kindergarten and first grade are continued as needed in grades two and three. The test and questionnaire methods of determining the child's reading level and reading needs and interests are used by the teacher at these higher grade levels early in the school year. The difference in education at these levels is more one of degree than of kind. The principles of basal reading instruction described in Chapter 22 are applicable in the primary grades, also.

Because children have learned to write many of the words they can read, and have learned to read many of the words they have wanted to write, the classroom reflects more written work than before, and writing has become a greater support for the learning activities in reading.

Because some children have not yet a good start in reading, while other children have been learning at varied rates, there is a greater span in accomplishment and level between the poorest reader and the best reader in the class. Because of differences in environment, including language background and family attitudes toward education, not to speak of native ability, some second grades look like third grades and some third grades look like second grades. The teacher knows that she can do something to overcome the language handicap, and that perhaps the environment she creates may compensate somewhat for the lack of incentive some children bring with them from home.

Ear Training

"Why do we say *an* anemometer instead of *a* anemometer?" the teacher asks. The reader may wonder why we say anemometer at all at the second-grade level, but that is only an evidence of his pre-World War II vintage. Globes, microscopes, and anemometers are the tools of second graders growing up in a smaller scientific world.

"Because it don't come out right?" ventures the willing Ernest.

"Because it . . ." the teacher waits.

"Because it doesn't come out right?" Ernest recovers.

"Listen," says the teacher. "Listen as I say it two ways and tell me what you notice." (The teacher sets a purpose for listening prior to the listening so that it will be more efficient. She does the same when she asks children to read. Knowing ahead of time what you are looking or listening for is a habit. It must be practiced to be established.) "A anemometer. An anemometer. A anemometer. An anemometer."

"An anemometer sounds better," says Jackie. "Anemometer starts with *an* too." What a trap! Now that the teacher has started something, she must see it through. She writes on the chalkboard, saying, "Look at the words I write, and be ready to say what you notice." She writes:

an apple	a car
an orange	a box
an elephant	a top
an Indian	a wagon

"Let's read down the first column of phrases and listen. . . . Now the second column. . . . What do you notice? What do all the words in the first column start with? What do all the words in the second column start with? What is the difference?" With luck, someone remembers that *a, o, e,* and *i* are vowels. The children at second-reader level are just learning about vowel sounds. Most of the children know consonants from last year.

"What rule can we remember? When a name starts with a vowel sound . . . ?" The children finish the rule. The teacher writes it on the chalkboard and all say it and prove it with other words. They roll on their tongues *an onion, an angel,* etc. Tomorrow the rule will appear on a chart and children will suggest words to be written on the chart as examples of the rule. They play a game. A child says a word like *box* or *ant* and another child has to say it with the proper *a* or *an*. Children (not the teacher) correct the mistakes and prove them by the chart. Their ears are assailed by the sound relationships and their attention is called to a basic fact of the English language. If children make a mistake as they speak and write, they will think it as they read.

Verbal Facility

Verbal facility is encouraged in many oral situations, one of which is the news period. But to speak well before a group, you need to be a good speaker and have a good audience.

"What are some of the things a speaker has to remember to make a good news period?" The children make suggestions. They also suggest a title: A Good News Period. The teacher writes, asking, "Do I capitalize this letter? Why? How do I spell this word?" She selects for her assistants the child who needs to be reminded about capitalizing important words in

a title, the child who is bursting to prove he does know how to spell *good*—
at last. She writes the contributions as they come:

> The speaker has something important to say.
> The speaker stands erect.
> The speaker looks at his audience.
> The speaker speaks clearly.

She herself may think of other ideas, but she writes the children's,
knowing that, as the year advances, she can make the class aware of other
attributes by such questions as, "Did you notice how Charles won our attention from the very first? What was it that he did that made us listen?"

In the same way she gathers the ideas about the good listener.

> The listener looks at the speaker.
> The listener asks good questions.
> The listener writes a report after class news.

But as a teacher of outlining she is dissatisfied with the form.

"Can anyone see how we can say these things in fewer words? Does
anyone notice anything about the way these sentences start?"

The first four all start with *the speaker*. The teacher shows how, by
erasing the last three "the speakers" she can save wording and still give
the same ideas:

"Now," she asks, "who thinks he can tell me how to change the last
three sentences." There are many volunteers for this, since the pattern has
been set, but the children have to do what thinking there is to be done.
The result looks like this:

A Good News Period

The speaker
1. has something important to say.
2. stands erect.
3. looks at the audience.
4. speaks clearly.

The listener
1. looks at the speaker.
2. asks good questions.
3. writes a report after class news.

Each child chooses one piece of news which caught his fancy, and writes
a brief news report for the day and illustrates it. By the end of the week
he has a booklet of News of the Week to take home to read to the family.
Buck's looks like this:

Monday

> Linda showed us a
> chart of the moon and
> the craters on it.

In the reading lessons the teacher notices that children confuse pairs of words: listen lesson, think thing, whole hold, wall walk, made make, snap snack, nail mail, cave cage, shark shot, must much, cold coal, when went, then than, sharp shark. Perhaps the trouble lies in recognition, but maybe it is basically a failure to differentiate the sounds.

"Rest your heads on your arms and close your eyes. I shall say two words. If they are the same, repeat the word to me; if they are different, be silent. Here are my words: listen listen . . . think thing . . ."

She notes the ones which cause confusion and tries to note which children are involved. On this basis she plans further ear training and opportunities for repetition of the words with emphasis upon good enunciation.

Another activity which helps children in verbal expression is hearing and making up poems. A prominent display in a classroom may be labelled: Read Our Poetry. A list of Songs We Like to Sing gives additional evidence of the teacher's effort to encourage clear enunciation and familiarity with language patterns.

Written expression reveals the poet, the deeply moved, or the matter-of-fact reporter. After a day of having the girls bring their dolls and show and tell about them, Esther writes with real feeling:

> My doll's name is Rosa.
> She is very beautiful.

Joe sizes up the situation and writes with as much male restraint as he can muster:

Doll Day

> Doll Day is a day for girls.
> Linda brought her doll to school.
> She talked a while. Then she sat
> down. And that's how Doll Day
> works.

The teacher decides that, while Joe may be learning tolerance, she may lose him entirely if she has many more ideas like Doll Day. She counters with Pocket Day, in which boys reveal the special treasures they carry all the time.

Once in a while the teacher needs to tape-record a class situation in which she herself is doing a great deal of speaking, and then compare her enunciation with the errors the children are making in discriminating the sounds of words. She may find an embarrassing similarity between their ear problem and her speech problems. And sometimes she discovers that long association with children of certain speech patterns has lowered her standards rather than elevated theirs. Dis happens alla time if ya doan watch, specially if ya talk too fas.

At the beginning of each day the children and the teacher plan the day, what they will attempt and what irregularities will require departures from the usual procedure. The teacher writes the program and gives information as she does so. The result in a third-grade room may look like this:

> Good morning circle: reporting
> Reading
>   Jo Ann's
>   Guide sheet: "Christmas with Stina Mor"
>   Workbook 74, 75, 76
>   Skills: Homonyms
>   Jason's
>   Skills: building new words
>   Workbook to 55
>   John's
>   Guide: "Visitor in a Camp"
>   Skills: visual clue to accent
>   Workbook to 64
> Writing Easter message
> Exploring Science books—solar system
> Weekly Reader
> Arithmetic: equal groups; multiplication
> Gym: new dances: Captain Jinx
>   Pop Goes the Weasel
> Art: painting Easter cards

Concept Building

Concepts are built in many ways. Observation of what a thing is good for (its function) is one of these.

"What can we do at Fleishacker Playground?"

1. Play on the swings.
2. Take a pony ride.
3. Go through Storyland.
4. Swim at the pool.

We have written 1, 2, 3, 4, and we refer to the first, second, third, fourth thing that we wrote. Comparison is another way of building concepts. Elsewhere in the room we have a reminder of these terms and their relationships to each other:

1	one	first
2	two	second
3	three	third
4	four	fourth
5	five	fifth

Study of what a thing is made of (composition) is another way of building a concept. A fish is made of flesh and blood and bone. The bone is made of calcium. The child writes: "I am made of calcium. I am part of a fish. What am I?"

The concept of friend can be enlarged through the teacher's reading of Joan Walsh Anglund's *A friend is someone who likes you* (New York: Harcourt, Brace and Company, 1958).

"A friend is someone who likes you," reads the teacher. "It can be a boy . . . It can be a girl . . . or a cat . . . or a dog . . . or even a white mouse . . . A tree can be a different kind of friend. It doesn't talk to you, but you know it likes you, because it gives you apples . . . or pears . . . or cherries . . . or, sometimes, a place to swing."

After the story is finished, the teacher may say, "Does anyone have a cat friend? How can you tell the cat is your friend?" Going along this vein, the children will review some of their friends—animals and objects—and the ways they know they are friends.

"Friends help each other. We are all friends in this room, aren't we, because we are always helping each other? What are some of the ways we help each other?

"Friends like to do things together. What are some of the things we like to do together?

"Think about this as you go home this afternoon. Tomorrow maybe you will have a story for us about one of your friends, how you know that a tree is your friend, or how you made friends with a dog or a bird."

In the process of writing their own story or poem or news report, children learn about form:

When You Write a Story

1. Make the title tell what the story is about.
2. Indent the first word in every paragraph.
3. Leave a margin.
4. Start each sentence with a capital letter.
5. End each statement with a period.
6. End each question with a question mark.

What the story should contain is suggested by questions the teacher asks when she discusses with the children a story they have read together.

"Who is the main character? What makes you think so?

"How can you tell where the story took place?

"How can you tell when the story took place?

"What happened in the story?"

Graph reading at higher grade levels will be easier for these children because they have kept their own graph of the high temperature each day of the month of March. Making it themselves, they know what it means. They interpret it as the teacher asks, "Which day had the highest temperature so far? What day was that? What was that temperature?" Each child has to prove his answer by finding the place on the graph. They grow a bean and chart its height every week on the same day of the week. Having made a temperature graph and a bean-height graph, they begin to know what a graph is, whatever it is about. They know how important it is to have it well labelled.

Map concepts are built on the classroom floor with chalk lines marking off the streets of the neighborhood. A wall becomes the north wall, another the east, etc. Children show on the floor map how they go home from school. Soon the floor map is translated into a wall map, and then the area represented by the homemade wall map of the neighborhood is found to be a small spot on the commercially made city map. The children have no trouble using this knowledge in locating on a world map the places represented by the stamps they have been collecting.

A child draws a picture of his house and writes:

> My address is 175 22nd Avenue.
> I walk to school. I go one block
> south and I stop.

Word Recognition and Meanings

Around the molding above the chalkboard are cards, each one containing a letter of the alphabet in lower-case and upper-case manuscript, and a picture of something beginning with that sound:

Ww

(picture of a wagon)

Words, sentences, and phrases label objects and displays around the room, helping children associate ideas with the correct verbal symbols:

> See my finger painting.
> Boris Rankov
> Our graph tells how fast wind travels.

There is a box of cards alphabetically arranged, containing words frequently asked for in writing. Another box labelled "Our Arithmetic Words" contains words like *how, much, more, difference,* which are used in original arithmetic problems.

A chart, to which additions are made as new words are encountered, lists the special words in the science vocabulary. One such chart looks like this:

Science Words

earth	direction
compass	caterpillar
evaporate	float
air	fog
atmosphere	gravity
clouds	helicopter
breathe	insect
barometer	heat
iron	hot

Each child keeps a booklet of arithmetic vocabulary, illustrating it with his own drawings and using the words in a defining sentence:

This is a *bunch* of grapes.

This is a *flock* of birds.

The children keep a calendar each month. Each child is selected to write the number of the day in the proper space. Another draws the symbol of the weather and chooses strips to complete the sentence. "Today is . . . It is a . . ." A list of words and symbols assists him:

The Days of the School Week	Our Weather Vocabulary	
Monday	warm	sunny
Tuesday		
Wednesday	hot	cloudy
Thursday		
Friday	windy	rainy
	cold	

A chart in one corner of the room shows colored balloons, each a different color (Black, red, green, yellow, blue, purple, brown, white, orange, and pink), with the name of the color written across the balloon. Association of the word with the color is further supported by a report the children have dictated:

Traffic Lights

Red lights mean danger.
Green lights say, "Go."
Yellow lights say, "Careful."
You had better go slowly
when walking or driving.

Words like *how* and *why* and *where*, so hard to recognize and remember, are seen in written questions: "Why are there so many different ways to travel and carry things?" In some cases they are questions dictated by the children. In others, they are teacher-made. But in both cases the teacher requires the children to read them silently and then aloud. She takes no chances that she is doing all the work while the children coast along on her efforts. She writes the words to be read and she sees to it that the children have reasons and opportunity for reading them. (How often has one seen a teacher laboriously write on the chalkboard and read aloud what she has written, while the children contemplate the fly on the ceiling?)

Sometimes a child comes upon a word in his reading and asks the teacher for help with it. He points to the word and looks up at the teacher. The teacher reads "elephant," and the child, looking at the teacher, a big motherly type, thinks "elephant." The wise teacher of whatever size has the child look at the word as she tells him the word, so that the visual and auditory impressions will occur simultaneously. Then she has him look at it again and repeat it. If he hears, says, and sees, he is more apt to learn. If he goes to his seat and writes the word from memory and puts it in his card file or vocabulary notebook, with a little picture of its meaning or a phrase showing its use, the learning is even more certain.

Deliberate explorations of word meanings through meanings of other words cause children to see the same words again and again in different situations.

Find the word in this sentence which means the opposite of *play:*

We like to work together.   (antonym)

Three of these words are about the same thing. One of them is about something different. Which one is about something different?

hammer   saw   carrot   nail   (association)

What were all of these three words about? (generalization)
What two words in this sentence are homonyms?

Is there no way to know?

What different meanings does the word *run* have in these sentences?

> I can run the machine.
> I took my dog for a run.
> I can run fast.   (multiple meanings)
> I will run for president.
> See the fence run around the field.

These sentences do not really mean what they say. What do they mean?

> Stop pulling my leg.
> Drop me off at the end of the block.
> Go to the corner and turn over on the next street.
>   (figurative language)

In which of these sentences can the words *scramble* and *scamper* both be used? In which can only one be used?

> ─────── my eggs.
> See the squirrel ─────── up the tree.
> ─────── the letters of this word.   (synonyms)

If this is all that the child knows about solving words, this is all that appears in his handbook. But if he has learned something about consonant sounds, a series of pages from A to Z records what he knows, such as:

> *Bb*
>
> big   (picture
> box   of dog)
> ball   Mac   Mac will not *bite* me.

On this page he sees three words he knows by sight, all beginning with *b*. If he has forgotten what *b* says, he can say the words to himself and recapture the sounds. Then he remembers, too, that he drew Mac's picture and wrote the sentence, with the teacher's help on the new word, "Mac will not bite me." The sentence reminds him that when you see a strange word in a sentence, beginning with a *b,* you read the sentence to see what word might make sense, and choose the word that starts with the *b* sound in *big, box,* and *ball.*

If he knows something about endings, there is a section in his handbook about them. One page may be devoted to the *s* at the end of a verb.

> *s*
>
> run   play   see   (picture of dog running)
> runs   plays   sees   Mac can run.
>   Mac runs.

Another set of pages shows what he knows about rhyme endings:

ake		
bake	(picture of piece of cake)	to
cake	May I *take* a piece of cake?	top
make		

The words *to* and *top* are words he knows which remind him what the first letter of *take* says, if he has forgotten.

This, then, is a book which gives him assurance and help. If the answer is in his book, he should not have to ask the teacher. He should learn to be independent. But because he has learned these facts inductively, the impressiveness of the learning means little forgetting and little asking. To a large extent the handbook is to the child what the word *Rumplesnitz* was to the knight in Heywood Broun's story of the "Fifty-First Dragon": a rabbit's foot, a symbol of confidence. To the child's parents it is proof that "something is being done about phonics." At the first of each year that such a book is kept, it is a means of reviewing the old learnings which may have suffered some slippage during the vacation. The child's writing it himself makes the handbook more effective than a commercial one, and, also, unfortunately, the commercial ones so far have been more authoritarian than inductive in their methods, often limiting a child's approach to a strange word so that he has to go to more trouble than is necessary in solving it. (Solving the word *something* by a purely phonetic approach, for instance.)

As the teacher has built knowledge of initial consonants, she has also made children aware of medial and final consonants. She has used listening games and games in which the children had to think of words ending with a certain sound. With Anita Wong she continues to work especially on hearing the final *l,* and on some other final consonants, too. If the family speaks Japanese at home, Gloria Matsumoto (Does she know that her name means "pine slope?") has trouble with many consonant endings, for most Japanese words end in a vowel.

The first-grade teacher has already found out that Rickie Sanchez does not produce a hard *ch* in his speech. She had to give him ear training and speech exercise before she attempted to teach him that *chair* and *choo* start with that sound. She was not fooled by Larry O'Doule's name when she heard the Spanish characteristics in his speech. Mothers often have more effect on their children's speech than the fathers.

The teachers in second and third grade do much to extend the knowledge of consonant blends, as two or more words containing a given blend appear in the sight vocabulary. First ear training: "I'm thinking of a word that begins like *black* and *blue* and it is something the duck hunters are using right now over by the lake." Then, when children can respond correctly to such a game, the teacher uses the same procedure as that described for the first-grade development of consonants.

Vowel study is preceded in the same way by ear training: "I'm thinking of a word that has the ă sound in it like *cat* and *bad* and it is something you lean against in a chair." (Notice that the words do not begin or end alike, and that they are short words with a minimum of sound interference in them.) Much training of this kind may be needed before the children successfully hear and can reproduce this sound in other words. Then the teacher writes the sight words and says, "Watch these words and be ready to tell me what they are." She writes:

>   cat
>   bad
>   back

"Let's read these words together aloud: cat, bad, back. What do you notice about the way these words sound? (Then, if no luck . . .) Do you hear a sound in the middle of each word? What is that sound? Yes, ă. (The teacher says ăăă, not "short A.") Now look at these words. What do you notice about the middle of each one?" A child sees that the middle contains an *a*. Fortunately, the teacher has chosen words of differing length so that he will not think this happens just in three-letter words. Ă is one of the sounds the letter *a* makes. When you see the letter *a* in the middle of a word like this, what sound may it make?" The children say "ăăă." Now the teacher draws a picture of a boy with a cap on his head. Then she writes, "See the cap." (Cap is a new word to the children, but they know the sounds of *c* and *p,* and have just learned the short *a* sound.) "Look at the picture. Look at the sentence. Who thinks he knows what the new word says? How do you know? Who will solve it for us?" A child reads, "See the cap." He says he knows it is cap because it begins like *cat* and ends like *top,* and has a short *a* in the middle. Another child says, "I know another way to solve it. It begins with a *c* and it rhymes with *tap*." Still another says, "It starts like cat. I just changed the *t* to a *p* sound." They are all right, but meanwhile they add a short *a* page to their handbooks.

A follow-up at their seats consists of independent work on worksheets which require them to draw a quick sketch of the meaning of the new word in each sentence. Now there is no picture to help them. They have to use the technique alone. Even the sentence contexts do not really identify the word. They simply make the setting more natural and remind the child that the word must make sense in the sentence.

>   The cat is having a *nap.*
>   See the pretty *fan.*

Other vowel sounds and sounds produced by two vowels together are similarly studied. A chart is often made of the different vowel combinations producing the same vowel sound (*ay ai ey,* etc.).

A few prefixes are developed in the same way, except that the meaning of the prefix is stressed. After ear training, the teacher writes:

> I am able to do it.
> I am unable to do it.

The children read the sentences and tell what they mean.

"What one thing makes the second sentence mean something different from the first? Who can underline that part and say it for us? What do you think un- means? Who can read the sentence using *not* instead of *un-*?"

At another time she may list:

like	unlike
able	unable
true	untrue

The children read across, and a child is chosen to write after *unlike* the two words it means (not like). Similar activity produces *not able* and *not true*. A child is then asked to underline the part of unlike which means *not,* and so on. Then the children are given new words, formed of sight words plus the prefix *un.*

Ear training for syllabification includes exercises such as: "I am going to beat out some words. Watch and listen and be ready to join me." The teacher claps two claps as she says, "Recess." As children catch on, they clap with her. The principal, hearing the applause, thinks, "I mustn't forget to recommend Miss Ruse for tenure." Then the teacher says, "Each clap is for a syllable of the word. (She writes.) Let's all say it: *syllable.* How many syllables or beats does *recess* have?" "It has two syllables," the children answer. "Who can prove it?" A child claps as he says, "Re-cess."

How do the children learn what it is that makes a syllable? The learning is a gradual process, covering different types of syllable. The children hear that *back, catch, go,* and *run,* have one syllable. Yet, when these words are written one below the other, the children see that they are of different lengths. If these words have just one syllable, then it isn't the number of consonants they have that decides it, because there are three in the first, four in the second, one in the third, and two in the fourth. What might it be? The children underline the vowel in each word. Each word has one vowel and each has one syllable. The vowel sound makes the syllable. When they discover this, they can go on to exercises showing that *have* has only one syllable because the *e* is silent, *boil* only one because the two vowels form one new sound together, *tail* only one because the *i* is silent.

The hard and soft sounds of *g* and *c* are studied. The children discover by this same inductive method that *g* or *c* followed by *e* or *i* is usually soft. Now Isadore can account for the spelling of a word like *changeable.* He collects examples of his discovery for the edification of his classmates.

The teacher writes *often, ghost,* and *toward* on the chalkboard, and asks why they are not pronounced of-ten, g-host, and to-ward. The children learn that vowels are not the only letters which can be silent. Consonants are sometimes, too. You can pretty much count on the *h* following *g* in a syllable to be silent, the *k* preceding *n* in a syllable (*know*), the *w* preceding *r* in a syllable (*wrong*).

In these and many other learnings which comprise a heavy word-analysis program for most children in grades two and three, the teacher stresses the method of approach as much as the learning itself. "How can we discover this for ourselves? What should we listen for? What should we look for? How shall we decide what our statement should be? How shall we prove that we are right? How can we remember?"

Frequently, when presenting the new spelling or reading words, which the children already know by ear but not by sight, the teacher will say, "Which of the kinds of words we have been studying are these words?" Up on a chart which she has developed with the children's help are these four classifications:

Kinds of Words We Know

1. Simple words like *stay*. Use phonics.
2. Compound words like *something*. Find the parts.
3. Prefixed words like *unlike*. Find the parts.
4. Words with endings like *going*. Find the parts.

The children refer to the chart when they discuss the words.

"The first one (*hold*) is a simple word like *stay*," says Joe.

"So how will Joe have to solve it?" asks the teacher.

"He'll have to use phonics," says Isadore, "think of the sound of *h* and the sound of *old*."

"*Old* is old," says George. "That's no trick."

"The next word (*buying*) is a word like *going*," volunteers Susie. "It has the *ing* ending. I solve it by seeing the *buy* that I know and adding the ending."

The word *toward,* they decide, after they are told what it is, is a mean one.

"It looks like a compound, but you pronounce it like t-o-r-d."

This kind of discussion helps children develop the ability to know by quick inspection of a new word what kind of word analysis to apply. Sometimes worksheets are given to the children, containing new words to be classified in columns as being of one of the four types. All of the words are words they know by ear, but none of them is a "mean" word like *toward.* In the follow-up, they tell what classification the word is in, and use it in a sentence, to show they know what it means.

Comprehension

Comprehension is a product of purposed listening and reading, and of creative imitation. The teacher has given some arithmetic problems orally:

"Listen to this problem and be ready to tell me what fact the author gives you first. 'There were 24 cookies in the sack.' . . . What next? 'There were 24 cookies in the sack. Eight boys and girls took one cookie each.' . . . Now what does the author ask? 'How many cookies were left in the sack?' "

Later the child reads such problems with his group. Later still, he reads some alone. Then he is encouraged to make up problems of his own:

Arithmetic

I weigh 59 pounds on
the earth. On the moon
I would weigh about 10
pounds. What is the
difference in these weights?
Joseph K.

Joseph has learned the form of an arithmetic problem, how to express arithmetic statements, how to stick to pertinent information, and the kind of vocabulary he will encounter in many future problems.

The understanding of the use of quotation marks is carefully developed as the teacher converts the usual information chart into direct-quotation form which the children dictate to her.

Starfish

"A starfish has five arms,"
said Rosa.
Velinda said, "It walks
with its five arms."
"Tube feet help it walk
on rocks," said Don.
Ben said, "Starfish are
the worst enemy of oysters."
"If a starfish loses an arm,
it will grow another," said Gregory.

Now the "said So-and-so's" which appear in the basal reader will not seem strange, and the comma-quotation marks, period-quotation marks sequence is impressed upon the child who sees it written before his eyes.

A report of a harbor cruise which the children took may result in the usual we-did-this-we-did-that chart if the teacher does not say, "Can anyone think of another way to begin our sentence?"

The children may have dictated, "We passed the prison. We saw where the watchmen and their families live."

The teacher asks, "Could we make one sentence of those two? Who thinks he could, starting the sentence with *as?*" With such promptings, a more mature product is achieved, which sounds more like the books and which helps children understand the books better.

Our Harbor Cruise

We took the Harbor Cruise.
The boat went by Fort Anza,
the Marina, and Alcatraz Prison.
As we passed the prison, we saw
where the watchmen and
their families live. From the
boat we could see Coit Tower
on Telegraph Hill.

On the chalkboard is a reminder of things to do when a child has finished his regular work. He helped dictate it in the first place and is able to read and understand what it says when he has forgotten some of the details.

Something to Do

Read a story.
Write a book report.
Write a science report.
Write a number story.
Play a number game.
Study spelling.

The initial reading of a story in the basal instruction always stresses meaning: "Let's read this page to find out . . . (silent reading) What did you find out about it, Jerry?" Rereading of the story for various purposes also emphasizes meaning: "Who thinks he can find on this page the reason Bill didn't want to come? . . . Are you sure, Eddie?" (The boy who always wants to have the floor but isn't always careful about being prepared.)

Interpretation

The poetry drawing book, edited by William Cole and Julie Colmore (New York: Simon and Schuster, 1960), gives the children the idea of listening to poems and then drawing or painting what they see. The anonymous poem, "Mr. Nobody," is good therapy for children trapped in the adults' china shop. It is fun to draw the kind of fellow he must be, with broken things all around him.

Mr. Nobody

I know a funny little man,
      As quiet as a mouse,
Who does the mischief that is done
      In everybody's house!
There's no one ever sees his face,
      And yet we all agree
That every plate we break was cracked
      By Mr. Nobody.

'Tis he who always tears our books,
      Who leaves the door ajar,
He pulls the buttons from our shirts,
      And scatters pins afar;
That squeaking door will always squeak,
      For, prithee, don't you see,
We leave the oiling to be done
      By Mr. Nobody.

The finger marks upon the door
      By none of us are made;
We never leave the blinds unclosed,
      To let the curtains fade.
The ink we never spill; the boots
      That lying round you see
Are not our boots—they all belong
      To Mr. Nobody.

The third-reader group reading "Christmas with Stina Mor" is asked questions which make the children do more than tell what happened in the story:

"What did Anna mean when she said of the straw goats, 'Maybe they seemed fine only because we made them.' " (point of view)

"Why would a letter from Oscar be the best present the children could bring their mother?" (human relationship)

"What is meant by 'The goats no longer seemed heavy?' " (attitude)

"There is a saying that when we help others, we help ourselves. Is this in any way true of this story? How?" (relevance)

Children enjoy dramatizing parts of this story, inventing conversation as they go along. In this way they demonstrate their grasp of the characters' feelings in the situation described in the story.

Study Skills

In the classroom are reference tools for the children's use. *The Golden Book Encyclopedia* is a limited, well-illustrated reference expressed in simple language. Isadore will ask more questions than it will answer, but he can consult a more challenging reference with the aid of the librarian. A picture dictionary for children shows pictures of many of the words they want to write, and uses large print. An elementary dictionary is available in multiple copies for children who can begin to study words listed in it.

In connection with the reading of a paragraph of information on Coit Tower, the words *memorial, mural, architect,* and *design* are encountered.

"In what part of the dictionary will we find the word *memorial?*" The children agree that it should be about halfway through. They open to a page and notice two words (guide words) at the top of the pages.

"Where do you see that first word again? (It reappears as the first word in the first column.) Where do you see the second word again? (It is the last word on the second page.) To be on this page, the word *memorial* would have to come in the alphabet between what two words? . . . Yes, so is it on this page?" Most of the children say no, and proceed to other pages to find it. When they do find it, they read the meaning that is given for the word. Then they fit that meaning back into the sentence in which *memorial* appeared.

George isn't catching on to any of this. He is shaky on the alphabet and needs deliberate exercises on alphabetizing. One of his special jobs from now on is to list his spelling words in alphabetical order and, when he is finished, find the number of the page in the dictionary on which each word appears. If the numbers increase in size, he knows he is probably right. This is something he can do at home, if the parent wishes to help by checking his finished work.

A box of cards in the corner of the room is labelled *Research Reading.* In it are cards which set reading tasks in science for the child who chooses them. A sample card looks like this:

The Wonder World of Science, Book I

1. Could anyone live on the moon? Why?
   page 67
2. Where does the moon get its light?
   page 68
3. Is the moon always round? Why?
   page 70
4. Why do the stars look little to us?
   page 72

The child reads the first question, finds the page on which its answer is to be found (page 67 for the first question), reads to find just that information (a low form of skimming at this level), and writes his answer to the question on a sheet of paper which goes into a folder of things he knows about science. If the same card is not to be used over and over again, the information may be given orally to the class. If it is to be used by other children, the information may be given privately to the teacher, as she reviews the independent activities.

Oral Reading

Much of the oral reading at this level is done in purposeful rereading of stories in the basal reader in answer to questions such as: "What part of the story made Jerry think that the children were unselfish?" (interpretation of character) "When Anna and Peter said, 'We can't go with you this time,' how do you suppose they felt? . . . Who will read it to show the way they felt?" (interpretation of feelings) "What words in the very first paragraph help you to see the kind of country Anna and Peter lived in?" (words descriptive of setting) "What clue in the story can you find to the kind of work Oscar did when he first left Sweden?" (My old neighbor, Oscar, is no longer sailing the seas.) "Do you think this story took place when your grandfather was a boy? Why or why not? Find a clue." (We make parts for helicopters.) "What do you think Oscar remembered about Sweden? What clues can you find?" (I can use this warm coat and this shawl . . .)

Some oral reading is done in a book club meeting as children share with the whole class parts of stories they have individually read. (Everybody belongs.) Some is done as children read information from the dictionary or from a science or social-studies reference for the benefit of the class. Occasionally, the teacher puts up a series of large pieces of unprinted newspaper on which she has printed in large manuscript letters a poem which the children like especially well. Following her pointer, they all read the poem. Familiarity makes it possible for all to be successful. Variations are thought of, the boys doing one line, the girls another, or individual soloists doing portions between choruses by the entire class. The children try to make their voices go up when a hill is climbed, their voices fade as something goes off into the distance. "Who can tell us how a train sounds as it goes off into the distance? . . . Now let's try to make our voices go off into the distance just the way that train did."

As in the very first reading the children did in the first grade, the first reading of practically everything in the second and third grades is silent. Once in a while, to test the child's fluency on easy material, the teacher may take him aside and ask him to read aloud. Or, if she wishes to test his level of reading, she may give him a series of paragraphs of increasing difficulty. One day a new boy comes into the class. When asked what reading level he is on, he says that in Vermont where he has lived his group read out of a green book. (Big help.) So the teacher has him read passages from the books used by her school system. He does well on the pre-primer passage, the primer, and first reader. He misses only a word or two on second-reader levels one and two, and when she asks him questions about what he read, he is able to tell very well. But when he comes to the horse story in the third-reader level, he has difficulty. This is the way he reads:

"He could . . . he could feel her . . . her mouth soft and wet as it . . . he could feel her mouth soft and wet as it t-t."

The teacher supplies the word *touched*.

"As it touched his hand. Andrew was . . . Andrew was afraid, but he did not . . . he did not move. Then the s . . . then the sss."

The teacher supplies the word *sugar*.

"Then the sugar was gone."

As the boy reads aloud, the teacher writes lightly in pencil on her copy of the same material. Her copy looks like this:

He could feel her mouth soft and wet as it touched his hand. Andrew

was afraid, but he did not move. Then the sugar was gone.

The wavy line means repetition. The straight line means the boy couldn't read that part of the word. The crossed-out letter and insertion mean a letter was substituted for the proper one in the word. The teacher sees that the words *feel, touched, afraid, move,* and *sugar* are words this child is unsure of. *Feel* and *afraid* are probably shady characters in his sight vocabulary, words he has learned but not well enough. The child mistook the word *move* for the word *more,* which he knows. Perhaps he knows *move* and confuses it with *more,* or perhaps he has never read *move* before. *Move* is not a word that can be solved phonetically, for it follows neither the pattern of *love* nor that of *cove.* It should be spelled *moov.* These mistakes suggest that the child probably should be started at second-reader level two, or possibly third-reader.

His attack on the words *sugar* and *touched* show that he knows the *t* and *s* sounds. He cannot be expected to sound out successfully the *sh* sound of the *s* or the short *u* sound of *ou* in *touched.* If he was attacking *feel,* he apparently knows those consonant sounds and the double-vowel sound of the *ee.* His attack on *afraid,* if it was not a sight word, shows that he knows the sound of a two-syllable word beginning with a single unaccented *a* in the first syllable, and that he knows what *fr* and *ai* say according to phonetic rules. He apparently has word-analysis skills typically taught in the first and second readers. The teacher decides that he encountered too much difficulty on the third-reader passage to start reading at that level. She plays safe and tries him in the second-reader level-two group. Meanwhile she gives him the second-reader level-one book to take home, and the parents co-operate in listening to him tell about the stories he reads silently in it and in telling him words for whose identity he asks. Studying the words he has not met before strengthens his progress with his group at the higher level.

Silent Reading and Speed

Since oral expression is the child's first introduction to language, he is tempted to read everything aloud. Even when the teacher says, "Read with your eyes, not with your mouth," many children still are thinking words or moving lips or throat muscles as they attempt to read silently. However, the teacher continues to tell children to read silently to find out such-and-such a thing, and practically never asks them to read aloud without their having read silently first. Some sentences she has them read only silently.

"I am going to put a sentence in the pocket chart. As soon as you have read it, look at me, and I shall call on someone to act it out."

Then she puts up a sentence such as, "My, how sleepy I am today!" Another may say, "I can hardly keep my eyes open."

Deliberate speed exercise is not ordinarily desirable for young children, who are tense enough over the hard task of learning to read. But there are activities which encourage children to read more rapidly than they might without such encouragement.

"Such good books we have here, and I have to take them back to the county library at the end of this week. I hope you will read as much in them as you can before then."

Speed is encouraged, too, by silent-reading purposes which require a minimal attention to detail and draw attention to main ideas or to one prominent fact.

"Read the next page to find out why they couldn't go."

"What did this make you wonder? . . . Read the next two pages to find out."

"The boy and girl in this story had a hard problem to solve. Read until you find out what the problem was, and stand when you have found it." People who are tired of sitting on their chairs find the problem fast and thus solve their own.

Content Fields

Incidentally throughout this chapter you have been seeing evidence of how a teacher tries to assist children in reading in the content fields. The appearance of the strange vocabulary is one of their problems. A science-vocabulary chart ("Our Science Vocabulary"), a list of social-studies words, and a card file of arithmetic words for original arithmetic problems are helpful. The meanings of the words constitute another part of the reading problem. So the teacher displays a chart illustrating and defining *bunch* and *flock* for arithmetic. A social-studies chart lists the new words *padres, expeditions, adobe,* and *settlement,* followed by the definitions the children have put into their own words from the information they have found: "Padres were priests and taught the Indians many things."

The child who finds out something for himself about the new word remembers it better. Clem reports that his father's dictionary at home says that *padre* came from the Latin word meaning *father*. Mary does her own thinking and says, "We call our priest Father."

Christine in a study of the cat flea brings one special delivery from her cat and puts it under the microscope at school. She writes:

> I saw a cat flea
> under a microscope.
> It looked like a
> brown bone.
>   Christine

In a study of the planets the children make their own model of the planetary system and label the planets. They use a strong light for the sun and two pieces of spherical fruit to show why the moon looks different at different times.

In a study of their own community children observe the materials from which their houses are made and the kinds of transportation they see on the streets.

> The buildings in our community are made of

brick	cement
wood	glass
plaster	plastic

The children discuss what they have seen and learn to summarize.

> The kinds of transportation are

busses	cars
trucks	motor scooters
bicycles	

Whenever they start a new topic, they consider what they want to know and how they can find out.

> Ways to Find Out
>
> observing
> listening
> reading books
> doing experiments
> hearing reports
> taking excursions
> seeing filmstrips

Trips to the library result in bringing into the classroom books to be used to obtain information of the type desired. A science table, for instance, may present a display of such books: *The first book of mammals, The first book of prehistoric animals, The first book of bugs.* If questions run from dinosaurs to cat fleas, this is not surprising.

Interest in outer space brings in a flood of clippings from the current news on outer-space exploration. A committee of children organizes a folder of clippings on the topic, with single-line explanations of what each section illustrates, for the clippings are mostly pictures. Reading about outer space is a difficult problem at this level, for many children still do not read well enough to meet the challenge of technical vocabulary. *My Weekly Reader,* however, is the type of material which is especially helpful, for it is issued on several grade levels and deals with current topics. Each week a child can receive his copy written at his level of reading achievement. With other children at his level he has a guided reading lesson on the news, the teacher dealing with new words and purposing the silent reading just as she would in basal-reader materials. Then, during the science period, the different groups of children can join to discuss together what their different articles contribute to knowledge of the subject.

The current news raises fundamental questions which are listed on the chalkboard and become a reason to refer to textbooks on science. How far is the moon from the earth? Is it always the same distance? The table of contents may have a chapter on the moon. The children look to see. Is anything said about the moon, the sky? If not, the children look in the index. How is the index organized?

"Look at the first letter of each word in the list. What do you notice?"

"It's just like the dictionary," says Alice.

"What do you mean by that?"

"Well, the A's come first, then the B's, like that," says Alice.

"What word shall we look for?"

Jack thinks *moon* would be a good one.

"How far through the index should we look for a word beginning with *m?*"

About halfway, is the consensus.

When *moon* is found, it looks like this: Moon, 29-31, 54, 62. What could that mean? The children turn to page 29. They see that there is something about the moon on page 29, 30, and 31.

"When the pages are written 29-31, then, what does that mean?"

"It means 29 and 30 and 31. No skipping," says Isadore.

Page 32 contains nothing about the moon. The children conclude that the comma means "no moon on the pages between."

The children then refer again to the questions they asked about the moon. Certain children are designated to read for the answer to just one question. If a sentence does not say anything about distance from the earth, for instance, the child who is looking for that information goes on looking. He looks for figures and words like *miles* and *earth* and *moon* as his signals.

The abler child may be reading much more difficult material from a more difficult science text or reference. He reports his findings as the others do, sometimes simply stating them, sometimes reading a part.

"What does that mean?" It is never well to assume that a passage expressively read is necessarily understood either by the reader or the audience. Words the children have heard commonly used sometimes confound the author's purpose. Children have been told that they themselves go through phases. So does the moon, but there is a difference! And Anita Wong must not think that a light year is the opposite of the Year of the Ox.

One of the major problems in reading in the content fields is noticing the signals the author gives. These signals are the clues which good students unconsciously use (and poor students never recognize) to grasp the relationships among ideas which are unfamiliar. The teacher starts with practice on material containing familiar ideas. She writes:

> We have a bean in our room.
> The bean is in a jar.
> The jar has soil and water in it.
> The soil and water will help the bean grow.

"*A* and *the* are two words that sometimes help us," says the teacher. "Let's see whether you can see what the *a*'s and *the*'s do in these sentences."

After the children have inspected the sentences silently, and individuals have read sentences aloud, she says, "Who will find the *a*'s for us? . . . the *the*'s for us?"

The children underline them from left to right.

"Which comes first, *a* bean or *the* bean?

"Which comes first, *a* jar or *the* jar?

"Which comes first, just soil and water or *the* soil and water?

"When something is first talked about, it may be called what?

"After that, what may it be called? *The* means a special one."

She scrambles pairs of sentences and has the children decide which sentence should come first, which second in each pair. The children find examples of the principle they have discovered, in experience charts around the room.

The teacher helps the children notice the function of referent words by writing two sentences and asking which should come first and what words tell them.

> This one is hers.
> Dick and Edith have new sleds.

The children say that *this one* means one of the sleds, and *hers* means Edith's. The first sentence needs the second one to precede it.

> The sleds are new.
> One is red and one is blue.

A child underlines *one* and *one,* and draws a line from *sleds* to each of them.

> Someone knocked at the door.
> "Who is it?" she asked.

Someone and *who* are underlined, and a line is drawn between them.

> Someone knocked at the door.
> It rattled.

It and *door* are underlined and connected.

The children discuss also the cause-and-effect relationship between the two sentences. You don't ask who someone is before you hear his knock, and a door doesn't rattle unless something shakes it.

Interests

There are a great many books at the present time written by skillful authors for good readers in the first grade. Many first graders cannot read them until they are in the second grade. Recently publishers have been furnishing children with stories, joke books, and factual accounts written in a deliberately controlled vocabulary. All kinds of interests typical of this age group seem to have been considered. (See about three hundred titles by many publishers in "Recent easy books for first-grade readers," by Patrick Groff, pages 521-527, *Elementary English,* 38, December, 1960.)

The whole class is spellbound over a discussion of the latest outer-space flight, all except one. Bert keeps looking down to one side as though he had a stiff neck. The teacher manoeuvers to see what is going on. He is peeking at a book. What is it? *Nobody listens to Andrew* by Elizabeth Guilfoile (Follett). By rights it should have been *You will go to the moon* by Mae Freeman (Random House), a fascinating account of what a visit to the moon will be like. But Bert, an old-fashioned boy, has problems. Nobody listens to him either. And isn't it wonderful to read about a boy nobody listens to, who has something really startling to tell that will make people sorry they didn't listen!

The second- and third-grade teachers continue the practice of having a file for recording the names of children who borrow books overnight. The librarian and teacher are helped to find books the children would like by keeping a list in the room, entitled, "What I'd Like to Read About Next." The names of the children are followed by the children's own writing, such as, "more bears." A bulletin board of book news tells what different children thought about the books they read: "This book was about whales. It told all the kinds and where they go." Once a week for a whole period or every day in snatches of time, children tell about the books they have been reading. Several who have happened to read about cowboys show the books they have read and describe some of the incidents or what they have learned about cowboys. Children who happen to have read the same story may act out a portion of it, tell it with hand puppets, or show an original picture interpreting the story.

"What are some interesting ways to share some of the ideas we are getting from our reading?"

If someone does something quite different from the usual presentation, the attention drawn by his technique means that more children will attempt such variations.

Beginners have no idea what they should tell people of their own experiences. Sometimes questions from the class will help them: "Who was in the story? What did the whale do? Why does it travel so far?" Later perhaps the class composes a list of things to remember to say when they introduce a book they liked: the title of the book, the part enjoyed most, the characters, the character liked best, what was found out (about whales, for instance).

The teacher cannot expect that the children and she will share the same interests entirely. A book which "leaves her cold" may send the children into stitches. The zany breed of book sired by the crazy cartoon movies, with their improbable events and chases and non sequiturs, gives hilarious enjoyment to many children. Sometimes there needs to be a formal waiting list of children who want to be the next to read the book. After Bill tells about his book, and several children say they would like to read it, they put their names on a list, and, as they finish reading it, cross their names off and pass the book on.

Taste

There are three major ways in which the teacher encourages taste: (1) by encouraging children to express themselves exactly and imaginatively; (2) by reading to them prose and poetry that are well written and varied in their kinds of appeal to children of the age, ability, and background concerned; (3) by asking them to listen for, to look for the ways an author makes us see, hear, feel, understand, and care. In the children's discussion of objects, for instance, the teacher does not accept a succession of "funny's"—a funny day, a funny nose, a funny sound.

"Can you think of a good word to describe that sound? (if no takers) Is it loud? soft? high? low? squeaky? deafening? scratchy? creaky? What does it remind you of? Is it like water? like a rusty hinge? like a mouse's voice? like a lion's roar?" Writing the children's suggestions on the chalkboard gives status to their contributions and acquaints the children with the visual forms of many more words than they may at the time know by sight.

What is it poets have done with sounds? Carl Sandburg has called the cricket's song before frost "so thin a splinter of singing" (from "Splinter" in Carl Sandburg's *Good morning, America,* New York: Harcourt, Brace and Company, Inc., 1928). Harry Behn in "Spring" says, "Cows begin lowing" (from *The little hill,* New York: Harcourt, Brace and Company, Inc., 1949). *Lowing* makes the very sound itself.

Summary

Teachers in the second and third grade continue many of the practices initiated by the first-grade teacher. Ear training and opportunities to use and analyze language are still prominent in the program. Setting standards for speaking, listening, reading aloud, and the like, the children learn something about parallelism of expression in outlining. Having children write favorite parts of the news is one way of encouraging the good listening which the speaker needs. Concepts are built through guided observation of objects and situations, through discussion, through reference charts, and through creative activities in which the child learns to use them.

Words which are relatively hard to learn are given more emphasis than others through both deliberate and incidental use. Extensive study of word meanings implies more opportunities to see word forms and remember them in connection with their meanings.

In teaching word analysis the teacher continues the methods used in the first grade, applying them to reviews of first-grade learnings and to new learnings such as the vowel sounds and the beginnings of the study of prefixes, suffixes, roots, and syllables. The child is made conscious of the method by which he, himself, can discover new facts about word forms and sounds, and is encouraged to use it independently as well as under guidance. He keeps a notebook or handbook which shows the kinds of word analysis he now knows.

Arithmetic, science, and social-studies material, as well as material in the basal readers, newspapers, and trade books, is used to develop comprehension of organized units of composition of various kinds. Here creative experiences in writing such material and listening experiences in hearing such material are used to support the learning. Interpretation of the meanings is constantly required, so that even at this level the child does not become a surface reader, satisfied with minimal understanding.

The children learn to use simple dictionaries and other reference tools, some of which, such as vocabulary boxes and cards with questions on them to be answered, keep the children actively needing and learning reference skills.

Purposeful oral reading is practiced in rereading situations in basal instruction and in reporting on stories children individually have read. Choral reading of familiar material serves to unite a class. The teacher tests a child occasionally on graded material to determine his level of reading. She learns to use quickly made notations which help her recall afterwards how the child read and what difficulties he encountered.

Efficiency in silent reading is likely to become more habitual if the teacher makes sure that the first reading of practically everything is silent reading for a purpose, that some reading is entirely silent, and that each child is given natural reasons for wanting to finish an easy story quickly.

At this level the hard job of learning to read is becoming worth the effort, for children more and more are able to explore independently in books of widely varied appeal. Giving time for the reading and some guidance in the selection of books, as well as help over trouble spots and time for enjoying the comments of other children on what they have read, providing books through a classroom collection and visits to the library, permitting overnight borrowing of books kept in the classroom, the teacher helps establish the reading habit and broad reading interests. Reading aloud to children well-written poems and stories, and having children think about the well-chosen word and its effect on the reader, she makes it possible for children to appreciate the products of skill and sensitivity.

Suggested Activities

Project. Select an arithmetic book, a science book, and a social-studies book written for this level. Study it for the words that would be new, the organization which would be new, the kinds of logical sequences which would have to be understood and followed, and make a plan of the way you would try to help the child with each of these difficulties.

Simplify a passage from one of these books for a retarded reader.

Select a story in a second or third reader, find the lesson for it in the manual, and plan how you would teach it. Teach it to a friend you don't mind losing! Have him make suggestions on your teaching if he doesn't mind losing you!

Further study. View filmstrips and recordings produced for the second and third grade by the Los Angeles City Schools, to see how basal, functional, and recreational reading programs are actually conducted in these schools.

Compare the second- or third-grade manuals and workbooks of two basal reader series to see the similarities and differences in the skills programs, with regard to the general areas of word recognition, word meaning, comprehension, interpretation, study skills. You will ordinarily find an index of skills at the back of the manual, inside the front or back cover of the workbook.

Notice that the manuals list children's literature of varied difficulty and topic for children using the basal reader. Get acquainted with some of these books and make a card file according to topic. Notice which books are recommended for the teacher to read aloud. Read some of these with considerable care, to see why the authors of the reader series believed these particularly worthy of such attention and of oral presentation.

See what articles you can find on reading at second and third grade levels in recent issues of *Elementary English* and *The Reading Teacher*. Sometimes an article on another aspect of the language arts, such as writing or listening, will give you ideas for ways in which you can use the same technique for reading purposes.

The children's literature references listed at the end of the previous chapter are not listed here but are applicable to this level.

Selected References

DeBoer, John J., and Dallmann, Martha, *The teaching of reading*. New York: Holt, Rinehart and Winston, Inc., 1960, Chap. 13.

Fox, Lorene K., and Brogan, Peggy, *Helping children to read*. New York: Holt, Rinehart and Winston, Inc., 1961.

Gray, Lillian, and Reese, Dora, *Teaching children to read*. New York: Ronald Press, 1957, Chap. 8.

Heilman, Arthur W., *Principles and practices of teaching reading*. Columbus: Charles E. Merrill Books, Inc., 1961, Chaps. 5 and 6.

McKee, Paul, *The teaching of reading in the elementary school*. Boston: Houghton Mifflin Company, 1948, Chap. 10.

McKim, Margaret, *Guiding growth in reading*. New York: The Macmillan Company, 1955, part 3.

Russell, David H., *Children learn to read*, 2nd ed. Boston: Ginn and Company, 1961, Chap. 7.

Siks, Geraldine Brain, *Creative dramatics for children*, Ginn and Company contributions in reading No. 26. Boston: Ginn and Company, 1961.

Triggs, Frances Oralind, *Reading: Its creative teaching and testing*. Mountain Home, North Carolina: The Author, 1960, part 1.

Films

Gregory learns to read. Detroit: Wayne State University, 1957.
They all learn to read. Chicago: International Film Bureau, Inc., 1955.

Filmstrips

Rhyme time, Fun with words, letters and sounds. Chicago: Scott, Foresman, and Company.

Using word boxes, Study skills in reading, *Reading*. Detroit: Jam Handy Organization, 1955. (Los Angeles City Schools reading program)

What's the word. Boston: Houghton Mifflin and Company, 1956.

22

Recommended Practices
in Grades Four, Five, and Six:
Diagnosis and Basal Instruction

Many of the concepts introduced in grades four, five, and six are remote from children's experience. The children are more mature in their thinking and interests, more experienced in types of classroom organization, and more able to work independently for longer periods of time. But the same processes which were used to develop and maintain skills at primary levels are valid here, and the skills which were important to reading at those levels continue to be so. This chapter attempts a sampling of what the teacher does to explore the child's reading achievement and needs and interests, and to maintain and extend skills in still more difficult basic instructional reading material. The chapter following this one will deal with the content fields and recreational aspects of reading at these same grade levels.

Learnings to be Extended and Maintained

The teacher in the intermediate grades must know what skills she is to maintain and extend. Paraphrased from statements in professional books on the teaching of reading and from indexes of skills in teacher's manuals for a reader series, she has a list of responsibilities such as this:

Word Meaning:
  Context clues to meaning (idea relationships, punctuation, capitalization, and organization)
  Figures of speech and choice of words
    simile (as soft as ——; like ——)
    metaphor (a *withered* old face)
    metonymy (from the cradle to the grave)
    synecdoche (all *hands* on deck)
    personification (*Truth* will lead us.)

idioms (to make friends)

colloquialisms (I'm in a pickle.)

Multiple meanings

(a band is a group, a musical organization, a ring of rubber)

Homonyms (pause, paws)

Antonyms (stop, go)

Related words (wool, bleat, flocks)

Abstract meanings (peace, democracy, co-operation)

Enriched word meanings (the many things that *home* means)

Synonyms (the meaning two words have in common; the meanings each has which are not shared with the other)

Definitions (*ascend* means to *climb up*)

Analogous words (If single means one, double means ———.)

Connotation and denotation (He *grunted* his reply. —a pig-like fellow?)

Effect of accent on word meaning (con' test, con test')

Sensory appeals (words reminding of taste, smell, sound, color, shape)

Comprehension

Ideas given by author

main ideas (of paragraph, section, chapter, whole story)

facts or details (supportive of main ideas)

Organization of ideas (sequence, logic, chronology)

Motive of author (as shown in his choice of ideas, manipulation of plot, comparisons and comments; illuminated by reader's knowledge of author's own life)

Interpretation of ideas

paraphrasing main ideas

paraphrasing facts

sensing effect of choice of words (imagery, vividness, repetition as a style technique, onomatopoeia, cadence, rhythm, stress by order, colloquialism, idiomatic expressions, sentence fragments)

gathering deeper meaning of sentence or story

(What was meant by ———? Why was it said? Why was that the reason? etc.)

(What kind of life was being shown? What was shown about this kind of life? What does it represent or symbolize? What meaning does it suggest for our own living?)

comparing or contrasting ideas (within a story, between stories, with life)

seeing cause and effect

seeing other types of relationship (in situation, time, character, plot)

Evaluation of ideas, organization, motive, and interpretation possible from these

judging validity (Are these true, right?)

judging choice (Are these slanted, less effective?)

judging relevance (Are these properly related to ———?)

Oral Reading

Setting standards and evaluating

Noting effect of punctuation

Studying stress appropriate to meaning

Using breath control to accommodate phrases

Altering voice for different characters, moods, meanings (volume, pitch, tone)

Study Skills

    Using reference tools
      a card catalogue
      a table of contents
      a telephone book
      an encyclopaedia
      a textbook
      an index
      a dictionary (alphabetical order, general location of word, guide words, base word as entry, pronunciation, derivation, part of speech, meanings) —use of pronunciation key in different dictionaries
      time tables
      menus
      radio and TV schedules
      informational posters
      signs
      maps
      charts
      graphs
      diagrams
    Adjusting reading method
      to type of material
      to purpose for reading material
        what to look for
        how fast to go
    Making use of material
      following directions
      selecting notes
      classifying notes
      outlining and planning a report
      making pictorial representations of data

The teacher knows that she will be working all year on all of these, reteaching them on easy material and helping the pupils apply them on harder material. All the teachers at the earlier school levels have actually been working on all of these, too, on simpler material—less abstract and less complicated and less remote from the children's experience. But in addition to these skills, she will be teaching skills of word analysis which the children have not yet been taught, and will be maintaining those they have been taught.

Some of her pupils may still be reading in primers or first readers, some in second, some in third. What skills of word analysis will she have to teach them? What won't they know that the average fourth, fifth, or sixth grader will know? She looks at a chart issued by the book company producing her basal reader series, showing the word-analysis skills taught in the manuals and workbooks at the different levels. This is what she sees (paraphrased in this case from the Ginn Basic Reader chart of skills accompanying the initial series):

Level	Phonetic Analysis	Structural Analysis
Readiness	Listening to sounds Identifying sounds Listening to rhymes	Seeing likenesses and differences in objects Observing picture details
Pre-primers	Reproducing sounds Hearing initial consonants	Recognizing basal vocabulary Noting capitals and small letters in words
Primer (Review all previous learnings)	Learning sound of initial consonants Learning sound of some ending consonants: *d, p, t, k* Learning sound of initial consonant digraph: *wh* Rhyming words	Noting parts of compound words Noting endings: *-s, -ed* Making a picture dictionary
First Reader (Review above)	Noting initial consonants Noting ending consonants Learning digraphs: *ch, sh, th* Learning blends: *br, fr, gr,* *tr, fl, bl, pl, sl* Rhyming words: *at, ay, an,* *ed, ook, et, ill, ow, out,* *en, ate, ox, ing, og, ound,* *other*	Noting parts of compound words Noting endings: *s, -ed, -ing* Using picture dictionary
Second Reader (Review above)	Noting double consonants Noting blends: *nk, sn, st,* *ck, qu, sc* Noting phonograms: *ight,* etc. Noting digraphs: *ng, kn* Noting variant sounds: *c, g* Noting short and long vowels Noting vowel rules: silent letter in digraph *ai*; medial vowel short; short vowel in two letter words (*it*); silent *e* and long medial vowel (*take*); sounds governed by *r* (ar, ir, or, ur, er); long vowel in two letter words (me); sounds governed by *l* (all) Noting digraphs: *ee, ay,* etc. Noting diphthongs: *ow, ou,* *ew, aw* Noting variant vowel sounds	Noting plural forms: *-s, -es* Noting verb variants: *tak(e)ing, step-ping,* *hurr(y)ied* Noting suffix: *-er* in *happ(y)ier* Noting contractions Using a picture or elementary dictionary

Level	Phonetic Analysis	Structural Analysis
Third Reader (Review above)	Noting consonant blends: *str, spr, thr* Noting silent letters in *gh, kn, wr* Noting variant sounds: *cks,* as *x; g* and *c* before *e, i, y; s* and *z, ed* as *t* Noting like sounds in different vowel digraphs: *stair, bear,* etc. Noting rules	Syllabic division of words: ear-training Noting prefixes: *un, ex* Noting suffixes: *ly, self, er, est, en, y,* etc. Dividing polysyllabic words by rule; compound: *post man;* double consonant: *bal loon;* single consonant: *la bor;* -le ending: *ta ble* Alphabetizing to first and second letter Using an elementary dictionary

Pupils who are reading at grade level in the fourth grade will need to review the preceding skills and add these:

Level	Phonetic Analysis	Structural Analysis
Fourth Reader (Review above)	Reviewing consonants; blends, digraphs, double, silent, variant-sounds Using principles or rules governing vowel sounds Reviewing vowel sounds, digraphs, diphthongs, double vowels Using diacritical markings of vowels Using pronunciation key in dictionary Noting vowel sound in open and closed syllables: open (*go*), closed (*got*) Noting relation of vowel sound to accent	Reviewing plural endings, verb endings, adjective endings Noting prefixes: *con, dis, ex, im, in, re, trans, un* Noting stems: un*coil*ing Noting suffixes: *able, er, est, ful, ish, ist, less, ly, ment, ness, or, tion, ward, y* Noting accent, effect on meaning Noting compound and hyphenated words Noting contractions and possessives Using rules of syllabication: *post man, bal loon, la bor, ta ble, un kind, like ly, float ing, car bon, an chor* (*ch, ph, th, sh*)

Aware that some especially capable children may be able to learn more skills than those of the grade level, the teacher looks at the rest of the list of skills for the higher reader levels.

Level	Phonetic Analysis	Structural Analysis
Fifth Reader	Reviewing variant sounds of consonants, double and silent consonants, digraphs, blends Reviewing principles governing vowel sounds	Reviewing prefixes, suffixes, stems Adding more prefixes, suffixes Using rules of syllabication Reviewing plurals, verb and adjective endings

Level	Phonetic Analysis	Structural Analysis
	Noting variant spellings of vowel sounds Noting vowel sounds in accented and unaccented syllables Reviewing diphthongs, digraphs, double vowels Reviewing diacritical marks	
Sixth Reader	Reviewing consonants and vowels as above Using pronunciation keys	Reviewing structural analysis as above Noting divisions of words at ends of lines Noting primary and secondary accents (de ter' min a' tion) Noting rules for accent
Seventh Reader	Reviewing consonant and vowel sounds Using phonetic symbols Using dictionary and glossary	Reviewing all of above Studying word derivations and word families Recognizing syllabication and accents
Eighth Reader	Reviewing all above	Reviewing all above Adding word derivations and word families

Diagnosis

The previous teacher who had these children last year has passed on some information about each child: the reading level he has just finished, his chief interests, and reading-test scores. Also she has indicated whether he has any special difficulties. "Fifth-reader comprehension, second-reader level-one vowels," tells the new teacher that this child does not have a phonetic background for the syllabication work of the fourth-reader level but apparently has considerable strength in understanding what he reads. In the first several days of the new term the teacher informally assesses the level at which each child can read, by having each child read a few sentences of different levels of material such as those in the oral reading tests mentioned in Chapter 16 or one in the reader manual. (See Allyn and Bacon manuals or *Manual for teaching the fourth reader,* Ginn and Company, 1961, pages 44-50, for examples.) When she sees that some children are at or above grade level, some at third, some at second, and some below second, she administers a test to discover more exactly the pupils' present status.

Perhaps she uses the readiness tests which accompany her basal series, and tests over a period of several days in regular reading time. To the children at second-reader level and below she may administer the second-grade readiness test; to the third-reader level children, the third-grade readiness test; to children evidently at grade level or above, the fourth-grade readiness test. She could give all children the fourth-grade readiness test to find their reading level, but several skills sections would be impossible for children reading at first- and second-reader level. If it happens to be the Ginn series of tests, the teacher will obtain three types of information: the level of reading in the Ginn books at which the child can work with ease, the vocabulary and comprehension strengths he has developed, and the child's mastery of the word analysis and study skills which have been taught *up to the level of test he is taking.* Thus, by giving poor readers a test for a lower grade, the teacher is testing them on skills they have probably been taught, not on skills they may not have been taught at all.

Here (Figure 10), for example, is the worksheet developed by Dr. Harold Weeks, Director of Research in the San Francisco Public Schools, on which the teacher may chart the test results for children who may have taken the second-grade readiness test of the Ginn series. Across the top of the sheet she puts each child's name. Under each child's name she puts a check for each error. Seeing the kinds of error a child makes and the level of words and paragraphs he read successfully, she determines and records at the bottom of the second page the reader level most appropriate for him. Looking across the pages at the mistakes of different children, she sees some things that all children need, some that several need, and some that need to be taught to individuals.

Early in the term, also, the teacher may give review tests of word analysis to determine in detail the strengths and weaknesses in this area. Her manual or workbook for the fourth reader may include a review test of all the initial consonant sounds ("I shall say two words beginning with the same letter. You are to find the letter that makes that sound and put a cross on it."), initial blends, phonograms, vowel sounds, and alphabetical order. Children who do badly on these tests may not have been taught these discriminations, and, still worse, may not even hear the sounds as different from other sounds. For such children the teacher will test further.

"Give me a word that begins like *trick* and *try.*" (consonant blend)

"Give me a word that begins like *took* and *team.*" (consonant)

"Give me a word that rhymes with *noon* and *soon.*" (phonograms)

"Say the sound that you hear in *rain* and *day.*" (vowel)

(Notice in each case that the two words sound completely different except for the sound being tested.)

Class Analysis of Ginn Second-Grade Readiness Test (Page 1)

Directions: Place scored tests in rank order by Total Test score. List names of pupils in column headings. Cross out(X) each item number omitted or incorrectly marked.

GINN SECOND-GRADE READINESS TEST Sections																			Total Correct
TOTAL TEST SCORE																			
TEST 2c: WORD ANALYSIS, STRUCTURAL ENDINGS s	1	1	1	1	1	1	1	1	1	1	1	1	1	1	1	1	1	1	
ing	2	2	2	2	2	2	2	2	2	2	2	2	2	2	2	2	2	2	
ed	3	3	3	3	3	3	3	3	3	3	3	3	3	3	3	3	3	3	
s	4	4	4	4	4	4	4	4	4	4	4	4	4	4	4	4	4	4	
s	5	5	5	5	5	5	5	5	5	5	5	5	5	5	5	5	5	5	
ing	6	6	6	6	6	6	6	6	6	6	6	6	6	6	6	6	6	6	
ed	7	7	7	7	7	7	7	7	7	7	7	7	7	7	7	7	7	7	
s	8	8	8	8	8	8	8	8	8	8	8	8	8	8	8	8	8	8	
(none)	9	9	9	9	9	9	9	9	9	9	9	9	9	9	9	9	9	9	
ing	10	10	10	10	10	10	10	10	10	10	10	10	10	10	10	10	10	10	
s	11	11	11	11	11	11	11	11	11	11	11	11	11	11	11	11	11	11	
ing	12	12	12	12	12	12	12	12	12	12	12	12	12	12	12	12	12	12	
TOTAL TEST 2c																			XX XX
TEST 3: COMPREHENSION (A=Main Idea; B=Details; C=Sequence; D=Creative Reading) Pre-Primer 1A	A	A	A	A	A	A	A	A	A	A	A	A	A	A	A	A	A	A	1A
1B	B	1B	1B	1B	1B	1B	1B	1B	1B	1B	1B	1B	1B	1B	1B	1B	1B	1B	1B
1C	C	C	C	C	C	C	C	C	C	C	C	C	C	C	C	C	C	C	1C
1D	D	D	D	D	D	D	D	D	D	D	D	D	D	D	D	D	D	D	1D
Primer 2A	A	A	A	A	A	A	A	A	A	A	A	A	A	A	A	A	A	A	2A
2B	2B	2B	2B	2B	2B	2B	2B	2B	2B	2B	2B	2B	2B	2B	2B	2B	2B	2B	2B
2C	C	C	C	C	C	C	C	C	C	C	C	C	C	C	C	C	C	C	2C
2D	D	D	D	D	D	D	D	D	D	D	D	D	D	D	D	D	D	D	2D
First Reader 3A	A	A	A	A	A	A	A	A	A	A	A	A	A	A	A	A	A	A	3A
3B	3B	3B	3B	3B	3B	3B	3B	3B	3B	3B	3B	3B	3B	3B	3B	3B	3B	3B	3B
3C	C	C	C	C	C	C	C	C	C	C	C	C	C	C	C	C	C	C	3C
3D	D	D	D	D	D	D	D	D	D	D	D	D	D	D	D	D	D	D	3D
4A	A	A	A	A	A	A	A	A	A	A	A	A	A	A	A	A	A	A	4A
4B	4B	4B	4B	4B	4B	4B	4B	4B	4B	4B	4B	4B	4B	4B	4B	4B	4B	4B	4B
4C	C	C	C	C	C	C	C	C	C	C	C	C	C	C	C	C	C	C	4C
4D	D	D	D	D	D	D	D	D	D	D	D	D	D	D	D	D	D	D	4D
Second Reader Level I 5A	A	A	A	A	A	A	A	A	A	A	A	A	A	A	A	A	A	A	5A
5B	5B	5B	5B	5B	5B	5B	5B	5B	5B	5B	5B	5B	5B	5B	5B	5B	5B	5B	5B
5C	C	C	C	C	C	C	C	C	C	C	C	C	C	C	C	C	C	C	5C
5D	D	D	D	D	D	D	D	D	D	D	D	D	D	D	D	D	D	D	5D
6A	A	A	A	A	A	A	A	A	A	A	A	A	A	A	A	A	A	A	6A
6B	6B	6B	6B	6B	6B	6B	6B	6B	6B	6B	6B	6B	6B	6B	6B	6B	6B	6B	6B
6C	C	C	C	C	C	C	C	C	C	C	C	C	C	C	C	C	C	C	6C
6D	D	D	D	D	D	D	D	D	D	D	D	D	D	D	D	D	D	D	6D
Second Lev. II 7A	A	A	A	A	A	A	A	A	A	A	A	A	A	A	A	A	A	A	7A
7B	7B	7B	7B	7B	7B	7B	7B	7B	7B	7B	7B	7B	7B	7B	7B	7B	7B	7B	7B
7C	C	C	C	C	C	C	C	C	C	C	C	C	C	C	C	C	C	C	7C
7D	D	D	D	D	D	D	D	D	D	D	D	D	D	D	D	D	D	D	7D
Third Lev. I 8A	A	A	A	A	A	A	A	A	A	A	A	A	A	A	A	A	A	A	8A
8B	8B	8B	8B	8B	8B	8B	8B	8B	8B	8B	8B	8B	8B	8B	8B	8B	8B	8B	8B
8C	C	C	C	C	C	C	C	C	C	C	C	C	C	C	C	C	C	C	8C
8D	D	D	D	D	D	D	D	D	D	D	D	D	D	D	D	D	D	D	8D
Third Lev. II 9A	A	A	A	A	A	A	A	A	A	A	A	A	A	A	A	A	A	A	9A
9B	9B	9B	9B	9B	9B	9B	9B	9B	9B	9B	9B	9B	9B	9B	9B	9B	9B	9B	9B
9C	C	C	C	C	C	C	C	C	C	C	C	C	C	C	C	C	C	C	9C
9D	D	D	D	D	D	D	D	D	D	D	D	D	D	D	D	D	D	D	9D
Fourth Reader 10A	A	A	A	A	A	A	A	A	A	A	A	A	A	A	A	A	A	A	A
10B	B	B	B	B	B	B	B	B	B	B	B	B	B	B	B	B	B	B	B
10C	C	C	C	C	C	C	C	C	C	C	C	C	C	C	C	C	C	C	C
10D	D	D	D	D	D	D	D	D	D	D	D	D	D	D	D	D	D	D	D
Tot. A's																			
Tot. B's																			
Tot. C's																			
Tot. D's																			
TOTAL TEST 3																			XX XX
Circle	PP	PP	PP	PP	PP	PP	PP	PP	PP	PP	PP	PP	PP	PP	PP	PP	PP	PP	
Reader	Pr	Pr	Pr	Pr	Pr	Pr	Pr	Pr	Pr	Pr	Pr	Pr	Pr	Pr	Pr	Pr	Pr	Pr	
Level	1	1	1	1	1	1	1	1	1	1	1	1	1	1	1	1	1	1	
Most	2I	2I	2I	2I	2I	2I	2I	2I	2I	2I	2I	2I	2I	2I	2I	2I	2I	2I	
Appropri-	2II	2II	2II	2II	2II	2II	2II	2II	2II	2II	2II	2II	2II	2II	2II	2II	2II	2II	
ate for	3I	3I	3I	3I	3I	3I	3I	3I	3I	3I	3I	3I	3I	3I	3I	3I	3I	3I	
Each	3II	3II	3II	3II	3II	3II	3II	3II	3II	3II	3II	3II	3II	3II	3II	3II	3II	3II	
Pupil	4	4	4	4	4	4	4	4	4	4	4	4	4	4	4	4	4	4	

Figure 10. (Reproduced by permission of the San Francisco Unified School District.)

Class Analysis of Ginn Second-Grade Readiness Test (Page 2)

Directions: Place scored tests in rank order by Total Test score. List names of pupils in column headings. Cross out (X) each item number omitted or incorrectly marked.

Figure 10. (cont.)

A log of out-of-school activities

For a week the teacher may have each child keep a log of his out-of-school activities, stating what he did with his time each day after school before dinner, and after dinner before bedtime. From this log the teacher sees what uses the child is making of reading and what interests he has that may lure him into more reading than he is now doing. She may find these classifications helpful in making for herself a picture of the out-of-school life of each child: (169)

Reading:	books	newspapers	magazines	letters
Listening:	radio	phonograph		
Watching:	television	movies	live theatre	
Speaking:	conversation	telephoning	reading aloud	
Writing:	letters			

Recreation:	active sports	having company
	games	construction, crafts
	visits to friends	church
	clubs	creative arts
	pets	collections
	fine arts	experiments
	taking trips	
Work:	doing homework	doing work outside home
	washing dishes	working in yard
	drying dishes	doing odd jobs around the
	preparing meals	home
	straightening own room	doing laundry
	cleaning house	care of siblings
	going shopping	care of clothing
	running errands	

Direct questions such as the following may give direct leads to interests, although the children, seeing pretty clearly the teacher's objective, may answer guardedly:

"What television programs do you like best?
"What is the best book you ever read?
"What movies do you like best?
"What radio programs do you like best?
"What newspaper do you read?
  "How often do you read it?
  "What do you read in it?
"What magazines do you read?
  "What do you like to read in them?
"What do you like to do best of all?"

The children will reveal themselves in creative writing on the subject: "If I Had a Day and Three Wishes."

From such pieces of evidence the teacher may learn that several children have something in common which they have never discussed, something which can build friendships and interest in reading.

Planning the Basal Program for Poorer Readers

Feeling a little as though she is between the devil and the deep blue sea, the teacher plans the basal program for her poorer readers. She knows that if she doesn't use a basal reader, she will have to plan the skills program entirely on her own; and she knows that what she plans alone will not turn out to be so complete or so wisely planned as a program she could plan with the help of a manual. If she uses a basal reader meant for younger children, she may lose the co-operation of her group. At least, this is what many teachers claim.

She reviews the reasoning of the people who are against the use of the easy basal reader. One point they make is that the stories insult the older children by their babyishness. She picks up the pre-primer of a different series. Are fourth graders still enjoying jumping rope, playing fetch with the dog, balancing, racing, playing marbles, masquerading, flying model airplanes, high-jumping? That's what the children in the pre-primer are doing. Then she remembers how a smart teacher named Vera Nofftz had retarded sixth graders reading a first reader with great satisfaction. She remembered now, how it was done. Vera had shifted the whole focus of the questioning to the younger children of the neighborhood and younger members of the family.

"Does your little sister ever get into a trunk of old clothes? What does she like to do?" These older brothers and sisters know. The answer is: "Dress up and trip around in Mother's old slippers and big hats." With the focus shifted, the children can be amused at the story and enjoy it. The teacher remembers, too, that Vera had the children try to perfect their reading of each story and compete for the honor of reading it to the first grade, who didn't have this book. Just the way *adults* read to little children.

That was another point. This wasn't the old book the children had seen in the lower grades. It was new to them, new to everybody. The teacher had selected a new one because the children's reading level was so low that shifting to another book could scarcely be called a hardship. Ordinarily it would have been one.

Vera held a couple more trumps. She told the children that the only sure way of learning any job was to start at the bottom and work your way up. She would take them as fast as they could go, and she was sure that now they could make real progress. She let them in on the secret that the more they used the words they were learning, the more they wrote them in sentences, stories, reports, etc., the better they would learn them. She gave them reasons for pride in their progress: frequent quizzes, a set of completed worksheets, a vocabulary notebook of words they now knew (get-

Use the children as resources
  Drawing on child's experiences—individual, group
  Consulting preferences
  Asking how they would feel if—
  Consulting wishes ("Have you ever wished that—?")
  Drawing on child's knowledge of books, TV, movies, magazines, news-
    papers, radio.
  Eliciting questions about the topic ("What would you want to know
    about——?")
Use the story itself as a clue
  Reading title and subtitles, comparing with unit title
  Looking at pictures on first page, other pages if it will not spoil story
  Reading a few lines from first of story to provoke questions (Have chil-
    dren do the reading silently.)
Use other books as stimuli
  Reading a poem related to the idea
  Showing books which may be read later on same topic, using pictures
  Having library display of related books
  Showing other books by same author, which may be read later
Use audio-visual aids
  Showing pictures (for information or to set mood)
  Showing slides, motion pictures, maps, actual objects, experiments
  Having child find place on map, in picture, etc.
  Using a time line to locate time of story
  Using a diagram or rough blackboard sketch
  Using recordings of sounds or music to suggest background (or make
    own noises)

Introducing words

She remembers that in introducing new words she puts them in an oral or written context, and writes the word (in cursive writing if the children are now well accustomed to it) as the children watch, so that they see it at least once being developed from left to right. (A few children at this level are still having "left-to-right trouble.") Sometimes, to save time, she writes the sentence or phrase ahead of time, omitting the new word:

"Read the sentence and be ready to tell me what you think the missing word is. (pause) How many think you know?"

The sentence reads: The tiger's coat had orange and black _____.

The children agree with Harry, who reads: "The tiger's coat had orange and black stripes."

"Let's see whether he is right," says the teacher, and inserts, standing so that all can see the word as it is formed, *stripes*.

If the children have had their second-reader phonics rule about the silent *e*, the teacher will say, "Who can prove that the word is *stripes*?" Children contribute the information that it begins like *street* and *straw*, it has the *s* ending to form the plural of *stripe*, the *i* is long because the word *stripe* ends in a silent *e* preceded by a single consonant. Harry says he gets it another way: *str* and his father's *pipes. Pipes, ipes, stripes,* he said to himself. The teacher remembers what a rugged individualist Harry was.

If the word is something the children do not know the meaning of, the teacher writes it in a sentence and underlines the word. Before she meets with the children to discuss the word, the children individually look up the word in a dictionary or in the basal-reader glossary, see how it is pronounced, and what its meanings are. They write down the pronunciation, saying it softly to themselves, and write an original sentence using the meaning which the teacher has used in her sentence. Why does the teacher not write the word as the children watch? Because in looking the word up in the glossary and in writing it themselves, they have had to observe it carefully from left to right. A glossary does not list a word backwards!

If the word is *kayaks* or *plentiful,* the dictionary may list only the base forms, *kayak* and *plenty.* If so, she warns the children:

"Will you find this word as it is or will it be listed differently in the dictionary? What part of the first word may be left out? Why? (plural) What part of the second? Why? (a suffix *-ful*) What happens to the *i?*" (changes to *y.*)

Clarification of the meaning of the word is important. Looking up the word *cache,* the children see that it is pronounced *kash,* defined as a place for hiding or storing supplies, or the supplies so hidden or stored. Jerold's sentence is "I like to have ready cache." Has he looked carefully at the definitions? What does he really mean? What other way might his *cash* be spelled? Jerold looks it up and, sure enough, he had his cash in the wrong mental drawer. A homonym has tricked him.

As the teacher discusses the meanings of the new words, she uses the new words to discuss other new words. When she has introduced *cabin, wilderness, hidden,* and *dare,* she may say (introducing the word *attacked*), "What if you lived in a cabin in the wilderness and you heard that the enemy had *attacked* the fort. What would you know had happened? What does an enemy do when he attacks a fort?" All television-bred children respond. He shoots arrows or other weapons. He sets fire to the stockade. He surrounds it and lets no one out and no supplies in. He kills, etc.

"How would you feel? Would you go out at dusk for water at the stream? Would you leave your cabin without a care in the world? How would the wilderness seem to you now that the fort had been attacked? What might be hiding near you?" In her high moments this teacher knows that she has generated a real lather over the situation which the association of words can create. The children not only knew the meanings of the new words and what they looked like, but were churned up to a fine froth to read the story. She has not broken the handle off *her* motivator!

Establishing the sight vocabulary

The slow groups are slow because—they are slow. She has to spend more time introducing words, more time for everything. But what she teaches sticks because she attacks it from every angle she can think of. What are the angles for making the new words sight words, words known on sight?

1. First, she introduces the new words as she would with the average children. The words are on the chalkboard in phrases or sentences. Now what can she do?

2. *Rereading.* "Let's read together, now, the phrases and sentences on the chalkboard." She runs her hand under them as the children read. She doesn't permit a dead-run drone but insists on proper grouping of words and expression: The cabin stood alone/at the edge/of the woods. The unison reading revives some children who have lost track of some of the words. Looking at the word as it is said and heard, helps Mortimer.

3. *Comprehension clues.* "Who can find, frame, and read the line that tells where someone lives? Jerry?" She asks the question first, then names a child after all children in the group have taken the trouble to think. If the children have an idea that framing is babyish, she gives them the honor of using a pointer, standing aside and reading aloud as the other children look and listen. Meaning is attached to form. The child had to think the meaning of the word to identify it from the clue the teacher gave.

4. *Word-recognition check.* "Stand when you think you can find and read us one of our new words. Pat? . . . We read our words from left to right. Underline the new word from left to right as you say it." The eyes of the children watching are guided from left to right. When the children have identified all the word, "Now I shall point to words quickly. As I point to a word, see how quickly you can say it. You don't have to shout. Speak so that I can hear all the voices."

5. *Flash-card exercise.* The teacher takes flash cards of different words in the sight vocabulary of the children and adds to them the new words she has just introduced. "I am going to build a story with these flash cards in the pocket chart; but, instead of telling the story to you, I am going to have you read it to me. Watch carefully so that you will be ready to read my first sentence. Look at me when you know what it says." She sits at the right of the pocket chart so that she does not cover the cards as she puts them in, a word at a time, from left to right. She invents something like:

> Jake lived in a cabin.
> It was in a wilderness.
> The fort had been attacked.
> He did not dare to go outdoors.
> He remained hidden inside.

When the sitting becomes tiresome, "Stand when you think you know how to read the sentence," or, "Who will come up to read the whole chart?"

6. *Chalkboard exercise.* This is similar to the pocket-chart exercise above. Instead of a story, however, it may be a set of statements to be approved, disapproved, and changed orally. "Tell whether you think this is a true statement or not and be ready to prove your point."

> A fort welcomes an attack.
> A wilderness is empty grassland.
> A cabin is a safe place.

The teacher who hasn't chalkboard space can write on unprinted newspaper. This same material can be used for recognition of the new words in a review later: "Find a new word and read it to us."

7. *Creative variations.* The children make up their own stories using the new words, and try them out on each other. Or, the group makes up a story co-operatively with the same purpose. Or the children act out or draw stick figures on the chalkboard or present riddles whose answers are the new words.

8. *Flash-card test.* As a final test of the effectiveness of the learning, the teacher mixes up the flash cards containing the new words and has each child respond to them. She exposes the words from left to right by drawing the first card off with her *left* hand. As each child successfully names the words, he joins others in the group watching and being ready to help if a child miscalls a word. The help may be a clue to its meaning ("It is a kind of boat.") rather than a simple pronunciation of the word.

Of course, the teacher uses all of these techniques only if she must, but it is comforting at the beginning of the year to know that they are all there. And if a child in the group is clearly not in need of so much repetition as the others are, the teacher may have him work on something more important to his reading progress. If she has already set purposes for the silent reading, he may go to read the story silently.

Using the table of contents

The teacher remembers that if she doesn't have children develop certain routines, valuable learning time is eaten up in the mechanics of preparation. Passing out the books, for instance. If one child is appointed to do it for several days, time will be saved that might have been consumed appointing someone each day. If the number of books to be passed means two trips for one person, two people had better do it. Where could the books be kept to be easily obtained with a minimum disturbance?

And the table of contents minimizes the fumbling. Melissa, of course, has a special trick. She is always looking at the edge of the book to see where the soiled pages stop and the clean begin. She finds the place first.

But will she when she uses an older book? The teacher decides that you learn to read a table of contents by reading one, and you make it a habit by doing it every time you read a new story.

"Let's open our books to the table of contents. In front, George; that's right. Look down the page for the name of our new story, *Daniel Boone.* What page is it on? Lester?" If the children are still shaky on numbers, a child may be asked to write the number on the chalkboard. If not, it will be assumed that all can read the number and find its mate on the proper page. Because children will reach the page at different times, the teacher says, "When you have found the page, study the picture at the top of it. Be ready to tell what you think is happening."

Setting purposes for silent reading

As children grow older, they are more and more capable of thinking of good purposes for reading, themselves. The teacher invites their participation: "What would you like to find out in this story?" However, it is her business, also, to teach them to read for different purposes, and over a period of time throughout the reading of these stories she must give them a diet of reading in different ways for different purposes. What are the kinds of purpose she might set? If she thinks them all over now, perhaps she won't fall into a rut. She turns to her notes again (McCullough, Ibid.) and reads the possibilities:

Reading for Details or Facts
   Read to find out
      what discovery this character made.
      what the character did.
      what the surprise was.
      what the character had to do.
      answers to our questions (about Indian life).
      how the character surprised his family.
      what the character's experiences were.
      what happened to the _____ in the pictures of the story.
      how the unusual qualities of the character helped.
      answers to questions raised by the pictures.
      answers to questions on study-guide sheet.
      items to fill in outline in later discussion.
      what character did to have fun (help, etc.).
      as many things as possible that one character told another to do.
   Read to write a good fact question on the story.
   Read to make up riddles to fit the characters.
   Read to visualize the place.
   Read to recall as many things as possible about the conversation.
Reading for Main Ideas
   Read to find out
      why the character called it _____ (a real Thanksgiving).
      why it was a good title.

what connection this story has with the unit title.

what the problem in this story is.

the answer to the question the subtitle raises.

places in story that make it suitable for inclusion in unit.

what the character learned.

Read to summarize in one sentence what the character did to achieve his purpose.

Reading for Sequence or Organization

Read to find out

what happened in each of the parts of story.

the events in the order of their occurrence.

key events in order, and jot down phrases to remember sequence.

about life story of a ———.

what the character does to solve his problems, step by step; where the climax of the story comes.

steps in the process described in the story (harvesting a crop).

how the character became a hero.

how many stages there are in the life of a ———.

scenes and events and characters concerned, to dramatize story.

Reading for Inference

Read to find out

how the character's family felt about his surprise.

what the author is trying to say, make us think, about ———.

why the character felt as he did.

why the story has made people laugh, etc. (a classic).

how the character changed.

how the character felt about his environment.

the moral to the story (Aesop).

why the strong were strong and why the weak were weak.

what quality in the character made for success.

Read to identify with the character and tell how you feel in his place.

Read to write a good question of opinion to ask others.

Reading to Classify

Read to find out

what kind of success the character had.

what kind of person the character was.

what is unusual about the character.

how the character is important to our own living (earthworm).

what was funny and how the author made you laugh (by exaggeration, understatement, inappropriate juxtaposition, etc.)

as many points of exaggeration as you can.

the most surprising things in the story.

what was good, what was bad about the character.

evidence that the story could have happened; could not have happened.

Read to classify the story material under three headings: note page, paragraph, key word, for quick reference to prove points in discussion.

Read to make questions related to subheadings of story.

Reading to Compare or Contrast

Read to find out

how the character acted differently from that in previous story.

whether your guesses about the story were right.

how the character changed.

how two stories are alike or different.

whether character lives up to standards set by class for _____
(sportsmanship, etc.).

how the holiday in the story differs from ours.

evidence that the story could or could not have happened.

how the character's problem is like one you had.

Reading to Evaluate

Read to decide (*and be ready with reasons*)

whether the goal was worth the sacrifice.

whether the story was true to life.

whether the character was successful and why or why not.

why the character has been so long remembered (Johnny Appleseed).

whether you'd like the kind of work described in the story; why.

Reading to Determine Relevance

Read to decide (*and tell why you think so*)

whether this story proves or disproves the statement that _____
(All is not gold that glitters).

what bearing this story has on the problem of _____.

whether this story answers the question: _____; reasons.

what bearing the nature of the country, the times, had on the story.

Reading to Give Oral Interpretation

Read to read aloud one page of the funny story, stressing humor.

one page of the sad story, stressing sadness.

Read to take dramatic parts in story and read aloud.

The abler students contribute to the discussion of purposes for which to read the material silently. The teacher has them think ahead of time *how* they will read to achieve a particular purpose.

"Should you read rapidly or slowly for this purpose?

"What will you have to look for as you read? what ideas? what words?

"What will you have to do with the ideas (words) when you do find them?

"What will you have to do with the ideas in order to answer the purpose?"

Over a period of time the children develop a list of general ideas on how to read for a main idea, how to read for facts, how to select facts for a purpose, how to sense organization, etc. As new experiences extend their practice, they contribute new insights to the lists. Meanwhile, for them, the more able, the teacher gives time to complete the reading of the story silently and to answer the questions set.

Guided silent reading and discussion of purposes set

The less able children, usually those using texts designed for third grade and below, are guided through the story at a rate of one or two pages at a time, depending upon the amount of material they can successfully comprehend at a time and the natural breaks in the material. Each page or two is read silently after questions have been asked to purpose the reading.

As each page or two is completed, a child volunteers to answer the question. The teacher invites discussion of his opinion. Occasionally she will require proof that he is right by having him read aloud the place which made him think what he does. Other children are invited to agree or disagree. Conjectures are made about what will happen next, a purpose is set for further reading, and silent reading is engaged in.

Frequently with groups who read through a story in short stages, the teacher does not introduce all the new words in the story at once. She may start with only those which occur early. Then, as the story proceeds, she weaves into the discussion the new words which will soon be met, and writes them on the chalkboard, introducing them as she would have in the beginning. Or, having introduced them all at the beginning, she may reinforce memory of them by referring back to the chalkboard or newspaper on which they are displayed in context.

She runs her hand under the phrase as she says, "We said something *might be hidden* in the forest. Let's see whether we were right."

She notices the difficulties various children have in recognizing these words and perhaps even old words. These difficulties require a follow-up before they snowball into a major problem. One of her old standby techniques is to dismiss children from the reading group at the end of the period in a special way, one at a time. Before he leaves, Billy has to recognize the word *hidden* in the pocket chart. Jean, who should be able to figure it out for herself, is asked what kind of word it is and what two words she sees in it. (The teacher is always careful not to do this small-word-in-large type of analysis unless (1) the small parts are actually structural parts of the word (true syllabic units) and (2) the parts are pronounced in the resultant word in the same way they are pronounced as small words. Not the *cat* in *cathedral*, for instance.) A second old standby is that, before they go to their seats, they are given a follow-up assignment which requires the type of observation in which they need practice: writing their own story, using the new words; writing *hidden* in several sentences, to show meaning; tracing and writing *hidden* from memory, then writing it in some sentences; finding the sentences in the story in which *hidden* is used, and copying the sentences (rather wasteful, considering that the meaning and form of *hidden* are the main purpose); writing or telling the history of *hidden*. The history would look something like this:

> The word is *hidden*.
> It comes from *hide*.
> I *hide* it. It is *hidden*.
>   hid-d-en.
> In syllables it is *hid den*.
> It is divided between the double d's, following rule No.———.
> Both syllables are closed. (They end in consonants, not vowels.)

Therefore the vowels are probably short.
The accent is probably on the root word: *hid*.
Therefore, the vowel in the unaccented syllable is probably not
  short *e* but the schwa sound: a.
The Webster dictionary spells it: *hĭd' 'n*.
The Thorndike dictionary spells it *hĭd' ən*.

(The last four steps assume fourth-reader-level learnings.)

All this trouble about one word would seem stupid except that the teacher knows that one example illuminates the children's thinking about many other words, and may help to build habits of considering the origin, meaning, structure, and dictionary interpretation of words.

Purposeful rereading of the story

The rereading of the story is important for various reasons. The teacher thinks over what some of them are: (1) It gives the child practice in quick location of its parts, practice in skimming, which is a skill he must have for successful reading and study in many areas. (2) It is another chance to impress him with the visual symbols he is learning before he goes on to new symbols. (3) It is a way to teach points of story structure, literary techniques, and exactness of meaning and interpretation, which a child reading by himself would not bother to observe or learn. (4) It is an opportunity for oral reading. It is a way of sharing insights in a group, so that each child, not to speak of the teacher, goes away better for the understandings exchanged.

Back to the old notebook, the teacher sees these purposes which might be set for rereading the story: (McCullough, Ibid.)

To dramatize:	taking character parts
	having narrator and pantomime
	having committees apportion parts and plan presentation
To share:	part liked best
	dialogue
	the whole story in relays—with audience to enjoy the *way* a character said something
	a poem chorally
To note style:	unusual expressions
	use of *as* and *like* (similes)
	use of metaphor
	idiomatic expressions
	story told in first person
To note mood or tone:	evidence of humor
	means of creating apprehension in the reader

To perfect mechanical
  aspects of oral reading: to phrase groups of words properly for sentence
           meaning
          to emphasize words of particular significance
          to skim to find page, paragraph, and read aloud
           the line sought

Го prove: similarity or difference in two characters (in same
           story, different stories, or in life)
          a character's attitude
          a character's trait
          the kind of life led
          statements written on chalkboard, to be verified in
           story
          answers to questions from other pupils
          implications of story
          the meaning of a sentence

To find: how character benefitted in story and what qualities
           got him these benefits
          answers to questions about character's appearance,
           contribution to plot, kind of person he was, why
           he felt as he did, how he acted, how he changed
           and why, how he was treated, how people re-
           acted to his behavior; how the situation appeared
           to him, to others
          certain descriptive phrases and explain meaning
          synonyms for words written on chalkboard
          sensory appeals (sounds, tastes, smells, feelings,
           appearances)
          difficult moments in the story
          references to location
          where introduction ended
          the big events
          similarities in plot with other story
          problem, climax, moral
          paragraphs to fit titles
          data for classification
          how something was done
          a certain expression, preparatory to discussion of
           its meaning

The extent to which the rereading is oral depends upon the need of children for the oral practice. If their silent reading of easy material is slow, probably they would benefit from less emphasis upon oral reading.

Motivation, the teacher remembers, is not just something one grinds up for the beginning of the lesson, but something that must be recreated throughout. How can children be motivated to be interested in the rereading activities? Curiosity is challenged by "Why do you suppose—" questions. Interest in current events rather than the dead past makes it wise to tie the story to current interests whenever possible. "What did we see in the news yesterday about a _____ that made you think of this story? Why do you suppose it reminded you of it?" (If the teacher is interested herself, she will be aware of more of these tie-ins.) In the same way, the teacher reminds children of favorite television programs, baseball, pets, a story she read aloud to them—whenever these enjoyable associations are pertinent to the story at hand.

Ego-satisfaction comes from identifying with the hero, or heroine, and provides the motivation for discussion of his or her feats, feelings, effect on others, etc. Respect for peer opinion, which runs high at this age, makes group sharing of ideas especially enjoyable to the children, something worthy of their attention. Running their own show, having a greater degree of independence, is another strong motive at this time. For this reason, committee work, and group discussions led by a pupil are increasingly effective. In these cases, the teacher is a participant, ready with the question or suggestion which prods the children beyond the thinking they might be satisfied with.

The pupil chairman, Harry, asks: "Who has another question for us?"

Ann asks: "What did Jemima's friends say to her?"

Harry calls on Bill, who says, reading aloud, "Jemima is afraid, afraid, afraid."

The matter is about to be dropped. Ann asked a fact question, received a verbatim answer, and deserved no better. But the teacher decides to make the most of a bad start, to require insight into the situation.

"What difference did that make? . . . Why?" Here the daughter of Daniel Boone was being taunted for cowardice. As Boone's daughter, she could not back down. The teacher digs until she gets this understanding from the children. They've all been taunted in their time, and all have reacted in different ways: fighting, crying, returning the insult, or taking the dare. If their fathers have been astronauts, what has entered into their decision to take or not to take the dare?

"What do you suppose Jemima thought to herself as she debated the issue? Who will pretend to be Jemima thinking, and say what she was saying to herself?"

After the discussion, the teacher asks, "How could the question Ann gave us have been worded so that the answer would have involved Jemima's feelings and the reasons for them, rather than just what her friends said?" Over a period of time, the kinds of questions the children ask become more provocative of thought about the story and about their own living.

If two children disagree, it is not always proper to assume that one is right and one is wrong. What is the thinking behind their views? Are these good reasons for deciding as they have? In this process children learn to respect ideas and each other's rights to them.

Related reading activities

All the skills which the teacher has reviewed for fourth-reader level are introduced and maintained in short exercises in the manual and work-book pages related to the story read. If children need additional skill building besides that given in the manual and workbook, the teacher knows that, unless it is skill in solving new words, the material should be in the sight vocabulary of the children concerned. (Otherwise the learning is made unnecessarily difficult. This is one of the troubles with separate phonics texts.) Over the years she and her fellow teachers using these basal mate-rials have assembled exercises for various purposes, which they have made themselves or have appropriated from other basal series, with alterations of vocabulary where necessary. Some of these are duplicated and expend-able; others she has covered with clear plastic sheets and grouped accord-ing to the skill and level. Children use them independently as exercise, and check their results by an answer sheet, discussing afterwards the reasons for their wrong answers with the teacher or another child who can explain. Insights born in follow-up discussions are worth more than hours of endless exercise by oneself. (A thought for programmed learning.)

A child who easily forgets skills and needs more carefully treated reading than the teacher can provide, is started in such material as the *S.R.A. Reading Laboratory* (See Chapter 15.) on an easy level and given opportunity to exercise, test himself, and record his results. The amount of time spent on this depends upon how much of this particular type of exercise he needs, not how many cards the company has provided. The teacher frequently checks to have the child discuss his wrong answers, so that he is not continually making the same mistakes and cheerfully deepening bad habits. The teacher realizes that neither this nor any similar material will provide the breadth of experience to warrant its having a lion's share of the program.

A child who has difficulty getting the main idea of paragraphs may go through exercises such as the Gates and Peardon *Practice exercises in read-ing*, starting at a level below his usual reading and using only the Type-A materials, "Reading for general significance." He does this until his skill has reached a satisfactory level in the regular instructional material of his group, for the teacher knows that such a skill, if carried to the extreme, will ultimately mean a deficiency in reading for details and other techniques which must also be developed. As with the S.R.A. material, the child dis-cusses his progress with the teacher. Two children who need the same practice may discuss their results together and give each other help, but frequently need the teacher's counsel also. A team headed in the wrong direction or going in circles is not achieving much.

In judging materials, the teachers in the school have developed a set of standards. Here is the list of points they observe about worksheets and independent work materials:

1. Is it in keeping with good education in language and other fields? (Does it let the child draw his own illustration instead of coloring-in an adult product?)

2. Does it give directions which are clear and not too time-consuming?

3. Is it interesting without being mere entertainment? (It has to be good for reading development, not just likable.)

4. Has it only one or two types of response on a page? (Too great a variety of types of response means confusion for many children and interruption for the teacher.)

5. Does it devote several pages to a skill in order to develop and maintain it? (The skill should appear at increasing difficulty levels throughout a booklet.)

6. Does it teach as well as test or exercise? (For instance, does it help the child to discover the principle by which he is operating, or does it provide mere repetition? If it only repeats, then the teacher must first help the child develop the principle. See explanation of the inductive approach to word analysis in previous chapters.)

7. Does it cover all important aspects of reading, representing balanced development? (Few materials, if any, do; but it is important for the teacher to see what is missing and what is there, so that she will know for whom it is good and to what extent.)

8. Does it have clear illustrations and type of a size appropriate to the degree of maturity of the children who are to read it? (It would be too bad to make the child go blind for the sake of teaching him to read!)

9. Does it give a fairly true picture of the child's needs and strengths? (If it is a series of "yes, no" questions, the fifty-fifty chance of guessing makes it doubtful just what the child knew and what he didn't. Each exercise deserves a follow-up of diagnosis, with the child present.)

10. Does it fit the level of achievement of the child who will use it? (The teacher remembers that level of achievement is not simply a grade level but a sight vocabulary and a sequence of skills. The safest material is that designed to go with the basal book she is using. Other material must be studied carefully for its assumptions about the previous experiences of its readers.)

11. Does it give the child opportunity for individual, creative reaction in art or writing? (The learning is reinforced by creative activity and is more interesting because of it. The arts reinforce each other.)

12. Does it adhere to natural thought units as much as possible? (Words learned "in habitat" will be more readily recognized elsewhere, for both the visual impression and the association of meaning with the symbol are more impressive and typical.)

13. Does it contain some pages which can be used repeatedly? (An economy measure is to have some material which may be used for skimming, for word recognition, for outlining, for instance, instead of just for one kind of word analysis.)

14. Does it foster left-to-right sequence? The task of matching items makes children look up and down columns, not from left-to-right. Lists of words and crossword puzzles which have vertical items do not stress left-to-right reading. Such items should be used sparingly, particularly if the child is having directional difficulties or is particularly slow in rate of reading.

15. Does it employ many sense avenues of learning? (Workbooks requiring the child to see, hear, trace, say, and write are more apt to get results than are workbooks which utilize only one or two senses. Putting a cross or a check is less impressive learning than having to write the word.)

16. Is it constructed so that every answer requires thought? (If a set of two pictures is to be matched with a set of two sentences, the child has to read and match only one sentence; the other goes without saying. At least three sentences should accompany such an exercise. Why not three pictures and two sentences? Because this is the teaching of reading, not primarily art appreciation.)

17. This last one is the most important of all: Would it be better for the child to do something "on his own" instead of through published or dittoed worksheets? As Edgar Dale has written about teaching machines, "We must be careful lest we do better what should not be done at all."[2] The whole goal of reading is independence. Sometimes the skill the child needs to stress can be exercised in material he freely chooses, or by using the dictionary or the encyclopaedia instead of a worksheet.

The teacher asks herself similar questions when she evaluates reading games. Very often a pertinent addition is: "How much real reading is going on per minute of game time?" Waiting for someone to spin a wheel and then viewing the result upside down is scarcely worthy of precious school time. Seeing again and again words already well known is a waste of time. The teacher has found that one good use of children's time is in making materials for games. Children may make sentence strips for each other to read, containing words from the list of words they are trying to learn. They can make card games in which sentence cards are to be matched to word cards. For once a good handwriting will seem important and worth cultivating!

On her desk the teacher has the manuals for the basal series, from first grade on up. When she needs to be reminded how a skill was initiated, when a child or a group comes from another teacher without the previous learnings, she can look into the manual of the level at which, according to the company's skill chart, the skill was first taught, and use the same technique with the vocabulary the children now know.

The teacher looks in the manual at the series of exercises accompanying each story. Usually a story is accompanied by four types of exercise: word meaning, word analysis, comprehension and interpretation, and study skills. Using the index of skills at the back of the manual, the teacher can trace the development of each skill. The skill does not simply recur. Each new task is more demanding. She realizes that for some children much more exercise than that provided may be necessary. For others, some exercise will not be necessary, for these children are demonstrating daily their mastery of the skills involved. However, this does not mean that the teacher always

[2] Edgar Dale, "Self-instruction through programmed materials," *The News Letter*, February 1961, 26, page 4.

releases such children to other unrelated activities. Sometimes they can go more deeply into the skill. For example, a child who already knows certain prefixes may not need the exercise which reminds the other children of their appearance and meaning; but he can go on to find additional words or to build words showing the function of the known prefixes, and offer this information to the group. Or he may extend his exploration to the meanings of other prefixes and make a chart displaying this new information. He learns more, and some of the learning rubs off on the group.

Enrichment activities

Why bother with enrichment activities? The teacher knows why. There are two general types of enrichment activity, a creative reaction to the reading and an extension of reading activities. The creative reaction may be dramatic (puppet shows, shadow shows), graphic (mural, dioramas, maps, etc.), verbal (poetry, storytelling and writing, reporting, news writing), musical (making up a song to go with the words of a poem or story), or physical (a dance). Such activity requires the child to be more thoughtful about what he has read. For the teacher, it is a diagnostic device by which she can see the extent of the child's ability to recall and the nature of his misconceptions. (We can all remember the classic misconception attributed to a high school student interpreting "The stag at eve had drunk his fill.") Beyond the reading values, of course, lies the cultivation of the imagination, of expressing ideas, of individual endeavor and of group co-operation.

Where can the teacher find the time for such activities? "Bootlegging" will account for much of it. Some of it will be taken from "art time," some from "language time," some from "physical education time," some from "music time." Some of it the children may complete at home. And some of it will occur in "reading time" because, as the teacher realizes, reading is supported by thinking, by writing, by hearing language, by speaking. Language activities which are related to the material read are a legitimate use of "reading time."

Part of the time, however, the reading of a story or poem in the basal reader does not result in creative expression immediately, but in further reading. The story raises some questions in the children's minds.

"What did you wonder about India as you read this story?" Sometimes the children start reading a story after having listed some things they hope it will tell them—about India, for example. After reading the story, they tell what they found out, and discover that some of their questions remain unanswered.

"Where can we find the answers?" All sorts of reference books, maps, travel books, interviews with travel bureaus may be the result. Since the usual middle-grade basal reader assumes the reading of one story a week, there is plenty of time for such reference reading before the next week and the next story.

Children may have enjoyed the story so much that they would like to read another story on the same subject. In this way they will be exposed to some of the same new words again, and they will be learning more about the subject while they strengthen their vocabulary. Also, they will be experiencing the style of another author. Lists of books, appearing either at the end of a unit of stories in the book itself or at the end of the lesson plan or unit in the manual, are used. Different books may be read by different children and reported. Children capable of reading at a higher level than the basal book are given harder books for this related reading. The teacher gives individual help as this differentiated reading is done. For poorer readers, sometimes the teacher will supervise the reading of a similar story from another basal series, usually at a grade level below that of the children, and treat it as she would a story in the basal reader regularly used.

"How was your story different from the one in our reader?

"What did you learn about India from this story that you did not learn in the reader?"

Conflicting information sends the children to a study of the qualifications of the authors. Are they eyewitnesses? Was one writing of 1900 and the other of 1960? Was one writing of peasants and one of officials? Was one writing of the coastal cities and another of the mountain people?

Evaluation activities and individual help

The teacher sees in the manual that there are tests to be duplicated and administered at the ends of units of stories, as well as initial diagnostic tests. In the workbook there is a set of tests to be given at the end of every unit, and final tests are presented at the end of the workbook itself. Some publishers offer separate tests of achievement to be administered at the conclusion of the children's reader. They test the kinds of material the children have read in that reader, and the skills initiated at that reader level. Administering such a test at the end of the book, the teacher finds out what the children learned and what they did not master. If it is given the latter part of April, the teacher has a month to help the children with special deficiencies. She also has very good information to pass on to the next teacher, though summer may make a difference.

The teacher sees that individual help is suggested in each lesson plan. Children who have trouble pronouncing words correctly receive special help. At the end of each unit in the manual is a list of suggestions for the poor reader and for the superior reader.

The basal reader itself

Looking at the basal reader itself, the teacher sees that it centers its stories around eight topics of interest to children of this age group. Under each topic are stories, poems, perhaps plays. The manual lesson plans have suggested unit activities and unit culminations, so that the children are conscious of exploring an area of knowledge or of fun, and have a sense of what they have accomplished at the conclusion of each unit. One such unit activity may be the establishment of a temporary classroom collection of humorous stories they have enjoyed, and the classification of the type of humor indulged. The culminating activity for a unit may include dramatic presentation of favorite stories, a panel discussion, a quiz program.

The teacher looks at the end of a unit in the reader. Here is a list of things to think about and to do in relation to the stories the children have read. The relationship of one story to another, comparisons of plot, situation, and character are in order.

"These were all stories of courage. Which situation took the most courage? Why?" The ingredients of a rewarding philosophical discussion are here.

"Which character might have said, 'I was more clever than brave?' "

"What other story do you think might well have been included in this unit? Give your reasons for thinking so."

Looking down the list of authors, the teacher does not find the Pablum of which reader series are popularly accused. These are the works of major children's authors, many of whose autobiographical sketches appear in *The junior book of authors*. The presence of samples of their writing in the basal reader leads children to read the books from which these stories came, and other works by the same authors. Enjoying the story of "Becky and the Bandit" (in *Roads to everywhere,* Ginn Fourth Reader), children can go on to the book-length story, *Becky and the bandit* by Doris Gates. In the hands of a responsible teacher, a good basal reader creates a steady and increasing appetite for good literature and the habit of reading it at every opportunity.

As the teacher reads the stories, she finds, as one of her colleagues said, enough in them to read them fifteen times over. Each has the quality of being of interest to children. But, beyond that, it has something more for them to understand beneath its surface. And when the children are as old as the teachers, rereading, they will still find meanings which will illuminate their lives.

Looking at these excellent stories and the teaching aids which accompany them, the teacher recognizes the scope and depth of her responsibility. She is not there simply to expose children to stories. She is there to help them learn how to get more from their reading than they would have been able to get without her, and to learn to value the kinds of reward which intensive reading has to offer. She knows that if she were not constantly reminded by the manual, of the many skills and attitudes and appreciations and understandings to foster, and of the ways of doing so, she might tend to neglect many of them and to overemphasize a few. She realizes, too, that when she feels something must be omitted from a lesson, she had better be pretty sure that the omission is the right one.

First, she herself will read the story and ask herself what values she feels the children should certainly obtain from it. Then she will look at the manual to see what the authors tried to do. If she has to shorten discussion time, she will not, as a teacher friend of hers does, just ask the first four questions under "Discussion" in the manual. She will study each question to see of what type it is, and will decide upon a variety which will induce exercise in different types of thinking (comparison, judgment, generalization, etc.) and reach down to the heart of the meaning.

Summary

This chapter has dealt with a part of the task of the reading teacher in grades four, five, and six. It has been concerned with diagnosis of children's needs and interests and level of reading achievement at the first of the school year, and with the means of diagnosis and achievement testing throughout and at the conclusion of the basal reader. It has described in some detail the skills for which the middle-grade teacher of reading is responsible, and the ways in which she may partially fulfill her responsibility through the use of a basal reader.

The point of view of the chapter has been that one basal reader is a year-long diet which steadily builds skills while it *constantly* gives children reason to move out to other reading. It recognizes the importance of creative expression and language-arts activities to reading development. It proposes various ways of meeting individual differences without sacrificing continuity of learning.

In the interests of brevity, the authors have not discussed basal instruction elsewhere in Part II of this book. They have attempted so to deal with it in the present chapter that teachers of other levels can see the applications of principles to their own situations.

Readers are invited to proceed to the following chapter for suggestions of activities related to reading in the content fields and reading for recreation.

Suggested Activities

Select a basal-reader test from the school library file of reading tests. Try answering the questions yourself. In each case, notice what you have to do as a reader to answer the question. What kinds of thinking does the test require? Perhaps you disagree with the answer key on some of the answers. It is possible that it is wrong, but you had better reconsider the status of your own skill and learn more about the area of disagreement.

Make the same kind of self-analysis, using the questions in a basal-reader lesson plan, the questions in an exercise book, or the questions accompanying material such as the *S.R.A. Reading Laboratory*. How many kinds of thinking did the basal-reader lesson require as compared with the others? What are the differences in the kinds of learning offered in these different materials?

Now, compare these learnings with the list of skills at the first of this chapter. As a middle-grade teacher, what materials would you use, for what purposes, and to what extent? You have typically fifty minutes a day for reading instruction. Perhaps only a third of this time per week should be occupied in using instructional materials of the types described in this chapter.

Selected References

Filmstrips

Reading (Reading Experiences in Grades 5 and 6, Parts I, II, and III) film-strips and recordings. Jam Handy Organization, 2821 E. Grand Blvd., Detroit 11, Michigan, 1955.

Learning to use the dictionary. Pacific Productions, Inc., 414 Mason Street, San Francisco 2, California.

How to use the encyclopaedia. F. E. Compton and Company, 1000 N. Dearborn Street, Chicago 10, Illinois.

What is a graph? Visual Education Consultants, Inc., 2066 Helena Street, Madison 4, Wisconsin, 1954.

Introduction to maps. Jam Handy Organization, 2821 E. Grand Blvd., Detroit 11, Michigan, 1954.

Books

DeBoer, John J., and Dallmann, Martha, *The teaching of reading.* New York: Holt, Rinehart and Winston, Inc., 1960, Chap. 14.

Durrell, Donald D., *Improving reading instruction.* New York: Harcourt, Brace & World, Inc., 1956, Chaps. 7, 12, and 13.

Gray, Lillian, and Reese, Dora, *Teaching children to read.* New York: Ronald Press, 1957, Chap. 9.

Kunitz, Stanley, and Haycraft, Howard, *The junior book of authors.* New York: H. W. Wilson Company, 1951.

Russell, David H., *Children learn to read.* Boston: Ginn and Company, 1961.
—— *Manual for teaching the fourth reader.* Boston: Ginn and Company, 1961.

23

Recommended Practices
in Grades Four, Five, and Six:
Reading in the Content Fields
and Personal Reading Activities

Mrs. Sharp is the kind of teacher who puts things down in her notebook when she thinks they are important. These are day-to-day observations such as, "Check Billy on meaning of *un-*," or, "Jose—more on the Morse Code." But in the back of her notebook is her special gem collection—in the back of her notebook but in the forefront of her mind and in her teaching in these intermediate grades. Look over her shoulder and see what years of teaching and thinking have stressed to her:

We can't make people equal in reading ability. We can only meet their differences. (Are you reading slowly and thoughtfully? You should be.)

Avoid difficulty by using materials of suitable level.

Anticipate difficulty by building meanings and skills before the task requiring them is assigned.

Identify the holes in children's preparation by feeling them out first. (Do they know how to outline, read an index, etc.)

Reading requires the association of ideas with symbols. Be sure the idea means something to the child before expecting the symbol to. (Otherwise all you get is a symbol-minded child.)

Learning involves all the senses. Include as many as you can in teaching everything you expect the child to learn.

A clear purpose is essential to efficient learning. Let the child be fully aware of the purpose of his activity. Have a clear purpose yourself!

Explain something new and strange through something that is not strange. Have the child put the idea into his own words.

Help the child see the direction of his learning. (Outline of the course, or chapter; questions at first of chapter; ground to be covered.)

Milestones make hard work seem worthwhile. Have a child keep a record of what he knows. Let him pile up concrete evidence of his progress.

Practice is essential to the maintenance of learnings and the continuation of growth. Don't keep the nonreader a nonreader by constantly substituting nonreading activities for reading ones. Make him in some degree a reader in every field.

Practice by itself doesn't make perfect. Errors must be noted by the child and the teacher, and further practice geared to avoidance of these. Don't give the child more time to practice errors than you give him to practice what is right.

Testing is no substitute for teaching, and teaching is no substitute for testing. The teacher who never tests her effectiveness is a squirrel on a wheel.

If you want to know whether learning is taking place, ask, don't tell.

Proof of the effectiveness of reading is reaction: writing, speaking, portraying, using.

Reading is meaningless unless put to use, and of little use unless recalled. Strengthen recall by making it necessary in other activities.

If you think something is important, give it time, give it space; let the children know you think it is by the way you treat it. Pretty soon they will think it is, too.

Mrs. Sharp may sound a little too much like Polonius to suit some people's taste, but because she knows where she is going, she is likely to get there. After a year with a purposeless teacher, a child can emerge with vague learnings, half-learnings, and hash. The reading requirements in the content fields in the intermediate grades demand a teacher who knows her destination.

Reading in Arithmetic

Looking at the arithmetic book she is to use with some of the children, Mrs. Sharp sees that the first chapter is a review of skills supposedly previously learned. But do the children really know them? As an arithmetic teacher, she reviews the processes of addition, subtraction, multiplication, and division with the children before she expects them to read verbal problems involving these processes. But as a reading teacher, she has even more work to do.

How many ways does the text say "add?" Do the children know these ways? She first tries listening activities to test the group on these ways.

"I am going to say some words with some numbers. You tell me what the words mean that I should do with the numbers. Ready? Two and 4." Someone says, "You add." "Show me on the chalkboard" (flannelboard, magnetic board, on whatever is used), says the teacher. The child writes:

$$\begin{array}{r} 2 \\ 4 \\ \hline \end{array}$$

The teacher continues, "Jane and Bill were going to the movies *with* 3 other children." A child shows how that is written:

$$\begin{array}{r} 2 \\ 3 \\ \hline \end{array}$$

"What two ways have we said *add* so far?" Children volunteer *and* and *with*. The teacher writes: *These words say add*: 2 and 4, 2 with 3.

In this way she continues to review ways of saying *add*. She includes such expressions as, "*How many* were there *altogether*?" Reviewing substraction words, she has a similar listening activity. Such words as *paid, bought, left, less* are involved, as well as such common expressions as *take away from.*

She leads from these listening activities to little expression quizzes on the chalkboard at the first of a lesson. "Be ready to show how you wrote these on your paper." At their seats the children write the meaning of each expression. Then one child at a time comes up to write it next to the verbal expression the teacher has put on the chalkboard. They check their own papers while the teacher quickly notes what has happened to each child.

> Add 2 and 3.
> Take 1 from 5.
> Put 6 with 1.
> One apple cost 10 cents. Another cost 12.
> How much did *both* cost?

In these exercises the children are not necessarily required to do the operation, but simply to show that they know how the problem should be set up and what the process would be.

The children make up problems for each other. Sometimes pairs of children are at the chalkboard, one reading the problem, the other writing the problem in arithmetic form.

Preparation for a page of verbal problems

As the teacher looks at the first page of problems in the book, she sees that all of them are about a visit to a circus. Fortunately a picture of a circus is on the facing page; but, even so, it takes knowledge of a circus to understand that one pays to get in to see it, that it is held in a tent, that it starts and stops at regular times. Checking the words used on this page with the words the children have had in their other reading, the teacher notes that there are several new words: *circus, paid, ticket, dollar, clown, rider, dimes, nickel, prove, arrived, problems, examples, below,* and *tent.* Perhaps the children know these words and perhaps they do not. She will introduce these words and the idea of a circus just as she would in a regular basal-reader lesson.

Mrs. Sharp says, "Let's read the title of this page to ourselves. Who can read it aloud for us?" Someone reads. "What do you suppose *Under the Big Top* means?" With luck, someone knows. Some children have seen circuses in the movies, others on television. Some have had the good fortune to see a real one.

"I've really been to one," says August. As he tells what he saw, the teacher writes some of the wording on the chalkboard, utilizing the new words as he says them, and has the children repeat the statements written there.

He *paid* to get into the *circus.*
two for a *dollar*
The man gave him a *ticket.*
He went into the *tent* with his *ticket.*

The teacher involves the other children as August presents his information, drawing their attention to the picture in the book.

"How many of you see the *clowns*? What are the clowns doing? Who sees the girl *rider*? What is she doing?"

"What is *below* the *rider* in this picture?"

Fortunately the teacher's pay day has been recent enough for her to be able to produce at this moment one dollar bill, two fifty-cent pieces, ten dimes, and twenty nickels. The children help her make a chart of what they know about money. The chart says that 10 dimes make 1 dollar, 20 nickels make 1 dollar, etc., and the forms of the dimes and the nickels and the dollar bill are illustrated. Now any child who forgets what the word *dime* looks like can see it on the chart.

Teachers have spoken to the children about *problems* and *examples* before. But this time the teacher writes as she speaks, "Give me a *problem* about *dimes* and a *ticket* to the *circus.*"

Boris says, "If circus tickets are 50 cents, how many dimes will I need for a ticket?" The children solve Boris's problem.

"That was a good *example* of a problem," says Mrs. Sharp. "Now who will give us another example, using nickels this time?"

Preparation for the form of the problem

The first problem on the page in the arithmetic text requires the subtraction of 75 from 85. So that the children can accustom themselves to the form of the problem, the teacher first gives them a simple problem of the same type, minimizing the arithmetic process.

"Listen to my problem and be ready to tell me first what kind of problem it is. Is it an addition problem, a subtraction problem, a multiplication problem, or a division problem? Are you ready? Listen carefully: Jack and Jo went to the circus. They had 20 cents for something to eat. They paid 10 cents for some popcorn. How much did they have left?"

She calls on Abel. "It's a subtraction problem."

"How many think he is right?" She isn't going to give the right answer away to the nonthinkers. "Why do you think so?" If necessary, she reads the problem again, until the children can say that "How much did they have *left*?" suggests subtraction.

With questions like, "How much money did they have at first? How much did they spend? How many dimes does it take to make 20 cents?" and by having children put two dimes for 20 cents on the table and actually take one away, they *prove* that 10 from 20 leaves 10.

Discussing with the children what they did first to solve this problem, and next and next, Mrs. Sharp has them make a list of things to observe about a problem. (See page 234 in Chapter 12.) In their notebooks the children put this sequence of steps. As a group, they make up another arithmetic problem like the one the teacher made, and solve it by the steps. Then each child in his notebook writes an original problem of the same kind, and solves it and proves it by drawings of dimes, nickels, etc.

Another problem on the first page of the text requires the reading of a clock face. The teacher can take no chances with this, either. She sees whether the children can do this before she ever asks them to read a problem demanding it.

"At this rate," remarks the teacher next door to Mrs. Sharp, "you'll never get through the book."

Mrs. Sharp's reply is astute if not too popular. "I am not trying to get through the book, Bessie. I am trying to get what's in it through the children's heads." In the beginning, Mrs. Sharp may be a slow tortoise, but by the end of the year Bessie will be a sorry hare.

After a problem is solved

After a problem is solved, the teacher with the children holds a post-mortem on the bad answers. The big question is, "What don't we understand that we should know for next time?" Gerald and Estelle both had the answer 7 for the problem of how many times the girl rode around the ring if she rode 2 times on each of her 5 ponies. "What kind of problem was this? What were the clues (each . . . times . . . total number)? If it had been addition, what would the words have been? What will you look for next time? Who can show with ponies and circles on the chalkboard, while we count, what the answer should be?"

Three children couldn't do the fifth problem because they had forgotten what *half* of anything signals. One thought of dollars and thought *half* meant *fifty*. In the case of each error, the teacher helps the children pinpoint the reason for error, see the clues they should have noticed or learn the principle they should have known, and plan what to look for next time. Each child keeps a notebook of what he has learned and makes up his own illustrations and examples:

> Half of anything is one of two equal parts.
> Half of 6 is 3.
> Half of 14 is 7.
> Half a dollar is 50 cents.

Looking ahead in the book

The teacher sees that there are extra problems in the back of the book, for children needing extra exercise of that type. Probably some of her children can sharpen their skills on these while those who are having difficulty with a concept or a process may be working it out with her.

She sees also that there is an appendix containing charts showing the relationships among different kinds of measure. She knows from the back of her little notebook that it will mean more for the children to find these things out for themselves, make their own chart, and then use the index to find the author's chart and compare it with theirs. As these measures are going to be required in the activities in the class, the teacher and the children bring in the equipment necessary for the experiments which will make the relationships clear. They save milk cartons—half-pints, pints, quarts, gallons. Then they decide what they want to know:

> How many cups are in a pint?
> How many pints are in a quart?
> How many quarts are in a gallon?

Individuals pour water into cups, into pints, into quarts, into the gallon, and as each finding is made (and usually it is good to do something more than once if a scientist is to know for sure), the result is recorded. The children plan their chart, the wording, the illustrations.

Are they sure they are right? How can they find out? They look in the table of contents. At the very end it says, "Tables of Measure. . . . . . Page 341." What does *tables* of *measure* mean? They know that a time table is a sheet listing the trains or busses or planes or ships and the times of their arrival and departure at or from certain places. They look at page 341. This is a list of different ways of measuring. On page 342 they find *liquid measures*. They see the pictures the author used and the statements he made. They find that he says the same things they do, just a little differently. They like *their* pictures better!

What are liquid measures? Oscar looks *liquid* up in a dictionary. What letter does he look under? How far back in the dictionary will that be? He finds that *liquid* means *free flowing*.

"What is free flowing?"

"Water," someone says. Milk, syrup, gasoline, olive oil, are suggested.

"And what kind of measure do we use for these?"

"Liquid measure," everyone says. And the children find it in the tables of measure in the back of their arithmetic book.

"That's not the only place," says Oscar, still browsing; "it's in the appendix of the dictionary here, too." The world is full of riches for people with eyes.

More looking ahead

Bessie next door is having trouble with her fifth-grade group.

"They're having trouble reading their problems," says Bessie, the diagnostician.

"What problems?" asks Mrs. Sharp.

The problems they are supposed to work on now have tables in them too, but tables of another kind. The problems are like this:

Miss Smith's girl scouts were selling cookies in teams. There were seven teams of three girls each. These are the boxes of cookies they sold. How many boxes did they sell in all?

Team 1	Team 2	Team 3	Team 4	Team 5	Team 6	Team 7
5	3	10	6	4	2	12
4	8	2	7	10	3	1
8	6	4	1	4	3	8
—	—	—	—	—	—	—

By the time Mrs. Sharp got to the heart of the trouble, she said, "How about taking time off and having your students figure out a table of their own?" (Anticipate difficulty by building meanings and skills before the task requiring them is assigned, Mrs. Sharp's notebook says.)

"Such as?" asked Bessie.

"We're having a paper drive," answered Mrs. Sharp. "Why not have rows (tables) compete, and keep a record for a week of how many bundles each row of children brings in each day. By the end of the week, we find out what our total is."

Bessie did, and to her credit be it said that she didn't make the table herself. She had the children work it out.

"Let's have a column for each row and the five days down the side," they said. By the end of the week, they were ready to see the connection between their contest and their arithmetic problems. Bessie had lost a week, but she had also caught on to one of Mrs. Sharp's principles. "Look ahead in the book, Bessie," said Mrs. Sharp. "When you see trouble coming, head it off."

Using the text as a reference

One day an argument over a news clipping develops in Mrs. Sharp's room.

"It's a million," says Al.

"Anybody knows that's a billion," says Pete. "A million looks like this." He writes his version on the chalkboard. Al writes his. Who is right?

"Let's look at the table of contents in our arithmetic book," says Mrs. Sharp. "Why," she asks, "do you suppose I think we'll find help in the arithmetic book?" (She realizes too late that she *should* have said, "Where do you think we could find out?")

"Millions and billions are numbers, and numbers are arithmetic."

"Look at the very last thing on the page. What do you see?"

"Index," says Bill. "Page 343."

"Let's all turn to page 343 and see what is there," says Mrs. Sharp.

Isadore arrives first, as usual.

"I've looked all over the page," he reports, "and there's not a million or a billion anywhere in sight."

"How is the index arranged?" asks Mrs. Sharp.

"It's alphabetical." "It's a, b, c, like that."

"*B* is for *billion*," says Isadore, "and there's nothing but *bushel*." Then he turns the page cannily. "Oh, here it is. It says *million*, 288, 289."

"How many find what Isadore sees? Where is it on the page? Put your fingers on the spot so that I can see you have it. What do you suppose those numbers and commas mean?"

"The numbers are the pages you'd find *million* on." "The commas separate the numbers and the words." (Too bad there wasn't a hyphen or a *See trillion*. Better luck next time.)

The children turn to page 288.

"What did we want to know?" asks Mrs. Sharp.

"We wanted to know how to write a *million*."

"Then let's look to see whether anywhere on the page a *million* is written in numbers."

Oscar finds it: "We write one million like this: 1,000,000."

One experience with an index doesn't teach the use of the index, but it counts. The children have just finished a booklet on animals they have studied in science. The table of contents lists them by classification. Maybe the children could become interested in making an index so that visitors can find their favorite animal quickly. Soon a sign in the room says: "Have you a favorite animal? Look in our index to see whether you can find his story."

One day Mrs. Sharp smiles to herself as she passes Bessie's room, because there she sees little evidences of the propaganda she has been bombarding Bessie with all year. There is a vocabulary chart:

Our Arithmetic Vocabulary

dimensions   length   width   square
        rectangle   perimeter   area

Elsewhere in the room is a display which says:

> A perimeter is the distance around the outside.
> Area is the surface or space covered.
> What are the area and perimeter of these?

Below these sentences are shapes whose areas and perimeters are to be solved. Each day children put up new shapes to be solved by other children. Solution is followed by a discussion of how it was done.

Apparently Bessie is paying attention to processes, too. On another chart Mrs. Sharp sees this:

Long Division

1. Divide.
2. Multiply.
3. Subtract.
4. Bring down
5. Repeat.

Borden Bliss is at Bessie's elbow. "Mrs. Barker," he says, "I divided and multiplied and subtracted and brought down all right, but I forget how to repeat."

Reading in Science

"Look ahead in the book, Bessie. When you see trouble, head it off."

Mrs. Sharp looks ahead in the science text. First comes a study of the seasons, and soon the class will be dealing with the life span of plants. What words will trouble them when they try to read about it? Here are the words she sees which are beyond third reader vocabulary: *elm, autumn, sequoia, sleet, perennials, remain, bushes, shrubs, bloom, form, stem, dandelions, freeze.* The few children in her class who have only second-reader vocabulary will be troubled also with *forest, frost,* and *die.* Some of these words (*sleet, remain, bushes, shrubs, bloom, form, stem, freeze, forest*) those children with third-reader skills can sound out successfully, but the meanings of the words are the greater problem. What to do?

It is Autumn now. A study of what is happening to plants in the neighborhood and a discussion of the season can build that concept. Also, there is a good picture of autumn in the text. A sequoia is illustrated in the text also. But sleet? And dandelions may be common in the authors' part of the country but not in Mrs. Sharp's neighborhood. She is going to have to dig for dandelions, figuratively.

"What *season* of the year is it?" she asks the class.

"It's deer season," says Jasper.

"It's Fall," says Bruce.

Mrs. Sharp has the children all say *season,* which she has written on the chalkboard.

"Who sees two words in this word?" she asks. Margaret underlines the *sea* and the *son.* "What do you notice about the pronunciation of the s-o-n?" The children say that the *s* has a *z* sound, as it often does when it stands alone between two syllables. "Like *reason,*" says Betty. Mrs. Sharp writes *reason* under *season* and has the children note the likeness and difference.

"Let's come back to what Jasper and Bruce said," says Mrs. Sharp. "What made them answer differently?"

"Jasper was thinking about hunting season and Bruce was thinking about—well, just seasons."

The children finally come to the idea that a season is a time of year in which things happen to the *weather* that are different from what happens at other seasons.

"And because of this, what happens to people and plants and animals?" asks Mrs. Sharp. The lively discussion requires some guidance, and so she makes three columns: *People*—("What else?" she says.) *Plants—Animals.* "And down the side here what seasons shall I write?" The children dictate, "Spring, Summer, Fall, Winter." "There's another name for Fall. What is it?" The children say, "Autumn." (If they don't, here is a good chance for use of the dictionary.) Mrs. Sharp inserts it instead of *Fall,* and they all say, "*Autumn.*"

The children discuss what people wear and what they do about housing for the different times of year; how the time of year affects the farmer's work. They tell Mrs. Sharp short ways of saying what they mean, and she writes them. She insists that what is written down in parallel fashion is parallel in expression. Under *people,* for instance, if the children start by saying that people *wear light clothing* in spring, the other items in the column must assume the same subject, *people,* and must finish the sentence, starting with a verb.

As the children discuss plants and animals, the fact emerges that some of them seem to be more affected by the seasons than others.

"What makes the seasons?" asks Mrs. Sharp.

"The temperature," "The weather," "The sun," are answers.

"This is a question worth writing down," says Mrs. Sharp. "We shall have to study to find out the answer."

"What do you suppose the difference is between a scientist and a person who just wonders about something? What does a scientist do that many people do not bother to do?" Mrs. Sharp draws out the fact that a scientist observes carefully and records what he finds, he thinks of possible reasons for what he finds and tests each one for its truth, he looks to authentic sources for his information. Other people are likely just to guess and come out with plausible hunches or falsehoods which satisfy them. A scientist is satisfied only when he thinks he has found a truth. A truth? Another concept to be built!

The children decide that they can study the seasons through many reference tools in the classroom: the dictionaries (both elementary and advanced), the encyclopaedias, textbooks of science, pamphlets about scientific subjects, a globe. The librarian will be able to help them find other books when they come with specific questions. If they are going to be real scientists, they can study the seasons right where they are, too.

In her usual reading groups for basal instruction, Mrs. Sharp uses scientific material of different difficulty levels so that the children can find information about the seasons. One group uses the first few pages of the textbook of science, which has articles on heat and the seasons, on the difference between seasons near the equator and near the poles, and on an experiment the group can try with a flashlight, to show the effect of slanting and straight rays of the sun. Later, as one member of the group reads the directions, another child in the class follows the directions, and the class concludes what the effect is.

Another group reads from a book which shows the position of the earth in relation to the sun at different seasons of the year. The group makes a picture of these positions and shows it to the class, and a child labels the illustration as its parts are mentioned.

Another group looks in different dictionaries and encyclopaedias to find out what is said about the seasons.

At the end of the discussion of the seasons by the whole class, Mrs. Sharp asks, "Now, a good scientist would summarize what he had found out. What was our first question? What was one of our answers?" As the children mention the question and the answers, the teacher writes down what they have found. She insists on keeping to each point, so that the result is organized along these lines:

> What are the seasons?
> There are four seasons:
> > Spring
> > Summer
> > Autumn
> > Winter
> The seasons are caused by:
> > etc.
> They are different in different places on the earth:
> > In time of year:
> > > etc.
> > In temperature:
> > > etc.

Each child makes his own book about what he knows about the seasons, illustrating it with his own pictures or occasionally with one he has found in a discarded magazine or newspaper. The very poorest readers are helped during "reading time" to write down what they know. The general vocabulary is simple, but words like *temperature* and *equator* and *seasons* are there because they have been taught in oral and written context, and now appear on a vocabulary chart of "Our Science Words."

One day Mrs. Sharp has everyone look out the window at the things which are growing around the school. "What do you see growing?" she asks.

"There's a big tree." "There are some bushes." "That's no bush. My mother calls that a sweet-scented shrub." "There's grass. It's growing."

Mrs. Sharp puts up some pictures of trees. "Are these like the tree you see outside the window?" She has the children observe that these are all trees because they all "come up out of the ground the way a tree does" (More to learn!), but that they aren't like the one outside the window. "Does anyone know what the one outside the window is called? How can we find out?"

The children decide to look in an encyclopaedia. A dictionary would tell them what a tree was, probably, and about a few kinds of trees, but—.

"We could go to a book that is especially about trees. There's one I saw in the library," says Oscar. This is a good time for Oscar to get that book. He doesn't need the practice with the encyclopaedia that some of the others do. Bruce had better go along. If the librarian is running true to form, she will send back more than one tree book.

The investigation of the encyclopaedia means that Mrs. Sharp will have to get answers to several questions. Do the children remember how the volumes are organized? Do they know what the letters on the back of each volume mean? What likely topics might they find listed that would tell them about trees? Do they know that there is an index at the end of the last volume, which tells in which volumes they will find different things about trees? (They find, for instance, that the volume Th-V, in which they would look up the word *tree*, is only one of eleven volumes in which they could find something on this topic.) They must not lose sight of their objective. Which of the subheadings in the index would be likely to have the information they want about different kinds of trees?

Part of the children's problem in reference reading is to stick to a topic that they are investigating and not be beguiled by offshoots from their main objective. One technique Mrs. Sharp uses is to read a passage aloud to them from the encyclopaedia, with the preface, "Listen and be ready to tell me whether this is what we want to know. Raise your hand when you think we have found what we want, or part of what we want." She then reads, looking up after every sentence or two. If a child says that a sentence is pertinent, she has him tell why he thinks so, what it says that the class wanted to know.

"As I have read to you from this encyclopaedia, what have you learned about reference reading?"

"You have to read carefully when you come to something you think you might want."

"You have to keep thinking what you want so that you'll know it when you come to it."

She tries to have the children state in few words what they have found from her reading. She writes the offerings on the chalkboard and has the children compare them for exactness of meaning and economy of language. She doesn't take a vote on which they like best! She doesn't say, "No, this one is best." She makes *them think* until they see which is best, or how something can be doctored up to be best.

By studying the index in the encyclopaedia the children see that bold type is used to indicate main entries, light type for subordinate headings; that the numbers in color indicate the volume and page containing the main article on the topic; that the first number is the volume and the second is the page; that commas separate the volumes and semicolons separate the topics. By studying the articles themselves, they see such directions as "See herbs." They learn that this means that more about the topic they want may be found under this other heading. They also see that subheadings in black type within the article help the reader decide whether to read a whole division of the article or go down to another one. For example, if the article on trees is divided into subheadings like *classification* (plants), *structure, growth, uses, kinds,* and all the class wants is the discussion of *kinds,* the reader will skip to the last subheading.

By the time trees have been studied in the encyclopaedias and in the books Oscar and Bruce brought back from the library, the children are ready to say what a tree is and what kinds there are. Meanwhile Mortimer, who has been looking at the pictures of trees in the easier of the two encyclopaedias "gets the jump" on everybody. "Here's that tree in our schoolyard, Mrs. Sharp, and here's its name right under it."

"Cottonwood," says Oscar. "Whoever heard of a cottonwood?" There are all sorts of ways to express disappointment.

Synonyms and derivations

Mrs. Sharp hasn't forgotten the question of whether those are bushes or shrubs in the schoolyard. Out come the dictionaries. The easy dictionary says that a shrub is a bush and a bush is a shrub. The harder dictionary says that a shrub has many branches at or near the ground level. It says that a bush has several branches at or near ground level. Is this a useful difference? The dictionary for adults, which Isadore reads, having borrowed it from Mrs. Sharp's desk, says that a bush is a shrub, especially a thick, densely branched shrub; of *shrub* it says that it is a low, several-stemmed, woody plant; a bush!

Isadore finds something else that interests him, which he writes on the chalkboard for everyone to see: bush (ME.busch,busk); shrub (Ar.drink), colloq.(sharāb). Mrs. Sharp helps Isadore find the key to the meaning of *ME* and *Ar.* He finds that *ME* means Middle English, and, looking up *English,* he finds that *Middle English* was the English of 1100-1500 A.D. *Ar* means *Arabic.* So *bush* comes from an English word and *shrub* comes from an Arabic word. What would the Arabic word for bush have to do with a drink? This brings up the fact that drinks have been made from the leaves or bark or roots of bushes; tea, for example.

Mrs. Sharp still has a doubt in her mind. She looks at her science reference book which she keeps on her desk from teacher-training days (She really should invest in a later edition.) The word *bush* isn't even in it;

just *shrub*. She decides there is no further use in beating about the bush.

"In the English language we have many words which have come from different origins and mean the same thing. *Bush* and *shrub* are examples of this." This is just a beginning for Isadore. For weeks ahead he will be finding such relationships, digging into word origins and returning with fire in his eye and inspired irrelevancies like, "*Lamb* comes from the Anglo-Saxon and *mutton* from the French!" He doesn't need outer space for *his* excitement.

Before the children ever come to that part in the text about the life span of plants, they will be so full of freezes and sleet, bushes and shrubs, that the vocabulary won't trouble them. Just to make sure, Mrs. Sharp sows a few ideas around the classroom. There is, in one corner, a display of questions to answer, questions to whet the curiosity of the budding scientist: What is a perennial? What is an annual? Sometimes children who find something out, ask the questions themselves for others to find the answers to. They sign their questions, and the people who find the answers add their names. There is a special day when the answers are revealed.

Listening activities for structure

The teacher notices that the textbooks in science tend to use certain forms of paragraph structure. She helps children learn how to think with such structure by reading passages aloud for certain listening purposes. When the child demonstrated the slanting and straight rays of the sun with a flashlight, another child was reading the directions from the textbook. Sentence by sentence the paragraphs were read, and at the end of each sentence there was a pause to see what action should be taken. If questions arose, the sentence was restated.

At the end of such a session of following written directions which are read aloud, Mrs. Sharp says, "What did you notice that we had to do as thinkers as these directions were read?" The result of this discussion is a chart on what to do when reading directions. It looks like this:

> When reading directions
> 1. Think what the whole purpose is.
> 2. Think the meaning of each sentence.
> 3. Think what the facts are.
> 4. Think what comes first and next and next.
> 5. Compare your result with what the book says you will find.
> 6. If you disagree with the book, try it all again. Try to see where you made your mistake.

The explanation of different kinds of plants requires a different kind of thinking.

"I am going to read you something about different kinds of plants. When you think you have heard what one kind of plant is, raise your hand. Put your head on your desk and just listen, so that you will tell what you think and not just what someone else thinks, and so that you can just listen and concentrate on meaning." Mrs. Sharp then reads the first paragraph, which starts with a description of a kind of plant and then says in the last sentence that it is called an *annual*. The children raise their hands and say that one kind is an annual. Mrs. Sharp then continues with the second paragraph. It says that beans and tomatoes live only one year, that they are annuals, too. If a child says that this is a new kind, other children protest that these are annuals, too; they live only one year.

Mrs. Sharp reads the third paragraph. It tells how annuals come up the next year from seeds. This is still about annuals. But the fourth paragraph says that some plants live two years and are called *biennials*. Hands go up.

Now Mrs. Sharp has the children turn to the page in the textbook and look at the first paragraph she read and read it silently to decide what she should put down as a summary about its meaning. She does this for each paragraph, and has the children say whether a paragraph gives an additional idea (subheading) or a new idea. The result on the chalkboard looks something like this:

> Plants that live one year are called annuals.
> Beans and tomatoes are annuals.
> Annuals grow from seed.
> Plants that live two years are called biennials.
> etc.

Mrs. Sharp says, "These are the notes we can take on what we read in paragraphs like these. Now let's see how we could make an outline of what we know." With her guidance the children dictate the following:

> Kinds of Plants
> I. Annuals
>   A. Life span: one year
>   B. Examples
>   1. beans
>   2. tomatoes
>   C. Growth: from seed
> II. Biennials
>   A. Life span: two years
>   B. etc.

When the children discuss the kinds of paragraph they have been reading this time, they make these comments:

> Some paragraphs define something.
> Some paragraphs give examples of something.

ting fuller and fuller), a list of books they had read, a list of techniques they knew.

Enrichment activities in relation to the stories read also were altered to suit the maturity of the children. They used the art media they were learning to use in sixth grade, not the paints and crayons of the pre-primer level. Also, now that they were older, they could write more responses and so had to draw fewer. The worksheets could be longer because their attention span was longer, and the print didn't have to be quite so big.

The teacher decides that she will use a new pre-primer (if she has a group that low). She decides also that she will have to develop modified materials using the social-studies and science and arithmetic vocabulary. She will see to it that these children have something unique to offer the rest of the class in information about any topic studied, that they will be given prominent but manageable parts in anything undertaken by the class as a whole, and that they will make up booklets on the various fields (social studies, etc.), writing their own summaries of what they have learned and illustrating and labelling the new concepts. They will learn to read by reading, writing, speaking, and listening to the words they are learning, so help her!

To the more able readers who are still not reading at fourth-grade level, the teacher assigns a reader of a level on which it is possible for them to learn. If it is a book with which they have some bad associations (the previous teacher perhaps having used it too soon, too fast), the teacher may choose instead an "in-between book," belonging to the same series. For instance, Scott, Foresman is one of several publishers now offering such books. *Just imagine* is a book which reteaches all the skills through third reader in the Scott, Foresman series. It is accompanied by a manual and workbook. It appeals to older children as well as to the age group who might normally read third-reader material. *Fun and fancy* is the counterpart in the Ginn series. (See list of basal reader series on pages 000.) Even though the teacher may prefer the teaching program of one series over another, she tries to keep the children working in a series with which they are already familiar, for she knows that changes she wants to make mean unnecessary hardships for the children in vocabulary and skills sequences.

Planning the Basal Program for Better Readers

The average and above average readers in her class use the fourth reader and workbook. It is a level on which all can learn, and the fourth-reader manual contains work they have not had before, emphasized as it will not be at higher levels. She will not bore the abler readers with long sessions developing the meanings of words they already know or reviewing skills they already use well, but the things they need exposure to, they will get.

They will set reading purposes and learn to stick to them. They will engage in discussions of the ideas gained from the reading, the meanings of words as they are used in different contexts, the intentions of the author and his skill in getting his effects, and how the story is related to their own lives and to other stories they know. They will relearn techniques which are in danger of rusting and will learn new ones. They will go beyond other children in finding out the forms, meanings, and derivations of words. They will take leadership in reference work, and in dictionary exercises. They will invent exercises for other children to use, thus confirming their own skill.

The teacher notices that the reader manual contains an appendix listing books the children can read in relation to the stories in the reader. Some are classified as easy reading—for the poorer readers in the group. Some are average. Some are hard and may be read by the teacher or by the ablest readers. She also sees that the lesson plans in the manual list enrichment activities, many of which would challenge the better readers in the group, and that at the ends of units in the manual there are lists of activities to help the poorer reader and others to challenge the better reader. The teacher feels she is not going to starve for ideas. All she has to do is be a reader herself, use her training, and her good sense.

Reviewing Ways of Handling Basal Reading

By June of each year this teacher feels very smart. Each September she feels as though she knows nothing, as though she won't deserve the apples and the flowers or even her self-respect. That's due to the fact that she has forgotten how much she really knows. So now she refreshes her memory by looking over some of the things she has collected over the years. Perhaps she looks again at the "B" chapters in DeBoer and Dallmann's *The teaching of reading*, at the many ideas of Russell and Karp's *Listening aids through the grades* and *Reading aids through the grades*. She pulls out her yellowed notebook and reads:[1]

How to Introduce a Story in a Basal Reader

Use yourself as a resource
  Explaining
  Hinting
  Comparing strange idea with familiar one
  Giving problem to discuss well ahead of introduction (such as which of
    previous stories is preferred and why)
  Telling previous episode in book from which story is taken
  Using foreign phrases to put children in foreigner's place in strange land
  Relating story to previous story
  Giving background facts (such as author's life or story setting)
  Contrasting (then and now) if story is of another time, place

[1] Excerpts from Constance M. McCullough, *Handbook for teaching the language arts.* South San Francisco: Paragon Press, 1958.

When they define, you have to keep thinking
  what they are defining and
  what they are saying about it that is
    important to remember.
When they give examples, you have to remember
  what the examples are and
  what they are examples of.

When the children come to the paragraph on perennials, Mrs. Sharp says, "Read this paragraph and be ready to tell me whether this is a paragraph which defines something or a paragraph which gives examples of something. Be ready to prove your answer." These children will know their perennials, and they will know how to read science, too.

Reading pictorial material

As a science teacher Mrs. Sharp knows that she must help children derive meaning from the illustrations in the texts and references they use. One way she does this is by having the children make such illustrations themselves on the basis of things they know. In a spot where digging is permissible on the school grounds, she and the class have a digging session, to see how the side of the cut looks as they dig down. At first the soil is dark and loose. Then it is hard.

"We've come to clay," Joe says. "We've got plenty of that at home."

Perhaps they hit rock, perhaps not. They come back into the classroom and discuss how they might make a picture of what they saw down the side of the cut they made in the ground. Different children show on the chalkboard how they think it might be done. Ultimately they have a plan, and soon the classroom has another chart: this time a *cross-section* of the soil in the schoolyard, with each part labeled to show clearly the difference in composition of each layer. It is not just coincidence that they soon come to a picture in their textbook of a cross-section of the ground, showing the location of natural gas. Do they remember the cross-section they made a few weeks ago? Indeed they do. They easily read the picture, once they have determined the pronunciation and meaning of words like *sandstone, gravel, limestone, shale.*

Mrs. Sharp remembers the year the Pratts excavated for the basement of their big house across the street. What a wonderful year for cross-sections *that* was!

Related science readings

A science table has a display of books on science to read for the various purposes that become important during the year. The books are changed as the topics change. As Bruce and Oscar bring in an armful, other books may be taken back to the library. If children are to learn to read science material, much of their science reading should be of the straight informational type.

However, Mrs. Sharp does not miss an opportunity to bring aesthetic experience into the science interest. Changing seasons are a good excuse for reading aloud or leaving available in the room Mary and Conrad Buff's *Dash and dart*. The bibliographies list it for primary grades. But any child who has not seen its appealing illustrations and read what the changing seasons mean to two fawns should have that pleasure right now.

Some of the young scientists in the class may have read the d'Aulaires' *Benjamin Franklin*, and will chuckle over Robert Lawson's *Ben and me*.

Children interested in the structure of the earth will want to investigate the Schneiders' *Rocks, rivers and the changing earth*. The best readers can read it and poorer ones may persuade Mrs. Sharp to read parts. Zim's *What's inside the earth* is easier and can be read by the average reader in the fourth grade who wants to know what the cross-section farther down in the schoolyard would look like.

Children should know that poets have observed the seasons as carefully as scientists but with somewhat different eyes and a different result. Mrs. Sharp reads aloud Christina Rossetti's "The Months" and Thomas Bailey Aldrich's "Marjorie's Almanac" for sensitively recorded impressions of the various times of year.

"Everyone has special feelings about each time of year. Maybe you would like to write a poem of your own about yours," hints Mrs. Sharp. And very likely someone does. By the end of the year these children know that poets and scientists have much in common. They would like to be both.

Reading in the Social Studies

Reading in the social studies requires the ability to follow important sequences in time and logic, to get main ideas and to associate pertinent facts with them. Mrs. Sharp helps her pupils learn these techniques at first through ear training, then through reading and studying. She lets the children know what she is doing and why.

"When you read for information," she says, "you have to know what you are looking for. Here is a description of the way a farmer in Wisconsin grows feed for his cattle. First I am going to read to you the first phrases of each paragraph, and ask you to tell me how the author has organized his information."

Mrs. Sharp reads, "In the fall. . . . When the ground freezes. . . . In the spring. . . ."

"He's organized it by time," says Billy. "Fall, winter, spring."

"How many of you think Billy is right?" asks Mrs. Sharp. If there is disagreement, she reads slowly again.

"If you are going to outline what you find in this description, then, what may be the headings for the outline?" The children decide that Fall, Winter, and Spring, *may* be.

"Let's see what we might say would happen in the fall," says Mrs. Sharp. "I'll read that paragraph slowly, and you think very hard about what happened in the fall." After the reading, the children say:

"He begins the work he is going to do to feed his animals." (But what was that work? If we put that in the outline, we still don't know. This sentence tells what *kind* of information we are going to learn, not what we actually *do* learn.)

"He plows and gets manure and spreads it."

"He will plant in the spring and that's why he plows."

"The manure puts food into the soil for the plants to use."

With questions such as the following, Mrs. Sharp gets the children to see what the essential news is:

"Why does the author tell us that the farmer will plant in the spring, in a paragraph about what the farmer does in the fall?" (So that we'll know the *reason* for the plowing.)

"Why does he tell us that manure puts food into the soil?" (So that we'll know why the farmer spreads it.)

"How many things does the farmer actually do in the fall, according to this author? I'll read the paragraph again, and you listen carefully."

The children decide that the outline should look like this:

> I. In the fall, the farmer
>   A. plows.
>   B. spreads manure.

"If this is all you put in the outline, what are you going to have to remember?" (They are going to have to remember why he plows, where he got the manure, and why he spread it. By remembering the big news in a paragraph, the reader has "branches" to hang his memories on; otherwise he forgets the things that have no place to "hang.")

"Do you think you could try to read and outline the next paragraph for yourselves?"

While some of the children do this, Mrs. Sharp takes the children who would not be able to read this material and reads to them. They suggest notes which she writes down. Some children are invited to put their outlines on the chalkboard. When the whole class pools its decisions and the outline is completed, Mrs. Sharp says:

"Now, who thinks he can use this outline to tell us in his own words what he read? Billy? As Billy tells us, let's listen to hear whether he remembers the important things to say about the points we have listed."

The audience reminds Billy, at the end, of any big omissions.

"What have we learned today about reading material like this?" asks Mrs. Sharp prayerfully. "What did we do first?"

The result is a chart that may look like this, and becomes a guide in further reading:

> When we read for information,
>
> 1. we read the subheading and ask ourselves what it means.
> 2. we read the first part of each paragraph to see where the author is going.
> 3. we plan what the headings of our outline may be.
> 4. we read for the big message in each paragraph.
> 5. we think why the author told us the other things.
> 6. we write the big message of each paragraph and try to "hang our memories" on each one.
> 7. we review the outline and try to say to ourselves what the author told us.

The children who could not have read this material at all, have heard and seen the words as Mrs. Sharp has said them, as children have said them, and as they have been written in the outline. Now, using these same words, they write their own stories of the farmer individually, and with stick figures illustrate the meaning of each sentence. The room, of course, abounds with labelled pictures of manure spreaders, plows, and other concepts mentioned in the account.

The children have learned something about the way the author of one of their textbooks writes and something of how to read, but they have learned something else just as important. They have learned that in Mrs. Sharp's lessons you have to stay awake, because she not only gets you to do things but asks you to summarize what you did and how you did it. She not only has you discover something for yourself but makes you use the discovery. And Father says *he's* tired when he comes home from work!

Reading logically organized material

A little way ahead in the textbook Mrs. Sharp sees looming the study of large cities in the United States—one, Indianapolis. Here she sees some new problems and challenges to her teaching. A map of the plan of the city is placed artfully beside an aerial photograph of the same area—a prime opportunity to compare the two types of representation and to learn more about map symbols. In the article itself Mrs. Sharp sees three subheadings

—how the site for the city was chosen, how the city grew, and what the modern city is like.

If the children in her class were expert readers, she might simply give them these things to do:

Read this article and write down six reasons which the author gives for the amount of growth Indianapolis has achieved. (main points)

Outline the functions of this city in the life of the people of Indiana, as given by the author. (important facts)

What does the author not tell which you think important to know? (Measuring content against ideal image of a city.) Where could we find answers? (Reference resources.)

Decide whether or not you think the original plan for Indianapolis was a good one. Defend your point of view. (Matching facts with purposes.)

If she thought the children needed stress on sequence and main ideas, but were fairly capable of sensing sequences and main thoughts, she might give a scrambled list like the following:

Match the following statements with the ten paragraphs in the article on Indianapolis, and rearrange the statements in proper order:

> Roads lead to the city.
> People come for trade and entertainment.
> Manufacturing is carried on.
> A committee is appointed.
> People move in.
> The city outgrows the plan.
> Store owners save time and effort.
> Wholesale business is carried on.
> A plan is made.
> East-west cities are joined.

A top-notch high school student might be able to take the simple assignment: "Read this article and take notes on its important points. Find answers to the exercises at the end of the article. Be ready to tell why you think the author chose this particular city to write about. What did he omit in his effort to stress his major points? See what more you can find out for yourself about this city and be ready to make a special report, citing your references for the statements you make."

Actually, Mrs. Sharp does differentiate assignments according to the abilities in her class. But most of her pupils still need careful guidance, just as many at all levels do. So what does she do?

She gives the pupils who still need careful guidance a guided reading lesson in the material. They open the book to the index to find the pages on which there will be material about Indianapolis. Then, turning to the first page listed, they look at the two illustrations, the map and the aerial photograph.

"What do you see in these two pictures that is alike?" Mrs. Sharp asks.

"What is the difference between the *picture* of the railroad tracks and the *map* of the railroad tracks? Who will come to the board and draw real tracks and then map tracks, to show the difference?

"How are the buildings different in the map from the way they are in the picture? Where do the names of the buildings appear on the map?

"This map shows the plan of the original city. How does the map show the limits of the original city?

"In what direction do the streets run? In what direction do the avenues run?

"How can we tell how long and how wide the original city was?"

In this way, Mrs. Sharp has the children notice the features of the map, the location of labels in relation to the objects named, and the meaning of the key to the interpretation of symbols for streets, railroads, buildings, and parks, and for the scale of miles. (The children find Indianapolis, also, on a map of the Central States, on another page in the text. There the city has become a dot.)

The first paragraph reads like this:[1]

> *Choosing a place for a city.* The city of Indian-
> apolis owes much of its growth to the fact that it
> was planned and built to serve as the capital of the
> state. Soon after Indiana became a state in 1816,
> the legislature appointed a committee to find a
> place near the center of the state for a capital city.
> At that time few people lived in central Indiana,
> but they felt sure that their state would grow and
> would need a fine capital.

"The story of Indianapolis given here is packed with important information. We shall read it slowly together and think carefully about the ideas. Read the heading of the story to yourselves. (Indianapolis: Trade Center and State Capital) What does the heading say? What does it mean, Trade Center and State Capital?

"Now let us read to ourselves the heading of the first paragraph. What does it say? What does it make you wonder?"

The children suggest that it makes them wonder who did the choosing and why it was chosen. (Mrs. Sharp writes *who* and *why* on the chalkboard.)

"The first sentence tells us why it was chosen. Read it to yourselves and be ready to tell what you find."

Joel says that it was chosen for a capital of the state.

"What is the capital of our state?" asks Mrs. Sharp. "What is a capital for?"

[1] Katheryne Thomas Whittemore, *The United States and Canada.* Boston: Ginn and Company, 1957, page 54.

Then she continues, "The first sentence gives a hint of something else about Indianapolis. What happened to it because it was planned to be a capital?"

Billy says, "It grew to be a big city."

Mortimer says, "The picture shows it grew bigger than its plan."

"Now let's find out who did the choosing and when they did it. Read the next sentence," says Mrs. Sharp.

The children find out that a little after 1816 a committee was chosen by the legislature. They recall the meaning of *legislature*.

"What is the importance of 1816 to Indiana?" asks Mrs. Sharp. "What were the conditions in this part of the country in 1816? What did becoming a state mean to people living here?" (If the children lack the background to answer, Mrs. Sharp shows pictures of the country in those days, to suggest problems of the time.)

"The last sentence," says Mrs. Sharp, "answers another important question. This time, read the sentence and be ready to tell what question you think it answers." Here Mrs. Sharp is attempting to sharpen the children's awareness of the fact cited, by forcing them to focus on it in the formation of a question.

Isadore volunteers, "It tells why people thought they needed a capital."

Esther says, "They just believed it would grow. They didn't know for sure."

"Were they right?" asks Mrs. Sharp.

Mortimer agrees. "The picture shows they were," he says.

The teacher does not go over every paragraph in such detail. She does this only if she sees that the children need to think carefully of the meaning of the sentences. Similarly, she does not introduce new words unless she knows that the children are going to have difficulty with them. Nor would she ordinarily plow through a whole school year at this snail's pace. She knows, however, that children who do not learn to ask questions as they read, who do not stop to sense the important meanings the author is giving, who do not look up words that recur and are crucial to meaning, are never going to learn independence in reading this kind of material.

"I am going to write three questions on the board," explains Mrs. Sharp, "and then I shall ask you which sentence in this paragraph answers each one."

She writes: *Why? What? How?*

In the discussion which follows, the children point out that the first sentence tells what was done, the second tells how, and the third tells why.

"This is like a newspaper article," says Chester. "It tells who, when, where, what, right in the first paragraph." A lovely lead for related work!

A sleeping dog is never comfortable in Mrs. Sharp's room. She throws out such challenges as, "Here is a book about early days in Indiana—

about a boy and a couple of bear cubs," or, "We've found in the table at the back of our text the 1955 estimate of population in Indianapolis. Let's see whether we can find still later information, to see whether it is still growing," or, "The map of Indiana in our text shows us something about Indianapolis that the story didn't tell us. I wonder who can find it," or, "The text leaves out some pretty important things about the way people in Indianapolis live. What are some of those things? How do you think we could find out from boys and girls living there today?" When the month of May comes around, she doesn't let them forget what they found out about Indianapolis. They search the sports pages for the outcome of the Speedway race. All of these reading-thinking activities build reading skills.

Meeting Additional Reading Needs and Interests

The basal reading instruction introduces children to a wider variety of materials than they would be wise enough to select for themselves. It whets the appetite for more stories on the same topics or by the same authors. There must be time in school for finding such stories and time to read them, particularly if the homes from which the children come provide little room or time or encouragement for such activities. Moreover, children frequently need help in choosing and reading the materials they select on their own, and a teacher or someone else must be on hand to give that aid.

Basal instruction has also, along with reading in the content fields, revealed some special needs peculiar to each child, and these require attention, either by the teacher in individual conference or by the teacher meeting a small group of children having similar needs. There must also be follow-up by the child in independent activity and occasionally in a team with another child to overcome the difficulty. And then there must be time to go over the work with the child to see progress and to define next steps.

Reading in the content fields has raised a thousand questions for which the child is eager to find answers. There must be time to find these answers, help in locating them and reading them, and in preparing and making reports on the findings.

Besides these needs and interests, a child has hobbies and curiosities and "passions" that are all his own, and problems he will not speak about to anyone. A child's concerns are a little like fish in a pond. Some splash about near the surface for everyone to see. Some hide in the shadows and never come up, no matter what. The school must provide scope for the child's explorations and help him find the satisfaction he needs, through reading. Mrs. Sharp, from years of watching children and parents, has developed X-ray vision. It is rumored that once she even dropped a book so that the right child would have to pick it up! (Thereafter she may, of course, have given a five-minute lecture on the care of books.)

Time for these activities

How can the teacher find time for all these activities? By being realistic. Some of the children's activities will be social studies or science. Some will involve art or music or even dance. Some are writing or dramatizing or reporting or learning the meanings of words. These are activities of "other subject fields" and can legitimately be done in their time. Basal-reader instruction will account for only two or three reading periods a week at this level, so that periods on two or three other days a week may be scheduled for these other activities. This is what Mrs. Sharp does.

Selecting books for the classroom collection

Because she used the log of children's out-of-school activities early in the term, Mrs. Sharp formed some idea of the interests of the children even before she had parent conferences or telephone conversations for this purpose. The children discuss some of their hobbies and club activities and the things they like to read. As one outcome of such talks, groups of interested children go to the library on special assignment and return with an armload of books on the "Hobby of the Week." Or perhaps the science table some day sprouts a display of rocks from various children's collections, all labelled, and a group of books about rocks, such as Fenton and Adams' *Rocks and their stories*. Above the display is a sign which reads, "Rock Hounds of Room 26." Children interested in rocks have planned the display, and today they present a program for the rest of the class, introducing their friends to their special interest.

Gleanings from children's essays on "If I Had Three Wishes," autobiographies, and other clues, help Mrs. Sharp to identify some of the deeper needs of the children in bibliotherapy. Sometimes she brings a group of books in from the library, reads a bit out of each or tells a little about each or shows pictures, to suggest the flavor and then says, "Who would like to be the first to read it?" (First! Maybe no one wanted it at all, but *now* he does!) The book is held out to the group and somehow, on purpose, finds the hand of the child who needs it most. Sometimes on the bulletin board a waiting list for a certain popular book is posted.

So Annie Wong, who is sensitive about her "different" background, reads Baker's *Necessary Nellie* because she likes dogs, but finds in it proof that America is full of good differences that are nothing to be ashamed of. Jane Brown, whose father follows the crops, finds comfort during her short stay in Mrs. Sharp's room, reading books about children of other migratory workers, like Gates' *Blue willow*, and Lenski's *Strawberry girl*. Agnes Schnook, who has been a little intolerant and snobbish toward crop followers' children, reads with some envy about the interesting experiences which she is denied by living in the same place all her life.

The children make an initial visit to the library in the fall to find books which they think they would like in their classroom collection. Each child chooses three books he thinks he would like. Later, in the classroom, the children organize the books on the shelves according to topic, and make labels for the shelves and cards for the classroom use of the books. One child becomes the librarian for a time, and another an assistant librarian, to keep the shelves in order and the card record of books which are taken out overnight. When interest in one book is exhausted, it is returned to the library and replaced by others of fresher interest.

Each week every child in the class has an opportunity to visit the library to hear a story told by the children's librarian. Sometimes only a portion of the class attends, while Mrs. Sharp gives special help to certain children, who get their chance later. Two or more children often go to the library on special assignment. Sometimes it is for reference work, sometimes to help the librarian set up a display. There is always in the library a special exhibit of things children have done in relation to their reading: shoe-box peep shows, pictures, brief reports, ceramic or pipestem models of characters, dioramas. Occasionally an ambitious person like Isadore writes and organizes a puppet show based upon a book he has read, presses his friends into service, and presents the show as a dividend to a group of children in the library alcove. (It is in this same place that the librarian assembles groups of intermediate-grade children every week to tell them stories and acquaint them with new books.)

Some children belong to a book club, each month receiving a book of their choice. By planning to choose different books on the list, they have a variety to read. For a time they share these with other children, putting them in the classroom collection.

When the weekly newspapers come in different editions of different levels, Mrs. Sharp helps the less able readers with the difficulties they encounter, and sets aside time for discussion of the news by the whole class. When the magazines to which the room subscribes come, the contents are quickly reviewed and a waiting list of eager readers is made up.

Motivating personal reading

Every day Mrs. Sharp reads something aloud. One book she may read in its entirety over a period of days. In order to be so strongly featured, the book is one with great appeal to both boys and girls, well written and worthwhile in content. Other books she may only sample. Of these she reads enough to make certain youngsters want to read more. Often, such books describe a series of incidents, after any one of which it is easy to stop.

One of her purposes, of course, is to keep the less able reader thinking that his efforts are approaching a rich reward. Another is to introduce children to the contribution which the sound of English words makes to meaning and mood. Another is to help them learn the delights of different styles and moods and topics, and to feel at one with characters of every time and clime.

For fun she reads Atwater's *Mr. Popper's penguins,* Cleary's *Henry Huggins,* McCloskey's *Homer Price,* Travers' *Mary Poppins.* For the feeling of pioneer country she dips into Brink's *Caddy Woodlawn,* Wilder's *Little house in the big woods,* and Dalgleish's *The courage of Sarah Noble.* For what civilization means to wild life she reads a snatch of Lier's *An otter's story.* For devoted horse lovers she reads a sampling of Henry's *The king of the wind.* Fanciers of red-blooded folk tales have a treat in Pyle's *Some merry adventures of Robin Hood* and the Andrew Lang edition of *Arabian nights.* Mrs. Sharp cultivates the imagination with E. B. White's *Charlotte's web,* and comforts those who can't quite take it with Brooks' *Freddy, the detective.* Children who feel that nothing ever happens to them get a bit of Enright's *The Saturdays* and begin to suspect that they, too, have something to write about.

"I have some friends," Mrs. Sharp says one day, "who, year after year, go to the same place for their vacation. They have no relatives in that place, and they have enough money to go other places. What do you think of that?"

"They must like it," volunteers Sadie.

"They're missing a lot," says Carl.

"Carl," asks Mrs. Sharp, "what do you mean by 'They're missing a lot?' "

"Well," he answers, "think of all the other places they might see— Yosemite, Grand Canyon, the Tetons." (Carl is in a rut himself,—all gorges and mountains.)

"Some people read books this way, too," says Mrs. Sharp. "They read all funny stories or all dog stories or all adventure stories or all outer-space stories. It is as though they built walls around their minds to make sure they wouldn't experience all that the world holds."

With such obvious propaganda she encourages children to read a variety of things, and to keep a personal record of what they have read so that they can see by the end of the year where in the world they have been. These records are more or less elaborate, according to the personality of the child. Ellen entitles hers, "Books I've Read," other-worldly Harriet writes, "These Are Now Part of Me," while Jack entitles his, "Looks at Books." He is the one who wrote on the cover of his *Dictionary for boys and girls,* "Dictionary for boys and girls and men and women and baby and you and me."

Other sources of motivation which Mrs. Sharp provides include a monthly "Saturday Review" which the children ditto themselves. The children contribute reviews of books they have read, grouping them by type of content. Two editors assemble the material, one who helped last month, and one who is new at the job. Every week the class holds a book club meeting. Everyone belongs to the club. The purpose of the meeting is to share some of the ideas gained, the reactions the children have had to the books. The programs are chaired by a different child each time, and are varied in the way they are run. Sometimes there is a symposium on horse books. Sometimes a child who has read about outer space writes his own story of an outer-space adventure and shares it with his classmates. A group of children who enjoy poetry may read favorites aloud, and then read some they have written themselves. Isadore and Billy, having read Adams' *The Santa Fe trail*, pretend that the class is the wagon expedition and involve it in a re-enactment of an episode from the book.

Developing standards

Mrs. Sharp, however, does not spend time in school for pure entertainment. She challenges the thinking of the children about the books they read.

"What makes a book good?"

"What makes a character good?"

"What are the things your listeners will be interested in?"

"What makes a plot good?"

Around the room begin to appear charts of things to bring up in discussing a book. Chairmen keep an eye on the charts as they guide panel discussions. The audience, participating after a panel is finished, points out omissions.

A book with an important message is not glossed over. Four children who have read Estes' *Hundred dresses* tell their impressions of the book. One boy who has read it is unimpressed.

"Oh, this girl keeps lying about the dresses she has."

The girls say, "Well, she hasn't a hundred dresses. She just says she has." "She wants to impress people." "She wants them to think she has but she hasn't."

To the audience it is so much mush. Clearly the children have missed the point. So Mrs. Sharp probes.

"Why did she say she had a hundred dresses?"

"How had the other children been treating her?"

"What were the reasons that they treated her like this, or that she felt as she did?"

"What was she trying to achieve by saying she had a hundred dresses?"

"What is important about people? Is it what they wear? Where they live? What they have? What is it?"

"How do you think you would have felt if you had been Wanda? What would you have done?"

Mrs. Sharp does not condone the lie, but she wants the children to understand the provocation and to think how in their own behavior toward classmates they can prevent the feelings that caused the lie. Mrs. Sharp isn't building just readers; she is building people, and she never forgets it.

Relating to basal reading and content fields

When during basal-reader lessons the children have been discussing the way an author describes a character or situation so that the reader feels he knows the person or has been in the situation himself, Mrs. Sharp says, "Let's be on the lookout for effective descriptions. Perhaps if we share some of the fine descriptions we read, we shall learn something we can use in our own story writing." Thus there is a carryover from a lesson in the basal reader, and a passing observation becomes a more permanent learning. Mrs. Sharp encourages observation of introduction of stories, problems which create the meat of stories, and ways in which the feelings of characters are revealed or the plot advanced.

Words continue to be fascinating. Sometimes the children agree to be on the lookout for verbs packed with special meaning, words whose choice in sound and rhythm add to the mood and meaning of a passage. Words new to them are frequently encountered. Sometimes everyone is asked to present a new word he found in his material, write it on the chalkboard, have students pronounce it, discuss how they think it might be used and what it might mean, then listen to the way it was used in the original sentence and decide whether the meaning is clearly indicated by the use. The child then shows the dictionary pronunciation and tells its dictionary meanings, as the class thinks which meaning is appropriate to the original sentence. Children make a conscious effort to use the new words sometime during the day.

The relationship between this part of the reading program and basal reading and reading in the content fields is a two-way street. Learnings from basal instruction and the content fields are consciously employed as children read materials of their own choice. But also, as the teacher notices problems in the free-choice reading, such as excessively slow reading, difficulty with word identification, and inability to draw conclusions from the material read, she sees to it that follow-up emphases are given in the basal instructional periods or in reading in the content fields.

Sometimes Mrs. Sharp finds, to her dismay, that although she and previous teachers have taught phonetic and structural principles with great care, a good many children in the class do not really apply these principles when they meet new words. She attacks this problem in several ways. One is the new word study, described a couple of paragraphs above. Another is that, finding several children with the same problem, she takes them aside for small group work on it. A third is that, in the time for basal instruction, she finds opportunities for teaching exercises to children who are working together on a common instructional level. A fourth is that, in introducing new words in the basal reader, she is careful to have children solve for themselves the words which they have the skill to solve, and to tell them the identity of a word only if she is sure they cannot get it for themselves. A fifth is that she has each child enter into a notebook of the principles he has learned, new examples of words following those principles. Thus he is forced to observe the principle and to remind himself of his knowledge of it.

The individual conference

Probably the most valuable part of the self-selection time is the time of individual conference. Each child as often as possible is given special attention by the teacher. Mrs. Sharp listens to Joe tell what he would like to read, and helps him find the book. If she thinks he is going to have some initial trouble with the vocabulary in it, she gives him background information and word study, just as though she were introducing a story in the basal reader to a group. Perhaps she assigns Billy to be at his elbow in case of further trouble.

Mrs. Sharp discusses the contents of a book with a child when he has progressed into it, much as she would with an adult. What is it about? Where is it supposed to have happened? Who are the main characters? What are the child's feelings about them at the present time? (Feelings change as the reader advances through a story.) When a child has finished a story, Mrs. Sharp discusses it in the same way, but adds such questions as, "What do you think the author was trying to say about people who . . . ? Why do you think he laid his story in . . . ? What were the problems in this story? What would you say was the high point in the story? What made it particularly so? Do you think this story would be true about all people who live in . . . ? Why or why not? When did the leading character feel the worst, the best? Why do you think so? Would you have felt the same? What did you learn about (the country) that you didn't know before? What did you learn about people that you hadn't thought much about before? Were there any parts in the story which you felt were especially well expressed?—tricks worth remembering for your own writing?"

Frequently by means of such questions, Mrs. Sharp causes the child to read a passage aloud. The child thinks he is conveying meaning to her, but he is also demonstrating the status of his oral reading. Sometimes they read a conversational part together in a sort of alternating duet. By listening to her expression the child begins to use more expression in his own oral reading.

The individual conference is also a time for looking over exercises the child has done, finding mistakes, and seeing what the trouble is, planning new attacks on the old problem. The child and teacher are a team in this situation. The child, with her help, finds out what his problems are and plans, with her, an attack on them. He knows that she will check on his progress again and that she expects and believes in his ability to achieve. In basal instruction and in reading in the content fields, he knows that she is aware of his special problem, and he is not surprised when she requires something of him in these other situations which relates to it.

Mrs. Sharp keeps notes on her work with each child. She is almost too busy to review these notes very often or very thoroughly, but she knows that when she writes something down, she remembers it better. Sometimes she has a burgeoning consciousness of the need on the part of several children for the same learning. In that case, she quickly reviews recent history to see which children these are.

The individual conference is not a hurried rat race because Mrs. Sharp knows that she can deal with Joe's problems in many situations during a day. She reserves for it only those activities which cannot be dealt with easily in group and whole-class situations. For example, if she knows that tomorrow one of the reading groups will be dealing with a problem which Joe has, she invites him to the meeting of that group rather than teaching him separately the day before. She knows, with some professional pride, that there is only one Mrs. Sharp, and that she must make the most of her by planning for the efficient use of her time.

Out-of-school activities

During the two or three days of the week in which reading time is devoted to basal instruction, children keep their self-selected books in their desks, to read when they have free time during the day, and take out for home reading. Mrs. Sharp remembers, however, that some children in her class come from homes of only one room, and sleep in beds which give 24-hour service to different members of the family. There is no room for books. There is no peace for concentration.

For the sake of such children, Mrs. Sharp has helped the church or settlement house provide and equip a room as a reading room. After school, a college student in the neighborhood, sometimes a mother or a social worker or the minister's wife herself, supervises the room to see that good reading conditions are maintained and to give a child help with his reading, if he needs it. The children who live close to the public library, of course, use its facilities.

When Billy is going to have a birthday, Mrs. Sharp does not wait for opportunity to knock twice. She lets his parents know about a book that would delight him. And when Christmas is coming, lists go home. At the approach of summer vacation, she propagandizes for summer reading programs at the library, and in the fall when the children drop past her room to report on their activities, makes much of the reading completed during the summer.

Summary

This chapter has described typical activities, exclusive of basal-reader instruction, which promote reading growth in the intermediate grades. It recognizes that individual differences must be taken care of by individual conferences and individual activities, by group activities, and by providing different levels of material for children of different reading levels. It recognizes, also, however, that children have certain problems in common, which can be met through group instruction or in whole-class activities.

The chapter has attempted to demonstrate, through detailed illustrations of techniques, the kinds of problems which children encounter in reading in the content fields, and the ways in which a good teacher may prepare for, meet, and overcome such problems.

The point of view of the writers is that a sound reading program in the intermediate grades requires (1) systematic basic instruction to a greater or less extent for every child continuously throughout the school year, according to his demonstrated needs, (2) the teaching of skills with equal care and thoroughness in the fields of arithmetic, science, and social studies, (3) and careful guidance and encouragement of the child's personal reading.

Suggested Activities

Select a textbook in arithmetic, science, or social studies, and try to plan some of the activities which Mrs. Sharp demonstrated in this chapter. Look through courses of study or textbook libraries for supplementary materials which might be used by children who could not read the assigned text.

What problems do you remember of your own in studying such materials?

Find out the reading interests and reading level of a child and list the books you might wish to introduce to him. If he has a personal problem, what books would you recommend to him, to help him clarify his thinking on it?

Choose a passage in a story which has considerable depth of meaning. Write down the questions you would ask to evoke the child's thought to that depth.

Selected References

BOND, Guy L., and WAGNER, Eva B., *Teaching the child to read*, 3rd ed. New York: The Macmillan Company, 1960, Chaps. 13, 14, 15.

DARROW, Helen F., and HOWES, Virgil M., *Approaches to individualized reading*. New York: Appleton-Century-Crofts, 1960.

Russell, David H., *Arithmetic power through reading*, in the Twenty-fifth Yearbook of the National Council of Teachers of Mathematics, *Instruction in arithmetic*. Washington, D.C.: National Council of Teachers of Mathematics, 1960, 208-223.

Strang, Ruth M., and Bracken, Dorothy, *Making better readers*. Boston: D. C. Heath and Company, 1957, part 5.

Taba, Hilda, and others, *Reading ladders for human relations*, revised edition. Washington, D.C.: American Council on Education, 1949.

24

Recommended Practices
in Seventh and Eighth Grades

George Wright teaches the seventh grade in a junior high school. He is the core teacher, the one who teaches a long period combining the social studies and the language arts. He feels lucky because, out of all the teachers in his school, he is the one who happens to have had a course in the teaching of reading. Result? He knows what he is about. Yet all teachers are responsible for the reading development of the students they teach. The math teacher has to meet the reading problems in math just as Mrs. Sharp met them in grades four, five, and six. The home economics teacher, shop teacher, music teacher, and the rest, also, have reading problems to meet. The central office of the school system has organized a series of meetings, by departments, in which teachers of a given field may come together to study ways of meeting reading problems in their particular area. Attendance at these meetings is compulsory for new teachers, optional for teachers on tenure. But, meanwhile, George feels lucky, and his students know that they are.

Practices similar to those in the earlier grades

Mr. Wright conducts his classes very much as Mrs. Sharp did in the intermediate grades. He recognizes that there must be basal instruction, instruction in reading in the content fields—in his case, social studies—and opportunities for independent reading. (This chapter will not deal in detail with these similarities, since it is assumed the reader will have read about them in the preceding chapters.) His problem is that he must provide this instruction for more students than Mrs. Sharp handled, and that he gets a chance to know his pupils as persons and to become acquainted with them during only about one-third of a teaching day. Mrs. Sharp had them all day. Another problem, of course, is that while Mrs. Sharp had frequent encounters with the pupils' former teacher, Mr. Wright, being in another building, blocks away from each of the three elementary schools which feed the junior high school, has little opportunity to seek advice from the former teachers of his numerous students. With less time, more students, and little contact with former teachers, Mr. Wright remains remarkably cheerful!

The students

Probably his buoyancy stems from his enjoyment of the age group with which he works. To many teachers (who have not taught first grade), seventh graders have a special charm. They bristle with the skills which a series of conscientious teachers has laboriously developed, they have energy and zest for many activities, they have learned a good deal about how to work in groups—indeed, are accustomed to it—and they are reading more avidly than they ever have before. Like many generalizations, this is in certain individual cases an utter falsehood; but it is true of so many students of this age group that Mr. Wright prefers to let this view dominate his attitude toward his job. Perhaps an even more delightful characteristic of seventh graders is that most of them have a receptive attitude toward learning.

"I would rather teach the seventh grade than be superintendent," declares Mr. Wright, and both he and the superintendent know how right he is.

Preparing to live together

Mr. Wright knows that he is a key figure in the junior high school. Students are going to judge what is expected of them in behavior and endeavor during the junior high school years, according to the way he treats them. If he initiates everything, if he deals with them as a whole class, if he assumes they have lost their skills of group work and teacher-pupil planning, they will soon become irresponsible, work-dodging, teacher-baiting nightmares. Somehow he must get close to each student and beguile the best out of him.

He purposely has no books in evidence the first day of school. He asks the students in each class to help him with suggestions of the kinds of books they would like to have for pleasure reading, and the reference books they think they will need for social studies. Between whole-class discussion and individually written responses, he obtains ideas about the breadth of interests in the class and the kinds of reference reading which they learned in the elementary school. By having each student write the name and authorship (if he remembers) of the last book he read that he liked especially, Mr. Wright senses the level of taste as well as the kind of interest. A discussion of books read and enjoyed during the summer brings out further evidence. What newspapers and magazines do they read regularly? What parts of them do they read? These are all clues to the readers who sit before him.

Talking over the kinds of activity to be included in his course, Mr. Wright says, "If we are going to do our best this year and get the most out of it, we are going to have to live by certain rules. When we have group work, what are we going to have to be careful about?" With the students he sets up rules for conduct during silent-reading periods, during group-work periods, during whole-class periods. If one class thinks of a rule no other class has mentioned, he brings the rule to the attention of the others, who endorse it and add it to the list. These rules are written on charts and permanently displayed in the room. When a violation occurs, sometimes a strong look at the student and a glance at the chart are enough. Some-times, the whole class must stop and review the situation. Sometimes, a talk with an individual student settles it.

The nice thing about Mr. Wright is that he does not have a punitive attitude. He makes the students feel that he thinks they want to learn, want to help each other and be considerate of each other. When a child mis-behaves, Mr. Wright talks with him about it in this spirit: "How can you *avoid* doing this another time?" He encourages him for later good behavior. "Good work," he says. "Keep it up." Little by little, Mr. Wright shows himself to be fair but firm, reasonable but tenacious about his expectations. A class spirit of supportiveness begins to bolster him, and a good environ-ment for reading is established.

The presence of books in the room creates the need for a library com-mittee to see that the books are in proper order. Monitors for various classroom routines are appointed. Materials needed for certain purposes are put in places in the room most convenient for use in the related activity. Seeing his room organization, a visitor knows that Mr. Wright is not one to stand in the tub wondering which foot to put out first, or one to spend time deciding which shoestring to tie first. In both home and school life, Mr. Wright has organized and established routines so that he can give full attention to things that are really worth it. By example he is show-ing students how to form a habit of making the most of their abilities.

Diagnosing reading level

For diagnosing the reading level of each student in the social studies material used in the class, Mr. Wright has made up a test like that described in Chapter 12, selecting short excerpts from the easiest, the average, and the hard books available in that field and asking questions that will test vocabulary and comprehension. The cumulative record card sent him from the elementary school tells which basal readers the student has been taught. This information gives him a rough idea of the probable reading level on which this student should receive instruction. If this information is not available, or if he doubts the appropriateness of the levels at which the students have already received instruction, he administers a diagnostic test which includes as a feature passages of increasing difficulty (The sixth-grade readiness tests accompanying the basal readers of certain series do this.) Or, he has students select passages from the S.R.A. *Reading Labora-*

tory, (See Appendix), or similar material, and answer questions on it, continuing to higher and higher passages on a sampling basis until they come to a passage which is too difficult to read without help. Just below this point is their probable instructional level. (The risk the teacher takes here is that the S.R.A. passages will not exactly correspond to the books he will use, in difficulty of vocabulary and structure of composition.)

Assessing speed of reading

Having each student select a passage which he can read with success, Mr. Wright gives each student a speed test.

"When I say, 'Begin,'" says Mr. Wright, "start reading your selection. When I say 'Stop,' mark the place lightly with a pencil, and count the number of words you have read."

He gives the students two minutes to read. They count the number of words and divide by 2, finding the number of words per minute. The students make a note of this speed in their notebooks. Mr. Wright makes the same notation in his record of each student. Periodically he will give such timed tests, so that the students can see what progress they are making in rate of reading. However, the student is urged not to read so rapidly during the test that he cannot answer the comprehension questions correctly. His score on these questions is also included on the record.

By means of such tests, Mr. Wright encourages students to read rapidly when the material is easy and when their purposes are not of a detailed study-type. But by these means he also identifies the student who reads everything much more slowly than his comprehension warrants, the one who reads carelessly, and the one whose speed and comprehension are well developed. He sees how much he can expect of some students in assigned reading, how little of others.

Assessing skills development

In addition to speed and level of reading, Mr. Wright has to find out how well developed the students' word recognition, word meaning, comprehension, interpretation, and study skills are; how well they read aloud. Some of this information he derives from tests, such as the basal-reader readiness tests for sixth grade, some from review tests in workbooks and manuals of the reader series he uses. To the extent that it is possible, Mr. Wright enlists the students' help in marking and evaluating the tests. While other students read books of their selection, to discuss with him when their turn comes, he interviews a student about his test results, and plans with him a personal program of attack on his deficiencies.

Sometimes he suspects that a review by the whole class of a particular area of learning will refresh students in what they know, while it informs him of generally shared gaps in certain areas.

"I am going to write some words which you have never seen before. They will be phonetic spellings of words you know. What do I mean by that? . . .

"When I write the word, sound it out to yourself, and think whether you have heard a word like that before. Don't voice your word, because everyone should have the chance to do his own thinking. Ready?"

He writes *biet* on the chalkboard.

"Who knows what this word says? Albert?"

"Beet," says Albert.

Mr. Wright has him use it in a sentence: "I was red as a beet."

Mr. Wright writes *beet* on the chalkboard, as Albert dictates the spelling.

"It could be another kind of beat," says Jack. "My team *beat* yours."

"How is that spelled?" asks Mr. Wright. Jack spells it and Mr. Wright writes it.

"Now think carefully," warns Mr. Wright. "What things do you know about word sounds that made you know what my word said?"

Students bring out the facts that the word begins with the *b* sound, like *box* and *band*, ends like *bit* and *bat*.

"What about that *ie* sound?" asks Mr. Wright. "How did you know what it said? What vowel does it sound like, by the way?"

The students say that it has the long *e* sound, and is spelled *ie* as in *field* and *believe*. Tom says that the sound should be long *i* as in *tie*. But Joe reminds him that the *i* is long because of a *final* silent *e*. In *biet,* the *e* is in the middle of the word, very much alive.

To check some of the nonparticipants, Mr. Wright presents another word: *biest,* and has other students tell how they solved it. He begins to sense who knows and how many know and who is uncertain.

"I am going to give you a piece of paper, now, with some words listed on it. After each word, you are to write the word you think it sounds like."

By this means Mr. Wright reviews students' knowledge of sounds and of principles governing them. If there seems to be a general lack of ability to apply this knowledge, he administers a thoroughly diagnostic word-analysis test, such as the *Roswell-Chall* or the *McCullough Word Analysis Tests,* to pinpoint the nature of the need. Do the students hear the consonant and vowel sounds? Do they know which letters make the sounds? Can they blend the sounds and apply the rules? Do they pronounce these sounds accurately in the first place?

(If you, the reader, are ready to fit into Mr. Wright's shoes, you should know words which sound like these: trak, groop, sturn, chare, crall, flud, praze, sleap, smawl, frend, shert, bleass, skil, spayd, plou, scowt, quien, cleen, thaught, bruze, whot, gloe, thoa, drewp, swai, knoock, phor, schar, streight, throwt.)

Each student, with the teacher, goes over the results of the tests. For example, in the *McCullough Word Analysis Tests* booklet on administering the tests, there is a chart beginning like this:

	Test IV	Test I	Test II	Test III
1.	trak	1	3	2

If the student missed *trak,* the teacher looks at Item 1 in Test I to see whether the student knew the sound which *tr* makes, at Item 3 in Test II, to see whether he could hear the short *a* sound, and at Item 2 in Test III to see whether he could tell which vowel made the sound (short *a*). Of course, chance errors and successes make such observations of doubtful reliability, but they are better than nothing, which is Mr. Wright's alternative. If the student failed one or more of these items, Mr. Wright sees what the probable trouble is. If the student has them all right, but still missed *trak,* Mr. Wright narrows the possibilities down to inability to use the knowledge by blending, or ignorance of the English word *track.* Often he finds that, although some students come with an excellent knowledge of phonics, they do not apply it. When this is the case, he seizes every opportunity to put them into word-solving situations. And there are plenty of them in the new vocabulary of the social studies.

Teaching the Class

Just as previous teachers of the earlier grades have done, Mr. Wright looks at all the data on the students and makes a plan of attack on their difficulties. The difference is that he can enlist their help in teaching each other and in taking more initiative in their learning. He uses the same techniques and principles previous teachers have used, but he expects students to engage in more independent efforts, evidence of which they then show to student helpers and to the teacher.

Materials for skill building

The students in one of his classes are variously ready to read at third-, sixth-, and seventh-grade levels. So, for basal instruction Mr. Wright chooses the seventh reader from the series most of those now at seventh-grade level have had in the previous grade. On a similar basis he selects readers for the other groups. Because he wishes as much as possible not to insult the lowest group with immature content, he chooses a book like *Just imagine* or *Fun and fancy* for their basal reader, for these readers are of third-reader difficulty and are consistent in method and expectation with other readers of the series in which they are found (Scott, Foresman; Ginn) but appeal well beyond the grade level in content.

Each of the three newspaper publishers in his area co-operates with the schools by delivering a free copy to each seventh-grade classroom every

Friday. These newspapers become the material for lessons on news reading, propaganda analysis, vocabulary development, composition, and paragraph structure. For students clearly unable to read the adult news, Mr. Wright uses newspapers issued especially for schools, such as *Newstime.*

Mr. Wright uses the workbooks belonging to the basal series as skill-building materials in basal instruction. For individual cases and some whole-class activity Mr. Wright uses such additional materials as the *Reader's Digest Skill Builders,* Gates' and Peardon's *Practice exercises in reading,* Guiler's *Reading for meaning* (different levels of which can be used by an entire class), N. B. Smith's *Be a better reader* (which reviews major skills in material representing the major content areas), and study-skill builders like S.R.A.'s *Study Skills Kit.*

For reference skills Mr. Wright has copies of a senior high, junior high, and elementary dictionary, an encyclopaedia, an almanac, an atlas, maps, and a globe.

Attention to principles

One of the major emphases in his teaching at this level is upon the principles governing a situation. In word learning, he encourages students to observe carefully from left to right, to say the word in syllables slowly, looking at the parts as they do this, and to write the word from memory, thinking the parts. If a student can do without some of these steps, he does; but Mr. Wright makes sure that the student knows how he best learns, and uses that method.

Knowing that story material is built upon one or more problems and developed through the solution of them, the students talk in terms of problems. Knowing that English words are derived from various languages, they identify new words by the telltale signs of their origin. Knowing that contexts reveal word meanings in several distinctive ways, they identify the context by type (See Chapter 6). Knowing that word structures are unitary or affixed, they learn to recognize a word as a base form which cannot be fragmented, as a compound, or as a form which has been given a prefix or suffix. Knowing that there are various types of paragraph structure, they begin to identify a paragraph by type (See Chapter 12). A chart in the room may read:

What Kind of Paragraph Is It?

Does it list or enumerate?
Does it relate or show time-sequence?
Does it compare ideas?
Does it explain an idea?

Thus, many lessons are concerned with the signals by which a student can be alerted to the kind of material he is encountering, and the ways of handling each type.

Word meanings

In the intermediate grades Isadore was a lone scout in reading books like Laird's *Tree of language* and delving into the dictionary for the derivations of English words. Now it is everybody's business. In the elementary school the children learned that when words are broken up into syllables, words beginning with *be, de, pro, pre, con,* etc., are usually divided after the last letter of those forms. Now they find out something new.

Mr. Wright says, "I am going to write some words on the chalkboard. Be ready to tell me what you think they mean."

He writes: *demand*
         decay
         defrost

Bill says, "When you demand something, you say you have to have it."

Alice says, "Decay means to rot."

Bruce says, "Defrost means to take off the frost."

"In an adult dictionary," explains Mr. Wright, "right after the pronunciation of the word, you will find brackets (he draws them to show what he means) around something. It is an explanation of the foreign words from which the English words we use were derived. What do you notice about these three words?"

"They all begin with *de,*" offers Geraldine.

"Tomorrow," warns Mr. Wright, "I'm going to ask you what you found out about the derivations of these words in a dictionary for adults. Besides, I'm going to expect each of you to be smart enough to find another word beginning with *de,* which has the same meaning for *de* that these words have. Any questions? Mortimer, what are you going to do?"

Mortimer tells, and everyone has it straight. Tomorrow the students show up with their loot. Demand—to get a commitment *from*; decay—to fall *from*; defrost—to take the frost *from*.

The class does similar work on other forms, and each student keeps in his notebook a section on what he is finding out about words. Then Mr. Wright is ready for the next shock and discovery. With the now known prefixes, he puts a common Latin root.

"We have learned about many prefixes lately," he begins. "Without looking into your notebooks, let's see how many prefixes and meanings for them we can remember."

As the students name them, Mr. Wright has another student write them on the chalkboard. Students suggest any corrections of the writing which may be necessary.

"Now I am going to see whether you can learn something from these prefixes."

He writes: *import*
    export
    transport
    report
    deport

"What do these words mean?" he asks.

The students tell what they think. The wording is varied.

"What are you noticing about these words?" he asks.

The students see that the root is the same in all of these words.

"What do you suppose that root means?"

There are guesses.

"How could we find out? . . . Tomorrow I am going to ask you what you found out about all of these words in the brackets after the words in the dictionary. Also, without saying anything to anyone else, be ready to tell me a word with that root and a suffix, and what it means."

The students, of course, come back with the knowledge that *port* is from the Latin meaning *to carry* (*portare*).

"The nice thing about knowledge is that it's *portable,*" says Ricky. Mr. Wright enjoys the joke because he knows that the creative act, even a joke, makes learning more memorable. Besides, he thinks it wasn't bad.

Mr. Wright doesn't carry the whole burden of teaching his students Latin roots and prefix and suffix meanings. He assigns certain roots and prefixes to different students who, one by one, take responsibility for presiding over an exercise similar to the ones he has presented. This means that all of his students have to use the dictionary and study the roots and prefixes and learn the method of discovery. After all, it is *their* education, not his.

In their social studies reading, their basal reading, and their independent reading, the students are constantly encountering new words. To stimulate interest in learning as many as possible of these, Mr. Wright uses all the tricks of previous teachers in the elementary school. But in addition to these he makes students aware of the facets of word meaning. After a discussion of synonyms, the students decide that one thing they can consider about a word is what synonym for it they know. After a discussion of antonyms, they now add the antonym idea. Soon a chart in the room and a page in their notes remind them that when they encounter a new word and discuss it in class, some good questions to consider are: What is a good definition of it? What is a synonym for it? What is an antonym for it? Does it have more than one common meaning? Has it a technical meaning in math, science, etc.? What is its function? (A *chair* is for sitting.) What are its characteristics? (Four legs, seat, back, etc.) How is it related to other ideas? (A chair is *furniture, lumber,* something *manufactured,* often associated with a *table,* etc.)

Sentence meanings

"Who would like to act out this meaning for us?" asks Mr. Wright.

He writes: *He staggered into the room.*

Ricky enjoys the opportunity to stagger into the room, dramatically weaving his way.

Mr. Wright modifies the sentence: *Holding his head, he staggered into the room.* Someone else dramatizes this.

Again Mr. Wright modifies this: *Holding his head and grimacing with pain, he staggered slowly into the room.*

The students learn that modifiers modify, enrich the image. Many a dull day thereafter is cheered by a sequence of sentence modifications, planned by a student, expurgated by the teacher, and dramatized by various individuals in the class.

When a sentence creates a problem, it is written on the chalkboard, stripped of its modifiers, and built, in meaning, from the skeleton out.

Sometimes sentence interrupters are the villains: *When no one was about—and this was often—he played his ukelele.*

"What happened?" asks Mr. Wright.

"He played his ukelele," answers Joan.

"When did he do it?" asks Mr. Wright.

"When no one was about."

"What do you mean by *about*?"

"Near, around, close so that he could hear."

"What does that interrupting clause, 'and this was often,' do?" asks Mr. Wright. "What does it tell?"

"It tells how frequently he did it."

By discussing the questions that different parts of a sentence answer (when, where, how, why, who, what), Mr. Wright helps students see the function of each part, the principal message, and the way the modifiers suggest cause and effect, parallelism (while . . .), etc. As a label in the allotment of school time, he calls it oral and written expression, but he knows that it fosters better reading comprehension, too.

The meanings of sentences and paragraphs whose message is mainly emotional are discussed, too: *Her face turned scarlet. "I absolutely refuse!"* That she refused is important. The color of her face is, too. But the main point is that she *feels*.

"How does she feel?" asks Mr. Wright. Indignant, angry, insulted, etc.— whatever the preceding material along with one's own experiences would lead one to suspect.

Paragraph organization

The ease with which we follow the ideas of the author depends in part upon the cue words which establish the relationships between sentences and paragraphs. Yet many students fail to notice these cues. Mr. Wright forces attention toward them and a realization of their importance and nature by giving the students scrambled paragraphs to reorganize.

For example, in the preceding paragraph, *these cues* in the second sentence provide the cue to the relationship with the first sentence; and *toward them* and *their* in the third sentence again cue the student in to the relationship of the second sentence to the third. Now look at the sentences Mr. Wright presents to his students and see whether you can unscramble them:

"These sentences," says Mr. Wright, "belong in the same paragraph, but are out of order. Write the number 1 before the first, number 2 before the one which should be second, and numbers 3 and 4 before the ones which belong next and last. Then underline the parts of the sentences that made you know the order."

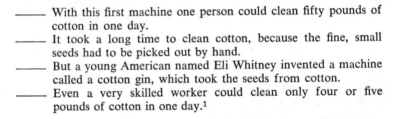

_____ With this first machine one person could clean fifty pounds of cotton in one day.
_____ It took a long time to clean cotton, because the fine, small seeds had to be picked out by hand.
_____ But a young American named Eli Whitney invented a machine called a cotton gin, which took the seeds from cotton.
_____ Even a very skilled worker could clean only four or five pounds of cotton in one day.[1]

It is quite possible that a student could reorganize the paragraph if he could read it, but cannot read the hard words in the material. So Mr. Wright chooses material carefully to be suitable to the skills of the students he asks to read it, and he has a volunteer read it aloud to everyone before all students start to work on it.

When the students are finished, Mr. Wright does not permit individuals to hide their opinions in the anonymity of the class. He asks, "What did you put down?" And he lists the sequence of answers (1342, 3214, 4321, 4132, etc.) and indicates with lines after each arrangement the number of students selecting it. He gets from the class practically every permutation and combination known to man! Doubtless, here is a class that needs to learn cues to paragraph organization.

The students discuss the cues: *this first machine . . . fifty pounds, long time . . . by hand, but . . . a machine, even . . . skilled worker . . . only four or five.* Taking those expressions and mating *machine* with *machine,* knowing that *a machine* would precede mention of *this machine,* that *hand* work came before *machine* work, that *but* indicates a change in direction (hand to machine), and that *even* introduces an example following a generaliza-

[1] Scrambled from page 174 in *Your world and mine* by Grace S. Dawson. Boston: Ginn and Company, 1958.

tion, they decide which arrangement is right After this exercise, each student knows whether he needs more exercise of this kind to heighten his sensitivity to sentence relationships within paragraphs, and the words which signal them.

This is another way Mr. Wright has students study structure: This selection comes from page 237 of Dawson's *Your world and mine* (ibid.)

Paris is also a great industrial and commercial center. Over a million people in the city and its suburbs are employed in manufacturing. Factories make machinery, tools, glass, chemicals, soaps, and automobiles. Smaller workshops produce leather goods, furniture, and the other fine products for which France is famous.

"What does the first sentence tell us?" asks Mr. Wright.

"What does the second sentence do for the first sentence?" It proves that the word *great* is appropriate, for over a million people are involved.

"What does the next sentence do?" It tells what kinds of manufacturing are done in factories. It gives concrete evidence of *manufacturing*.

"What does the last sentence do?" It gives more concrete evidence of the same thing.

"What would an outline of this paragraph look like?" asks the teacher. With the students' suggestions, he writes:

Paris—a great industrial and commercial center
  Industries
      employ over 1,000,000 people
      produce in
         factories
            machinery
            tools
            glass
            chemicals
            soaps
            automobiles
         smaller workshops
            leather goods
            furniture
            etc.

Once Mr. Wright has gone through such a process with the students, he gives another illustration and has them try it individually. Then outlines are compared and discussed. He is working on the principle that students must first have the help of the class and teacher in understanding a process before they try it alone, but that then they must try it alone to prove that they are learning, not merely enjoying a rest while others carry the class discussion. Students who cannot read such difficult material are given easier passages on which to learn. In fact, Mr. Wright usually chooses an easy passage for the whole class and then has groups and individuals turn to work at examples which are more appropriate to their levels of reading ability.

Gradually students realize that paragraphs illustrate all of the organized thought processes of which man is capable. Some ramble as the thoughts ramble in the wool-gathering mind. Others go like the crow to their pre-determined destination. But all can be classified by the type or hybrid type that they exemplify. Mr. Wright frequently reads paragraphs of selected types aloud, saying, "Be ready to tell me which kind, or combina-tion of kinds, this paragraph is." Sometimes, for example, it will be not only a time-sequence type but a cause-and-effect type as well.

Mr. Wright has the students take a further step in learning. He has them write paragraphs of designated types. Sometimes he hands out slips of paper with the first sentence of a potential paragraph of a particular type. Students write them. Then individuals read them aloud and others state what kinds they are.

A stand-up paragraph is popular. Five students volunteer to stand in a row. A topic is given. The first student gives a sentence containing the main idea. Other students in the row, in sequence, must give sentences which appropriately follow. The listening judges are severe as well as helpful.

Relationships among paragraphs are also a concern of the seventh grade. *Reader's Digest* passages, basal-reader passages, newspaper articles, and social studies articles from a textbook, all provide material for such exer-cise. Précis writing, the writing of a one-sentence summary of each para-graph, using cue words to show the relationships of ideas to each other, tends to clarify these relationships. Making titles for each paragraph and putting titles in outline form is another way of suggesting over-all structure.

The reverse process is illuminating also. Mr. Wright tries to have students realize that an article is merely the enlargement of a single thought, that the first paragraph usually introduces the thought, and succeeding para-graphs explain, justify, illustrate, or debate it, while a final statement con-sisting of one or more paragraphs comes to a conclusion regarding it— puts a period to it, so to speak. He gives the students a sentence and asks them to build a paragraph on it. Then he asks how the paragraph might be expanded, perhaps each sentence in it becoming the seed of another paragraph. Students find that, while a sentence may contain a world of meaning, to write paragraphs on the idea requires much more detailed knowledge.

Ricky, however, lets his imagination go in doggerel, and starts an epi-demic of verse writing which turns out to be a good discipline, for every line has to make sense and contribute to the thought. Meaning cannot be distorted for the sake of rhyme.

My Nice Dog

My dog is nice.
 His name is Butch,
And people like
 Him very much.

He's nice to Sal,
 He's nice to Flo,
And he's even nice
 To my Uncle Joe.

He wags his tail
 At Sal and Flo
And harder yet
 At my Uncle Joe.

What Ricky's rhyme may lack in literary quality it makes up in beat. Volunteers add verses, each of which *must* illustrate just one way a dog can be nice (such as not jumping on the sofa). Pete invents a tune, Rita brings a ukelele, and the principal is a little nonplussed when he pokes his head in the door and is told that the class is studying structural relationships in verbal material. Hmmm!

Refining thought processes

To see implications, to make correct inferences, to sense propaganda, to suspend judgment, to hold one's mind to the purpose of one's reading—these are disciplines important to the development of the mature reader. Opportunities for stressing these learnings lurk in every assignment.

One day the headlines in the three different newspapers are not only on the same topic but vastly different in the impression they give the reader. Mr. Wright has the students discuss each headline.

"What does each one make you think? . . . What will you have to look for in the articles to find out which is right, or if any is right?" And after the students have listened to the articles being read by other students and have noted the needed points, he asks, "What further evidence would you need to know for sure which is right? Where could you find it?"

Mr. Wright puts the students on the lookout for slanted news:

"This paper says the attorney intervened on behalf of his client," reports Evelyn.

"This other one doesn't say intervened. It says interfered," says Albert.

"What's the difference?" asks Mr. Wright. This remark sends students to the dictionaries and to conclusions about the attitudes of the different writers.

Facts are sifted from opinions: A "spokesman close to the President" is not the President. Furthermore, why is he not identified by name or position? Statements of fact are distinguished from value judgments: "He won the Olympics" versus "He is the greatest player of all time." Cause and

effect are examined: "If you want to ruin the country you will vote the
_____ ticket."

Another approach to the understanding of propaganda techniques is a
creative one.

"Suppose somebody borrowed your umbrella and brought it back to you
turned inside out. How would you write two sentences about that, naming
the person by his proper name—Jim, Bill,—?" The students write the information and read their sentences aloud for approval of the straight
reporting.

"Now, suppose you didn't like the person. Write your sentence from that
point of view." Again the students write.

"Now suppose you like him."

"What would you write if you think he is nice but clumsy with mechanical things? nice but careless? deliberately mean? unappreciative of the
value of what he ruined?"

Mr. Wright makes some attempts of his own, for the students to classify
according to the feelings he reveals by his wording.

One day Mr. Wright writes a statement on the chalkboard and asks
students to tell whether it is fact or opinion. The statement is: "Since the
new administration has been in office, 500,000 more people are out of
work." The students say that it sounds like a fact.

"We'd have to check to see whether it was true or not, though," Ed
reminds the class. "Somebody just might want you to think it."

"What if this statement appears in mid-June?" asks Mr. Wright. "What
happens in early June that sends a lot of new people into the world looking
for work, some of whom don't get jobs?"

"Graduation," says Isadore. "Some graduates get work and some don't."

"If there are more graduates looking for work than there are people
retiring from jobs, what happens?" asks Mr. Wright.

"What else besides graduation might affect these figures?" he asks. Such
matters as strikes, seasonal unemployment, the effects of automation are
considered. It is an easy step from this kind of analysis to the analysis of
the true situation behind the statement, "Since the _____s have been in,
governmental expenditures have gone up _____ billion dollars." The
teacher's purpose is not to develop students who discredit everything they
hear but students who are not satisfied with implied relationships and
oversimplifications or distortions of them. A chart developed by the students reads:

> Statements to be believed should be
> > accurate
> > fact, not opinion
> > made by reliable authorities
> > uncolored by emotional language or bias
> > not slanted by omissions

Developing sensitivity to effective writing (See Chapter 2.)

Mr. Wright uses contrast a good deal in his attempt to make students sensitive to effectiveness in writing. He also encourages students to find examples similar to those he has shown them and to make up examples of their own. By studying a particular type of quality at a time, and by learning or applying a term to it, the students are able to say, "This is a good example of vividness (etc.)" Mr. Wright often finds examples in the basal reader, and clues to them in the lesson plans appearing in the teacher's manual. These are some examples of his techniques.

"Here are two descriptions," says Mr. Wright. Read them to yourselves and be ready to tell me which gives you the better picture." He writes:

> He was a tall man in a uniform.
> A tall, dignified figure he was, in the familiar uniform of
>   blue and buff.

Lena volunteers. "The second one gives me the better picture."

"How many of you agree?" asks Mr. Wright. Everybody must think. "Why do you think it does?"

"It's longer," says Mortimer. Mr. Wright cringes within himself. Boob that he was to permit this difference, when he could have filled the first sentence with fluff: There he stood, a tall sort of man in a uniform of some kind. Well, he will make the best of it. "Even if it weren't longer, what else is different?" asks Mr. Wright. "What does the first one help you to see and know, as compared with the second?"

"Well," answers Julian, "both of them say he's tall and in a uniform."

Mr. Wright crosses out *tall* and *uniform* in both so that he won't keep getting answers like that.

Beverly says, "I see colors: blue and buff."

"And it says it's a *familiar* uniform," adds Peter, "not one of some other country."

"What else?" asks Mr. Wright.

Alice says, "He's dignified. That gives me the idea he is kind of—I mean, rather formal. He's holding himself straight and looking serious. Proper."

"What is a good word for what the second sentence has that the first one hasn't?" asks Mr. Wright.

"Color?"

"Detail?"

"The facts?"

Mr. Wright says, as he writes the word on the chalkboard, "The critics call it *vividness*. As you read today, find a good example of vividness to share with us, and be ready to tell why you think it is a good example."

Frequently Mr. Wright draws on the students' own experiences to clarify a concept.

"Have you ever had to go to a meeting of some kind just before you were to go to a movie or a dance or some other activity you had looked forward to?" asks Mr. Wright. Many heads agree. "In the story Billy was reading today, a character named Tom was in a meeting, and the author made this comment."

The teacher writes on the chalkboard: The bench seemed harder than usual.

"What did the author mean by that?"

Almost everyone in the class knows the answer. Joe speaks for all. "It was harder for him to sit in the meeting because he was so anxious to get to the next place where he really wanted to be."

"It was his attitude," concludes Isadore. "He *thought* the bench was harder."

"What is a word for his attitude?" asks Mr. Wright.

"Impatient."

"The author wrote about the hardness of the bench just to show what?" asks the teacher.

"He wanted to show how Tom felt about having to wait."

"This technique of saying one thing to reveal another," explains Mr. Wright, "has a special name." If no one can offer it, he writes it: *Suggestion.* "Good authors don't tell you everything. They give you a chance to fill in, to come to the correct conclusions from what they have said. Good authors describe things vividly, but they often suggest when they know that to explain in detail would be to state the obvious and insult the reader's intelligence. See whether you can find some good examples of suggestion today. Even if you don't happen to find an example in a book, you will probably be able to find one right at home in the things your family says."

The technique of suggestion is well understood in homes in which "Junior!" means, "Mind your manners," and "This rug just came from cleaners," means, "The first person who puts a spot on it is a dead duck."

Mr. Wright takes aside students who are temporarily or chronically puzzled, for further study of the technique, before he sends them off to find examples of their own in material he is sure contains obvious examples. Meanwhile, Isadore is not only finding examples but writing his own. He even makes up a special little plan which he tries on the class, describing a situation and then saying, "The author then might have said this or this. In which case would he have been using suggestion?" He has caught on to Mr. Wright's use of contrast. Step aside, Mr. Wright. Here come the Future Teachers of America!

Increasing speed of reading (See Chapter 11.)

Mr. Wright exposes all of the students to certain techniques of increasing their efficiency in reading. In introducing a textbook he spends at least one lesson on the SQ3R system, going through each step of the system and applying it to the reading assignment. Here is SQ3R: (S) The students skim with him through the headings and illustrations to size up the general nature of the content and general structure of the composition, (Q) they raise *questions* about the headings, one at a time, (R) give the material a first careful silent *reading,* (R) *review* the material to see whether the questions have been answered and the needed information has been identified, and (R) *recite* what they have found out, in the form most likely to be required. Students who do not catch this on the first bounce are given additional opportunities, sometimes working with Mr. Wright in a small group while others read assignments silently, sometimes one student working with another student who can show him how he does it, and sometimes a student working by himself, following an outline of the things he must do in relation to reading the particular assignment (a kind of programmed learning).

In a summer workshop on social studies, Mr. Wright used his textbooks to make plans for guided study of the introductory chapters, with poorer learners particularly in mind. He made tape recordings of what he would normally say, with pauses for the student's response, and worksheets on which the students could show that he was following the material and understanding. Using tape-recorder jacks and earphones, several students needing this help now sit in a corner of the room getting needed guidance in an assignment, while Mr. Wright is free to give individual attention to students of greater ability. Mr. Wright discusses the worksheet with them either before the period is over, or at the earliest opportunity, so that he can make sure his system is successful.

Further experience in skimming is given to all students in the course of many activities—finding a word in a dictionary, looking for the exact wording in an assignment previously read, looking through pages on a general topic for a subordinate topic dealt with somewhere in them.

When the students study different kinds of paragraph structure, Mr. Wright encourages quick inspection for the type of development. This may be rapid reading or actually a kind of skimming. For example, a passage may say: "The Soandsos made a kind of cake called _____ for their special feasts. First they . . . . Then they . . . . Finally. . . ." The students do not have to read it all to know that here is a recipe, but if they want to make the cake themselves, they had better reread carefully for facts and sequence. On the other hand, they may read: "The people of _____ were engaged in many different occupations. Some were . . . . Others. . . ." Here is clearly a paragraph of enumeration, of description, going nowhere in time but filling out a picture of occupations. Here they do not have to remember which occupation was mentioned first. They *may* have to remember which was predominant or unusual.

Using simple articles like those found in the *Reader's Digest* at different levels of difficulty, and seeing to it that the group using them has reading ability somewhat above that required by the articles, Mr. Wright gives students both speed and skimming experience. Sometimes he has them skim to find out one or two general ideas about the article, with, "Let's see who can tell me in less than two minutes." They read quickly through the first paragraph, and read parts of first sentences all through, then the concluding paragraph, if, by that time, they do not know the answers. At other times Mr. Wright has the students read several questions for which they must find answers in an article (only *important* details and important main ideas), while he writes on the chalkboard 1 .... 2 .... ticking off the minutes it takes them. Each student notes the time it has taken him to read for the answers, and records it in his notebook. Then he writes his answers, and the answers are discussed. If his answers are wrong, he draws a line through his notebook notation to show that he read too fast on that occasion. Next time he will have to go more slowly.

Mr. Wright also encourages the skimming of newspaper headlines and articles for specific purposes, and gives students chances to tell what their experiences with particular articles are—whether the headline was misleading, what the structure of the article was. An example is Gerald's report:

> I saw this big headline saying the Giants had beaten the Dodgers. I knew there would be a lot of guff at the first of such a long article, and I wanted to see just what the exciting plays were; so I skimmed down to a subheading that said, "How They Won", and sure enough, there it all was.

Mr. Wright advises students whose reading speed is clearly too slow for the quality of their comprehension and vocabulary knowledge, to do some exercises to increase their speed. He suggests books of light reading matter and also simple purposes for which the students might read them, a quiet place to do it when they are not too tired, and doing it for only a short period of time, such as fifteen minutes or half an hour. They can set an alarm clock and keep track each day of the number of pages they can tick off in this way. The results are often initially spectacular and encouraging. When this does not happen, Mr. Wright sends the student to practice in the reading laboratory (which may only be a well-lighted alcove in the principal's office) with a reading accelerator or similar mechanical device to force speed and concentration. The appeal and pace of a mechanical device and the forcing of concentration may jolt the stubborn case of Snail's Pace out of his rut. A session with this, at regular intervals, followed by the recommended exercises with light reading, may do the trick. Preferably this exercise is on the student's own time and does not take him away from other profitable experiences in the class, which he needs.

Summary

This chapter has dealt with some of the activities in which an upper-grade teacher engages to develop and improve reading ability. However, since good reading methods are applicable in more than one grade level, and since for the sake of brevity we have not repeated in this chapter what has been said in previous chapters that applies here also, the reader is encouraged to examine the two preceding chapters on grades four, five, and six, which deal in greater detail with basal instruction, reading in the content fields, and personal reading.

The teacher of the upper grades must diagnose his class for level of reading ability and skills development. Then he must, with the students, discuss what must be done to keep their skills growing and to improve sagging ones. He selects materials to help achieve these ends. He puts considerable emphasis on principles and techniques, so that students not only learn how to read but are conscious of the types of meaning and structure with which they are dealing. Both the teacher and the student keep records of the student's progress. In addition, the student takes notes on what he learns, in order to refer to them and to feel cheered by the progress they represent.

Writing, speaking, and listening activities support the reading program at this level, as they have before. Creativity is encouraged in making a learning "stick." (See Ricky's poem.) As before, also, speed is encouraged by natural means and deliberate exercise. In special cases, mechanical means are used in moderation both to beguile and hoist the student out of his rut.

Meanwhile, the student is receiving systematic basal instruction (See Chapter 22.), guidance by all of his teachers in reading in the content fields (See Chapter 23.), and help in selecting and in improving his selection of materials for personal reading (See Chapter 23.)

It is hoped that Mr. Wright's example has shown the reader that a teacher can be creative without violating either the principles of learning or what can be considered the firmly established principles of teaching reading.

Suggested Activities

Find in the library the latest booklist for junior high school students, published by the National Council of Teachers of English. It is probably under the title of *Your Reading*. First look through it for books you have read yourself, and try to recall what you enjoyed in them. Then select a few books from each interest category and read them. Try to put yourself in the place of a modern twelve-year-old, and watch as you read for the values this youngster is going to meet in these books and for the kinds of help (questions, proposed activities) he will need from you to realize these values.

Imagine that you are introducing one of these books to the class. How would you go about it. How *will* you?

Selected References

BOARD OF EDUCATION OF THE CITY OF NEW YORK, *Reading, grades 7, 8, 9: A teacher's guide to curriculum planning.* Curriculum Bulletin 1957-58 Series, No. 11. Brooklyn: Board of Education of the City of New York, 1959.

HILDRETH, Gertrude, *Teaching reading.* New York: Holt, Rinehart and Winston, Inc., 1958, Chaps. 17, 20.

JEWETT, Arno, ed. *Improving reading in the junior high school*, Bulletin 1957 Number 10, U.S. Department of Health, Education and Welfare. Washington, D.C.: U.S. Government Printing Office, 1957.

STRANG, Ruth M., and BRACKEN, Dorothy, *Making better readers.* Boston: D. C. Heath and Company, 1957, Parts 3 and 5.

—— McCULLOUGH, Constance M., and TRAXLER, Arthur E., *The improvement of reading*, 3rd ed. New York: McGraw-Hill Book Company, 1961, Part 2.

WITTY, Paul A., ed. *Development in and through reading*, Sixtieth Yearbook, Part I, National Society for the Study of Education. Chicago: University of Chicago Press, 1961, Chaps. 7, 8, 17.

25

Remedial Reading in the Classroom

The ever-present task of the elementary school teacher of reading is to identify the needs of individual pupils and to provide such remedial measures in the classroom as are called for. In order to do this the teacher must have a well-organized program of instruction, one that puts emphasis upon the prevention of reading disability, and she must be constantly alert to give individual help where it is needed. Although good teaching can and does reduce the incidence of reading difficulties, it could never eliminate them altogether. Even with the best of teaching, one or another child may fail to acquire some particular skill at the time it is taught to the others, and so later corrective work will be necessary. A child can fall behind in any one of the reading skills, or, as noted by Robinson (208), reading progress may be arrested at any stage in the sequence of development. So corrective or remedial reading will be needed wherever and as often as the progress of a child is blocked by one or another difficulty.

Responsibility for remedial work

The degree of difficulty in reading that a child is having determines who can most effectively give the remedial work. Such difficulties range from relatively mild and uncomplicated ones to those that are severe and complicated. There are ordinarily three places in which remedial work can be given: the classroom, the school reading center, and the clinic.

The classroom. The regular classroom teacher can and should give remedial instruction to the majority of children, for theirs will be the mild to moderate disabilities. The teacher will be limited to the solution of the less complicated reading problems by such conditions as the size of her class, her other responsibilities, and her lack of specialized training. Nevertheless, if she can employ good techniques of appraisal, is efficient in managing her class, and uses appropriate materials, she will be able to detect and correct most reading difficulties. But at times any teacher will require the help of an expert to aid her in diagnosing a particular case and in setting up the best possible remedial exercises.

The school reading center. Such a center, located right in the school, is usually a room well stocked with materials for reading and for special practice exercises. A technically trained remedial teacher is in charge. She works with small groups of children who need more specialized and individual attention than the classroom teacher can give. The size of the groups given instruction in these centers depends upon the needs of the children and the number of pupils in the school requiring exceptional teaching. If the groups are small, each child will profit more. But there seems to be little advantage in restricting groups to fewer than about 6 children unless their disabilities are rather severe. The remedial teachers who work in school reading centers need special training to qualify them to handle the variety of problems they will meet. It is desirable that they should be selected from among successful classroom teachers and then given additional training in the fundamentals of reading instruction and in diagnosing and treating reading disability. Besides their duties in the reading center, such remedial teachers will on occasion help in diagnosing the less complex reading disabilities and also offer the regular teachers suggestions for helping those children who are to be treated in the classroom.

The reading clinic. A reading clinic is usually located in a university, teachers college, or in the child-study center of a sizeable school system. The really complex and severe reading problems can be best diagnosed and treated in such clinics. These clinics are qualified to make more thorough diagnoses and to supply more intensively individualized treatment than can be obtained elsewhere (Bond and Tinker, 26).

Severe reading disability

When a child fails to respond to the best efforts of the teacher, a situation that may occur in any classroom, the origin of the difficulty may be complex. The causal factors may involve a physiological deficiency in hearing or vision, difficulties in emotional and personal adjustment, or the child may have been instructed by teaching techniques not suited to him. Ordinarily a pattern of factors, rather than a single cause is involved. The disability may have progressed far before the teacher recognizes how serious the condition is. Obviously the classroom teacher is not able to deal successfully with the more extreme cases. They should be referred to a specialist in remedial reading who is equipped by training and experience to handle such cases and who will diagnose the difficulty and carry out the indicated remedial work. In certain cases a complete diagnosis may be reached only after special physical or psychiatric examinations. In addition to the analysis of the child's handicaps in reading, the diagnosis includes the essential facts concerning his or her physiological condition, emotional adjustment, mental capacity, interest patterns, educational history, and background of experience. The diagnosis will state the most probable sources of the reading difficulty. Then the remedial program, based upon this diagnosis, will ordinarily improve the child's reading. It should be continued until the child is able to handle adequately the regular classroom work with only the normal amount of individual attention. The duration of the remedial work may vary from a few months to a year or more with various children. Although remedial reading consists of the type of developmental tutelage found in any good classroom program, the instruction and materials are in greater measure adjusted to the needs of a particular child and he receives more of the teacher's individual attention. The child should emerge from a course of remedial teaching with the greater motivation that comes with successful performance.

To qualify for diagnosing relatively severe reading disability and to do remedial teaching requires special training and clinical practice. Its precise description is a subject outside the province of the present book. Here we need only emphasize that the classroom teacher will occasionally encounter a severe reading-disability case. As soon as such a case is identified, or as soon as a reasonable length of time has elapsed during which a pupil fails to respond to the best efforts of the classroom teacher, she should refer the pupil to the appropriate specialist. For further discussion of severe reading disability see Bond and Tinker (26), and Harris (122).

Minor reading difficulties

In any reading program, a pupil may, and ordinarily does encounter minor difficulties such as deficiencies in word meanings or some inability to master the use of phonics as an aid to word recognition. Bond and Handlan (25) state that the detection and correction of such difficulties should be an essential part of individualized instruction in reading. As a matter of fact, teachers are rather consistently doing certain kinds of remedial instruction and we shall therefore devote space here to those aspects of remedial reading which should be carried out in the classroom. In a class of 30 pupils, the number and variety of individual difficulties that arise during the teaching of reading over a school year are large.

Understanding the Child

A sound basis for diagnosing the difficulties which pupils have in reading can only be found when the teacher is thoroughly acquainted with their capacities, physiological handicaps, if any, and their personality traits and behavior patterns. During the first few weeks of a school year, the teacher should as far as possible collect, assemble, co-ordinate, and study all the information she has available on her pupils. Some of this information will be passed to her from the teacher of the previous grade. Other materials will have to be collected by means of observation, inventories, and standardized tests. From a comparison of scores on mental tests and reading tests, the degree to which reading ability corresponds to capacity in each child is ascertained. The school nurse's or a doctor's report on hearing and visual status will indicate whether special seating and instructional adjustments are necessary to prevent interference with progress in learning. Data concerning the social and emotional adjustment in the personality of the child are obtained from information on home conditions and from teacher observation of adjustment to the school, to class participation, and to other pupils in work and play activities. Closely related to the personality structure are the behavior patterns arising from attitudes toward reading and toward the teacher as well as from the degree of self-confidence as expressed by individual responses and group participation. Observations of the child's interests, study habits, and work habits should be recorded.

These data constitute the minimum information she should have about the pupil. From time to time the teacher will find occasion to add other relevant items. Acquaintance with a pupil's record is not only useful in adjusting instruction to the individual, but it also provides an excellent fund of information which will aid in diagnosing and correcting the reading difficulties that arise from day to day and which the teacher should handle in the classroom. The fact that a teacher knows a child's capacities and his behavior and personality patterns will provide an *individual* slant to her diagnosis and corrective measures which are *more likely* to yield quick results than can be obtained with less complete information.

The above statement implies that a teacher through careful study of her pupils can come to know intimately their strengths and weaknesses, their behavior, interest, and personality patterns, along perhaps with other factors. Now the teacher, as a matter of fact, cannot find time for a thorough study of every child in her class each year. She can, however, realize the importance of the goal of a comprehensive understanding of the child. Furthermore, she can know some important facts about each child and, as opportunity occurs, extend her information. The more knowledge a teacher has about a given child, the more effective can be her diagnosis and correction of his difficulties. In any case, the teacher will ordinarily have accumulated enough material so that she has a fair background for understanding the major strengths and weaknesses of each child.

When to Do Remedial Work

Difficulties should be corrected as soon as they appear. Remedial work by the classroom teacher begins, therefore, soon after reading instruction is started in grade one and continues throughout the grades. The teacher's relatively frequent appraisal of pupil progress will reveal any lack of expected improvement. When in course of doing so, a difficulty is located, the reason for the deficiency is determined, and a technique for teaching what has not been learned is outlined and put into effect. Prompt detection of difficulties ordinarily makes their correction by remedial teaching relatively simple and easy. In most cases, all that is necessary is individual concentration for a short period on the specific needs of the child. In other words, group teaching becomes temporarily individual instruction until the child has achieved adequate mastery of the skill being taught.

Specific Difficulties

The child in difficulty is the one who is not progressing at the rate expected in terms of his capacity. If the class grouping is satisfactory, this means that the pupil is not keeping up with his group in learning a particular skill. A first step in diagnosis is to review the accumulated information about the pupil. This information on capacities and behavior patterns, as discussed above, will be helpful in both the diagnosis and in deciding upon the corrective procedures. With this basis, the teacher now searches for reasons why the child is not learning the specific skill that is being taught.

Within any class it is to be expected that there will be a wide range of proficiency in any aspect of reading and that there will be grouping for instruction. Where two or more pupils are deficient in a specific skill, as in some phase of word-recognition techniques, it is frequently desirable to form a special group for appropriate remedial instruction. When this is done, there is still need for adjusting instruction to the individual needs of pupils in this special group. In fact it is likely that part of this instruction will have to be individual teaching of a single pupil. Except for the instruction to remedy a specific deficiency, the pupils participate in the activities of the group to which they are regularly assigned.

After discovering that a child is in difficulty, therefore, prompt diagnosis of the deficiency and plans for remedy are in order. In addition to the observations of daily responses and teacher evaluation of progress noted above, the teacher may employ various aids in her diagnosis. These special aids are used to gather additional and more specific evidence concerning a difficulty tentatively inferred from the day-by-day evaluation of progress.

The basic sight vocabulary

The habitual responses of the child may suggest he lacks an adequate sight vocabulary. The status of his sight vocabulary is readily checked by means of the Dolch basic lists (62) given in Tables 4 and 5. Children with second-grade reading *capacity* should know about half of these words and those with third-grade *capacity* should know practically all of them. When a child is found deficient, the words he does not know can

Table 4
The Dolch Basic Sight Vocabulary of 220 Service Words[1]

a	could	had	may	said	under
about	cut	has	me	saw	up
after		have	much	say	upon
again	did	he	must	see	us
all	do	help	my	seven	use
always	does	her	myself	shall	
am	done	here		she	very
an	don't	him	never	show	
and	down	his	new	sing	walk
any	draw	hold	no	sit	want
are	drink	hot	not	six	warm
around		how	now	sleep	was
as	eat	hurt		small	wash
ask	eight		of	so	we
at	every	I	off	some	well
ate		if	old	soon	went
away	fall	in	on	start	were
	far	into	once	stop	what
be	fast	is	one		when
because	find	it	only	take	where
been	first	its	open	tell	which
before	five		or	ten	white
best	fly	jump	our	thank	who
better	for	just	out	that	why
big	found		over	the	will
black	four	keep	own	their	wish
blue	from	kind		them	with
both	full	know	pick	then	work
bring	funny		play	there	would
brown		laugh	please	these	write
but	gave	let	pretty	they	
buy	get	light	pull	think	yellow
by	give	like	put	this	yes
	go	little		those	you
call	goes	live	ran	three	your
came	going	long	read	to	
can	good	look	red	today	
carry	got		ride	together	
clean	green	made	right	too	
cold	grow	make	round	try	
come		many	run	two	

[1] Reprinted with permission of the author and the Garrard Press.
These basic service words may be taught with the Basic Sight Vocabulary Cards or with the Group Word Teaching Game (both published by the Garrard Press, Champaign, Ill.).

Table 5

The Dolch List of Ninety-five Common Nouns[2]

apple	dog	horse	Santa Claus
	doll	house	school
baby	door		seed
back	duck	kitty	sheep
ball			shoe
bear	egg	leg	sister
bed	eye	letter	snow
bell			song
bird	farm	man	squirrel
birthday	farmer	men	stock
boat	father	milk	street
box	feet	money	sun
boy	fire	morning	
bread	fish	mother	table
brother	floor		thing
	flower	name	time
cake		nest	top
car	game	night	toy
cat	garden		tree
chair	girl	paper	
chicken	goodbye	party	watch
children	grass	picture	water
Christmas	ground	pig	way
coat			wind
corn	hand	rabbit	window
cow	head	rain	wood
	hill	ring	
day	home	robin	

[2] Reprinted with permission of the author and the Garrard Press. These widely used nouns may be taught with the Picture Word Cards, Garrard Press, Champaign, Ill.

be taught by games like those suggested at the bottom of the lists, or by other means common in classroom practice (see Chapter 7).

The basic character of the 220 *service words* is revealed by the frequency with which they occur. About two-thirds of the words that occur in the reading material of the primary grades are from this list. And close to 60 per cent of the running words in most of the books examined in grades four to six are in the basic list of 220. The 95 most common nouns (Table 5) are listed separately by Dolch because they are not what he classifies as *service words*.

The Dolch basic lists of words continue to serve a useful purpose as indicated above. A desirable supplementary vocabulary is given in the recent report by Fullmer and Kolson (90). This list of 184 words, given in Table 6, has certain advantages not possessed by the Dolch lists:

Table 6

A Beginning Reading Vocabulary[3]

List I	down	asked	ran	just
	from	baby	red	laughed
a	fun	back	run	let's
and	funny	ball	school	liked
at	get	basket	something	made
away	give	birthday	surprises	many
can	he	black	take	milk
come	help	blue	that	must
fast	her	but	want	name
for	here	call	wanted	noise
go	him	children	water	oh
had	his	could	where	other
has	jump	day	who	our
have	like	dinner	will	pets
I	look	dog	work	picnic
in	looked	eat	yellow	played
is	may	father	your	please
it	me	feet		pony
little	mother	find	List IV	ready
make	no	girl		say
now	not	going	about	sleep
one	ride	goodby	after	so
said	saw	green	another	some
the	see	happy	ask	soon
there	she	home	book	street
up	stop	house	bump	thank
with	they	how	cake	them
you	this	hurry	called	then
out	to	into	car	three
	too	kitten	cat	time
List II	two	know	daddy	tree
	was	laugh	faster	uncle
all	we	let	flower	us
are	went	man	found	wagon
be	yes	may	goat	were
big		new	got	white
box	List III	of	guess	
came		on	head	
did	am	put	high	
do	as			

[3] Adapted with permission of the publisher from D. W. Fulmer and C. J. Kolson, A Beginning Reading Vocabulary, *Journal of Educational Research*, 1961, 54, 370-372.

(1) The level of application is the first grade and the list is up-to-date. The words are derived from all the 11 basic-reading series published during the period 1954-1959. They were tabulated from pre-primers, primers, and first readers. As with the Dolch lists, only the words that occurred most frequently are included, i.e., frequency of use was 50 per cent or greater. (2) The words are presented in groups according to frequency of use: List I, most frequent; List IV, least frequent (50 per cent). (3) All the words listed are in the child's speaking and understanding vocabulary.

The possible applications of this list of words include: (1) *As an aid in determining deficiencies in sight vocabulary.* When a deficiency is discovered the list can then be used for individual corrective instruction with the child. (2) *As a guide in developing experience charts.* It is likely that the teacher can employ to advantage both the Dolch words and the Fullmer-Kolson vocabulary in her diagnostic and remedial work.

Left-to-right orientation

A left-to-right progression of perception in reading words and sentences is essential in all reading. This must be learned. Occasionally a pupil will have difficulty in mastering this orientation during the course of regular classroom teaching. Gross difficulty in left-to-right progression along a line of print is readily diagnosed by direct observation of a pupil's eyes while he is trying to read. Lack of proper orientation of perceptual sequence in reading words results in errors of response due to observing letters in a reverse order or a partial reverse order. A full reversal is illustrated by reading *saw* for *was*, *on* for *no;* a partial reversal by reading *won* for *own*. Sometimes a single letter is reversed as in reading *big for dig*. Any serious tendency toward reversals is readily diagnosed by recording the errors while the child reads aloud series of words, or sentences which include several words that produce other familiar words when wholly or partially reversed, such as *now, was, no, dog, big, split*, and *who*. An indication that the child is directing his attention primarily to the ends of words is when errors of pronunciation tend to concentrate at the beginning of words while the ending is correct.

It is entirely normal for all children to make some reversals when learning to read. As the child progresses through the primary grades, reversals ordinarily become less frequent. Even in the upper elementary grades, an occasional reversal error is normal.

Corrective instruction for faulty left-to-right orientation consists of highly individualized application of the techniques described in Chapter 5. It involves an explanation of how words and lines are printed. Full, careful, and detailed demonstration of how the teacher reads words and lines of print is given. It is helpful to slide the finger or a pointer along the word or line as she demonstrates. Much repetition is usually necessary. Left-to-right orientation may well receive additional emphasis as phonetic analysis is taught.

In general, difficulties of proper orientation do not constitute a major problem for the classroom teacher. As noted earlier, while teaching reading during the early primary grades, the teacher should frequently give direct as well as incidental training in left-to-right orientation in perceiving words and sequences of words in sentences. Only a few children will fail to "catch on" so that they need the individual attention classed as remedial instruction. Persistence of marked reversal tendencies by a child in an individualized program beyond the second grade would probably indicate a severe reading disability complicated by other factors. Referral to the remedial specialist would be indicated.

Word recognition

Lack of satisfactory progress in learning one or another of the word-recognition skills is rather common. These skills involve use of picture, word-form, and context clues, phonetic analysis, and the various aspects of structural analysis such as syllabification and identification of known word roots. Observation of a child's responses from day to day may indicate to the teacher that the child is not making desirable progress in learning to use a clue or a technique that is being taught. Some individual checking with the child will more clearly identify the source of the trouble and determine the seriousness of the difficulty.

Undoubtedly the most satisfactory method of diagnosing difficulties in word-recognition techniques is from observation of oral reading by the child. Gray's Oral Reading Paragraphs (110) or material from a carefully graded series of readers may be used. The Gray paragraphs range from first-grade to high-school difficulty and are prepared to reveal tendencies to make specific kinds of errors. A method of recording errors is illustrated in Figure 11.

Every error should be recorded so that examination of the marked material will supply a satisfactory picture of a child's difficulties. The teacher may want to work out her own method of indicating errors. For instance, a wavy underline to indicate repetitions, a check mark to indicate hesitation, a "P" over words pronounced by the teacher, a circle around words omitted, and parenthesis marks around self-corrected mistakes. All mispronunciations, substitutions, and insertions should be written on the copy where they occur.

If the Gray paragraphs are not available, satisfactory results can be obtained by using Smith's (229) *Graded selections for informal reading diagnosis,* or selections of six to eight lines from each level of the graded readers. If graded readers are used, the materials for grade one should be typed in primer type, and for the higher levels in regular (smaller) type.

The child is started at an easy level and continues with succeeding levels until he makes one error in every six or seven words. As the child reads, the teacher takes down a complete record of his errors as described above. When the child finishes each paragraph or selection, the teacher takes notes on the characteristics of the reading performance, noting such items as too slow or too fast reading, word-by-word reading without phrasing, failure

The sun pierced into my *many* large windows. It was the opening of October, and the *clear* sky was of a dāzzling blue. I looked out of my window and down the street. The white houses of the long, straight street were almost painful to the eyes. The clear atmos-phere allowed full play to the sun's brightness.

> If a word is wholly mispronounced, underline it as in the case of ''Atmosphere.'' If a portion of a word is mispro-nounced, mark appropriately as indicated above: ''pierced'' pronounced in two syllables, sounding long *a* in ''dazzling,'' omitting the *s* in ''houses'' or the *al* from ''almost,'' or the *r* in ''straight.'' Omitted words are marked as in the case of ''of'' and ''and''; substitutions as in the case of ''many'' for ''my''; insertions as in the case of ''clear''; and repe-titions as in the case of ''to the sun's.'' Two or more words should be repeated to count as a repetition.
> It is very difficult to record the exact nature of each error. Do this as nearly as you can. In all cases where you are un-able to define clearly the specific character of the error, under-line the word or portion of the word mispronounced. Be sure you put down a mark for each error. In case you are not sure that an error was made, give the pupil the benefit of the doubt. If the pupil has a slight foreign accent, distinguish carefully between this difficulty and real errors.

Figure 11. Directions for recording errors on the *Gray Oral Reading Paragaphs.* (Reproduced with permission of the Bobbs-Merrill Company, Inc., Indianapolis, Indiana.)

to correct errors by use of meaning context, distinctness of enunciation, unwillingness to try or inability to adequately carry out phonetic analysis, indications of nervousness, and any other behavior which might seem of importance.

Analysis of the errors and observations on reading behavior will furnish ample data for diagnosing those word-recognition difficulties that can be corrected by the classroom teacher. Furthermore, corrective measures are usually indicated by the analysis. Use of this information may be illustrated by a few examples. For details see Bond and Tinker (26).

When book material is read, failure to make use of picture context as an aid to correct word recognition may be noted. Frequently clues to the correct word are indicated by things or action represented in the accompanying picture. Failure to use such clues suggests need of some additional training in "reading" pictures (Chapters 5 and 7).

Failure to employ satisfactorily the clues found in verbal context is frequently revealed either by refusal to hazard a "guess" at a word when its meaning is clearly indicated by the meaning of the rest of the sentence, or by giving a word that does not fit the context and then not seeing that it is an error. Elimination of the deficiency is achieved by individual training which directs the child's attention to contextual meanings and by encouragement to "guess" a word that makes sense.

Other errors may indicate an overdependence on verbal context without simultaneously using word-form clues to check accuracy of the guess. The guessed word may fit the context but still be the wrong word. For instance, the correct word might be *brother* and the guess *boy*. Further training in attending to familiar word forms and how the word forms can be employed to check a guess is indicated (Chapter 7).

Still other errors may indicate inadequate or inappropriate use of word-form clues. As noted earlier, word-form clues aid in word recognition when the child becomes familiar with the total configuration of printed words. A moderate amount of individual drill specifically directed toward attending to characteristic word forms ordinarily will correct this deficiency. Other errors may indicate too great a dependence on word form alone, so that different words with similar total form are confused, as *horse* and *house*, or *there* and *these*. If verbal context does not furnish the clue to correct recognition, it is frequently necessary to note more carefully the details or separate letters which make up the word. In correcting this difficulty, the drill to encourage more careful discrimination of letters in words should emphasize the proper left-to-right *sequence* or perception. Otherwise, an irregular examination of the word may lead to reversals. Occasionally a child will note some detail of a word and guess at the rest in terms of the general shape or configuration. The resulting errors may tend to occur at the beginning, at the end, in the middle, or in more than one place in the words. Corrective training for ineffective use of word form in recognizing words consists of guidance in how to discover the distinctive parts (tall and short letters, ascenders and descenders, wide and narrow letters, shape of letters, length of word) and how these are combined into a characteristic total pattern which is unique for that word. Development of a habitual attitude of perceiving an accurate picture of the word form is desirable. Care must be exercised in this guidance to emphasize the contribution of the essential features to the total configuration so that the result is clear perception of a total word form and not of unrelated parts. Timely guidance in getting the child on the right track in the use of word-form clues is very important.

If, during the oral reading of the paragraphs, the child refuses to try sounding out the word, or employs an ineffective sounding procedure, lack of progress in mastering phonetic or structural analysis is probably at the root of the trouble. Additional checking is necessary for diagnosis of specific aspects of the difficulty. Careful observation of procedure and recording of errors while the child attempts to sound out words met in reading aloud some additional material will reveal whether there are difficulties with initial and final consonants, other consonants and vowels, syllabification, the identification of compound forms, endings in inflected forms, root words, prefixes, suffixes, or other aspects of analysis. The child may employ overanalysis by breaking up a word into the component sounds and then not be able to recombine them into a word whole. When the difficulty or difficulties in word recognition are diagnosed, corrective work involves individual guidance following procedures outlined in Chapter 7.

Phrasing

Deficiencies in phrasing during oral reading are often associated with word-recognition difficulties. Or the inadequate phrasing may be due either to the habit of word calling, a monotonous word-by-word type of reading, or to grouping wrong words due to a disregard of punctuation and thought units. Lack of proper comprehension may accompany word-by-word reading.

Phrasing inadequacies are readily detected in the day-to-day performance in oral reading. Some individual observation of the child's oral reading may be necessary to diagnose more exactly the nature of the difficulty. If there are word-recognition difficulties, these should be corrected first. Word calling as a habit may occur in the absence of difficulties in recognition or may persist after these have been corrected.

In addition to group work, a child may need some individual attention to overcome imperfect phrasing. Ordinarily this calls for concentrated individual instruction using the customary methods of teaching phrasing rather than resorting to new methods. If this does not bring about progress the child's difficulty is severe enough for referral to the remedial specialist.

To develop phrasing skill, material which offers no difficulty in recognition should be employed. Attention is directed to meaningful thought units and the aid provided by punctuation. Demonstration should be given by the teacher. Aid in recognizing the proper phrases may be provided by separating them by short vertical lines or typing material with additional space between phrases. When progress is made by these aids, the pupil does the marking of the phrases in regular sentences and then is gradually led to do the phrasing without marking or other artificial aids. Details of these and other techniques for developing phrasing are given by Bond and Tinker (26).

It might be noted that the child with overdependence upon context may manifest good phrasing but be inaccurate in his reading due to omission and addition of words. Correction here involves remedial work in word-recognition techniques, slower reading, and greater attention to details.

Word meanings

Deficiencies in understanding the meaning of words necessarily results in lack of comprehension of what is being read. In addition to observation of daily performance in the reading situation, deficiencies in word meanings are checked by standardized tests and teacher-made tests (Chapter 16). When a child is deficient in word meanings, the first things to check are the data employed for determining what group the child belongs in, for example, intelligence, language development, experience background, and so on. The improvement of word meanings tends to be a rather extended program and naturally belongs in individualized group teaching. After re-evaluation to check whether the child is in the proper group, he is taught along with others who have a similar reading status. If he is deficient also in word-recognition techniques, individual training as outlined above is given simultaneously with vocabulary instruction. The individualized program for development of a meaningful vocabulary, outlined in Chapter 6, is followed. In the day-to-day instruction, the teacher will of course develop the concepts needed to comprehend meanings of all new words introduced. At the same time, the long-range program is carried on for development of word meanings by expanding the background of experience, training in the use of language, wide reading, use of the dictionary, and direct study of word meanings as previously outlined. The general emphasis in this remedial work is development of the concepts needed for adequate comprehension of material to be read. To a large degree this involves, therefore, an extension of the reading-readiness program up through the grades with the customary adaptation to individual needs. In all this program, of course, stress is placed upon development of strong motivation.

Comprehension

Deficiencies in various aspects of comprehension are detected by observation of the child's daily responses as he reads and by his scores on tests, both teacher-made and standardized (Chapter 16). Any failure to make satisfactory progress in quality and degree of comprehension will raise practically the same problems that come up in connection with deficiencies in word meanings. They are dealt with in a similar manner (see previous section). But shortcomings in sentence and paragraph comprehension as well as in comprehension and study skills are specific and require appropriate corrective training. Having discovered that a child is not making the expected progress in one of these skills, the teacher must apply some of the procedures outlined in Chapter 8 or 9 in order to bring the child up to the level of achievement where he can make normal progress under group instruction.

Oral reading

Detection and correction of deficiencies in oral reading involve use of the techniques discussed in Chapter 10. In addition, many of the methods of diagnosis and remedial work outlined earlier in this chapter are applicable. For instance, difficulties in word recognition, phrasing, word meanings, and basic comprehension ability will need correction.

Evidence of progress

As noted earlier in this chapter, many minor reading difficulties are easily corrected if they are spotted early enough. A few children in any class, however, may tend to run into one difficulty after another. Unless the teacher devotes special attention to such children they may lose confidence in themselves, become frustrated, and in consequence develop an aversion to reading. It is desirable, of course, that all children feel a surge of success as they read, and for this reason such success must be openly referred to by the teacher. This is especially important to any child who encounters more than average difficulty in learning to read. A good way to encourage such a child is to dramatize each bit of evidence that he is making progress. For instance, when a child has an inadequate sight vocabulary, stress should be placed upon how well he is doing in mastering the words in the Dolch lists and in the beginning vocabulary given in the above tables. Children tend to respond well to any recognition of their progress and to each bit of approval.

Adjusting to Special Handicaps[4]

In a relatively few cases, reading difficulties are complicated by one or another special sort of handicap. Several different types of handicaps will now be considered briefly. Some can be aided by adjustments in the classroom; others need to be referred to appropriate specialists.

1. *Emotionally disturbed children.* The milder cases such as the shy, retiring child who reaches school somewhat immature in social and per-

[4] Part of this discussion is based upon material written by M. A. Tinker in Chapter 18 of G. L. Bond and M. A. Tinker, *Reading difficulties.* New York: Appleton-Century-Crofts, Inc., 1957.

sonal development can be aided by the sympathetic guidance of the class-room teacher. For techniques of diagnosis and methods of guidance see Chapters 3, 4, and 5. All children with severe emotional maladjustment, whether apparently caused by reading disability, or more probably by unfortunate conditions at home or constitutional instability, should be referred for diagnosis and treatment to the appropriate specialist, who may be a reading clinician, a psychiatric social worker, or a psychiatrist.

2. *Slow learners.* If slow learners are recognized as such early in their school careers, the classroom program of instruction can be adjusted to their needs so that they will progress at least according to their own capabilities. See Chapter 13. If a slow learner has become an outright reading-disability case, he should be referred to the school reading center or a reading clinic for diagnosis and remedial treatment. But when the slow learner encounters only minor and rather specific difficulties, as in some aspect of word recognition, his difficulty can be diagnosed and corrected by the classroom teacher herself. Such correction of course is likely to require more intensive individual attention than will be needed by most of the normal pupils in the class.

3. *The visually handicapped.* The visual status of all children in the classroom should be known by the teacher from the beginning of the school year. If it can be arranged, a new screening test should be given to the children each year (see Chapter 4). If the screening tests indicate possible visual deficiencies, the child should be sent to a specialist, an oculist or optometrist, for diagnosis and correction by means of glasses or by other means if this is indicated and is possible. A small number of children have visual deficiencies which cannot be fully corrected either by glasses or treatment. When recommended by a competent eye specialist, a sight-conservation program should be set up for such children.

Whether a child with an uncorrectable visual defect that is relatively severe spends all his time in a sight-saving class, or part of it in a regular classroom and part in the sight-saving class, depends upon local practice. In general, the main objective in teaching children with severe visual deficiencies to read is to put them in a situation that will promote as much progress in reading as possible without harm to their eyes. Material to be read by these children should be printed in large-size type, and the illumination under which they read should be relatively bright.

Many children suffer from only a mild degree of visual deficiency, making their problem less serious. Practically all of these children can participate in the regular reading program provided for normal children. It is probably desirable for them to rest their eyes periodically and to do somewhat less extensive reading than the habitual reader. As with the more serious cases, they should be taught to recognize words by phonetic analysis, combining this with attention to larger units and the use of context (Fendrick, 83).

4. *Hearing deficiency*. Every child should be given an adequate hearing test early in his school life. This is especially important since many cases of severe hearing disability can be prevented if there is early diagnosis and treatment. See Chapter 4. Hearing difficulties range from the slightly hard-of-hearing to the partly deaf (severe hard-of-hearing) and to deaf-mutes who are totally deaf. The partly deaf and deaf-mute children are taught to read by specially trained instructors. Once a hard-of-hearing child has acquired skill in lip reading and a good start in reading, he can usually participate in normal class activities without too much difficulty when classroom adjustments are made similar to those for children with mild hearing deficiencies.

5. *Mild hearing deficiency*. The child with mild hearing deficiency will ordinarily adjust rather readily to the normal classroom situation when given a moderate amount of special aid. Such pupils should be given favorable seats close to the place from which the teacher does most of her talking to the class. Special emphasis should be placed upon clear enunciation in all situations which involve the hard-of-hearing child. Some training in lip reading will be helpful. He will then be able to follow oral discussions more accurately by watching the lips of the speaker. To avoid embarrassing the hard-of-hearing child, the discussion or recitation group should be so arranged that he can watch the lips of each speaker without obviously turning his head. Seating the children in a semicircle or around a table, with the hard-of-hearing child at one end, does this nicely.

It is likely that the hard-of-hearing child will have considerable difficulty in auditory discrimination. Because of this, in the teaching of word perception, there should be emphasis upon the visual approach to word identification and word recognition rather than phonics (Bond, 23). This does not imply a total neglect of word sounds but merely that more emphasis than usual is placed upon the visual characteristics of words and upon the use of visual analysis along with context clues for recognizing words previously met and for identifying unfamiliar words. The amount of this emphasis will be determined by how much difficulty the child has with auditory discrimination. If these precautions are taken, any child with a relatively mild hearing defect should be able to make normal progress in learning to read.

Remedial procedures

Pupils with mild emotional disturbances, visual defects, and auditory deficiencies do learn to read if the classroom adjustments outlined above are carried out. But, as with normal children, specific difficulties will occur from time to time, as with some aspect of word recognition, vocabulary meaning, phrasing, and oral reading. When such difficulties arise, they are diagnosed and remedied as described in earlier sections of this chapter.

Deficiencies in understanding English

Children who come from a home where a foreign language is spoken may be unable at first to understand or speak English well enough to participate much in ordinary classroom activities. The procedures customarily employed in teaching beginning reading in our schools are based on the assumption that each child has already learned to understand and speak our language. Language-handicapped children need first of all a program designed to improve their knowledge of English. Usually a preparatory instructional period should be concerned with: (1) building a basic vocabulary for understanding and speaking; (2) improvement of facility in oral communication; (3) providing a background of meaningful experiences. The words and concepts associated with these experiences must be in English. In this way the child learns to speak and understand a vocabulary before he encounters it in reading. It is probably best that most of the training in the understanding and use of oral English should be carried out in sessions not concerned with reading, particularly during the early stages of such instruction. The development of an adequate background in English is pretty certain to be gradual. In some cases such instruction may need to be continued throughout the elementary school years.

Language-handicapped children need not become severe reading-disability cases if an appropriate teaching program is organized early in their school careers. But as long as a child has a language handicap, he will be at a disadvantage in reading activities. Progress in learning to read will necessarily be slow until the language difficulty is cleared up. The teacher, therefore, must adjust her instruction to slow improvement somewhat as she does for a slow learner. At the same time she must be alert to note and remedy specific difficulties (word recognition, phrasing, etc.) as they arise just as she does with the rest of her pupils.

Summary

There are certain general considerations which apply to all remedial work in the classroom. In the first place, it is neither necessary nor desirable that the classroom teacher become a specialist in remedial reading. The role of the classroom teacher, with regard to remedial work, is to detect and correct promptly the relatively minor deficiencies that arise during the step-by-step progress in her program of instruction. During this program, certain pupils will fail to make the expected gain in using one or another of the *specific skills* being taught.

Ordinarily, observation of pupil responses during the day-by-day and week-by-week classes, plus performance on the rather frequent teacher-made tests employed to check progress in the skills being taught, will suggest the nature and degree of the difficulty. At times, some additional individual diagnosis is necessary for a clearer definition of the deficiency. This is followed by the corrective instruction indicated by the diagnosis. The difficulty, if promptly identified, is ordinarily cleared up rather promptly by individual instruction adjusted to the specific needs of the child. The only difference between such instruction and group instruction adapted to individual differences is that the teacher works temporarily with the pupil, employing the regular teaching methods but concentrating more intensely upon the skill wherein the child is deficient. In other words, the teacher, while carrying out her program of adapting reading instruction to individual differences, will give a moderate amount of special corrective help to any child needing it.

Every classroom teacher, to be successful in teaching developmental reading, which necessarily involves adapting reading instruction to individual differences, must do remedial teaching of the kind described here. She is not required, however, to be equipped by training, facilities, or time to handle the more severe, deep-seated, and complicated cases of reading disability. They should be referred to the remedial-reading specialist.

If the reading program throughout the grades were organized so that difficulties with specific skills could be promptly detected and corrected, there would be fewer severe disability cases. Such a program, of course, would be one which put the emphasis on prevention of reading difficulties as a major objective in teaching reading throughout the grades.

Vocabulary

What did these terms mean?

corrective instruction	reading pictures
school reading center	phrasing
reading clinic	day-to-day instruction
remedial teacher	visual deficiency
severe reading disability	hearing deficiency
basic sight vocabulary	foreign-language handicap
service words	oral communication
reversals	special handicaps

Suggested Activities

Observation: Visit an elementary school classroom. Note the kinds of specific skills the pupils are having difficulty with and how the teacher proceeds in her correction of each difficulty. Can you suggest any procedures that might supplement those she is using?

Further study: Read, in the Robinson reference listed below, the sections dealing with the elementary grades. Take notes for your future use on diagnostic and corrective techniques suggested.

Selected References

BOND, Guy L., and TINKER, Miles A., *Reading difficulties.* New York: Apple-ton-Century-Crofts, Inc., 1957, Chaps. 7, 8, 10, 14.

DEBOER, John J., and DALLMANN, Martha, *The teaching of reading.* New York: Holt, Rinehart and Winston, Inc., 1960, Chap. 12.

DURRELL, Donald D., *Improving reading instruction.* New York: Harcourt, Brace & World, Inc., 1956, Chap. 16.

GATES, Arthur I., *The improvement of reading,* 3rd ed. New York: The Macmillan Company, 1947.

GRAY, Lillian, and REESE, Dora, *Teaching children to read,* 2nd ed. New York: The Ronald Press Company, 1957, Chap. 12.

HARRIS, Albert J., *How to increase reading ability,* 4th ed. New York: Longmans, Green and Company, 1961, Chaps. 9, 10, 11, 14, 19.

HENRY, Nelson B. (ed.), *Development in and through reading.* The Sixtieth Yearbook of the National Society for the Study of Education, Part I, Section V. Chicago: University of Chicago Press, 1961, Chaps. 20, 21.

HEILMAN, Arthur W., *Principles and practices of teaching reading.* Columbus, Ohio: Charles E. Merrill Books, Inc., 1961, Chaps. 12, 13.

HILDRETH, Gertrude, *Teaching reading.* New York: Holt, Rinehart and Winston, Inc., 1958, Chap. 23.

KIRK, Samuel A., *Teaching reading to slow-learning children.* Boston: Houghton Mifflin Company, 1940.

LARRICK, Nancy (ed.), *Reading in action.* International Reading Association Conference Proceedings, Vol. 2. New York: Scholastic Magazines, 1957, 114-120; 156-167.

ROBINSON, Helen M. (ed.), *Corrective reading in classroom and clinic.* Suppl. Educ. Monog. No. 79. Chicago: University of Chicago Press, 1953.

STRANG, Ruth, and BRACKEN, Dorothy K., *Making better readers.* Boston: D. C. Heath and Company, 1957, Chap. 6.

—— McCULLOUGH, Constance M., and TRAXLER, A. E., *Problems in the improvement of reading,* 3rd ed. New York: The McGraw-Hill Book Company, 1961, Chap. 14.

Bibliography

1. AARON, I. E., Comparisons of good and poor readers in fourth and eighth grades. *Journal of Educational Research*, 1960, 54, 34-37.
2. —— GOODWIN, Frances, and KENT, Vada, Fourth grade teachers experiment with cross-class grouping for reading instruction. *Elementary English*, 1959, 36, 305-307.
3. ADDY, M. L., Development of a meaning vocabulary in the intermediate grades. *Elementary English Review*, 1941, 18, 22-26; 30.
4. ALLEN, W. H., *Teaching machines* (a filmstrip). Pasadena, Calif.: Basic Skill Films.
5. ANDERSON, I. H., and DEARBORN, W. F., *The psychology of teaching reading*. New York: The Ronald Press Company, 1952.
6. —— HUGHES, B. A., and DIXON, W. R., Age of learning to read and its relation to sex, intelligence and reading achievement in the sixth grade. *Journal of Educational Research*, 1956, 49, 447-453.
7. ANDERSON, Robert H., HAGSTROM, Ellis A., and ROBINSON, Wade M., Team teaching in an elementary school. *The School Review*, 1960, 68, 71-84.
8. ARBUTHNOT, M. H., *Children and books*, rev. ed. Chicago: Scott, Foresman and Company, 1957.
9. —— and others, *Children's books too good to miss*, revised. Cleveland: Western Reserve University Press, 1959.
10. ARTLEY, A. S., Teaching word meaning through context. *Elementary English Review*, 1943, 20, 68-74.
11. BAHNER, John M., Planning for teaching different groups in grades 4 through 6, in Helen M. Robinson (ed.), *Reading instruction in various patterns of grouping*. Chicago: University of Chicago Press, 1959, 95-98.
11a. BAKER, E. V., Reading readiness is still important. *Elementary English*, 1955, 32, 17-23.
12. BAKER, W. D., *Reading skills*. Englewood Cliffs, N.J.: Prentice-Hall, Inc., 1953.
13. BAMMAN, H. A., and DAWSON, Mildred A., *Teaching reading*. San Francisco: Howard Chandler, Publisher, 1958.
14. BEERY, A., Development of reading vocabulary and word recognition. *Reading in the elementary school*. The Forty-Eighth Yearbook of the National Society for the Study of Education, Part II. Chicago: University of Chicago Press, 1949, 172-292.
15. BEHN, Helen, Comparison of the pre-primer vocabularies in eight basal reader series. Unpublished report, 1960.
16. BENNETT, C. C., *An inquiry into the genesis of poor reading*. New York: Bureau of Publications, Teachers College, Columbia University, 1938.

17. *Best books for children.* New York: Junior Libraries (62 W. 45th Street, New York 36), 1961.
18. BETTS, E. A., *Foundations of reading instruction.* New York: American Book Company, 1957.
19. —— Phonics: syllables. *Education,* 1959, 79, 557-564.
20. BEVINGTON, W. G., Effects of age at time of entrance into grade one on subsequent achievement. *Alberta Journal of Educational Research,* 1958, 4, 6-16.
21. BLAIR, G. M., *Diagnostic and remedial teaching,* rev. ed. New York: The Macmillan Company, 1956.
22. BOND, Eva, *Reading and ninth-grade achievement.* New York: Bureau of Publications, Teachers College, Columbia University, 1938.
23. BOND, G. L., *Auditory and speech characteristics of poor readers.* New York: Bureau of Publications, Teachers College, Columbia University, 1935.
24. —— and BOND, E., *Developmental reading in high school.* New York: The Macmillan Company, 1941.
25. —— and HANDLAN, B., *Adapting instruction in reading to individual differences.* Minneapolis: University of Minnesota Press, 1948.
26. —— and TINKER, M. A., *Reading difficulties.* New York: Appleton-Century-Crofts, Inc., 1957.
27. —— and WAGNER, Eva B., *Child growth in reading.* Chicago: Lyons and Carnahan, 1955.
28. —— and WAGNER, Eva B., *Teaching the child to read,* 3rd ed. New York: The Macmillan Company, 1960.
29. BOTEL, M., *How to teach reading.* State College, Pa.: Penns Valley Publishers, Inc., 1959.
30. —— and SMITH, Margaret H., *The multi-level reading skill text.* State College, Pa.: Penns Valley Publishers, Inc., 1959.
31. BRADLEY, B. E., An experimental study of the readiness approach to reading. *Elementary School Journal,* 1956, 56, 262-267.
32. BREEN, L. C., Vocabulary development by teaching prefixes, suffixes, and word derivatives. *The Reading Teacher,* 1960, 14, 93-97.
33. BREMER, N., Do readiness tests predict success in reading? *Elementary School Journal,* 1959, 59, 222-224.
34. BROWN, J. I., Teaching reading with the tachistoscope. *Journal of Developmental Reading,* 1958, 1 (No. 2), 8-18.
35. BRUECKNER, L. J., and BOND, G. L., *The diagnosis and treatment of learning difficulties.* New York: Appleton-Century-Crofts, Inc. 1955.
35a. BRYAN, F. E., How large are children's vocabularies? *Elementary English,* 1954, 31, 210-216.
36. BUROS, O. K. (ed.), *The fifth mental measurements yearbook.* Highland Park, N. J.: The Gryphon Press, 1959.
37. BURTON, D. L., and LARRICK, Nancy, Literature for children and youth. *Development in and through reading.* The Sixtieth Yearbook of the National Society for the Study of Education, Part I. Chicago: University of Chicago Press, 1961.
38. BURTON, W. H., KIMBALL, R. B., and WING, R. L., *Education for effective thinking.* New York: Appleton-Century-Crofts, Inc., 1960.
39. CARLSON, T. R., The relationship between speed and accuracy of comprehension. *Journal of Educational Research,* 1949, 42, 500-512.
40. CARTER, L. B., The effect of early school entrance on the scholastic

achievement of elementary school children in the Austin public schools. *Journal of Educational Research*, 1956, 50, 91-113.

41. CASON, E. B., *Mechanical methods for increasing the speed of reading.* New York: Bureau of Publications, Teachers College, Columbia University, 1943.

42. CENTER, Stella S., *The art of book reading.* New York: Charles Scribner's Sons, 1952.

43. CLEMENT, J. A., *Manual for analyzing and selecting textbooks.* Champaign, Ill.: The Garrard Press, 1942.

44. —— *Score sheet for analysis and approval of textbooks.* Champaign, Ill.: The Garrard Press, 1942.

45. CLYMER, T., A study of the validity of the California Test of Mental Maturity, Elementary, Non-Language Section. *The Seventeenth Yearbook of the National Council on Measurement Used in Education.* Ames, Iowa: Published by the Council, 1960, 123-139.

46. —— A study of the California Test of Mental Maturity, Elementary, Language Section. *The Eighteenth Yearbook of the National Council of Measurement Used in Education.* Ames, Iowa: Published by the Council, 1961 (in press).

46a. —— The utility of phonic generalization in the primary grades. In *Changing Concepts of Reading Instruction,* International Reading Association Proceedings, Vol. 6. New York: Scholastic Magazines, Inc., 1961 (in press).

47. COOK, W. W., *Grouping and promotion in the elementary school.* Minneapolis: University of Minnesota Press, 1941.

48. DAHL, L. A., *Public school audiometry.* Danville, Ill.: The Interstate Printers and Publishers, 1949.

49. DALE, E. W. (ed.), *Readability.* Chicago: National Council of Teachers of English, 1949. Reprinted from *Elementary English*, January to May, 1949.

50. —— and CHALL, J. S., A formula for predicting readability. *Educational Research Bulletin*, 1948, 27, 11-20; 28.

51. DARROW, H. F., and HOWES, V. M., *Approaches to individualized reading.* New York: Appleton-Century-Crofts, Inc., 1960.

52. DAVIDSON, H. P., *An experimental study of the bright, average and dull children at the four-year mental level. Genetic Psychology Monographs*, 1931, 9, 119-289.

53. DAVIS, F. B., Comprehension in reading. *Baltimore Bulletin of Education*, 1951, 28, 16-24.

54. DAWSON, Grace S., *Your world and mine.* Boston: Ginn and Company, 1958.

55. DAWSON, M. A., and BAMMAN, H. A., *Fundamentals of basic reading instruction.* New York: Longmans, Green and Company, Inc., 1959.

56. —— and ZOLLINGER, Marian, *Guiding language learning.* New York: Harcourt, Brace & World, Inc., 1957.

57. DeBOER, J. J., and DALLMANN, Martha, *The teaching of reading.* New York: Holt, Rinehart and Winston, Inc., 1960.

58. DELACATO, C. H., *The treatment and prevention of reading problems: The neuro-psychological approach.* Springfield, Ill.: Charles C. Thomas, 1959.

59. DENECKE, L., Fifth-graders study the comic books. *Elementary English Review*, 1945, 22, 6-8.

60. DEPUTY, E. C., *Predicting first grade reading achievement: a study in*

reading readiness. New York: Bureau of Publications, Teachers College, Columbia University, 1930.

61. DOLCH, E. W., *Graded reading difficulty worksheet.* Champaign, Ill.: The Garrard Press, 1948.

62. —— *Problems in reading.* Champaign, Ill.: The Garrard Press, 1948.

63. —— *Psychology and teaching of reading,* 2nd ed. Champaign, Ill.: The Garrard Press, 1951.

64. —— Self-survey of a school program for the teaching of reading. *Elementary School Journal,* 1949, 49, 230-233.

64a. —— and BLOOMSTER, M., Phonic readiness. *Elementary School Journal,* 1937, 37, 201-205.

65. DUNKLIN, H. T., *The prevention of failure in first grade reading by means of adjusted instruction.* New York: Bureau of Publications, Teachers College, Columbia University, 1940.

66. DURKIN, D., A study of children who learned to read prior to first grade. *California Journal of Educational Research,* 1959, 10, 109-113.

67. —— The precocious reader: a study of pre-school reading ability. *California Journal for Instructional Improvement,* 1959, 2, 24-28.

68. DURRELL, D. D., Development of comprehension and interpretation. *Reading in the elementary school.* Forty-eighth Yearbook of the National Society for the Study of Education, Part II. Chicago: University of Chicago Press, 1949, 193-204.

69. —— First-grade reading success study: a summary. *Journal of Education,* 1958, 140, 2-6.

70. —— *Improving reading instruction.* New York: Harcourt, Brace & World, Inc., 1956.

71. —— and MURPHY, H. A., The auditory discrimination factor in reading readiness and reading disability. *Education,* 1953, 73, 556-560.

72. ——, SULLIVAN, Helen B., and MURPHY, Helen A., *Building word power in primary reading,* rev. ed. New York: Harcourt, Brace & World, Inc., 1945.

73. EDMISTON, R. D., and PEYTON, B., Improving first grade achievement by readiness instruction. *School and Society,* 1950, 71, 230-232.

74. EDMON, M., Criteria for selecting literature in the middle and upper grades, *The appraisal of current practices in reading.* Suppl. Educ. Monog. No. 61. Chicago: University of Chicago Press, 1946, 209-215.

75. EPHRON, Beulah K., *Emotional difficulties in reading.* New York: The Julian Press, Inc., 1953.

76. EURICH, A. C., The relation of speed of reading to comprehension. *School and Society,* 1930, 32, 404-406.

76a. FALLON, M. E., The pre-reading program. *Chicago Schools Journal,* 1939, 21, 10-12.

77. FARGO, L. F., *Activity book for school libraries.* Chicago: American Library Association, 1945.

78. FAST, I., Kindergarten training and grade one reading. *Journal of Educational Psychology,* 1957, 48, 52-57.

79. FAY, Leo C., The relationship between specific reading skills and selected areas of sixth-grade achievement. *Journal of Educational Research,* 1950, 43, 453-465.

80. FELDMANN, Shirley C., and MERRILL, Kathleen K., *Ways to read words.* New York: Bureau of Publications, Teachers College, Columbia University, 1959.

81. —— and MERRILL, Kathleen K., *More ways to read words*. New York: Bureau of Publications, Teachers College, Columbia University, 1959.

82. FENDRICK, P. A., *Visual characteristics of poor readers*. New York: Bureau of Publications, Teachers College, Columbia University, 1935.

83. —— and McGLADE, C. A., A validation of two prognostic tests of reading aptitude. *Elementary School Journal*, 1938, 39, 187-194.

84. FERNALD, Grace M., *Remedial techniques in basic school subjects*. New York: McGraw-Hill Book Company, 1943.

85. FIELD, Rachel, This afternoon, from *Poems*. New York: The Macmillan Company, 1934.

85a. FIGUREL, J. A., The vocabulary of underprivileged children. *University of Pittsburgh Bulletin*, 1949, 45, 1-10.

86. FLESCH, R., A new readability yardstick. *Journal of Applied Psychology*, 1948, 32, 221-233.

87. —— *How to test readability*. New York: Harper and Brothers, 1951.

88. —— *Why Johnny can't read*. New York: Harper and Brothers, 1955.

89. FLOYD, Cecil, Meeting children's reading needs in the middle grades: a preliminary report. *Elementary School Journal*, 1954, 55, 99-103.

90. FULLMER, D. W., and KOLSON, C. J., A beginning reading vocabulary. *Journal of Educational Research*, 1961, 54, 370-372.

91. GAMMON, A. L., Comprehension of words with multiple meanings. *California Journal of Educational Research*, 1952, 3, 228-232.

92. GANS, Roma, *A study of critical reading comprehension in the intermediate grades*. New York: Bureau of Publications, Teachers College, Columbia University, 1940.

93. GATES, A. I., An experimental evaluation of reading readiness tests. *Elementary School Journal*, 1939, 39, 497-508.

94. —— A further evaluation of reading readiness tests. *Elementary School Journal*, 1940, 40, 577-591.

95. —— *Gates reading readiness tests*, New York: Bureau of Publications, Teachers College, Columbia University, 1940.

96. —— *Interest and ability in reading*. New York: The Macmillan Company, 1945.

97. —— *The improvement of reading*, 3rd ed. New York: The Macmillan Company, 1947.

98. —— The necessary mental age for beginning reading. *Elementary School Journal*, 1937, 37, 497-508.

99. —— and BOND, G. L., Reading readiness. *Teachers College Record*, 1936, 37, 679-685.

100. —— and BOND, G. L., Relation of handedness, eye-sighting, and acuity dominance to reading. *Journal of Educational Psychology*, 1936, 27, 455-456.

101. —— BOND, G. L., and RUSSELL, D. H., assisted by others, *Methods of determining reading readiness*. New York: Bureau of Publications, Teachers College, Columbia University, 1939.

101a. —— and CASON, E. B., An evaluation of tests for diagnosis of ability to read by phrases or "thought units." *Elementary School Journal*, 1945, 46, 23-32.

102. —— and RUSSELL, D. H., The effects of delaying beginning reading. *Journal of Educational Research*, 1939, 32, 321-328.

103. GAVEL, S. R., June reading achievements of first grade children. *Journal of Education*, 1958, 140, No. 3, 37-43.

104. GILBERT, Doris Wilcox, *Power and speed in reading.* Englewood Cliffs, New Jersey: Prentice-Hall, Inc., 1956.

105. GOINS, J. T., *Visual perceptual abilities and early reading progress.* Suppl. Educ. Monog. No. 87. Chicago: University of Chicago Press, 1958.

106. GOLDSTEIN, H., *Reading and listening comprehension at various controlled rates.* New York: Bureau of Publications, Teachers College, Columbia University, 1940.

107. GRAY, Lillian, and REESE, Dora, *Teaching children to read,* 2nd ed. New York: The Ronald Press Company, 1957.

108. GRAY, W. S. (ed.), *Improving reading in all curriculum areas.* Suppl. Educ. Monog. No. 76. Chicago: University of Chicago Press, 1952.

108a. ——*On their own in reading,* rev. ed. Chicago: Scott, Foresman and Company, 1960.

109. —— New approaches to the study of interpretation in reading. *Journal of Educational Research,* 1958, 52, 65-67.

110. —— *Standardized oral reading paragraphs.* Bloomington, Ill.: Public School Publishing Company, 1916. (Now a Division of the Bobbs, Merrill Company, Inc., Indianapolis 6, Indiana.)

111. —— The measurement of understanding in the language arts: the receptive language arts. *Measurement of understanding,* Forty-fifth Yearbook of the National Society for the Study of Education, Part I. Chicago: University of Chicago Press, 1946, 189-200.

112. —— and HOLMES, E., *The development of meaning vocabularies in reading.* Chicago: University of Chicago Press, 1938.

113. —— and LEARY, B. E., *What makes a book readable?* Chicago: University of Chicago Press, 1935.

114. —— and ROGERS, Bernice, *Maturity in reading: its nature and appraisal.* Chicago: University of Chicago Press, 1956.

115. GRAYUM, Helen S., An analytic description of skimming: Its purpose and place as an ability in reading. *Studies in Education* (Theses Abstract Series). Bloomington, Ind.: School of Education, Indiana University, 1952, 137-143.

116. HAEFNER, R., Casual learning of word meanings. *Journal of Educational Research,* 1932, 25, 267-277.

117. —— *The educational significance of left-handedness.* New York: Bureau of Publications, Teachers College, Columbia University, 1929.

118. HAMPLEMAN, R. S., A study of the comparative reading achievement of early and late school starters. *Elementary English,* 1959, 34, 331-334.

119. —— Comparison of listening and reading comprehension ability of fourth and sixth grade pupils. *Elementary English,* 1958, 35, 49-53.

120. HANSEN, Carl W., Factors associated with successful achievement in problem solving in sixth grade arithmetic. *Journal of Educational Research,* 1944, 38, 111-118.

121. HARRINGTON, Sister M. J., and DURRELL, D. D., Mental maturity versus perception abilities in primary reading. *Journal of Educational Psychology,* 1955, 46, 375-380.

122. HARRIS, A. J., *How to increase reading ability,* 4th ed. New York: Longmans, Green and Company, 1961.

123. HARRISON, M. L., *Reading readiness,* rev. ed. Boston: Houghton Mifflin Company, 1939.

124. HAY, Julie, and WINGO, C. E., *Teacher's manual for reading with phonics,* rev. ed. Chicago: J. P. Lippincott Company, 1954.

125. HEIL, Louis, POWER, Marion, and FEIFER, Irwin, *Characteristics of teacher behavior related to the achievement of children in several elementary grades* (mimeographed). Brooklyn, N. Y.: Brooklyn College, May, 1960.

126. HENIG, M. S., Predictive value of a reading-readiness test and of teachers' forecasts. *Elementary School Journal*, 1949, 50, 41-46.

127. HERR, Selma E., *Effective reading for adults*. Dubuque, Iowa: William C. Brown Company, 1959.

128. HERRICK, V. E., ANDERSON, D., and PIERSTOFF, Lola, Basal instruction materials in reading. *Development in and through reading*. The Sixtieth Yearbook of the National Society for the Study of Education. Chicago: University of Chicago Press, 1961, 165-188.

129. HERSEY, John, *A single pebble*. New York: Alfred A. Knopf, 1956, 15.

130. HILDRETH, Gertrude, *Personality and interest inventory, elementary form*. New York: Bureau of Publications, Teachers College, Columbia University, 1936.

131. —— *Educating gifted children at Hunter College Elementary School*. New York: Harper and Brothers, 1952, Chap. 4.

132. —— *Readiness for school beginners*. New York: Harcourt, Brace & World, Inc., 1950.

133. —— *Teaching reading*. New York: Holt, Rinehart and Winston, Inc., 1958.

134. HILLIARD, G. H., and TROXELL, E., Informational background as a factor in reading readiness and reading progress. *Elementary School Journal*, 1937, 38, 255-263.

135. HOLLOWELL, Lillian (ed.), *A book of children's literature*, 2nd ed. New York: Holt, Rinehart and Winston, Inc., 1950.

136. HOWELL, Wallace J., Work-study skills of children in grades 4 to 8. *Elementary School Journal*, 1950, 50, 384-389.

137. HUEY, E. B., *The psychology and pedagogy of reading*. New York: The Macmillan Company, 1909.

138. HYATT, A. V., *The place of oral reading in the school program*. New York: Bureau of Publications, Teachers College, Columbia University, 1943.

139. ILG, F. L., and AMES, L. B., Developmental trends in reading behavior. *Journal of Genetic Psychology*, 1950, 76, 291-312.

140. *Iowa elementary teachers handbook, Vol. II. Reading*. Des Moines: Department of Public Instruction, State of Iowa, 1943.

141. JENKINS, E. M., Ready to read? *Grade Teacher*, 1954, 71, 56; 90; 92; 94.

142. KARLIN, R., Physical growth and success in undertaking beginning reading. *Journal of Educational Research*, 1957, 51, 191-201.

143. —— The prediction of reading success and reading-readiness tests. *Elementary English*, 1957, 34, 320-322.

144. KIRK, S. A., *Teaching reading to slow-learning children*. Boston: Houghton Mifflin Company, 1940.

145. KLARE, G. R., and BUCK, B., *Know your reader*. New York: Hermitage House, 1954.

146. KNOX, G. E., Classroom symptoms of visual difficulty. *Clinical studies in reading: II,* Suppl. Educ. Monog. No. 77. Chicago: University of Chicago Press, 1953, 97-101.

147. KRANTZ, L. L., The relationship of reading abilities and basic skills of the elementary school to success in the interpretation of the content ma-

terials in the high school. *Journal of Experimental Education,* 1957, 26, 97-114.

148. LaBRANT, Lou, The larger context: setting. *The Reading Teacher,* 1958, 11, 234-238.

149. LARRICK, Nancy, *A parent's guide to children's reading.* Garden City: Doubleday and Company, Inc., 1958. (Also published by Pocket Books, Inc.)

150. —— *A teacher's guide to children's books.* Columbus, Ohio: Charles E. Merrill Books, Inc., 1960.

151. —— Making the most of children's interests. *Education,* 1953, 73, 523-531.

152. LAZAR, May, *The place of reading in the elementary school program.* Educational Research Bulletin No. 7. New York: Board of Education, City of New York, 1944.

153. —— *The retarded reader in the junior high school.* Bureau of Educational Research Publication No. 31. New York: Board of Education, City of New York, 1952.

154. LEESTMA, R., *Audio-visual materials for teaching reading.* Ann Arbor, Michigan: Slater's Book Store, 1954.

155. *Let's go to kindergarten: handbook for parents of children in kindergarten.* Tulsa, Oklahoma: Tulsa Public Schools (no date).

156. LEWIS, Claudia, Children's current book choices, in Nancy Larrick (ed.), *Reading in action,* International Reading Association Proceedings, Volume 2, 1957. New York: Scholastic Magazines, 1957, 69-70.

157. LINEHAN, E. B., Early instruction in letter names and sound as related to success in beginning reading. *Journal of Education,* 1958, 140, 44-48.

158. LINK, H. C., and HOPF, H. A., *People and books: a study of reading and book-buying habits.* New York: Book Industry Committee, 1946.

159. LORGE, I., *Estimating structure in prose* (mimeographed). New York: Irving Lorge, Teachers College, Columbia University, October 1960.

160. —— Predicting readability. *Teachers College Record,* 1944, 45, 404-419.

161. —— and Blau, R., Reading comprehension of adults. *Teachers College Record,* 1941, 43, 189-198.

162. MACKINTOSH, Helen K., Children's interests in literature and the reading program. *The Reading Teacher,* 1957, 10, 138-145.

163. MALTER, M. S., Children's ability to read diagrammatic materials. *Elementary School Journal,* 1948, 49, 98-102.

164. MANEY, Ethel, Literal and critical reading in science. *Journal of Experimental Education,* 1958, 27, 57-64.

164a. MANOLAKES, G., The effects of tachistoscopic training in an adult reading program, *Journal of Applied Psychology,* 1952, 36, 410-412.

165. MARIAM, Sister, Context clues in primary reading. *The Reading Teacher,* 158, 11, 230-234.

166. McCALLISTER, James M., Reading ability of junior college freshmen II: in relation to survey sources. *Chicago School Journal,* 1936, 18, 79-82.

167. —— Reading difficulties in studying content subjects. *Elementary School Journal,* 1930, 31, 191-201.

168. McCULLOUGH, Constance M., About practices in teaching reading. *English Journal,* 1957, 46, 475-490.

169. —— A log of children's out-of-school activities. *Elementary School Journal,* 1957, 58, 157-165.

170. —— Conditions favorable to comprehension. *Education*, 1959, 79, 533-536.
171. —— Context aids in reading. *The Reading Teacher*, 1958, 11, 225-229.
172. —— *Handbook for teaching the language arts.* South San Francisco, Calif.: Paragon Publications, 1958.
173. —— Implications of research on children's concepts. *The Reading Teacher*, 1959, 13, 100-107.
174. —— The recognition of context clues in reading. *Elementary English Review*, 1945, 22, 1-5.
175. —— What's behind the reading score? *Elementary English,* 1953, 30, 1-7.
176. —— and RUSSELL, D. H., *Reading readiness tests for each level* (pre-reading through the six grades), rev. ed. Boston: Ginn and Company, 1952-1957.
177. McHUGH, Walter, *Comparison of primary reader vocabularies.* Unpublished report, 1960.
178. McKEE, P., *The teaching of reading in the elementary school.* Boston: Houghton Mifflin Company, 1948.
179. McLAREN, V. M., Socio-economic status and reading ability—a study in infant reading. *Studies in Reading.* London: University of London Press, 1950, 1-62.
180. MEEK, L. H., *Study of learning and retention in young children.* New York: Bureau of Publications, Teachers College, Columbia University, 1925.
181. MILNER, E., A study of the relationship between reading readiness in grade one school children and patterns of parent-child interaction. *Child Development*, 1951, 22, 95-112.
182. MOE, I. L., and NANIA, F., Reading deficiencies among able pupils. *Journal of Developmental Reading*, 1959, 3 (No. 1), 11-26.
183. MONROE, Marion, *Children who cannot read.* Chicago: University of Chicago Press, 1932.
184. —— *Growing into reading.* Chicago: Scott, Foresman and Company, 1951.
185. MOREAU, M. C., Long-term prediction of elementary reading achievement. *California Journal of Educational Research*, 1950, 1, 173-176.
186. MORPHETT, M. V., and WASHBURNE, C., When should children begin to read? *Elementary School Journal*, 1931, 31, 496-503.
187. MOTT, C., and BAISDEN, L. B., *The children's book on how to use books and libraries.* New York: Charles Scribner's Sons, 1955.
188. MUNKRES, A., *Helping children in oral communication.* New York: Bureau of Publications, Teachers College, Columbia University, 1959.
189. NICHOLSON, A., Background abilities related to reading success in first grade. *Journal of Education*, 1958, 140, No. 3, 7-24.
190. NILA, Sister Mary, *Foundations of a successful reading program. Education*, 1953, 73, 543-555.
191. O'DONNELL, Mabel, and COOPER, J. Louis, *From codes to captains.* Evanston: Row, Peterson Company, 1960.
192. OLSON, A. V., Growth in word perception abilities as it relates to success in beginning reading. *Journal of Education*, 1958, 140, No. 3, 25-36.
193. OLSON, W. C., Reading as a function of total growth of the child, in *Reading and pupil development.* Suppl. Educ. Monog. No. 51. Chicago: University of Chicago Press, 1940, 233-237.

194. —— and HUGHES, B. O., Growth of the child as a whole, in *Child behavior and development*, edited by R. G. Barker and others. New York: McGraw-Hill Book Company, Inc., 1943, 199-208.

195. —— and HUGHES, B. O., The concept of organismic age. *Journal of Educational Research*, 1942, 35, 525-527.

196. OREAR, M. L., Social maturity and first grade achievement. *California Journal of Educational Research*, 1951, 2, 84-88.

197. ORME, Lillian, Building readiness for reading in first grade children thru special instruction. *The National Elementary Principal*, 1955, 35, 43-46.

198. ORTON, S. T., *Reading, writing and speech problems in children*. New York: W. W. Norton and Company, Inc., 1937.

199. PARKE, Margaret B., Picture dictionaries. *Elementary English*, 1955, 32, 519-524.

200. PARKER, Bertha Morris, *The golden encyclopedia*. New York: Simon and Schuster, Inc., 1959.

201. PEI, M., *The story of English*. Philadelphia: J. B. Lippincott Company, 1953.

202. PIEKARZ, Josephine A., Getting meaning from reading. *Elementary School Journal*, 1956, 56, 303-309.

203. PRATT, W. E., A study of the differences in the prediction of reading success of kindergarten children and non-kindergarten children. *Journal of Educational Research*, 1949, 42, 183-188.

204. PRESTON, R. C., and BOTEL, M., *How to study*. Chicago: Science Research Associates, 1956.

205. REHAGE, Kenneth J., News and comment. *Elementary School Journal*, 1960, 61, 1-3.

206. ROBERTS, C., *Word attack*. New York: Harcourt, Brace and Company, 1956.

207. ROBINSON, F. P., and HALL, W. E., *Concerning reading readiness tests*. Bulletin of the Ohio Conference on Reading, No. 3. Columbus, Ohio: Ohio State University Press, 1942.

208. ROBINSON, Helen M., Corrective and remedial instruction. *Development in and through reading*. The Sixtieth Yearbook of the National Society for the Study of Education, Part I. Chicago: University of Chicago Press, 1961, 357-375.

209. —— (ed.), *Materials for reading*. Suppl. Educ. Monog. No. 86. Chicago: University of Chicago Press, 1957.

210. —— (ed.), *Promoting maximum reading growth among able learners*. Suppl. Educ. Monog. No. 81. Chicago: University of Chicago Press, 1954.

211. —— *Why pupils fail in reading*. Chicago: University of Chicago Press, 1946.

212. RUDOLF, Kathleen Brady, *The effect of reading instruction on achievement in eighth-grade social studies*. New York: Bureau of Publications, Teachers College, Columbia University, 1949.

213. RUSSELL, D. H., *Children learn to read*, 2nd ed. Boston: Ginn and Company, 1961.

214. —— *Children's thinking*. Boston: Ginn and Company, 1956.

215. —— Inter-class grouping for reading instruction in the intermediate grades. *Journal of Educational Research*, 1946, 39, 462-470.

216. —— Reading for effective living, in J. Allen Figurel, (ed.), *Reading for*

effective living, International Reading Association Proceedings, Volume 3, 1958. New York: Scholastic Magazines, 1958, 12-17.

217.   —— *The basic reading program in the modern school.* Contributions to Reading No. 1. Boston: Ginn and Company, 1949.

218.   —— *The dimensions of children's meaning vocabularies in grades four through twelve.* Publications in Education, Vol. 11, No. 5. Berkeley: University of California Press, 1954.

219.   —— and KARP, E. E., *Reading aids through the grades*, rev. ed. New York: Bureau of Publications, Teachers College, Columbia University, 1951.

220.   —— and OUSLEY, O., *Manual for teaching the reading readiness program*, rev. ed. (Ginn basic readers). Boston: Ginn and Company, 1957.

221.   SARTAIN, Harry W., The Roseville experiment with individualized reading. *The Reading Teacher*, 1960, 13, 277-281.

222.   SCHMIDT, W. H. O., An investigation to determine the optimum mental age for commencing reading instructions under conditions at present obtaining in certain schools in Pietermaritzburg and in Durban. *Journal of Social Research* (Union of South Africa), 1954, 5, 119-128.

223.   SCHUBERT, Delwyn G., The relationship between reading ability and literary appreciation. *California Journal of Educational Research*, 1953, 4, 201-202.

224.   SCOTT, C. M., An evaluation of training in readiness classes. *Elementary School Journal*, 1947, 48, 26-32.

225.   SHAW, Phillip B., *Effective reading and learning.* New York: Thomas Y. Crowell Company, 1955.

225a.   SHIBLES, B. H., How many words does a first-grade child know? *Elementary English*, 1959, 36, 42-47.

226.   Sixtieth Yearbook of the National Society for the Study of Education, *Development in and through reading.* Chicago: University of Chicago Press, 1961.

227.   SMITH, D. V., Literature and personal reading. *Reading in the elementary school.* Forty-eighth Yearbook of the National Society for the Study of Education, Part II. Chicago: University of Chicago Press, 1949, 205-232.

228.   SMITH, Nila B., *Be a better reader*, Books 1, 2, and 3. Englewood Cliffs, New Jersey: Prentice-Hall, Inc., 1958.

229.   —— and others, *Graded selections for informal reading diagnosis, grades 1 through 3.* New York: New York University Press, 1959.

230.   —— Readiness for reading. *Elementary English*, 1950, 27, 31-39; 91-106.

231.   —— Teaching study skills in reading. *Elementary School Journal*, 1959, 60, 158-162.

232.   SOCHOR, E., Readiness and the development of reading ability at all school levels. *Education*, 1954, 75, 555-560.

233.   SPACHE, G. D., A new readability formula for primary grade materials. *Elementary School Journal*, 1953, 53, 410-413.

234.   —— Auditory and visual materials. *Development in and through reading.* The Sixtieth Yearbook of the National Society for the Study of Education, Part I. Chicago: University of Chicago Press, 1961, 209-225.

235.   —— Problems in primary-book selection. *Elementary English Review*, 1941, 18, 5-12; 52-59; 139-148; 154; 175-181.

236.   —— *Resources in teaching reading.* Gainesville, Florida: The Author, 1955.

237. —— and BERG, Paul C., *The art of efficient reading*. New York: The Macmillan Company, 1955.

238. SPARKS, P. E., and FAY, L. C., An evaluation of two methods of teaching reading. *Elementary School Journal*, 1957, 57, 386-390.

239. STANLEY, J. C., *Ross's measurement in today's schools*, 3rd ed. Part II. Englewood Cliffs, N.J.: Prentice-Hall, Inc., 1954.

240. STAUFFER, R. G. (ed.), *Individualized reading instruction*. Newark, Delaware: The Reading-Study Center, School of Education, University of Delaware, 1959.

241. STEWART, Robert S., Personality maladjustment and reading achievement. *American Journal of Orthopsychiatry*, 1950, 20, 410-417.

242. STORM, G. E., Criteria for selecting literature for school use and for judging methods of presenting or using it: primary grades. *The appraisal of current practices in reading*, Suppl. Educ. Monog. No. 61. Chicago: University of Chicago Press, 1946, 202-208.

243. STRANG, Ruth, Relationships between certain aspects of intelligence and certain aspects of reading. *Educational and Psychological Measurement*, 1943, 3, 355-359.

244. —— McCULLOUGH, Constance M., and TRAXLER, A. E., *The improvement of reading*, 3rd ed. New York: McGraw-Hill Book Company, Inc., 1961.

245. STROM, I. M., Does knowledge of grammar improve reading? *English Journal*, 1956, 49, 561-570.

246. SUTTON, R. S., A study of certain factors associated with reading readiness in the kindergarten. *Journal of Educational Research*, 1955, 48, 531-538.

247. SWENSON, Esther J., A study of the relationships among various types of reading scores on general and science material. *Journal of Educational Research*, 1942, 36, 81-90.

248. TAYLOR, C. D., The effect of training on reading readiness. *Studies in reading* II. London, England, E. C. 4: University of London Press, Ltd., 1950, 63-80.

249. TEMPLIN, M. C., *Certain language skills in children*. Minneapolis: University of Minnesota Press, 1957.

250. TERMAN, L. M., and ODEN, Melita H., *The gifted child grows up*. Stanford, Calif.: Stanford University Press, 1947.

251. TERMAN, Sibyl, and WALCUTT, C. C., *Reading: chaos and cure*. New York: McGraw-Hill Book Company, 1958.

251a. THAYER, L. O., and PRONKO, N. H., Some psychological factors in the reading of fiction. *Journal of Genetic Psychology*, 1958, 93, 113-117.

252. THORNDIKE, E. L., The vocabulary of books for children in grades 3 to 8. *Teachers College Record*, 1936-37, 38, 196-205; 316-323; 416-429.

253. THURSTONE, T. G., *Reading for understanding*. Chicago: Science Research Associates, Inc., 1958.

254. TINKER, M. A., Eye movements in reading. *Journal of Educational Research*, 1936, 30, 241-277.

255. —— Rate of work in reading performance as measured in standardized tests. *Journal of Educational Psychology*, 1945, 36, 217-228.

256. —— Recent studies of eye movements in reading. *Psychological Bulletin*, 1958, 54, 215-231.

257. —— Speed versus comprehension in reading as affected by level of difficulty. *Journal of Educational Psychology*, 1939, 30, 81-94.

258. —— The relation of speed to comprehension in reading. *School and Society*, 1932, 36, 158-160.

259. —— The study of eye movements in reading. *Psychological Bulletin*, 1946, 43, 93-120.

260. —— and RUSSELL, W. A., *Introduction to methods in experimental psychology*. New York: Appleton-Century-Crofts, Inc., 1958.

261. TRAXLER, A. E., *The nature and use of reading tests*. Educational Records Bulletin No. 34. New York: Educational Records Bureau, 1941.

262. —— and JUNGEBLUT, Ann, *Research in reading during another four years*. Bulletin No. 75. New York: Educational Records Bureau, 1960.

263. —— with the assistance of SEDER, Margaret, *Ten years of research in reading*. Bulletin No. 32. New York: Educational Records Bureau, 1941.

264. —— and TOWNSEND, Agatha, *Another five years of research in reading*. Bulletin No. 46. New York: Educational Records Bureau, 1946.

265. —— and TOWNSEND, Agatha, *Eight more years of research in reading*. Bulletin No. 64. New York: Educational Records Bureau, 1955.

266. TREACY, John P., The relationship of reading skills to the ability to solve arithmetic problems. *Journal of Educational Research*, 1944, 37, 86-96.

267. TRIGGS, Frances O., A comparison of auditory and silent presentations of reading comprehension tests. *The 14th Yearbook, National Council on Measurements Used in Education*. Princeton, N. J.: Educational Testing Service, 1957, 1-7.

268. —— *Reading*. Mountain Home, N. C.: The Committee on Diagnostic Reading Tests, Inc., 1960.

269. TRONSBERG, Josephine, The place of phonics in basal reading instruction. *The Reading Teacher*, 1954, 8, 18-20; 38.

270. University Elementary Demonstration School Faculty, *Illustrative teaching units for the elementary grades*. Minneapolis: University of Minnesota Press, 1941.

271. University Elementary Demonstration School Faculty, *Using community resources: Illustrative experience units for grades one to six*. Minneapolis: University of Minnesota Press, 1948.

272. VERNON, M. D., *Backwardness in reading*. Cambridge: Cambridge University Press, 1957.

273. WEBB, W. B., and WALLON, E. J., Comprehension by reading versus hearing. *Journal of Applied Psychology*, 1956, 40, 237-240.

274. WESTOVER, F. L., A comparison of listening and reading as a means of testing. *Journal of Educational Research*, 1958, 52, 23-26.

275. —— *Controlled eye movements versus practice exercises in reading*. New York: Bureau of Publications, Teachers College, Columbia University, 1946.

276. WHIPPLE, Gertrude, Desirable materials, facilities and resources for reading, *Reading in the elementary school*. Forty-eighth Yearbook of the National Society for the Study of Education, Part II. Chicago: University of Chicago Press, 1949, 147-171.

277. WILLIAMS, G. H., What does research tell us about readiness for beginning reading? *The Reading Teacher*, 1953, 6, 34-40.

278. WITTY, P. (ed.), *Development in and through reading*, Sixtieth Yearbook of the National Society for the Study of Education, Part I. Chicago: University of Chicago Press, 1961.

279 —— *How to become a better reader*. Boston: D. C. Heath and Company, 1949.

280. —— Improving the reading ability of gifted pupils, in *Better readers for our times*. New York: Scholastic Magazines, 1956, 147-150.

281. —— Phonics study and word analysis. *Elementary English*, 1953, 30, 296-305.

282. —— *Reading in modern education*. Boston: D. C. Heath and Company, 1949.

283. —— and GOLDBERG, S., The army's training program for illiterate, non-English speaking and educationally retarded men. *Elementary English Review*, 1943, 20, 306-311.

284. —— and KOPEL, D., *Reading and the educative process*. Boston: Ginn and Company, 1939.

285. —— and KOPEL, D., Sinistrad and mixed manual-ocular behavior in reading disability. *Journal of Educational Psychology*, 1936, 27, 119-134.

286. —— and SIZEMORE, R. A., Studies in listening, I. Relative values of oral and visual presentations. *Elementary English*, 1958, 35, 583-592.

287. —— and SIZEMORE, R. A., Studies in listening, II. Realtive values of oral and visual presentations. *Elementary English*, 1959, 36, 59-70.

288. —— and SIZEMORE, R. A., Studies in listening, III. The effectiveness of visual and auditory presentations with changes in age and grade levels. *Elementary English*, 1959, 36, 130-140.

289. WOODS, E. I., A study of entering B1 children in the Los Angeles city schools. *Journal of Educational Research*, 1937, 21, 9-19.

290. WRIGHTSTONE, J. W., *Appraisal of growth in reading*. Educational Research Bulletin No. 2. New York: Board of Education, City of New York, 1941.

291. YOAKAM, G. A., *Basal reading instruction*. New York: McGraw-Hill Book Company, 1955.

292. YOUNG, William E., Recent research on reading in the social studies. *Education*, 1941, 62, 18-26.

Appendix I: Tests

Note: Name of publisher is abbreviated. The key to abbreviations is given below. Prices may be obtained from the most recent catalogues, which publishers will send upon request. The prices are not quoted here because they change frequently. Representative tests rather than a complete list are given.

Key to Publishing Companies

APC   Acorn Publishing Company, Inc., Rockville Center, N. Y.

BEM   Bureau of Educational Measurements, Kansas State Teachers College, Emporia, Kansas.

BP   Bureau of Publications, Teachers College, Columbia University, 525 W. 120 St., New York 27, N. Y.

CDRT   Committee on Diagnostic Reading Tests, Inc., Mountain Home, N. C.

CTB   California Test Bureau, 5916 Hollywood Blvd., Los Angeles 28, Calif.

CTD-ETS   Cooperative Test Division, Educational Testing Service, Princeton, N. J.

EMH   E. M. Hale and Co., 320 S. Barstow St., Eau Claire, Wis.

ERB   Educational Records Bureau, 21 Audubon Ave., New York 32, N. Y.

ETB   Educational Test Bureau, 720 Washington Ave., S. E., Minneapolis 14, Minn.

GC   Ginn and Company, P. O. Box 191, Boston 17, Mass.

GP   Garrard Press, 119 W. Park Ave., Champaign, Ill.

HBW   Harcourt, Brace & World, Inc., New York 17, N. Y.

HM   Houghton Mifflin Co., 2 Park St., Boston 7, Mass.

LC   Lyons and Carnahan, 2500 Prairie Ave., Chicago 16, Ill.

NPC   C. H. Nevins Printing Co., Pittsburgh, Pa.

OSUP   Ohio State University Press, Columbus, Ohio.

PC   Psychological Corporation, 522 Fifth Ave., New York 18, N. Y.

PSP   Public School Publishing Co., Division of the Bobbs-Merrill Co., Inc., 1720 E. 38th St., Indianapolis 6, Ind.

SC   Stech Co., Austin, Tex.

SPS   Seattle Public Schools, Seattle, Wash.

SRA   Science Research Associates, Inc., 57 W. Grand Ave., Chicago 10, Ill.

ST   C. H. Stoelting Co., 424 N. Homan Ave., Chicago, Ill.

STS   Scholastic Testing Service, Inc., 3774 West Devon Ave., Chicago 45, Ill.

SUP   Stanford University Press, Stanford University, Calif.

VW   Van Wagenen, Psycho-Educational Research Laboratories, 1729 Irving Ave. S., Minneapolis 5, Minn.

WPC   Webster Publishing Co., 1808 Washington Ave., St. Louis 3, Mo.

A. Representative Intelligence Tests

Arthur Point Scale of Performance Tests. ST, 1943 (Form I), also PC. Ages 4.5 or 5.5 to superior adults. Two forms. Time: 45-90 minutes. Individual test.

California Test of Mental Maturity. CTB. Grades kgn-1, 1-3, 4-8, 7-9, 9-13, 10-16, and adults. One form. Time: 48-92 minutes. Three scores: total mental, language, nonlanguage.

Chicago Non-Verbal Examination. PC. Age 7-adult. One form. Time: about 55 minutes. Group test.

Chicago Tests of Primary Mental Abilities. SRA. Ages 11-17. One form for long test, two for shortened version. Time: 25 minutes, short form; 240 for long form. Group test.

Cornell-Coxe Performance Scale. ST. Ages 6-15. One form. Time: about 50 minutes. A nonverbal performance scale. Individual test.

Davis-Eells Test of Intelligence or Problem-Solving Ability. PC. Grades 1, 2, 3-6. One form. Time: 60-100 minutes. No reading involved. Group test.

Detroit Beginning First-Grade Intelligence (Revised). HBW. Beginning grade 1. One form. Time: 30-35 minutes. No reading required. Group test.

Detroit Advanced First-Grade Intelligence Test. HBW. High first grade or beginning grade 2. One form. Time: 30-35 minutes. No reading required. Group test.

Detroit Primary Intelligence Test. PSP. Grades 2-3. Two forms. Time: about 35 minutes. No reading required. Group test.

Detroit Tests of Learning Aptitude. PSP. Ages 4-adult. One form. Individual test.

Henmon-Nelson Tests of Mental Ability, rev. ed. HM. Grades 3-6, 6-9, 9-12. Two forms. Time: 30 minutes. Group test.

Junior Scholastic Aptitude Test, rev. ed. ERB. Three forms. Time: 60 minutes. Group test.

Kuhlmann-Anderson Intelligence Tests, 6th ed. ETB. Grades 1, 2, 3, 4, 5, 6, 7-8, 9-12. One form. Time: 40-45 minutes. Group test.

Kuhlmann-Finch Intelligence Tests. ETB. Grades 1, 2, 3, 4, 5, 6, 7-9. Time: 25-30 minutes. Group test.

Lorge-Thorndike Intelligence Test. HM. Grades kgn-12. Time: 27-34 minutes. Group test.

New Rhode Island Intelligence Test. PSP. Ages 3-6. Two forms. Time: 30 minutes. Group test.

Otis Quick Scoring Mental Ability Tests. HBW. Grades 1-4, 4-9, 9-16. Two forms. Time: 30-40 minutes. Group test.

Pintner General Ability Tests. HBW. Grades kgn-2, three forms; 2.5-4.5, two forms; 4.5-9.5, two forms. Time: 45 minutes. Group tests.

Revised Stanford-Binet Scale, 3rd ed. HM. Age 2-adult. Two forms. No time limit. Individual test.

Scholastic Mental Ability Tests. STS. Grades kgn-1, 2-3, 4-9. One or two forms at different levels. Time: 26-60 minutes. Group test.

SRA Primary Mental Abilities. SRA Grades 5-7, 7-11. One form. Time: 60-70 minutes. Group test.

Wechsler Intelligence Scale for Children. PC. Ages 5-15. Verbal and performance scores. One form. Time: 40-60 minutes. Individual test.

B. Representative Reading Readiness Tests

American School Reading Readiness Test. PSP. Grade 1. One form. Time: about 45 minutes. Vocabulary, visual discrimination of various kinds, recognition of words, following directions, memory for geometric forms.

Binion-Beck Reading Readiness Tests for Kindergarten and First Grade. APC. Grades kgn-1. One form. Time: about 40 minutes. Picture vocabulary and discrimination, following directions, memory for story, motor control.

Checklist for Reading Readiness. SPS. One form. Physical development, work habits and attitudes, skills, language abilities.

Diagnostic Reading Tests: Reading Readiness. CDRT. Grades kgn-1. One form. Untimed. Relationships, co-ordination, left-to-right approach, visual discrimination, vocabulary.

Gates Reading Readiness Tests. BP. Grades kgn-1. One form. Time: about 50 minutes. Picture directions, word matching, word-card matching, rhyming, letters, and numbers.

Harrison-Stroud Reading Readiness Profiles. HM. Grades kgn-1. One form. Time: 76 minutes. Using symbols, visual discrimination, using the context, auditory discrimination, using context and auditory cues, naming letters.

Lee-Clark Reading Readiness Tests. CTB. Grades kgn-1. One form. Time: about 15 minutes. Letter symbols, concepts, word symbols.

Metropolitan Readiness Tests. HBW. Grades kgn-1. Two forms. Time: about 60 minutes. Reading readiness, number readiness, drawing a man.

Monroe Reading Aptitude Tests. HM. Grade 1. One form. Time: about 50 minutes. The 17 subtests include visual functions, auditory discrimination, memory for a story, motor control, vocabulary knowledge, length of sentences used, and laterality preferences.

Murphy-Durrell Diagnostic Reading Readiness Test. HBW. Grade 1. One form. Time: parts 1-2, about 60 minutes; part 3, about 35-50 minutes. Auditory, visual, and learning-rate scores.

Van Wagenen Reading Readiness Scales. VW. Grades kgn-1. One form. Part I: Listening vocabulary; Part II: Range of information, perception of relations, opposites, memory span for ideas, word discrimination. Part I and Part II may be obtained separately.

C. Representative Reading and Study Skill Tests

Ability to Interpret Reading Materials in the Natural Sciences: Iowa Tests of Educational Development, Test 6. SRA. Grades 9-13. One form. Time: 60 minutes. Interpreting reading materials in natural sciences.

Ability to Interpret Reading Materials in the Social Studies: Iowa Tests of Educational Development, Test 5. SRA. Grades 9-13. One form. Time: 60 minutes. Interpreting social studies materials.

American School Achievement Tests. PSP. Grades 1, 2-3, 4-6, 7-9. Three forms. Reading and arithmetic; reading vocabulary, arithmetic and spelling; paragraph meaning and vocabulary; paragraph meaning and vocabulary, respectively, at successive levels.

Bennett Use of Library Test. BEM. High school and college. Two forms. Time: 50 minutes. Questions concerning library rules and practices.

Brown-Carlsen Listening Comprehension Test. HBW. Grades 9-13. Two forms. Time: about 50 minutes. Immediate recall, following directions, recognizing transitions, word meanings, lecture comprehension.

California Reading Test. CTB. Grades 1, 2, 3, lower 4, 4-6, 7-9, 9-14. Four forms. Time: 20-50 minutes. Vocabulary, comprehension, total score.

Chapman-Cook Speed of Reading Test. ETB. Grades 4-8. Two forms. Time: 2½ minutes. Speed of reading easy material with check on comprehension.

Chicago Reading Tests. EMH. Grades 1-2, 2-4, 4-6, 6-8. Three forms. Time: 31-45 minutes. Comprehension of words, sentences, and paragraphs. Comprehension of maps and graphs added in grades 4-8.

Cooperative Dictionary Test. CTD-ETS. Grades 7-12. One form. Time: 30 minutes. Alphabetizing, spelling, pronunciation, meaning.

Detroit Reading Tests. HBW. Grades 2-9. Two to four forms. Time: 5-8 minutes. Comprehension and rate.

Detroit Word Recognition Test. HBW. Grades 1-3. Four forms. Time: 4-6 minutes. Word recognition.

Developmental Reading Tests: Primary Reading. LC. Grades 1-3 (three levels: primer reading, lower primary reading, upper primary reading). One form. Time: 10-15 minutes on each part. Part I, basic vocabulary; Part II, general comprehension; Part III, specific comprehension.

Developmental Reading Tests: Intermediate Reading. LC. Grades 4-6. One form. Time: 32 minutes. Part I, basic vocabulary; Part II, factual reading: Part III, reading to organize; Part IV, reading to evaluate—interpret; Part V, reading to appreciate.

Diagnostic Reading Tests. CDRT. Grades kgn-4, 4-6, 7-13. Two to 8 forms. Time: 15-60 minutes on different parts. Survey test: rate, narrative comprehension, vocabulary and textbook-type comprehension. Diagnostic tests: vocabulary, comprehension, rate, word attack.

Doren Diagnostic Reading Test. ETB. Any grade for analysis of word-recognition difficulties. One form.

Dolch Basic Sight Word Test. GP. Assigned to no specific grade. Untimed. Recognition of the 220 words in the Dolch Basic Word List.

Durost-Center Word Mastery Test. HBW. Grades 9-13. Two forms. Time: two class periods. Meanings for isolated words and words in context.

Durrell Analysis of Reading Difficulty. HBW. Grades 1-6. Time: 30-90 minutes. Materials for individual diagnosis of reading difficulties.

Durrell-Sullivan Reading Capacity and Achievement Tests. HBW. Grades 2.5-4.5; 3-6. Two forms. Time: 30-45 minutes. Word and paragraph meaning, spelling, written recall.

Dvorak-Van Wagenen Diagnostic Examination of Silent Reading Abilities. VW. Grades 4-6, 7-9, 10-12. One form. Untimed except rate test. Rate of comprehension, perception of vocabulary in isolation, range of information, paragraph comprehension.

Gates Primary Reading Test. BP. Grades 1-2. Three forms. Time: 15-20 minutes each part. Word recognition, sentence and paragraph reading.

Gates Advanced Primary Reading Test. BP. Grades 2-3. Three forms. Time: 15-25 minutes. Word recognition and paragraph reading.

Gates Basic Reading Test. BP. Grades 3-8. Four forms: Time: about 35 minutes. Reading to appreciate general significance, predict outcomes, understand directions, note details.

Gates Reading Survey. BP. Grades 3-10. Two forms. Time: 45-60 minutes. Vocabulary and comprehension plus measures of rate and accuracy.

Gates Reading Diagnostic Test. BP. Grades 1-8. Two forms. Time: 60-90 minutes. Materials for individual diagnosis of difficulties.

Gilmore Oral Reading Test. HBW. Grades 1-8. Two forms. Time: 15-20 minutes. Comprehension, rate, and accuracy of oral reading. Analysis of errors used to diagnose reading difficulties.

Gray Standardized Oral Reading Paragraph Test. PSP. Grades 1-8. One form. Time: about 5-10 minutes. Rate and accuracy of oral reading. Analysis of errors used to diagnose reading difficulties.

Gray Standardized Oral Reading Check Tests. PSP. Grades 1-8. Five forms. Time: about 1-3 minutes. Rate and accuracy of oral reading.

High School Reading Test. APC. Grades 7-12. Two forms. Time: 40 minutes. Vocabulary, word discrimination, sentence meaning, paragraph comprehension.

Iowa Every-Pupil Tests of Basic Skills. HM. Grades 3-5, 5-9. Four forms. Time: 55-90 minutes. Test A: vocabulary and paragraph comprehension. Test B: reading maps, use of references, index, dictionary, and alphabetizing (3-5) or reading graphs, charts, and tables (5-9).

Iowa Silent Reading Test. HBW. Grades 4-8, 9-13. Four forms. Time: 45-60 minutes. Directed reading, comprehension of words, sentences, paragraphs, rate of reading, skill in alphabetizing and indexing.

Kelley-Greene Reading Comprehension Test. HBW. Grades 9-13. Three forms. Time: 63 minutes, three sessions. Paragraph comprehension, directed reading (finding answers), retention of details, rate.

Leavell Oral Reading Test. ETB. Grades 1-high school. One form. Individual test.

Lee-Clark Reading Test—First Reader. CTB. Grades 1-2. Two forms. Time: about 25 minutes. Auditory and visual stimuli, following directions, completion, inference.

Los Angeles Elementary Reading Test. CTB. Grades 3-9. Four forms. Time: 30 minutes. Paragraph comprehension.

Los Angeles Primary Reading Test. CTB. Grades 1-3. Four forms. Time: 10 minutes. Comprehension of sentences and paragraphs.

McCullough Word Analysis Tests. GC. Grades 4 through college. One form. Untimed. Diagnoses 7 types of word-analysis skills, 210 items.

McGuffey Diagnostic Reading Tests. ETB. Grades 4-6. One form: Time: two class periods. Syllabication, sound recognition, vocabulary, appreciation, speed, understanding. Group test.

Metropolitan Achievement Tests: Reading. HBW. Grades 1, 2, 3, 3-4, 5, 6, 7, 8. Three forms. Time: about 45 minutes. Paragraph comprehension and vocabulary.

Michigan Speed of Reading Test. PC. Grades 6-16. Two forms. Time: 7 minutes. Rate of reading easy material.

Monroe Diagnostic Reading Examination. ST. Grades 1-6. One form. Time: about 45 minutes. Materials for individual diagnosis of difficulties.

Monroe Revised Silent Reading Tests. PSP. Grades 3-5, 6-8, high school. Three and two forms respectively. Time: 4-5 minutes. Rate and comprehension.

Monroe-Sherman Group Diagnostic Reading and Achievement Tests. NPC. Grade 3 and up. One form. Achievement tests: paragraph meaning, speed, word discrimination, arithmetic, and spelling; aptitude tests: visual memory, auditory memory and discrimination, motor speed, vocabulary. Group test.

Nelson Silent Reading Test. HM. Grades 3-9. Two forms. Time: 30 minutes. Vocabulary and comprehension.

Nelson-Lohmann Reading Test. PSP. Grades 4-8. Two forms. Reading comprehension.

Primary Reading Test. HM. Grade 1. One form. Untimed, two sittings. Recognition of word forms, meaning of words, meaning of sentences, meaning of paragraphs.

Reading Comprehension: Cooperative English Test. CTD-ETC. Grades 7-12, 11-16. Four forms. Time: 40 minutes. Vocabulary, speed, and level of comprehension.

Reading Test: National Achievement Tests. APC. Grades 3-6, 6-8. Two forms. Time: 33 minutes. Following directions, sentence and paragraph meaning, rate.

Sangren-Woody Reading Test. HBW. Grades 4-8. Two forms: Time: 27 minutes. Word meaning, rate, fact material, total meaning, central thought, following directions, organization.

Schrammel-Gray High School and College Reading Test. PSP. Grades 7-13. Two forms. Time: 25 minutes. Paragraph comprehension.

Silent Reading Diagnostic Tests. LC. Grades 2.5-6 and for retarded pupils in junior and senior high school. One form. Time: about 90 minutes in two sessions. Recognition of words in isolation and in context, recognition of reversible words in context, locating elements, syllabification, locating root words, word elements, beginning sounds, rhyming sounds, letter sounds, and word synthesis.

SRA Achievement Series: Reading. SRA. Grades (reading) 1, 2; 2-4; 4-6; 6-9; (work-study skills) 4-6; 6-9. One form grades 1, 2; two forms other grades. Verbal-pictorial association, language perception, comprehension, vocabulary in grades 1, 2; comprehension and vocabulary in grades 2-9; work-study skills in grades 4-9.

SRA Reading Record. SRA. Grades 7-12. One form. Time: 40 minutes. Rate, comprehension, sentence and paragraph meaning, general and technical vocabulary, graph and other specialized reading.

Stanford Achievement Test: Reading. HBW. Grades 2-3, 4-6, 7-9. Three (primary) to five forms. Time: 30-40 minutes. Paragraph and word meaning.

Stroud-Hieronymus Primary Reading Profiles. HM. Grades 1-2. One form. Aptitude for reading, auditory association, word recognition, word attack, reading comprehension.

Study-Habits Inventory. SUP. Grades 12-16. One form. Time: 10-20 minutes. Check-list of study habits.

Survey of Study Habits, Experimental Edition. ERB. Grades 8-14. One form. Time: 30 minutes. Self-analysis of study habits.

Test of Study Skills. SC. Grades 4-9. Two forms. Time: 60 minutes. Use of references, reading graphs, tables, maps, critical inference.

Test on the Use of Books and Libraries: General Education Series. CTD-ETS. Grades 7-12. Two forms. Time: about 50 minutes. Use of library, books, an index, card catalog, dictionary, and various kinds of reference sources.

Tests of Natural Sciences: Vocabulary and Interpertation of Reading Materials: Cooperative Inter-American Tests. CTD-ETS. Grades 8-13. Two forms. Time: 35 minutes. Vocabulary, interpretation.

Tests of Reading: Cooperative Inter-American Tests. CTD-ETS. Grades 1-3, 4-7, 8-13. Two forms. Time: about 25-50 minutes. Vocabulary and comprehension.

Tests of Social Studies: Vocabulary and Interpretation of Reading Materials: Cooperative Inter-American Tests. CTD-ETS. Grades 8-13. Two forms. Time: 35 minutes. Vocabulary, interpretation.

Tests of Study Skills. SC. Grades 4-9. Two forms. Time: 60 minutes. Use of reference books, indexes, and dictionary, reading graphs, tables and maps, critical inference.

Thorndike-Lorge Reading Test. BP. Grades 7-9. Two forms. Time: 40 minutes. Measures a variety of factors in silent reading including ability to interpret idioms and figures of speech.

Traxler Silent Reading Test. PSP. Grades 7-10. Four forms. Time: 46 minutes. Rate, story comprehension, word meaning, paragraph meaning.

Use of Sources of Information: Iowa Tests of Educational Develpment, Test 9. SRA. Grades 9-13. One form. Time: 27 minutes. Use of sources of information.

Van Wagenen Analytical Reading Scales. VW. Grades 4-6, 7-9, 10-12. One form. Untimed. Comprehension: central thought, details, ideas spread over several sentences, and interpretation. Each division may be obtained separately.

Van Wagenen Comprehensive Reading Scales. VW. Grades 4-12 (separate for each grade 4-8, 9 and 10 in one, 11 and 12 in one). One form. Untimed. Paragraph comprehension: grasping central thoughts, noting details, ideas spread over several sentences, inferences and interpretation. Each division may be obtained separately.

Van Wagenen Listening Vocabulary Scales. VW. Grades 2-6 (separate for each grade). One form. Untimed. Listening vocabulary knowledge.

Van Wagenen Primary Reading Scales. VW. Grades 1, 2, 3. One form. Untimed. Vocabulary and comprehension.

Williams Primary Reading Tests. PSP. Grades 1-3. Two forms. Time: 20 minutes. Vocabulary and sentence comprehension.

Wide Range Vocabulary Test. PC. Grades 3-16. Two forms. Time: about 10 minutes. Vocabulary knowledge. May be used for quick estimate of intelligence.

Work-Study Skills: Iowa Every-Pupil Tests of Basic Skills. HM. Grades 3-5, 5-9. Four forms. Time: 47-77 minutes. Map reading, alphabetizing (or graphing in advanced battery), and use of references, index, and dictionary.

Appendix II: Texts and Monographs

A. Representative Books on Teaching Reading and Remedial Instruction

ABRAHAM, W., *A new look at reading: A guide to the language arts.* Boston: Porter Sargent, 1956.

Adult reading. The Fifty-fifth Yearbook of the National Society for the Study of Education, Part II. Chicago: University of Chicago Press, 1956.

ANDERSON, I. H., and DEARBORN, W. F., *The psychology of teaching reading.* New York: The Ronald Press Company, 1952.

ARTLEY, A. S., *Your child learns to read.* Chicago: Scott, Foresman and Company, 1953.

AUSTIN, Mary C., BUSH, C. L., and HUEBNER, Mildred H., *Reading evaluation: appraisal techniques for school and classroom.* New York: The Ronald Press Company, 1961.

BAMMAN, H. A., HOGAN, Ursula, and GREENE, C. E., *Reading instruction in the secondary school.* New York: Longmans, Green and Company, Inc., 1961.

BARBE, Walter B., *Educator's guide to personalized reading instruction.* Englewood Cliffs, N. J.: Prentice-Hall, Inc., 1961.

BETTS, E. A., *Foundations of reading instruction.* New York: American Book Company, 1957.

BLAIR, G. M., *Diagnostic and remedial teaching,* Part I. New York: The Macmillan Company, 1956.

BOND, G. L., and TINKER, M. A., *Reading difficulties.* New York: Appleton-Century-Crofts, Inc., 1957.

—— and WAGNER, Eva B., *Child growth in reading.* Chicago: Lyons and Carnahan, 1955.

—— and WAGNER, Eva B., *Teaching the child to read,* 3rd ed. New York: The Macmillan Company, 1960.

BROOM, M. E., DUNCAN, M. A. A., EMIG, D., and STUEBER, J., *Effective reading instruction,* 2nd ed. New York: McGraw-Hill Book Company, Inc., 1951.

BURTON, W. H., BAKER, C., and KEMP, G. K., *Reading in child development.* Indianapolis: Bobbs-Merrill Company, Inc., 1956.

CARTER, H. J. L., and McGINNIS, Dorothy J., *Learning to read: A handbook for teachers.* New York: McGraw-Hill Book Company, 1953.

CAUSEY, O. S. (ed.), *The reading teacher's reader.* New York: The Ronald Press Company, 1958.

DARROW, Helen F., and HOWES, V. M., *Approaches to individualized reading.* New York: Appleton-Century-Crofts, Inc., 1960.

DAWSON, Mildred A., and BAMMAN, H. A., *Fundamentals of basic reading instruction*. New York: Longmans, Green and Company, 1959.

DEBOER, J. J., and DALLMANN, Martha, *The teaching of reading*. New York: Holt, Rinehart and Winston, Inc., 1960.

DELACATO, C. H., *The treatment and prevention of reading problems: The neuropsychological approach*. Springfield, Ill.: Charles C. Thomas, 1959.

Development in and through reading. The Sixtieth Yearbook of the National Society for the Study of Education, Part I. Chicago: University of Chicago Press, 1961.

DOLCH, E. W., *Psychology and teaching of reading*, 2nd ed. Champaign, Ill.: The Garrard Press, 1951.

—— *Teaching primary reading*, 2nd ed. Champaign, Ill.: The Garrard Press, 1950.

—— *Problems in reading*. Champaign, Ill.: The Garrard Press, 1948.

DUKER, S., and NALLY, T. P., *The truth about your child's reading*. New York: Crown Publishers, Inc., 1956.

DUNCAN, J., *Backwardness in reading*. London: George G. Harrap and Company, 1953.

DURRELL, D. D., *Improving reading instruction*. New York: Harcourt, Brace & World, Inc., 1956.

EPHRON, Beulah K., *Emotional difficulties in reading*. New York: The Julian Press, Inc., 1953.

FOX, Lorene K., and BROGAN, Peggy, *Helping children read*. New York: Holt, Rinehart and Winston, Inc., 1961.

GRAY, W. S., *On their own in reading*, 2nd ed. Chicago: Scott, Foresman and Company, 1960.

HARRIS, A. J., *How to increase reading ability*, 4th ed. New York: Longmans, Green and Company, 1961.

HARRISON, M. L., *Reading readiness*, rev. ed. Boston: Houghton Mifflin Company, 1939.

HEILMAN, A. W., *Principles and practices of teaching reading*. Columbus, Ohio: Charles E. Merrill Books, Inc., 1961.

HESTER, K. B., *Teaching every child to read*. New York: Harper and Brothers, 1955.

HILDRETH, Gertrude, *Readiness for school beginners*. New York: Harcourt, Brace & World, Inc., 1950.

—— *Teaching reading*. New York: Holt, Rinehart and Winston, Inc., 1958.

HUNNICUTT, C. W., and IVERSON, W. J. (eds.), *Research in the three R's*, Part I. New York: Harper and Brothers, 1958.

JUDSON, H., *Techniques of reading*. New York: Harcourt, Brace & World, Inc., 1954.

KIRK, S., *Teaching reading to slow-learning children*. Boston: Houghton Mifflin Company, 1940.

KOTTMEYER, W., *Teacher's guide for remedial reading*. St. Louis: Webster Publishing Company, 1959.

LAZAR, M. (ed.), *The retarded reader in the junior high school*. Publication No. 31. New York: Board of Education, City of New York, Bureau of Educational Research, 1952.

—— DRAPER, M. K., and SCHWIETERT, L. H., *A practical guide to individualized reading*. Publication No. 40. New York: Board of Education, City of New York, Bureau of Educational Research, 1960.

McKEE, P., *The teaching of reading in the elementary school*. Boston: Houghton Mifflin Company, 1948.

McKIM, M. G., *Guiding growth in reading*. New York: The Macmillan Company, 1955.

MONROE, M., *Children who cannot read*. Chicago: University of Chicago Press, 1932.

—— *Growing into reading*. Chicago: Scott, Foresman and Company, 1951.

MOORE, E. H., *Fives at school: Teaching in the kindergarten*. New York: G. P. Putnam's Sons, 1959.

Reading in high school and college. Forty-seventh Yearbook of the National Society for the Study of Education, Part II. Chicago: University of Chicago Press, 1948.

Reading in the elementary school. Forty-eighth Yearbook of the National Society for the Study of Education, Part II. Chicago: University of Chicago Press, 1949.

ROBINSON, H. M., *Why pupils fail in reading*. Chicago: University of Chicago Press, 1946.

RUSSELL, D. H., *Children learn to read*, 2nd ed. Boston: Ginn and Company, 1961.

SCHONELL, F. J., *The psychology and teaching of reading*, 3rd ed. Toronto, Canada: Clarke, Irwin and Company, Ltd., 1951.

SHAW, P. B., *Effective reading and learning*. New York: Thomas Y. Crowell Company, 1955.

SIMPSON, E. A., *Helping high-school students read better*. Chicago: Science Research Associates, Inc., 1954.

SMITH, D. E. P., and CARRIGAN, Patricia, *The nature of reading disability*. New York: Harcourt, Brace & World, Inc., 1960.

SMITH, H. P., and DECHANT, Emerald, *Psychology in teaching reading*. Englewood Cliffs, N. J.: Prentice-Hall, Inc., 1961.

SPACHE, G. D., and BERG, P. C., *The art of efficient reading*. New York: The Macmillan Company, 1955.

SPALDING, Romalda B., and SPALDING, W. T., *The writing road to reading*. New York: Whiteside, Inc., and William Morrow and Company, 1957.

STEWART, L. Jane, HELLER, Frieda M., and ALBERTY, Elsie J., *Improving reading in the junior high school*. New York: Appleton-Century-Crofts, Inc., 1957.

STONE, C. R., *Progress in primary reading*. St. Louis: Webster Publishing Company, 1950.

STRANG, Ruth, and BRACKEN, Dorothy K., *Making better readers*. Boston: D. C. Heath and Company, 1957.

—— and LINDQUIST, D. M., *The administrator and the improvement of reading*. New York: Appleton-Century-Crofts, Inc., 1960.

—— McCULLOUGH, Constance M., and TRAXLER, A. E., *The improvement of reading*, 3rd ed. New York: McGraw-Hill Book Company, 1961.

TRIGGS, Frances O., *Reading: Kindergarten through college*. Mountain Home, N. C.: The Author (Chairman: Committee on Diagnostic Reading Tests, Inc.), 1960.

VEATCH, Jeannette, *Individualizing your reading program*. New York: G. P. Putnam's Sons, 1959.

VERNON, M. D., *Backwardness in reading*. New York (Branch): Cambridge University Press, 1957.

WITTY, P., *Reading in modern education.* Boston: D. C. Heath and Company, 1949.

YOAKAM, G. A., *Basal reading instruction.* New York: McGraw-Hill Book Company, Inc., 1955.

WOOLF, M. D., and WOOLF, Jeanne A., *Remedial reading: Teaching and treatment.* New York: McGraw-Hill Book Company, Inc., 1957.

B. Selected Monographs and Conference Reports

AUSTIN, Mary C., Director, and others, *The torch lighters: Tomorrow's teachers of reading.* Cambridge, Mass.: Graduate School of Education, Harvard University (distributed by Harvard University Press), 1961.

BOND, G. L., and HANDLAN, Bertha, *Adjusting instruction in reading to individual differences.* Minneapolis: University of Minnesota Press, 1948.

BONEY, C. DeWitt, and others, *Children learn to read.* Chicago: Committee on Reading in the Elementary Grades, National Council of Teachers of English, 1949.

CHALL, Jeanne, *Readability: An appraisal of research and applications.* Columbus, Ohio: Ohio State University, Bureau of Educational Research, 1958.

Child development through reading in the content fields. Kent State University Bulletin, Vol. 39, No. 11. Kent, Ohio: College of Education, Kent State University, 1952.

Conference Proceedings of the International Reading Association. Contains papers presented at annual meetings beginning 1956. New York: Scholastic Magazines (33 West 42nd Street).

Diagnostic reading tests: A history of their construction and validation. Mountain Home, N. C.: Committee on Diagnostic Reading Tests, Inc., 1952.

Five steps to reading success in mathematics, science and social studies. New York: Institute of Administrative Research (525 West 120th St.), 1959.

GANS, Roma, *Guiding children's reading through experiences.* New York: Bureau of Publications, Teachers College, Columbia University, 1941.

GRAY, W. S. (ed.), *Reading in an age of mass communication.* New York: Appleton-Century-Crofts, Inc., 1949.

—— *The teaching of reading and writing.* Chicago: Scott, Foresman and Company, 1956.

—— and ROGERS, Bernice, *Maturity in reading: Its nature and appraisal.* Chicago: University of Chicago Press, 1956.

MACDOUGALL, Ursula C., *If your child has reading difficulties.* New York: The Dalton School, 1952.

Proceedings of the Annual Conferences on Reading at the University of Chicago. Edited earlier by W. S. Gray and recently by Helen M. Robinson. Published as Supplementary Educational Monographs. Chicago: University of Chicago Press.

Reading in the content subjects. Kent State University Bulletin, Vol. 39, No. 5. Kent, Ohio: College of Education, Kent State University, 1951.

Reports of the Annual Conferences on Reading. Pittsburgh: University of Pittsburgh. Annual monographs which include papers and abstracts of papers given at the reading conferences.

ROBINSON, Helen M. (ed.), *Clinical studies in reading: I.* Chicago: University of Chicago Press, 1949.

—— (ed.), *Clinical studies in reading: II.* Chicago: University of Chicago Press, 1953.

STAUFFER, R. G. (compiler), *Reading instruction in the total school program.* Newark, Delaware: Reading Clinic, School of Education, University of Delaware, 1951.

Using the essay to teach reading, writing, thinking. New York: Institute of Administrative Research (525 W. 120th St.), 1957.

WILLIAMS, Dorothy (chairman), *The improvement of reading in the content subjects.* Albany Area Committee on Reading. Albany, N. Y.: Capital Area School Development Association, State University of New York State College, 1950.

WILLSON, Margaret F., and SCHNEYER, J. W. (prepared by), *Developmental reading in the junior high school.* Danville, Ill.: Interstate, 1959.

Yearbooks of the Claremont Reading Conferences. Claremont, Calif.: Claremont College Curriculum Library. Monographs which include papers given at the annual conferences.

Appendix III:

Sources of Graded Book Lists

A basic book collection for the elementary grades, 6th ed. Chicago: American Library Association, 1956.

A basic book collection for junior high schools. Chicago: American Library Association, 1956.

A graded list of library books and supplementary readers for elementary and high school. New York: Charles Scribner's Sons, 1954-55.

BEUST, N. (compiler), *Graded list of books for children*. Chicago: American Library Association, 1936. Brief description of books for grades 1-3, 4-6, and 7-9.

Bibliography of books for children. Washington, D. C.: Association for Childhood Education International, 1956. Books for ages 5 to 14.

BLAIR, G. M., *Diagnostic and remedial teaching*, rev. ed. New York: The Macmillan Company, 1956, 180-198. Various book lists for retarded readers in high school with grade levels indicated for some.

CARPENTER, H. McC., *Gateways to American history: An annotated graded list of books for slow learners in junior high school*. New York: H. W. Wilson Company, 1942. List of 200 books for social studies and English.

CARTER, H. L. J., and McGINNIS, D. J., *Learning to read*. New York: McGraw-Hill Book Company, Inc., 1953, 92-114. Reading materials classified according to various grade and interest levels. Also a graded list of books of interest to retarded readers, pp. 115-118.

Catalog of the best books for children. Wellesley Hills, Mass.: Junior Reviewers, 1956. Two thousand books classified by age and subject.

COLBURN, E., *Books and library reading for pupils of the intermediate grades*. Chicago: University of Chicago Press, 1942. An annotated and graded list classified as to subject matter.

COOKE, D. E. (chairman), and FRIER, E. A. (co-ordinator), *The road to better reading*. Albany, N. Y.: New York State Education Department, 1953. Texts for reading classes, pp. 64-66; adapted, simplified editions, pp. 69-70.

DAWSON, M. A., and BAMMAN, H. A., *Fundamentals of basic reading instruction*. New York: Longmans, Green and Company, Inc., 1959. Selected series of books with reading and interest levels indicated.

DEBOER, J. J., and DALLMANN, M., *The teaching of reading*. New York: Holt, Rinehart and Winston, Inc., 1960. Lists of book lists, some graded, pp. 260-262; award-winning books, pp. 262-265; lists of books for retarded readers, pp. 286-288.

DURRELL, D. D., *Improvement of basic reading abilities*. New York: Harcourt, Brace & World, Inc., 1940, 86-97. Graded list of books for teaching units at various grade levels. Also a selected list of books for remedial reading with vocabulary level and interest level indicated, pp. 112-114.

GRAY, L., and REESE, D., *Teaching children to read,* 2nd ed. New York: The Ronald Press Company, 1957. List of graded books, pp. 364-370.

HARRIS, A. J., How to increase reading ability, 4th ed. New York: Longmans, Green and Company, 1961, 594-607. A graded list of books for remedial reading; levels: grades 1-6.

HILDRETH, G., *Teaching reading.* New York: Holt, Rinehart and Winston, Inc., 1958, 547-550. Lists of booklists and other sources of information on children's books.

HILL, M. K. (compiler), *A bibliography of reading lists for retarded readers.* Extension Bulletin, College of Education Series, No. 37. Iowa City: State University of Iowa, 1953.

HOLLOWELL, L., *A book of children's literature,* 2nd ed. New York: Holt, Rinehart and Winston, Inc., 1950. Classified and graded book lists, pp. 623-657.

KINGERY, R. E., *How-to-do-it books.* New York: R. R. Bowker Company, 1954. List of books arranged from easy to advanced reading levels.

KIRK, S. A., *Teaching reading to slow-learning children.* Boston: Houghton Mifflin Company, 1940, 195-210. A bibliography of children's books suitable for slow-learning children. Pre-primer level through grade four.

LARRICK, N., *A teacher's guide to children's books.* Columbus, Ohio: Charles E. Merrill Books, Inc., 1960. Several graded lists of books.

LAZAR, May (ed.), *The retarded reader in the junior high school.* Bureau of Educational Research Bulletin, No. 31. New York: Board of Education, City of New York (110 Livingston St., Brooklyn 2, N. Y.), 1952, 122-124. Fiction, simplified classics, and informational books, grade levels 1-6.

—— DRAPER, M. K., and SCHWIETERT, L. H., *A practical guide to individualized reading.* Bureau of Educational Research Bulletin No. 40. New York: Board of Education, City of New York, 1960, 141-153. Books suggested for individualized reading, grades 1-2, 2-3, 4, and above.

LEARY, B. E., and SMITH, D. V., *Growing with books, a reading guide.* Eau Claire, Wis.: E. M. Hale, 1952-53.

McCONNELL, M. L., and WEST, D. H. (compilers), *Children's catalog,* 9th ed. New York: H. W. Wilson Company, 1956; supplement to 9th ed., 1957-59. Classified and graded lists.

McCULLOUGH, C. M., *Handbook for teaching the language arts.* South San Francisco, Calif.: Paragon Publications, 1958. Lists of basic series of readers, pp. 51-53; other books graded in levels: primer to third reader.

Roos, J. C., *Patterns in reading: an annotated book list for young people.* Chicago: American Library Association, 1954. Arranged according to interest areas and roughly as to difficulty.

RUE, E., *Subject index to books for primary grades.* Chicago: American Library Association, 1943. Arranged according to reading difficulty, pre-primer to third grade. (First supplement of 225 additional titles in 1946.)

—— *America, past and present: an annotated bibliography of children's stories.* New York: H. W. Wilson Company, 1948. Books for normal, retarded, and accelerated readers in junior high school age group.

—— *Subject index to books for intermediate grades.* Chicago: American Library Association, 1950. Books range from third to sixth grade in reading level.

RUSSELL, D. H., *Children learn to read,* 2nd ed. Boston: Ginn and Company, 1961. List of selected book lists, some graded, pp. 452-453.

SLATER, R., *Books for youth who dislike reading.* Columbus, Ohio: Ohio State University, 1941. A master list of lists.

SPACHE, G. D., *Basic reading materials graded by a new readability formula for primary materials* (mimeographed). Gainesville, Fla.: Reading Laboratory and Clinic, University of Florida. Grade levels of books in many basic reading series are given.

—— *Good books for poor readers.* Gainesville, Fla.: The Author, 1954. Titles arranged according to reading and interest levels, pp. 1-36; narrative materials adapted for poor readers (graded), pp. 37-49; graded books for boys and girls, pp. 76-79.

—— *Good reading for poor readers*, rev. ed., Champaign, Ill.: The Garrard Press, 1960. Graded and classified lists.

STRANG, R., and others, *Gateways to readable books.* New York: W. H. Wilson Company, 1952. Graded list of books for retarded readers of high school age.

—— McCULLOUGH, C. M., and TRAXLER, A. E., *The improvement of reading*, 3rd ed. New York: McGraw-Hill Book Company, Inc., 1961, Appendix C. Reading materials for grades 7-16.

SULLIVAN, H. B., and TOLMAN, L. E., high interest, low vocabulary reading materials. *Journal of Education* (published by Boston University School of Education), 1956, vol. 139, No. 2, pp. 1-132. A graded book list classified as to subject matter. The December, 1956 issue of the Journal.

WILKINSON, M. S., and others, *The right book for the right child.* New York: John Day Company, 1942. Lists of graded books, pre-primer to high school levels.

WOOLF, M. D., and WOOLF, J. A., *Remedial reading.* New York: McGraw-Hill Book Company, Inc., 1957. Lists of graded books for retarded readers, pp. 385-394.

Appendix IV:

Representative Sources of Materials[1]

ADAMS, B. P., *About books and children*. New York: Holt, Rinehart and Winston, Inc., 1953.

ADSHEAD, G. L., and DUFF, A., *An inheritance of poetry*. Boston: Houghton Mifflin Company, 1948. Anthology.

Aids in selection of materials for children and young people. Chicago: American Library Association.

ARBUTHNOT, M. H. (compiler), *Time for poetry*. Chicago: Scott, Foresman and Company, 1952. Poetry anthology.

—— *Children and books*, 2nd ed. Chicago: Scott, Foresman and Company, 1957. This annotated bibliography provides an excellent selected list of books for children up to 15 years. Reviews and comments are given in the preceding chapters.

—— and others, *Children's books too good to miss*. Cleveland: Western Reserve University Press, 1948.

Association of Children's Book Editors, *A selected list of books for boys and girls*. New York: The Children's Book Council and the New York Times, 1948.

BENNET, R., *Story-teller poems*. Philadelphia: The John C. Winston Company, 1948. Anthology.

Bibliography of books for children. Washington: Association for Childhood Education. An annual pamphlet.

BLAIR, G. M., *Diagnostic and remedial teaching*, rev. ed. New York: The Macmillan Company, 1956, 173-211. Materials and practice exercises.

BOND, G. L., and TINKER, M. A., *Reading difficulties*. New York: Appleton-Century-Crofts, Inc., 1957, 461-477. Annotated lists of tests and sources of book lists and materials.

The Booklist: a guide to new books. Chicago: American Library Association. This bimonthly journal has a section devoted to children's books.

Books of the year for children. New York: Child Study Association of America. A pamphlet dealing with books for boys and girls published annually.

BREWTON, J. E., and BREWTON, S. W., *Index to children's poetry*. New York: H. W. Wilson Co., 1942; first supplement, 1952.

BREWTON, S., and BREWTON, J. E., *Bridled with rainbows*. New York: The Macmillan Company, 1949. Poetry anthology.

Bulletin of Children's Book Center. Chicago: Center for Children's Books, University of Chicago Library. Issued monthly.

[1] This list is selected from the more recent publications. See also Appendix III.

BUROS, O. K. (ed.), *The fifth mental measurements yearbook*. Highland Park, N. J.: The Gryphon Press, 1959. Reviews and evaluations of mental tests, reading tests, machines used in reading.

CARTER, H. L. J., and McGINNIS, D. J., *Learning to read*. New York: McGraw-Hill Book Company, Inc., 1953, 71-120. Materials of various kinds to aid teaching of reading.

Children's books around the world. Washington: American Association of University Women. List of 265 children's books from 52 countries.

Children's Book Council. Twelve recommended booklists in *The world of children's books*. New York: Children's Book Council.

COLE, W., *Humorous poetry for children*. Cleveland: The World Publishing Company, 1955. Anthology.

CONDIT, M. A., *Trade books for beginning readers*. New York: H. W. Wilson Company, 1960. Books for children in grades 1, 2 and 3.

COOK, D. E., EATON, A. T., and WEST, D. H., *Standard catalog for high school libraries*, 5th ed. with supplements. New York: H. W. Wilson Company, 1947. Lists for grades 7-12.

COOKE, D. E. (chairman), *The road to better reading*. Albany, N. Y.: New York Education Department, 1953. Films useful in developmental reading program, pp. 77-83.

Coronet Instructional Films. Chicago 1: Coronet Films, Coronet Building. A wide variety of teaching films.

DAWSON, M. A., and BAMMAN, H. A., *Fundamentals of basic reading instruction*. New York: Longmans, Green and Company, 1959, 281-295. Book lists, tests, films and film strips, magazines and newspapers, and other teaching aids. See especially pp. 298-299 for distributors of films, records, and other teaching aids.

DAWSON, M. A., and PFEIFFER, L., *A treasury of books for the primary grades*. San Francisco: Howard Chandler, 1959. List of 300 choice books with annotations.

DOLCH, E. W., *Dolch materials for better teaching of reading*. Champaign, Ill.: The Garrard Press. A variety of devices and other materials for developing word recognition, sight vocabulary, etc. Request catalog from publisher.

DUFF, A., *Longer flight: a family grows up with books*. New York: The Viking Press, Inc., 1955. About children's literature.

DURRELL, D. D., and SULLIVAN, H. B., *High interest—low vocabulary book list*. Boston: Boston University, School of Education, 1950.

EAKIN, M. K., *Good books for children*. Chicago: University of Chicago Press, 1960.

EATON, A. T., *Treasure for the taking*, rev. ed. New York: The Viking Press, Inc., 1957. About children's literature.

The EDL study skills library. Huntington, N. Y.: Educational Developmental Laboratories, 1961. A sequential, developmental program of reading for independently learning the study skills, grades 4-9.

FENNER, P., *Proof of the pudding: what children read*. New York: The John Day Company, 1957. Lists classified, annotated, and grouped by children's ages.

—— *Something shared: children and books*. New York: The John Day Company, 1959.

FERRIS, H., *Favorite poems, old and new*. Garden City: Doubleday and Company, 1957. Anthology.

GATES, A. I., and PEARDON, C. C., *Gates-Peardon practice exercises in reading*.

New York: Bureau of Publications, Teachers College, Columbia University. Exercises to develop various kinds of reading skills.

GILES, R., COOKE, D. E., WEST, D. H., and others (eds.), *Children's catalog*, 7th ed. with supplements. New York: W. H. Wilson Company, 1946. Book lists for all grades up through 9th.

GRAY, L., and REESE, D., *Teaching children to read*, 2nd ed. New York: The Ronald Press Company, 1957, 364-372. Graded books, practice materials, recreational books, word-analysis materials, source materials.

The Horn Book Magazine. Boston: Horn Book, Inc. A monthly magazine devoted to books and reading material for young children.

HUFFARD, G. T., CARLISLE, L. M., and FERRIS, H. J., *My poetry book,* rev. ed. Philadelphia: The John C. Winston Company, 1956. Anthology.

HUGHES, R., *Let's enjoy poetry*. Boston: Houghton Mifflin Company, 1958. Anthology.

JACOBS, L. B., *Bibliography of books for children*. Washington: Association for Childhood Education International, 1952.

JOHNSON, Edna, SICKELS, Evelyn R., and SAYERS, Frances C., *Anthology of children's literature*, 3rd ed. Boston: Houghton Mifflin Company, 1959.

LARRICK, Nancy, *A parent's guide to children's books*. Garden City: Doubleday and Company, Inc., 1958 (also in Pocket Books edition).

—— *A teacher's guide to children's books*. Columbus, Ohio: Charles E. Merrill Books, Inc., 1960. Books for children throughout the grades and how to use them.

LAZAR, May (ed.), *The retarded reader in the junior high school*. Bureau of Educational Research, Publication No. 31. New York: Board of Education, City of New York (110 Livingston St., Brooklyn 2, N. Y.), 1952, 121-125. Practice materials, magazines and newspapers, pupil reference material.

—— (ed.), *Source material for the improvement of reading*. Bureau of Educational Research Bulletin No. 37. New York: Board of Education, City of New York, 1956. References on reading, lists of sources for materials.

LEESTMA, R., *Audio-visual materials for teaching reading*. Ann Arbor, Michigan: Slater's Book Store, 1954.

MARKEY, L. R., *Books are vacations*. Boston: Horn Book, Inc., 1956. Annotated, for ages 8-12 years.

MARTIGNONI, M. F. (ed.), *The illustrated treasury of children's literature*. New York: Grosset and Dunlap, 1955.

MARTIN, L. K., *Magazines for school libraries*. New York: H. W. Wilson Company, 1950.

MCCONNELL, M. L., and WEST, D. H., *Children's catalog*, 9th ed. New York: H. W. Wilson Co., 1956. Annotated list, graded and classified.

MCCULLOUGH, C. M., *Handbook for teaching the language arts*. South San Francisco, Calif.: Paragon Publications, 1958, 49-50. Sources for children's reading material.

MCDONALD, G. D., *A way of knowing*. New York: Thomas Y. Crowell Company, 1959. Poetry anthology.

MCGINLEY, P., *All around the town*. Philadelphia: J. B. Lippincott Company, 1948. Poetry anthology.

National Council of Teachers of English, *Adventures with books: a reading list for elementary schools*. Chicago: National Council of Teachers of English, 1960.

OPIE, I., and OPIE, P. (eds.), *The Oxford dictionary of nursery rhymes.* New York: Oxford University Press, Inc., 1951. Anthology.

ROBINSON, H. M. (ed.), *Materials for reading.* Chicago: University of Chicago Press, 1957. Discussions of materials to use at successive grade levels.

RUSSELL, D. H., *Children learn to read,* 2nd ed. Boston: Ginn and Company, 1961, 444-453. Classified lists of books, magazines, and papers, poetry anthologies, children's literature, current reviews of children's books, and book clubs.

—— and KARP, E. E., *Reading aids through the grades: Three hundred developmental reading activities,* rev. ed. New York: Bureau of Publications, Teachers College, Columbia University, 1951.

SECHRIST, E. H., *One thousand poems for children.* Philadelphia: Macrae-Smith Company, 1946. Anthology.

SELL, V., and others, *Subject index to poetry for children and young people.* Chicago: American Library Association, 1957.

SMITH, L. H., *The unreluctant years: a critical approach to children's literature.* Chicago: American Library Association, 1953.

SMITH, N. B., HART, H. C., and BAKER, C. B. (compilers and editors), *The best of children's literature.* Indianapolis, Ind.: The Bobbs-Merrill Company, Inc., 1960. Supplementary reading materials, grades 1-6.

SNOW, M. B. (chairman), *A basic book collection for the elementary grades.* Chicago: American Library Association, 1951.

SPACHE, G. D., *Resources in teaching reading.* Gainesville, Fla: The Author, Reading Laboratory and Clinic, University of Florida, 1955. A multitude of teaching materials including book lists and visual and auditory aids.

SRA Reading Laboratory (elementary ed.). Chicago: Science Research Associates, 1959. A multilevel reading program for individualized reading, grades 4-6.

SRA Reading Laboratory (secondary ed.). Chicago: Science Research Associates, 1959. A multilevel individualized reading program for grades 7-12.

STRANG, R., and BRACKEN, D. K., *Making better readers.* Boston: D. C. Heath and Company, 1957, 345-355. Lists of tests; sources of films, slides and records; texts and other books.

—— McCULLOUGH, C. M., and TRAXLER, A. E., *The improvement of reading,* 3rd ed. New York: McGraw-Hill Book Company, Inc., 1961, Chapter 18. Information on booklists, practice exercises, magazines, and teaching aids.

TAYLOR, S. E., and FRACKENPOHL, H., *A core vocabulary.* EDL Research and information Bulletin No. 5. Huntington, N. Y.: Educational Developmental Laboratories, 1960. A basic vocabulary for grades 1-8; an advanced vocabulary for grades 9-13.

—— *The EDL Skimmer* (with teacher's guide). Huntington, N. Y.: Educational Developmental Laboratories, 1961. A program for teaching skimming with aid of the skimmer.

THOMPSON, Jean, *Books for boys and girls,* rev. ed. Toronto, Canada: Ryerson Press, 1959. Classified according to interest.

TOOZE, R., *Your children want to read, a guide for teachers and parents.* Englewood Cliffs, N. J.: Prentice-Hall, Inc., 1957.

—— *Storytelling.* Englewood Cliffs, N. J.: Prentice-Hall, Inc., 1959.

Appendix V:

Bibliographies of Reading Literature

BETTS, E. A., and BETTS, T. M., *An index to professional literature on reading and related topics*. New York: American Book Company, 1945.

CLYMER, T., and ROBINSON, H. M., Reading. *Review of Educational Research*, 1961, 31, 130-144.

DALE, E. (ed.), *Bibliography of vocabulary studies*. Columbus, Ohio: Bureau of Educational Research, Ohio State University, 1949.

GILBERT, L. C., and HOLMES, J. A., Reading: Psychology. *Review of Educational Research*, 1955, 25, 77-91.

GRAY, W. S., Summary of investigations relating to reading. *Supplementary Educational Monographs*, No. 28. Chicago: University of Chicago Press, 1924.

—— Summary of reading investigations (July 1, 1924 to June 30, 1925). *Elementary School Journal*, 1926, 26, 449-459; 507-518; 574-584; 662-673. See also successive annual summaries in same journal up through 1932.

—— Summary of reading investigations (July 1, 1931 to June 30, 1932). *Journal of Educational Research*, 1933, 26, 401-424. See also successive annual summaries in same journal up through 1960. Author of series from 1961 on is Helen M. Robinson.

KEYSER, Margaret L., Research in reading in the elementary school. *Review of Educational Research*, 1952, 22, 65-75.

McCULLOUGH, Constance M., Reading. *Review of Educational Research*, 1958, 28, 96-106.

Proceedings of the annual conference on reading held at the University of Chicago. Chicago: University of Chicago Press, 1961. Contains list of noteworthy books published during preceding year suitable for primary, intermediate, and upper grades. See also preceding and subsequent annual proceedings.

ROBINSON, Helen M., Summary of investigations relating to reading. *Journal of Educational Research*, 1961, 54, 203-220; see also *The Reading Teacher*, Research Issue, 1962, Vol. 15.

SHELDON, W. D., Reading: Instruction. *Review of Educational Research*, 1955, 25, 92-106.

The Reading Teacher, published by the International Reading Association, 5835 Kimbark Ave., Chicago 37, Illinois. In each issue see sections: (*a*) "What research says to the reading teacher;" (*b*) "What other magazines say about reading;" (*c*) "Interesting books for the reading teacher."

TINKER, M. A., Eye movements in reading. *Journal of Educational Research*, 1936, 30, 241-277.

—— The study of eye movements in reading. *Psychological Bulletin*, 1946, 43, 93-120.

—— Recent studies of eye movements in reading. *Psychological Bulletin*, 1958, 54, 215-231. (These three articles contain all materials in the field up to 1958.)

TRAXLER, A. E., and SEDER, M., *Ten years of research in reading: Summary and bibliography.* New York: Educational Records Bureau (21 Audubon Ave.), Bulletin No. 32, 1941.

—— and TOWNSEND, A., *Another five years of research in reading: Summary and bibliography.* New York: Educational Records Bureau (21 Audubon Ave.), Bulletin No. 46, 1946.

—— and TOWNSEND, A., *Eight years more of research in reading: Summary and bibliography.* New York: Educational Records Bureau (21 Audubon Ave.), Bulletin No. 64, 1955.

—— and JUNGEBLUT, Ann, *Research in reading during another four years.* New York: Educational Records Bureau (21 Audubon Ave.), Bulletin No. 75, 1960.

WITTY, P. A., and SIZEMORE, R. A., Reading the comics: A summary of studies and an evaluation—I, II, III. *Elementary English*, 1954, 31, 501-506; 1955, 32, 43-49; 109-114.

Appendix VI:

Glossary of Statistical Terms

Note: The explanations are simplified to meet the needs of students with a limited background in statistics. For further clarification of terms and their usage, see an elementary statistics textbook such as B. J. Underwood, C. P. Duncan, J. A. Taylor, and J. W. Cotton, *Elementary statistics,* New York: Appleton-Century-Crofts, Inc., 1954; or H. E. Garrett, *Elementary statistics,* New York: Longmans, Green and Company, 1956.

arithmetic mean (M). The sum of a set of scores divided by their number.

average (or measure of central tendency). A measure that is typical of a number of like things, e.g., the average score on a reading test. There are three kinds of averages in common use: the *arithmetic mean*, the *median*, the *mode*. The arithmetic mean (the mean) is commonly called the average.

average deviation (AD). The average of deviations of the scores from the mean, the average size of the distance of individual scores from the average score.

bar graph. A chart made up of a series of vertical bars (rectangles) of equal width; the heights of the bars represent the size of scores or frequencies. Also called *bar chart* and *bar diagram*.

centile. Same as percentile, "per hundred."

control. Any procedure introduced into the experimental plan (design) to eliminate the effect of a factor (stimulus variable) or to insure that it remains constant in its effect on the responses measured (dependent variable). Examples: control of sex is to use all boys or all girls; control of age is to use pupils all the same age.

critical ratio (CR). The difference between two means divided by the standard error of the difference; the size of the CR indicates whether the obtained difference between means is "real" (significant) or just a matter of chance (see Garrett reference). If the CR is 3.0 or larger you are "very sure" that the difference is significant; if the CR is between 2.0 and 2.9, you are "pretty sure" that the difference is significant.

correlation (r, for product-moment; ρ, rho, for rank difference method). This measure shows whether a high score on one test will usually mean that an individual will get a high score on another test. If a correlation coefficient (r) is 1.00, the prediction of one test score by another is assured; .80 is considered a very high correlation, a good predictive relationship; .40 is substantial but not high enough for assurance that any one individual's scores will be comparable on the two tests.

derived score. A score derived from another score by statistical means. It describes a person's position in a group, e.g., a percentile score, a standard score, a T-score. Contrasted with *raw score.*

distribution. Same as frequency distribution.

frequency curve. Same as frequency polygon.

frequency distribution. A tabulation which shows the frequency of scores when these scores are arranged in order of size in a frequency table.

frequency polygon. A graphic representation of frequency distribution.

heterogeneous. Refers to distributions with wide (large) variability, the opposite of homogeneous.

histogram. A graphic representation of a frequency distribution; a rectangular frequency polygon.

homogeneous. Refers to distributions with small and regular variability, the opposite of heterogeneous.

line graph. A diagram to show the trend of performance, such as learning new words, over a period of time. Successive days are given on the base line and accumulation of words learned on the vertical axis. Increases in speed of reading may be shown similarly. Also called *line diagram.*

matched groups (samples). Two equated groups are used: one the control and the other the experimental. The two groups are matched on all factors (such as age, intelligence, teacher experience) that might obscure responses that are being measured. Or groups equal in learning ability may be obtained by random selection (see random sample). Also see Sartain experiment in Chapter 2.

mean (M). Same as arithmetic mean.

mean deviation (MD). Same as the average deviation.

median (Mdn). The point or value on a scale of measurements, arranged in order of size, that divides the series of scores into two equal groups, i.e., in a frequency distribution, 50 per cent of the scores are above and 50 per cent below the median; the same as the second quartile. Half the individuals tested have a score above this, and half have a score below this. In a class of 35, it is the score of the 18th student from the top or bottom of the list of scores arranged in order of size.

mode (Mo). The value in a distribution of scores that occurs the greatest number of times. If more students get a score of sixty on a test than get any other score, the modal score is sixty.

normal curve. The symmetrical, bell-shaped curve depicting the normal distribution.

normal distribution. A theoretical distribution in which the number of scores is taken to be infinitely large.

overlapping. The extent to which the scores in one distribution are the same as those of another distribution; the percentage of one set of scores which exceeds the mean or median of another set.

percentile. A point measured along the scale of scores in a distribution below which a given per cent of the scores occurs, i.e., 10 per cent are below the 10th percentile.

population. Any group of individuals who are alike in at least one specific way, e.g., all third-grade pupils in a city school system.

profile. A line diagram which depicts the standing or relative position of an individual or a group in each of several traits or test scores to show variation from trait to trait and the general trend of the scores or ratings (also called *proficiency profile* and *profile graph*).

quartile. One of three points, Q1, Q2 (median), Q3, in a series of scores which divide the frequency distribution into four parts, each part containing exactly one-fourth of the scores.

quartile deviation (Q). Half the difference between the third and the first quartiles, i.e., half the distance between the 75th and the 25th percentiles.

random sample. A sample selected in a purely random manner from the population which it is to represent. A sample made up by taking every n-th (as every 10th) name in a city directory is approximately random.

range. The distance in score values between the highest and the lowest measures in a distribution.

raw score. Untreated score, the original score obtained by measurement, as a score of 32 on a reading test.

representative sample. A sample obtained by systematic selection so that no factor which might influence the ability or trait being measured is given undue weight, i.e., a miniature image of the population from which the sample is drawn.

sample. A group drawn from a larger entity called a population, as a sample of 10-year-old school children, i.e., any number of cases less than the total number of cases in the population from which it is drawn.

sampling error. Deviation, due to chance, as of a mean (or other statistic) from the true value of the mean it is intended to represent. The true value is theoretical, based upon a hypothetical population of infinite size.

significance of correlation. Determined by computing the standard error of the coefficient (SE); reference to a table will show if the coefficient of correlation is or is not significant at the 5% level (some significance), or at the 1% level (highly significant). See Garrett reference.

skewness. Scores or values that extend farther above than below the peak of the distribution, or vice versa, indicate a skewed distribution; unusually low scores (to the left) indicate negative skewness; to the right, positive skewness.

standard deviation (SD). A measure of variability of scores around the mean (the square root of the mean of the squared deviations taken from the arithmetic mean of the distribution).

standard error (SE). A measure of the variability of a statistic as standard error of a mean (SE_M) and a standard error of a difference (SE_D).

standard score (z). The value that indicates how far a raw score deviates from the mean in SD units or distances.

statistic. A value such as the mean, the standard deviation, a correlation, or any other measure that characterizes a specific series of scores.

t. Same as critical ratio.

T-score. A derived score used in connection with educational, achievement, and intelligence tests. The mean is 50, the SD is 10, and the range of scores stretches from 0 to 100. A T-score gives an individual's exact location in a group, e.g., his T-scores of 57 in arithmetic and 57 in history express the same degree of achievement relative to performance in his group. See Garrett reference.

variable. A term that refers to any condition in a scientific investigation which may in any way affect the observations made; it also refers to the thing observed or measured (independent variable), and to responses, as score on a test (dependent variable).

variability. The dispersion of scores in a distribution, i.e., the spread of the scores above and below the mean or average.

z-score. Same as standard score.

Appendix VII:

Root Derivatives, Prefixes, and Suffixes[1]

A. Greek Root Derivatives

	Root Word	Frequency	Root Stem	Meaning	Example, English
1.	graph	22	graph (gram)	to write	barograph, graph, phonograph
2.	syn	14	syn (syl, sym)	together	synthesis, synthetic
3.	kyklos	11	(cir, circl, cycle)	ring	circle, circumference, cyclone
4.	organon	11	org, organ	organ	organ, organize
5.	phonos	11	phon, phone	sound	phonetic, telephone
6.	monos	10	mon, mono	one	monotone, monotonous, monologue
7.	tele	9	tel, tele	far off	telephone, television
8.	polis	9	pol, poli	city	metropolis, politics
9.	auto	8	auto	self	automobile, automatic
10.	phos	8	phos (phot)	light	phosphate, phosphorus, photograph
11.	mousa	7	(muse)	muse, to think	muse, museum, musical
12.	para	7	para	beside	parallel, paraphrase
13.	physis	7	phys	nature	physics, physical
14.	logos	7	log	word, reason	logical, biology
15.	dia	6	dia	through	dia, diameter
16.	mikros	6	(micro)	small	microbe, microscope
17.	prakticos	6	(pract)	to do	practice, practical
18.	character	5	chara	engraving	character, characteristics
19.	hydor or hydra	5	hydra	water	hydrogen, hydromatic

[1] Reproduced with permission of the publisher from L. C. Breen, Vocabulary development by teaching prefixes, suffixes and root derivatives, *The Reading Teacher*, 1960, 14, 93-97.

B. Latin Root Derivatives

Infinitive	Frequency	Meaning	Participle	Root Stem	Examples, English
1. facare	105	to do, to make	factus	fac, fact, fic, fy, fied, fash	face, fact, factory, benefit, feat, fashion, purify
2. stare	89	to stand	status	sta, sti, stat, sist, st	station, status, insist, rest
3. ponere	63	to place	positus	pos, pose, pon, pound	pose, post, opposite, opponent, compound
4. ferre	50	to bear, to carry	tuli, latus	fer, ferre, lat, tol	coniferous, ferry, oblation, tolerate
5. regere	41	to rule	rectus	reg, rect, reign, roy, rul	direct, regal, ruler, regular, royal
6. mittere	40	to send	missus	mit, mis, miss, mes, mise	emit, mission, submit, surmise
7. tendere	38	to stretch	tensus	tend, tens	tend, tendor, tension
8. cedere	36	to go, to happen	cessus	ced, ces, cess, ceed	sede, session, secede
9. videre	36	to see	visus	vid, vis, view, vise	video, vision, visa, visit, advise
10. movere	33	to move	motus	mov, mot, mob	move, motivation, mobility
11. spectare	33	to see	spectus	spect, spic or pic	expect, spectacle, suspicion
12. venire	33	to come	ventus	ven, vent	event, vent, convenience
13. tenere	30	to hold	tentus	ten, tent, tain, tin	tent, tentacle, tenant, attain, continent
14. parare	29	to get ready	paratus	par, para, pair	apparent, prepare, repair
15. portare	29	to carry	portatus	port	port, export, report
16. capare	28	to take, to head	captus	cap, capt	cape, caption, captor, capital, capitol
17. ducere	26	to lead	ductus	duc, duct, duit	duct, conduct, conduit
18. quaerere	26	to question, to ask	quaesitus	quire, quis, quer, quest	acquire, requisition, conquer, conquest
19. servire	25	to serve	servitus	serv, serf	reserve, servant, service, serf
20. finire	24	to end	finis	fin	fine, finish, refinish
21. dare	23	to give	datus	da, don, der, di, dote	data, donate, add, pardon, render, antidote
22. parsicapere	23	to share, to participate	partcaptus[1]	part	depart, particle, participate
23. significare	23	to indicate, to notify, to mark	significatus[2]	signific, sign, less, fic	significant, sign, signify
24. trahere	23	to pull, to draw	tractus	tra, tract, trait, treat	trace, traction, trait, retreat
25. genere	23	cause to be, to begin	generatus	gen, gener	generate, Genesis, generation
26. ligere	22	to choose	lectus	lect	elect, re-elect, select
27. agere	21	to act	actus	ag, act	agent, act, action
28. plicare	21	to fold	plicatus	pli, plic, ply	apply, complicated, duplicate, reply
29. jacere or iacere	21	to throw	jactus, iactus	ject	eject, dejection, project
30. premere	20	to press	pressus	press	depress, press, impress
31. struere	19	to build	structus	struct, stroy, stru	construct, instrument, destroy, structure
32. vertere or versare	19	to turn	versus	vert, vers, verse	advertise, convert, reverse, verse
33. cadere	18	to fall, to happen	caesus	cid, cide	accident, decide, incident
34. cordare[3]	17	heart	cordatus	cord, cour	accord, concord, cordially, discourage
35. fortis[4]	17	strong		fort, force	comfort, effort, force, fort

[1] Note that this word has as a basis the infinitive *capere* (to head, to lead).
[2] Note that this word is made up of two parts. In Latin *signe* meant sign and *ficare* mean to show.
[3] The Greek word was *chorde* and meant either gut or string.
[4] This is a Latin adjective.

C. PREFIXES

Prefix	Frequency	Total frequency for groups	Meaning
1. in	(203)		in, into, and not
en	(83)		
im	(42)		
em	(21)	349	
2. re	(209)	209	again
3. a	(149)		to, toward
ad	(53)		
ap	(47)		
at	(29)	278	
4. de	(146)		from, away from, apart
dis	(82)	228	
5. ex	(145)		out of, out from
e	(63)	208	
6. con	(145)	145	together
7. com	(95)		together with
col	(29)	124	
8. o	(65)		against, away from
op	(22)		
of	(15)		
ob	(12)	114	
9. pro	(58)		before, for
pre	(35)	93	
10. al	(40)		pertaining to, like
ar	(39)	79	
11. an	(68)	68	belonging to
12 ac	(56)	56	pertaining to
13. be	(45)	45	around, all over, act of being, action
14. for	(44)	44	away, off
15. di	(43)	43	doubly, to separate
		Total 2,083	

D. SUFFIXES

Suffix	Frequency	Total frequencies for groups	Meaning	Example, English
1. er	(323)		action or a process, something that does something	teller, grocer, teacher
or	(114)	337		
2. tion	(210)		action	temptation (the word action means literally the action of acting)
tions	(56)			
sion	(24)			
cion	(9)	289		
3. ty	(95)	95	condition	empty, safety
4. al	(84)	84	pertaining to	musical, practical
5. ble, able,			capable of being	adaptable, preventable,
ible	(82)	82		sociable
6. ment	(73)	73	action or the result of action	judgment, supplement
7. full	(44)	44	full, complete	forceful, meaningful
8. man	(43)	43	human, man	foreman, superman
9. ic or	(34)			
ics	(7)	41	pertaining to	tellic,[1] phonetic
10. ous	(34)	34	full of, like	delicious, joyous
ious				
eous[2]				
11. ence	(16)		action, state of being, relating to, state of quality	assistance, distance, romance, persistence
ance	(13)	29		
		Total 1,151		

[1] The ic followed by al is an example of what might be termed a double syllable combined as one, as each syllable has the same meaning (pertaining to).
[2] The syllables ious and eous are to be considered as forms of ous.

INDEX